Quantum Models of Cognition and Decision

Much of our understanding of human thinking is based on probabilistic models. This innovative book by Jerome R. Busemeyer and Peter D. Bruza argues that, actually, the underlying mathematical structures from quantum theory provide a much better account of human thinking than traditional models. They introduce the foundations for modelling probabilistic-dynamic systems using two aspects of quantum theory. The first, "contextuality," is a way to understand interference effects found with inferences and decisions under conditions of uncertainty. The second, "quantum entanglement," allows cognitive phenomena to be modelled in non-reductionist ways. Employing these principles drawn from quantum theory allows us to view human cognition and decision in a totally new light. Introducing the basic principles in an easy-to-follow way, this book does not assume a physics background or a quantum brain and comes complete with a tutorial and fully worked-out applications in important areas of cognition and decision.

Jerome R. Busemeyer is a Professor in the Department of Psychological and Brain Sciences at Indiana University, Bloomington, USA. His research includes mathematical models of learning and decision making, and he has formulated a dynamic theory of human decision making called decision field theory. Professor Busemeyer has published over 100 articles in cognitive and decision science journals, including *Psychological Review*, and was Chief Editor of the *Journal of Mathematical Psychology* from 2005 to 2010.

Peter D. Bruza is a Professor in the Faculty of Science and Technology at Queensland University of Technology, Brisbane, Australia. His research intersects information retrieval, cognitive science, and applied logic. He is a pioneer and co-instigator of the field of quantum interaction (QI) and serves on the steering committee of the quantum interaction symposia. Professor Bruza also serves on the editorial boards of *Information Retrieval, Journal of Applied Logic, The Logic Journal of the IGPL*, and the "Information Science and Knowledge Management" book series.

Quantum Models of Cognition and Decision

Jerome R. Busemeyer   Peter D. Bruza

CAMBRIDGE
UNIVERSITY PRESS

CAMBRIDGE UNIVERSITY PRESS
Cambridge, New York, Melbourne, Madrid, Cape Town,
Singapore, São Paulo, Delhi, Mexico City

Cambridge University Press
The Edinburgh Building, Cambridge CB2 8RU, UK

Published in the United States of America by Cambridge University Press, New York

www.cambridge.org
Information on this title: www.cambridge.org/9781107011991

First published 2012
Reprinted 2012

Printed and Bound in the United States of America by Edwards Brothers

A catalogue record for this publication is available from the British Library

Library of Congress Cataloguing in Publication data
Busemeyer, Jerome R.
Quantum models of cognition and decision / Jerome R. Busemeyer and Peter D. Bruza.
pages cm
Includes bibliographical references.
ISBN 978-1-107-01199-1 (Hardback)
1. Decision making–Mathematical models.   2. Statistical decision.
3. Cognition–Mathematical models.   4. Quantum theory.
I. Bruza, Peter David, 1962–   II. Title.
QA279.4.B87 2012
530.12–dc23

2011051232

ISBN 978-1-107-01199-1 Hardback

《周易》有云：穷则变、变则通、通则久。

⟨⟨Yi Jing⟩⟩ Book states: ANY circumstance hitting a limit will begin to change. Change will in turn lead to an unimpeded state, and then lead to continuity.

This book is dedicated to the person who inspired this amazing journey, the first author's wife.

Contents

Preface

Rationale

The purpose of this book is to introduce the application of quantum theory to cognitive and decision scientists. At first sight it may seem bizarre, even ridiculous, to draw a connection between cognition and decision making – research lying within the realm of day-to-day human behavior – on the one hand and quantum mechanics – a highly successful theory for modelling subatomic phenomena – on the other hand. Yet there are good scientific reasons for doing so, which is leading a growing number of researchers to examine quantum theory as a way to understand perplexing findings and stubborn problems within their own fields. Hence this book. Given the nascent state of this field, some words of justification are warranted. The research just mentioned is not concerned with modelling the brain using quantum mechanics, nor is it directly concerned with the idea of the brain as a quantum computer. Instead it turns to quantum theory as a fresh conceptual framework for explaining empirical puzzles, as well as a rich new source of alternative formal tools. To convey the idea that researchers in this area are not doing quantum mechanics, various modifiers have been proposed to describe this work, such as quantum-like models of cognition, cognitive models based on quantum structure, or generalized quantum models.

There are two aspects of quantum theory which open the door to addressing problems facing cognition and decision in a totally new light. The first is known as "contextuality" of judgments and decisions, which is captured in quantum theory by the idea of "interference": the context generated by making a first judgment or decision interferes with subsequent judgments or decisions to produce order effects, so that judgments and decisions are non-commutative. The second aspect relates to "quantum entanglement." Entanglement is a phenomenon whereby making an observation on one part of the system instantaneously affects the state in another part of the system, even if the respective systems are separated by space-like distances. The crucial point about entanglement relevant to this book is that entangled systems cannot be validly decomposed and modelled as separate subsystems. This opens the door to developing quantum-like models of cognitive phenomena which are not decompositional in nature. For example, the semantics of concept combinations would seem to be non-compositional, and quantum theory provides formal tools to model these as non-decomposable interacting systems. Similar applications appear in human memory. Most models consider words as separate entities – new models are made possible by going beyond this assumption and, for example, modelling a network of word associates as a non-decomposable system.

It is important to note the authors are agnostic toward the so-called "quantum mind" hypothesis, which assumes there are quantum processes going on in the brain. We motivate the use of quantum models as innovative abstractions of existing problems. That is all. These abstractions have the character of idealizations in the sense there is no claim as to the validity of the idealization "on the ground." For example, modelling concept combinations as quantum entangled particles involves no claim as to whether there is associated physical entanglement going on somewhere in the brain. This may seem like an easy way out, but is not that different than idealizations employed in other areas of science. For example, in neural dynamical models of the brain, continuous state and time differential equations are used to model growth of neural activation, even though actually there are only a finite number of neurons and each one only fires in an all or none manner. In short, we apply mathematical structures from quantum mechanics to cognition and decision without attaching the physical meaning attributed to them when applied to the human behavioral phenomena. In fact, many areas of inquiry that were historically part of physics are now considered part of mathematics, including complexity theory, geometry, and stochastic processes. Originally they were applied to physical entities and events. For geometry, this was shapes of objects in space. For stochastic processes, this was statistical mechanics of particles. Over time they became generalized and applied in other domains. Thus, what happens here with quantum mechanics mirrors the history of many, if not most, branches of mathematics.

The cognitive revolution that occurred in the 1960s was based on classical computational logic, and the connectionist/neural network movements of the 1970s were based on classical dynamic systems. These classical assumptions remain at the heart of both cognitive architecture and neural network theories, and they are so commonly and widely applied that we take them for granted and presume them to be obviously true. What are these critical but hidden assumptions upon which all traditional theories rely? Quantum theory provides a fundamentally different approach to logic, reasoning, probabilistic inference, and dynamic systems. For example, quantum logic does not follow the distributive axiom of Boolean logic; quantum probabilities do not obey the law of total probability; quantum reasoning does not obey the principle of monotonic reasoning; and quantum dynamics can evolve along several trajectories in parallel rather than be slave to a single trajectory as in classical dynamics. Nevertheless, human behavior itself does not obey all of these restrictions. This book will provide an exposition of the basic assumptions of classic versus quantum models of cognition and decision theories. These basic assumptions will be examined, side by side, in a parallel and elementary manner. For example, classical systems assume that measurement merely observes a preexisting property of a system; in contrast, quantum systems assume that measurement actively creates the existence of a property in a system. The logic and mathematical foundation of classic and quantum theory will be laid out in a simple and elementary manner that uncovers the mysteries of both theories. Classic theory will emerge to be seen as a possibly overly restrictive case of the more general quantum theory. The fundamental implications of these contrasting assumptions will be examined closely with concrete examples and applications to cognition and decision making. New research programs in cognition and decision making, based on quantum theory, will be reviewed.

Book chapters

Chapter 1 provides the motivation for why one might be interested in applying quantum theory to cognition and decision making. In this chapter, we give a quick glance at several applications, including perception, conceptual judgments, decision making, and information retrieval. Also, this chapter briefly reviews some of the previous history and connections made between psychology and quantum physics and places the current ideas within this larger framework of research. Chapter 2 provides a simple and intuitive introduction to the basic axioms of quantum probability theory, alongside a comparison with the basic axioms of classic probability theory, and we also provide a clear *psychological* interpretation of the quantum axioms. The chapter includes simple numerical examples, calculations, and simple computer programs that provide clear and concrete ideas about how to use quantum theory to compute probabilities for cognitive and decision-making applications. Only linear algebra is needed for this introduction, which will be introduced and explained in a simple tutorial manner. No physics background is required. The next five chapters describe applications of the theory presented in Chapter 2. This includes applications to order effects on attitude judgments in Chapter 3, explanations for human probability judgment errors in Chapter 4, quantum models of conceptual combination judgments in Chapter 5, a detailed application of a quantum model to the conjoint memory recognition paradigm in Chapter 6, and a quantum model of the human mental lexicon in Chapter 7. Chapter 8 introduces the dynamic principles of quantum theory in a simple step-by-step manner with numerical examples and simple-to-use computer programs. This chapter also identifies fundamental differences between simple classical dynamic systems and quantum dynamic systems by presenting a parallel development of classic Markov and non-classic quantum processes. Chapter 9 applies the dynamic principles of the previous chapter to several paradoxical findings of decision making that cannot be easily explained by traditional decision models, including Markov models. Chapter 10 introduces some basic concepts of quantum computing and contrasts these ideas with production rule systems, connectionist networks, fuzzy set theory, and Bayesian inference theory. Computer code for analyzing various logic inference problems under uncertainty using quantum computing are provided. Chapter 11 introduces the problem of learning with quantum systems and reviews work on quantum neural networks. Finally, Chapter 12 summarizes the progress made toward applying quantum theory to cognitive and decision sciences thus far, and provides a view of future possibilities. This chapter also includes a debate with a skeptic (actually previous reviewers) about the advantages and disadvantages of using a quantum approach to cognition and decision making, as well as different ways to understand the biological basis of quantum computations by the brain. An appendix is included to review some additional mathematics needed for understanding and using more advance parts of quantum theory, and to present technical proofs that are too long to be included in the main text.

In our experience thus far, people either love or hate these ideas, but no one remains unaffected. We challenge you to make your own opinion.

Jerome R. Busemeyer, Indiana University, USA
Peter Bruza, Queensland University of Technology, Australia

Acknowledgments

We were greatly helped by many of our colleagues who provided numerous useful comments, corrections, and thought-provoking dialogues in the subject area of this book. This includes Diederik Aerts, Sven Aerts, Harald Atmanspacher, Acacio de Barros, Reinhard Blutner, Charles Brainerd, Daoyi Dong, Riccardo Franco, Liane Gabora, Andrei Khrennikov, Kirsty Kitto, Peirofrancesco La Mura, Ariane Lambert-Mogiliansky, Shimon Malin, Cathy McEvoy, Douglas Nelson, Emmanual Pothos, Brentyn Ramm, Keith van Rijsbergen, Dawei Song, Laurianne Sitbon, Richard Shiffrin, Jennifer Trueblood, Giuseppe Vitiello, Zheng Wang, Dominic Widdows, John Woods, Eldad Yechiam, Guido Zuccon, and several other anonymous reviewers. The book is much improved by their efforts. The first author's efforts were supported by a grant from the United States National Science Foundation, and the second author's efforts were supported by a grant from the Australian Research Council.

1

Why use quantum theory for cognition and decision? Some compelling reasons

Why should you be interested in quantum theory applied to cognition and decision? Perhaps you are a physicist who is curious whether or not quantum principles can be applied outside of physics. In fact, that is one purpose of this book. Perhaps you are a cognitive scientist who is interested in representing concepts by vectors in a multidimensional feature space. This is essentially the way quantum theory works too. Perhaps you are a decision scientist who is trying to understand how people make decisions under uncertainty. Quantum theory could provide some interesting new answers. Generally speaking, *quantum theory is a new theory for constructing probabilistic and dynamic systems*, and in this book we apply this new theory to topics in cognition and decision. Later in this chapter we will give some specific examples, but let us step back at this point and try to understand the more general principles that support a quantum approach to cognition and decision.

1.1 Six reasons for a quantum approach to cognition and decision

Quantum physics is arguably the most successful scientific theoretical achievement that humans have ever created. It was created to explain puzzling findings that were impossible to understand using the older classical physical theory, and it achieved this by introducing an entirely new set of revolutionary principles. The older classical physical theory is now seen as a special case of the more general quantum theory. In the process of creating quantum mechanics, physicists also created a new theory of probabilistic and dynamic systems that is more general than the previous classic theory (Pitowski, 1989). This book is not about quantum physics per se, but instead it explores the application of the probabilistic dynamic system created by quantum theory to a new domain – the field of cognition and decision making. Almost all previous modelling in cognitive and decision sciences has relied on principles derived from classical probabilistic dynamic systems. But these fields have also encountered puzzling findings that also seem impossible to understand within this limited framework.

Quantum principles may provide some solutions. Let us examine these principles to see why they may be applicable to the fields of cognition and decision.

1.1.1   Judgments are based on indefinite states

According to many formal models (computational or mathematical) commonly used in cognitive and decision sciences (such as Bayesian networks, or production rules, or connectionist networks), the cognitive system changes from moment to moment, but at any specific moment it is in a definite state with respect to some judgment to be made. To make this clearer, let us take a simple example. Suppose you are a member of a jury and you have just heard conflicting evidence from the prosecutor and defense. Your job is to weigh this evidence and come up with a verdict of guilty or not. Suppose your subjective probability of guilt is expressed on a $p \in [0,1]$ probability scale. Formal cognitive models assume that at each moment you are in a definite state with respect to guilt – say a state that selects a value p such that $p > 0.50$ or a state that produces p such that $p \leq 0.50$ (in other words, p is a function of the current state of the system). Of course, the model does not know what your true state is at each moment, and so the model can only assign a probability to you responding with $p > 0.50$ at that moment. But the model is stochastic only because it does not know exactly what trajectory (definite state at each time point) you are following. A stochastic model postulates a sample space of trajectories, along with a measure that assigns probabilities to sets of trajectories. But according to a stochastic model, once a trajectory is sampled (e.g., once a seed is selected to start a computer simulation), then the system deterministically jumps from one definite state (e.g., respond with $p > 0.50$) to another (e.g., respond with $p \leq 0.50$) or stays put across time. The states are pointwise and dispersion free and probabilities only arise from sampling different trajectories across new replications (e.g., starting the computer simulation over again with a new seed). In this sense, cognitive and decision sciences currently model the cognitive system as if it was a *particle* producing a definite sample path through a state space.

Quantum theory works differently by allowing you to be in an *indefinite* state (formally called a *superposition* state) at each moment in time before a decision is made. Strictly speaking, being in an indefinite or superposition state means that the model *cannot* assume either (a) you are definitely in a guilty state (e.g., a state that responds with $p > 0.50$) or (b) you are definitely in a not guilty state (e.g., respond with $p \leq 0.50$) at some moment. You may be in an indefinite state that allows both of these definite states to have *potential* (technically called state amplitudes) for being expressed at *each* moment (Heisenberg, 1958). (This does *not* mean you are definitely in both states simultaneously at each moment.) Intuitively, if you are in an indefinite state, then you do not necessarily think the person is guilty and at the same time you do not necessarily think the person is not guilty. Instead, you are in a superposition state that leaves you *conflicted, or ambiguous, or confused, or uncertain* about the guilty status. The potential for guilt may be greater than the potential for not guilty at one moment, and these potentials (amplitudes) may change from one moment to the next moment, but both answers are potentially available at *each* moment. In quantum theory, there is *no* single trajectory or sample path across time before making a decision, but instead there is a smearing of potentials across states that flows across time. In this sense, quantum theory allows one to model the cognitive system as if it was a *wave* moving across time over the state space until a decision is made. However, once a decision is reached, and uncertainty is resolved, the state becomes definite as if the wave collapses to a point like a particle. Thus, quantum systems require *both* wave (indefinite) and particle (definite) views of a cognitive system.

We argue that the wave nature of an indefinite state captures the psychological experience of conflict, ambiguity, confusion, and uncertainty; the particle nature of a definite state captures the psychological experience of conflict resolution, decision, and certainty.

1.1.2 Judgments create rather than record

According to many formal models, the cognitive system may be changing from moment to moment, but what we record at a particular moment reflects the state of the system as it existed immediately before we inquired about it. So, for example, formal cognitive models assume that if a person watches a disturbing scene and we ask the person a question such as "Are you afraid?", then the answer reflects the state of the person regarding that question just before we asked it. If instead we asked the person "Are you excited?" then the answer again reflects the state regarding this other question just before we asked it.

One of the more provocative lessons learned from quantum theory is that taking a measurement of a system creates rather than records a property of the system (Peres, 1998). Immediately before asking a question, a quantum system can be in an indefinite state. For example, the person may be ambiguous about his or her feelings after watching a disturbing scene. The answer we obtain from a quantum system is constructed from the interaction of the indefinite state and the question that we ask (Bohr, 1958). This interaction creates a definite state out of an indefinite state. For example, the person may have been ambiguous about their feelings after the disturbing scene, but this state becomes more definite after answering the question about being afraid. If the answer is "Yes, I feel afraid," then the person acts accordingly. This is, in fact, the basis for modern psychological theories of emotion (Schachter & Singer, 1962). Decision scientists also argue that beliefs and preferences are constructed on line rather than simply being read straight out of memory (Payne *et al.*, 1992). For example, a person may initially be in an indefinite state about a set of paintings on display, but if the person is asked to choose one as a gift, then a preference order is constructed on line for the purpose.

We do not wish to argue that every answer to every question involves the construction of an opinion. For many questions you do have a stored answer that is simply retrieved on demand (e.g., Have you ever read a certain book?). But other questions are new and more complex and you have to construct an answer from your current state and context (e.g., Did you like the moral theme of that book?). So we argue that the quantum principle of constructing a reality from an interaction between the person's indefinite state and the question being asked actually matches psychological intuition better for complex judgments than the assumption that the answer simply reflects a preexisting state.

1.1.3 Judgments disturb each other, introducing uncertainty

According to quantum theory, if one starts out in an indefinite state, and is asked a question, then the answer to this question will change the state from an indefinite state to one that is more definite with respect to the question that was asked. But this change in state after the first question then causes one to respond differently to subsequent questions so that the order of questioning becomes important. Consider the following popular example from social psychology. Suppose a teenage boy is directly asked "How happy are you?" the typical answer is "Everything is great." However, if this teenager is first asked "When was the last time you had a date?" then the answer tends to be "Seems like a long time ago." Following this sobering answer, a later question about happiness tends to produce a second answer that is not so sunny and rosy. Thus, the first question sets up a context that changes the answer to the next question. Consequently, we cannot define a joint probability of answers to question A and question B, and instead we can only assign a probability to the sequence of answers to question A followed by question B. In quantum physics, if A and B are two measurements and the probabilities of the outcomes depend on the order measurement, then the two measurements are non-commutative. In physics, for example, measurements of position and momentum along the same direction are non-commutative, but measurements of positions along the horizontal and vertical coordinates are commutative. Many of the mathematical properties of quantum theory arise from developing a probabilistic model for non-commutative measurements, including Heisenberg's (1927) famous uncertainty principle (Heisenberg, 1958).

Order effects are also responsible for introducing uncertainty into a person's judgments. If the first question A produces an answer that creates a definite state with respect to that question, the state created by A may be indefinite with respect to a different question B. Consider the following consumer choice example. Suppose a man is considering the purchase of a new car and two different brands are in contention: a BMW versus a Cadillac. If he directly asks himself what he prefers, he definitely answers with the BMW. But if he first asks himself what his wife prefers (she definitely wants the Cadillac) and subsequently asks himself what he prefers (after taking on his wife's perspective), then he becomes uncertain about his own preference. In this example, the question about his wife's preference disturbs and creates uncertainty about his own preference. Thus, it may be *impossible* to be in a definite state with respect to two different questions, because a definite state (technically speaking an eigenstate) for one is an indefinite state (superposition) for another. In this case, the questions are said to be *incompatible* and the incompatibility of questions is mathematically implemented by the non-commutativity of quantum measurements. Question order effects are a major concern for attitude researchers, who seek a theoretical understanding of these effects similar to that achieved in quantum theory (Feldman & Lynch, 1988).

1.1.4 Judgments do not always obey classic logic

The classic probability theory used in current cognitive and decision models is derived from the Kolmogorov axioms (Kolmogorov, 1933/1950). These axioms assign probabilities to events defined as sets. Consequently, the family of sets in the Kolmogorov theory obeys the Boolean axioms of logic. Thus, Boolean logic lies at the foundation of current probabilistic models of cognition and decision making. One important axiom of Boolean logic is the distributive axiom: if $\{G, T, F\}$ are events then $G \cap (T \cup F) = (G \cap T) \cup (G \cap F)$. Consider, for example, the concept that a boy is good (G) and the pair of concepts the boy told the truth (T) and the boy did not tell truth (falsehood, F). Suppose you are trying to decide if the boy is good but you do not know if he is truthful. According to Boolean logic, the event G can only occur in one of two ways: either $(G \cap T)$ occurs or $(G \cap F)$ exclusively. This means there are only two mutually exclusive and exhaustive ways for you to think the boy is good: he is good and truthful or he is good and he is not truthful.

From this distributive axiom, one can derive the law of total probability. Define $p(G)$ as the probability of event G, $p(T)$ is the probability of event T, $p(F)$ is the probability of event F, $p(G|T)$ is the probability of event G conditioned on knowing event T, and $p(G|F)$ is the probability of event G conditioned on knowing event F. Then the law of total probability follows from

$$p(G) = p\left((G \cap T) \cup (G \cap F)\right) = p\left(G \cap T\right) + p(G \cap F))$$
$$= p(G)p(G|T) + p(F)p(G|F).$$

This law provides the foundation for inferences with Bayes nets. The law of total probability is violated by the results of the disjunction experiment and the category – decision-making experiment in psychology and the two-slit type of experiments in physics, all of which we describe later in this chapter.

Quantum probability theory is derived from the von Neumann axioms (von Neumann, 1932/1955). These axioms assign probabilities to events defined as subspaces of a vector space (more on this in Chapter 2). The definite states form the basis for the vector space, and an indefinite or superposition state can be any point within this vector space. An important consequence of using subspaces is that the logic of subspaces does not obey the distributive axiom of Boolean logic (Hughes, 1989). For example, according to quantum logic, when you try to decide whether a boy is good without knowing if he is truthful or not, you are *not* forced to have only two thoughts: he is good and he is truthful or he is good and he is not truthful. You can have other ambiguous thoughts represented by a superposition over the truthful or not truthful attributes.

The fact that quantum logic does not always obey the distributive axiom implies that the quantum model does not always obey the law of total probability (Khrennikov, 2010). This is why the quantum model can explain the results of the disjunction experiment in psychology and the two-slit experiment in physics. Thus, quantum logic is a generalization of classic logic and quantum probability is a generalized probability theory. We argue that classic logic and classic probability theory are too restrictive to explain human judgments and decisions.

1.1.5   Judgments do not obey the principle of unicity

The classic (Kolmogorov) probability theory, which is used in current cognitive and decision models, is based on the principle of *unicity* (Griffiths, 2003). A single sample space is proposed which provides a complete and exhaustive description of all events that can happen in an experiment.[1] This follows from the Boolean algebra used in classic theory: if A is an event and B is another event from an experiment, then $A \cap B$ must be an event too, and repeated application of this principle leads to intersections that cannot be broken down any further (the atoms or elements or points of the sample space). All events can be described by unions of the atoms or elements or points of the sample space. If you think about this for a while, this is a tremendous constraint on a theory. We argue that it is oversimplifying the extremely complex nature of our world.

Let us examine the consequence of assuming unicity for experiments on human probability judgments. Suppose we do an experiment in which we ask a person to describe the likelihood of various future events with respect to future political history. Perhaps a person has the knowledge to do this within a single sample space. But then we can also ask the same person to describe the likelihood of future events with respect to progress in science. Now it becomes quite a stretch to imagine that the person is able to assign joint probabilities to all historical and scientific events. Instead, the person might need to fall back on one description of events (one sample space) for political futures, but use a different description of events (another sample space) for future scientific progress. To go even further, we could ask about the likelihood of events concerning the romantic and marital relations of Hollywood movie stars. Surely we have passed the capacity of the person who would have little or no idea about how to combine all three of these topics into a unified sample space that assigns joint probabilities to all three kinds of events.[2]

Quantum probability does not assume the principle of unicity (Griffiths, 2003). This assumption is broken as soon as we allow incompatible questions into the theory which cause measurements to be non-commutative (Primas, 2007).

---

[1] Kolmogorov realized that different sample spaces are needed for different experiments, but his theory does not provide a coherent principle for relating these separate experiments. This is exactly what quantum probability theory is designed to do.

[2] One could try to assume independence between questions about history, science, and Hollywood movie stars. But independence is also an overly severe restriction to impose on human judgments.

Incompatible questions cannot be evaluated on the same basis, so that they require setting up separate sample spaces. Quantum theory allows one to use a partial Boolean algebra: one sample space can be used to answer a first set of questions in a Boolean way and another sample space can be used to answer a different set of questions in a Boolean way, but both Boolean subalgebras are pasted together in a coherent but non-Boolean way. This provides more flexibility for assigning probabilities to events, and it does not require forming all possible joint probabilities, which is a property we believe is needed to understand the full complexity of human cognition and decision.

1.1.6   Cognitive phenomena may not be decomposable

In cognitive science, researchers often take the approach to model a cognitive process for a task by proposing a large collection of random variables, but what is actually observed only corresponds to a small subset of these variables for any single experimental condition. A single *complete* joint distribution, which is a joint probability distribution across all the random variables, is then assumed to exist that can be used to determine the observed marginalized distributions for any subset of variables. This seemingly straightforward and innocuous theoretical approach is what the quantum physicists questioned when trying to experimentally test the existence of quantum entanglement. Entanglement is a surprising phenomenon in which two seemingly distinct and separated systems behave as one – these systems are sometimes referred to as "quantum correlated." It turned out that when systems are entangled it is not possible to construct such a *complete* joint distribution. Intuitively, this result suggests there is an extreme form of dependencies between the systems which goes beyond the dependencies derived from traditional probability theory. Since the initial probabilistic models were developed for the entanglement experiments, there has been a large body of literature explaining the general probabilistic foundations of quantum correlations. This has resulted in analysis methods that are general enough for application to cognitive science. A note of caution, however: assuming the existence of quantum correlations in cognitive phenomena is certainly highly speculative. There is, however, a steadily growing body of pioneering literature putting forward this view. But what do these quantum correlations entail for our cognitive models?

In cognitive science, and science in general, reductionism has been a powerful background philosophy underlying model development. By this we mean the assumption that phenomena can be analyzed by considering their different components separately, and then synthesizing the results obtained. Phenomena, or systems, that can be understood this way are deemed "decomposable." Non-decomposable systems cannot be so straightforwardly understood. The majority of models in cognitive science are decomposable, as they are understood in terms of their constituent parts and how these are related. For example, consider the spreading activation model of words in human memory. Even though the network structure may feature a high degree of interrelationship, the nodes (i.e., the words) are still considered as discrete components in the model. Many models in cognitive science are like this. However, is reductionism always appropriate when modelling cognition? Quantum correlations which appear in cognitive phenomena suggest that this assumption can at least be questioned in specific situations. For example, when a word is studied in a memory experiment, there is a view that a word's associative network arises in synchrony with the word being studied. The intuition behind this view is very similar to that of quantum entanglement – the study word and its associates are behaving as one. The existence of quantum correlations suggests the cognitive model in question is not decomposable in the way we initially assumed and formalized via a particular set of random variables. It forces us to rethink very differently the nature of the phenomena being modelled.

Now that we have identified some general reasons for considering a quantum approach to cognition and decision, let us take a quick look at some simple examples of paradoxical findings from cognition and decision and give a brief idea about how quantum theory can be applied.

1.2   Four examples from cognition and decision

1.2.1   The disjunction effect

The first example is a phenomenon discovered by Amos Tversky and Eldar Shafir called the disjunction effect (Tversky & Shafir, 1992). It was discovered in the process of testing a rational axiom of decision theory called the sure thing principle (Savage, 1954). According to the sure thing principle, if under state of the world X you prefer action A over B, and if under the complementary state of the world ˜X you also prefer action A over B, then you should prefer action A over B even when you do not know the state of the world. For example, suppose you are trying to decide whether or not to make a risky investment right before a presidential election with only two parties, Democrat versus Republican. Assume that if the Democrats win, then you prefer to invest; also, if the Republicans win, then you prefer to invest. Therefore, you should invest without knowing the election outcome. Tversky and Shafir experimentally tested this principle by presenting students with a two-stage gamble; that is, a gamble which can be played twice. At each stage the decision was whether or not to play a gamble that has an equal chance of winning $200 or losing $100 (the real amount won or lost was actually $2.00 and $1.00 respectively). The key result is based on the decision for the second play, after finishing the first play. The experiment included three conditions: one in which the students were informed that they already won the first gamble, a second condition in which they were informed that they lost the first gamble, and a third in which they did not know the outcome of the first gamble. If they knew they won the first gamble, the majority (69%) chose to play again; if they knew they lost the first gamble, then again the majority (59%) chose to play again; but if they did not know whether they won or lost, then the majority chose not to play (only 36% wanted to play again). What went wrong here? Only one of two

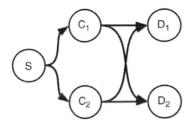

Figure 1.1 Diagram of double-slit experiment showing that a photon, starting from state S, can travel two channels (C_1 or C_2) before hitting one of two detectors (D_1 or D_2).

possible events can occur during the first play: win or lose. These students generally preferred to play if they won and they also preferred to play if they lost. So why do they prefer not to play when they do not know whether they won or lost?

Tversky and Shafir explained the finding in terms of choice based on reasons as follows. If the person knew they won, then they had extra house money with which to play and for this reason they chose to play again; if the person knew they had lost, then they needed to recover their losses and for this other reason they chose to play again; but if they did not know the outcome of the game, then these two reasons did not emerge into their minds. Why not? If the first play is unknown, it must definitely be either a win or a loss, and it cannot be anything else. We try to explain this in more detail in Chapter 9, but let us give a hint here.

Researchers working with quantum models see this finding as an example of an interference effect similar to that found in the double-slit type of experiments conducted in particle physics. Although we do not wish to present a whole lot of physics here, it is worthwhile to briefly discuss this one simple example to compare the experimental design and the statistical results produced by the disjunction experiment in psychology and the double-slit experiment in physics (technically, this description corresponds to a Mach–Zehnder interferometer experiment). Referring to Figure 1.1, a *single* photon is dispersed from a light source (S in the figure) and it is split by a beam splitter off into one of two channels (C_1 and C_2 in the figure) from which it eventually can reach one of two detectors (D_1 or D_2 in the figure). Two conditions are examined: for one condition, the channel through which the photon passes is observed, and for the other condition it is not. The results are the following. When the channels are observed, a single photon either definitely goes through the upper channel or definitely goes through the lower channel, and you never find parts of photons going through both channels. If the photon is observed to pass through the upper channel C_1, then there is a 50% chance of reaching the upper detector D_1; likewise, if the photon is observed to pass through the lower channel C_2, then again there is a 50% chance of reaching the upper detector D_1.

Now consider what happens when the channels are unobserved. Only a single particle ever enters and exits this system, and according to classic probability there is a 0.5 chance of it reflecting off in either direction; so when the channel is not observed, we still should expect 50% of the photons to reach detector D_1. However, in fact, the probability of reaching the upper detector D_1 drops to zero and the probability of reaching the lower channel rises to one. Something is wrong again here! But experimental results are never wrong, so it is our classic thinking that is wrong. Instead, what happens when the channel is unobserved is that the photon enters a superposition state – it is superposed between the two channels. From this superposition state, it cannot make the transition to detector D_1 and must always go to detector D_2. This is an example of an extreme case of interference, and less extreme cases can occur depending on the phases assigned to two channels. We will not go further into the physics to show how this is computed here. Instead, we will wait to see how the probability for the superposition state is computed in a later decision-making example.

By observing the channel through which the photon passes, we break down the superposition state into one of the definite states. The difference between the probability obtained under conditions of no observation versus the probability obtained under conditions of observation is called the *interference* effect. The main point is that interference lowers the probability of being detected at D_1 for the unobserved case far below each of the probabilities for each of the observed conditions. Quantum probability theory was designed to explain these bizarre statistics, which it succeeds in doing extremely well.

At this point, the analogy between the disjunction experiment and the double-slit type of experiment should be clear. Both cases involve two possible paths: in the disjunction experiment, the two paths are inferring the outcome of either a win or a loss with the first gamble; for the double-slit experiment, the two paths are splitting the photon off into the upper or lower channel by a beam splitter. In both experiments, the path taken can be known (observed) or unknown (unobserved). Finally, in both cases, under the unknown (unobserved) condition, the probability (of gambling for the disjunction experiment, of detection at D_1 for the double-slit experiment) falls far below each of the probabilities for the known (observed) cases. So can we speculate that for the disjunction experiment, under the unknown condition, instead of definitely being in the win or loss state, the student enters a superposition state that prevents finding a reason for choosing the gamble? One cannot help but wonder whether the mathematical model that succeeds so well to explain interference statistics in physics could also explain interference statistics in psychology. Let us look at another example to broaden the range of application a little and go into a bit more detail about how the quantum model mathematically works.

1.2.2   Interference of categorization on decision making

James Townsend (Townsend *et al.*, 2000) introduced a new paradigm to study the interactions between categorization and decision making, which we

Table 1.1 Empirical results for narrow face condition

C-then-D					D-alone
$p(G)$	$p(A\|G)$	$p(B)$	$p(A\|B)$	$p_\text{T}(A)$	$p(A)$
0.17	0.41	0.83	0.63	0.59	0.69

discovered is highly suitable for testing Markov and quantum models. We (Busemeyer *et al.*, 2009) recently replicated and extended their earlier work using the following experimental methods. On each trial, participants were shown pictures of faces, which varied along two dimensions (face width and lip thickness). Two different distributions of faces were used: on average, a "narrow" face distribution had a narrow width and thick lips; on average, a "wide" face distribution had a wide width and thin lips. The participants were asked to categorize the faces as belonging to either a "good guy" or "bad guy" group, and/or they were asked to decide whether to take an "attack" or "withdraw" action. The primary manipulation was produced by using the following two test conditions, presented on different trials, to each participant. In the C-then-D condition, participants made a categorization followed by an action decision; in the D-alone condition, participants only made an action decision. In total, 26 undergraduate students from a Midwest university participated in the study, and each person participated for six blocks of C–D trials with 34 trials per block, and one block of D-alone trials with 34 trials per block. Little or no learning was observed (because instructions provided all of the necessary information) and so the C–D trials were pooled across blocks. This example is discussed in more detail in Chapter 8, but the empirical results for the narrow face condition are shown in Table 1.1.

The columns labeled $p(G)$ and $p(B)$ show the probability of categorizing the narrow face as a "good guy" versus "bad guy" and the columns labeled $p(A|G)$ and $p(A|B)$ show the probability of attacking conditioned on being a "good guy" or a "bad guy" respectively. The last column, labeled $p(A)$, shows the probability of attacking under the D-alone condition. The column labeled $p_\text{T}(A)$ is the total probability, which is computed by the well-known formula

$$p_\text{T}(A) = p(G) \cdot p(A|G) + p(B) \cdot p(A|B). \tag{1.1}$$

Townsend and colleagues originally proposed a very simple Markov model for this task, and Figure 1.2 illustrates the basic idea (which is just the double-slit figure with the labels changed). The person starts in a state labeled S determined by the presentation of the narrow face. From this state the person can transit $S \to G$ to the "good guy" state labeled G with probability $p(G|S)$ or transit $S \to B$ to the "bad guy" state labeled B with probability $p(B|S)$. From state G the person can transit $G \to A$ to the "attack" state A with probability $p(A|G)$, or transit $G \to W$ to the "withdraw" state labeled W with probability $p(W|G)$. Alternatively, from the B state the person can transit $B \to A$ to the "attack" state A with probability $p(A|B)$, or transit $B \to W$ to the "withdraw" state labeled W with probability $p(W|B)$.

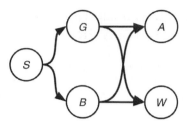

Figure 1.2 Diagram representing category – decision-making task. Starting from a face, the person can categorize it as good or bad and then decide to attack or withdraw.

These transition probabilities can all be estimated from the C–D conditions and the results are shown in Table 1.1. The critical prediction concerns the probability of attacking in the D-alone condition. According to the Markov model, this cognitive system can only travel through one of two definite paths. Thus, the probability should equal the probability of the path $S \rightarrow G \rightarrow A$ plus the probability of the path $S \rightarrow B \rightarrow A$. The path probability for $S \rightarrow G \rightarrow A$ equals the product of the transition probabilities along the branches, $p(G|S){\cdot}p(A|G)$; in the same manner, the path probability for $S \rightarrow B \rightarrow A$ equals $p(B|S) \cdot p(A|B)$; and the total probability is then given by Eq. (1.1). According to the law of total probability, the attack probability in the D-alone condition should be a weighted average of the two probabilities of attacking conditioned on each categorization state. In other words, we should always find $p(A|G) \leq p(A) \leq p(A|B)$. However, when we look at the results in Table 1.1, we see that $p(A)$ substantially exceeds $p_T(A)$. More dramatic is the fact that the probability of attacking in the D-alone condition is even greater than the probability of attacking after categorizing the face as a "bad guy" so that $p(A) > p(A|B)$. What went wrong here? This is a case where we have a positive interference effect. (Of course, the probability of withdrawal, $p(W) = 1 - p(A)$, exhibits a negative interference effect as found earlier, and so the sign simply depends on which final response we select.)

How does a quantum model explain these results? The quantum model works in a manner very similar to the Markov model if we replace the probability of transiting from X to Y, denoted $p(Y|X)$, with something called the amplitude for transiting from X to Y, denoted $\langle Y|X \rangle$. The strange thing about an amplitude is that it can be a complex number (more on this in Chapter 2), which is clearly not a probability. In the end, however, a complex amplitude can be converted into a probability by taking its squared magnitude, $p(Y|X) = |\langle Y|X \rangle|^2$, which by design is always between zero and one inclusive.

A very simple quantum model for this task is also based on Figure 1.2. The person starts in a state labeled S determined by the presentation of the narrow face. From this state the person can transit to either the "good guy" state labeled G with amplitude $\langle G|S \rangle$ or the "bad guy" state labeled B with amplitude $\langle B|S \rangle$. From state G the person can transit to the "attack" state A with probability $\langle A|G \rangle$, or transit to the "withdraw" state labeled W with amplitude $\langle W|G \rangle$. Alternatively, from the B state the person can transit to the "attack" state A with amplitude $\langle A|B \rangle$, or transit to the "withdraw" state labeled W with amplitude $\langle W|B \rangle$.

Let us initially analyze the quantum model using Feynman's path diagram rules (Feynman *et al.*, 1965), which provide more of a dynamic view of the quantum model (the next example will use geometric rules, which are mathematically equivalent). Feynman's first rule asserts that the amplitude for a path is the product of the amplitudes for each transition along the path. Therefore, the amplitude for the $S \to G \to A$ path equals $\langle G|S \rangle \cdot \langle A|G \rangle$ and the amplitude for the $S \to B \to A$ path equals $\langle B|S \rangle \cdot \langle A|B \rangle$. So far this is just like the Markov model with amplitudes replacing probabilities.

Feynman's next two rules concern the way to compute the probability of transiting from a state S to another state A by way of many possible paths. In our example, we only have the two paths shown in Figure 1.2.

Feynman's second rule asserts that if we do not observe which path was followed from a state S to a state A (i.e., the system remains in a superposition state over paths, which is true for condition D-alone in this application), then first we sum the path amplitudes across all possible paths and then we take the squared magnitude of this sum. In this case we sum the two path amplitudes and square this to obtain

$$p(S \to A) = |\langle G|S \rangle \cdot \langle A|G \rangle + \langle B|S \rangle \cdot \langle A|B \rangle|^2 \qquad (1.2)$$
$$= |\langle G|S \rangle|^2 \cdot |\langle A|G \rangle|^2 + |\langle B|S \rangle|^2 \cdot |\langle A|B \rangle|^2$$
$$+ 2 \cdot |\langle G|S \rangle \langle A|G \rangle \langle B|S \rangle \langle A|B \rangle| \cdot \cos(\theta).$$

(The expansion of the first line into the second line of the above equation will be explained in more detail in Chapter 2.) This is the formula that should be used in the D-alone condition, because we do not observe the path that the person takes to make the final decision. The quantity $\langle A|S \rangle = \langle G|S \rangle \cdot \langle A|G \rangle + \langle B|S \rangle \cdot \langle A|B \rangle$ is called the law of total amplitude (Gudder, 1988).

Feynman's third rule asserts that if we observe the path that was followed (i.e., we break down the superposition state into one of the definite paths), then the probability of the transition from $S \to A$ is obtained by first converting each path amplitude into a path probability and then summing the path probabilities across all possible paths. In our example, we simply sum path probabilities across the two paths in Figure 1.2 to obtain

$$p(S \to A) = |\langle A|S \rangle|^2 = |\langle G|S \rangle \cdot \langle A|G \rangle|^2 + |\langle B|S \rangle \cdot \langle A|B \rangle|^2 \qquad (1.3)$$
$$= |\langle G|S \rangle|^2 \cdot |\langle A|G \rangle|^2 + |\langle B|S \rangle|^2 \cdot |\langle A|B \rangle|^2.$$

This is the formula that should be used for the C–D condition, because we observe the path that the person takes to make the final decision. Well this is just the law of total probability written down in terms of squared amplitudes.

The result in the second line of Eq. (1.2) almost looks like the law of total probability expressed as squared amplitudes as in Eq. (1.3), except for the third term, which is called the interference term. The cosine part of that term comes from the phase of the complex product $\langle G|S \rangle \langle A|G \rangle \langle B|S \rangle \langle A|B \rangle$, which we will discuss more in Chapter 2. For now we just point out that this cosine can range from -1 to 0 to $+1$, producing negative, zero, or positive interference. If the cosine is zero, then the quantum model reduces to the Markov model and they make exactly the same predictions. By the way, this is exactly the same mathematics used to determine the interference effect for the double-slit example from physics presented earlier.

Thus, the law of total probability applies when we observe the paths, but the law of total amplitude applies when we do not. This probability law may seem strange, but Feynman recommends that you do not ask why it works this way or "you will go down the drain." It just works, and because he cannot explain why, he recommends making it an axiom.

Let us plug in some numbers to see how this works more concretely. We can set $\langle G|S \rangle = \sqrt{0.17}$ and $\langle B|S \rangle = \sqrt{0.83}$ to reproduce $p(G)$ and $p(B)$ exactly; we can also set $\langle A|G \rangle = \sqrt{0.40}$ and $\langle A|B \rangle = \sqrt{0.60}$, which then implies that $\langle W|G \rangle = \sqrt{0.60}$ and $\langle W|B \rangle = \sqrt{0.40}$ (because $|\langle A|G \rangle|^2 + |\langle W|G \rangle|^2 = 1 = |\langle A|B \rangle|^2 + |\langle W|B \rangle|^2$). This reproduces the results for $p(A|G)$ and $p(A|B)$ from the C–D condition fairly accurately (we cannot fit these results perfectly with this quantum model because these amplitudes must satisfy a unitary property discussed later in Chapter 2). The critical issue is to reproduce the results obtained from the D-alone condition using Eq. (1.2). This is achieved by solving for the cosine term. If we set $\cos(\theta) = 0.33$, and plug this into Eq. (1.2), along with the other amplitudes that we selected earlier, then the model reproduces $p(A)$ in Table 1.1. Mathematically speaking, this is how the quantum model reproduces the interference effect.

Of course, we do not expect you to be very impressed at this point for several good reasons. First and foremost is that we simply post hoc fit the parameters to the data. (Initially, this is what quantum physicists had to do to determine the cosine for spin.) Surely we need more conditions to really test the model. However, once the cosine has been determined, we can manipulate any one of the probabilities for the C–D condition in the task to obtain a number of new experimental conditions, and then we can obtain stronger a priori tests of the model for the D-alone condition.

A second reason for questioning this analysis is that we did not gain much psychological insight yet from the model. All we know is that, for condition D-alone, we cannot assume the person follows a definite path (definitely infer good guy or definitely infer bad guy), and instead we postulate that the person enters a superposition state which is superposed over good and bad. But how does this determine the transition amplitudes and the cosine? The next example tries to give more insight into the way transition amplitudes are constructed.

1.2.3   The conjunction fallacy

For a third example, let us consider an important probability judgment error, called the conjunction fallacy, which is based on the famous "Linda" problem

(Tversky & Kahneman, 1983). (Many different types of stories have been used in past research, but this story is the most famous of all.) Judges are provided a brief story about a woman named Linda, who used to be a philosophy student at a liberal university and who used to be active in an anti-nuclear movement. Then the judge is asked to rank the likelihood of the following events: that Linda is now (a) active in the feminist movement, (b) a bank teller, (c) active in the feminist movement and a bank teller, (d) active in the feminist movement and not a bank teller, and (e) active in the feminist movement or a bank teller. The conjunction fallacy occurs when option c is judged to be more likely than option b (even though the latter contains the former), and the disjunction fallacy occurs when option a is judged to be more likely than option e (again, the latter contains the former). Surprisingly, people (students from Stanford, professional medical doctors, etc.) frequently produce conjunction and disjunction fallacies for the Linda problem and many other problems as well (Tversky & Kahneman, 1983). We focus on the conjunction fallacy here, but both fallacies as well as other probability judgment errors are analyzed with more generality in Chapter 4.

For this application, we will use a geometric approach to quantum theory, which is mathematically equivalent to Feynman's rules, but gives more insight about how to assign amplitudes to transitions between states.[3] We will use a very simple two-dimensional model here (Franco, 2009a), but see Chapter 4 for a more general N-dimensional model. Figure 1.3 provides a simple geometric model for the conjunction fallacy. In this problem there are two questions: the feminism question and the bank teller question. For each question, there are two answers: yes or no.

The first principle is to represent the two answers to the feminism question by two orthogonal rays that span a two-dimensional space. In the figure, the answer yes to feminism is represented by the ray labeled F and the answer no to the feminism question is represented by an orthogonal ray labeled $\tilde{\ }F$. The person's initial belief about the feminism question, which is generated from the Linda story, can then be represented as a (unit-length) vector (labeled S in the figure) within the two-dimensional space spanned by these two rays. Note that the initial state vector S is close to the ray for yes to feminism, which matches the description in the Linda story.

The second principle is that the amplitude $\langle F|S \rangle$ for transiting from the initial state S to the ray F equals the projection of the state S onto the F ray, which is the point on the F ray that intersects with the line extending up from the S state in the top panel. The squared amplitude equals the probability of saying yes to the feminism question starting from the initial state, and this is equal to $|\langle F|S \rangle|^2 = 0.9755$ in the figure.

The advantage of using a vector space is that we can rotate the axes to form a new basis for representing the bank teller question within the same two-dimensional space. In the figure, the bank teller question is represented by two

---

[3]Sloman (1993) earlier introduced the idea of using geometric projections to model probability judgments.

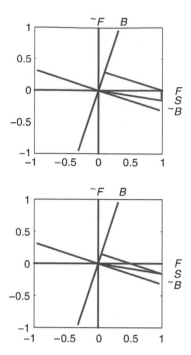

Figure 1.3 The top panel shows projections for feminist and bank teller conjunction event; the bottom panel is for single bank teller event. $F =$ yes to feminist, $\tilde{\ }F =$ no to feminist, $B =$ yes to bank teller, $\tilde{\ }B =$ no to bank teller, $S =$ initial state.

orthogonal rays labeled B and $\tilde{\ }B$ which are rotated so that $\tilde{\ }B$ is 20° below F. This means that being a feminist and not being a bank teller are also close in this belief space. Note that the same initial state S, which is close to F, is also far away from the B ray (S is close to the orthogonal ray $\tilde{\ }B$). The amplitude $\langle B|S\rangle$ for transiting from the initial state S to the ray B equals the projection of the state S onto the B ray, which is illustrated by the point along the B ray that intersects with the line segment extending from S up to B in the bottom figure. The squared amplitude equals the probability of saying yes to the bank teller question starting from the initial state, and this is equal to $|\langle B|S\rangle|^2 = 0.0245$ in the figure.

Now let us consider the sequence of answers in which the person says yes to the feminism question and then says yes to the bank teller question in that order. The order that questions are processed is critical for quantum theory, and here we are assuming that the more likely event is evaluated first. The third principle is that the amplitude for this sequence of answers equals the amplitude for the path $S \to F \to B$, and the latter equals the product of amplitudes $\langle B|F\rangle \cdot \langle F|S\rangle$. The first transition is from the initial state S to the ray F, and the second transition is from the state F to the state B. The path $S \to F \to B$ is illustrated in the top figure. The amplitude $\langle F|S\rangle$ is the projection from S to F in the figure, which has a squared magnitude equal to $|\langle F|S\rangle|^2 = 0.9755$; and the amplitude $\langle B|F\rangle$ is the projection from the (unit-length) basis vector aligned with F to the B ray in the figure, which has a squared magnitude equal to $|\langle B|F\rangle|^2 = 0.0955$. The probability for the sequence equals the squared amplitude for the path $|\langle B|F\rangle \cdot \langle F|S\rangle|^2 = (0.9755)(0.0955) = 0.0932$. Note that this probability exceeds the probability of saying yes to bank teller when starting from the initial state based on the story, $|\langle B|S\rangle|^2 = 0.0245$. In conclusion, this simple geometric model reproduces the basic facts about the conjunction fallacy. What does this mean psychologically?

Psychologically speaking, starting from the Linda story, it is very difficult to think of Linda as a bank teller, and thus the transition directly from S to B is very low. But if the person first judges whether or not Linda is a feminist and the answer is likely to be yes, then, from this feminist perspective, it becomes easier to imagine a feminist as a bank teller. Thus, the indirect path $S \to F \to B$ is more likely than the direct path $S \to B$.

The direct transition $S \to B$ does not force the person to become definite about the feminism question. Thus, the person can remain in a superposed state with respect to this question. The conjunction forces the person to become definite about the feminism question before answering the bank teller question. Thus, this example again demonstrates negative interference with respect to the bank teller question: if we compare (a) the probability of saying yes to the bank teller question without forcing any definite answer to the question about feminism with (b) the likelihood of saying yes to the bank teller question after forcing a definite answer to the question about feminism, then we find the latter is greater than the former. In other words, the conjunction question forces the person to form a definite opinion about feminism which breaks down the superposition state between yes versus no to feminism, which eventually increases the likelihood of saying yes.

This example also shows how the quantum model produces question order effects that are observed in attitude research. Note that the probability of the sequence for the order "yes to bank teller and then yes to feminism" is quite different than the probability for the opposite order. The bank teller first sequence has a probability equal to $|\langle F|B\rangle \cdot \langle B|S\rangle|^2 = (0.0955)(0.0245) = 0.00234$, which is much smaller than the feminism first sequence $|\langle B|F\rangle \cdot \langle F|S\rangle|^2 = (0.9755)(0.0955) = 0.0932$. This order effect follows from the fact that we introduced a property of incompatibility between the feminism question and the bank teller question. This was introduced by assuming that the person is able to answer the feminism question using one basis $\{F, \tilde{F}\}$, but the person requires using a different basis $\{B, \tilde{B}\}$ for answering the bank teller question (as shown in Figure 1.3). This representation implies that if we are definite with respect to the feminism question (in other words our belief state vector S is lined up with the ray F), then we must be indefinite with respect to the bank teller question (because F and B are not orthogonal). Similarly, if we are definite with respect to the bank teller question, then we must be indefinite with respect to the feminism question. This is essentially the Heisenberg uncertainty principle.

Given that the questions are treated as incompatible, we must also be violating unicity. We are assuming that the person is unable to form a single description (i.e., sample space) containing all of the possible conjunctions $\{F \wedge B, F \wedge {}^{\sim}B, {}^{\sim}F \wedge B, {}^{\sim}F \wedge {}^{\sim}B\}$. In other words, perhaps the person never thought about conjunctions involving feminism and bank tellers sufficiently to assign probabilities to all these conjunctions. Instead, the person relies on two separate sample spaces: one based on elementary events $\{F, {}^{\sim}F\}$ for which they are familiar and a second based on elementary events $\{B, {}^{\sim}B\}$ for which they are also familiar. If we did assume unicity in this example, then we could not explain the conjunction fallacy, because the joint probabilities can be defined under unicity, and they will always be less than (or equal to) the marginal probabilities. Therefore, to explain the results, we require a violation of unicity.

1.2.4   Modelling the semantics of concept combinations

Conceptual processing lies at the basis of a range of cognitive information processing functions; for example, classifying instances into categories, inference, explanation, planning, for language understanding and production. Research into concepts has generally focused on gaining an understanding of how concepts play a role in these functions. Key to this research is how concepts are represented; for example, as exemplars, prototypes, definitions. In cognitive science, as well as in fields such as computational linguistics, information retrieval, and machine learning, vector representations have been used to represent individual words corresponding to concepts. The principle of semantic compositionality states the meaning of a (syntactically complex) whole is a function only of the meanings of its (syntactic) parts together with the manner in which these parts were combined. As it is often assumed that language adheres to this principle, it is then also assumed that semantics of concept combinations must be compositional. Therefore, the semantics of concept combinations should be some function of the semantics of its constituent concepts. The "principle of compositionality" has been attributed to philosopher and logician Gottlob Frege and underpins the semantics of logical languages, and by this fact has made its way into logical approaches to natural language semantics; for example, Montague semantics. Aligned with this are positions held in cognitive science that concepts, as basic cognitive constructs, are and must be compositional.

Consider the bi-ambiguous concept combination "Apple suit." Seen in isolation it could refer to a suit made of apples, or a legal procedure against the Apple corporation. Assume that "apple" (fruit or computer) and "suit" (clothing or computer corporation) are ambiguous concepts. Possible interpretations can be modelled as a joint probability distribution across senses by running experiments asking subjects to give their interpretation. This idea could be extended to include priming the subjects before they are asked to give an interpretation;

		suit		
		B1(vest)	B2(scandal)	
		+1 −1	+1 −1	
A1(computer)	+1	0.13 0	0.31 0.08	
	−1	0.87 0	0 0.61	
A2(banana)	+1	1 0	0 1	
	−1	0 0.	0 0	

apple

$$\begin{array}{c} \\ A1\text{(computer)} \\ \\ A2\text{(banana)} \end{array} \begin{array}{c} +1 \\ -1 \\ +1 \\ -1 \end{array} \left(\begin{array}{cc|cc} 0.13 & 0 & 0.31 & 0.08 \\ 0.87 & 0 & 0 & 0.61 \\ \hline 1 & 0 & 0 & 1 \\ 0 & 0. & 0 & 0 \end{array} \right)$$

Figure 1.4 "Apple suit" $(n = 116)$.

for example, a subject may be asked to study the word "banana," which would prime the fruit sense of the concept "apple." In this way, pairwise joint probability distributions across the senses can be constructed whether the prime influenced the sense of the given concept $(+1)$ or not (-1). Figure 1.4 depicts four joint probability distributions based on such priming. For example, when the subjects have been primed with "banana" and "clothing," there is a a 100% chance they will interpret the combination "apple suit" with "apple" being interpreted as fruit and "suit" as clothing, e.g., a suit made of apples, or a suit with apple color, etc. Thus far, there is nothing particularly unusual about such an experimental framework. What is unusual in the framework is that the same idea is used to analyze the entanglement of quantum particles where polarizer settings for photons have the role of primes. It turns out that "apple suit" exhibits a quantum statistical profile. As a consequence, "apple" and "suit" cannot be validly modelled as separate parts, which is at odds with the principle of semantic compositionality. The issue of compositionality and concepts will be further taken up in Chapter 5.

This concludes our preview showing how the same quantum principles can help explain four completely different puzzling phenomena: the disjunction effect, the categorization–decision interference effect, the conjunction fallacy, and conceptual entanglements. There are other findings as well, including interference effects found in perception (Conte *et al.*, 2009) and overextension effects found in category membership judgments (Aerts & Gabora, 2005). These findings have remained puzzling for many years; and, moreover, they have never been linked together by a common theory before this. We realize that these are just a handful of examples, and by themselves this may not be so convincing yet. Certainly we can never *prove* that a quantum model is necessary to explain these phenomena, and we can only compare the quantum model with other competitors and build an accumulation of support across empirical applications. In the remainder of this book, we examine these problems in more depth as well as present numerous other applications to build a stronger case for the quantum model. At this point let us position this program of building quantum models for cognition and decision within a larger scope of previous research programs relating neuroscience, psychology, and computer science to quantum theory.

1.3   Some history and a broader picture

1.3.1   A brief history

The history of quantum physics makes an amazingly interesting story.[4] Because many cognitive and decision scientists may be unfamiliar with it, we provide a very brief synopsis here. The story begins in 1900 with Max Planck's explanation for black body radiation. Planck tried to unify the known radiation laws of Wien and Rayleigh–Jeans for the limits of high and low frequencies, respectively, and saw that this unification was only possible by introducing discrete energies, ultimately boiling down to the so-called Planck action h. With his very conservative personality, Planck was reluctant to put this revolutionary idea forward. Only because it turned out to be without alternative – an "act of desperation" as he himself later called it – he published it in 1900. Another decisive step was Albert Einstein's explanation for the photo-electric effect based on Planck's energy quanta hypothesis. Long ago Isaac Newton argued that light was made of discrete particles, called corpuscles, but Robert Hooke proposed a wave theory that was later elaborated in detail by Christopher Huygens and others. Experiments demonstrating interference effects by Thomas Young provided convincing evidence supporting the hypothesis that light was better characterized as a wave than a particle. In 1905 Einstein boldly resurrected the particle hypothesis by the interpretation of light in terms of photons to explain the photoelectric effect (the release of electrons from metal surfaces by light radiation, known since 1839). Initially scientists were skeptical because there was much evidence against particles in favor of waves and he was even criticized for being premature and not taking into consideration all of the other evidence against particles in favor of waves. But this did not deter Einstein, who insisted that the idea was too important to wait until he could explain all past results. He eventually won the Nobel Prize for this paper rather than his groundbreaking work on relativity theory. The momentum for quantum ideas was slowly gaining.

Several years later, Niels Bohr adopted the quantum idea to try to explain the discrete energy levels of the hydrogen atom. Classical theory had to predict that the atom would always collapse in on itself. This was the early stage of the so-called "old quantum theory" when everyone was still very confused by lots of puzzling experimental findings without a clear or a coherent theory from which to move forward. A window was opened by Louis de Broglie, who used Einstein's earlier ideas to make the creative link that, just as light can be viewed as particles rather than waves, matter could be viewed as waves rather than particles. Then, in the mid 1920s, two independent breakthroughs occurred due to Erwin Schrödinger and Werner Heisenberg.

When Schrödinger gave a lecture on de Broglie's ideas at a scientific meeting in Switzerland, someone in the audience asked him, "if matter is a wave, then what is its wave equation?" During the following Christmas vacation (with his young female companion) he proposed the now famous Schrödinger equation for the time evolution of a quantum state. The second major step happened at

---

[4]Special thanks to Harald Atmanspacher for help with these last two sections.

the island of Helgoland, where Heisenberg developed his matrix formulation of quantum theory, later published with Max Born and Paul Jordan at Göttingen. Now physicists were confronted with two different solutions of the quantum riddle. Which one was right? Schrödinger soon showed that they were mathematically equivalent, and a completely rigorous proof of this equivalence was given by John von Neumann in 1932.

In 1927 Heisenberg went on to work with Niels Bohr in Copenhagen to find a plausible physical interpretation of the new theory. (In this period he wrote his famous paper on the uncertainty principle, published in 1927.) But although more and more experimental results matched the mathematical theory extremely precisely, quantum phenomena still were highly perplexing to the quantum community. Their conceptual understanding, the meaning of the mathematical framework, was the issue which Bohr, Pauli, and Heisenberg were deeply concerned with at Copenhagen. The result of their intense discussions is today known as the Copenhagen interpretation of quantum theory – an interpretation emphasizing observable facts and being as abstinent as possible from ontological issues. This interpretation became the prevailing opinion; but this is still a controversial topic today, and other competing interpretations have been proposed.

Moreover, the mathematical theory itself, though empirically successful without precedent, also appeared in a somewhat disorganized shape. In the 1930s it was mostly John von Neumann's merit to axiomatize the theory with a first coherent set of fundamental principles. By doing this, he discovered (together with Francis Murray and Garrett Birkhoff) that quantum theory implies a new type of algebra of (non-commutative) observables and a new kind of (non-distributive) logic, briefly called quantum logic, entailing a generalized theory of probability. (This is particularly important for researchers who wish to employ the abstract principles of quantum theory to problems outside of physics, like we are doing in this book.)

In 1928, Dirac formulated the first steps toward a quantum electrodynamics to merge quantum mechanics with Einstein's special theory of relativity. The story continued with the accomplishments by Richard Feynman, Freeman Dyson, Shin-Ichiro Tomonoga, and Julian Schwinger in the 1940s. Later, quantum chromodynamics was formulated as an even more comprehensive quantum field theory in the 1960s by Murray Gell-Mann and many others. Further progress was initiated by Daniel Kastler and Rudolf Haag, whose algebraic approach to quantum field theory, based on the work of von Neumann and Murray, laid the foundations of modern quantum statistical mechanics.

Einstein, who was one of the instigators of quantum theory, was never content with the interpretation that Bohr and his friends had proposed. He was deeply convinced that random quantum events have an underlying reason (later called "hidden variables") which needs to be unveiled – "God does not play dice with the universe." In this sense, he insisted that quantum theory was incomplete. Together with Boris Podolsky and Nathan Rosen, he published the famous EPR paper in 1935, which showed that quantum theory leads to paradoxical conclusions if quantum states are assumed to be local "elements of reality" (Einstein's parlance). Nonlocal correlations between quantum states, as predicted by the theory, would introduce what Einstein derided as "spooky action at a distance" and, in his view, would make science impossible.

Still in the same year 1935, Schrödinger turned this argument upside down and pointed out that it is precisely the nonlocality that makes quantum theory so radically different from classical physics. He coined the notion of "entanglement," which since then has appeared on millions of pages in physics journals. In the 1950s, David Bohm, who had his own controversial interpretation of quantum theory, recast the EPR thought experiment in terms of spin. This greatly simplified the argument so that eventually John Bell in the 1960s could present a fundamental inequality that must not be violated if reality is local as in classical physics. (More precisely, Bell's inequality sets limits for correlations between subsystems which cannot be exceeded if these subsystems behave classically.)

Quantum theory predicts that the Bell inequality is violated indeed, so that it is now possible to actually conduct an experimental test that could distinguish between classic and quantum conceptions of reality. After some first experimental results, the ultimately convincing study was done by Allen Aspect and collaborators in 1982. Their results showed beyond any doubt that physical systems systematically violate the Bell inequality precisely as predicted by quantum theory.

At this point, Einstein's original intention to challenge quantum theory had ironically turned into its opposite and paved the way to discover a decisive feature of the theory: the nonlocal nature of entangled states. Today, entanglement is the key to many developments that have even entered the domain of engineering – for quantum cryptography, quantum computation, superconductivity, and many other experimental hot spots in physics, the notion of entanglement has become crucial.

In 1982, Richard Feynman published a paper proposing that quantum computers should be built in order to carry out quantum calculations. This started a new field of quantum computation. The most exciting feature of quantum computing is quantum parallelism produced by operations on superposition states. In 1985, David Deutsch formulated a universal quantum computer, proving that it could be made to simulate any physical system using operations called quantum "gates." The field really took off with the discovery by Peter Shor in 1994 of a quantum algorithm that could search and factor prime numbers in polynomial time. This is critical for our encryption systems, because they rely on this factoring taking exponential time. Shor's algorithm opened the doors to much more effort aimed at realizing the quantum computers' potential. Significant progress has been made by numerous research groups around the world. The field of quantum computing has grown rapidly with the search for other highly efficient algorithms and most importantly for the development of real quantum computers (Nielsen and Chuang, 2000). But it still remains in doubt whether it is possible to build sufficiently large quantum computers to do practical large-scale computations.

1.3.2   A broader perspective

Some of the leading figures in the development of quantum theory had a long-standing interest in psychology. This stems from three issues that arise in the theory. The first is the effect of observation on quantum systems. The second concerns the possibility that the brain is a quantum system. The third concerns prevalence of complementary descriptions of nature beyond physics.

1.3.2.1   Quantum measurements and consciousness

As we discussed earlier with regard to Figure 1.1, one of the key features of quantum theory is that observing the system changes the behavior of the system. Observation causes a superposition state, containing the disposition for many states to be measured, to reduce to one definite state that will be observed in the actual measurement. (The superposition state of the system before observation is sometimes viewed as a "quantum wave" and the transition from a superposition state to definite state associated with the observed outcome is often called the "collapse of the wave.")

When and how does an observation occur? Some quantum theorists (e.g., von Neumann, London and Bauer, Wigner) occasionally speculated that human consciousness plays a role to cause the reduction of superposition states. The current mainstream position, however, is that measurement is properly described by a physical interaction with a physical recording device. Questions about when and how the state reduction (sometimes called "collapse") occurs, and how the outcome gets selected, are called the quantum measurement problem.

Volumes have been written on this topic in philosophy of science and the issue is far from settled. One point of view proposes to regard quantum measurement as a Bayesian type of updating process, so that collapse simply reflects a revision of the state (and consequently the probabilities) conditioned on new information (Caves *et al.*, 2002). This is the point of view that resonates strongly with what we present in the subsequent chapters of this book.

Let us reconsider the four examples described earlier to see how this idea can be applied. In the first example, the player is informed by the experimenter about the first play of a gamble before the second play of the same gamble. In this case, the experimenter provides information that prepares the initial state of the player before acting on the second gamble. If we view the state as a superposition of the outcomes of the first play, and we assume that the person actually *accepts* the experimenter's statement about the outcome of the first gamble, then the superposition should break down, aligning the initial state with the known outcome. If the initial state is aligned with the outcome of the first gamble, then this has the same effect as a measurement that collapses the state on the first outcome. Next consider the second example, which required inferring a category prior to taking an action. In the C-then-D condition, the experimenter requests a categorization and records a response from the person, and so it seems rather clear that an observation or measurement took place.

By doing this, however, we are assuming that the superposition state over categories is broken down and *revised* so that it aligns with the output category response before taking the next action. In other words, it is assumed that if the person categorizes the face as a "bad guy" then the person acts accordingly. What about the third example on the conjunction fallacy? For the conjunction question, we assume that the person first answers a question about feminism and, conditioned on that answer, the person then answers a question about bank tellers. In this case, it is assumed that the person is taking a measurement on him or herself *implicitly*. In other words, the person must implicitly ask him or herself the feminism question, which forces a breakdown of the superposed state with respect to the feminism question. In the last example with the ambiguous concepts, it is assumed that the prime (banana) causes an ambiguous idea (is apple a suit or a company?) to break down to a particular interpretation (fruit). From these four examples we see that the question of when a measurement is taken or, alternatively, when a state is revised conditioned on new information is a very important issue even beyond physics.

The idea that human consciousness and quantum theory have a lot to do with each other has been put forward intensely by Henry Stapp, a theoretical physicist at University of California at Berkeley (Stapp, 2009). Stapp proposes that physical brain functioning can be characterized as a quantum superposition state over possible "self-world" schemas that evolves across time according to an evolutionary quantum process. Conscious attention is responsible for a self-measurement action that breaks down a superposition state into one definite state "self-world" schema. The resulting conscious state can then be recorded physically in memory. His book is deeply concerned with the problem of mind–body relations and tries to provide an entry point for consciousness in the material world. We will not be going into these deeper philosophical issues in this book, but rather stick closely to empirical results from concrete experiments from cognitive and decision sciences – an issue that Stapp leaves largely unaddressed.

1.3.2.2 The quantum brain

Several other proposals have been made to understand consciousness in terms of quantum theory (for a review, see the Atmanspacher's 2004 entry in the *Stanford Encyclopedia of Philosophy*). Quite popular among them is the approach by the physicist and mathematician Roger Penrose (Penrose, 1989), complemented and advocated by the anesthesiologist Stuart Hameroff (Hameroff, 1998). In their picture, consciousness also has to do with a "collapse" of a superposition state in the brain, which changes an indeterminate state into a definite state of deliberate intention. Different from Stapp, they propose a specific quantum physical model of this brain process in terms of the microtubule cytoskeleton of neurons. An influential web-based course on quantum consciousness has been put up by Hameroff (at the University of Arizona at Tucson) for years now, and since 1994 UA Tucson hosts international conferences on the topic.

The hypothesis by Penrose and Hameroff has received a lot of criticism, because it is argued that within the "hot and wet" highly interacting brain, decoherence (the breakdown of the superposition state) occurs much too fast to allow any relevant effects of quantum states for comparably slow brain processes, and even more so for psychological thought processes. Nevertheless, the idea of modelling the brain by quantum physics continues to be vigorously pursued. Early on in 1966, Karl Pribram (Pribram, 1993) proposed using holography to model perception and memory, and in 1967 Hideki Umezawa and Luigi Ricciardi published a quantum field model for memory that was later refined by others (Jibu & Yasue, 1995). More recently, related ideas have been used to describe basic findings concerning electroencephalographic (EEG) frequency patterns (Freeman & Vitiello, 2006). Guido Vitiello, a quantum field physicist, wrote a popular book to make this work more accessible (Vitiello, 2001).

An independent but somewhat related line of research is the use of artificial quantum neural networks to model complex perceptual–motor systems of both humans and robots (Ivancevic & Ivancevic, 2010). For example, a real-time quantum neural network model was developed that could learn to perform complex eye-tracking movements (Behera *et al.*, 2005). Quantum neural networks have the same computational power as classic neural nets but provide the possibility of significant increases in speed of computation (Gupta & Zia, 2001). However, these quantum neural networks are designed more for the purpose of modelling complex information processing, rather than attempting to understand the neurophysiological mechanisms of the brain (and even less about cognition and decision).

This book is *not* concerned with the biological basis of quantum computations. It may be that cognitive processes are implemented in the brain by a physical quantum field model, or it may be that the brain is a very complex classical neural net involving hidden states and our coarse measures of this system produce statistics that are well captured by quantum probability theory. We remain agnostic with respect to this question, and instead focus more on the application of the mathematics, of the formal core of quantum theory, to the behavioral results obtained from cognition and decision experiments. Only our final chapter, Chapter 12, will make a modest attempt to build some bridges to neuroscience.

1.3.2.3 Complementarity and incompatibility

Neils Bohr and Wolfgang Pauli intensively discussed the option of different ways of describing nature that are mutually incompatible but equally valid and together necessary for a complete description. In physics, position and momentum are complementary ways of describing the state of a particle. In finance, price and derivatives have been interpreted as complementary ways to describe the value of a stock option (Haven, 2002). In psychology, perhaps personality and intelligence, or cognition and emotion, should be treated as complementary ways of characterizing an individual (Blutner & Hochnadel, 2010). Both Bohr and Pauli speculated that the concepts of complementarity and incompatibility are applicable beyond physics to human knowledge. In fact, from the start, Bohr was heavily influenced by the writings of the psychologist William James, who wrote about these issues much earlier from a psychological perspective. Bohr learned about the work by James from his Danish friend Edgar Rubin, who invented the "Rubin face" (an ambiguous image which causes perception to switch between figure and ground from a face to a vase). Thus, we see that our third reason for applying quantum theory to cognition and decision actually does not have its origin in physics – instead, physics imported complementarity as a concept that first emerged within psychology.

Today it is well recognized that complementarity and, more generally, incompatibility abound in descriptions of classical systems and are by far not unique to quantum theory. One well-known example is the uncertainty relation between duration and frequency bandwidth in signal processing theory (Primas, 2007). Incompatibility can also arise in classical systems whose states cannot be characterized sharply, e.g., if only coarse measurements of the system are possible (Graben & Atmanspacher, 2006). These coarse measurements induce a partition of the classic state space, and two descriptions of the system are incompatible if they are based on two partitions that do not share a common refinement. Thus, it is possible for neural as well as mental descriptions to be classical and yet exhibit complementarity (Grossberg, 2000) and incompatibility (Barros & Suppes, 2009).

These generalizations of quantum theory (by physicists working at the foundations of physics) inspired the exploration of applications using the mathematics of quantum theory to fields outside of physics. The pioneers that paved this path include Diederich Aerts (Aerts & Aerts, 1994), who describes his research as using "quantum structure," Andrei Khrennikov (1999), who calls these approaches "quantum like," and Harald Atmanspacher (Atmanspacher et al., 2002), who refers to them as "generalized quantum theory." Even earlier, Elio (Conte, 1983) suggested applying quantum theory outside physics to fields such as psychology, and another early exploration into applications of quantum theory to decision making was started by Robert Bordley (Bordley, 1998; Bordley & Kadane, 1999).

A related pioneering effort was the development of quantum game theory by Meyer (1999) and Eisert (Eisert et al., 1999). Shortly afterward, a series of more detailed applications began to appear, including applications to probability judgments (Bordley, 1998), human conceptual judgments (Gabora & Aerts, 2002), information retrieval (van Rijsbergen, 2004), game theory (Piotrowski & Sladkowski, 2002), semantic analysis (Bruza & Cole, 2005), perception of impossible figures (Conte et al., 2007), decision making in psychology (Busemeyer et al., 2006a), preferential choice (Lambert-Mogiliansky et al., 2009), utility theory (La Mura, 2009), finance (Baaquie, 2004), human motivation (Ivancevic & Aidman, 2007), and again economic decision making (Yukalov & Sornette, 2008).

A special issue on quantum cognition and decision making has recently appeared (Bruza *et al.*, 2009a), and three edited volumes of collected research from proceedings have been published by Bruza *et al.* (2007, 2008, 2009b). Most recently, Andrei Khrennikov wrote a book summarizing applications of his contextual (quantum-like) probability approach to psychological, social, and economic sciences (Khrennikov, 2010).

2

What is quantum theory? An elementary introduction

What can you learn about quantum theory in one chapter without knowing any physics? A complete presentation of quantum theory requires an entire textbook, but our goal for this chapter is to provide only the essential elements of the theory that we feel are relevant for modelling behavioral phenomena.[1] Just like classical probability theory, quantum theory is based on a small set of axioms used to assign probabilities to events. This chapter is limited to what is called the structural principles of quantum theory, whereas Chapter 8 will set out the dynamic principles. For simplicity, only finite state systems will be described, although quantum theory can also be applied to continuous state systems. Even though this book is limited to finite dimensions, the number of dimensions can be arbitrarily large.

For finite state systems, the structural part of quantum theory is expressed in the formalism of linear algebra (for continuous state systems, it is expressed in the formalism of functional analysis). Consequently, a brief tutorial of linear algebra is presented along with our elementary introduction to quantum theory. Various notations are used to describe linear algebra, depending on the application field. Physicists like to use Dirac notation, invented by one of the founders of quantum theory, Paul Dirac (Dirac, 1958). Although the Dirac notation will be unfamiliar to many cognitive scientists, we will still use it as it is a succinct notation for expressing linear algebra. It helps the reader to see relations that are more difficult to identify using other formalisms.

The general plan for this chapter is to start out with a conceptual overview of quantum probability theory along with some simple and concrete examples. Thereafter, a tutorial on linear and matrix algebra is presented, which provides the mathematical tools needed to describe the theory more rigorously. Finally, the formal representation of quantum probability axioms is given and compared against the formal representation of the axioms governing classical probability theory. At the very end of this chapter, some references to books on quantum theory are provided.

---

[1] Recall from our discussion in Section 1.3 that we are not proposing a quantum physical model of neural brain mechanisms. We are only applying the mathematical principles of quantum probability theory to explain the statistical properties of human behavior.

The conceptual overview describes two different ways for building quantum probability models: the geometric approach and the path diagram approach. They are mathematically equivalent, but for some problems one approach is more intuitive and, therefore, easier to use than the other. The path diagram approach is convenient for representing sequences of state transitions, but the geometric approach is useful for determining the values to assign to each state transition. The chapter begins with the geometric approach, but if you prefer you can proceed to the path diagram approach. Alternatively, you may skip over the conceptual overview and proceed directly to the general principles that appear in the last section. These sections are all self-contained.

2.1 Geometric approach

2.1.1 General overview

Amazingly, around the same time in the 1930s, two different sets of axioms were formulated for probability theory. One was the Kolmogorov axioms (Kolmogorov, 1933/1950), which organized the principles underlying the probabilistic applications already used for several centuries in classical physics. The other was the von Neumann axioms (Von Neumann, 1932/1955), which organized the principles underlying the newly created probabilistic application in quantum physics. By axiomatizing these theories, they become abstract and can thus be applied in domains outside of physics, such as economics or psychology. The four quantum postulates are introduced below and compared with the corresponding postulates found in classic probability. At a conceptual level, a key difference is that classic probability theory relies on a set-theoretic representation, whereas quantum theory uses a vector space representation. In order to help the reader build up a clear understanding of the similarities and differences of the two approaches, a small model is developed based on a simple preferential choice situation. The model is based on a previous theory developed by Lambert-Mogiliansky (Lambert-Mogiliansky *et al.*, 2009), but the example is hypothetical to keep the application fairly simple:

> Suppose a man is considering buying a new car and has narrowed his options down to three, which for concreteness are labeled as follows: A for Audi, B for BMW, and C for Cadillac. The first two cars are sporty European makes and the third is a luxurious American type. The man must decide on only *one* car from this set. In this situation, there is a single categorical variable M (i.e., "man chooses a car") that can produce one of three possible outcomes (M chooses car A, M chooses car B, M chooses car C).

2.1.1.1 Events

Both classic and quantum theories are concerned with the problem of assigning probabilities to events. For example, what is the probability that the man will

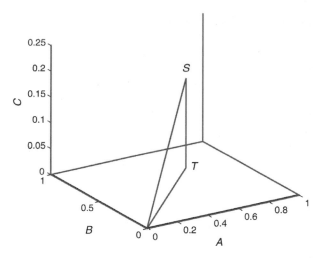

Figure 2.1 Three-dimensional real vector space: each orthogonal axis represents one car; S is the preference state, T is the projection on the A, B plane.

choose car A from the set? What is the probability that the man chooses the sporty car (A or B) from the set? So both theories are founded on assumptions about how to represent events.

Classic theory begins by assuming a sample space, which is a set of points or elementary outcomes, or events. Each elementary event represents one of the unique outcomes that can be observed (such as M choosing car A), and these outcomes cannot be broken down into more refined outcomes. In general, the sample space contains a set of N elementary events, where N can be arbitrarily large. In the running example, however, $N = 3$ as there are three outcomes, denoted by the set $\{A, B, C\}$. These outcomes are *mutually exclusive*, meaning M choosing A excludes the choice of another car. In addition, the sample space is *exhaustive*, meaning the sample space includes all the possible outcomes.

Using the set of elementary events, more complex events can be described; for example, the event corresponding to choosing a European sports car. In other words, this corresponds to the event "M chooses A" OR "M chooses B." Events correspond to subsets of the set of elementary events, so the previous event corresponds to the set union of the corresponding elementary events: $\{A\} \cup \{B\} = \{A, B\}$. In general, the rules for combining events in classic probability obey the logic of set theory: the conjunction of two events is represented by set intersection $(A \cap B)$, and the disjunction of two events is represented by the union of sets $(A \cup B)$. Also, these events are governed by the distributive axiom of set theory: $A \cap (B \cup C) = (A \cap B) \cup (A \cap C)$.

Events in quantum theory are not modelled as sets but rather as subspaces. Quantum theory begins by assuming a set of basis vectors (Figure 2.1 is an example with three axes corresponding to the three cars A, B, C). Each basis vector corresponds to an elementary outcome. For example, there is one basis vector denoted $|C\rangle$ corresponding to "M choosing C," which is represented by the vertical axis in Figure 2.1. The basis vectors corresponding to the elementary outcomes are orthogonal; that is, at right angles to each other. This is a geometric expression of the constraint mentioned above that the elementary events should be mutually exclusive.

Recall that events in classic probability theory are represented as arbitrary subsets of the sample space. The counterparts in quantum theory are subspaces. For example, the event corresponding to "M choosing a European car" corresponds to the *plane* spanned by the basis vectors $|A\rangle$ and $|B\rangle$. In Figure 2.1, this is the horizontal plane defined by the A, B axes. Because events are defined as subspaces, the rules for combining events obey the logic of subspaces: the conjunction of two events is represented by the intersection of subspaces, and the disjunction of two events is represented by the span of the subspaces. For example, the span of the rays formed by $|A\rangle$ and $|B\rangle$ includes every point on the entire horizontal plane. A fundamentally important point of distinction between classic probability theory and quantum theory is that the logic of subspaces *does not obey* the distributive axiom of set theory. This point will hopefully become clear as more of the detail is revealed.

2.1.1.2   System state

Both classic and quantum theories refer to a system, which is the person, animal, or thing that eventually generates the events that we observe. Also, they both postulate that the system has a state, which determines the probabilities of the events that the system generates. For example, the system may be a person, which has a state that determines the probabilities of choosing the various cars in the choice set.

In classic theory, the state is a probability *function,* denoted by $p(\cdot)$, that directly maps elementary events into probabilities. In our example, the state is the probability function that assigns a probability of choosing each car. For example, the probability function p assigns the probability $p(A)$ to event A. Probabilities for all other events are then generated by adding the probabilities of the elementary outcomes that are contained in the event. The empty set receives a probability of zero, whereas the sample space has a probability of one.

In quantum theory, the state is a unit-length *vector* in the N-dimensional vector space, symbolized as $|S\rangle$ that is used to map events into probabilities, but the mapping from the state to probabilities is indirect. The state in Figure 2.1 is the line attached to the letter S located at 0.696 units along the A axis, 0.696 units along the B axis, and 0.175 units up the C axis. The state is projected onto the subspace corresponding to an event, and the squared length of this projection equals the event probability. For example, the probability of choosing car A simply equals $0.696^2 = 0.4844$ and the probability of choosing car C equals $0.175^2 = 0.0306$. The probability of choosing a sporty car (M chooses A or B) is determined by the squared length of the projection of the state vector S down onto the horizontal plane representing the choice of car A or B. In Figure 2.1, the projection is the vector T, which equals the line reaching from zero to the point T on the plane. This mapping from the state into probabilities is nonlinear (because it involves squaring a magnitude), which is important for later applications. Projections onto the zero point are mapped onto a probability of zero, and projections onto the entire vector space are mapped onto a probability equal to one.

2.1.1.3   State revision

Both classic and quantum theories provide a rule for updating the state based on observations. Suppose that an event is observed or concluded to be true, and we now want to determine the probabilities of other events after observing or assuming this fact. For example, we may learn from a website that a person just purchased a product: given this fact, what is the probability that this person will purchase some other products?

Classic theory changes the original probability function into a new *conditional* probability function by (a) determining the joint probability between the observed event and each of the elementary events and (b) dividing each joint probability by the sum over all of the joint probabilities. The normalization produced by the second step guarantees that the new revised probability function sums to one across the elementary events. This reduces the state to have nonzero probabilities assigned only to events consistent with the observed event.

Quantum theory changes the original state vector into a new state vector by (a) projecting the original state onto the subspace representing the observed event and (b) dividing the projection by the length of the projection. For example, if car A is chosen, then the state is changed from $|S\rangle$ to $|A\rangle$. The normalization produced by the second step guarantees that the revised state has length one. This is called the *collapse* of the state vector onto the subspace corresponding to the observed event.

2.1.1.4   Compatibility

The issue of compatibility is new and unique to quantum theory, and it is never raised within classic theory. To introduce this issue we need to include a second categorical variable into our example. Suppose now that we have two categorical variables: one is the man's choice of a car from the set {A,B,C} and the second is his prediction about what his wife would choose from this same set. For example, he might prefer car B, but he might predict that his wife will prefer car C. The first categorical variable M has three outcomes {MA, MB, MC} and the second categorical variable W has three outcomes {WA, WB, WC}. Both are measured within the same experiment.

Can all events be described within a single sample space? Classic theory assumes that the answer is yes, which is called the unicity assumption (Griffiths, 2003). Classic probability theory assumes a closure property, if A and B are events then so is A AND B. Therefore, we can form all combinations of the three outcomes from the categorical variable M with the three outcomes from W to produce nine combinations. For example, the event (MA AND WC) is one of the nine combinations; the event (MB AND WC) is another combination.

Quantum theory does not necessarily assume unicity (Griffiths, 2003). Some events may be compatible and share a common basis, but other events may be incompatible and do not share a common basis. Events that do not share a common basis cannot be combined into one combination event and instead they must be evaluated sequentially.[2] For example, suppose the man cannot think of his own preference and at the same time think about his wife's preference, so they must be evaluated sequentially, and the order of evaluation affects the final result. In that case, a first event (such as man chooses car A) can correspond to a subspace spanned by one basis vector (using the basis that provides the man's perspective), but a second event (such as the woman wants car C) can correspond to a ray spanned by a non-orthogonal basis vector (using the basis that provides the woman's perspective), and a common basis cannot span both subspaces. More intuitively, one way of describing events is needed to identify the first event, but a different way of describing events is needed to identify the second set event. There is no common way to describe them both. If all events are compatible, then quantum theory is equivalent to classic theory (Gudder, 1988). Thus, incompatibility (also known as complementarity) is a key new idea that distinguishes quantum probability from classic probability.

A simple example of incompatible events was used to account for the conjunction fallacy described in Section 1.2.3 (refer back to the simple two-dimensional model illustrated in Figure 1.3). In this case, one basis was used to describe the events "feminist" versus "not feminist" for the feminism question, but a different basis was used to describe the events "bank teller" versus "not bank teller" for the bank teller question. The bank teller basis lies within the same two-dimensional space as the feminism basis, but the feminism basis is rotated to produce the bank teller basis. Using this representation of events, the "feminist" event is incompatible with the "bank teller" event. Accordingly, the person cannot evaluate the likelihood of feminism and bank teller events simultaneously. In this case the reason is because the person never experienced or thought about these unusual combinations before. Consquently, the person first needs to evaluate the feminism question and, once that is resolved, turn to a new basis to evaluate the bank teller question. As pointed out in Section 1.1, the order of this evaluation makes a big difference in the final judgment.

These four principles are the essential ideas that make up quantum probability theory. Next we present some concrete examples of these principles. Later we present some of the mathematics needed to make these principles more rigorous.

---

[2]The original quantum logic approach defined the meet (A ∧ B) of two events as the intersection of the two subspaces, and the join (A ∨ B) as the span of the two subspaces; see Hughes (1989). This makes sense when the events are compatible, but not when they are incompatible; see Griffiths (2003) and Neistegge (2008).

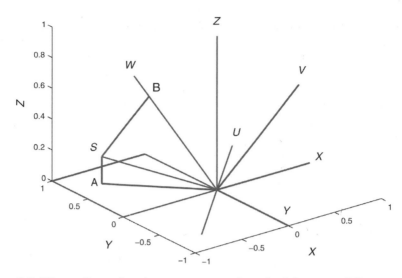

Figure 2.2 Three-dimensional vector space described by two different sets of basis vectors. One basis is defined by $\{X, Y, Z\}$ and the other basis is defined by $\{U, V, W\}$. The initial state equals S. The points A and B are projections onto different subspaces.

2.1.2 Concrete example for geometric approach

We continue with the example based on a simple preferential choice task (Lambert-Mogiliansky *et al.*, 2009). Suppose a man is thinking about buying a new car, and he has narrowed his options down to three, which for concreteness we will call Audi (A), BMW (B), and Cadillac (C).

2.1.2.1 Analysis of a single categorical variable

A three-dimensional vector space, such as illustrated in Figure 2.2, can be used to model the man's personal preferences.[3] For this more complex example, we do not wish to label the axes (A, B, C) as we did before, because we now need to represent two categorical variables, variable M with values MA, MB, MC and variable W with values WA, WB, WC. Therefore, the ray labeled X in the figure represents the event "man prefers BMW," the ray labeled Y in the figure represents the event "man prefers Audi," and the ray labeled Z in the figure represents the event "man prefers Cadillac." Note that these three rays are orthogonal. We (the theorists) can choose a unit-length basis vector to span the X-ray that starts at zero and extends out to one unit in the positive direction of the X-ray. Using Dirac notation, the basis vector for the X-ray is called a "ket" and it is symbolized as $|X\rangle$. The use of the word span in the earlier sentence

---

[3]If we assigned real numbers to the categorical outcomes, then this categorical variable becomes a random variable in classic theory and it becomes an observable in quantum theory. However, nothing is gained by assigning meaningless numbers to the categories, and so we avoid this.

refers to the fact that any point on the X-ray can be reached by $a \cdot |X\rangle$, where a is a scalar (in this example, a scalar is a real number). Similarly, we can choose a unit-length basis vector to span the Y-ray that starts at zero and extends one unit along the positive direction of the Y-ray, which is denoted by the ket $|Y\rangle$. Finally, we can choose a unit-length basis vector to span the Z-ray that starts at zero and extends one unit along the positive direction of the Z-ray, which is denoted by the ket $|Z\rangle$.

Any arbitrary vector that lies within this three-dimensional space can be reached by a linear combination of the three basis vectors, $\{|X\rangle, |Y\rangle, |Z\rangle\}$, and therefore we say these three basis vectors span the three-dimensional space. For example, the vector labeled S in the figure is another vector in this space which is symbolized by the ket $|S\rangle$. In our quantum model, we refer to this as the state vector. In this figure, the state $|S\rangle$ is described by the following coordinates with respect to the $\{|X\rangle, |Y\rangle, |Z\rangle\}$ basis:

$$|S\rangle = (-0.6963) \cdot |X\rangle + (0.6963) \cdot |Y\rangle + (0.1741) \cdot |Z\rangle.$$

The state is interpreted geometrically as follows. To reach the vector $|S\rangle$ we start at 0 and we first travel 0.6963 units in the negative direction of the basis vector $|X\rangle$; then, continuing from that first point, we travel 0.6963 units in the positive direction of the vector $|Y\rangle$, and continuing from the second point we travel 0.1741 units in the positive direction of vector $|Z\rangle$. We will provide a psychological interpretation of these coordinates shortly, but for the time being let us simply continue with the linear algebra. The 3-tuple $[-0.6963, 0.6963, 0.1741]$ is called the coordinate representation of the vector $|S\rangle$ with respect to the $\{|X\rangle, |Y\rangle, |Z\rangle\}$ basis. This correspondence between the abstract vector $|S\rangle$ and its coordinates with respect to the $\{|X\rangle, |Y\rangle, |Z\rangle\}$ basis is symbolized by

$$|S\rangle \rightarrow \begin{bmatrix} -0.6963 \\ 0.6963 \\ 0.1741 \end{bmatrix} = \begin{bmatrix} \psi_1 \\ \psi_2 \\ \psi_3 \end{bmatrix} = \psi. \tag{2.1}$$

The symbol ψ represents the 3×1 (single column) matrix of coordinates for the abstract vector $|S\rangle$ when represented in terms of the $\{|X\rangle, |Y\rangle, |Z\rangle\}$ basis. For example, $\psi_2 = 0.6963$ is the coordinate for the state with respect to the $|Y\rangle$ basis vector. The squared length of the vector $|S\rangle$, which is denoted $|| \, |S\rangle \, ||^2$, is defined by the sum of the squared magnitudes of its coordinates. In this case, the squared length equals $|| \, |S\rangle \, ||^2 = ||\psi||^2 = (|-0.6963|)^2 + |0.6963|^2 + |0.1741|^2) = 1$, so the vector has unit length. What about the coordinates of $|X\rangle$ with respect to the $\{|X\rangle, |Y\rangle, |Z\rangle\}$ basis? What about $|Y\rangle$ and $|Z\rangle$? The answers to these questions simply correspond to the standard canonical coordinate system

$$|X\rangle \rightarrow \begin{bmatrix} 1 \\ 0 \\ 0 \end{bmatrix}, \ |Y\rangle \rightarrow \begin{bmatrix} 0 \\ 1 \\ 0 \end{bmatrix}, \ |Z\rangle \rightarrow \begin{bmatrix} 0 \\ 0 \\ 1 \end{bmatrix}.$$

Clearly, these vectors are orthogonal and they also each have unit length.

Note that the coordinate assigned to each basis vector can be obtained from the inner product between the basis vector and the state vector. The inner product between two real vectors is obtained by multiplying the corresponding coordinates and then summing across coordinates. For example, with respect to the $\{|X\rangle, |Y\rangle, |Z\rangle\}$ basis, the inner product between $|X\rangle$ and $|S\rangle$ is computed from the matrix formula

$$\langle X|S\rangle = \begin{bmatrix} 1 & 0 & 0 \end{bmatrix} \cdot \begin{bmatrix} -0.6963 \\ 0.6963 \\ 0.1741 \end{bmatrix}$$

$$= 1 \cdot (-0.6963) + 0 \cdot (0.6963) + 0 \cdot (0.1741)$$

$$= -0.6963 = \psi_1.$$

This inner product $\langle X|S\rangle$ also represents what Feynman calls the transition amplitude from state $|S\rangle$ to state $|X\rangle$; that is, the amplitude for a transition from the initial state to the state in which the man decides to choose the BMW.

How can this vector space be used to compute choice probabilities? According to quantum theory, the probability of an individual event is obtained by first projecting the state vector onto the ray representing that event and then squaring the magnitude of this projection. The probability of choosing the BMW is obtained by projecting the state vector onto the ray corresponding to the BMW (which is the X-ray) and squaring the length of this projection. The projection of $|S\rangle$ on the X-ray equals $|X\rangle\langle X|S\rangle = -0.6963 \cdot |X\rangle$ and its squared length is $|| -0.6963 \cdot |X\rangle ||^2 = |-0.6963|^2 \cdot || \,|X\rangle\, ||^2 = (0.4848) \cdot 1$. In a similar manner, the projection of $|S\rangle$ on the Y-ray is $|Y\rangle\langle Y|S\rangle = 0.6963 \cdot |Y\rangle$ and its squared length is $|0.6963|^2 = 0.4848$, and so Audi has the same probability to be chosen as the BMW. Finally, the projection of $|S\rangle$ on the Z-ray is $|Z\rangle\langle Z|S\rangle = 0.1741 \cdot |Z\rangle$ and its squared length is $|0.1741|^2 = 0.0303$ and this is the probability of the man choosing the Cadillac (from his personal perspective). These three choice probabilities sum to unity because the length of the state equals one.

Why does a negative coordinate for the BMW produce the same probability as a positive coordinate for the Audi? Does a negative coordinate not imply that the BMW has a negative evaluation? No! The negative coordinate is an arbitrary choice that the authors made to display the figure. We could simply reverse the direction of the basis vector used to represent the X-ray by using $-|X\rangle$ instead of $|X\rangle$ as the basis vector. Note that $-|X\rangle$ and $|X\rangle$ span the same ray, and we can express $|S\rangle$ equally well by the basis $\{-|X\rangle, |Y\rangle, |Z\rangle\}$ as follows:

$$|S\rangle = (0.6963) \cdot (-|X\rangle) + (0.6963) \cdot |Y\rangle + (0.1741) \cdot |Z\rangle.$$

Thus, the sign of the basis vector is arbitrary and only the square magnitude is meaningful, and this is the same for the BMW and Audi.

We can also compute the probability for more general events using this model. For example, what is the probability that the man chooses either the BMW or the Audi? The event "Audi or BMW" is a subspace spanned by two basis vectors $\{|X\rangle, |Y\rangle\}$, which is the entire X–Y plane in Figure 2.2.

The probability for this event is obtained by projecting the state $|S\rangle$ onto this subspace, which is shown by the letter A in Figure 2.2. Formally, this projection equals $(|X\rangle\langle X| + |Y\rangle\langle Y|)\,|S\rangle = |X\rangle\langle X|S\rangle + |Y\rangle\langle Y|S\rangle = (-0.6963)\cdot|X\rangle + (0.6963)\cdot|Y\rangle$. The probability of this event equals the squared length of this projection: $||(-0.6963)\cdot|X\rangle + (0.6963)\cdot|Y\rangle||^2 = 2\cdot(0.6963)^2 = 0.9697$. Orthogonality of $|X\rangle, |Y\rangle$ guarantees that the squared length of the sum equals the sum of squared lengths.

The negation of the event "BMW or Audi" (i.e., the event that the man does not choose either the BMW or the Audi) is determined by the complementary subspace that is orthogonal to the X–Y plane, which is the Z-ray. The squared magnitude of the projection on the Z-ray equals $|0.1741|^2 = 0.0303 = 1 - 0.9697$.

In summary, there is not much difference between a quantum model and a classic probability model at this point. We have three outcomes and the state assigns a probability to each outcome, and the probabilities sum to unity. Therefore, we shall now address more clearly the advantages of a vector-based approach to probabilities.

2.1.2.2 Analysis of two categorical variables

To see why we need a vector space, we now make the problem a bit more complex (like real life). Now consider two perspectives. One perspective we already described is the man's own personal view, but a second perspective is from his wife's point of view, who does not necessarily agree with his personal point of view.

At this point, we have two different types of preferences to measure. The first type is a measure of the man's personal preferences, which can result in one of three mutually exclusive and exhaustive outcomes: $M = \{$man prefers BMW, man prefers Audi, man prefers Cadillac$\}$. The second type is a measure of (what the man thinks are) his wife's preferences, which can result in one of three mutually exclusive and exhaustive outcomes: $W = \{$woman prefers BMW, woman prefers Audi, woman prefers Cadillac$\}$.

Now a quantum theorist is faced with an important question. Should these two variables be represented as compatible or incompatible? In general, the answer depends on whether or not the person has sufficient knowledge of and experience with the various events to form a compatible representation. If unusual combinations of events are involved, the person may need to rely on different bases for evaluating the events. Alternatively, the events may be incompatible because, as in this particular example, they require evaluations from completely different perspectives or points of view, which have to be viewed sequentially. A compatible representation requires us to assume that it is meaningful to assign probabilities to conjunctions of events, and an incompatible representation assumes that this cannot be done, and instead we need to assign probabilities to ordered sequences of events.

Initially for this example we assume the man *cannot* think about his preference at the same time as thinking about his wife's preference. Thus, we start by analyzing the events from the man's perspective as incompatible with the events from the women's perspective. Consequently, we must also postulate an order of processing because the probability of two answers depends on the order that the questions are asked. Later we change our assumption and treat the two variables as compatible to see the difference that this assumption makes in the calculation of quantum probabilities.

2.1.2.3   Incompatible representation

First we assume that the man's and woman's preferences are *incompatible* and the order of evaluation matters. In this case, we return to use the same $\{|X\rangle,$ $|Y\rangle, |Z\rangle\}$ basis as shown in Figure 2.2 to represent the car choice from the man's perspective. However, now we need to use a *new* basis within the same space to represent what the man views as his wife's preferences. The ray labeled U in the figure represents the event "wife wants BMW" spanned by a unit-length vector $|U\rangle$, the ray labeled V in the figure represents the event "wife wants Audi" spanned by a unit-length vector $|V\rangle$; and the ray labeled W in the figure represents the event "wife wants Cadillac" spanned by the unit-length vector $|W\rangle$. Note that these three rays are also orthogonal and they span the same three-dimensional space as the $\{|X\rangle, |Y\rangle, |Z\rangle\}$ basis. Any point within the three-dimensional vector space can also be reached by a linear combination of the $\{|U\rangle, |V\rangle, |W\rangle\}$ basis vectors. In particular, now the state vector $|S\rangle$ can be represented in terms of either the $\{|X\rangle, |Y\rangle, |Z\rangle\}$ basis or the $\{|U\rangle, |V\rangle, |W\rangle\}$ basis as follows:

$$|S\rangle = (-0.6963) \cdot |X\rangle + (0.6963) \cdot |Y\rangle + (0.1741) \cdot |Z\rangle$$
$$= 0 \cdot |U\rangle + (-0.5732) \cdot |V\rangle + (0.8194) \cdot |W\rangle.$$

The coordinates for the state $|S\rangle$ with respect to the $\{|U\rangle, |V\rangle, |W\rangle\}$ basis are given by the 3×1 (single column) matrix

$$|S\rangle \rightarrow \begin{bmatrix} 0 \\ -0.5732 \\ 0.8194 \end{bmatrix} = \varphi, \tag{2.2}$$

which again has unit length: $\| \,|S\rangle\, \|^2 = \|\varphi\|^2 = 0^2 + (-0.5732)^2 + (0.8194)^2 = 1$. So we see that the same state $|S\rangle$ can be referred to different bases, and each basis produces a new coordinate representation. Now we can see why we need to think about $|S\rangle$ as an abstract vector: it is impossible for $|S\rangle$ to be equal to ψ (2.1) and at the same time be equal to φ (2.2) because ψ is not equal to φ. However, ψ and φ both refer to the same vector $|S\rangle$ with respect to different bases.

At this point, we have two different types of preferences to measure. The first type is a measure of the man's personal preferences, which can result in one of three mutually exclusive and exhaustive outcomes: $M = \{$man prefers BMW, man prefers Audi, man prefers Cadillac$\}$. These three outcomes are represented by the X-ray, Y-ray, and Z-ray respectively. The coordinates in ψ representing the state $|S\rangle$ with respect to the man basis are used to assign probabilities to the man's three outcomes. The second type is a measure of the wife's preferences, which can result in one of three mutually exclusive and exhaustive outcomes: $W = \{$woman prefers BMW, woman prefers Audi, woman prefers Cadillac$\}$. These three outcomes are represented by the U-ray, V-ray, and W-ray respectively. The coordinates in φ representing the state $|S\rangle$ with respect to the woman basis are used to assign probabilities to the wife's three possible outcomes.

We have already shown how the the probabilities of the three outcomes are computed from the man's perspective. Now let us consider the probability of choosing the BMW from what the man views as his wife's preferences. From this other perspective, the wife's view is based on the $\{|U\rangle, |V\rangle, |W\rangle\}$ basis. For example, to compute the probability that the man thinks his wife wants the Cadillac, we project the state $|S\rangle$ onto the basis vector $|W\rangle$, which is shown as the letter B in Figure 2.2. Formally, the projection of $|S\rangle$ on the W-ray is $|W\rangle\langle W|S\rangle = 0.8194 \cdot |W\rangle$ and its squared magnitude is $|0.8194|^2 = 0.6714$, and so the Cadillac has a high probability (from the wife's perspective). The probability of choosing the BMW is obtained by projecting the state vector onto the ray corresponding to the BMW (which is now the U-ray) and squaring the magnitude of this projection. The projection of $|S\rangle$ on the U-ray is $0 \cdot |U\rangle$ and its squared magnitude is 0, and so there is zero probability of choosing the BMW from the wife's point of view. In a similar manner, the projection of $|S\rangle$ on the V-ray is $-0.5732 \cdot |V\rangle$ and its squared magnitude is $|-0.5732|^2 = 0.32856$, and so the Audi is more likely to be chosen than the BMW.

2.1.2.4   Law of reciprocity

A very important restriction on transitions between basis states is the principle that the probability of transiting $|X\rangle \rightarrow |W\rangle$, from one basis state $|X\rangle$ to another basis state $|W\rangle$, equals the probability of the transition in the opposite direction $|W\rangle \rightarrow |X\rangle$. In other words, $|\langle W|X\rangle|^2 = |\langle X|W\rangle|^2$, which is called the *law of reciprocity*, and transition probabilities between basis states in quantum theory must obey this law (Peres, 1998). This property follows from the fact that the probability of a transition from one basis state to another equals the squared magnitude of the inner product between two vectors, and the magnitude of an inner product is the same regardless of the direction in which it is formed. In our simple example, the event "woman wants Cadillac" is spanned by the basis vector $|W\rangle$ and the event "man wants BMW" is spanned by the basis vector $|X\rangle$. So for this example, the probability of event "woman wants Cadillac" conditioned on the event "man chooses BMW" is predicted to be equal to the conditional probability "man chooses BMW" conditioned on "woman chooses Cadillac." It is important to note that this law only applies to events that are represented by unidimensional rays. Later we show how events represented by multiple dimensions (spanned by more than one basis vector) do not imply this symmetry condition. Conditional probabilities from classic probability theory do not have to obey this restriction. Also note that the simple example presented here is only hypothetical; more realistically, the events described in this example may require multidimensional subspaces for their representations.

2.1.2.5   Uncertainty principle

The incompatible representation used in Figure 2.2 forces us to accept a form of uncertainty that is the essence of Heisenberg's famous uncertainty principle. Note that the three vectors $\{|U\rangle, |V\rangle, |W\rangle\}$ can be reached by linear combinations of the $\{|X\rangle, |Y\rangle, |Z\rangle\}$ basis. Specifically, we can describe the three vectors $\{|U\rangle, |V\rangle, |W\rangle\}$, with respect to the $\{|X\rangle, |Y\rangle, |Z\rangle\}$ basis, as follows:

$$|U\rangle = \frac{1}{\sqrt{2}}|X\rangle + \frac{1}{\sqrt{2}}|Y\rangle + 0 \cdot |Z\rangle,$$

$$|V\rangle = \frac{1}{2}|X\rangle + \frac{-1}{2}|Y\rangle + \frac{1}{\sqrt{2}} \cdot |Z\rangle,$$

$$|W\rangle = \frac{-1}{2}|X\rangle + \frac{1}{2}|Y\rangle + \frac{1}{\sqrt{2}} \cdot |Z\rangle.$$

For example, to reach the vector $|V\rangle$ we start at 0 and travel $1/2$ unit in the positive direction of $|X\rangle$ and continuing from that first point we travel another $1/2$ unit in the negative direction of $|Y\rangle$, and continuing from the second point we travel $1/\sqrt{2}$ units in the direction of $|Z\rangle$. Therefore, the coordinates for these three vectors, $\{|U\rangle, |V\rangle, |W\rangle\}$ with respect to the $\{|X\rangle, |Y\rangle, |Z\rangle\}$ basis are described by

$$|U\rangle \rightarrow \begin{bmatrix} 1/\sqrt{2} \\ 1/\sqrt{2} \\ 0 \end{bmatrix}, \ |V\rangle \rightarrow \begin{bmatrix} 1/2 \\ -1/2 \\ 1/\sqrt{2} \end{bmatrix}, \ |W\rangle \rightarrow \begin{bmatrix} -1/2 \\ 1/2 \\ 1/\sqrt{2} \end{bmatrix}.$$

These coordinates have the following important meaning. If the man is convinced that his wife wants the Cadillac (i.e., his state $|S\rangle$ aligns with $|W\rangle$), then he must be uncertain about what he personally chooses: there is a $(-1/2)^2 = 0.25$ chance he chooses the BMW, there is a $(1/2)^2 = 0.25$ chance he chooses the Audi, and there is a $\left(1/\sqrt{2}\right)^2 = 0.50$ chance he chooses the Cadillac. In other words, if the man becomes definite about his wife's preference, then he must be indefinite about his own.

Alternatively, we could describe the three vectors $\{|X\rangle, |Y\rangle, |Z\rangle\}$, with respect to the $\{|U\rangle, |V\rangle, |W\rangle\}$, basis as follows:

$$|X\rangle = \frac{1}{\sqrt{2}}|U\rangle + \frac{1}{2}|V\rangle + \frac{-1}{2} \cdot |W\rangle,$$

$$|Y\rangle = \frac{1}{\sqrt{2}}|U\rangle + \frac{-1}{2}|V\rangle + \frac{1}{2} \cdot |W\rangle,$$

$$|Z\rangle = 0 \cdot |U\rangle + \frac{1}{\sqrt{2}}|V\rangle + \frac{1}{\sqrt{2}} \cdot |W\rangle.$$

Therefore, the coordinates for these three vectors $\{|X\rangle, |Y\rangle, |Z\rangle\}$ with respect to the $\{|U\rangle, |V\rangle, |W\rangle\}$ basis are described by

$$|X\rangle \rightarrow \begin{bmatrix} 1/\sqrt{2} \\ 1/2 \\ -1/2 \end{bmatrix}, \quad |Y\rangle \rightarrow \begin{bmatrix} 1/\sqrt{2} \\ -1/2 \\ 1/2 \end{bmatrix}, \quad |Z\rangle \rightarrow \begin{bmatrix} 0 \\ 1/\sqrt{2} \\ 1/\sqrt{2} \end{bmatrix}.$$

These coordinates imply the following. If the man becomes definite that he wants the BMW (i.e., his state $|S\rangle$ aligns with $|X\rangle$), then there is a $\left(1\sqrt{2}\right)^2 = 0.50$ chance that he thinks his wife wants the BMW, there is a $(1/2)^2 = 0.25$ chance he thinks his wife wants the Audi, and there is a $(-1/2)^2 = 0.25$ chance that he thinks his wife wants the Cadillac. In short, the man can be definite about his own preference, but then he is forced to be indefinite about his wife's preferences. There is no way to be definite about both at the same time.

2.1.2.6   Order effects

The order that the man considers his own preference and his wife's preference can be interchanged. What effect does this order have on the probability of judgments for these two incompatible variables? Order effects pose a difficulty for classic probability theory because the conjunction of two events is defined as the intersection of two sets which commute, so that for example $p(\text{WC} \cap \text{MB}) = p(\text{MB} \cap \text{WC})$.

Suppose the man first evaluates his wife's preferences and then his own. Let us compute the probability that the man first thinks his wife prefers the Cadillac (event WC represented by the ray $|W\rangle$) and then he prefers the BMW (event MB represented by the ray $|X\rangle$), which is the probability for the path $|S\rangle \rightarrow |W\rangle \rightarrow |X\rangle$. For this section, we consistently use the coordinates expressed in terms of the $\{|X\rangle, |Y\rangle, |Z\rangle\}$ basis for all of the computations. This provides an opportunity to practice computing some more inner products. The probability that the man thinks his wife prefers the Cadillac is obtained by projecting the initial state $|S\rangle$ onto the W-ray spanned by the basis vector $|W\rangle$ and squaring its length. This projection equals $\langle W|S\rangle \cdot |W\rangle$, and the inner product between the vectors $|W\rangle$ and $|S\rangle$ (represented in coordinates of the $\{|X\rangle, |Y\rangle, |Z\rangle\}$ basis) is computed by the matrix formula

$$\langle W|S\rangle = \begin{bmatrix} -1/2 & 1/2 & 1/\sqrt{2} \end{bmatrix} \cdot \begin{bmatrix} -0.6963 \\ 0.6963 \\ 0.1741 \end{bmatrix}$$

$$= (-1/2) \cdot (-0.6963) + (1/2) \cdot (0.6963) + \left(1/\sqrt{2}\right) \cdot (0.1741) = 0.8194.$$

(This equals the coordinate φ_3 for $|S\rangle$ with respect to the $|U\rangle$ basis mentioned earlier.) The probability of this first event then equals $|\langle W|S\rangle|^2 = |0.8194|^2 = 0.6714$. Now we need to revise the state conditioned on this observation. The revised state conditioned on the wife wanting the Cadillac equals $|W\rangle$, and using this revised state, the probability that the man chooses the BMW is obtained by projecting the state $|W\rangle$ onto the X-ray and squaring its length. This projection equals $\langle X|W\rangle \cdot |W\rangle$, and the inner product between $|X\rangle$ and $|W\rangle$ is computed again from the matrix formula

$$\langle W|X\rangle = \begin{bmatrix} -1/2 & 1/2 & 1/\sqrt{2} \end{bmatrix} \cdot \begin{bmatrix} 1 \\ 0 \\ 0 \end{bmatrix}$$

$$= (-1/2) \cdot 1 + (1/2) \cdot 0 + \left(1/\sqrt{2}\right) \cdot 0 = -1/2.$$

Thus, the inner product is $\langle X|W\rangle = -1/2$, and so the probability equals $|\langle X|W\rangle|^2 = |-1/2|^2 = 0.25$. Thus, the probability of the path $|S\rangle \to |W\rangle \to |X\rangle$ equals $|\langle W|S\rangle|^2 \cdot |\langle X|W\rangle|^2 = (0.6714)(0.25) = 0.16785$.

Now let us compute the probability for the reverse order; that is, the probability that the man first prefers the BMW (event MB represented by ray $|X\rangle$), and then he thinks his wife prefers the Cadillac (event WC represented by ray $|W\rangle$), which is the probability for the path $|S\rangle \to |X\rangle \to |W\rangle$. The probability for this other path equals the probability of the first event (a transition from $|S\rangle$ to $|X\rangle$) times the probability of the second event given the first (a transition from $|X\rangle$ to $|W\rangle$), which is given by $|\langle X|S\rangle|^2 \cdot |\langle X|W\rangle|^2$. The inner product $\langle X|S\rangle$ (which we calculated earlier) equals $\langle X|S\rangle = -0.6963$, and so $|\langle X|S\rangle|^2 = |-0.6369|^2 = 0.4848$. The inner product $\langle X|W\rangle$ (which we just recently calculated) equals $\langle X|W\rangle = -1/2$, and so the probability that the man thinks his wife wants the Cadillac, given that he chooses the BMW, equals $|\langle W|X\rangle|^2 = |-1/2|^2 = 1/4$. Finally, the probability for the path $|S\rangle \to |X\rangle \to |W\rangle$ equals $|\langle X|S\rangle|^2 \cdot |\langle W|X\rangle|^2 = (0.4848) \cdot (1/4) = 0.1212$. Thus, the path $|S\rangle \to |W\rangle \to |X\rangle$ is more likely than the opposite path from $|S\rangle \to |X\rangle \to |W\rangle$ because of the difference in the probabilities produced by the first link: $|\langle W|S\rangle|^2 > |\langle X|S\rangle|^2$. This order effect reflects the incompatible representation that underpins this example.

2.1.2.7   Interference effect

The example model shown in Figure 2.2 also produces an interference effect that violates the classic law of total probability. Let us compare the probability that the man thinks his wife wants the BMW without deciding what he prefers (denoted $p(\text{WB})$) with the probability that he thinks his wife wants the BMW after deciding what he prefers (denoted $p_T(\text{WB})$). According to classic probability theory, the event $\text{WB} = (\text{WB} \cap \text{MB}) \cup (\text{WB} \cap \text{MA}) \cup (\text{WB} \cap \text{MC})$, which implies the law of total probability, $p(\text{WB}) = p_T(\text{WB})$, with the latter defined by

$$p_T(\text{WB}) = p(\text{MB}) \cdot p(\text{WB}|\text{MB}) + p(\text{MA}) \cdot p(\text{WB}|\text{MA}) + p(\text{MC}) \cdot p(\text{WB}|\text{MC}).$$

What is the quantum probability for the event WB = "man thinks his wife wants BMW" without first deciding what he prefers? That is, what is the quantum version for $p(WB)$? Recall that this event corresponds to ray $|U\rangle$. So this probability is obtained by projecting the initial state $|S\rangle$ onto the U-ray, which equals $\langle U|S\rangle \cdot |U\rangle$ and then taking the squared length. Using the coordinates expressed in terms of the $\{|X\rangle, |Y\rangle, |Z\rangle\}$ basis, the inner product $\langle U|S\rangle$ is computed from the matrix formula

$$\langle U|S\rangle = \begin{bmatrix} 1/\sqrt{2} & 1/\sqrt{2} & 0 \end{bmatrix} \cdot \begin{bmatrix} -0.6963 \\ 0.6963 \\ 0.1741 \end{bmatrix}$$

$$= \left(1/\sqrt{2}\right) \cdot (-0.6963) + \left(1/\sqrt{2}\right) \cdot (0.6963) + 0 \cdot (0.1741) = 0.$$

(This equals the coordinate $\varphi_1 = 0$ for $|S\rangle$ with respect to the $|U\rangle$ basis mentioned earlier.) The inner product is zero, which means that these two vectors are orthogonal, and so the transition probability directly from $|S\rangle \rightarrow |U\rangle$ is also zero. Thus, the probability that the man thinks his wife wants the BMW (before he decides himself) is simply $p(WB) = |\langle U|S\rangle|^2 = 0$.

Now what is the quantum probability for the same event WB after the man decides what he wants? In this case, the man is forced to break down his superposition state into one of the three definite preference states before thinking about his wife's preference. This results in only three possible indirect paths to get to the conclusion that the wife wants the BMW: $|S\rangle \rightarrow |X\rangle \rightarrow |U\rangle$, $|S\rangle \rightarrow |Y\rangle \rightarrow |U\rangle$, or $|S\rangle \rightarrow |Z\rangle \rightarrow |U\rangle$. The man must take one of these three paths. Each path has its own probability; therefore, the total probability that the man thinks his wife wants the BMW (when he is forced to resolve his own preferences first) equals the sum of each of these three path probabilities:

$$p_T(WB) = |\langle X|S\rangle|^2 \cdot |\langle U|X\rangle|^2 + |\langle Y|S\rangle|^2 \cdot |\langle U|Y\rangle|^2 + |\langle Z|S\rangle|^2 \cdot |\langle U|Z\rangle|^2$$

$$= (0.4848)(1/2) + (0.4848)(1/2) + (0.0303)(0) = 0.4848.$$

As $p_T(WB)$ *does not equal* $p(WB)$, the law of total probability does not hold for this example.

In summary, it is impossible for the man to think his wife wants the BMW if the man's personal preference remains indefinite, but if the man breaks down his superposition state into a definite state first, then it is more likely that he can imagine his wife also wanting the BMW. The probability produced by the direct path (before resolving the man's preference) falls below the total probability (after resolving the man's preference), so the interference is negative. Even more dramatic is the fact that the probability of a single path with two links, say $|S\rangle \rightarrow |X\rangle \rightarrow |U\rangle$, which equals 0.2424, is greater than the probability of the direct path $|S\rangle \rightarrow |U\rangle$, which is zero.

2.1.2.8   Unitary transformations

In Section 2.1.2.5 on the uncertainty principle, we expressed the coordinates for the three basis vectors $\{|U\rangle, |V\rangle, |W\rangle\}$ in terms of the basis vectors $\{|X\rangle, |Y\rangle, |Z\rangle\}$. We can collect these columns together to form a 3×3 transformation matrix

U_{MW} shown below that relates the man and woman coordinate systems: the first column contains the coordinates of $|U\rangle$, the second column contains the coordinates of $|V\rangle$, and the third column contains the coordinates of $|W\rangle$, all with respect to the basis vectors $\{|X\rangle, |Y\rangle, |Z\rangle\}$. The first row contains the coordinates of $|X\rangle$, the second row contains the coordinates of $|Y\rangle$, and the third row contains the coordinates of $|Z\rangle$, all with respect to basis vectors $\{|U\rangle, |V\rangle, |W\rangle\}$.

The unitary property is important for the following reason. Transformations produced by a unitary matrix preserve inner products. We saw this earlier when we computed the inner product $\langle W|S\rangle$ two different ways. One was based on the coordinates using the $\{|X\rangle, |Y\rangle, |Z\rangle\}$ basis and the other was based on coordinates using the $\{|U\rangle, |V\rangle, |W\rangle\}$ basis, and they gave the same answer. This is because the coordinates using the $\{|X\rangle, |Y\rangle, |Z\rangle\}$ basis are a unitary transformation of the coordinates using the $\{|U\rangle, |V\rangle, |W\rangle\}$ basis.

Suppose we start with the state $|S\rangle$ expressed initially in the coordinate vector φ (2.2) corresponding to the $\{|U\rangle, |V\rangle, |W\rangle\}$ basis, and we wish to transform this into the vector ψ (2.1) that describes $|S\rangle$ in terms of the $\{|X\rangle, |Y\rangle, |Z\rangle\}$ basis. This can easily be done by matrix multiplication. We multiply the 3×3 matrix U_{MW} by the 3×1 matrix φ as follows:

$$\psi = U_{MW} \cdot \varphi$$

$$\begin{bmatrix} \psi_1 \\ \psi_2 \\ \psi_3 \end{bmatrix} = \begin{bmatrix} \langle X|U\rangle & \langle X|V\rangle & \langle X|W\rangle \\ \langle Y|U\rangle & \langle Y|V\rangle & \langle Y|W\rangle \\ \langle Z|U\rangle & \langle Z|V\rangle & \langle Z|W\rangle \end{bmatrix} \cdot \begin{bmatrix} \varphi_1 \\ \varphi_2 \\ \varphi_3 \end{bmatrix}$$

$$\begin{bmatrix} -0.6963 \\ 0.6963 \\ 0.1741 \end{bmatrix} = \begin{bmatrix} \frac{1}{\sqrt{2}} \cdot (0) + \frac{1}{2} \cdot (-0.5732) + \frac{-1}{2} \cdot (0.8194) \\ \frac{1}{\sqrt{2}} \cdot (0) + \frac{-1}{2} \cdot (-0.5732) + \frac{1}{2} \cdot (0.8194) \\ 0 \cdot (0) + \frac{1}{\sqrt{2}} \cdot (-0.5732) + \frac{1}{\sqrt{2}} \cdot (0.8194) \end{bmatrix}.$$

In other words, the result ψ_i in row i on the left-hand side is obtained by taking the inner product of the ith row of U_{MW} with φ. Notice that if the state is equal to $|S\rangle = |V\rangle$ so that $\varphi_2 = 1$, then $U_{MW} \cdot \begin{bmatrix} 0 & 1 & 0 \end{bmatrix}^\dagger$ equals the coordinates for $|V\rangle$ expressed in the $\{|X\rangle, |Y\rangle, |Z\rangle\}$ basis. The unitary matrix U_{MW} transforms the woman's coordinates into the man's coordinates.

Alternatively, suppose we start with the state $|S\rangle$ expressed initially in the coordinate vector ψ (2.1) corresponding to the $\{|X\rangle, |Y\rangle, |Z\rangle\}$ basis, and we wish to transform this into the vector φ (2.2) that describes $|S\rangle$ in terms of the $\{|U\rangle, |V\rangle, |W\rangle\}$ basis. This is done by the matrix product

$$\varphi = U_{MW}^\dagger \cdot \psi$$

$$\begin{bmatrix} \varphi_1 \\ \varphi_2 \\ \varphi_3 \end{bmatrix} = \cdot \begin{bmatrix} \langle U|X\rangle & \langle U|Y\rangle & \langle U|X\rangle \\ \langle V|X\rangle & \langle V|Y\rangle & \langle V|Y\rangle \\ \langle W|X\rangle & \langle W|Y\rangle & \langle W|Z\rangle \end{bmatrix} \begin{bmatrix} \psi_1 \\ \psi_2 \\ \psi_3 \end{bmatrix}$$

$$\begin{bmatrix} 0 \\ -0.5732 \\ 0.8194 \end{bmatrix} = \begin{bmatrix} \frac{1}{\sqrt{2}} \cdot (-0.6963) + \frac{1}{\sqrt{2}} \cdot (0.6963) + 0 \cdot (0.1741) \\ \frac{1}{2} \cdot (-0.6963) + \frac{-1}{2} \cdot (0.6963) + \frac{1}{\sqrt{2}} \cdot (0.1741) \\ \frac{-1}{2} \cdot (-0.6963) + \frac{1}{2} \cdot (0.6963) + \frac{1}{\sqrt{2}} \cdot (0.1741) \end{bmatrix}.$$

Recall that the "adjoint" † operation indicates the transpose–conjugate operation on a matrix. Transpose means change rows to columns. Conjugation means we reverse the inner product from $\langle X|Y \rangle$ to $\langle Y|X \rangle$. Note that if the state is equal to $|S\rangle = |Y\rangle$ so that $\psi_2 = 1$, then $U_{MW}^{\dagger} \cdot [0 \quad 1 \quad 0]^{\dagger}$ equals the coordinates for $|Y\rangle$ expressed in the $\{|U\rangle, |V\rangle, |W\rangle\}$ basis. For convenience we can define $U_{MW}^{\dagger} = U_{WM}$ as the unitary matrix that represents changes from the man's to the woman's coordinates.

These transformations are called unitary matrices for the following reasons. First, the sum of squared magnitudes within each column of U_{MW} must sum to one; given that one is in a column state, the person must transit to one of the row states. Also, the sum of squared magnitudes of the columns of U_{WM} must sum to one. Using the law of reciprocity, this also implies that the sum of squared magnitudes of the rows of each matrix must sum to one as well. Third, the columns of U_{MW} are pairwise orthogonal; this follows from the fact that it is impossible to transit from one of the states in the set $|X\rangle, |Y\rangle$, or $|Z\rangle$ directly to a different member of this set. The columns for U_{WM} are also orthogonal; again, this is because it is impossible to transit from one of the states in the set $|U\rangle, |V\rangle$, or $|W\rangle$ directly to a different member in this set. Of course, these orthogonal properties also apply to the rows, because the row for one matrix is the column for the other. All of these properties are conveniently summarized by matrix algebra: $U_{MW} \cdot U_{MW}^{\dagger} = I = U_{MW}^{\dagger} \cdot U_{MW}$, where I is an identity matrix.

2.1.2.9   Coarse and complete measurements, pure and mixed states

In quantum theory, it is important to distinguish a complete measurement from a coarse measurement. For a *complete* measurement, the set of mutually exclusive and exhaustive events that are used to record the outcome of an experiment are defined by rays (one-dimensional subspaces) spanned by each of the basis vectors. These events cannot be broken down or refined into more specific outcomes. For a *coarse* measurement, some of the events are not rays; instead, they are subspaces of dimension greater than one. It is possible to break down the coarse measurement into more specific outcomes. The law of reciprocity is defined in terms of transitions between state vectors (spanning one-dimensional rays) and so this law can only be tested with complete measurements.

Transitioning from a pure state   Referring to the example in Figure 2.2, suppose the man considers a choice between the category of sporty car (which includes BMW, Audi) and luxurious car (Cadillac). From this task, we can obtain two conditional probabilities. One is the probability of the event "man chooses a sporty car" given that he thinks "the woman desires a luxurious one" and the other is the probability that he thinks the "woman desires the luxurious car" given that "the man chooses a sporty car."

Let us first compute the probability that the man either chooses a car from the category of sporty cars or he chooses a luxurious car, given that his wife told him she wants a luxurious car. For this problem, we compute the probability of observing the event spanned by $\{|X\rangle \cup |Y\rangle\}$ given that the event spanned by $|W\rangle$ has been observed. Note that $|X\rangle, |Y\rangle$ are orthogonal as in Figure 2.2 because the man can only choose one car. According to our quantum model, given the observation about the wife, the original state $|S\rangle$ changes to the revised state $|W\rangle$. In quantum theory, $|W\rangle$ is called a *pure* state – it is a basis vector in the $\{|U\rangle, |V\rangle, |W\rangle\}$ basis, but it is a superposition state with respect to the $\{|X\rangle, |Y\rangle, |Z\rangle\}$ basis. The probability equals the squared length of the projection of $|W\rangle$ onto the plane spanned by $\{|X\rangle, |Y\rangle\}$, which equals

$$|| \, |X\rangle\langle X|W\rangle + |Y\rangle\langle Y|W\rangle \, ||^2 = || \, \langle X|W\rangle|X\rangle \, ||^2 + || \, \langle Y|W\rangle|Y\rangle \, ||^2$$

$$= |\langle X|W\rangle|^2 + |\langle Y|W\rangle|^2 = \left(\frac{-1}{2}\right)^2 + \left(\frac{1}{2}\right)^2 = \frac{1}{2}.$$

Transitioning from a mixed state   Now suppose the man records a definite choice of one car from the set of three cars {BMW, Audi, Cadillac}, and then he considers the probability that his wife wants a luxurious car. However, the on-line site only happens to record the categories of sporty (BMW or Audi) versus luxurious (Cadillac). So, for example, the man may choose the BMW, but this is categorized by the web logging system as a sporty car, which discards information about exactly which sporty car was actually chosen. In this case, the man's preference for a car has become definite before he judges whether or not his wife wants the Cadillac. For this problem, we have what is called a *mixed* state. Either the man definitely chose the BMW or the man definitely chose the Audi, and there is no other possibility. The probability he chose the BMW, given that he chose one of these two options, equals $|\langle X|S\rangle|^2/(|\langle X|S\rangle|^2 + |\langle Y|S\rangle|^2)$; similarly, the probability he chose the Audi, given that he chose one of these two options, equals $|\langle Y|S\rangle|^2/(|\langle X|S\rangle|^2 + |\langle Y|S\rangle|^2)$. The probability that he thinks his wife wants the luxury car (Cadillac) given that he definitely chose the BMW equals $|\langle W|X\rangle|^2$; similarly, the probability that he thinks his wife wants the luxury car (Cadillac) given that he definitely chose the Audi equals $|\langle W|Y\rangle|^2$. Thus, the total probability that the event spanned by $|W\rangle$ occurs given that either the event spanned by $|X\rangle$ was recorded or the event spanned by $|Y\rangle$ was recorded equals

$$\frac{|\langle X|S\rangle|^2}{|\langle X|S\rangle|^2 + |\langle Y|S\rangle|^2} \cdot |\langle W|X\rangle|^2 + \frac{|\langle Y|S\rangle|^2}{|\langle X|S\rangle|^2 + |\langle Y|S\rangle|^2} \cdot |\langle W|Y\rangle|^2$$

$$= \frac{1}{2} \cdot \left(\frac{-1}{2}\right)^2 + \frac{1}{2} \cdot \left(\frac{1}{2}\right)^2 = \frac{1}{4}.$$

So we see that, in this simple case of coarse measurements, the conditional probability of p(man chooses a sporty car|wife chooses a luxury car) $= 1/2$ does not equal the conditional probability p(wife chooses a luxury car|man chooses a sporty car) $= 1/4$. Appendix B describes a more elegant way to treat mixed states based on what is called the density matrix representation of states.

2.1.2.10 Compatible representation

Now consider forming a compatible representation. In this case we are assuming that the man can simultaneously view his own preference as well as his wife's preference, and the order of evaluation does not matter. Using this representation, we define nine different events formed by all possible combinations of the man's three outcomes × the woman's three outcomes: {(man prefers BMW ∧ woman prefers BMW), (man prefers BMW ∧ woman prefers Audi), ..., (man prefers Cadillac ∧ woman prefers Cadillac)}. To represent these nine combined events, we form a nine-dimensional vector space, with nine orthogonal rays, and each ray corresponds to one of the nine combined events. For the time being, we have to abandon Figure 2.2, and we cannot make a graph of this representation. The nine rays are spanned by nine basis vectors that form the basis $MW = \{|AA\rangle, |AB\rangle, |AC\rangle, |BA\rangle, |BB\rangle, |BC\rangle, |CA\rangle, |CB\rangle, |CC\rangle\}$, where the first index represents the man's preference and the second the woman's preference. In particular, the basis vector $|BC\rangle$ represents the event that the man prefers the BMW and the man thinks his wife prefers the Cadillac. The state is represented within this nine-dimensional space as

$$|S\rangle = \psi_{AA} \cdot |AA\rangle + \psi_{AB} \cdot |AB\rangle + \psi_{AC} \cdot |AC\rangle$$
$$+ \psi_{BA} \cdot |BA\rangle + \psi_{BB} \cdot |BB\rangle + \psi_{BC} \cdot |BC\rangle$$
$$+ \psi_{CA} \cdot |CA\rangle + \psi_{CB} \cdot |CB\rangle + \psi_{CC} \cdot |CC\rangle,$$

which has nine coordinates, one for each basis vector. The probability of one of the nine events is obtained by projecting the state $|S\rangle$ onto the basis for an event. In particular, the probability that the man prefers the BMW and the woman prefers the Cadillac equals $\| \psi_{BC} \cdot |BC\rangle\|^2 = |\psi_{BC}|^2$.

An interesting special case for the state is one in which the man blissfully believes that he and his wife will always agree, but they are equally likely to agree on choosing either the BMW or the Cadillac:

$$|S\rangle = \frac{1}{\sqrt{2}} \cdot |BB\rangle + \frac{1}{\sqrt{2}} \cdot |CC\rangle.$$

As discussed earlier, the inner product between a basis vector and the state vector produces the coefficient assigned to that basis vector by the state vector. We can numerically represent each basis vector, with respect to the basis MW, by a 9×1 matrix with zeros in all rows except a one in the row corresponding to the basis vector. Then the inner product between a basis vector, say $|BB\rangle$ (man prefers BMW, woman prefers BMW) and the state $|S\rangle$ simply equals $\langle BB|S\rangle = \psi_{BB} = 1/\sqrt{2}$ (using the above blissful example). Using Feynman's transitions terminology, $\langle BB|S\rangle$ is the transition amplitude from the initial state $|S\rangle$ to the basis state $|BB\rangle$ and the probability of this transition equals the squared magnitude of the amplitude $|\langle BB|S\rangle|^2 = |\psi_{BB}|^2 = 1/2$.

We can also compute probabilities for more general events within this setting. The probability that the man prefers the BMW (ignoring the wife's preference) is obtained by projecting the state on the subspace spanned by vectors

path. This sounds a lot like the product rule for the Markov model except that it applies to amplitudes rather than probabilities. In fact, the probability of a single path is the squared magnitude of the amplitude, which equals the product of squared magnitudes of the amplitudes for each transition step along the path. Therefore, the quantum probability for a single path is essentially the same as the Markov probability for a single path.

2.2.3 Multiple indistinguishable paths

Now consider the second rule, which concerns starting from an initial state $|S\rangle$ and transiting to a final state $|Z\rangle$ through multiple possible paths, such as for example $|S\rangle \to |X_1\rangle \to |Z\rangle$ or $|S\rangle \to |X_2\rangle \to |Z\rangle$ or $|S\rangle \to |X_3\rangle \to |Z\rangle$, and one does not resolve or cannot observe which path is taken to get from $|S\rangle$ to $|Z\rangle$, so that the paths remain indistinguishable. For example, when choosing a car, the man can pass through three different possible states of thought about his wife's preferences (she may want the Audi, or BMW, or Cadillac) before arriving at his own conclusion about the BMW. If he is not forced to decide about his wife before making his own choice, then these three paths are not resolved or observed and they remain indistinguishable.

According to a Markov model, the probability of starting in state $|S\rangle$ and arriving at state $|Z\rangle$ by multiple paths is simply the sum of the individual path probabilities. This is essentially the law of total probability applied to Markov models.

Feynman's *second* rule states that the amplitude for the transition from a beginning state $|S\rangle$ to a final state $|Z\rangle$ passing through multiple indistinguishable paths equals the sum of the path amplitudes. This is called the law of total amplitude, and resembles the law of total probability for Markov models, except that it applies to amplitudes rather than probabilities. The magnitude of the amplitudes must be squared in order to determine the probability, and this is where the quantum probability deviates from the Markov probability. The final answer is different because the quantum *probability* obtained from squaring the sum of the path amplitudes does not equal the Markov probability obtained by summing the path probabilities (e.g., if a and b are two amplitudes for two different paths, then $|a + b|^2 = |a|^2 + |b|^2 + (a^*b + b^*a)$.

2.2.4 Observations along the path

Now consider the third rule for the more complex case in which we wish to compute the probability of starting from an initial state $|S\rangle$ and ending at some state $|Z\rangle$, but we resolve the state at some intermediate point. For example, suppose we observe one of three possible intermediate states ($|U\rangle$, $|V\rangle$, $|W\rangle$) along the way from $|S\rangle$ to $|Z\rangle$. Referring to our car choice example, what is the probability that the man starts in state $|S\rangle$ and finally decides he wants a BMW, if we first ask him to determine what his wife wants before he makes his personal choice?

According to both the quantum and Markov models, we first compute the probability of starting at $|S\rangle$ and ending at each one of the intermediate states ($|U\rangle$, $|V\rangle$, $|W\rangle$) that we observe. Then we compute the probability of starting at each one of the intermediate states ($|U\rangle$, $|V\rangle$, $|W\rangle$) and ending at the final state $|Z\rangle$. Finally, we compute the total probability by taking the product of the previous two probabilities for each intermediate state and then summing these products across all of the intermediate states ($|U\rangle$, $|V\rangle$, $|W\rangle$). Note that the probability of starting at a state $|S\rangle$ and passing through multiple unobserved states to reach an intermediate $|U\rangle$ will differ for the quantum and Markov models if there are multiple paths from $|S\rangle$ to $|U\rangle$ because of the second rule for multiple paths. So will the probability of going from an intermediate state $|U\rangle$ to the final state $|Z\rangle$ if there are multiple indistinguishable paths from $|U\rangle$ to $|Z\rangle$. Deciding when to use the second rule is the tricky part of applying quantum theory – we have to use the second rule whenever the paths that can be taken are indistinguishable. If we distinguish the path by identifying which path was taken, then we use Feynman's third rule stated above, which is just like the Markov model. Let us take a look at some concrete examples which demonstrate the application of these rules.

2.2.5   Concrete example for path diagrams

Once again the plan for this example is to build a simple quantum model for a preferential choice task (Lambert-Mogiliansky *et al.*, 2009). Suppose a man is thinking about buying a new car and he has narrowed his options down to three: BMW, Audi, and Cadillac. But he makes this choice from two different perspectives: one is from his own personal view, but a second perspective originates from his wife's point of view.

2.2.5.1   Single transitions

First, let us focus only on the probabilities that the man chooses the BMW, or Audi, or Cadillac. The choice process starts with an initial state denoted $|S\rangle$, and it can end at one of the three preference states $|X\rangle$, $|Y\rangle$, or $|Z\rangle$ generating three possible transitions from initial to final states: $|S\rangle \rightarrow |X\rangle$ with amplitude $\langle X|S\rangle$, or $|S\rangle \rightarrow |Y\rangle$ with amplitude $\langle Y|S\rangle$, or $|S\rangle \rightarrow |Z\rangle$ with amplitude $\langle Z|S\rangle$. The probability of each transition equals the squared magnitude of the amplitude. Given the state $|S\rangle$, the man must choose one of these three, so that we require $|\langle X|S\rangle|^2 + |\langle Y|S\rangle|^2 + |\langle Z|S\rangle|^2 = 1$. Of course, we need to determine these amplitudes somehow, and in the geometric approach we discuss methods for doing this, but for now we simply assume that $\langle X|S\rangle = -0.6963$, $\langle Y|S\rangle = 0.6963$, and $\langle Z|S\rangle = 0.1741$. Then using Feynman's rule we obtain the path probabilities by taking the squared amplitudes of each path to produce $|\langle X|S\rangle|^2 = 0.4848$ as probability of choosing the BMW, $|\langle Y|S\rangle|^2 = 0.4848$ as the probability of choosing the Audi, and $|\langle Z|S\rangle|^2 = 0.0303$ as the probability of choosing the Cadillac.

Given that $|X\rangle, |Y\rangle$, or $|Z\rangle$ are states, we can also ask what the amplitude is of transiting from state $|X\rangle$ to state $|Y\rangle$ represented by the amplitude $\langle Y|X\rangle$. If the man chooses the BMW, then he cannot choose the Audi as he may only choose one. Thus, $\langle Y|X\rangle = 0$ and for the same reason any transition from one of these three states to a different one is impossible and has zero amplitude. However, if the man decides he chooses the BMW, then he chooses the BMW (unless something happens over time to make him change his mind, which we ignore for the time being) and so $\langle X|X\rangle = \langle Y|Y\rangle = \langle Z|Z\rangle = 1$.

Now let us consider only what the man thinks his wife wants. Once again the initial state is represented by $|S\rangle$, but three new states of preferences, $|U\rangle, |V\rangle$, or $|W\rangle$, are used to represent what the man thinks his wife wants concerning the BMW, Audi, or Cadillac respectively. From the initial state the man can make a transition to one of the three final states of preference for his wife: $|S\rangle \rightarrow |U\rangle$ with amplitude $\langle U|S\rangle$, or $|S\rangle \rightarrow |V\rangle$ with amplitude $\langle V|S\rangle$, or $|S\rangle \rightarrow |W\rangle$ with amplitude $\langle W|S\rangle$. Given the state $|S\rangle$, the wife must choose one of these three, so that we require $|\langle U|S\rangle|^2 + |\langle V|S\rangle|^2 + |\langle W|S\rangle|^2 = 1$. Again, we need to determine these amplitudes somehow, and we discussed a method in the geometric approach, but for now we simply assume that $\langle U|S\rangle = 0$, $\langle V|S\rangle = -0.5732$ and $\langle W|S\rangle = 0.8194$. Using Feynman's rule we obtain the path probabilities by taking the squared amplitudes of each path to produce $|\langle U|S\rangle|^2 = 0$ as the probability of choosing the BMW, $|\langle V|S\rangle|^2 = 0.32856$ as the probability of choosing the Audi, and $|\langle W|S\rangle|^2 = 0.6714$ as the probability of choosing the Cadillac.

What about transitions between the three states $|U\rangle, |V\rangle$, or $|W\rangle$? If the man thinks his wife would choose the Cadillac then he cannot think his wife would choose the BMW, because she may only choose one. So the transition from one of these states to a different one must be zero; e.g., $\langle U|V\rangle = 0$. However, if the man decides his wife wants the Cadillac, then that conclusion is final (unless some new information comes along to change this conclusion, which we ignore for the time being) and so $\langle W|W\rangle = 1$. For the same reason, $\langle U|U\rangle = 1 = \langle V|V\rangle$.

At this point, it may seem that nothing special happens with a single transition from one state to another, and the quantum model behaves exactly like a Markov model. However, recall the following surprising property of transitions required by the geometric approach.

2.2.5.2   Law of reciprocity revisited

It is possible for the man to think his wife wants the Cadillac but he chooses the BMW for himself. In other words, $\langle X|W\rangle$ is not zero. If we wish to interpret the transition amplitude $\langle X|W\rangle$ as an inner product between two vectors as discussed in the geometric approach, then we must impose the restriction implied by inner products on quantum transitions. The probability of transiting $|X\rangle \rightarrow |W\rangle$, from one state $|X\rangle$ to another state $|W\rangle$, equals the probability of the transition in the opposite direction $|W\rangle \rightarrow |X\rangle$. In other words, $|\langle W|X\rangle|^2 = |\langle X|W\rangle|^2$. Markov models, from classic probability theory, do not have to obey this restriction, and they allow $p(X|W) \neq p(W|X)$ for Markov states. Note, however, that quantum probabilities only obey the law of reciprocity for transitions between quantum states (events represented by unidimensional rays). If X, Y are general events (coarse measurements), and each event contains several possible states, then quantum theory no longer entails that $p(X|Y) = p(Y|X)$.

2.2.5.3 Unitary amplitude transition matrices

In fact any transition from the states $|U\rangle, |V\rangle$, or $|W\rangle$ to the states $|X\rangle, |Y\rangle$, or $|Z\rangle$ is possible. Thus, we can form a 3×3 table or matrix of transitions representing transitions from each of the $|U\rangle, |V\rangle$, or $|W\rangle$ states to each of the $|X\rangle, |Y\rangle$, or $|Z\rangle$ states, which is given below. Earlier, we discussed how to determine these from the transformation between basis vectors shown in Figure 2.2.

$$U_{MW} = \begin{bmatrix} \langle X|U\rangle & \langle X|V\rangle & \langle X|W\rangle \\ \langle Y|U\rangle & \langle Y|V\rangle & \langle Y|W\rangle \\ \langle Z|U\rangle & \langle Z|V\rangle & \langle Z|W\rangle \end{bmatrix} = \begin{bmatrix} 1/\sqrt{2} & 1/2 & -1/2 \\ 1/\sqrt{2} & -1/2 & 1/2 \\ 0 & 1/\sqrt{2} & 1/\sqrt{2} \end{bmatrix}. \quad (2.3)$$

Each cell entry in the transformation matrix represents the amplitude for transiting from a column state to a row state. For example, the entry in row 2 and column 1 is $\langle Y|U\rangle = 1/\sqrt{2}$, which is the amplitude for transiting from state $|U\rangle$ to state $|Y\rangle$.

What about the other direction? This would be a new table formed by flipping rows to columns and reversing the transitions of the previous matrix, which is called the Hermitian transpose (an operation symbolized by the dagger representing adjoint)

$$U_{MW}^\dagger = U_{WM} = \begin{bmatrix} \langle U|X\rangle & \langle U|Y\rangle & \langle U|Z\rangle \\ \langle V|X\rangle & \langle V|Y\rangle & \langle V|Z\rangle \\ \langle W|X\rangle & \langle W|Y\rangle & \langle W|Z\rangle \end{bmatrix} = \begin{bmatrix} 1/\sqrt{2} & 1/\sqrt{2} & 0 \\ 1/2 & -1/2 & 1/\sqrt{2} \\ -1/2 & 1/2 & 1/\sqrt{2} \end{bmatrix}.$$
$$(2.4)$$

To conform with the geometric approach, these amplitude transformation matrices must be unitary matrices, which satisfy the unitary property $U_{MW} \cdot U_{MW}^\dagger = I = U_{MW}^\dagger \cdot U_{MW}$, where I is an identity matrix.

2.2.5.4 Double stochasticity

If we square the magnitude of an amplitude in a cell of the unitary transition matrix U_{MW}, then we obtain the probability of the transition for that cell:

$$T_{MW} = \begin{bmatrix} |\langle X|U\rangle|^2 & |\langle X|V\rangle|^2 & |\langle X|W\rangle|^2 \\ |\langle Y|U\rangle|^2 & |\langle Y|V\rangle|^2 & |\langle Y|W\rangle|^2 \\ |\langle Z|U\rangle|^2 & |\langle Z|V\rangle|^2 & |\langle Z|W\rangle|^2 \end{bmatrix} = \begin{bmatrix} 1/2 & 1/4 & 1/4 \\ 1/2 & 1/4 & 1/4 \\ 0 & 1/2 & 1/2 \end{bmatrix}.$$

For example, in the second row and first column of U_{MW}, we have $\langle Y|U\rangle = 1/\sqrt{2}$; therefore, $|\langle Y|U\rangle|^2 = 0.50$ is the probability of the transition $|U\rangle \rightarrow |Y\rangle$. We can construct a new transition matrix T_{MW} by taking the squared magnitude of all the cells in U_{MW}. As we noted previously, the squared magnitudes within a column must sum to unity. This makes sense, because a transition must occur to one of the row states from a given column. This is a property that all transition matrices must obey. Markov models also require the use of transition matrices with columns that sum to unity. In addition, however, if we impose the law of reciprocity required by the geometric approach, then the quantum model also requires that the squared magnitudes of the rows must sum to unity. Therefore, the transition matrix T_{MW} generated from a unitary transformation matrix U_{MW} must satisfy a property called *double stochasticity*: both the rows and columns of the transition matrix must sum to one (Peres, 1998). This is a restriction that quantum models must obey, but Markov models do not have to obey. This marks another facet where quantum theory is more restricted than Markov theory.

2.2.5.5   Analysis of single paths

Let us consider the probability for a sequence of two choices. What is the probability that the man thinks that the wife wants the BMW (represented by state $|U\rangle$) and then he himself also chooses the BMW (represented by state $|X\rangle$)? That is, what is the probability of the path $|S\rangle \to |U\rangle \to |X\rangle$? According to Feynman's first rule, we compute the product of the amplitudes $\langle X|U\rangle\langle U|S\rangle = \frac{1}{\sqrt{2}} \cdot 0 = 0$ and the probability equals the squared magnitude, $|\langle X|U\rangle\langle U|S\rangle|^2 = 0$. So, in this example, this sequence of choices is impossible.

Now what is the probability that the man wants the BMW (represented by state $|X\rangle$) and then he thinks his wife wants the BMW too (represented by state $|U\rangle$)? That is, what is the probability for the reverse path $|S\rangle \to |X\rangle \to |U\rangle$. Again, according to Feynman's rule, we obtain $\langle U|X\rangle\langle X|S\rangle = \frac{1}{\sqrt{2}} \cdot (-0.6963)$ and the probability of this path equals $|\langle U|X\rangle\langle X|S\rangle|^2 = \left|\frac{1}{\sqrt{2}} \cdot (-0.6963)\right|^2 = 0.2424$. Therefore, it makes a difference which preference is established first – a well-established fact within psychology. It may be impossible to immediately think the wife wants the BMW, but if the man first becomes convinced that he wants the BMW, then it becomes possible for him to think of reasons that his wife wants it too.

A Markov model can also produce this order effect. According to the Markov model, the probability of the first sequence equals $p(X|U) \cdot p(U|S)$, and if we set $p(U|S) = 0$, then we obtain the same as the quantum model for the first order. For the reverse sequence, the Markov model produces the path probability $p(U|X) \cdot p(X|S)$ and if we set $p(U|X) = 0.50$ and $p(X|S) = 0.4848$, then we again obtain the same result as the quantum model for the second order. In short, both quantum and Markov models exhibit order effects for sequences of events.

2.2.5.6   Analysis of multiple paths

Recall that quantum and Markov models differ most dramatically when multiple indistinguishable paths are possible from a start to an end state. The Markov model must obey the law of total probability, but the quantum model obeys the law of total amplitude, and the probability is the squared amplitude. Below, we consider two different choice conditions: the first condition is when the man makes his choice without considering his wife's preference and the second condition is when he makes his choice after taking into consideration his wife's preference. For both conditions, we examine the probability that the man chooses the Cadillac (represented by state $|Z\rangle$). For the first condition, this is a single probability of the man choosing the Cadillac denoted as $p(\mathrm{MC})$; for the second condition it is the total probability for the man choosing the Cadillac denoted by $p_\mathrm{T}(\mathrm{MC})$.

For the first condition, suppose the man does not think about what his wife wants (he does not resolve whether she wants the BMW, Audi, or Cadillac). Recall that "man chooses Cadillac" corresponds to the basis vector $|Z\rangle$. In this case, there are three indeterminate paths starting from $|S\rangle$ and ending at $|Z\rangle$: one is $|S\rangle \to |U\rangle \to |Z\rangle$ with amplitude $\langle Z|U\rangle\langle U|S\rangle = 0$, a second is $|S\rangle \to |V\rangle \to |Z\rangle$ with amplitude $\langle Z|V\rangle\langle V|S\rangle = \frac{1}{\sqrt{2}}(-0.5732)$, and a third is $|S\rangle \to |W\rangle \to |Z\rangle$ with amplitude $\langle Z|W\rangle\langle W|S\rangle = \frac{1}{\sqrt{2}}(0.8194)$. According to Feynman's second rule, the transition amplitude for starting at $|S\rangle$ and transiting through these unresolved paths and ending at $|Z\rangle$ equals the sum of the amplitudes: $\langle Z|S\rangle = \langle Z|U\rangle\langle U|S\rangle + \langle Z|V\rangle\langle V|S\rangle + \langle Z|W\rangle\langle W|S\rangle$. The probability of the path equals the squared magnitude of this sum $|\langle Z|S\rangle|^2 = \left|0 + \frac{1}{\sqrt{2}}(-0.5732) + \frac{1}{\sqrt{2}}(0.8194)\right|^2 = |0.1741|^2 = 0.0303$. Thus, we obtain $p(\mathrm{MC}) = |\langle Z|S\rangle|^2 = 0.0303$. This is exactly the same as the probability for the direct path from $|S\rangle \to |Z\rangle$ described earlier when single transitions were discussed.

For the second condition, suppose that the man makes up his mind about what he thinks his wife wants first and afterwards he makes his own personal choice. In this case, he must conclude that she prefers the BMW, or Audi, or Cadillac, and these are the only three conclusions he can reach when forced to decide. According to Feynman's third rule, the probability of starting at $|S\rangle$ and ending at $|Z\rangle$ after first resolving either $|U\rangle, |V\rangle$, or $|W\rangle$ equals the sum of three path probabilities: (a) the probability of taking the $|S\rangle \to |U\rangle \to |Z\rangle$ path ($|\langle Z|U\rangle\langle U|S\rangle|^2 = 0$), (b) the probability of taking the $|S\rangle \to |V\rangle \to |Z\rangle$ path ($|\langle Z|V\rangle\langle V|S\rangle|^2 = \left(\frac{1}{2}\right)(0.32856) = 0.16428$), (c) the probability of taking the path $|S\rangle \to |W\rangle \to |Z\rangle$ ($|\langle Z|W\rangle\langle W|S\rangle|^2 = \left(\frac{1}{2}\right)(0.6714) = 0.3357$), and so the sum equals $|\langle Z|U\rangle\langle U|S\rangle|^2 + |\langle Z|V\rangle\langle V|S\rangle|^2 + |\langle Z|W\rangle\langle W|S\rangle|^2 = 0 + 0.16428 + 0.3357 = 0.50$. Therefore, $p_\mathrm{T}(\mathrm{MC}) = 0.50 > p(\mathrm{MC}) = 0.0303$, and so the total probability of the man choosing the Cadillac when the man resolves what he thinks his wife wants first is much greater than the probability that he chooses the Cadillac when he remains unresolved about what his wife wants. Again, not surprising from a psychological point of view – forcing the man to think first about what his wife wants increases the probability that he chooses what she wants too.

What about the Markov model? For the first condition, the man's state concerning what he believes about his wife is left in some unknown state. The

as it is required to understand the introduction to the quantum principles. The matrix operations can involve complex numbers, so these are also given due consideration. Matrix algebra programs such as Mathematica, Matlab, Gauss, R, etc. can easily and quickly carry out all of these computations with a single programming function or symbol that corresponds to one of the symbols used below. See Strang (1980) for a good matrix algebra textbook.

A matrix is a table containing real or complex numbers in the cells, such as X, Y, P, Q, R shown below:

$$X = \begin{bmatrix} x_1 \\ x_2 \\ x_3 \end{bmatrix}, \quad Y = \begin{bmatrix} y_1 \\ y_2 \\ y_3 \end{bmatrix}, \quad P = \begin{bmatrix} p_{11} & p_{12} & p_{13} \\ p_{21} & p_{22} & p_{23} \\ p_{31} & p_{32} & p_{33} \end{bmatrix},$$

$$Q = \begin{bmatrix} q_{11} & q_{12} & q_{13} \\ q_{21} & q_{22} & q_{23} \end{bmatrix}, \quad R = \begin{bmatrix} r_{11} & r_{12} & r_{13} \\ r_{21} & r_{22} & r_{23} \end{bmatrix}.$$

The matrices X and Y are both 3×1 (single-column) matrices, P is a 3×3 square matrix, and both Q and R are 2×3 matrices. The elements in the matrices can be complex numbers.

Later, a more comprehensive review of complex numbers is provided. For now, a complex number is a number such as $x = (0.3 - 0.2i)$, where $i^2 = -1$ (conventionally interpreted as $i = \sqrt{-1}$) and 0.3 is the real part, and -0.2 is the imaginary part. The complex conjugate of x is the number $x^* = (0.3 + 0.2i)$. The squared magnitude of $x = (0.3 - 0.2i)$ equals $|x|^2 = x \cdot x^* = (0.3 - 0.2i)(0.3 + 0.2i) = (0.3^2 + 0.2^2) = 0.13$. Complex numbers can be added, such as $(-0.5 + 0.1i) + (0.3 - 0.2i) = (-0.2 - 0.1i)$; they can also be multiplied: $(-0.5 + 0.1i) \cdot (0.3 - 0.2i) = (-0.15 + 0.10i + 0.03i - 0.02i^2) = (-0.13 + 0.13i)$, where we used the fact that $i^2 = -1$. They can also be divided, such as $(-0.5 + 0.1i) \div (0.3 - 0.2i) = \frac{(-0.5 + 0.1i) \cdot (0.3 + 0.2i)}{(0.3^2 + 0.2^2)} = (-1.3077 - 0.5385i)$, and the latter has the property that $(0.3 - 0.2i) \cdot (-1.3077 - 0.5385i) = (-0.5 + 0.1i)$.

For example, in Matlab we can set r11 $= 0.2 + 0.3 * i$, r12 $= -0.3 + 0.7 * i$, r13 $= 0.50$, etc. to create complex or real numbers. We can use abs(r11) to get the absolute value or magnitude of a complex number, and abs(r11)^2 gives the squared magnitude. In Matlab for example, after defining r11, r12, etc., we can write R = [r11 r12 r13 ; r21 r22 r23] to form a 2×3 matrix.

2.3.1   Special matrices

A diagonal matrix is a square matrix with nonzero values only on the diagonal elements. For example:

$$D = \begin{bmatrix} d_{11} & 0 & 0 \\ 0 & d_{22} & 0 \\ 0 & 0 & d_{33} \end{bmatrix}.$$

It is convenient to write this as $D = \text{diag}[d_{11}, d_{22}, d_{33}]$ to save space. An identity matrix is a diagonal matrix with all ones on the diagonal, such as

$$I = \begin{bmatrix} 1 & 0 & 0 \\ 0 & 1 & 0 \\ 0 & 0 & 1 \end{bmatrix}.$$

As we shall see when we get to matrix multiplication, the identity matrix acts like the number one, in the sense that $I \cdot P = P = P \cdot I$. An indicator matrix is a diagonal matrix with ones in some of the rows that we design to keep and zeros in the remaining rows we design to eliminate. For example, the following indicator matrix picks out the second row:

$$\begin{bmatrix} 0 & 0 & 0 \\ 0 & 1 & 0 \\ 0 & 0 & 0 \end{bmatrix} \cdot \begin{bmatrix} x_1 \\ x_2 \\ x_3 \end{bmatrix} = \begin{bmatrix} 0 \\ x_2 \\ 0 \end{bmatrix}.$$

In Matlab, for example, `eye(3)` is used to form a 3×3 identity matrix and `D=[ d11; d22; d33]; diag(D)` forms a diagonal matrix (`diag` turns a vector into a diagonal matrix). Also in Matlab, `diag` applied to a diagonal matrix returns a vector.

2.3.2 Adjoint (conjugate transpose) of a matrix

Rows and columns of a matrix can be flipped by applying the "adjoint" operation

$$X^\dagger = \begin{bmatrix} x_1^* & x_2^* & x_3^* \end{bmatrix}$$

$$Q^\dagger = \begin{bmatrix} q_{11}^* & q_{21}^* \\ q_{12}^* & q_{22}^* \\ q_{13}^* & q_{23}^* \end{bmatrix}.$$

Notice that the dagger operation also changes the original complex numbers into their complex conjugates. For example, if $x_1 = 0.3 + 0.2i$ then $x_1^* = 0.3 - 0.2i$. This is important to remember when complex numbers are used. If the matrices only contain real numbers, then we can ignore conjugation. In Matlab, `Q'` is used to compute the conjugate transpose.

2.3.3 Hermitian matrices

A matrix H is called Hermitian if it satisfies $H^\dagger = H$. In other words, it is self-adjoint. For example, the following matrix is Hermitian:

$$\begin{bmatrix} a & c \\ c^* & b \end{bmatrix}^\dagger = \begin{bmatrix} a & c \\ c^* & b \end{bmatrix}.$$

And note that the diagonal values, a, b, must be real for this to be true. The following matrix is not Hermitian:

$$\begin{bmatrix} a & d \\ c^* & b \end{bmatrix}^\dagger = \begin{bmatrix} a & c \\ d^* & b \end{bmatrix}.$$

If all the elements of the Hermitian matrix H are real, then this corresponds to a symmetric matrix. Hermitian matrices play an important role in quantum theory, because they are used to represent what is called an observable. This is covered in more detail after spectral decomposition is introduced below.

2.3.4 Multiply by a scalar

A new matrix is formed by multiplying a scalar (a complex number) and a matrix. For example

$$a \cdot Q = \begin{bmatrix} a \cdot q_{11} & a \cdot q_{12} & a \cdot q_{13} \\ a \cdot q_{21} & a \cdot q_{22} & a \cdot q_{32} \end{bmatrix}.$$

Multiplication by a scalar is used to expand or shrink a vector or reverse its direction. In Matlab, this is computed by `a*Q`, assuming `a` is a number and `Q` is a matrix which are already defined. Matlab can perform element-wise multiplication. For example, in `P.*Q`, the dot before * tells Matlab to perform element-wise multiplication (multiply corresponding cells). If the dot is removed, as in `P*Q`, then Matlab does matrix multiplication (described later).

2.3.5 Adding and subtracting matrices

Two matrices can be added as long as they have the same number of rows and columns:

$$Q + R = \begin{bmatrix} q_{11} + r_{11} & q_{12} + r_{12} & q_{13} + r_{13} \\ q_{21} + r_{21} & q_{22} + r_{22} & q_{32} + r_{23} \end{bmatrix}.$$

Two matrices can be subtracted in the same manner because $Q - R = Q + (-1) \cdot R$. In Matlab the sum would be expressed as written above: `S = Q+R`.

2.3.6 Matrix inner product

Quantum theory draws heavily on the concept of the inner product between two vectors defined earlier and denoted $\langle X | Y \rangle$. The inner product is computed by taking two $N \times 1$ column matrices and converting them into a scalar (a complex number). Consider the inner product for the ordered pair of 3×1 matrices (X, Y) defined earlier. The matrix formula for the inner product for this ordered pair is

$$\langle X|Y\rangle = X^\dagger \cdot Y = \begin{bmatrix} x_1^* & x_2^* & x_3^* \end{bmatrix} \cdot \begin{bmatrix} y_1 \\ y_2 \\ y_3 \end{bmatrix}$$

$$= x_1^* \cdot y_1 + x_2^* \cdot y_2 + x_3^* \cdot y_3.$$

More generally, if X is an $N \times 1$ column matrix with element x_i in the ith row and Y is another $N \times 1$ column matrix with element y_i in the ith row, then the inner product equals

$$\langle X|Y\rangle = \sum_{i=1}^{N} x_i^* \cdot y_i.$$

If the inner product is zero, $\langle X|Y\rangle = 0$, then the two vectors are orthogonal. Note that $\langle X|Y\rangle = (X^\dagger \cdot Y)$ but $\langle Y|X\rangle = (Y^\dagger \cdot X) = (X^\dagger \cdot Y)^*$, so that $\langle Y|X\rangle = \langle X|Y\rangle^*$. They are equivalent only if both column matrices contain only real numbers. Matrix inner products provide a measure of similarity between two vectors. For example, in statistics they are used to compute correlations between two variables. If X, Y are two standardized variables (each has mean zero and standard deviation one) and they are each represented by a column with N rows, then the correlation equals the inner product divided by N. In Matlab for example, X'*Y computes the inner product, assuming X and Y are $N \times 1$ matrices as defined previously.

The inner product of a vector with itself equals the squared length of the vector $||X||^2 = \langle X|X\rangle = X^\dagger \cdot X$. (The conjugation produced by the adjoint operation is critical here to make the final result a real number.) The squared length of the difference between two vectors is equal to the distance between the two vectors:

$$||X - Y||^2 \geq 0 \text{ and}$$

$$||X - Y||^2 = (X - Y)^\dagger \cdot (X - Y)$$

$$= X^\dagger \cdot X + Y^\dagger \cdot Y - X^\dagger \cdot Y - Y^\dagger \cdot X$$

$$= ||X||^2 + ||Y||^2 - (X^\dagger \cdot Y) - (X^\dagger \cdot Y)^*$$

$$= ||X||^2 + ||Y||^2 - 2 \cdot \text{Re} [X^\dagger \cdot Y].$$

So it follows that

$$||X||^2 + ||Y||^2 - 2 \cdot \text{Re} [X^\dagger \cdot Y] \geq 0,$$

which then implies that

$$||X||^2 + ||Y||^2 \geq 2 \cdot \text{Re} [X^\dagger \cdot Y].$$

If X and Y are normalized so that $||X||^2 = ||Y||^2 = 1$, then $1 \geq \text{Re} [X^\dagger \cdot Y]$. Alternatively, if X and Y are not normalized, then $U = \frac{1}{||X||} X$ and $V = \frac{1}{||Y||} Y$ are normalized, so that

$$1 \geq \mathrm{Re}\left[U^\dagger \cdot V\right] = \mathrm{Re}\left[\left(\frac{1}{||X||}X\right)^\dagger \cdot \left(\frac{1}{||Y||}Y\right)\right] = \frac{1}{||X||} \cdot \frac{1}{||Y||}\,\mathrm{Re}\left[X^\dagger \cdot Y\right],$$

$$\rightarrow ||X|| \cdot ||Y|| \geq \mathrm{Re}\left[X^\dagger \cdot Y\right].$$

Another inequality is derived from the property

$$||X + Y||^2 \geq 0.$$

A similar line of reasoning as above leads to the conclusion

$$||X|| \cdot ||Y|| \geq -\mathrm{Re}\left[X^\dagger \cdot Y\right].$$

Together these imply

$$||X|| \cdot ||Y|| \geq \left|X^\dagger \cdot Y\right|.$$

The last expression is called the Cauchy–Schwartz inequality.

2.3.7   Matrix outer product

Quantum theory also heavily uses a concept called an outer product. The outer product takes two $N \times 1$ (single-column) matrices and converts them into an $N \times N$ matrix. The outer product for the ordered pair of 3×1 column matrices (X, Y) defined earlier equals

$$X \cdot Y^\dagger = \begin{bmatrix} x_1 \\ x_2 \\ x_3 \end{bmatrix} \cdot \begin{bmatrix} y_1^* & y_2^* & y_3^* \end{bmatrix}$$

$$= \begin{bmatrix} x_1 \cdot y_1^* & x_1 \cdot y_2^* & x_1 \cdot y_3^* \\ x_2 \cdot y_1^* & x_2 \cdot y_2^* & x_2 \cdot y_3^* \\ x_3 \cdot y_1^* & x_3 \cdot y_2^* & x_3 \cdot y_3^* \end{bmatrix}.$$

Outer products are important for forming projectors in quantum theory: $P_X = X \cdot X^\dagger$ is the matrix representation of the projector for the unit-length vector $|X\rangle$ and $P_X \cdot Y = (X \cdot X^\dagger) \cdot Y = (X^\dagger \cdot Y) \cdot X$ is the matrix representation of the projection of the vector $|Y\rangle$ onto the ray spanned by the vector $|X\rangle$. In Matlab, the outer product is computed by X*Y', assuming X and Y are $N \times 1$ column matrices.

2.3.8   Matrix multiplication

An $M \times N$ matrix S multiplied by an $N \times K$ matrix R gives rise to an $M \times K$ matrix $T = S \cdot R$. (The inner dimension N must be equal for S and R.) The value in row i and column j equals

$$T_{ij} = \sum_{j=1}^{N} s_{ij} \cdot r_{jk}.$$

For example, matrix multiplying the 3×3 square matrix P and the 3×1 column matrix X defined earlier produces

$$P \cdot X = \begin{bmatrix} p_{11} \cdot x_1 + p_{12} \cdot x_2 + p_{13} \cdot x_3 \\ p_{21} \cdot x_1 + p_{22} \cdot x_2 + p_{23} \cdot x_3 \\ p_{31} \cdot x_1 + p_{32} \cdot x_2 + p_{33} \cdot x_3 \end{bmatrix}.$$

An inner product is a special case of matrix multiplying a $1 \times N$ row matrix times an $N \times 1$ column matrix. An outer product is a special case of multiplying an $N \times 1$ column matrix times a $1 \times N$ row matrix. Matrix multiplication is *not* commutative and so, for example, $P \cdot X \neq X \cdot P$; in fact, $X \cdot P$ does not even exist, because the inner dimension does not match. Matrix multiplication is distributive so that, for example, $(Q + R) \cdot X = Q \cdot X + R \cdot X$ and $Q \cdot (X + Y) = Q \cdot X + Q \cdot Y$. The identity matrix I has the property that, if it is multiplied by another matrix, the product is just the other matrix, such as for example $I \cdot X = X$ and $I \cdot P = P$. As we shall see later, matrix multiplication is the matrix representation of linear transformations. Matrix multiplication is used in statistics to describe linear sets of equations, such as in multiple regression analysis. In Matlab, `C = P*X` is used, assuming P is defined as an $M \times N$ matrix and X is defined as an $N \times K$ matrix.

2.3.9 Unitary matrices

Suppose a vector $|S\rangle$ can be represented in terms of an orthonormal basis $\{|V_i\rangle, i = 1, N\}$ by an $N \times 1$ column matrix of coordinates α (e.g., $\alpha_i = \langle V_i | S \rangle$); also suppose the same vector $|S\rangle$ can be represented in terms of an orthonormal basis $\{|W_i\rangle, i = 1, N\}$ by an $N \times 1$ column matrix of coordinates β (e.g., $\beta_i = \langle W_i | S \rangle$). We can transform one set of coordinates into the other by using the unitary matrix that relates the two sets of basis vectors. The unitary matrix U is an $N \times N$ matrix with an element in row i column j equal to $\langle V_i | W_j \rangle$, which represents the amplitude to transit from state $|W_j\rangle$ to state $|V_j\rangle$. For example, with $N = 3$, we have

$$U = \begin{bmatrix} \langle V_1|W_1\rangle & \langle V_1|W_2\rangle & \langle V_1|W_3\rangle \\ \langle V_2|W_1\rangle & \langle V_2|W_2\rangle & \langle V_2|W_3\rangle \\ \langle V_3|W_1\rangle & \langle V_3|W_2\rangle & \langle V_3|W_3\rangle \end{bmatrix}.$$

Starting with β, we obtain α by the matrix product $\alpha = U \cdot \beta$; starting with α, we obtain β by the matrix product $\beta = U^\dagger \cdot \alpha$. The unitary matrix satisfies the unitary property $U^\dagger U = I = UU^\dagger$, where I is the identity matrix. In Matlab, assuming U and alpha and beta are defined, we just write alpha = U*beta, or beta = U'*alpha, and U'*U will produce an identity matrix.

2.3.9.1 Position and momentum example

To see again how this works, consider the following example. Suppose a person is tracking a target that is randomly walking left or right along a horizontal line

indicator matrix $P_{BC} = \text{diag}\,[0, 0, 0, 0, 0, 1, 0, 0, 0]$; that is, a diagonal matrix with zeros in all of the rows, except a one is placed in the diagonal of the row corresponding to the coordinate ψ_{BC}. Then we can express the projection as $P_{BC} \cdot \psi$, which is simply a vector filled with zeros except for the row that contains ψ_{BC}. The probability of this event is then computed by $||P_{BC} \cdot \psi||^2 = |\psi_{BC}|^2$. Note that the projectors for the rays corresponding to the basis vectors are mutually orthogonal ($P_{ij} \cdot P_{mn} = 0$ if $(i, j) \neq (m, n)$).

Next, consider a more general event such as "the man prefers the BMW," which is a three-dimensional subspace spanned by the three vectors $\{|BB\rangle, |BA\rangle, |BC\rangle\}$. The matrix representation of this projector is $P_B = (P_{BB} + P_{BA} + P_{BC})$, which is simply an indicator matrix $P_B = \text{diag}\,[0, 0, 0, 1, 1, 1, 0, 0, 0]$ with zeros in all rows, except that ones are placed in the diagonal of the rows corresponding to the coordinates ψ_{BB}, ψ_{BA}, ψ_{BC}. The projection then equals $P_B \cdot \psi = (P_{BB} + P_{BA} + P_{BC}) \cdot \psi$, and the probability of this event equals

$$||P_B \cdot \psi||^2 = ||(P_{BB} + P_{BA} + P_{BC}) \cdot \psi||^2$$
$$= ||P_{BB} \cdot \psi||^2 + ||P_{BA} \cdot \psi||^2 + ||P_{BC} \cdot \psi||^2$$
$$= |\psi_{BB}|^2 + |\psi_{BA}|^2 + |\psi_{BC}|^2.$$

The squared sum breaks down into a sum of separate squares because of the orthogonality between the different projectors.

Note that the sum of the projectors over all of the basis states equals the identity matrix denoted I, which has the property that $I \cdot \psi = \psi$. This allows us to easily identify the projector for the negation of an event. For example, the probability for the event "man does not choose BMW" equals $I - P_B$, and the probability of this event equals $||(I - P_B) \cdot \psi||^2 = 1 - ||P_B \cdot \psi||^2$.

Finally, note that the projectors for a conjunction event such as the event spanned by $|BC\rangle$ can be derived from the product of coarse projectors: $P_{BC} = P_B \cdot P_C$, where $P_B = (P_{BB} + P_{BA} + P_{BC})$ and $P_C = (P_{BC} + P_{AC} + P_{CC})$.

2.3.10.2   Projectors for the incompatible representation

Projectors for incompatible events are complicated by the introduction of the change of bases across the incompatible variables. Here, we study the states and projections when expressed by using a common basis, the $\{|X\rangle, |Y\rangle, |Z\rangle\}$ basis, for all events. Suppose the state $|S\rangle$, when expressed in the $\{|X\rangle, |Y\rangle, |Z\rangle\}$ basis, is the 3×1 column matrix

$$|S\rangle \rightarrow \begin{bmatrix} \psi_1 \\ \psi_2 \\ \psi_3 \end{bmatrix} = \begin{bmatrix} -0.6963 \\ 0.6963 \\ 0.1741 \end{bmatrix} = \psi.$$

First, we compute the probability of the event "man chooses BMW." To do this, we project the state onto the X-ray spanned by $|X\rangle$. With respect to the $\{|X\rangle, |Y\rangle, |Z\rangle\}$ basis, the matrix representation of the basis vector $|X\rangle$ is simply

$$|X\rangle \rightarrow \begin{bmatrix} 1 \\ 0 \\ 0 \end{bmatrix} = X.$$

The projector for the event spanned by $|X\rangle$ is obtained from the outer product

$$P_X = X \cdot X^\dagger = \mathrm{diag}[1, 0, 0] = \begin{bmatrix} 1 & 0 & 0 \\ 0 & 0 & 0 \\ 0 & 0 & 0 \end{bmatrix}.$$

Using this projector, the projection then equals

$$P_X \cdot \psi = X \cdot (X^\dagger \cdot \psi) = \begin{bmatrix} \psi_1 \\ 0 \\ 0 \end{bmatrix} = \begin{bmatrix} -0.6963 \\ 0 \\ 0 \end{bmatrix}$$

and the probability equals $||P_X \cdot \psi||^2 = |\psi_1|^2 = |\langle X|S\rangle|^2 = |-0.6963|^2$.

Now let us compute the probability for the event "woman wants Cadillac" using the $\{|X\rangle, |Y\rangle, |Z\rangle\}$ basis. Recall from Eq. (2.3) that, in the $\{|X\rangle, |Y\rangle, |Z\rangle\}$ basis,

$$|W\rangle \rightarrow \begin{bmatrix} \langle X|W\rangle \\ \langle Y|W\rangle \\ \langle Z|W\rangle \end{bmatrix} = \begin{bmatrix} -1/2 \\ 1/2 \\ 1/\sqrt{2} \end{bmatrix} = W.$$

Recall that W is simply the third column from the unitary operator U (see Eq. (2.3)) that transforms coordinates of the $\{|U\rangle, |V\rangle, |W\rangle\}$ basis into coordinates of the $\{|X\rangle, |Y\rangle, |Z\rangle\}$ basis (and we are currently using the latter). The projector for the W-ray, when expressed in the $\{|X\rangle, |Y\rangle, |Z\rangle\}$ basis, is obtained from the outer product

$$P_W = W \cdot W^\dagger = \begin{bmatrix} \frac{-1}{2} \cdot \frac{-1}{2} & \frac{-1}{2} \cdot \frac{1}{2} & \frac{-1}{2} \cdot \frac{1}{\sqrt{2}} \\ \frac{1}{2} \cdot \frac{-1}{2} & \frac{1}{2} \cdot \frac{1}{2} & \frac{1}{2} \cdot \frac{1}{\sqrt{2}} \\ \frac{1}{\sqrt{2}} \cdot \frac{-1}{2} & \frac{1}{\sqrt{2}} \cdot \frac{1}{2} & \frac{1}{\sqrt{2}} \cdot \frac{1}{\sqrt{2}} \end{bmatrix},$$

which produces the desired projection

$$P_W \cdot \psi = W \cdot (W^\dagger \cdot \psi) = W \cdot \varphi_3 = 0.8184 \cdot W$$

and probability $||P_W \cdot \psi||^2 = |\varphi_3|^2 = |\langle W|S\rangle|^2 = |0.8194|^2$. Recall from Section 2.1.2.3 that this is exactly the same answer we obtain if we use the $\{|U\rangle, |V\rangle, |W\rangle\}$ basis to repesent the state instead of the $\{|X\rangle, |Y\rangle, |Z\rangle\}$ basis.

Now let us compute the probability for a sequence of events "man chooses BMW" and then "woman wants Cadillac." We already computed the probability of the first event, which is $||P_X \cdot \psi||^2 = |\psi_1|^2 = |\langle X|S\rangle|^2 = |-0.6963|^2$. The revised state, conditioned on this first event, equals the projection $P_X \cdot \psi$ divided by its length $||P_X \cdot \psi|| = |\psi_1| = 0.6963$:

$$\psi_X = \frac{P_X \cdot \psi}{||P_X \cdot \psi||} = \begin{bmatrix} -1 \\ 0 \\ 0 \end{bmatrix} = -X.$$

The probability of the second event, conditioned on the first, then equals

$$||P_W \cdot \psi_X||^2 = |\langle W|X\rangle|^2 = \left|\frac{1}{2}\right|^2.$$

Finally, the probability for the sequence is

$$||P_X \cdot \psi||^2 \cdot ||P_W \cdot \psi_X||^2$$

$$= ||P_X \cdot \psi||^2 \cdot ||P_W \cdot \frac{P_X \cdot \psi}{||P_X \cdot \psi||}||^2$$

$$= ||P_X \cdot \psi||^2 \cdot \frac{1}{||P_X \cdot \psi||^2} \cdot ||P_W \cdot P_X \cdot \psi||^2$$

$$= ||P_W \cdot P_X \cdot \psi||^2 = ||W \cdot W^\dagger \cdot X \cdot X^\dagger \cdot \psi||^2$$

$$= ||W \cdot (W^\dagger \cdot X) \cdot (X^\dagger \cdot \psi)||^2$$

$$= ||W||^2 \cdot |(W^\dagger \cdot X) \cdot (X^\dagger \cdot \psi)|^2$$

$$= 1 \cdot \left|\frac{1}{2} \cdot (0.6963)\right|^2.$$

Thus, the probability of the path $|S\rangle \to |X\rangle \to |W\rangle$ equals $||P_W \cdot P_X \cdot \psi||^2 = |\frac{1}{2} \cdot (0.6963)|^2 = 0.1212$. If we compute the probability of the opposite order $|S\rangle \to |W\rangle \to |X\rangle$, then we obtain a different answer: $||P_X \cdot P_W \cdot \psi||^2 = |-0.4097|^2 = 0.1679$. The two answers differ because the projectors do not commute:

$$P_W \cdot P_X - P_X \cdot P_W = \begin{bmatrix} 0 & 0.25 & 0.3536 \\ -0.25 & 0 & 0 \\ -0.3536 & 0 & 0 \end{bmatrix} \neq \mathbf{0}$$

More generally, the projectors for the X-ray, Y-ray, and Z-ray events do not commute with any of the projectors spanned by the U-ray, V-ray, and W-ray. This non-commutative property of the projectors is the key mathematical property that distinguishes quantum probability from classic probability.

Let us summarize the construction of projectors a little bit more generally. Recall the earlier target-tracking example used in relation to Figure 2.4. Suppose the state $|S_t\rangle$ can be expressed either in terms of the position X-basis

$\{|x_1\rangle, |x_2\rangle, \ldots, |x_N\rangle\}$ by the $N \times 1$ matrix α or in terms of the momentum Y-basis $\{|y_1\rangle, |y_2\rangle, \ldots, |y_N\rangle\}$ by the $N \times 1$ matrix β, and the coordinates are related by the unitary matrix $\alpha = U \cdot \beta$ given in Eq. (2.6). Suppose we wish to consistently express both the state and the projectors all in terms of the position X-basis. The projector for any event Q spanned by the X-basis is simply an indicator matrix P_Q that picks out the appropriate rows of α. For example, the projector for the event spanned by positions $\{|x_{j-1}\rangle, |x_j\rangle, |x_{j+1}\rangle\}$ equals $P_Q = (P_{j-1} + P_j + P_{j+1})$, where P_j is simply a diagonal matrix with zeros everywhere except a one in row j. The probability of event Q equals $p(Q) = \|P_Q \cdot \alpha\|^2 = \|(P_{j-1} + P_j + P_{j+1}) \cdot \alpha\|^2$. Next consider the construction of the projector for an event R spanned by velocities $\{|y_{k-1}\rangle, |y_k\rangle, |y_{k+1}\rangle\}$ in the momentum Y-basis. Now the projector for the question R in the Y-basis is simply $(P_{k-1} + P_k + P_{k+1})$, where P_k is once again a diagonal matrix with zeros everywhere except the number one in row k. The probability of event R equals $p(R) = \|(P_{k-1} + P_k + P_{k+1}) \cdot \beta\|^2$. But if we wish to express this projector in terms of the X-basis, then we use the unitary matrix U to transform it to the X-basis as follows: $P_R = U \cdot (P_{j-1} + P_j + P_{j+1}) \cdot U^\dagger$. The operation of $U^\dagger$ changes the coordinates of the state from the X-basis to the Y-basis, the operation of $(P_{j-1} + P_j + P_{j+1})$ picks the coordinates in the Y-basis, and the operation of U changes the projector back to the X-basis. The probability of event R equals

$$
\begin{aligned}
p(R) &= \left\| U \cdot (P_{k-1} + P_k + P_{k+1}) \cdot U^\dagger \cdot \alpha \right\|^2 \\
&= \left\| U \cdot (P_{k-1} + P_k + P_{k+1}) \cdot \beta \right\|^2 \\
&= \left\| (P_{k-1} + P_k + P_{k+1}) \cdot \beta \right\|^2,
\end{aligned}
$$

where the last step follows from the fact that unitary transformations do not change the lengths of vectors.

2.3.11   Matrix inverse

Suppose P is a square $N \times N$ matrix. Define P_i as the ith column of this matrix and define Q as the $N \times (N-1)$ matrix containing all the remaining columns in P after deleting P_i. If there exists an $(N-1) \times 1$ column vector β such that $P_i = Q \cdot \beta$, then P_i is linearly dependent on the remaining columns in Q; otherwise it is linearly independent. If all of the columns are linearly independent, then the matrix P is of full rank; otherwise it is less than full rank or singular. If a matrix is of full rank, then the inverse P^{-1} exists so that $P \cdot P^{-1} = I = P^{-1} \cdot P$. Note that for orthonormal (unitary) matrices $U^{-1} = U^\dagger$.

The inverse matrix can be used to solve linear equations. For example, suppose we wish to obtain the least-squares estimates for the $K \times 1$ matrix of coefficients β given the $N \times 1$ matrix of criteria Y and the $N \times K$ matrix of predictors X in the regression equation $Y = X \cdot \beta + E$, where E is the residual vector whose squared length we wish to minimize. Then the solution is $\beta = (X^\dagger \cdot X)^{-1} \cdot X^\dagger \cdot Y$. The projection of Y onto the subspace spanned by X equals the prediction $\hat{Y} = X \cdot \beta = \left[X \cdot (X^\dagger \cdot X)^{-1} \cdot X^\dagger \right] \cdot Y = P_X \cdot Y$, where

$P_X = \left[X \cdot (X^\dagger \cdot X)^{-1} \cdot X^\dagger \right]$ is the orthogonal projector for the subspace spanned by X. In Matlab, the inverse can be obtained either by `IP = inv(P)` or by `IP = P^-1`. So, for example, one can solve for the regression coefficients in Matlab by the formula `b = inv(X'*X)*X'*Y`; the prediction is `Yh = X*b` and the residual is `E=Y-Yh`.

2.3.12   Spectral decomposition of a matrix

An $N \times 1$ column matrix V_i is an eigenvector of an $N \times N$ square matrix H if $H \cdot V_i = \lambda_i \cdot V_i$, where λ_i is a scalar called the eigenvalue corresponding to the eigenvector V_i. Suppose the $N \times N$ matrix H is Hermitian; that is, $H^\dagger = H$. Then we can decompose this matrix into an $N \times N$ orthonormal matrix V containing eigenvectors ($V^\dagger V = I$) and another diagonal matrix $\Lambda = \mathrm{diag}[\lambda_1, \ldots, \lambda_N]$ with real-valued eigenvalues so that

$$H = V \cdot \Lambda \cdot V^\dagger$$

$$= \sum_{i=1}^{N} \lambda_i \cdot V_i \cdot V_i^\dagger.$$

The second line follows from the first line using matrix multiplication. In the second line, V_i is the ith column of the matrix V; in other words, it is the ith eigenvector, corresponding to the ith eigenvalue λ_i. Spectral analysis, when applied to a real-valued and symmetric variance–covariance matrix, is used in statistics to perform principal component analysis.

In quantum theory, the variables that an experimenter can measure are called observables. Each such observable is represented by a Hermitian matrix. Using the example matrix H defined immediately above, the eigenvalue λ_i represents one of the possible real values that can be observed when measuring this observable, and the probability of this value is determined by its projector $P_i = V_i \cdot V_i^\dagger$.

Often we work with square matrices that are not Hermitian. For example, when working with Markov models, the transition matrix T is a real $N \times N$ matrix but non-symmetric. If all of the eigenvalues of the square matrix are unique (not repeated), then it is still possible to form an eigenvector decomposition as follows:

$$T = Q \cdot \Lambda \cdot Q^{-1},$$

where Q is an $N \times N$ matrix of eigenvectors and Λ is a diagonal matrix of eigenvalues. However, the columns of Q are linearly independent but not orthogonal, so we must use the inverse matrix for this decomposition. Also, the eigenvalues are not required to be real in this more general case and they are usually complex values. If Q is Hermitian, then the eigenvectors are orthogonal, so that $Q^\dagger Q = I$ and then $Q^{-1} = Q^\dagger$.

All matrix algebra programming languages can carry this out easily with a single function. In Matlab, you can use `[V,L] = eig(H)`, for a Hermitian matrix H, where V contains the orthonormal eigenvectors (in the columns) and L contains the eigenvalues (which may or may not be repeated). If an eigenvalue is unique, then the eigenvector is unique (except that it can contain an arbitrary phase factor $e^{i\theta}$ which has no effect). If an eigenvalue is repeated, then the eigenvectors corresponding to the repeated eigenvalue are not unique. For a non-symmetric transition matrix T with unique eigenvalues, you can also use [V,L] = eig(T) and this will give a matrix of eigenvectors, but they will not be orthogonal and the eigenvalues may be complex.

2.3.13   Matrix representation of observables

Classic probability theory is enriched by the concept of a *random variable*. A discrete random variable X is a function that maps the N points in the sample space into $M \leq N$ real numbers. Suppose $p(X = x_i)$ is the probability of obtaining the value x_i from the random variable X. In other words, p describes the probability distribution for the random variable X. Two important statistics are used to characterize this distribution. The mean, denoted μ, is a statistic used to represent the central tendency and the variance σ^2 is used to measure the variability. The mean of this random variable is defined as

$$\mu = E(X) = \sum_x p(X = x_i) \cdot x_i$$

and the variance of this random variable is defined as

$$\sigma^2 = V(X) = E(X - \mu)^2$$
$$= \sum_x p(X = x_i) \cdot (x_i - \mu)^2$$
$$= \sum_x p(X = x_i) \cdot x_i^2 - \mu^2.$$

As mentioned earlier, in quantum theory a Hermitian matrix H is used to represent an observable, which is the quantum analogue of a random variable in classic probability theory. Recall our earlier target-tracking example discussed in connection with Figure 2.4 referred to in Section 2.3.9 on unitary matrices. There, we introduced the idea of a person estimating either the position or the momentum (actually velocity) of a target moving along a horizontal line. In that example, the position of a target at some moment in time is one observable and the momentum of the target at any moment is another observable.

Suppose all the eigenvalues are unique so that there is only one V_i such that $H \cdot V_i = \lambda_i \cdot V_i$, and this is true for every eigenvalue of H. Each eigenvalue is considered one of the possible real values that can be observed in an experiment investigating this variable. The probability of observing a value is determined by the projector $P_i = V_i \cdot V_i^\dagger$ for the eigenvalue λ_i. If ψ is an $N \times 1$ vector of amplitudes that represents the state, then the probability of observing the value λ_i equals

$$||P_i \cdot \psi||^2 = (P_i \cdot \psi)^\dagger \cdot (P_i \cdot \psi)$$
$$= \psi^\dagger \cdot P_i^\dagger \cdot P_i \cdot \psi$$
$$= \psi^\dagger \cdot P_i \cdot P_i \cdot \psi$$
$$= \psi^\dagger \cdot P_i \cdot \psi.$$

The mean value, denoted μ, of the observable is defined as the sum of the products formed by multiplying each probability by each value:

$$\mu = \sum \lambda_i \cdot ||P_i \cdot \psi||^2$$
$$= \sum \lambda_i \cdot \left(\psi^\dagger \cdot P_i^\dagger \cdot P_i \cdot \psi \right)$$
$$= \sum \lambda_i \cdot \left(\psi^\dagger \cdot P_i \cdot \psi \right)$$
$$= \psi^\dagger \cdot \left(\sum \lambda_i \cdot P_i \right) \cdot \psi$$
$$= \psi^\dagger \cdot H \cdot \psi.$$

The variance of the observable equals

$$\sigma^2 = \sum (\lambda_i - \mu)^2 \cdot ||P_i \cdot \psi||^2$$
$$= \psi^\dagger \cdot (H - \mu \cdot I)^2 \cdot \psi$$
$$= \psi^\dagger \cdot H^2 \cdot \psi - \mu^2.$$

We can illustrate these formulae with the position and momentum observables as discussed in relation to Figure 2.4 on unitary transformations. The discrete analogue of the position observable, described in terms of the position basis, is represented by an $N \times N$ diagonal matrix $H_x = \text{diag}[-m, \ldots, -1, 0, +1, \ldots, +m]$ with diagonal values defined by the N observable positions in the set Ω. If we set $N = 101$ and use the state represented by the distribution shown in Figure 2.4, then the mean position equals $\psi^\dagger \cdot H_x \cdot \psi = 0$ and the variance of the position observable equals $\psi^\dagger \cdot H_x^2 \cdot \psi = 50$; in other words, the standard deviation equals 7.0711 on the -50 to $+50$ scale.

The discrete analogue of the momentum observable, described in terms of the position basis, is represented by an $N \times N$ matrix $H_y = U \cdot H_x \cdot U^\dagger$, where the unitary matrix, defined in Eq. (2.6), is used to describe the momentum projector in terms of the position coordinates. If we again set $N = 101$ and use the state represented by the distribution in Figure 2.4, then the mean momentum equals $\psi^\dagger \cdot H_y \cdot \psi = 16.075$ and the variance of the momentum observable equals $\psi^\dagger \cdot H_y^2 \cdot \psi - (16.075)^2 = 1.292$; in other words, the standard deviation equals 1.1366, which is much smaller than the position standard deviation. Once again, the psychological intuition is that if a person allocates attention to momentum, then these judgments are more precise, but there is less capacity left for attending to position.

2.3.13.1 Matrix functions

The functions of a matrix can be computed using the spectral decomposition theorem introduced below. Suppose H is Hermitian. The matrix function of H is defined by

$$f(H) = V \cdot \text{diag}[f(\lambda_1), \ldots, f(\lambda_N)] \cdot V^\dagger.$$

This is also easily computed by matrix language programs. For example, in Matlab, $H\text{\^{}}3$ = $H*H*H$, logm(H) computes the log of a matrix H, expm(H) computes the matrix exponential, and sqrtm(H) computes the square roots of a matrix H.

One particularly important example of a matrix function is the problem of generating a unitary matrix. A unitary matrix can be constructed from a Hermitian matrix as follows:

$$\begin{aligned} U = \exp(i \cdot H) &= V \cdot \exp(\Lambda) \cdot V^\dagger \\ &= V \cdot \text{diag}[..e^{\lambda_i}..] \cdot V^\dagger \\ &= \sum e^{\lambda_i} \cdot V_i \cdot V_i^\dagger. \end{aligned}$$

First, a Hermitian matrix is chosen and then the complex matrix exponential function of this matrix is computed to create the unitary matrix. To prove the matrix is unitary,

$$\begin{aligned} U^\dagger U = \exp(-i \cdot H) \cdot \exp(i \cdot H) &= I \\ &= U U^\dagger = \exp(i \cdot H) \cdot \exp(-i \cdot H). \end{aligned}$$

Also, starting with a unitary matrix U, the Hamiltonian can be constructed by the transformation

$$\begin{aligned} H = -i \cdot \ln(U) &\rightarrow \exp(i \cdot H) \\ &= \exp(-i \cdot i \cdot \ln(H)) = U. \end{aligned}$$

It is much more efficient to use the abbreviated notation for the matrix exponential:

$$U = \exp(i \cdot H) = e^{iH},$$

but one needs to remember that H is a matrix and not a scalar when using this notation. Try to remember that later chapters make use of this abbreviated notation. In physics, the Hermitian matrix, which is used to determine the unitary matrix, is often called a Hamiltonian matrix. In Matlab, for example, U =expm(i*H) can be used.

Matrix powers and exponentials can also be computed for non-Hermitian matrices, such as transition matrices used in a Markov model, by using the eigenvector decomposition. If T is a square non-symmetric transition matrix, then

$$\begin{aligned} T^2 = Q \cdot \Lambda \cdot Q^{-1} \cdot Q \cdot \Lambda \cdot Q^{-1} \\ = Q \cdot \Lambda^2 \cdot Q^{-1}. \end{aligned}$$

Repeated application of this principle implies $T^n = Q \cdot \Lambda^n \cdot Q^{-1}$. If K is a square matrix that has all unique eigenvalues, then the matrix exponential of K equals $T = \exp(K) = Q \cdot \text{diag}[\ldots e^{\lambda_i} \ldots] \cdot Q^{-1}$. The same Matlab function can be used to compute these too: `T = expm(K)`, `Tn = T^n`.

2.3.14   Commuting Hermitian matrices

Suppose A and B are both Hermitian matrices with rank N. If $A \cdot B = B \cdot A$ then the two matrices commute and if $A \cdot B \neq B \cdot A$ then they do not commute. If the two matrices commute then they are simultaneously diagonalizable: $V^\dagger \cdot A \cdot V = \Lambda_A$ and $V^\dagger \cdot B \cdot V = \Lambda_B$, with $V^\dagger V = I$ and Λ_A and Λ_B are diagonal matrices. Alternatively, if $A \cdot B = B \cdot A$ then we can find a common eigenmatrix V such that

$$A = V \cdot \Lambda_A \cdot V^\dagger = \sum_{k=1,N} a_k \cdot V_k \cdot V_k^\dagger$$

$$B = V \cdot \Lambda_B \cdot V^\dagger = \sum_{k=1,N} b_k \cdot V_k \cdot V_k^\dagger,$$

where V is the same matrix of eigenvectors for both matrices. When the Hermitian matrices A and B commute, then they are called commuting observables. For example, in quantum physics, the x and y positions of a particle form two observables that commute. They can be measured simultaneously and order has no effect. For example, psychologically it seems reasonable to assume that questions about simple well-known facts, such as a person's age and gender, would not affect each other and therefore be commutative.

Usually in this case, the eigenvalues are repeated. Consider this important but simple example. Suppose A is a 4×4 Hermitian matrix and B is another 4×4 Hermitian matrix and $A \cdot B = B \cdot A$. Consider the case in which A has only two unique eigenvalues $A \cdot V_1 = a_1 \cdot V_1$ and $A \cdot V_2 = a_1 \cdot V_2$ and $A \cdot V_3 = a_2 \cdot V_3$ and $A \cdot V_4 = a_2 \cdot V_4$. The corresponding projectors are $P_{a_1} = V_1 \cdot V_1^\dagger + V_2 \cdot V_2^\dagger$ for the event that the value a_1 is observed and $P_{a_2} = V_3 \cdot V_3^\dagger + V_4 \cdot V_4^\dagger$ for observing value a_2. Likewise, consider the case where B has only two unique eigenvalues $B \cdot V_2 = b_2 \cdot V_2$ and $B \cdot V_4 = b_2 \cdot V_4$ and $B \cdot V_1 = b_1 \cdot V_1$ and $B \cdot V_3 = b_1 \cdot V_3$. The corresponding projectors are $P_{b_1} = V_1 \cdot V_1^\dagger + V_3 \cdot V_3^\dagger$ for observing b_1 and $P_{b_2} = V_2 \cdot V_2^\dagger + V_4 \cdot V_4^\dagger$ for observing b_2. The joint event that a_1 is observed and b_1 is observed is represented by the product of projectors $P_{a_1} \cdot P_{b_1} = V_1 \cdot V_1^\dagger$; likewise, $P_{a_1} \cdot P_{b_2} = V_2 \cdot V_2^\dagger$ is the projector for observing a_1 and b_2 and $P_{a_2} \cdot P_{b_1} = V_3 \cdot V_3^\dagger$ is the projector for observing a_2 and b_1. Finally, $P_{a_2} \cdot P_{b_2} = V_4 \cdot V_4^\dagger$ is the projector for observing the a_2 and b_2 joint event. This implies that we can construct another observable

$$C = \sum_{k=1,N} c_k \cdot V_k \cdot V_k^\dagger,$$

with $c_1 = f_C(a_1, b_1)$, $c_2 = f_C(a_1, b_2)$, $c_3 = f_C(a_2, b_1)$, and $c_4 = f_C(a_2, b_2)$, that has four unique eigenvalues. The observable C corresponds to a compatible representation of the two variables represented by A and B. The eigenvalues of the A observable can be written as a function of the eigenvalues of the C observable: $a_1 = f_A(c_1) = f_A(c_2)$ and $a_2 = f_A(c_3) = f_A(c_4)$. The same can be done for the B observable: $b_1 = f_B(c_1) = f_B(c_3)$ and $b_2 = f_B(c_2) = f_B(c_4)$. Then we can write $A = \sum_{k=1,N} f_A(c_k) \cdot V_k \cdot V_k^\dagger$ and $B = \sum_{k=1,N} f_B(c_k) \cdot V_k \cdot V_k^\dagger$.

More generally, if A, B are commuting observables and A has n unique eigenvalues and B has m unique eigenvalues, then we require an $N = n \cdot m$-dimensional space to represent all the mutually exclusive and exhaustive compatible combinations, and form an N-dimensional observable C for this compatible representation.

There is one other important property to mention concerning commuting observables. If observable A commutes with the observable B then a matrix function of A commutes with any matrix function of B because

$$
\begin{aligned}
f_1(A) \cdot f_2(B) &= \left(V \cdot f_1(\Lambda_A) \cdot V^\dagger\right) \cdot \left(V \cdot f_2(\Lambda_B) \cdot V^\dagger\right) \\
&= V \cdot f_1(\Lambda_A) \cdot f_2(\Lambda_b) \cdot V^\dagger \\
&= V \cdot \mathrm{diag}\,(..f_1(\lambda_{Ai})..) \cdot \mathrm{diag}\,(..f_2(\lambda_{Bi})..) \cdot V^\dagger \\
&= V \cdot \mathrm{diag}\,(..f_1(\lambda_{Ai}) \cdot f_2(\lambda_{Bi})..) \cdot V^\dagger \\
&= V \cdot \mathrm{diag}\,(..f_2(\lambda_{Bi}) \cdot f_1(\lambda_{Ai})..) \cdot V^\dagger \\
&= V \cdot \mathrm{diag}\,(..f_2(\lambda_{Bi})..) \cdot \mathrm{diag}\,(..f_1(\lambda_{Ai})..) \cdot V^\dagger \\
&= V \cdot f_2(\Lambda_B) \cdot f_1(\Lambda_A) \cdot V^\dagger \\
&= \left(V \cdot f_2(\Lambda_B) \cdot V^\dagger\right) \cdot \left(V \cdot f_1(\Lambda_A) \cdot V^\dagger\right) \\
&= f_2(B) \cdot f_1(A).
\end{aligned}
$$

If the observables commute, then the matrix exponential of the sum equals the product of matrix exponentials:

$$
\begin{aligned}
e^{A+B} = \exp(A + B) &= \exp\left(\left(V \cdot \Lambda_A \cdot V^\dagger\right) + \left(V \cdot \Lambda_B \cdot V^\dagger\right)\right) \\
&= \exp\left(V \cdot (\Lambda_A + \Lambda_B) \cdot V^\dagger\right) \\
&= V \cdot \exp(\Lambda_A + \Lambda_B) \cdot V^\dagger \\
&= V \cdot \mathrm{diag}\left[..e^{(\lambda_{Ai}+\lambda_{Bi})}..\right] \cdot V^\dagger \\
&= V \cdot \mathrm{diag}\left[..e^{\lambda_{Ai}} \cdot e^{\lambda_{Bi}}..\right] \cdot V^\dagger \\
&= V \cdot \exp\Lambda_A \cdot \exp\Lambda_B \cdot V^\dagger \\
&= \left(V \cdot \exp\Lambda_A \cdot V^\dagger\right) \cdot \left(V \cdot \exp\Lambda_B \cdot V^\dagger\right) \\
&= \exp(A) \cdot \exp(B) = e^A \cdot e^B = e^B \cdot e^A.
\end{aligned}
$$

Alternatively, if observables A and B do not commute, then $e^{(A+B)} = e^{(B+A)} \neq e^A \cdot e^B \neq e^B \cdot e^A$.

2.3.15   Kronecker product

The Kronecker product is another kind of product that is useful when working with complex quantum systems. Consider the Kronecker product of the 2×3 matrix Q with the 3×3 matrix P defined earlier. The Kronecker product

$$Q \otimes P = \begin{bmatrix} q_{11} \cdot P & q_{12} \cdot P & q_{13} \cdot P \\ q_{21} \cdot P & q_{22} \cdot P & q_{23} \cdot P \end{bmatrix}$$

forms a new larger matrix with $(2 \times 3) = 6$ rows by $(3 \times 3) = 9$ columns. In Matlab, this is done by using the code `kron(Q,P)`. For example, one of the cells in the above table equals

$$q_{12} \cdot P = q_{12} \cdot \begin{bmatrix} p_{11} & p_{12} & p_{13} \\ p_{21} & p_{22} & p_{23} \\ p_{31} & p_{32} & p_{33} \end{bmatrix}$$

$$= \begin{bmatrix} q_{12} \cdot p_{11} & q_{12} \cdot p_{12} & q_{12} \cdot p_{13} \\ q_{12} \cdot p_{21} & q_{12} \cdot p_{22} & q_{12} \cdot p_{23} \\ q_{12} \cdot p_{31} & q_{12} \cdot p_{32} & q_{12} \cdot p_{33} \end{bmatrix}.$$

The Kronecker product

$$P \otimes Q = \begin{bmatrix} p_{11} \cdot Q & p_{12} \cdot Q & p_{13} \cdot Q \\ p_{21} \cdot Q & p_{22} \cdot Q & p_{23} \cdot Q \\ p_{31} \cdot Q & p_{32} \cdot Q & p_{33} \cdot Q \end{bmatrix}$$

forms a different matrix. So it does not follow the commutative rule $A \otimes B \neq B \otimes A$ and the order matters. In Matlab this is computed using `kron(P,Q)`. The Kronecker product is associative and distributive, so that $A \otimes (B \otimes C) = (A \otimes B) \otimes C = A \otimes B \otimes C$ and $A \otimes (B + C) = A \otimes B + A \otimes C$.

Often the Kronecker product is used to form a matrix representation of a tensor product of two column vectors as in the next example:

$$X \otimes Y = \begin{bmatrix} x_1 \\ x_2 \\ x_3 \end{bmatrix} \otimes \begin{bmatrix} y_1 \\ y_2 \\ y_3 \end{bmatrix} = \begin{bmatrix} x_1 \cdot y_1 \\ x_1 \cdot y_2 \\ x_1 \cdot y_3 \\ x_2 \cdot y_1 \\ x_2 \cdot y_2 \\ x_2 \cdot y_3 \\ x_3 \cdot y_1 \\ x_3 \cdot y_2 \\ x_3 \cdot y_3 \end{bmatrix}.$$

One last important example is the following. Suppose I is a 2×2 identity matrix. The Kronecker product

$$I \otimes P = \begin{bmatrix} P & 0 \\ 0 & P \end{bmatrix}$$

is a 6×6 matrix with P copied along the diagonals and zeros in the off-diagonals.

2.4 Linear algebra

Having the foundations of matrix algebra in place, we are now in a position to understand some of the linear algebra background that is used to formalize quantum theory. This is somewhat more abstract than matrix algebra, but it forms the theoretical basis for matrix algebra. We begin with a more extensive review of complex numbers. A good book on linear algebra is by Paul Halmos (Halmos, 1993).

2.4.1 Complex numbers

Quantum theory is sometimes considered exotic because it uses complex numbers. What is so exotic about complex numbers? They were invented in 1545 by Gerolamo Cardano to solve polynomial equations, which is not so exotic. Fourier analysis is a commonly used tool in all sciences, which is also based on complex numbers. Complex numbers are useful and important in a variety of applications, including signal processing theory, time series analysis, automated control theory, and many other applications, all of which are used to describe data collected from humans. Complex numbers are not unique to quantum theory. Given their proven utility, it is worthwhile to learn a little bit about them.

René Descartes gave i the name "imaginary" and Gauss gave these numbers the controversial name "complex," which is at least a better name than "irrational number." But more importantly, Gauss came up with the idea of representing them as points in a two-dimensional complex plane. A complex number is usually first described as a sum of a real and imaginary part, $a = x + i \cdot y$, where by definition $i^2 = -1$ or more commonly it is described as $i = \sqrt{-1}$ (also note that $i^{-1} = 1/i = -(i \cdot i)/i = -i$). For example, setting the real part to $x = 0.6472$ and the imaginary part to $y = 0.4702$ produces the scalar $a = 0.6472 + i \cdot 0.4702$. Gauss had the brilliant idea of viewing this as a point in a two-dimensional space, produced by plotting the real part on the horizontal axis and the imaginary part on the vertical axis, as shown in Figure 2.5.

The magnitude of the vector in this figure equals $|a| = \sqrt{x^2 + y^2} = \sqrt{0.64} = 0.80$. Now we can redescribe our original complex number as $a = |a| \cdot \left[\frac{x}{|a|} + i \cdot \frac{y}{|a|}\right]$ $= (0.8) \cdot [0.809 + 0.5978 \cdot i]$. Furthermore, we can re-code $\frac{x}{|a|} = \cos(\theta)$ and $\frac{y}{|a|} = \sin(\theta)$ by setting $\theta = 0.2\pi$ because $\cos(0.2\pi) = 0.809$ and $\sin(0.2\pi) = 0.5978$. Thus, we can redescribe our complex number now as $a = |a| \cdot [\cos(\theta) + i \cdot \sin(\theta)]$. Finally, if we expand $[\cos(\theta) + i \cdot \sin(\theta)]$ by its Taylor series then it is equivalent to

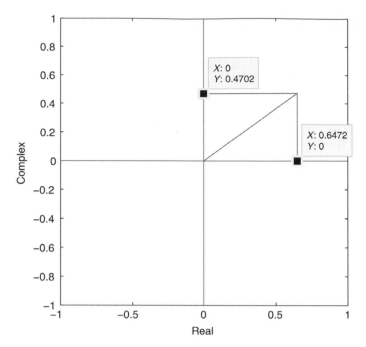

Figure 2.5 Representation of a complex number as a vector in the complex plane. Horizontal is the real component; vertical is the complex component.

expanding $\exp(i \cdot \theta)$ by its Taylor series, and so we equate the two expansions to obtain $\exp(i \cdot \theta) = [\cos(\theta) + i \cdot \sin(\theta)]$. We have now arrived at the final expression for our complex number: $a = |a| \cdot \exp(i \cdot \theta)$, with $|a|$ defined as the magnitude and θ defined as the phase angle of the complex number.

It is important to know the conjugate of a complex number. Suppose $a = x + i \cdot y = |a| \cdot [\cos(\theta) + i \cdot \sin(\theta)] = |a| \cdot e^{i\theta}$. The conjugate of this number is $a^* = x - i \cdot y = |a| \cdot [\cos(\theta) - i \cdot \sin(\theta)] = |a| \cdot e^{-i\theta}$. The conjugate is used in several important ways. First note that $(a + a^*)/2 = x = |a| \cos(\theta)$ and that $(a - a^*)/2i = y = |a| \cdot \sin(\theta)$. Also, we have $(a \cdot a^*) = |a|$, which is the modulus or magnitude of a. If a is strictly real, then of course $a^* = a$.

Sometimes we will call a complex number a *scalar*. Remember that a complex number could be a real number if the imaginary part is zero. So scalars include real numbers as a special case. How do we interpret these complex numbers when used in quantum theory to describe cognition and decision making? We will postpone answering this question until after we see how they are used in quantum theory. However, let us make one preliminary comment. Nothing is gained by restricting the theory to real numbers. The beauty of complex numbers is that the formulae retain their simplicity and elegance whether they are based on real or complex numbers. So why tie one hand behind one's back when both hands are needed for finding answers to complex scientific questions?

2.4.2 Hilbert space and vectors

Quantum theory is expressed within a Hilbert space, which is a vector space with an inner product operation, and it is a complete metric space. Since the vector spaces presented in this book are finite, they are always complete.

A vector space is composed of a set of abstract points, $\mathbf{X}$, and each point, such as $|X\rangle$, is called a vector. Quantum theorists prefer to call this vector a "ket." Furthermore, we can take any pair of vectors say $\{|X\rangle, |Y\rangle\}$ from $\mathbf{X}$ and sum them $|X\rangle + |Y\rangle$ to produce another vector in the set $\mathbf{X}$; we can also take any vector $|X\rangle$ from $\mathbf{X}$ and multiply it by a scalar a (i.e., a complex number) to produce a new vector $a \cdot |X\rangle$ in the set $\mathbf{X}$. There is a unique zero point, $\mathbf{0}$, which when added to any vector $|X\rangle$ just returns the same vector $|X\rangle + \mathbf{0} = |X\rangle$, and a scalar multiplication of the zero point produces $a \cdot \mathbf{0} = \mathbf{0}$. As described later, the ket can be represented by an $N \times 1$ column matrix. But a ket is a more general object.

A set of vectors $\{|X_i\rangle, \ i = 1, \ldots, N\}$ is linearly independent if the following is true: $\sum_{i=1}^{N} a_i \cdot |X_i\rangle = \mathbf{0}$ implies $\{a_i = 0, \ i = 1, \ldots, N\}$. A set of vectors spans the vector space if every point in the space can be reached by a linear combination of the set of vectors. The dimension of a vector space equals the number of linearly independent vectors that span the entire space.

2.4.3 Inner products between vectors

The inner product is a key new idea introduced to create a Hilbert space. The abstract idea is much deeper than the final formula that we eventually derive for inner products. An inner product is a *linear functional* that assigns a scalar to a pair of vectors $[|X\rangle, |Y\rangle]$ in the Hilbert space. The linear functional operates on the second vector or ket $|Y\rangle$ taken from the Hilbert space. The linear functional itself is defined by the first vector $|X\rangle$ taken from the Hilbert space. The term "linear functional" is too long and it needs to be replaced by a symbol, and so it is symbolized as another kind of vector $\langle X|$ which is called a "bra." Bras form another vector space, called the dual space, because they can also be added to form a new bra $\langle Z| = \langle X| + \langle Y|$, or multiplied by a scalar to form a new bra $\langle W| = a \cdot \langle X|$ in the dual space. As we shall see, the bra can be represented by a $1 \times N$ row matrix. But like a ket, a bra is a more general object.

Then the inner product is denoted by the "bra–ket" $\langle X|Y\rangle$ for the bra $\langle X|$ operating on the ket $|Y\rangle$. Linearity refers to the property that the inner product for the bra $\langle X|$ operating on the ket $|Y\rangle = (a \cdot |V\rangle + b \cdot |W\rangle)$ equals $\langle X|Y\rangle = a \cdot \langle X|V\rangle + b \cdot \langle X|W\rangle$. The order used to define the inner product matters, such as $\langle X|Y\rangle$ with $\langle X|$ as the bra $|Y\rangle$ as the ket. The order makes a difference because the inner product is by definition anti-symmetric: $\langle X|Y\rangle = \langle Y|X\rangle^*$. In other words, the inner product $\langle X|Y\rangle$ is a complex number and $\langle Y|X\rangle = \langle X|Y\rangle^*$ is the complex conjugate of $\langle X|Y\rangle$. Only if the inner product is real do we obtain $\langle Y|X\rangle = \langle X|Y\rangle$. As we shall see later, the abstract inner product corresponds to the matrix inner product presented earlier.

The inner product is used to define orthogonality: two vectors are defined to be orthogonal if $\langle Y|X \rangle = \langle X|Y \rangle = 0$. The inner product also defines a norm or length for a vector $|X\rangle$ as $|| \, |X\rangle \, || = \sqrt{\langle X|X \rangle}$. Using the norm, the normalized (unit-length) vector is constructed by $|x\rangle = \frac{1}{|| \, |X\rangle \, ||} \cdot |X\rangle$, so that $\langle x|x \rangle = 1$. This norm is also used to define a distance metric between a pair of vectors $\{|X\rangle, |Y\rangle\}$: define the difference vector $|D\rangle = |X\rangle - |Y\rangle$, then $\mathrm{dist}(|X\rangle, |Y\rangle) = || \, |D\rangle \, || = \sqrt{\langle D|D \rangle}$. At this stage, the linear algebraic foundations are not sufficient to compute an inner product, but definitions are in place for the norm of a vector, orthogonality between two vectors, and distance between vectors.

2.4.4   Outer product operators

An outer product is a special kind of linear operator that maps one vector into another vector in Hilbert space. Suppose $[|X\rangle, |Y\rangle]$ is an ordered pair of vectors in the Hilbert space. An outer product for this pair, symbolized as $|Y\rangle\langle X|$, is a linear operator that takes another vector $|Z\rangle$ and maps it into

$$|Y\rangle\langle X| \cdot |Z\rangle = |Y\rangle\langle X|Z\rangle = \langle X|Z\rangle \cdot |Y\rangle.$$

The linearity refers to the property that if $|Z\rangle = (a \cdot |U\rangle + b \cdot |V\rangle)$ then $|Y\rangle\langle X| \cdot |Z\rangle = (a \cdot \langle X|U\rangle + b \cdot \langle X|V\rangle) \cdot |Y\rangle$. If all the vectors are unit length, then $|Y\rangle\langle X| \cdot |X\rangle = |Y\rangle\langle X|X\rangle = |Y\rangle$, in which case we call $|Y\rangle\langle X|$ the transition operator from $|X\rangle$ to $|Y\rangle$. The outer product operator corresponds to the matrix outer product presented earlier.

An important special case of an outer product is a projector defined by the outer product $\mathbf{P}_X = |X\rangle\langle X|$ assuming that $|X\rangle$ is unit length. The projection of $|Y\rangle$ onto the subspace spanned by $|X\rangle$ equals $\mathbf{P}_X|Y\rangle = |X\rangle\langle X| \cdot |Y\rangle = |X\rangle\langle X|Y\rangle = \langle X|Y\rangle \cdot |X\rangle$. In particular, if $|X\rangle$ is unit length, then $\mathbf{P}_X \cdot |X\rangle = |X\rangle\langle X| \cdot |X\rangle = |X\rangle$. So each vector $|X\rangle$ has a projector $\mathbf{P}_X = |X\rangle\langle X|$. Two important properties of an orthogonal projector are that it is Hermitian $\mathbf{P}_X = \mathbf{P}_X^\dagger$ and idempotent:

$$\begin{aligned}
\mathbf{P}_X \cdot \mathbf{P}_X &= |X\rangle\langle X| \cdot |X\rangle\langle X| \\
&= \langle X|X\rangle \cdot |X\rangle\langle X| = |X\rangle\langle X| = \mathbf{P}_X,
\end{aligned}$$

where we are assuming that $|X\rangle$ has unit length so that $\langle X|X\rangle = 1$. The Hermitian property implies that if $|e\rangle = |Y\rangle - \mathbf{P}_X|Y\rangle$ then $\langle e|\mathbf{P}_X|Y\rangle = 0$.

2.4.5   Linear operators

The action of a linear operator $\mathbf{A}$ is the transformation from one point to another point in the Hilbert space, and it satisfies the basic linear rule

$$\mathbf{A}(a \cdot |X\rangle + b \cdot |Y\rangle) = a \cdot \mathbf{A}|X\rangle + b \cdot \mathbf{A}|Y\rangle.$$

We can take linear combinations of outer products to form linear operators such as $\mathbf{A} = a \cdot |Y\rangle\langle X| + b \cdot |V\rangle\langle U|$, which produces

$$\begin{aligned}
|W\rangle = \mathbf{A} \cdot |Z\rangle &= (a \cdot |Y\rangle\langle X| + b \cdot |V\rangle\langle U|) \cdot |Z\rangle \\
&= a \cdot \langle X|Z\rangle \cdot |Y\rangle + b \cdot \langle U|Z\rangle \cdot |V\rangle.
\end{aligned}$$

If we first apply a linear transformation to generate $|Y\rangle = \mathbf{A}|X\rangle$ and then operate on this with $\langle Z|$, then the resulting inner product equals $\langle Z|Y\rangle = \langle Z|\mathbf{A}|X\rangle$. As we shall see later, a linear operator can be represented by a matrix.

There is a special linear operator, called the identity operator, denoted $\mathbf{I}$, that has the property $\mathbf{I}|X\rangle = |X\rangle$ for any $|X\rangle$. The inverse of a linear operator $\mathbf{A}$, if it exists, is symbolized as $\mathbf{A}^{-1}$, which is defined by the inverse map: if $|Y\rangle = \mathbf{A}|X\rangle$, then $|X\rangle = \mathbf{A}^{-1}|Y\rangle = \mathbf{A}^{-1}\mathbf{A}|X\rangle$, and so $\mathbf{A}^{-1}\mathbf{A} = \mathbf{I}$.

Suppose we apply two linear operators in a series, such as $|Z\rangle = (\mathbf{BA})|X\rangle = \mathbf{B}(\mathbf{A}|X\rangle) = \mathbf{B}|Y\rangle$. The order can make an important difference, so that $\mathbf{BA}$ does not necessarily have the same effect as $\mathbf{AB}$. The commutator, symbolized as $[\mathbf{A}, \mathbf{B}]$, is defined as the difference $[\mathbf{A}, \mathbf{B}] = \mathbf{AB} - \mathbf{BA}$. If the commutator is zero, then the linear operators commute: $\mathbf{AB} = \mathbf{BA}$, and if the commutator is nonzero, then they do not commute $\mathbf{AB} \neq \mathbf{BA}$. The inverse can also be defined by the property $\mathbf{AA}^{-1} = \mathbf{I} = \mathbf{A}^{-1}\mathbf{A}$, and so these two commute.

2.4.6 Adjoint operation

The adjoint operator † (dagger) is used to flip the role of a ket such as $|X\rangle$ into the role of bra such as $\langle X|$ and vice versa. In particular, $|X\rangle^{\dagger} = \langle X|$ and $\langle X|^{\dagger} = (|X\rangle^{\dagger})^{\dagger} = |X\rangle$. We can apply the dagger to the inner product to obtain $((\langle X|Y\rangle)^{\dagger} = \langle Y|X\rangle = \langle X|Y\rangle^{*}$. The dagger operation also can be used to flip the outer product: $(|Y\rangle\langle X|)^{\dagger} = |X\rangle\langle Y|$. Note also that we can flip back to the original $(((|Y\rangle\langle X|)^{\dagger})^{\dagger} = |Y\rangle\langle X|$. However, the dagger operation is defined to be anti-linear. If $\mathbf{A} = a \cdot |Y\rangle\langle X| + b \cdot |V\rangle\langle U|$, then $\mathbf{A}^{\dagger} = (a \cdot |Y\rangle\langle X| + b \cdot |U\rangle\langle V|)^{\dagger} = a^{*} \cdot |X\rangle\langle Y| + b^{*} \cdot |V\rangle\langle U|$.

If we first apply a linear transformation to generate $|Y\rangle = \mathbf{A}|X\rangle$ and then apply the dagger to change this into a bra, then we obtain $|Y\rangle^{\dagger} = (\mathbf{A}|X\rangle)^{\dagger} = \langle X|\mathbf{A}^{\dagger}$, which is the linear transformation $\mathbf{A}^{\dagger}$ applied to the bra $\langle X|$. This linearly transformed bra operates on $|Z\rangle$ to produce the inner product $\langle X|\mathbf{A}^{\dagger}|Z\rangle$. If we apply the dagger to the product $\mathbf{BA}|X\rangle = \mathbf{B}|Y\rangle$ to change this into a bra, then $\langle Y|\mathbf{B}^{\dagger} = \langle X|\mathbf{A}^{\dagger}\mathbf{B}^{\dagger}$; then this bra applied to $|Z\rangle$ produces the inner product $\langle X|\mathbf{A}^{\dagger}\mathbf{B}^{\dagger}|Z\rangle$. Thus, the dagger applied to the product of linear operators equals $(\mathbf{BA})^{\dagger} = \mathbf{A}^{\dagger}\mathbf{B}^{\dagger}$. Obviously, the adjoint operation corresponds to the conjugate transpose for matrices.

For a given linear operator, $\mathbf{A}$, it generally makes an important difference whether: (a) we first transform a ket to $\mathbf{A}|Y\rangle$ and then apply the bra $\langle X|$ to form the inner product $\langle X|\mathbf{A}|Y\rangle$; or (b) we first transform a bra to $\langle X|\mathbf{A}^{\dagger}$ and then operate on the ket $|Y\rangle$ to obtain the inner product $\langle X|\mathbf{A}^{\dagger}|Y\rangle$. For a special type of linear operator, called a Hermitian operator, this does not matter, because if $\mathbf{A}$ is Hermitian then $\mathbf{A}^{\dagger} = \mathbf{A}$. Note that a second important property of an orthogonal projector is that it is Hermitian: $\mathbf{P}_X^{\dagger} = (|X\rangle\langle X|)^{\dagger} = |X\rangle\langle X| = \mathbf{P}_X$.

2.4.7 Orthogonal decomposition

An N-dimensional Hilbert space has a set of N linearly independent vectors that by definition span the entire space. An arbitrary set of linearly independent vectors can be transformed into a set of orthonormal vectors by using the Gram–Schmidt orthogonalization procedure (Strang, 1980). The latter is called an orthonormal basis for the space. We will skip the actual procedure and assume that we have selected an orthonormal basis $\{|V_i\rangle,\ i=1,\ldots,N\}$, and each vector $|V_i\rangle$ in this set is called a basis vector.

Each basis vector corresponds to a projector $\mathbf{P}_i = |V_i\rangle\langle V_i|$ that projects an arbitrary vector onto the ray spanned by that basis vector $\mathbf{P}_i|X\rangle = |V_i\rangle\langle V_j|X\rangle$. Note that each pair of projectors is orthogonal $(i \neq j)$:

$$\mathbf{P}_i\mathbf{P}_j = |V_i\rangle\langle V_i| \cdot |V_j\rangle\langle V_j| = \langle V_i|V_j\rangle|V_i\rangle\langle V_j| = 0 \cdot |V_i\rangle\langle V_j| = \mathbf{0}.$$

A subset of basis vectors, say $\{|V_i\rangle, |V_j\rangle, |V_k\rangle\}$, spans a subspace of the Hilbert space, say $\mathbf{S}$, and the projector for this subspace is $\mathbf{P}_S = (\mathbf{P}_i + \mathbf{P}_j + \mathbf{P}_k)$. The projector for the entire Hilbert space is simply

$$\sum_{i=1}^{N}\mathbf{P}_i = \mathbf{I},$$

where $\mathbf{I}$ is the identity operator $\mathbf{I}\cdot|X\rangle = |X\rangle$.

A partition of the space is formed by a set of projectors $\{\mathbf{Q}_1,\ldots,\mathbf{Q}_K\}$ such that $\mathbf{Q}_i$ is a projector on a subspace, the $\mathbf{Q}_i$ are pairwise orthogonal so that $\mathbf{Q}_i\mathbf{Q}_j = \mathbf{0}$ for $i \neq j$, and $\sum_k \mathbf{Q}_k = \mathbf{I}$. Note that if two projectors are orthogonal, then they commute because $\mathbf{Q}_i\mathbf{Q}_j = \mathbf{0} = \mathbf{Q}_j\mathbf{Q}_i$.[4]

Let us examine an arbitrary point $|X\rangle$ in the Hilbert space with respect to the basis $\{|V_i\rangle,\ i=1,\ldots,N\}$ by expanding the identity

$$|X\rangle = \mathbf{I}\cdot|X\rangle = \sum_{i=1}^{N}\mathbf{P}_i \cdot |X\rangle$$

$$= \sum_{i=1}^{N}|V_i\rangle\langle V_i| \cdot |X\rangle = \sum_{i=1}^{N}\langle V_i|X\rangle \cdot |V_i\rangle.$$

What we have done is described the vector $|X\rangle$ in terms of coordinates $\langle V_i|X\rangle$ defined by the basis $\{|V_i\rangle,\ i=1,\ldots,N\}$. The $N \times 1$ column matrix α of coefficients

$$|X\rangle \rightarrow \begin{bmatrix} \langle V_1|X\rangle \\ \cdot \\ \langle V_i|X\rangle \\ \cdot \\ \langle V_N|X\rangle \end{bmatrix} = \begin{bmatrix} \alpha_1 \\ \cdot \\ \alpha_i \\ \cdot \\ \alpha_N \end{bmatrix} = \alpha$$

is a representation of the vector with respect to the $\{|V_i\rangle,\ i=1,\ldots,N\}$ basis. So we now see the difference between an abstract ket and its column matrix. The column matrix is a special case where we have chosen a particular basis to represent the ket. The ket is more general because it can be represented by

---

[4]If $\mathbf{Q}_i\mathbf{Q}_j = \mathbf{0}$, then $\langle X|\mathbf{Q}_i\mathbf{Q}_j|Y\rangle = 0 = \langle X|\mathbf{Q}_i\mathbf{Q}_j|Y\rangle^* = \langle Y|\mathbf{Q}_j\mathbf{Q}_i|X\rangle$ for any $|X\rangle, |Y\rangle$, which implies $\mathbf{Q}_j\mathbf{Q}_i = \mathbf{0}$.

differerent column matrices by changing the basis. The ket itself is an object that is free of any particular basis.

2.4.8 Orthogonal projections

Suppose we wish to project a vector on to a subspace spanned by a subset, say $\{|V_i\rangle, |V_j\rangle, |V_k\rangle\}$, of orthonormal basis vectors $\{|V_i\rangle, \; i = 1, \ldots, N\}$. The goal is to find the projection $|y\rangle$ that fits optimally in the sense that the residual $|e\rangle = |Y\rangle - |y\rangle$ has minimum squared length. The optimal projection is

$$|y\rangle = \mathbf{P}_S|Y\rangle = (\mathbf{P}_i + \mathbf{P}_j + \mathbf{P}_k)|Y\rangle.$$

with $\mathbf{P}_i = |V_i\rangle\langle V_i|$, which produces the unique residual $|e\rangle = |Y\rangle - |y\rangle = (\mathbf{I} - \mathbf{P}_S)|Y\rangle$, with $\langle e|y\rangle = \langle Y|(\mathbf{I} - \mathbf{P}_S)\mathbf{P}_S|Y\rangle = 0$.

To prove this, suppose we choose an arbitrarily selected projection $|z\rangle$ on this subspace. Given that $|z\rangle$ is on the subspace and $\{|V_i\rangle, |V_j\rangle, |V_k\rangle\}$ span the subspace, we can reach it by $|z\rangle = a_1 \cdot |V_i\rangle + b_2 \cdot |V_j\rangle + b_3|V_k\rangle$, which corresponds to the projection $|z\rangle = (a_1 \cdot \mathbf{P}_i + a_2 \cdot \mathbf{P}_j + a_3 \cdot \mathbf{P}_k)|Y\rangle$ on this subspace. For convenience, define $|d\rangle = |y\rangle - |z\rangle$. Now $|y\rangle$ produces a residual $|e\rangle = |Y\rangle - |y\rangle$ and $|z\rangle$ produces a residual $|r\rangle = |Y\rangle - |z\rangle = |e\rangle + |d\rangle$. The residual for $|z\rangle$ has a squared length equal to

$$\langle r|r\rangle = (|e\rangle + |d\rangle)^\dagger (|e\rangle + |d\rangle) = \langle e|e\rangle + \langle d|d\rangle + \langle e|d\rangle + \langle d|e\rangle,$$

where $\langle e|d\rangle = \langle Y|(\mathbf{I} - \mathbf{P}_S)(\mathbf{P}_S - a_1 \cdot \mathbf{P}_i - a_2 \cdot \mathbf{P}_j - a_3 \cdot \mathbf{P}_k)|Y\rangle = 0$ because $(\mathbf{I} - \mathbf{P}_S)$ is orthogonal to each of the projectors $\mathbf{P}_i, \mathbf{P}_j, \mathbf{P}_k$. For example, $(\mathbf{I} - (\mathbf{P}_i + \mathbf{P}_j + \mathbf{P}_k)) \cdot \mathbf{P}_j = ((\mathbf{I} - \mathbf{P}_j) - \mathbf{P}_i - \mathbf{P}_k) \cdot \mathbf{P}_j = 0$. Thus, $\langle r|r\rangle = \langle e|e\rangle + \langle d|d\rangle \geq \langle e|e\rangle$.

2.4.9 Spectral decomposition of linear operators

Recall that a Hermitian linear operator $\mathbf{A}$ is one that satisfies $\mathbf{A}^\dagger = \mathbf{A}$. These operators play a crucial role in quantum theory. In particular, recall that orthogonal projectors are Hermitian. An eigenvector of the linear operator $\mathbf{A}$ is defined as a vector that has the special property

$$\mathbf{A}|V\rangle = \lambda \cdot |V\rangle$$

for some scalar λ called the eigenvalue associated with the eigenvector $|V\rangle$.

One of the most important theorems of linear algebra is that any Hermitian operator can be decomposed in terms of a set of orthonormal eigenvectors $\{|V_i\rangle, \; i = 1, .., N\}$ and real-valued eigenvalues λ_k as follows

$$\mathbf{A} = \sum_{i=1}^{N} \lambda_i \cdot \mathbf{P}_i,$$

where $\mathbf{P}_i = |V_i\rangle\langle V_i|$ for $k = 1, \ldots, N$ eigenvectors. If all N eigenvalues are unique, then the projectors are unique.

Clearly, this last expression for the inner product is invariant to the choice of basis, because we can expand in another orthonormal basis $\{|W_i\rangle,\ i=1,\ldots,N\}$ and obtain the same result,

$$\sum_{i=1}^{N}\langle X|W_i\rangle\langle W_i|Y\rangle = \langle X|\left(\sum_{i=1}^{N}|W_i\rangle\langle W_i|\right)|Y\rangle = \langle X|\mathbf{I}|Y\rangle = \langle X|Y\rangle,$$

so any basis is equally good for defining it. This implies the following simple matrix algebra formula for the inner product. Suppose $|X\rangle \to \alpha$ and $|Y\rangle \to \beta$ with respect to the $\{|V_i\rangle,\ i=1,\ldots,N\}$ basis. Then the inner product for the pair $[|X\rangle, |Y\rangle]$ is defined as

$$\langle X|Y\rangle = \sum_{i=1}^{N}\langle X|V_i\rangle\langle V_i|Y\rangle$$

$$= \sum_{i=1}^{N}\alpha_i^* \cdot \beta_i,$$

where α_i^* is the conjugate of α_i. Suppose once again that $|X\rangle \to \alpha$ and $|Y\rangle \to \beta$ with respect to the $\{|V_i\rangle,\ i=1,\ldots,N\}$ basis. The conjugate transpose of the $N \times 1$ column matrix α is denoted $\alpha^\dagger$, which produces a $1 \times N$ row matrix

$$\alpha^\dagger = \begin{bmatrix} \alpha_1^* & . & \alpha_i^* & . & \alpha_N^* \end{bmatrix} \to \langle X|.$$

The $1 \times N$ row matrix $\alpha^\dagger$ corresponds to the bra $\langle X|$. This allows us to rewrite the inner product as a matrix product:

$$\langle X|Y\rangle = (\alpha^\dagger \cdot \beta) = \sum_{i=1}^{N}\alpha_i^* \cdot \beta_i.$$

As we mentioned earlier, quantum theorists like to call a vector $|X\rangle$ which corresponds to the $N \times 1$ column matrix α of coefficients a "ket"; and they like to call the dual vector $\langle X|$ which corresponds to the $1 \times N$ row matrix of coefficients $\alpha^\dagger$ a "bra." Thus, the inner product $\langle X|Y\rangle$ is called a "bra | ket." In general, this will be a complex number. The inner product is invariant to the choice of orthonormal basis, and so any orthonormal basis can be used to compute the inner product.

Once again using the $\{|V_i\rangle,\ i=1,\ldots,N\}$ basis, the squared length of a vector equals $||\,|X\rangle\,||^2 = \langle X|X\rangle = \sum_{i=1}^{N}\alpha_i^* \cdot \alpha_i$. (This squared length is also invariant to choice of basis.) The critical role of the conjugate can be clearly seen here. If we did not use the conjugate, then the length would remain complex. By using the conjugate, the length is forced to be a real number.

2.4.14   Matrix formula for linear transformations

Suppose $\mathbf{A}$ is an arbitrary linear operator which produces the linear transformation that maps an arbitrary vector $|X\rangle$ into a new vector $|Y\rangle$ by the operation $|Y\rangle = \mathbf{A}|X\rangle$. Now let us examine the coordinates of $|Y\rangle$ with respect to the $\{|V_j\rangle, \; j = 1, \ldots, N\}$ basis. The coordinate of $|Y\rangle$ associated with basis vector $|V_i\rangle$ is

$$\langle V_i|Y\rangle = \langle V_i|\mathbf{A}|X\rangle$$

$$= \left\langle V_i|\mathbf{A} \cdot \sum_{j=1}^{N} \langle V_j|X\rangle \cdot |V_j\right\rangle$$

$$= \sum_{j=1}^{N} \langle V_j|X\rangle\langle V_i|\mathbf{A}|V_j\rangle.$$

Recall that $\alpha_j = \langle V_j|X\rangle$ is the jth coordinate of $|X\rangle$ with respect to the $\{|V_j\rangle, \; j = 1, \ldots, N\}$ basis, and these coefficients form an $N \times 1$ column matrix α. Also define $\beta_i = \langle V_i|Y\rangle$ as the ith coordinate of $|Y\rangle$ with respect to the $\{|V_j\rangle, \; j = 1, \ldots, N\}$ basis, and these coefficients form another $N \times 1$ column matrix β. We can define a matrix element $a_{ij} = \langle V_i|\mathbf{A}|V_j\rangle$ that forms a table or matrix of coefficients $A = [a_{ij}]$ with $a_{ij} = \langle V_i|\mathbf{A}|V_j\rangle$ in row i and column j. Then we can express the effect of the linear transformation in terms of the coordinates as

$$\beta_i = \sum_{j=1}^{N} a_{ij} \cdot \alpha_j.$$

This allows us to define matrix product $\beta = A \cdot \alpha$, where the ith row of β is defined by the above matrix formula.

The unitary transformation $\mathbf{U}$ used to transform from one basis to another can be expressed in terms of the $\{|V_i\rangle, \; i = 1, \ldots, N\}$ basis as a matrix with cell entries

$$\langle V_i|W_j\rangle = \langle V_i|\mathbf{U}|V_j\rangle.$$

2.4.15 Matrix formula for a sequence of linear transformations

Let us examine the matrix representation of the product operator $\mathbf{C} = \mathbf{B}\mathbf{A}$ with respect to the $\{|V_j\rangle, \; j = 1, \ldots, N\}$ basis. Define γ as the $N \times 1$ column matrix containing the coordinates of $|Z\rangle$ with respect to the $\{|V_j\rangle, \; j = 1, \ldots, N\}$ basis. We already know that $|Y\rangle = \mathbf{A}|X\rangle$ corresponds to $\beta = A \cdot \alpha$ with $A = [a_{jk}]$ and $a_{jk} = \langle V_j|\mathbf{A}|V_k\rangle$. Following the same arguments leads to the conclusion that $|Z\rangle = \mathbf{B}|Y\rangle$ corresponds to $\gamma = B \cdot \beta$, where $B = [b_{ij}]$ is a matrix of coefficients used to represent $\mathbf{B}$ in the $\{|V_j\rangle, \; j = 1, \ldots, N\}$ basis and $b_{ij} = \langle V_i|\mathbf{B}|V_j\rangle$ in row i and column j. Therefore, we obtain $\gamma = B \cdot \beta = B \cdot A \cdot \alpha$, with probabilities to all events of the experiment. This is called the principle of unicity (Griffiths, 2003).

Quantum probability assumes that there is only one Hilbert space and all events are contained in this single Hilbert space. For a single fixed basis, such as $V = \{|V_i\rangle, i = 1, \ldots, N\}$, the meet and the join of two events spanned by a common set of basis vectors in V are always well defined, and a probability function q_V can be used to assign probabilities to all the events defined with respect to the basis V. When a common basis is used to define all the events, then the events are compatible.

The beauty of a Hilbert space is that there are many choices for the basis that one can use to describe the space. For example, suppose $W = \{|W_i\rangle, i = 1, \ldots, N\}$ is another orthonormal basis for the Hilbert space. If event A is spanned by $V_A \subset V$ and event B is spanned by $W_B \subset W$, then the meet for these two events is not defined; also, the join for these two events is not defined either (Griffiths, 2003). In this case, the events are not compatible, the projectors for these two events do not commute, $\mathbf{P}_A\mathbf{P}_B \neq \mathbf{P}_B\mathbf{P}_A$, and the projectors for these two events do not share a common set of eigenvectors. In this case, it is not meaningful to assign a probability simultaneously to the pair of events $\{A, B\}$ (Dirac, 1958).

For incompatible events, probabilities are assigned to histories or sequences of events using Lüder's rule (Niestegge, 2008). Suppose A is an event spanned by $V_A \subseteq V$ and event B is spanned by $W_B \subseteq W$. Consider the probability for the sequence of events A followed by B. The probability of the first event, A equals $q_V(A) = ||\mathbf{P}_A|S\rangle||^2$; the revised state, conditioned on observing this event equals $|S_A\rangle = \frac{\mathbf{P}_A|S\rangle}{||\mathbf{P}_A|S\rangle||}$; the probability of the second event, conditioned on the first event, equals $q_W(B|A) = ||\mathbf{P}_B|S_A\rangle||^2$; therefore, the probability of event A followed by event B equals $q_V(A) \cdot q_W(B|A)$. These steps can be compressed into a single step as follows (Nielsen & Chuang, 2000: 86). The probability of the sequence A and then B equals

$$q_V(A) \cdot q_W(B|A) = ||\mathbf{P}_A|S\rangle||^2 \cdot ||\mathbf{P}_B|S_A\rangle||^2 \tag{2.7}$$

$$= ||\mathbf{P}_A|S\rangle||^2 \cdot \left|\left|\mathbf{P}_B \frac{\mathbf{P}_A|S\rangle}{||\mathbf{P}_A|S\rangle||}\right|\right|^2$$

$$= ||\mathbf{P}_A|S\rangle||^2 \cdot \frac{1}{||\mathbf{P}_A|S\rangle||^2}||\mathbf{P}_B\mathbf{P}_A|S\rangle||^2$$

$$= ||\mathbf{P}_B\mathbf{P}_A|S\rangle||^2.$$

Recall that we can express $||\mathbf{P}|S\rangle||^2$ as the inner product $||\mathbf{P}|S\rangle||^2 = \langle S|\mathbf{P}^\dagger\cdot\mathbf{P}|S\rangle = \langle S|\mathbf{P}|S\rangle$. Then we can rewrite Eq. (2.7): as an inner product as follows:

$$||\mathbf{P}_B\mathbf{P}_A|S\rangle||^2 = \langle S|\mathbf{P}_A\mathbf{P}_B \cdot \mathbf{P}_B\mathbf{P}_A|S\rangle = \langle S|\mathbf{P}_A\mathbf{P}_B\mathbf{P}_A|S\rangle. \tag{2.8}$$

2.5.5 Implications

2.5.5.1 Gleason's theorem

A skeptic might question whether the fundamental quantum probability rule, $p(A) = \|P_A|S\rangle\|^2$ that assigns probabilities to events defined as subspaces, is somehow arbitrary or ad hoc. Are there other rules that one could use? And if so, why choose this one? Well, this turns out not to be the case, and in fact the fundamental quantum probability rule is the *only* way to assign probabilities to events defined as subspaces (at least for vector space of dimension greater than 2). One of the great mathematical achievements in quantum probability theory is Gleason's theorem (Gleason, 1957), which proves that each additive probability measure defined on a projective lattice has a unique extension defined by the fundamental quantum probability rule.

2.5.5.2 Not A

The probability of the negation of an event A follows directly from the above axioms. Suppose A is a subspace that corresponds to the projector $\mathbf{P}_A$, which has probability $q_V(A) = \|\mathbf{P}_A|S\rangle\|^2$. Then the projector for the event $\bar{A}$ is the projector for the complementary subspace, which equals $\mathbf{I} - \mathbf{P}_A$. The probability for the event $\bar{A}$ equals

$$\|(\mathbf{I} - \mathbf{P}_A)|S\rangle\|^2 = \langle S|(\mathbf{I} - \mathbf{P}_A)|S\rangle$$
$$= \langle S|S\rangle - \langle S|\mathbf{P}_A|S\rangle = 1 - q_V(A).$$

2.5.5.3 A or then B

What about the probability for a sequence that event A occurs or then event B occurs for incompatible events? Well this sequence is the negation of the sequence that event A does not occur (denoted by the event $\bar{A}$) and then event B does not occur (denoted by the event $\bar{B}$). Therefore, the probability event A occurs or then event B occurs equals

$$1 - q_V(\bar{A}) \cdot q_W(\bar{B}|\bar{A}) = 1 - \|\mathbf{P}_{\bar{B}}\mathbf{P}_{\bar{A}}|S\rangle\|^2. \tag{2.9}$$

2.5.5.4 Compatible events

Suppose the two events are compatible; that is, A is spanned by $V_A \subseteq V$ corresponding to projector $\mathbf{P}_A$ and B is spanned by $V_B \subseteq V$ corresponding to projector $\mathbf{P}_B$. Then they are described by a common basis V, which implies that $\mathbf{P}_B$ commutes with $\mathbf{P}_A$. The meet $A \wedge B$ is well defined and it has a projector spanned by $V_A \cap V_B$, which equals $\mathbf{P}_A\mathbf{P}_B = \mathbf{P}_B\mathbf{P}_A$; but this projector produces exactly the same probability as Eq. (2.7). Additionally, assuming compatibility, the join $A \vee B$ is well defined and it is spanned by $V_A \cup V_B$, which corresponds to the projector $\mathbf{I} - \mathbf{P}_{\bar{A}}\mathbf{P}_{\bar{B}}$; but this projector produces exactly the same probability as Eq. (2.9). Therefore, Eqs (2.7) and (2.9) can be used consistently for both compatible and incompatible events.

2.5.5.5   Violation of the distributive axiom

According to classic probability theory, the distributive axiom asserts that $A = A \cap (B \cup \bar{B}) = (A \cap B) \cup (A \cap \bar{B})$, where $\bar{B}$ is the complement of B. This axiom implies the law of total probability:

$$\begin{aligned} p(A) = p(A \cap \mathbf{X}) &= p(A \cap (B \cup \bar{B})) \\ &= p((A \cap B) \cup (A \cap \bar{B})) \\ &= p(A \cap B) + p(A \cap \bar{B}) \\ &= p(B)p(A|B) + p(\bar{B})p(A|\bar{B}). \end{aligned}$$

This law is key to much of the work done in Bayesian analysis. Essentially this axiom assumes that if event A occurs, then it can only occur in two mutually exclusive and exhaustive ways. Either event A occurs with event B, or event A occurs without event B. You might wonder, how can it be otherwise? Why does quantum probability violate this law?

The problem for quantum theory does not arise for the left-hand side of the distributive axiom; that is, $A = A \wedge (B \vee \bar{B})$. In particular, the projector $\mathbf{P}_B$ corresponding to the event B commutes with the projector $\mathbf{P}_{\bar{B}}$ corresponding to the event $\bar{B}$, and so the event B is compatible with the orthogonal complement $\bar{B}$. Therefore, the disjunction event $B \vee \bar{B}$ is well defined, and it equals the span of the two subspaces, corresponding to the projector $(\mathbf{P}_B + \mathbf{P}_{\bar{B}}) = \mathbf{I}$, which projects onto the entire Hilbert space. The projector $\mathbf{P}_A$ corresponding to the event A commutes with $(\mathbf{P}_B + \mathbf{P}_{\bar{B}}) = \mathbf{I}$, and so event A is compatible with the event $B \vee \bar{B}$. Therefore, the conjunction $A \wedge (B \vee \bar{B})$ is well defined and is equal to the intersection of A with $(B \vee \bar{B})$, which equals the event A. Therefore, according to quantum theory, $A = A \wedge (B \vee \bar{B})$, and in fact the projectors satisfy the distributive rule for linear operators:

$$\mathbf{P}_A = \mathbf{P}_A \cdot \mathbf{I} = \mathbf{P}_A \cdot (\mathbf{P}_B + \mathbf{P}_{\bar{B}}) = \mathbf{P}_A \cdot \mathbf{P}_B + \mathbf{P}_A \cdot \mathbf{P}_{\bar{B}}.$$

The problem arises with the right-hand side of the distributive axiom; that is, $(A \wedge B) \vee (A \wedge \bar{B})$. The root of the problem goes back to the issue of incompatible events or non-commuting projectors. Suppose the event A is spanned by $V_A \subseteq V = \{|V_i\rangle, i = 1, \ldots, N\}$ and event B is spanned $W_B \subseteq W = \{|W_i\rangle, i = 1, \ldots, N\}$. Then the projector for event A (that is, $\mathbf{P}_A$) does not commute with the projector for event B (that is, $\mathbf{P}_B$). The conjunction is defined to be commutative $A \wedge B = B \wedge A$, and so we cannot identify this definition with a non-commutative product such as $\mathbf{P}_A \mathbf{P}_B$. It is impossible to define a single projector for $A \wedge B = B \wedge A$ because $\mathbf{P}_A \mathbf{P}_B \neq \mathbf{P}_B \mathbf{P}_A$. The conjunction does not even make sense here because only a sequence such as A *and then* B is observable. In this situation, it is possible to have an event A that is a nontrivial subspace spanned by V_A, but it has zero intersection with the subspace spanned by B, and at the same time it has zero intersection with the subspace spanned by $\bar{B}$ (the orthogonal complement of the space spanned by B). For example, refer back to Figure 2.2. The event U spanned by the vector $|U\rangle$ is contained in the three-dimensional space spanned by $|X\rangle, |Y\rangle, |Z\rangle$ so that $U = U \wedge (X \vee Y \vee Z)$.

But $U \wedge X = 0$ and $U \wedge Y = 0$ and $U \wedge Z = 0$, so that $(U \wedge X) \vee (U \wedge Y) \vee (U \wedge Z) = 0$. This is a case where the event U (woman wants BMW) can occur but we *cannot* assume that it must occur under only one of three mutually exclusive and exhaustive ways – we cannot assume that U (woman wants BMW) only occurs in conjunction with event X (man wants BMW) or in conjunction with event Y (man wants Audi) or in conjunction with event Z (man wants Cadillac). Somehow the event U (woman wants BMW) can occur another way.[8]

2.5.5.6   Total probability and interference

The violation of the distributive axiom by quantum theory leads to a violation of the law of total probability. To see this, consider two different experiments. The first simply records whether or not event B occurs. The second first observes whether A occurs or not A, and then records whether or not B occurs. For both experiments we are mainly interested in the probability of the event B. For the first experiment, this is simply $p(B) = ||\mathbf{P}_B|S\rangle||^2$. For the second experiment, we could observe the sequence with event A and then event B with probability $||\mathbf{P}_B\mathbf{P}_A|S\rangle||^2$, or we could observe the sequence with event $\bar{A}$ and the event B with probability $||\mathbf{P}_B\mathbf{P}_{\bar{A}}|S\rangle||^2$, and so the total probability for event B in the second experiment equals the sum of these two ways: $p_T(B) = ||\mathbf{P}_B\mathbf{P}_A|S\rangle||^2 + ||\mathbf{P}_B\mathbf{P}_{\bar{A}}|S\rangle||^2$. The interference produced in this experiment is defined as the probability of event B observed in the first experiment minus the total probability of event B observed in the second experiment. According to quantum probability the interference equals $\text{Int}_B = p(B) - p_T(B)$. To analyze this more closely, let us decompose the probability from the first experiment as follows:

$$p(B) = ||\mathbf{P}_B|S\rangle||^2 = ||\mathbf{P}_B\mathbf{I}|S\rangle||^2 \tag{2.10}$$

$$= ||\mathbf{P}_B \left(\mathbf{P}_A + \mathbf{P}_{\bar{A}}\right) |S\rangle||^2 \tag{2.11}$$

$$= \langle S| \left(\mathbf{P}_A + \mathbf{P}_{\bar{A}}\right) \mathbf{P}_B\mathbf{P}_B \left(\mathbf{P}_A + \mathbf{P}_{\bar{A}}\right) |S\rangle$$

$$= \langle S|\mathbf{P}_A\mathbf{P}_B\mathbf{P}_A|S\rangle + \langle S|\mathbf{P}_{\bar{A}}\mathbf{P}_B\mathbf{P}_A|S\rangle$$

$$\quad + \langle S|\mathbf{P}_A\mathbf{P}_B\mathbf{P}_{\bar{A}}|S\rangle + \langle S|\mathbf{P}_{\bar{A}}\mathbf{P}_B\mathbf{P}_{\bar{A}}|S\rangle$$

$$= ||\mathbf{P}_B\mathbf{P}_A|S\rangle||^2 + ||\mathbf{P}_B\mathbf{P}_{\bar{A}}|S\rangle||^2$$

$$\quad + [\langle S|\mathbf{P}_{\bar{A}}\mathbf{P}_B\mathbf{P}_A|S\rangle + \langle S|\mathbf{P}_A\mathbf{P}_B\mathbf{P}_{\bar{A}}|S\rangle]$$

$$= p_T(B) + \text{Int}_B.$$

So we see that we predict interference whenever the cross product term $\text{Int}_B = [\langle S|\mathbf{P}_{\bar{A}}\mathbf{P}_B\mathbf{P}_A|S\rangle + \langle S|\mathbf{P}_A\mathbf{P}_B\mathbf{P}_{\bar{A}}|S\rangle]$ is nonzero. There is also an interference term for the event $\bar{B}$, which is denoted $\text{Int}_{\bar{B}}$ but these two must cancel out because $p(B) + p(\bar{B}) = 1 = p_T(B) + p_T(\bar{B})$ so that $\text{Int}_B + \text{Int}_{\bar{B}} = 0$. If $\mathbf{P}_B\mathbf{P}_A = \mathbf{P}_A\mathbf{P}_B$, then $\mathbf{P}_{\bar{B}}\mathbf{P}_A = (\mathbf{I} - \mathbf{P}_B)\mathbf{P}_A = \mathbf{P}_A - \mathbf{P}_B\mathbf{P}_A = \mathbf{P}_A - \mathbf{P}_A\mathbf{P}_B = \mathbf{P}_A\mathbf{P}_{\bar{B}}$ and so all the

---

[8]This section benefited from discussions with Brian Busemeyer.

projectors commute. If they all commute, then $\mathbf{P}_A\mathbf{P}_B\mathbf{P}_{\bar{A}} = \mathbf{P}_A\mathbf{P}_{\bar{A}}\mathbf{P}_B = \mathbf{0}$, and so $\mathrm{Int}_B = 0 = \mathrm{Int}_{\bar{B}}$. Therefore, interference only occurs if the projectors do not commute. In the latter case it may be positive or negative, thus violating the law of total probability.

It is informative to decompose $\mathrm{Int}_B = [\langle S|\mathbf{P}_{\bar{A}}\mathbf{P}_B\mathbf{P}_A|S\rangle + \langle S|\mathbf{P}_A\mathbf{P}_B\mathbf{P}_{\bar{A}}|S\rangle]$ into its parts using our rules for complex numbers summarized earlier. Note that $\langle S|\mathbf{P}_A\mathbf{P}_B\mathbf{P}_{\bar{A}}|S\rangle = \langle S|\mathbf{P}_{\bar{A}}\mathbf{P}_B\mathbf{P}_A|S\rangle^*$, so that

$$\mathrm{Int}_B = \langle S|\mathbf{P}_{\bar{A}}\mathbf{P}_B\mathbf{P}_A|S\rangle + \langle S|\mathbf{P}_{\bar{A}}\mathbf{P}_B\mathbf{P}_A|S\rangle^*$$
$$= 2 \cdot |\langle S|\mathbf{P}_{\bar{A}}\mathbf{P}_B\mathbf{P}_A|S\rangle| \cdot \cos(\theta),$$

where θ is the phase angle of the inner product $\langle S|\mathbf{P}_{\bar{A}}\mathbf{P}_B\mathbf{P}_A|S\rangle$. We see that there are two ways for the interference to be zero. One way is that $|\langle S|\mathbf{P}_{\bar{A}}\mathbf{P}_B\mathbf{P}_A|S\rangle| = 0$, which would occur if the projectors commute. Excluding this, we must have $\cos(\theta) = 0$ (i.e., $\theta = \pi/2$ or $\theta = -\pi/2$, the complex axis in Figure 2.5). The interference is most positive when $\cos(\theta) = 1$ ($\theta = 0$), and it is most negative when $\cos(\theta) = -1$ ($\theta = \pi$) (the real axis in Figure 2.5).

2.5.5.7   Path diagram rules

It is worthwhile pointing out that the quantum probability axioms are completely consistent with Feynman's path rules. Consider two paths, each starting from state vector $|S\rangle$ and each ending at state vector $|E\rangle$, and traveling through states $|V_i\rangle$ for $i = 1, N$, which we will assume exhaust the possible intermediate paths. Each path is denoted $|S\rangle \to |V_i\rangle \to |E\rangle$. If we observe the location of the intermediate state, then according to Feynman's third rule (see Section 2.2.4), the probability of starting at $|S\rangle$ and each ending at state vector $|E\rangle$ equals

$$\sum_{i=1}^{N} |\langle V_i|S\rangle|^2 \cdot |\langle E|V_i\rangle|^2 . \tag{2.12}$$

If we do not observe the intermediate state, then according to Feynman's second rule (see Section 2.2.3), the probability of starting at $|S\rangle$ and each ending at state vector $|E\rangle$ equals

$$\left| \sum_{i=1}^{N} \langle V_i|S\rangle \cdot \langle E|V_i\rangle \right|^2 . \tag{2.13}$$

Now let us analyze the same situation according to the quantum axioms. Using Eq. (2.7), the probability of the sequence $|S\rangle \to |V_i\rangle \to |E\rangle$ equals

$$\langle S|\mathbf{P}_{V_i}\mathbf{P}_E\mathbf{P}_{V_i}|S\rangle = \langle S|V_i\rangle\langle V_i|E\rangle\langle E|V_i\rangle\langle V_i|S\rangle = |\langle V_i|S\rangle|^2|\langle E|V_i\rangle|^2,$$

which is exactly the same as Feynman's path probability for an individual path. When the path is observed, we compute the total probability, which equals the sum of path probabilities across the paths, which reproduces Eq. (2.12). When the path is not observed, then we simply have the probability

$$||\mathbf{P}_E|S\rangle||^2 = ||\mathbf{P}_E\mathbf{I}|S\rangle||^2 = \left\|\mathbf{P}_E\sum_{i=1}^{N}\mathbf{P}_{Vi}|S\rangle\right\|^2$$

$$= \left\|\sum_{i=1}^{N}\mathbf{P}_E\mathbf{P}_{Vi}|S\rangle\right\|^2 = \left\|\sum_{i=1}^{N}|E\rangle\langle E|V_i\rangle\langle V_i|S\rangle\right\|^2$$

$$= \left|\sum_{i=1}^{N}\langle E|V_i\rangle\langle V_i|S\rangle\right|^2 \cdot || \,|E\rangle\,||^2$$

$$= \left|\sum_{i=1}^{N}\langle E|V_i\rangle\langle V_i|S\rangle\right|^2 \cdot 1,$$

which is exactly the same result as Eq. (2.13) for the unobserved condition.

2.5.6 Observables as linear operators

As mentioned earlier in the matrix algebra section, classic probability theory uses a concept of a *random variable,* which is defined as a function that maps a set of points in the sample space into real numbers. The probability $p(X = x)$ that the random variable X is assigned the value x equals the probability of sampling a point from the sample space that is assigned the value x. Two important statistics used to characterize this probability distribution are the mean μ measuring central tendency and the variance σ^2 measuring variability.

In quantum theory, the concept of an *observable* is used in place of a random variable. An observable linear operator $\mathbf{X}$ is represented by a Hermitian linear operator defined on a (finite in our applications) Hilbert space. Because the observable is Hermitian, it has a spectral decomposition with real eigenvalues

$$\mathbf{X} = \sum x_i \cdot \mathbf{P}_i, \tag{2.14}$$

where $\mathbf{P}_i = V_i V_i^\dagger$ is the projector on the eigenvalue x_i and V_i is an eigenvector corresponding to x_i. The state vector $|\psi\rangle$ determines the probability distribution for the values of the observable as follows: $p(\mathbf{X} = x_i) = ||\mathbf{P}_i|\psi\rangle||^2 = \langle\psi|\mathbf{P}_i|\psi\rangle$. The mean of the observable equals

$$\mu = \langle\psi|\mathbf{X}|\psi\rangle$$

$$= \langle\psi|\sum x_i \cdot \mathbf{P}_i|\psi\rangle$$

$$= \sum x_i \cdot \langle\psi|\mathbf{P}_i|\psi\rangle$$

$$= \sum x_i \cdot p(\mathbf{X} = x_i).$$

The variance of the observable equals

$$\sigma^2 = \langle\psi|(\mathbf{X} - \mu \cdot \mathbf{I})^2|\psi\rangle$$

$$= \langle\psi|\sum (x_i - \mu)^2 \cdot \mathbf{P}_i|\psi\rangle$$

$$= \sum (x_i - \mu)^2 \cdot \langle\psi|\mathbf{P}_i|\psi\rangle$$

$$= \sum (x_i - \mu)^2 \cdot p(\mathbf{X} = x_i).$$

Physicists use the principle of quantization to form observables using Eq. (2.14), and then they can work directly from the observable on the left-hand side to define the projectors and eigenvalues on the right-hand side. That is, they map classical dynamic variables (such as classical position and momentum variables) into the corresponding quantum linear operators (a process called quantization) to form observables (such as position and momentum observables). This is difficult to do at this point in cognition and decision making. In the latter fields, it is easier to start with outcomes of an experiment, then form orthogonal projectors to represent the mutually exclusive outcomes, and if the outcomes are assigned real numbers, then one can form observables from a complete orthonormal set of projectors and the corresponding real-valued outcomes. In other words, it is easier for cognition and decision researchers to use Eq. (2.14) by working from projectors and outcome values on the right-hand side to form the observable on the left-hand side.

2.5.7   Heisenberg uncertainty principle

One of the most famous principles of quantum physics is the celebrated uncertainty principle. We briefly referred to this principle in Section 1.1.3, and we again talked about this principle in Sections 2.1.2.5 and 2.3.9.1. Is this principle limited to physics or does it apply more generally outside of physics? The answer is that the uncertainty principle is a general property of the mathematics used in quantum probability theory. Therefore, if we use quantum probability theory to describe human judgments, then we must face the same uncertainty relations as confront physicists. The uncertainty principle follows from the Cauchy–Schwartz inequality; see Nielsen and Chuang (2000: 89).

Suppose $\mathbf{X}$ and $\mathbf{Y}$ are two observables and $\hat{\mathbf{X}} = \mathbf{X} - \mu\mathbf{I}$ and $\hat{\mathbf{Y}} = \mathbf{Y} - \mu\mathbf{I}$ and $|\psi\rangle$ is a state vector. The inner product $\langle\psi|\hat{\mathbf{X}}\hat{\mathbf{Y}}|\psi\rangle$ is a complex number which can be written as $\langle\psi|\hat{\mathbf{X}}\hat{\mathbf{Y}}|\psi\rangle = x + i \cdot y$. Also note that

$$\langle\psi|\hat{\mathbf{X}}\hat{\mathbf{Y}} - \hat{\mathbf{Y}}\hat{\mathbf{X}}|\psi\rangle = \langle\psi|\hat{\mathbf{X}}\hat{\mathbf{Y}}|\psi\rangle - \langle\psi|\hat{\mathbf{Y}}\hat{\mathbf{X}}|\psi\rangle$$

$$= \langle\psi|\hat{\mathbf{X}}\hat{\mathbf{Y}}|\psi\rangle - \langle\psi|\hat{\mathbf{X}}\hat{\mathbf{Y}}|\psi\rangle^*$$

$$= (x + i \cdot y) - (x + i \cdot y)^* = 2 \cdot i \cdot y$$

and $\langle\psi|\hat{\mathbf{X}}\hat{\mathbf{Y}} + \hat{\mathbf{Y}}\hat{\mathbf{X}}|\psi\rangle = (x + i \cdot y) + (x + i \cdot y)^* = 2x$, so that

$$\left|\langle\psi|\hat{\mathbf{X}}\hat{\mathbf{Y}} - \hat{\mathbf{Y}}\hat{\mathbf{X}}|\psi\rangle\right|^2 + \left|\langle\psi|\hat{\mathbf{X}}\hat{\mathbf{Y}} + \hat{\mathbf{Y}}\hat{\mathbf{X}}|\psi\rangle\right|^2$$

$$= |2 \cdot i \cdot y|^2 + |2x|^2 = 4 \cdot \left(x^2 + y^2\right)$$

$$= 4 \cdot |x + i \cdot y|^2$$

$$= 4 \cdot \left|\langle\psi|\hat{\mathbf{X}}\hat{\mathbf{Y}}|\psi\rangle\right|^2,$$

and by the Cauchy–Schwarz inequality:

$$\left|\langle\psi|\hat{\mathbf{X}} \cdot \hat{\mathbf{Y}}|\psi\rangle\right|^2 \leq \langle\psi|\hat{\mathbf{X}}^2|\psi\rangle \cdot \langle\psi|\hat{\mathbf{Y}}^2|\psi\rangle.$$

Combining the above two lines, we obtain the inequality

$$\left|\langle\psi|\hat{\mathbf{X}}\hat{\mathbf{Y}} - \hat{\mathbf{Y}}\hat{\mathbf{X}}|\psi\rangle\right|^2 \leq \left|\langle\psi|\hat{\mathbf{X}}\hat{\mathbf{Y}} - \hat{\mathbf{Y}}\hat{\mathbf{X}}|\psi\rangle\right|^2 + \left|\langle\psi|\hat{\mathbf{X}}\hat{\mathbf{Y}} + \hat{\mathbf{Y}}\hat{\mathbf{X}}|\psi\rangle\right|^2$$

$$= 4 \cdot \left|\langle\psi|\hat{\mathbf{X}}\hat{\mathbf{Y}}|\psi\rangle\right|^2 \leq 4 \cdot \langle\psi|\hat{\mathbf{X}}^2|\psi\rangle \cdot \langle\psi|\hat{\mathbf{Y}}^2|\psi\rangle.$$

The last line implies

$$b = \frac{\left|\langle\psi|\hat{\mathbf{X}}\hat{\mathbf{Y}} - \hat{\mathbf{Y}}\hat{\mathbf{X}}|\psi\rangle\right|}{2} \leq \sqrt{\langle\psi|\hat{\mathbf{X}}^2|\psi\rangle} \cdot \sqrt{\langle\psi|\hat{\mathbf{Y}}^2|\psi\rangle},$$

which is the Heisenberg uncertainty relation. On the right-hand side we have the product of the standard deviations of observables $\mathbf{X}$ and $\mathbf{Y}$, and this product must exceed the positive bound produced by the commutator on the left-hand side. If we prepare a person's state $|\psi\rangle$ for a task in such a way that the preparation decreases the variance of one observable below the bound, then this same state $|\psi\rangle$ must increase the variance of the other observable to exceed the bound. This provides a critical method for testing a basic principle of quantum probability theory. Psychologically, this inequality may reflect a basic limit on human capacity to attend to two incompatible observables, and attention to one or the other variable could be manipulated by task instructions.

A concrete example is helpful here. As we mentioned earlier, for a task in which a person has to judge either the position or the momentum of a rapidly moving target, this inequality may reflect an intrinsic limit on attention capacity that has to be distributed to these two incompatible tasks. Recall that when expressed in the position basis, the position operator is represented by the matrix $H_x = \mathrm{diag}\,[-m, \ldots, -1, 0, 1, \ldots, m]$ and the momentum operator is represented by the matrix $H_y = U \cdot X \cdot U^\dagger$, where U is defined by Eq. (2.6). Then the Heisenberg bound equals

$$b = \frac{\left|\psi^\dagger \cdot (H_x \cdot H_y - H_y \cdot H_x) \cdot \psi\right|}{2}.$$

Using the distribution shown in Figure 2.4, the bound equals $b = 8.037$ and recall that $\sigma_x = 7.0711$ and $\sigma_y = 1.1366$, so the product of standard deviations equals $\sigma_x \cdot \sigma_y = (7.0711)(1.1366) = 8.037$, which is exactly equal to the bound. Explorations using other states produce the same product and bound whenever the variances are less extremely different than this example. The difference $\sigma_x \cdot \sigma_y - b > 0$ only becomes large and positive for very large discrepancies in σ_x versus σ_y.

This concludes our presentation of the basic quantum axioms and the relation to classic probability theory. The remaining chapters show how these axioms can be applied to problems of interest to researchers in cognitive and decision sciences.

2.6   Some further reading on quantum theory

There are many excellent introductions to quantum theory. Here is a list of a few references that may be helpful for the purposes of this book. A few of the standard quantum physics books are the Feynman introductory lectures (Feynman *et al.*, 1965), an introductory course by Sakurai (1994), lectures by Isham (2004), and a more advanced course by Peres (1998). Another good physics book, but one written with more emphasis on probability theory, is by Griffiths (2003). A more advanced book on quantum probability theory is the one by Gudder (1988). Another option is to read a book written from a philosophy of science perspective, and one good reference for this type is by Hughes (1989). There are several quantum logic books, including a classic one by Beltrametti and Cassinelli (1981) and a more modern one that addresses problems with the definitions of join and meet for incompatible events (Engesser *et al.*, 2009). Alternatively, an excellent book to read written from a quantum computing perspective is by Nielsen and Chuang (2000). Recently, two books have been written with applications to psychology, one by Khrennikov (2010) and another by Ivancevic and Ivancevic (2010).

3

What can quantum theory predict? Predicting question order effects on attitudes

Can one really predict something new and interesting using quantum theory in the social or behavioral sciences? Consider the law of reciprocity described in Chapter 2: according to this law, the probability of transiting from one state to another is equal to the probability of making this transition in the opposite direction. Now this symmetrical property is a pretty bold prediction to make in the social and behavioral sciences. Does this really work?

To answer this question, in this chapter we empirically test this law by applying the quantum principles to an important empirical problem concerning the effects of question order on attitude judgments. For example, suppose you are asked "How happy are you with life in general?" This question could be preceded or followed by the question "How happy are you with your marriage?" If the marriage question comes first, then the happiness rating for the general life question tends to be substantially depressed, producing a large order effect (Tourangeau *et al.*, 1991). Quantum physics was originally developed to understand how measurement affects the system under investigation, which led to Heisenberg's famous uncertainty principle. The potential reactivity to measurement by the person being measured has an even longer history in psychology (Tourangeau *et al.*, 2000).

The effects of question order have been an important issue to survey researchers interested in studying beliefs and attitudes (Schuman & Presser, 1981). Measurement of a belief or attitude directs attention to a subset of a person's knowledge, which is then used in guiding subsequent judgments. Central to this issue is whether the constructs of belief or attitude even exist before a question is asked – if not, then the act of asking the question *creates* an answer instigating attitude formation and even forming future intentions (Feldman & Lynch, 1988). Furthermore, just asking a person to state an intention to perform a behavior increases the likelihood of actually performing that behavior (Sherman, 1980).

Why do order effects challenge classic attitude theories? Suppose people have well-defined attitudes in memory and answering a question is just a matter of retrieving this stored information. Then the probability of selecting a person who says yes to question A and then yes to question B equals $p(A) \cdot p(B|A) = p(A \cap B) = p(B \cap A) = p(B) \cdot p(A|B)$ and the latter is the same as the probability of saying yes to question B and then saying yes to question A. In other words, the joint event is commutative and thus no order effect is predicted.

The commonly held explanation for order effects by social psychologists is the following: when question A is asked first, the person relies on a subset of knowledge he or she can retrieve from memory related to this question; but if question A is preceded by another question B, then the person incorporates thoughts retrieved from the previous question B into answering the second one about A. This intuitive explanation is NOT necessarily a classical reasoning explanation. In fact, it is completely consistent with a quantum judgment viewpoint. Only it lacks a rigorous formulation, which is what quantum probability theory can provide. What can be gained by providing a more rigorous formulation of this intuitive explanation? The answers are (a) exact quantitative predictions that can be directly tested with empirical data and (b) new theoretically derived methods for measuring similarity relationships between survey questions.

The earliest attempt to explain question order effects using quantum probability principles was by Aerts and Aerts (1994). This was followed by ideas proposed by Andrei Khrennikov (Khrennikov, 2004), and early empirical tests of these ideas were reported by Elio Conte (Conte *et al.*, 2009). In this chapter we describe a quantum model previously developed to explain and predict question order effects by Wang and Busemeyer (2012); see also Busemeyer and Wang (2010). The quantum model described here is applied to four different types of order effects reviewed by Moore (2002), including the assimilation, contrast, additive, and subtractive effects (described later).

3.1   A simple example

Before introducing the general quantum model, it will be helpful to have a concrete example in mind. One of the four examples presented by Moore (2002) concerned public opinions on the characters of Bill Clinton and Al Gore. In a Gallup poll conducted during September 6–7, 1997, half of the 1002 respondents were asked "Do you generally think Bill Clinton is honest and trustworthy?" and then asked the same question about Al Gore. The other half of respondents answered exactly the same questions but in the opposite order. The results exhibited a striking order effect. When presented as the first question, Clinton received a 53% agreement rate and Gore received 76%, which shows a gap of 23%; however, when presented as the second question, the agreement rate for Clinton increased to 59% while for Gore it decreased to 67% – that is, the gap decreased to 8%.[1] Moore (2002) defines this as a consistency (assimilation) effect: the difference between the objects becomes significantly smaller in the comparative context (second presentation) than in the non-comparative context (first presentation). Now we describe how to apply the quantum axioms from Chapter 2 to this application.

---

[1]These proportions only include agree or disagree counts into the total count, and they do not include "don't know" responses. They differ slightly from those presented by Moore (2002), who included "don't know" counts in the total count.

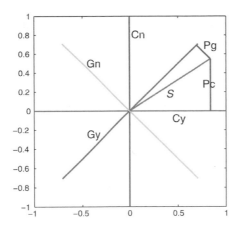

Figure 3.1 Two-dimensional model for the Clinton and Gore questions. Cy = yes to Clinton, Cn = no to Clinton, Gy = yes to Gore, Gn = no to Gore, S = initial state. Two projections are shown, one from S to Cy, another from S to Gy.

Let us start with a very simple model for this situation before presenting the more general theory. To fix ideas, Figure 3.1 provides a simple geometric example of the model described next, but the general theory is formalized to accommodate a much more realistic N-dimensional space with a much higher number of dimensions. We first analyze the situation in which a question is asked first before any other question is asked.

3.1.1 Analysis of first question

First, we assume that a person's belief can be represented by a vector in a feature space. In this simple example, there is only one feature (honesty) for Clinton with two values (yes,no); and there is only one feature (honesty) for Gore with two values (yes,no). In Figure 3.1, the feature space has $N = 2$ dimensions and the initial belief state vector is represented in the figure by the line next to the symbol S. There are two pairs of dimensions displayed in this figure. One pair of orthogonal axes is displayed horizontally and vertically. The horizontal axis is used to represent the event that a person answers "yes" to the Clinton question and the vertical axis represents the "no" answer. But there is another pair of orthogonal axes, rotated 45° from the horizontal and vertical axes. These other two axes represent the event "yes" and "no" to the Gore question. Now a key idea is that the belief vector $|S\rangle$, on the one hand, can be described in terms of the basis defined by Cy–Cn rays. The vector $|C_Y\rangle$ is a basis vector extending from $(0,0)$ to $(1,0)$ along the horizontal axis and $|C_N\rangle$ is a basis vector extending from $(0,0)$ to $(0,1)$ on the vertical axis. Using this basis, $|S\rangle$ represents the respondent's beliefs about agreeing or not with the question of "whether Clinton is honest and trustworthy" and the coordinates (amplitudes) for the (yes,no) answers are $(0.8367, 0.5477)$. These coordinates tell us to travel 0.8367 units in the direction of $|C_Y\rangle$ and then continue another 0.5477 units in the direction of $|C_N\rangle$. On the other hand, $|S\rangle$ can be defined by the Gy–Gn rays rotated 45° with respect to the Clinton basis. The vector $|G_Y\rangle$ is a basis vector extending from $(0,0)$ to $(1/\sqrt{2}, 1/\sqrt{2})$ (45° up from horizontal on the positive side) and $|G_N\rangle$ is a basis vector extending from $(0,0)$ to $(-1/\sqrt{2}, 1/\sqrt{2})$ (45° up from horizontal on the negative side). Using this other basis, $|S\rangle$ represents the respondent's belief about agreeing or not with the question of "whether Gore is honest and trustworthy" and the (yes,no) coordinates (amplitudes) are $(0.9789, -0.2043)$. These coordinates tell us to travel 0.9789 units in the direction of $|G_Y\rangle$ and then continue another -0.2043 in the direction of $|G_N\rangle$. Note that the state vector is designed to always have a length equal to one. As shown later, this guarantees that the probabilities across answers sum to one.

At this point, you might wonder what the negative coordinate for Gore means on the second coordinate. This simply means that we arbitrarily fixed the direction for the basis vector $|Gn\rangle$ to be a unit-length vector that starts at $(0,0)$ and ends at $(-1/\sqrt{2}, 1/\sqrt{2})$. We could reverse the direction of this basis vector and use $-|Gn\rangle$ as the basis, in which case the coordinates become $(0.9789, 0.2043)$. This sign depends on the arbitrary orientation of the basis vector and so it is not meaningful.

As mentioned above in our example shown in Figure 3.1, the answer to each question is represented by a line, more technically called a ray, which is a one-dimensional subspace. The ray labeled Cy in the figure is spanned by the basis vector $|C_Y\rangle$, which means any point on the ray can be reached by multiplying $|C_Y\rangle$ by a scalar, and this ray represents responding "yes" to the Clinton question. The ray labeled Cn in the figure represents responding "no" to the Clinton question; similarly, the Gy and Gn rays respectively represent rays of answering "yes" and "no" to the Gore question. Note that the two rays for Clinton are orthogonal, as are the two rays for Gore. This is because the pair of responses (yes, no) are mutually exclusive and the probability of their conjunction should be zero. With the same reasoning, each of the Clinton rays is at an acute (45°) angle with respect to each of the Gore rays. This represents the fact that answering one question (yes versus no) does not lead to a certain answer (yes versus no) to the other question.

The key idea of quantum theory is that the probability of responding to a question is determined by projecting the state S in the figure onto a ray that represents an answer. The probability of the answer equals the squared length of this projection. In Figure 3.1, the symbol Pc represents the projector for the "yes" answer to Clinton (the Cy ray), and the matrix representation of this projector is a simple 2×2 diagonal matrix, $P_C = \text{diag}[1, 0]$ (when expressed in terms of the Clinton basis). We know that $|S\rangle$ is represented by $(0.8367, 0.5477)$ in the Clinton basis and P_C picks the first coordinate; hence, the probability of saying "yes" to Clinton equals $p(\text{Cy}) = ||\ \mathbf{P}_C|S\rangle\ ||^2 = |0.8367|^2 = 0.70$. The probability of saying "no" to the Clinton question equals the squared magnitude of the second coordinate, $|0.5477|^2 = 0.30$. Likewise, in the figure, the symbol Pg represents the projector for the "yes" answer to Gore (the Gy ray), and the matrix representation is again a 2×2 diagonal matrix, $P_G = \text{diag}[1, 0]$ (when expressed in terms of the Gore basis). Likewise, we know that $|S\rangle$ is represented by $(0.9789, -0.2043)$ in the Gore coordinates, and P_G picks the first Gy coordinate, and so the probability of saying "yes" to the Gore question is $p(\text{Gy}) = || \, \mathbf{P}_G|S\rangle \, ||^2 = |0.9789|^2 = 0.9582$, and the probability of saying "no" to Gore equals $|-0.2043|^2 = 0.0417$. Apparently in this example, when asked in a non-comparative context, Gore was favored more than Clinton. Note that the probabilities for yes and no answers sum to one, and this follows from the requirement that the state vector must be unit length.

3.1.2 Analysis of second question

In our example, if the Clinton question is asked first and a respondent answers "yes," then, given this answer, the initial belief vector $|S\rangle$ is revised to become $|C_Y\rangle$, which is consistent with a positive first answer to the Clinton question. Alternatively, if the Clinton question is asked first and a respondent answers "no," then the initial belief vector $|S\rangle$ is revised to $|C_N\rangle$, which is the state that is consistent with a negative first answer. Using the same principle, the revised state after saying "yes" to the Gore question equals $|G_Y\rangle$ and the revised state after saying "no" first to Gore question equals $|G_N\rangle$. Thus this new revised state represents the change in the belief induced by expressing an opinion, and incorporates updated information consistent with the expressed opinion.

The revised state is then used to determine the probabilities for the second question. The probability of saying "yes" to Gore after saying "yes" to Clinton equals the squared length of the projection of $|C_Y\rangle$ on to the ray Gy in the figure. Similarly, the probability of saying "yes" to Clinton after saying "yes" to Gore equals the squared length of the projection of $|G_Y\rangle$ on the Cy ray. In Figure 3.1, the squared lengths of these two projections are both equal to 0.50. This is easy to tell from the figure because the Cy–Gy rays share the same angle of $45°$. The $45°$ angle is used in the example for simplicity, because it represents equal probability to the alternative response patterns.

Now let us compute the total probability of saying "yes" to Clinton in the comparative context – that is, the probability of saying "yes" to Gore and then "yes" to Clinton plus the probability of saying "no" to Gore and then "yes" to Clinton. Using the example in Figure 3.1, the total probability of saying "yes" to Clinton in the comparative context equals $p_T(C_Y) = (0.96)(0.50) + (0.04)(0.50) = 0.50$. Again using the example in Figure 3.1, the total probability of saying "yes" to Gore in the comparative context equals $p_T(G_Y) = (0.70)$ $(0.50) + (0.30)(0.50) = 0.50$, which turns out to be exactly the same as the total probability for Clinton.

Thus, according to the simplified two-dimensional model in Figure 3.1, there is a large difference between the agreement rates to the two politicians in the non-comparative context: 0.70 for Clinton and 0.96 for Gore; but there is no difference in the comparative context: 0.50 for both. So, as we intentionally designed, this example reproduces the pattern of the assimilation effect that occurred in the Clinton and Gore survey reported by Moore (2002).

3.1.3   Summary of example

This simple example illustrates some of the basic ideas used in quantum probability theory to explain order effects. It shows how a simple geometric representation of questions in a two-dimensional space provides a compelling and intuitive explanation for assimilation types of question order effects. In Figure 3.1, it is easy to tell that the assimilation order effect is a result of the geometry of the feature space – particularly, the positions of the initial belief state and the two "yes" response subspaces. First, the initial belief state $|S\rangle$ starts out closer to the subspace for saying "yes" to Gore (the Gy ray) than to Clinton (the Cy ray). This represents the initial favoring of Gore in the non-comparative context. However, in the comparative context, the updated belief state is equally distant from these two rays, which causes the agreement rates to equalize in the comparative context.

You might complain that this simple example only represents a special case, and so it does not really provide any strong test of the general principles. This is absolutely true, and for this reason we develop a completely general model for N-dimensional spaces. Furthermore, we derive a strong test of the theory that does not make any specialized assumptions about the position of the start vector and the relation between the basis vectors for different questions. But before we go into the mathematical details of this derivation, let us take a look at the predictions that the theory makes and how well these predictions stand up to empirical results.

3.2   Empirical tests of reciprocity

Later in this chapter we derive a fundamental theorem that provides a parameter-free test of the quantum theory for arbitrarily high-dimensional spaces. But let us examine the accuracy of the prediction before we go into all of the technical mathematical details. The prediction concerns the probabilities for sequences of answers to questions. Suppose A is a question with two answers (yes,no) and B is a second question with two answers (yes,no). Empirically, this produces observable estimates of probabilities for response sequences such as $p(\text{AyBy})$ representing the probability of saying yes to A and then yes to B, or $p(\text{AyBn})$ representing the probability of saying yes to A and then no to B, or $p(\text{BnAy})$ representing the probability of saying no to B and then yes to A, etc. The theorem states that if two questions are answered one immediately after another with no information inserted in between, then the quantum probabilities must satisfy a test that we call the q-test:

$$q = [p(\text{AyBn}) + p(\text{AnBy})] - [p(\text{ByAn}) + p(\text{BnAy})] = 0. \qquad (3.1)$$

Table 3.1 The q-test applied to four data sets

Statistic	C–G	G–D	W–B	R–J
$p(\mathrm{Ay})$	0.5347	0.4760	0.4161	0.6621
$p(\mathrm{By})$	0.7616	0.6870	0.4609	0.4827
$p_\mathrm{T}(A_\mathrm{Y})$	0.5880	0.4085	0.5391	0.5390
$p_\mathrm{T}(B_\mathrm{Y})$	0.6667	0.7140	0.5599	0.3557
θ	0.8409	0.6634	0.7866	0.7771
q	-0.0031	-0.0031	-0.0189	0.1514
z	-0.1541	-0.1270	-1.0497	7.5068

Note: these results do not include "don't know" responses in the total count.

The q test value can range from $+1$ to -1. For example, if $p(\mathrm{AyBy}) = 0.1060$, $p(\mathrm{AyBn}) = 0.0791$, $p(\mathrm{AnBy}) = 0.2455$, $p(\mathrm{AnBn}) = 0.5693$, and $p(\mathrm{ByAy}) = 0.1012$, $p(\mathrm{ByAn}) = 0.2605$, $p(\mathrm{BnAy}) = 0.1678$, $p(\mathrm{BnAn}) = 0.4696$ then $q = -0.1045$. A q statistic can be computed by inserting the observed relative frequencies, and the above null hypothesis can be statistically tested by using a standard z-test for a difference between two independent proportions.

Essentially, this prediction is a test of the law of reciprocity. The derivation follows from the fact that the probability of transiting from the projection on to question A to the projection on to question B must equal the probability of transiting in the opposite direction. In other words, the probability of the transition $|S_\mathrm{A}\rangle \rightarrow |S_\mathrm{B}\rangle$ is the same as the probability of a transition in the opposite direction $|S_\mathrm{B}\rangle \rightarrow |S_\mathrm{A}\rangle$. We also derive a simple formula for an index of the similarity between questions, which we denote by θ, which represents the cosine between the projections on to each question:

$$\theta = \frac{p(\mathrm{ByAy}) + \frac{\mathrm{Int}_A}{2}}{\sqrt{p(\mathrm{Ay})p(\mathrm{By})}} = \frac{p(\mathrm{AyBy}) + \frac{\mathrm{Int}_B}{2}}{\sqrt{p(\mathrm{Ay})p(\mathrm{By})}}. \tag{3.2}$$

where $-\mathrm{Int}_A = p_\mathrm{T}(A_\mathrm{Y}) - p(\mathrm{Ay})$ is the order effect produced by question A, and $-\mathrm{Int}_B = p_\mathrm{T}(B_\mathrm{Y}) - p(\mathrm{By})$ is the order effect produced by question B (see below for details).

Wang & Busemeyer (2012) tested the law of reciprocity (using the q-test) on four different types of order effects reviewed in Moore (2002), which we summarize below. As we shall see, for the first three data sets, the key assumption of back-to-back measurements was satisfied, but for the last data set this key assumption was not satisfied. Thus, we predict that the q-test will be satisfied in the first three but violated in the last data set. The data sets were provided by David Moore, and each complete data set consisted of $2 \times 2 = 4$ response sequence frequencies for each of two orders, producing a total of eight relative frequencies. The results for the marginal probabilities are summarized in Table 3.1. See Wang and Busemeyer (2011) for the complete table containing the relative frequencies for the response sequences.

3.2.1 Assimilation effects

The first data set in Table 3.1, under the column labeled "C–G," refers to a Gallup poll conducted during September 6–7, 1997, in which 1003 respondents were asked "Do you generally think Bill Clinton/Al Gore is honest and trustworthy?" The empirical results produced an assimilation effect because there was a large gap favoring Gore when each candidate was presented in the non-comparative context (presented first), but the gap shrunk in the comparative context (presented second). As shown, the prediction for the q-test by the quantum model is surprisingly accurate: $q = -0.0031$, and the corresponding z-statistic equals $z = -0.1541$, which is obviously not statistically significant. (Recall that $z = 1.96$ corresponds to a significant deviation at the 0.05 level of significance, and recall that $-1 \leq q \leq +1$.) The similarity index is $\theta = 0.8408$ in this case, which is high (recall that $-1 \leq \theta \leq +1$) and this is expected because of the high similarity of the two equally liberal candidates.

3.2.2 Contrast effects

The second data set refers to the question "Do you think Newt Gingrich/Bob Dole is honest and trustworthy?" collected in a Gallup pole involving a sample of 1016 participants during March 27–29, 1995. These data are presented in the column labeled "G–D" in Table 3.1. In this case, within the non-comparative context, there was an initial difference favoring Dole; but within the comparative context, the difference became more exaggerated. In other words, the order effect was positive for Dole and negative for Gingrich. This is a completely different kind of order effect which is called a contrast effect. Once again, the prediction of the quantum model is extremely accurate. Clearly, the prediction error, $q = -0.0031$, is not statistically significantly different from zero. It is also interesting to note that the similarity index is lower in this Gingrich–Dole example, as compared to the Clinton–Gore example, which seems reasonable when considering that Dole is a moderate conservative and Gingrich is a more extreme conservative.

3.2.3 Additive effects

The third data set, showing an "additive" effect, refers to the pair of questions on perceptions of racial hostility collected from the Aggregate of Racial Hostility Poll involving 1005 participants during June 27–30, 1996. In the poll, respondents were asked "Do you think that only a few white people dislike blacks, many white people dislike blacks, or almost all white people dislike blacks?" preceding or following the same question asked about black hostility toward whites. For both questions, the percentage responding "all or many" versus "few" increased from the non-comparative context to the comparative context – hence, the reason this is called the "additive" order effect. The prediction of the quantum model is shown to be very accurate again: the prediction error $q = -0.0189$ is small and not significantly different from zero.[2]

3.2.4   Subtractive effects

The fourth data set refers to the pair of questions about baseball players Pete Rose and Shoeless Joe Jackson: "Do you think he [Rose/Jackson] should or should not be eligible for admission to the Hall of Fame?" (1060 participants, July 13–14, 1999). These data are presented in the column labeled "R–J." The survey results show that the favorable rate for both baseball players decreased in the comparative context; thus, this shows a subtractive pattern. Interestingly, our quantum model is predicted not to fit this data set because this case violates an important assumption of the model.

Recall that our prediction for the quantum model was based on the assumption that only the question order influences the question context (i.e., the belief state prior to answering the question). This assumption is violated in this Rose/Jackson data set. Respondents lacked sufficient knowledge about the baseball players in the questions, and so it was necessary to provide some background information prior to each question. Thus, the initial belief state when Rose/Jackson was asked first was affected by the information provided about the particular player. Furthermore, the context for the second question was changed not only by answering the first question, but also by the additional background information on the player in the second question.

As seen in Table 3.1, the Rose/Jackson data indeed show that the prediction error is highly statistically significant using the z statistic to evaluate the significance of the q-test. Thus, the quantum model does not accurately predict the Rose/Jackson data set. Note that, as shown in Wang and Busemeyer (2012), it is clearly possible for the quantum model to produce a subtractive order effect. It is just that it cannot reproduce these particular results because the key assumption was violated. It is expected to accurately predict subtractive effects as long as only the order of questions influences the question context.

3.2.5   Summary of tests

The q-test is a parameter-free exact quantitative prediction derived from the general N-dimensional quantum theory for order effects. This test depends on one key assumption; that is, that questions are asked back to back with no information inserted in between. Four empirical tests were performed using four data sets exhibiting four different types of question order effects. The first three data sets were obtained under conditions that satisfied the key assumption and the last data set was obtained using procudures that clearly

---

[2]The model is developed for binary responses; and following Moore (2002), the data for "all" or "many" were categorized together to fit this binary structure. However, this categorization could cause some failure of the model, and we ultimately need to extend the model to include more than two options.

did not. The predictions regarding the q-test provided by the general quantum theory were extremely accurate for the three data sets satisfying the assumptions, and the predictions were clearly violated by the data set that did not satisfy the assumption. We regard this as fairly convincing evidence supporting the model so far; but, of course, more tests need to be conducted to build this confidence. Now it is time to present the general theory and the mathematical derivation of the test. We also derive a new index for measuring similarity between questions, which has practical applications for question-order researchers.

3.3   General quantum model

The model in Figure 3.1 is much too simple, being based on a single feature with only two values. Realistically, there are many features and combinations of features that a person needs to consider when making a complex moral judgment such as honesty. It is not very difficult to recast this whole idea in an arbitrary N-dimensional vector space, which is described next.

3.3.1   Analysis of first question

Our first assumption is that a person's belief of the object in question is represented by a state vector $|S\rangle$ in an N-dimensional feature space (a Hilbert space). Each dimension corresponds to a feature pattern; that is, a combination of properties that the person believes about the object. This use of feature vectors to represent belief or knowledge is consistent with many other cognitive models of memory and categorization. For example, a feature pattern may include a conjunction of features such as "age over 50 and married to Hillary and good politician and honest, etc." The state vector $|S\rangle$ determines how likely a person is to agree with such a combination of features. In addition, the belief vector $|S\rangle$ is assumed to have unit length, $\||S\rangle\| = 1$.

As we discussed in Chapter 2, the initial state is a vector $|S\rangle$, and different choices can be made for the basis that is used to describe this vector. One basis, $C = \{|C_i\rangle, i = 1, N\}$ may be used to describe Clinton, but a different basis $G = \{|G_i\rangle, i = 1, N\}$ may be used to describe Gore. Some of the features may overlap (e.g., the feature "good politician") but not others (Hillary is a feature used only with Clinton, Tennessee is a feature used only for Gore).

Our second assumption is that a potential response to a question such as yes to "Is Clinton honest and trustworthy?" is represented by a subspace of the feature space. The subspace for the answer yes to the Clinton question is spanned by a subset $C_Y \subset C = \{|C_i\rangle, i = 1, N\}$ of the basis vectors, and the answer no to the Clinton question is spanned by the orthogonal complement. For example, regarding the answer yes to the honesty question about Clinton, the pattern "age over 50 and married to Hillary and good politician and honest, etc." would be included and so would the pattern "age over 50 and married to Hillary and not a good politician and honest, etc." because both include honest, but the pattern "age over 50 and married to Hillary and good politician and not honest, etc." would not be included. Corresponding to the subspace spanned by C_Y is the projector $\mathbf{P}_C$ which projects vectors onto this subspace, and the projector for the complement is $\mathbf{P}_{\bar{C}} = \mathbf{I} - \mathbf{P}_C$, where $\mathbf{I}$ is the identity operator that projects on the entire Hilbert space.

Similarly, the subspace for the answer yes to the Gore question is spanned by a subset $G_Y \subset G = \{|G_i\rangle, i = 1, N\}$ of the basis vectors, which corresponds to a projector $\mathbf{P}_G$. The answer no to the Gore question is spanned by the orthogonal complement, which corresponds to the projector $\mathbf{P}_{\bar{G}} = \mathbf{I} - \mathbf{P}_G$, where $\mathbf{I}$ is the identity operator. Although some of the features used to describe the Gore question may overlap with those used to describe the Clinton question (e.g., good politician), others may not (e.g., marriage to Hillary is a feature only relevant to the Clinton question, Tennessee is a feature relevant only to the Gore question). Therefore, different features are used for each question, which makes the projectors incompatible.

Our third assumption is that the probability of responding yes to a question is determined by the following process. The judge first projects his or her belief state vector down onto the subspace for that response to the question, and the probability equals the squared length of this projection. Specifically, the probability of saying yes to the Clinton question is determined by (a) projecting the belief state $|S\rangle$ onto the subspace for yes, which produces the projection $\mathbf{P}_C|S\rangle$, and then (b) the probability of saying yes equals the squared length, $p(C_Y) = ||\ \mathbf{P}_C|S\rangle||^2$. Similarly, the probability of saying yes to the Gore question equals $p(G_Y) = ||\ \mathbf{P}_G|S\rangle||^2$. The probability of saying no to the Clinton question equals $p(C_N) = ||\mathbf{P}_{\bar{C}}|S\rangle||^2 = ||(\mathbf{I} - \mathbf{P}_C)|S\rangle||^2 = 1 - ||\mathbf{P}_C|S\rangle||^2$, and the probability of saying no to the Gore question equals $p(G_N) = 1 - ||\mathbf{P}_G|S\rangle||^2$. These comprise the probabilities for the Clinton and Gore questions obtained under the non-comparative context for the first question.

3.3.2 Analysis of second question

Our fourth assumption concerns the change in the belief state after answering an opinion question, and it is critical for generating order effects. This assumption is consistent with research on measurement effects on belief, attitude, intention, and behavior (Feldman & Lynch, 1988). This line of research has supported that survey measurement itself can change the measured evaluation and cognition.

In our example, if the Clinton question is asked first and a respondent answers "yes," then, given this answer, the initial belief vector $|S\rangle$ is revised to become $|S_C\rangle = \frac{\mathbf{P}_C|S\rangle}{||\mathbf{P}_C|S\rangle||}$, which is a normalized state that is consistent with a positive first answer. Alternatively, if the Clinton question is asked first and a respondent answers "no," then the initial belief vector $|S\rangle$ is revised to $|S_{\bar{C}}\rangle = \frac{(\mathbf{I} - \mathbf{P}_C)|S\rangle}{||(\mathbf{I} - \mathbf{P}_C)|S\rangle||}$, which is the normalized state that is consistent with a negative first answer. Using the same principle, the revised state after saying "yes" to the Gore question equals $|S_G\rangle = \frac{\mathbf{P}_G|S\rangle}{||\mathbf{P}_G|S\rangle||}$, and the revised state after saying "no" first to the Gore question equals $|S_{\bar{G}}\rangle = \frac{(\mathbf{I} - \mathbf{P}_G)|S\rangle}{||(\mathbf{I} - \mathbf{P}_{CG})|S\rangle||}$. Thus, this new revised state represents the change in the belief induced by expressing an opinion, and incorporates updated information consistent with the expressed opinion.

The subsequent question must be evaluated based upon the updated belief, which has been changed by the answer to the preceding question. After updating the belief state, the process used to determine probabilities of opinion responses to the next question is exactly as outlined above in the non-comparative context. Given that the person already said "yes" to the Clinton question and, thus, the belief has been updated to $|S_C\rangle$, the conditional probability of saying "yes" to the Gore question equals $||\mathbf{P}_G|S_C\rangle||^2$; likewise, given that the person already said "no" to the Clinton question, the conditional probability of saying "yes" to the Gore question equals $||\mathbf{P}_G|S_{\bar{C}}\rangle||^2$. The same principle applies when the Gore question is asked first: the probability of saying "yes" to the Clinton question conditioned on saying "yes" to the Gore question equals $||\mathbf{P}_C|S_G\rangle||^2$; likewise, the probability of saying "yes" to the Clinton question conditioned on saying "no" to the Gore question equals $||\mathbf{P}_C|S_{\bar{G}}\rangle||^2$.

Now we can calculate all the probabilities needed for the second question that arise in the comparative context. Consider the total probability of saying yes to Clinton after answering the Gore question, which we denote as $p_T(C_Y)$. This equals the probability of saying "yes" to Gore and then "yes" to Clinton, denoted $p(\text{GyCy})$, plus the probability of saying "no" to Gore and then "yes" to Clinton, denoted $p(\text{GnCy})$. That is, $p_T(C_Y) = p(\text{GyCy}) + p(\text{GnCy})$. According to our quantum model,[3]

$$p(\text{GyCy}) = ||\mathbf{P}_G|S\rangle||^2 \cdot ||\mathbf{P}_C|S_G\rangle||^2 = ||\mathbf{P}_C\mathbf{P}_G|S\rangle||^2$$

$$p(\text{GnCy}) = ||\mathbf{P}_{\bar{G}}|S\rangle||^2 \cdot ||\mathbf{P}_C|S_{\bar{G}}\rangle||^2 = ||\mathbf{P}_C\mathbf{P}_{\bar{G}}|S\rangle||^2.$$

Next, we consider the total probability of saying "yes" to the Gore question after answering the Clinton question. This equals the probability of saying "yes" to Clinton and then "yes" to Gore, denoted $p(\text{CyGy})$, plus the probability of saying "no" to Clinton and then "yes" to Gore, denoted $p(\text{CnGy})$. That is, $p_T(G_Y) = p(\text{CyGy}) + p(\text{CnGy})$. Again, according to our quantum model,

$$p(\text{CyGy}) = ||\mathbf{P}_C|S\rangle||^2 \cdot ||\mathbf{P}_G|S_C\rangle||^2 = ||\mathbf{P}_G\mathbf{P}_C|S\rangle||^2$$

$$p(\text{CnGy}) = ||\mathbf{P}_{\bar{C}}|S\rangle||^2 \cdot ||\mathbf{P}_G|S_{\bar{C}}\rangle||^2 = ||\mathbf{P}_G\mathbf{P}_{\bar{C}}|S\rangle||^2.$$

3.3.3 Summary

The theory above was described in terms of specific questions about Clinton and Gore. More generally, suppose A is a question with two answers (yes,no) and B

---

[3]Recall from Chapter 2 that the sequential probability of A then B equals $||\mathbf{P}_A \cdot |S\rangle||^2 \cdot ||\mathbf{P}_B \cdot |S_A\rangle||^2 = ||\mathbf{P}_B\mathbf{P}_A|S\rangle||^2$.

is a second question with two answers (yes,no). Empirically, this produces observable estimates of probabilities for response sequences such as $p(\text{AyBy})$ representing the probability of saying yes to A and then yes to B, or $p(\text{AyBn})$ representing the probability of saying yes to A and then no to B, or $p(\text{BnAy})$ representing the probability of saying no to B and then yes to A, etc. The following list summarizes the probabilities derived from the quantum model:

$$p(\text{Ay}) = p(\text{AyBy}) + p(\text{AyBn}) = ||\mathbf{P}_A|S\rangle||^2 \qquad (3.3)$$

$$p(\text{By}) = p(\text{ByAy}) + p(\text{ByAn}) = ||\mathbf{P}_B|S\rangle||^2$$

$$p_{\text{T}}(A_{\text{Y}}) = p(\text{ByAy}) + p(\text{BnAy}) = ||\mathbf{P}_A\mathbf{P}_B|S\rangle||^2 + ||\mathbf{P}_A\mathbf{P}_{\bar{B}}|S\rangle||^2$$

$$p_{\text{T}}(B_{\text{Y}}) = p(\text{AyBy}) + p(\text{AnBy}) = ||\mathbf{P}_B\mathbf{P}_A|S\rangle||^2 + ||\mathbf{P}_B\mathbf{P}_{\bar{A}}|S\rangle||^2.$$

The order effects for each question are defined as

$$-\text{Int}_A = p_{\text{T}}(A_{\text{Y}}) - p(\text{Ay})$$

$$-\text{Int}_B = p_{\text{T}}(B_{\text{Y}}) - p(\text{By}).$$

3.4 Order effect predictions

Now that we have a theoretical structure, we can use it to derive three empirically testable predictions from the model with increasing precision with regard to the predictions. In the appendix, we prove the results using a more general density matrix representation of the state, which allows a mixture of individual differences.

3.4.1 Non-commutativity

The very first prediction that we must make is that an order effect can only occur if the subspace used to describe one question is incompatible with the subspace used to describe the other. In other words, the person does not use a single set of features for describing both questions. One question is described by one set of features, but the other question is described by a different set of features. For if the subspaces were compatible and described by a single basis, then the projectors commute and $\mathbf{P}_B\mathbf{P}_A - \mathbf{P}_A\mathbf{P}_B = \mathbf{0}$ so that it does not matter which question was asked first or second. We will return to the meaning and implications of this first prediction in the discussion after we have derived some more precise predictions from the model.

3.4.2 Similarity between questions

Next, we derive the following simple formulae for predicting order effects:

$$-\text{Int}_A = 2 \cdot p(\text{ByAy}) - 2 \cdot \theta \cdot \sqrt{p(\text{Ay})} \cdot \sqrt{p(\text{By})}$$

$$-\text{Int}_B = 2 \cdot p(\text{AyBy}) - 2 \cdot \theta \cdot \sqrt{p(\text{By})} \cdot \sqrt{p(\text{Ay})},$$

where $-1 \leq \theta \leq 1$ is an index that we derive below that measures the similarity between the normalized projections onto each question. We can solve for θ:

$$\theta = \frac{p(\text{ByAy}) + \frac{\text{Int}_A}{2}}{\sqrt{p(\text{Ay})p(\text{By})}} = \frac{p(\text{AyBy}) + \frac{\text{Int}_B}{2}}{\sqrt{p(\text{Ay})p(\text{By})}}. \tag{3.4}$$

For example, in Figure 3.1, $\theta = 1/\sqrt{2}$, reflecting the $45°$ angle between the Cn and Gn rays in the figure. Before we derive this prediction, note that the signed value of the order effect is predicted to be a decreasing function of this similarity index θ. According to the quantum model, the squared similarity index θ^2 is determined by the probability of transiting from the normalized projection on the subspace for question A to the normalized projection on the subspace for question B. Low similarity indices produce positive order effects and high similarity indices produce negative order effects. Some readers may wish to skip the derivation of this formula and jump to the most important prediction, which leads to a precise empirical test of the model.

Theorem 3.1 $-\text{Int}_A = 2 \cdot p(\text{ByAy}) - 2 \cdot \theta \cdot \sqrt{p(\text{Ay})} \cdot \sqrt{p(\text{By})}.$

Proof. First we obtain from Eq. (3.3) that

$$p_{\text{T}}(A_{\text{Y}}) = ||\mathbf{P}_A\mathbf{P}_B|S\rangle||^2 + ||\mathbf{P}_A\mathbf{P}_{\bar{B}}|S\rangle||^2.$$

Next we compare $p_{\text{T}}(A_{\text{Y}})$ with $p(\text{Ay})$ by expanding the latter expression:

$$\begin{aligned}
p(\text{Ay}) &= ||\mathbf{P}_A|S\rangle||^2 = ||\mathbf{P}_A\mathbf{I}|S\rangle||^2 = ||\mathbf{P}_A(\mathbf{P}_B + \mathbf{P}_{\bar{B}})|S\rangle||^2 \\
&= \langle S|(\mathbf{P}_B + \mathbf{P}_{\bar{B}})\mathbf{P}_A\mathbf{P}_A(\mathbf{P}_B + \mathbf{P}_{\bar{B}})|S\rangle \\
&= \langle S|\mathbf{P}_B\mathbf{P}_A\mathbf{P}_B|S\rangle + \langle S|\mathbf{P}_B\mathbf{P}_A\mathbf{P}_{\bar{B}}|S\rangle \\
&\quad + \langle S|\mathbf{P}_{\bar{B}}\mathbf{P}_A\mathbf{P}_B|S\rangle + \langle S|\mathbf{P}_{\bar{B}}\mathbf{P}_A\mathbf{P}_{\bar{B}}|S\rangle \\
&= ||\mathbf{P}_A\mathbf{P}_B|S\rangle||^2 + ||\mathbf{P}_A\mathbf{P}_{\bar{B}}|S\rangle||^2 + \text{Int}_A.
\end{aligned}$$

From the comparison we find that

$$\begin{aligned}
\text{Int}_A &= p(\text{Ay}) - p_{\text{T}}(A_{\text{Y}}) \\
&= \langle S|\mathbf{P}_B\mathbf{P}_A\mathbf{P}_{\bar{B}}|S\rangle + \langle S|\mathbf{P}_{\bar{B}}\mathbf{P}_A\mathbf{P}_B|S\rangle \\
&= \langle S|\mathbf{P}_B\mathbf{P}_A\mathbf{P}_{\bar{B}}|S\rangle + \langle S|\mathbf{P}_B\mathbf{P}_A\mathbf{P}_{\bar{B}}|S\rangle^* \\
&= 2 \cdot \text{Re}[\langle S|\mathbf{P}_B\mathbf{P}_A\mathbf{P}_{\bar{B}}|S\rangle] \\
&= 2 \cdot \text{Re}[\langle S|\mathbf{P}_B\mathbf{P}_A(\mathbf{I} - \mathbf{P}_B)|S\rangle] \\
&= 2 \cdot \text{Re}[\langle S|\mathbf{P}_B\mathbf{P}_A|S\rangle - \langle S|\mathbf{P}_B\mathbf{P}_A\mathbf{P}_B|S\rangle] \\
&= 2 \cdot \text{Re}[\langle S|\mathbf{P}_B\mathbf{P}_A|S\rangle] - 2 \cdot ||\mathbf{P}_A\mathbf{P}_B|S\rangle||^2.
\end{aligned} \tag{3.5}$$

The term $\mathrm{Re}[\langle S|\mathbf{P}_B\mathbf{P}_A|S\rangle]$ is the real part of the inner product $\langle S|\mathbf{P}_B\mathbf{P}_A|S\rangle$, which is a complex number in general (see Section 2.4.1 on complex numbers). This inner product can be re-expressed as

$$\langle S|\mathbf{P}_B\mathbf{P}_A|S\rangle = (\mathbf{P}_B|S\rangle)^\dagger\,(\mathbf{P}_A|S\rangle)$$

$$= ||\mathbf{P}_B|S\rangle|| \cdot ||\mathbf{P}_A|S\rangle|| \cdot \left(\frac{\mathbf{P}_B|S\rangle}{||\mathbf{P}_B|S\rangle||}\right)^\dagger \left(\frac{\mathbf{P}_A|S\rangle}{||\mathbf{P}_A|S\rangle||}\right)$$

$$= ||\mathbf{P}_B|S\rangle|| \cdot ||\mathbf{P}_A|S\rangle|| \cdot \langle S_B|S_A\rangle.$$

The real part of the inner product can be expressed as

$$\mathrm{Re}[\langle S|\mathbf{P}_B\mathbf{P}_A|S\rangle] = ||\mathbf{P}_B|S\rangle|| \cdot ||\mathbf{P}_A|S\rangle|| \cdot (|\langle S_B|S_A\rangle| \cdot \cos(\phi)),$$

where ϕ is the phase angle for this inner product. Then we define the similarity index as $\theta = \cos(\phi) \cdot |\langle S_B|S_A\rangle|$, and this index is bounded by $-1 \leq \theta \leq 1$. Inserting this definition we obtain

$$-\mathrm{Int}_A = 2 \cdot ||\mathbf{P}_A\mathbf{P}_B|S\rangle||^2 - 2 \cdot \theta \cdot ||\mathbf{P}_B|S\rangle|| \cdot ||\mathbf{P}_A|S\rangle||. \qquad \blacksquare$$

3.4.3　Law of reciprocity

Finally, we derive a precise prediction from the quantum model that directly tests the law of reciprocity. The derivation follows from the fact that θ derived from order effect $-\mathrm{Int}_A$ must be the same as θ derived from $-\mathrm{Int}_B$ (even though $-\mathrm{Int}_A$ is not necessarily equal to $-\mathrm{Int}_B$). This equality follows from the property $|\langle S_B|S_A\rangle| = |\langle S_A|S_B\rangle|$, where $|S_A\rangle$ is the normalized projection of the initial state onto the subspace for the yes answer to question A and $|S_B\rangle$ is the normalized projection of the initial state onto the subspace for the yes answer to question B. In other words, the probability of the transition $|S_A\rangle \to |S_B\rangle$ is the same as the probability of a transition in the opposite direction $|S_B\rangle \to |S_A\rangle$. This property is called the law of reciprocity in quantum theory. This constraint implies the following simple but precise prediction, which we call the q-test:

$$q = [p(\mathrm{AyBn}) + p(\mathrm{AnBy})] - [p(\mathrm{ByAn}) + p(\mathrm{BnAy})] = 0. \qquad (3.6)$$

The q-test value can range from $+1$ to -1. As we mentioned earlier, a q statistic can be computed by inserting the observed relative frequencies, and the above null hypothesis can be statistically tested by using a standard z-test for a difference between two independent proportions; see Wang and Busemeyer (2012) for details. This is an exact prediction that has no free parameters and the prediction holds for any dimension N. The model does not predict that $p(\mathrm{AyBn}) = p(\mathrm{BnAy})$, because of non-commutativity of projectors. Nor does it predict that $p(\mathrm{Ay}|\mathrm{Bn}) = p(\mathrm{Bn}|\mathrm{Ay})$ as we demonstrate later in a remark.

　　A key assumption underlying the q-test prediction is that the only factor to change the state from one judgment to the next is the question itself. No new information can be inserted in between the questions. If the latter occurs, the model no longer makes this prediction because we must update the state in between questions on the basis of the new information. Of course, this leads to new predictions from the model, but the q-test is expected to be violated in the case of new information inserted in between questions. Earlier, we presented the results of four different statistical tests of the q-statistic. Below, we derive this prediction from the model.

Theorem 3.2 *If two questions are answered one immediately after another with no information inserted in between, then the quantum model must satisfy Eq. (3.6).*[4]

Proof. Starting from the numerator of Eq. (3.4), we obtain

$$0 = (2 \cdot p(\text{ByAy}) + \text{Int}_A) - (2 \cdot p(\text{AyBy}) + \text{Int}_B)$$

$$= [2 \cdot p(\text{ByAy}) - p(\text{ByAy}) - p(\text{BnAy}) + p(\text{Ay})]$$

$$- [2 \cdot p(\text{AyBy}) - p(\text{AyBy}) - p(\text{AnBy}) + p(\text{By})]$$

$$= p(\text{ByAy}) - p(\text{BnAy}) + p(\text{AyBy}) + p(\text{AyBn})$$

$$- p(\text{AyBy}) + p(\text{AnBy}) - p(\text{ByAy}) - p(\text{ByAn})$$

$$= p(\text{AyBn}) + p(\text{AnBy}) - p(\text{ByAn}) - p(\text{BnAy}) = q. \qquad \blacksquare$$

Remark 3.3 *The q-test is not the same as testing the difference between two conditional probabilities obtained by reversing the events:*

$$p(\text{Ay}|\text{By}) = ||\mathbf{P}_A|S_B\rangle||^2 = \frac{||\mathbf{P}_A\mathbf{P}_B|S\rangle||^2}{||\mathbf{P}_B|S\rangle||^2}$$

$$p(\text{By}|\text{Ay}) = ||\mathbf{P}_B|S_A\rangle||^2 = \frac{||\mathbf{P}_B\mathbf{P}_A|S\rangle||^2}{||\mathbf{P}_A|S\rangle||^2}.$$

The quantum model does not require these conditional probabilities to be equal to each other. For example, if $\mathbf{P}_A\mathbf{P}_B = \mathbf{P}_B\mathbf{P}_A$ (commutative projectors) and $||\mathbf{P}_B|S\rangle||^2 \neq ||\mathbf{P}_A|S\rangle||^2$, then $p(\text{Ay}|\text{By}) \neq p(\text{By}|\text{Ay})$, just like classical probability theory. Alternatively, if $||\mathbf{P}_B|S\rangle||^2 = ||\mathbf{P}_A|S\rangle||^2$ and $\mathbf{P}_A\mathbf{P}_B \neq \mathbf{P}_B\mathbf{P}_A$, then again $p(\text{Ay}|\text{By}) \neq p(\text{By}|\text{Ay})$, unlike classical probability theory.

3.4.4   Summary

The quantum model incorporates the intuitive explanation for order effects given by social psychologists, but it takes this explanation much further. From the model, we derived a parameter-free prediction that allows one to test the law of reciprocity. The derivation was based on very general assumptions. The

---

[4]In the appendix, we prove this theorem using more general density matrices. We recently discovered that this theorem is the same as Axiom 1 in Niestegge's (2008) axiomatic development of quantum probability theory.

dimension of the space does not need to be specified, nor is it necessary to specify the features, and it is not necessary to specify the transformation that relates one basis to another. The test only requires one to assume that the projectors representing each question are non-commuting and that the questions are asked back to back. From this general theory we derive this very demanding prediction represented by the q-test. It is amazing that it worked so well in the three data sets in which the key assumption of back-to-back questions was satisfied. The last data set, in which the assumption was violated, shows that very substantial deviations from this prediction can be realized. This shows that the q-test is not a trivial test that is always satisfied. It is only satisfied when the assumptions of the theory are satisfied. We find these results to be very encouraging for the application of quantum theory to important issues in the social and behavioral sciences.

According to this quantum model, the sign of the order effect, whether it is positive or negative, depends on the similarity index θ that represents the similarity of projections onto answers to each question. Furthermore, the sign of the order effect for each question determines whether assimilation, contrast, additive, or subtractive effects occur. Wang and Busemeyer (2012) provide a complete table outlining the conditions under which each type of order effect is predicted to occur.

3.5 Concluding thoughts

The quantum approach agrees very well with the constructionist view of belief, attitude, and intention proposed by social psychologists (Schwarz, 2007). Because of cognitive economy, our beliefs, attitudes, and intentions are not simply stored in memory as properties; instead, they are constructed when needed. Information about attitudes that have been previously measured may be retrieved with some additional influences from the current context, and this context affects the construction process of subsequent judgments. Many researchers have investigated the effects of measurements themselves on measured cognition, such as mere measurement effects and self-generated validity theory (Feldman & Lynch, 1988). The quantum model presented here extends these ideas by formalizing and quantifying these theories. It provides precise and empirically testable hypotheses and can account for strikingly different question order effects, such as consistency and contrast effects.

At the heart of the quantum model is the assumption that questions are incompatible. Why is this reasonable? Why, you might ask, cannot people form a compatible space for Clinton and Gore questions? The answer is that the respondents never thought about these two questions together before, and each question is actually quite complex in a unique way, because each one requires the recruitment of a lot of personal details. Only a subset of this knowledge can be recruited at any time for answering a single question. When considering all the various types of questions that can be asked, the cost of forming a large compatible representation space may exceed the cognitive capacity of an individual. Thus, cognitive limitations may force an individual to rely on a lower dimensional incompatible representation of many novel questions for the sake of cognitive economy (Tourangeau *et al.*, 2000).

A compatible representation may form after sufficient experience with the combinations of the questions/dimensions. If a person has a great deal of experience with a combination, then the person may have sufficient knowledge to form a compatible representation as a result of cognitive adaptation to the environment. Therefore, order effects are expected to occur for pairs of incompatible questions, especially uncommon pairs involving complex details, which must be (partially) constructed on the spot to answer them.

4

How to apply quantum theory? Accounting for human probability judgment errors

How can we use quantum theory to model other phenomena of interest to researchers in cognition and decision making? Quantum theory is not easy for researchers in cognition and decision making to accept. In fact, quantum mechanics was not easy for physicists to accept either, but it was forced on them by several paradoxical findings that could not be explained using classical physics. We have a similar problem in cognition and decision making – there are numerous paradoxical findings that just seem irrational according to classic probability theory. For example, under some conditions, people judge the probability of event A and B to be greater than the probability of event B, which is called the conjunction fallacy (Tversky & Kahneman, 1983). Also, under the same conditions, they judge the probability of A or B to be less than the probability of event A (Carlson & Yates, 1989), which is called the disjunction fallacy. In this chapter we examine how quantum probability theory explains these and other puzzling results from human probability judgment research. This chapter has two main parts. In the first part, we use a quantum model to derive qualitative predictions for conjunction errors, disjunction errors, and other closely related findings. The first section provides a general set of predictions that do not depend on specific assumptions about the features used to represent events, and the predictions are parameter free. In the second part, we examine the quantitative predictions of the quantum model for a Bayesian inference task, which we use to explain order effects on inference. The second section provides precise quantitative predictions based on specific assumptions about features, and parameters are fit to the data. Both sections also compare the quantum model with other competing explanations for these probability judgment errors.

4.1 Conjunction and disjunction errors

To introduce the issues for the first section, let us consider the famous "Linda" problem which has been used to demonstrate the conjunction fallacy. (Many different types of stories have been used in past research, but this story is the most famous of all.) Judges are provided a brief story about a woman named Linda:

> Linda is 31 years old, single, outspoken and very bright. She majored in philosophy. As a student, she was deeply concerned with issues of discrimination and social justice, and also participated in anti-nuclear demonstrations.

Then the judge is asked to rank the likelihood of the following events: that Linda is now (a) active in the feminist movement, (b) a bank teller, (c) active in the feminist movement and a bank teller, (d) active in the feminist movement and not a bank teller, and (e) active in the feminist movement or a bank teller. The conjunction fallacy occurs when option c is judged to be more likely than option b (even though the latter contains the former), and the disjunction fallacy occurs when option a is judged to be more likely than option e (again, the latter contains the former).

There is now a large empirical literature establishing the findings of both conjunction fallacies (Sides *et al.*, 2002) and disjunction fallacies (Fisk, 2002). These findings are very robust and occur with various types of stories (e.g., female philosophy students who are now feminist bank tellers, high-pressure business men who are over 50 and have heart disease, Norwegian students with blue eyes and blond hair, state legislatures that increase cigarette taxes and reduce teenage smoking), and various types of response measures (e.g., choice, ranking, probability ratings, monetary bids). These fallacies are not simply the result of misunderstanding the meaning of probability, because they even occur with bets in which the word "probability" never appears. For example, Sides *et al.* (2002) found that participants preferred to bet on the future event "cigarette tax will increase and teenage smoking will decrease" over betting on the single event "teenage smoking will decrease."

Moreover, both fallacies have been observed to occur at the same time (Morier & Borgida, 1984). For example, Morier and Borgida (1984) used the Linda story and found that the mean probability judgments were ordered as follows (where $J(A)$ denotes the mean judgment for event A): $J(\text{feminist}) = 0.83 > J(\text{feminist or bank teller}) = 0.60 > J(\text{feminist and bank teller}) = 0.36 > J(\text{bank teller}) = 0.26$ ($N = 64$ observations per mean, and all pair-wise differences are statistically significant). These results violate classic probability theory, which is the reason why they are called fallacies.

Various attempts have been made to explain conjunction errors and disjunction errors using quantum principles. The earliest effort was made to explain disjunction effects by Richard Bordley (Bordley, 1998). Next, Riccardo Franco (first appearing in 2007 on the physics archives) proposed a simple two-dimensional model for the conjunction fallacy (Franco, 2009). Afterwards, other versions were developed by Andrei Khrennikov (Khrennikov, 2010), Yukulov and Sornette (2010), Aerts (2009), and Blutner (2009). This chapter is based on a comprehensive model of conjunction and disjunction and other related errors by Busemeyer *et al.* (2011). Although there are important variations in

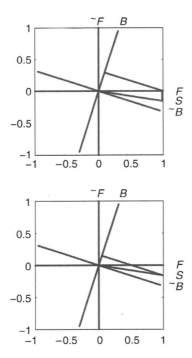

Figure 4.1 Two-dimensional representation of the Linda problem. $F =$ yes to feminism, $\tilde{\ } F =$ no to feminism; $B =$ yes to bank teller, $\tilde{\ } B =$ no to bank teller; $S =$ initial state. Top panel shows projection for feminism and then bank teller; bottom panel shows projection for bank teller.

all of these modelling attempts, they all share most of the basic assumptions described below.

4.1.1 A simple example

Now we describe how to apply the quantum axioms from Chapter 2 to this application. To make ideas concrete, Figure 4.1 provides a simple two-dimensional representation of the judgment problem, but the general theory is formalized to accommodate a much more realistic N-dimensional space with a much higher number of dimensions. In Figure 4.1 there is only one feature, feminism, defined by two values (true,false) for the feminist question. Similarly, there is only one feature, bank teller profession, defined by two values (yes,no) for the bank teller question. The figure contains two pairs of axes. The horizontal–vertical axis is used to represent the answers "yes" versus "no" to the question "Is Linda a feminist?" with "yes" on the horizontal axis labeled by the letter F and "no" on the vertical axis labeled with $\tilde{\ } F$. The other pair of axes is rotated counterclockwise with respect to the horizontal–vertical axes. This other pair of axes is used to represent "yes" versus "no" answers to the question "Is Linda a bank teller?" with the "yes" answer labeled by the letter B and the "no" answer labeled by

$\tilde{}B$. In Figure 4.1, the state vector is the vector labeled S which lies in between the F and the $\tilde{}B$ axes.

4.1.1.1   Probability for a single question

The horizontal ray labeled F in Figure 4.1 is spanned by a basis vector $|F\rangle$ that starts at $(0,0)$ and ends at $(1,0)$, representing the feature value "feminist property is true." The vertical ray labeled $\tilde{}F$ in the figure is spanned by a basis vector $|\bar{F}\rangle$ that starts at $(0,0)$ and ends at $(0,1)$, and represents the feature value "feminist property is false." With respect to this basis, the state vector labeled S in the figure is located at coordinates $(0.987, -0.1564)$. Using this basis, the state is then described by $|S\rangle = (0.987) \cdot |F\rangle + (-0.1564) \cdot |\bar{F}\rangle$.

The line labeled B in the figure is a ray that corresponds to the answer "yes" to the bank teller question, and the ray labeled $\tilde{}B$ in the figure corresponds to the "no" answer to this question. The basis vector $|B\rangle$ spans the B-ray, and the orthogonal basis vector $|\bar{B}\rangle$ spans the $\tilde{}B$-ray. These two basis vectors are obtained by rotating the feminism basis vectors by $0.4 \cdot \pi$ radians counterclockwise. The coordinates of the state with respect to this bank teller basis are $(0.1564, -0.9877)$. Using this basis, the state is described by $|S\rangle = (0.1564) \cdot |B\rangle + (-0.9877) \cdot |\bar{B}\rangle$.

One might wonder what the negative coordinates mean in the representation shown in Figure 4.1. As we have pointed out earlier, this simply reflects the arbitrary direction picked for representing a ray by a basis. For example, the -0.9877 coefficient reflects the fact that we (the theorist) chose the direction for the $|\bar{B}\rangle$ basis to start at $(0,0)$ and end at $(-0.9511, 0.3090)$ (using the horizontal–vertical axes). Instead, we could choose the opposite direction and define the basis that spans the $\tilde{}B$-ray in Figure 4.1 to be $-|\bar{B}\rangle$ which starts $(0,0)$ and now ends at $(0.9511, -0.3090)$. Using the basis $\{|B\rangle, -|\bar{B}\rangle\}$, the state is described by $|S\rangle = (0.1564) \cdot |B\rangle + (0.9877) \cdot (-|\bar{B}\rangle)$. Thus, the sign depends on the arbitrary choice of the direction of the basis, and it is not meaningful.

The ray labeled F in Figure 4.1 is orthogonal to the ray labeled $\tilde{}F$ in the figure, because they represent mutually exclusive events. For the same reason, the ray labeled B in the figure and ray labeled $\tilde{}B$ in the figure are also orthogonal. However, the rays for the feminism question are oblique with respect to the rays for the bank teller question because these are not mutually exclusive events.

Referring still to the simple example in Figure 4.1, the probability of saying "yes" to the feminism question equals the squared projection of the state labeled S on to the ray labeled F for "yes" to the feminism question – the projection equals $|S\rangle = (0.987) \cdot |F\rangle$ and the squared length equals $0.987^2 = 0.97553$. This projection is shown in the top panel of Figure 4.1 by the point along the F-ray where the line going up from the S-ray meets the F-ray. Similarly, the probability of saying "yes" to the bank teller question equals the squared length of the projection of the state S on to the B-ray – the projection of the state on to the "yes" to B-ray equals $|S\rangle = (0.1564) \cdot |B\rangle$ and the squared length equals $0.1564^2 = 0.024472$. This projection is shown in the bottom panel of

Figure 4.1 by the point along the B-ray where the line coming from the S-ray meets the B-ray.

4.1.1.2 Probability for conjunction

Now suppose the person considers the feminism question and resolves that the answer is "yes." Referring back to our example in Figure 4.1, if the person implicitly answers "yes" to the feminism question, then the revised state changes from $|S\rangle$ to $|F\rangle$ and then the probability of saying "yes" to the bank teller question is the squared length of the projection $|B\rangle\langle B|F\rangle$, which equals $|\langle B|F\rangle|^2 = |0.3090|^2 = 0.0955$.

The top panel in Figure 4.1 illustrates the transitions $|S\rangle \rightarrow |F\rangle \rightarrow |B\rangle$ that determine the probability of "yes to feminist and then yes to bank teller." Given the previous results, the probability for this sequence equals $||\mathbf{P}_F|S\rangle||^2 \cdot ||\mathbf{P}_B|F\rangle||^2 = (0.97553)(0.0955) = 0.093155 > 0.024472 = ||\mathbf{P}_B|S\rangle||^2$. Thus, the simple geometric model shown in Figure 4.1 reproduces the conjunction fallacy. The direct path from $|S\rangle \rightarrow |B\rangle$ has a smaller squared amplitude than the product of squared amplitudes produced by the indirect path $|S\rangle \rightarrow |F\rangle \rightarrow |B\rangle$. Psychologically, given the story about Linda, it is very hard to imagine that she is a bank teller; but it is easy to imagine that Linda is a feminist, and once you are thinking about feminists, it is easier to think of a feminist as a bank teller. Thinking about feminism facilitates thinking about bank tellers; or, in other words, thinking about feminism increases the availability of bank teller features.

4.1.1.3 Probability for disjunction

Now let us see how the example illustrated in Figure 4.1 works out for the disjunction of events. Note that the probability of "yes" to the disjunction equals the probability that "no" to the bank teller and then "no" to the feminist question does not occur. The probability for the sequence "no to bank teller and then no to feminist" equals $||\mathbf{P}_{\bar{B}}|S\rangle||^2 \cdot ||\mathbf{P}_{\bar{F}}|S_{\bar{B}}\rangle||^2 = (0.9877)^2 (0.3090)^2 = 0.0931$. Therefore, the quantum probability for "yes" to bank teller or "yes" to feminist then equals $1 - ||\mathbf{P}_{\bar{B}}|S\rangle||^2 \cdot ||\mathbf{P}_{\bar{F}}|S_{\bar{B}}\rangle||^2 = 1 - 0.0931 = 0.9069 < 0.97553 = ||\mathbf{P}_F|S\rangle||^2$, and so this simple geometric example also reproduces the disjunction fallacy. Thus, the same principles work in this particular example to produce both fallacies.

4.1.2 Quantum model

The two-dimensional example is much too simple and needs to be generalized. In particular, the two-dimensional model assumes that each answer to a question is represented by a single dimensional ray. This is problematic, because it implies that the conditional probablity of saying "yes" to a question B, given "yes" to question A equals $|\langle B|A\rangle|^2 = |\langle A|B\rangle|^2$, which is equal to the conditional probability in the opposite order. This equality may hold for a few chosen examples, but not in general. For a counter example, consider the probability of a person dying given that the person was lethally poisoned by a rare snake (which is high), versus the probability that a person was lethally poisoned by a rare snake given the person is dying (which is low). The equivalence between conditional probabilities in reverse order does not hold for higher dimensional spaces because, as described in Chapter 2, the answers are coarse measurements represented by subspaces with dimensions greater than one dimension. This and other problems that arise with simple two-dimensional models force us to consider higher dimensional spaces. Also, it is more realistic to assume that a person relies on a large number of features and their combinations to judge complex issues such as feminism and professions. Besides, generalizing the model to higher dimensional spaces is not very difficult to do, and so we now present a more general N-dimensional theory.

4.1.2.1   Belief state

To apply the general quantum probability theory to this problem, our first assumption is that the Linda story generates a state of belief represented by a state vector $|S\rangle$ that lies within a high-dimensional vector space (a Hilbert space). Each dimension of the vector space corresponds to a basis vector from an orthonormal basis that spans the space. Psychologically, each basis vector represents a unique conjunction of properties or feature values, called a feature pattern, which is used to describe the situation under question. For example, the Linda question may call to mind conjunctions of features such as the feature pattern "older woman, feminist, mother of a child, etc." or the feature pattern "younger woman, not feminist, unmarried with no children, etc." If there were m features and each feature had n values, then the space would have $N = m^n$ dimensions. The state vector is a unit-length vector in this space, $\| \, |S\rangle \, \| = 1$, that represents the judge's beliefs about whether or not to agree with a particular feature pattern. Our use of feature vectors to represent cognitive states follows other related cognitive research (Dougherty et al., 1999), whereby information is represented as vectors in high-dimensional spaces.

As described in Chapter 2, the state vector can be described by different choices for the basis that spans the space. One basis, $F = \{|F_i\rangle, i = 1, N\}$, is used to represent the feature patterns that describe the question about feminism; another basis, $B = \{|B_i\rangle, i = 1, N\}$, is used to represent the feature patterns that describe the question about the bank teller. Some of the features may overlap (e.g., young or older woman), but others may not (e.g., political affiliation may be relevant only for feminism, salary may be relevant only for bank teller).

4.1.2.2   Events

Our second assumption is that an event (i.e., an answer to a question) is represented by a subspace of the vector space, and each subspace has a projector that is used to evaluate the event. The subspace for the event "yes" to the feminism question is spanned by a subset $F_Y \subset F$ of the basis vectors for the feminism basis, which corresponds to a projector $\mathbf{P}_F$; the subspace for the event "no" to the feminism question corresponds to the projector $\mathbf{P}_{\bar{F}} = (\mathbf{I} - \mathbf{P}_{F})$ that projects onto the orthogonal complement. For example, a basis vector corresponding to the feature pattern "young woman, politically liberal, feminist, etc." would be included in F_Y as well as the basis vector corresponding to the feature pattern "older woman, conservative, feminist, etc." But the basis vector for the feature pattern "young woman, politically liberal, not feminist, etc." would not be included in F_Y and instead it would be in the orthogonal complement.

Similarly, the subspace for event "yes" to the bank teller question is spanned by a subset $B_Y \subset B$ of the basis vectors for the bank teller basis, which corresponds to a projector $\mathbf{P}_B$; the subspace for the event "no" to the bank teller question corresponds to the projector $\mathbf{P}_{\bar{B}} = (\mathbf{I} - \mathbf{P}_B)$ that projects onto the orthogonal complement. Although some of the features used to describe the feminism question (e.g., age may be relevant to both) may overlap between the projectors for the feminism and bank teller questions, others may not (e.g., political affiliation may only be relevant to feminism, salary may only be relevant to bank teller). Thus, the projectors are hypothesized to be incompatible in general and they do not commute.

4.1.2.3   Probability

Our third assumption is that the probability of an event is obtained by first projecting the state vector onto the subspace representing the event and then taking the squared length of this projection. The probability of the event "yes" to the feminism question equals $||\mathbf{P}_F|S\rangle||^2$; and likewise, the probability of "yes" to the bank teller question equals $||\mathbf{P}_B|S\rangle||^2$. This projective approach to probability agrees with the intuitive idea of representativeness. The idea of a match in the representativeness heuristic is formalized by the projection in quantum theory. However, the projector in quantum theory can correspond to a multidimensional subspace, rather than a single dimensional prototype vector (as assumed in the past).

4.1.2.4   State revision

Our fourth assumption concerns the revision in the state that occurs after a person resolves a previous question. Suppose the person concludes in his or her mind that the answer to a question is yes. Then the original state vector changes to a new conditional state vector, which is the projection onto the subspace representing yes to the question, but now normalized to have unit length. For example, if the implicit answer to the feminism question is yes, then a new revised state is the projection on to this answer $\mathbf{P}_F|S\rangle$ divided by the length of this projection, $||\mathbf{P}_F|S\rangle||$, which produces the revised state $|S_F\rangle = \frac{\mathbf{P}_F|S\rangle}{||\mathbf{P}_F|S\rangle||}$, so that the new conditional state vector has unit length. This corresponds to the normalization used to form conditional probabilities in classic probability theory. Similarly, if the implicit answer to the feminism question is "no," then the new state becomes $|S_{\bar{F}}\rangle = \frac{\mathbf{P}_{\bar{F}}|S\rangle}{||\mathbf{P}_{\bar{F}}|S\rangle||}$. Of course, the same principle holds for revising the state after implicitly answering the bank teller question. The conditional state vector is then used to answer subsequent questions. For example, if the person first implicitly answers "yes" to the feminism question, then the new state equals $|S_F\rangle = \frac{\mathbf{P}_F|S\rangle}{||\mathbf{P}_F|S\rangle||}$; and following this revision, the probability of saying "yes" to a subsequent bank teller question equals $||\mathbf{P}_B|S_F\rangle||^2$.

4.1.2.5   Order of processing

Our fifth assumption concerns the order of processing of the conjunction question. According to quantum theory, if the feminism and bank teller questions are incompatible, then the order that questions are answered is critical. So when a person is asked "What is the probability that Linda is a feminist bank teller?" we assume that one question (either feminism or bank teller) is implicitly answered before the other. In Section 4.2 on quantitative tests we present an experiment in which we directly manipulate this order. However, in other problems the order of processing is not controlled, and the individual is free to choose an order. Sometimes there is a causal order implied by the questions that are being asked. For example, when asked to judge the likelihood that "the cigarette tax will increase and a decrease in teenage smoking occurs" it is natural to assume that the causal event "increase in cigarette tax" is processed first. But for questions with no causal order, such as "feminist and bank teller," we assume that individuals tend to consider the more likely of the two events first. Note that a person can easily rank order the likelihood of individual events (feminism versus bank teller) before going through the more extensive process of estimating the probability of a sequence of events (feminism and then bank teller conditioned on the answer to the question about feminism). There are several ways to justify the assumption that the more likely event is processed first. One is that the more likely event matches the story better and so these features are more quickly retrieved and available for consideration. A second reason is that individuals sometimes conform to a confirmation bias and seek questions that are likely to be confirmed first.

Given the Linda story, the event "Linda is a feminist" is more likely than "Linda is a bank teller." Therefore, according to our order of processing assumption, the probability of "yes" to the question "Is Linda a feminist bank teller?" is determined by the probability of saying "yes" to the feminism question times the probability of saying "yes" to the bank teller question conditioned on the implicit answer of "yes" to the feminism question. Therefore, it follows that the judged probability for the conjunction is predicted by

$$J(F \text{ and then } B) = ||\mathbf{P}_F|S\rangle||^2 \cdot ||\mathbf{P}_B|S_F\rangle||^2 = ||\mathbf{P}_B\mathbf{P}_F|S\rangle||^2.$$

The last assumption also has implications for the processing of the disjunction question. As described in Chapter 2, the quantum probability of event X or then event Y equals the probability that "not X and then not Y" does not occur. Formally, the probability of "event X or then Y" equals $1 - ||\mathbf{P}_{\bar{X}}|S\rangle||^2 \cdot ||\mathbf{P}_{\bar{Y}}|S_{\bar{X}}\rangle||^2 = 1 - ||\mathbf{P}_{\bar{Y}}\mathbf{P}_{\bar{X}}|S\rangle||^2$. Once again, if the events are incompatible, then the order matters. Regarding the disjunction "feminist or bank teller" the principle of applying the more likely event first implies that, when computing the probability for the sequence "not X and not Y," the event "not a bank teller" is applied before "not a feminist," because, given the Linda story, "not a bank teller" is more likely than "not a feminist." Therefore, the judged probability for the disjunction is predicted by

$$J(B \text{ or then } F) = 1 - ||\mathbf{P}_{\bar{B}}|S\rangle||^2 \cdot ||\mathbf{P}_{\bar{F}}|S_{\bar{B}}\rangle||^2 = 1 - ||\mathbf{P}_{\bar{F}}\mathbf{P}_{\bar{B}}|S\rangle||^2.$$

4.1.3 Qualitative model predictions

The simple example based on Figure 4.1 demonstrated that the quantum model is capable of predicting conjunction and disjunction errors using a specific set of vectors within a two-dimensional space. However, we have yet to determine the general conditions under which the model predicts these effects, and these qualitative predictions are presented next.

4.1.3.1 Conjunction fallacy

For the conjunction fallacy, we need to compare the probability of the event "yes" to bank teller with the conjunction "yes to feminist bank teller." Formally, we need to compare $||\mathbf{P}_B|S\rangle||^2$ with $||\mathbf{P}_B\mathbf{P}_F|S\rangle||^2$. To do this we expand the probability for the "yes" to bank teller event:

$$
\begin{aligned}
||\mathbf{P}_B|S\rangle||^2 = ||\mathbf{P}_B\mathbf{I}|S\rangle||^2 &= ||\mathbf{P}_B(\mathbf{P}_F + \mathbf{P}_{\bar{F}})|S\rangle||^2 \\
&= \langle S|(\mathbf{P}_F + \mathbf{P}_{\bar{F}})\mathbf{P}_B\mathbf{P}_B(\mathbf{P}_F + \mathbf{P}_{\bar{F}})|S\rangle \\
&= \langle S|\mathbf{P}_F\mathbf{P}_B\mathbf{P}_F|S\rangle + \langle S|\mathbf{P}_F\mathbf{P}_B\mathbf{P}_{\bar{F}}|S\rangle \\
&\quad + \langle S|\mathbf{P}_{\bar{F}}\mathbf{P}_B\mathbf{P}_F|S\rangle + \langle S|\mathbf{P}_{\bar{F}}\mathbf{P}_B\mathbf{P}_{\bar{F}}|S\rangle \\
&= ||\mathbf{P}_B\mathbf{P}_F|S\rangle||^2 + ||\mathbf{P}_B\mathbf{P}_{\bar{F}}|S\rangle||^2 \\
&\quad + \langle S|\mathbf{P}_F\mathbf{P}_B\mathbf{P}_{\bar{F}}|S\rangle + \langle S|\mathbf{P}_F\mathbf{P}_B\mathbf{P}_{\bar{F}}|S\rangle^* \\
&= p_{\mathrm{T}}(B) + \mathrm{Int}_B,
\end{aligned}
$$

where the total probability for event B equals

$$p_{\mathrm{T}}(B) = ||\mathbf{P}_B\mathbf{P}_F|S\rangle||^2 + ||\mathbf{P}_B\mathbf{P}_{\bar{F}}|S\rangle||^2$$

and the interference for event B equals

$$
\begin{aligned}
\mathrm{Int}_B &= \langle S|\mathbf{P}_F\mathbf{P}_B\mathbf{P}_{\bar{F}}|S\rangle + \langle S|\mathbf{P}_{\bar{F}}\mathbf{P}_B\mathbf{P}_F|S\rangle \\
&= \langle S|\mathbf{P}_F\mathbf{P}_B\mathbf{P}_{\bar{F}}|S\rangle + \langle S|\mathbf{P}_F\mathbf{P}_B\mathbf{P}_{\bar{F}}|S\rangle^* \\
&= 2 \cdot |\langle S|\mathbf{P}_F\mathbf{P}_B\mathbf{P}_{\bar{F}}|S\rangle| \cdot \cos(\theta).
\end{aligned}
$$

Note that there is also an expansion for $||\mathbf{P}_{\bar{B}}|S\rangle||^2 = p_{\mathrm{T}}(\bar{B}) + \mathrm{Int}_{\bar{B}}$, but $||\mathbf{P}_B|S\rangle||^2 + ||\mathbf{P}_{\bar{B}}|S\rangle||^2 = 1 = p_{\mathrm{T}}(B) + p_{\mathrm{T}}(\bar{B})$, so that $\mathrm{Int}_B + \mathrm{Int}_{\bar{B}} = 0$. One of these interference terms must be negative; given the Linda story, we argue that $\mathrm{Int}_B < 0$, making it less likely to judge Linda as a bank teller. If this interference is sufficiently negative, so that $\mathrm{Int}_B < -||\mathbf{P}_B\mathbf{P}_{\bar{F}}|S\rangle||^2$, then a conjunction fallacy occurs. The latter is plausible with the Linda story because Linda is likely to be a feminist and so $||\mathbf{P}_B\mathbf{P}_{\bar{F}}|S\rangle||^2$ is small.

4.1.3.2   Disjunction fallacy

Next consider the disjunction probability, in which case we evaluate the probability of saying no to "Linda is neither a bank teller nor a feminist." First note that when processing the two events "Linda is not a bank teller" versus "Linda is not a feminist" the former is more likely than the latter, and so the former is processed first. In this case, we need to compare the single event $||\mathbf{P}_F|S\rangle||^2$ with $1 - ||\mathbf{P}_{\bar{F}}\mathbf{P}_{\bar{B}}|S\rangle||^2$ and the disjunction fallacy is predicted when $||\mathbf{P}_F|S\rangle||^2 = 1 - ||\mathbf{P}_{\bar{F}}|S\rangle||^2 > 1 - ||\mathbf{P}_{\bar{F}}\mathbf{P}_{\bar{B}}|S\rangle||^2$, or equivalently when $||\mathbf{P}_{\bar{F}}|S\rangle||^2 < ||\mathbf{P}_{\bar{F}}\mathbf{P}_{\bar{B}}|S\rangle||^2$. To do this, we mathematically decompose the quantum probability that Linda is not a feminist as follows:

$$||\mathbf{P}_{\bar{F}}|S\rangle||^2 = ||\mathbf{P}_{\bar{F}}\mathbf{I}|S\rangle||^2 = ||\mathbf{P}_{\bar{F}}(\mathbf{P}_B + \mathbf{P}_{\bar{B}})|S\rangle||^2$$

$$= ||\mathbf{P}_{\bar{F}}\mathbf{P}_B|S\rangle||^2 + ||\mathbf{P}_{\bar{F}}\mathbf{P}_{\bar{B}}|S\rangle||^2$$

$$+ \langle S|\mathbf{P}_B\mathbf{P}_{\bar{F}}\mathbf{P}_{\bar{B}}|S\rangle + \langle S|\mathbf{P}_B\mathbf{P}_{\bar{F}}\mathbf{P}_{\bar{B}}|S\rangle^*$$

$$= p_{\mathrm{T}}(\bar{F}) + \mathrm{Int}_{\bar{F}}.$$

Once again there is also an expansion for $||\mathbf{P}_F|S\rangle||^2 = p_{\mathrm{T}}(F) + \mathrm{Int}_F$, and $\mathrm{Int}_F + \mathrm{Int}_{\bar{F}} = 0$. In this case it is reasonable to argue that, given the Linda story, $\mathrm{Int}_F > 0$, making it more likely to agree that Linda is a feminist. If the interference Int_F is sufficiently positive, so that $||\mathbf{P}_{\bar{F}}\mathbf{P}_B|S\rangle||^2 < -\mathrm{Int}_{\bar{F}} = \mathrm{Int}_F$, then a disjunction fallacy occurs. The latter is likely to happen because Linda is not likely to be a bank teller and so $||\mathbf{P}_{\bar{F}}\mathbf{P}_B|S\rangle||^2$ is small.

4.1.3.3   Simultaneous explanation

To complete the analysis of conjunction and disjunction fallacies, we must check to see what the quantum model predicts for the remaining ordinal relations reported by Morier and Borgida (1984). It follows from $0 \le ||\mathbf{P}_B|S_F\rangle||^2 \le 1$ that $||\mathbf{P}_F|S\rangle||^2 \ge ||\mathbf{P}_F|S\rangle||^2 \cdot ||\mathbf{P}_B|S_F\rangle||^2 = ||\mathbf{P}_B\mathbf{P}_F|S\rangle||^2$, which satisfies the inequality $J(\text{feminist}) > J(\text{feminist and bank teller})$ found by Morier and Borgida (1984).

Now consider the order of the conjunction versus disjunction. The Linda story is designed so that the probability $||\mathbf{P}_{\bar{B}}\mathbf{P}_F|S\rangle||^2$ corresponding to the conjunction "Linda is a feminist and she is not a bank teller" is more likely than the probability $||\mathbf{P}_{\bar{F}}\mathbf{P}_{\bar{B}}|S\rangle||^2$ corresponding to the conjunction "Linda is not a bank teller and she is not a feminist." This design implies that

$$||\mathbf{P}_{\bar{F}}\mathbf{P}_{\bar{B}}|S\rangle||^2 < ||\mathbf{P}_{\bar{B}}\mathbf{P}_F|S\rangle||^2 + ||\mathbf{P}_{\bar{F}}|S\rangle||^2 = 1 - ||\mathbf{P}_B\mathbf{P}_F|S\rangle||^2$$

$$\rightarrow ||\mathbf{P}_B\mathbf{P}_F|S\rangle||^2 < 1 - ||\mathbf{P}_{\bar{F}}\mathbf{P}_{\bar{B}}|S\rangle||^2,$$

and the last line implies that the conjunction is less likely than the disjunction. This last prediction is important because, even though human judgments tend to satisfy this constraint, there is no requirement for them to do so. Therefore, if both the conjunction and disjunction fallacies occur, then the quantum model must produce the order reported by Morier and Borgida (1984). This is not true of theoretical explanations that we present later, which are free to produce consistent or inconsistent orders of disjunction and conjunction events depending on free parameters.

At this point, the quantum model is forced to make a very strong qualitative a priori prediction. To simultaneously explain both the conjunction and disjunction fallacies, the model requires the following order constraint: $||\mathbf{P}_B\mathbf{P}_F|S\rangle||^2 > ||\mathbf{P}_F\mathbf{P}_B|S\rangle||^2$. This constraint exactly fits our previous psychological explanation of order effects that we presented earlier – the first likely event increases availability of the second unlikely event. Processing the likely event first facilitates retrieving relevant thoughts for the second event, which then increases the likelihood of the conjunction. By contrast, if the unlikely event is processed first, it is hard to imagine any thoughts at all in favor of this unlikely event from the very beginning, which lowers the probability of the conjunction.

Theorem 4.1 *To simultaneously explain both the conjunction and disjunction fallacies, the quantum model requires the order constraint* $||\mathbf{P}_B\mathbf{P}_F|S\rangle||^2 > ||\mathbf{P}_F\mathbf{P}_B|S\rangle||^2$.

Proof. The conjunction and disjunction fallacies require the following two inequalities to be satisfied simultaneously:

$$\mathrm{Int}_F = \langle S|\mathbf{P}_B\mathbf{P}_F\mathbf{P}_{\bar{B}}|S\rangle + \langle S|\mathbf{P}_B\mathbf{P}_{\bar{F}}\mathbf{P}_{\bar{B}}|S\rangle^* > ||\mathbf{P}_{\bar{F}}\mathbf{P}_B|S\rangle||^2$$

$$-||\mathbf{P}_B\mathbf{P}_{\bar{F}}|S\rangle||^2 > \langle S|\mathbf{P}_F\mathbf{P}_B\mathbf{P}_{\bar{F}}|S\rangle + \langle S|\mathbf{P}_F\mathbf{P}_B\mathbf{P}_{\bar{F}}|S\rangle^* = \mathrm{Int}_B.$$

Recall from Eq. (3.5) that, for an arbitrary pair (A, B), $\langle S|\mathbf{P}_B\mathbf{P}_A\mathbf{P}_{\bar{B}}|S\rangle + \langle S|\mathbf{P}_B\mathbf{P}_A\mathbf{P}_{\bar{B}}|S\rangle^* = 2 \cdot \mathrm{Re}[\langle S|\mathbf{P}_B\mathbf{P}_A|S\rangle] - 2 \cdot ||\mathbf{P}_A\mathbf{P}_B)|S\rangle||^2$. Substituting the latter into the two inequalities implies

$$2 \cdot \mathrm{Re}[\langle S|\mathbf{P}_B\mathbf{P}_F|S\rangle] - 2 \cdot ||\mathbf{P}_F\mathbf{P}_B|S\rangle||^2 >$$

$$2 \cdot \mathrm{Re}[\langle S|\mathbf{P}_F\mathbf{P}_B|S\rangle] - 2 \cdot ||\mathbf{P}_B\mathbf{P}_F)|S\rangle||^2$$

$$\rightarrow ||\mathbf{P}_B\mathbf{P}_F|S\rangle||^2 > ||\mathbf{P}_F\mathbf{P}_B|S\rangle||^2. \qquad \blacksquare$$

4.1.3.4   Order effects

The quantum explanation for conjunction and disjunction errors must predict that order of processing is a critical factor for determining whether or not the fallacy will occur. One effective way to manipulate this order is to ask people to judge the conjunction first or last when judging the likelihood of events. For example, suppose U is an unlikely event and L is a likely event. A person could be asked to judge an unlikely event U first, and then judge the conjunction "U and L"; or they could be asked these questions in the opposite order. The quantum model predicts smaller effects when the conjunction is presented last, because in this case the person evaluates the probability $||\mathbf{P}_U|S\rangle||^2$ for the unlikely event first, and so the person is encouraged to use this probability estimate to determine the conjunction probability for "U and L." But in the latter case we must predict that $||\mathbf{P}_U|S\rangle||^2 \cdot ||\mathbf{P}_L|S_U\rangle||^2 = ||\mathbf{P}_L\mathbf{P}_U|S\rangle||^2$ and mathematically it follows that $||\mathbf{P}_U|S\rangle||^2 > ||\mathbf{P}_U|S\rangle||^2 \cdot ||\mathbf{P}_L|S_U\rangle||^2 = ||\mathbf{P}_L\mathbf{P}_U|S\rangle||^2$; therefore, no conjunction error can occur. This reduction does not happen in the reverse order when the conjunction is evaluated first, because in this case the "start with the higher probability event first" rule applies and the conjunction is always computed from the opposite order $|\mathbf{P}_L|S\rangle||^2 \cdot ||\mathbf{P}_U|S_L\rangle||^2 = ||\mathbf{P}_U\mathbf{P}_L|S\rangle||^2$, which produces conjunction errors as described earlier.

In fact, conjunction errors are significantly larger when the conjunction is rated first as opposed to being rated last. In the study by Stolarz-Fantino *et al.* (2003), when the single judgment for the unlikely event was made first, the mean judgment for the unlikely event was $J(U) = 0.14$ compared with $J(U$ and $L) = 0.17$ for the conjunction ($N = 105$, not significantly different); but when the conjunction was rated first, the mean judgment for the conjunction was $J(U$ and $L) = 0.26$ compared with $J(U) = 0.18$ for the unlikely event ($N = 102$, significantly different). Similar robust and large effects of order were reported by Gavanski and Roskos-Ewoldsen (1991). This order effect also explains why ratings produce fewer errors than rank orders (Wedell & Moro, 2008) – the latter procedure does not require any estimates of the constituent events ahead of time.

4.1.3.5   Event dependencies

The quantum model makes another strong prediction concerning the effect of dependencies between events on the conjunction fallacy. Suppose event U by itself is an unlikely event and L by itself is a likely event. However, these two events can be dependent so that the likelihood of one changes depending on the occurrence of the other. In classic probability theory, if $p(U|L) > p(U)$ so that the occurrence of event L increases the probability of event U, then there is a positive dependency of event L on event U. Similarly, according to the quantum model, an event L has a positive dependency on an event U if $||\mathbf{P}_U|S_L\rangle||^2 > ||\mathbf{P}_U|S\rangle||^2$. To produce a conjunction fallacy, the quantum model requires

$$||\mathbf{P}_U\mathbf{P}_L|S\rangle||^2 = ||\mathbf{P}_L|S\rangle||^2 \cdot ||\mathbf{P}_U|S_L\rangle||^2 > ||\mathbf{P}_U|S\rangle||^2$$

$$\rightarrow ||\mathbf{P}_U|S_L\rangle||^2 > \frac{||\mathbf{P}_U|S\rangle||^2}{||\mathbf{P}_L|S\rangle||^2} \geq ||\mathbf{P}_U|S\rangle||^2 .$$

Thus, the quantum model is forced to predict that conjunction errors occur only when there is a positive dependency of the unlikely event on the likely event. For example, according to the quantum model, knowing that Linda is a feminist increases the likelihood that she is a bank teller. In fact, the presence of dependencies between events A and B has been shown to affect the rate of conjunction fallacies – a positive conditional dependency generally increases the frequency of conjunction errors (Fisk, 2002). Thus, on the one hand, the quantum model provides an explanation for the effect of event dependencies on the conjunction error. On the other hand, the quantum model cannot explain conjunction errors obtained with independent events (at least not without assuming that the judge infers some dependency where none actually exists).

A competing explanation for conjunction and disjunction errors is the averaging model (Wyer, 1976), but this model fails to account for event dependencies. According to the averaging model, the judged probability of a conjunction is a weighted average of the likelihood assigned to the individual events:

$$J(A \text{ and } B) = w \cdot L(A) + (1 - w) \cdot L(B), 0 \leq w \leq 1.$$

The same rule is used to explain disjunction effects, except that the weight is allowed to change across tasks. Thus, this model is not required to predict any particular ordering for conjunction and disjunction events. Instead, to reproduce the finding that disjunctions are judged to be more likely than conjunctions, it is assumed that more weight is placed on the less likely event for the conjunction task, but more weight is placed on the more likely event for the disjunction task. A key idea, however, is that the likelihood $L(A)$ that enters the average is independent whether event A is averaged with event B or averaged with another event B'. This assumption fails to explain the effect of event dependency on the conjunction error.

A strong test of the independence assumption was reported by Miyamoto *et al.* (1995). In their design, judges evaluated four conjunctions of events including "A and X," "A and Y," "B and X," "B and Y." Contrary to an averaging model, violations of independence were observed: $J(A \text{ and } X) > J(B \text{ and } X)$ but $J(A \text{ and } Y) < J(B \text{ and } Y)$. According to the averaging model, the common likelihood $L(X)$ in the first comparison cancels out and so the first inequality implies that $L(A) > L(B)$; similarly, the common likelihood $L(Y)$ in the second comparison cancels out and so the order established by the first comparison should be maintained for the second comparison (but it is not). According to both the classic and quantum models, for this case, the probability of event A conditioned on the state X is larger than B, but the opposite can occur conditioned on the state Y.

There are many more probability judgment errors that the quantum model can qualitatively predict, including averaging errors, unpacking effects, conjunction errors with three events, and other findings. But we need to stop here and refer you to more details appearing in Busemeyer *et al.* (2011).

4.1.4 Comparison with other explanations

Classic (Kolmogorov) probability theory fails to explain conjunction and disjunction fallacies because, when given a story S and two uncertain events U and L, it requires $p(U \cap L|S) \leq p(U|S)$ and $p(U \cup L|S) \geq p(L|S)$. However, it is possible that people evaluate the conditional in the wrong direction. Classic probability theory does allow $p(S|U \cap L) > p(S|U)$ and $p(S|U \cup L) < p(S|L)$. This explanation fails to predict any ordering for $p(S|U \cap L)$ versus $p(S|L)$, nor does it predict any ordering for $p(S|U \cup L)$ versus $p(S|U \cap L)$, which is problematic. A more serious deficiency is that this idea cannot explain why the fallacy occurs for a conjunction of future events that entail the current state. For example, given the current cigarette tax and teenage smoking rate, people tend to prefer to bet on the event that "an increase in cigarette tax from the current rate and a decrease in teenage smoking from the current rate" rather than the event "a decrease in teenage smoking from the current rate" (Sides *et al.*, 2002). In this case, if we let S represent the current state of the world, then we are asked to compare $p(S \cap U \cap L|S) = p(U \cap L|S)$ versus $p(S \cap U|S) = p(U|S)$ and people tend to judge the former as more likely. If the conditional is reversed, then we have $p(S|S \cap U \cap L) = p(S) = p(S|S \cap U)$, which fails to explain the findings.[1]

Support theory (Tversky & Koehler, 1994) proposes that unpacking an event into its component parts increases the availability of the components, and thus the unpacked event is judged to be more likely than the logically identical packed event. Tversky and Koehler (1994) explained conjunction errors as an effect of unpacking an unlikely event (e.g., bank teller). So far, however, support theory has not provided an explanation of disjunction errors. This may be difficult because a packed event (e.g., feminism) is judged greater than the explicit disjunction of this same event with another event (e.g., feminism or bank teller).

The most popular model for conjunction and disjunction fallacies is the averaging model (Wyer, 1976). The averaging model assumes that each item is assigned a likelihood value (zero to one), and the judgment for a conjunction or disjunction question equals the weighted average of these likelihoods. Different weights are used to explain differences between conjunction and disjunction tasks. But the averaging model has a serious deficiency because it fails to account for interdependence among events. An item is assigned a likelihood value independent of the other items with which it is paired. This independence assumption is falsified by empirical violations of independence.

The quantum judgment model provides a common simple explanation for both conjunction and disjunction errors, and it also makes a number of strong, testable, a priori predictions that are supported by the empirical results. This includes (a) the ordering of the most likely event compared with either

---

[1] But see von Sidow (2011) for a new challenge from a Bayesian modelling approach.

disjunction or disjunction events, (b) the ordering of judgments for conjunction and disjunction events, (c) order effects on conjunction errors, (d) the effect of event dependency on the conjunction fallacy, as well as other findings.

According to this quantum model, incompatibility is the source of both conjunction and disjunction fallacies, and it is critically here that quantum probabilities deviate from classic probabilities. The incompatibility between events implies order effects, which we argue are the source of many of these judgment errors. Consider the effect of asking the feminism and bank teller questions in different orders. Suppose we first ask about bank teller and then ask about feminism. Also suppose on the basis of the Linda story that the projection of the original state onto the bank teller subspace is close to zero. In other words, initially it is very difficult to think of Linda as a bank teller. Then the probability of first saying yes to the bank teller question and then saying yes to the feminism question is also close to zero. But now consider asking the feminism question first. Given the initial state produced by the Linda story, the projection on the feminism subspace will be large, making a yes answer very likely. Given that the answer is yes to the feminism question, the original state vector (which was initially almost orthogonal to the bank teller subspace) is now projected onto the feminism subspace, so that the new state vector exists entirely in the feminist subspace. But, the feminist subspace is not orthogonal to the bank teller subspace or any of the other profession subspaces (if they were, then the two sets of features would be compatible). The disturbance of the state vector produced by answering yes to the feminism question now makes it possible to transit to the bank teller subspace, and the probability of saying yes to both questions, one after the other, is now substantially greater than zero. Thus, the indirect path of thought from Linda to feminism to bank teller is a fair possibility even though the direct path from Linda to bank teller is almost impossible. In other words, asking first about feminism increases the availability of later thoughts about bank tellers.

What is the evidence for order effects and is there any reason to think that quantum theory provides a good explanation for them? First, as shown in Chapter 3, the quantum model makes surprisingly accurate predictions for the effects of question order on attitude judgments. Second, in the previous section on qualitative tests, we presented evidence for question order effects on conjunction fallacies. Finally, it is well established that presentation order affects human inference judgments (Hogarth & Einhorn, 1992). In the next section on quantitative tests we fit the quantum model to the results of a new study examining order effects on inference.

4.2   Order effects on inference

One of the oldest and most reliable findings regarding human inference is that the order in which evidence is presented affects the final inference (Hogarth & Einhorn, 1992). If judges are asked to make a sequence of judgments, one after each new piece of evidence, then recent evidence appearing at the end of the

Table 4.1 Results from eight order conditions

2nd judgment	3rd judgment	Anchor–adjust		Quantum	
WP = 0.651	WP,WD = 0.516	0.578	0.552	0.647	0.502
	WP,SD = 0.398		0.436		0.407
SP = 0.805	SP,WD = 0.687	0.748	0.587	0.870	0.689
	SP,SD = 0.54		0.4373		0.527
WD = 0.390	WD,WP = 0.619	0.499	0.589	0.390	0.639
	WD,SP = 0.779		0.747		0.758
SD = 0.278	SD,WP = 0.495	0.401	0.568	0.275	0.487
	SD,SP = 0.69		0.756		0.702

First judgment = 0.459. W = weak evidence, S = strong evidence, P = prosecution, D = defense.

sequence tends to have a bigger impact than early evidence appearing at the beginning of a sequence (Hogarth & Einhorn, 1992). One might suspect that these order effects arise from memory recall failures, but it turns out that memory recall is uncorrelated with order effects in sequential judgment tasks (Hastie & Park, 1988).

4.2.1   Empirical study

Trueblood and Busemeyer (2011) recently conducted a large study of order effects on inference that included a total of 291 students. Each one participated in a computer-controlled experiment in which they read fictitious criminal cases (robbery, larceny, or burglary) and made judgments of guilt or innocence on a zero to one probability scale. A sequence of three judgments was made for each case: one before presenting any evidence and two more judgments after presentations of evidence by a prosecutor and a defense. For a random half of the cases, the prosecution was presented before the defense and for the other half the defense was presented first. The strength of the evidence was also manipulated. For example, in one case, participants read a short story (one short paragraph) about a burglarized warehouse, made an initial judgment based on no information, read a strong prosecution (described by three sentences), made a second judgment based only on this prosecution, read a weak defense (described by one sentence), and made a third judgment based on both the prosecution and the defense. Altogether, each person was presented with eight cases based on the experimental design shown in Table 4.1. The assignment of orders to cases was different for each participant in a counterbalanced manner, which produces approximately 38 participants per order condition.

   The main results are shown in Table 4.1, which shows the mean judgment, averaged over participants and across the eight cases. The first judgment (prior to any information) produced a mean probability equal to 0.459 (this is not shown in the table). This small bias against guilt reflects an initial bias to assume innocence at the beginning. The column labeled "2nd judgment" in Table 4.1 shows the judgment after the first piece of information, which demonstrates a clear effect produced by manipulating the evidence. The column labeled "3rd judgment" shows the judgment after both pieces of evidence, which provides four tests for order effects. The strongest example is SP,SD $= 0.54 <$ SD,SP $= 0.69$, which is a recency effect equal to 0.15; the other three recency effects were approximately equal to 0.10. All four tests for order effects produced strong and statistically significant recency effects (all with $p < 0.001$).

4.2.2 Bayesian inference model

Before considering a quantum model, it is worthwhile to first formulate a classic probability model (i.e., a Bayesian inference model) for this task. To be specific, consider the condition in which the prosecutor first presents strong evidence, which is followed by weak evidence from the defense. There are two hypotheses, guilty or not, which are represented by events G versus $\bar{G}$. The strong prosecution evidence is represented by another event S and this event has a complement $\bar{S}$; the weak defense evidence is represented by another event W, and this event has a complement $\bar{W}$. Altogether we can form a sample space composed of eight joint events $\{G \cap S \cap W, G \cap S \cap \bar{W}, \ldots, \bar{G} \cap \bar{S} \cap \bar{W}\}$. According to classic probability theory, we assign a probability to each element of this sample space, e.g., $p(G \cap \bar{S} \cap W)$ is assigned a probability, and all eight of these elementary probabilities sum to one. The probability of a more general event is obtained from the elementary probabilities by summing the probabilities for the elements contained in the more general event, such as $p(S \cap W) = p(G \cap S \cap W) + p(\bar{G} \cap S \cap W)$. The conditional probability of an event G given a pair of the other two events is obtained by the conditional probability rule: $p(G | S \cap W) = \frac{p(G \cap S \cap W)}{p(S \cap W)}$. The latter implies Bayes' rule:

$$p(G | S \cap W) = p(G|S) \cdot \frac{p(W | G \cap S)}{p(W|S)} = p(G|W) \cdot \frac{p(S | G \cap W)}{p(S|W)} = p(G | W \cap S).$$

So this Bayesian model cannot explain the order effect because the events are commutative and order does not matter.

One can save the Bayesian model by including order as another event as follows. Define O_1 as the event "defense presented first," and O_2 as the event "prosecutor presented first." Then we can have a more complex Bayesian model that incorporates order information as follows:

$$p(G | S \cap W \cap O_j) = p(G|O_j) \cdot \frac{p(S \cap W | G \cap O_j)}{p(S \cap W | O_j)}.$$

On the surface, this may seem to solve the problem, but if one looks a bit deeper, this just creates bigger problems. How do we evaluate the terms on the right-hand side? If they are just free parameters, then the model simply just restates the empirical finding and does not explain anything. The participants in the study know that the order of presentation is random and independent

of the evidence. Thus, order should be independent of all other events. So far
we have not seen any theory that provides a way to derive this dependence on
order from rational principles for these types of experiments.

4.2.3   Anchor–adjustment model

To explain order effects on inference, Hogarth and Einhorn (1992) proposed a
heuristic model, according to which a new state of belief equals the previous
(anchor) state plus an adjustment:

$$p_n = p_{n-1} + w_n \cdot [s(E_n) - R_n],\ n = 1, 2,$$

where p_n is the new belief state after observing n pieces of information, p_{n-1}
is the previous belief state after observing $n - 1$ pieces of information, $s(E_n)$
is the evidence provided by the nth piece of information, w_n is a weight, and
R_n is a reference point for this serial position. Furthermore, Hogarth and Einhorn (1992) proposed the following principle for setting the serial position
weight: if $[s(E_n) - R_n] > 0$ then $w_n = (1 - p_{n-1})$ and if $[s(E_n) - R_n] < 0$ then
$w_n = p_{n-1}$.

Different versions of the model can be formed by imposing assumptions on
the evidence $s(E_n)$ and the reference point R_n. One important variation is the
averaging model, which is formed by assuming that $0 \leq s(E_n) \leq 1$ and setting
$R_n = p_{n-1}$. Hogarth and Einhorn (1992) proved that this model must produce
recency effects, which is consistent with the results in Table 4.1. Recall that
the averaging model is also a popular model for explaining conjunction and
disjunction effects, and to be consistent we will focus on this model in this
chapter (however, Trueblood and Busemeyer (2010) also examine other versions
of the anchor–adjust model).

The mean first judgment (before presenting any evidence) was used to ini-
tiate the averaging process, $p_0 = 0.459$ and then the model was fit to the remaining 12 conditions based on the second and third judgments. The averaging
model requires estimating four parameters to fit the 12 conditions in Table 4.1,
which are the four values of $s(E)$ corresponding to the four types of evidence
WD, SD, WP, SP. These were fit by minimizing the sum of squared errors
(SSE) between the predicted and observed mean probability judgments for each
of the 12 conditions, which produced SSE $= 0.0704$ (standard deviation of the
error $= 0.0766$, $R^2 = 0.9833$). The predictions are given under the two columns
labeled Anchor–adjust in Table 4.1. The model correctly predicts the recency effects, but, despite the high R^2, the model fit is only fair. For example, the model
severely overestimates the recency effect for the SDSP versus SPSD comparison (predicted effect equals 0.319, observed effect equals 0.15). Also, the model
fails to reproduce the correct ordering across all the conditions. For example,
the averaging model predicts that SDSP $= 0.756 >$ WDSP $= 0.747$ when in fact
SDSP $= 0.69 <$ WDSP $= 0.779$. There are many other substantial quantitative
prediction errors, which demonstrates the challenge of fitting all of these order
effects.

4.2.4 Quantum inference model

To formulate an explicit quantum model for this task, we need to make specific assumptions about the basis vectors used to define the vector space. One idea is to form an eight-dimensional vector space and assume each of the eight joint events from the Bayesian model is a feature pattern that is assigned to a basis vector. This produces a single compatible representation of all the events, and all the events commute. But this representation produces no order effects, just like the Bayesian model.

Instead, Trueblood and Busemeyer (2011) used a smaller four-dimensional space based on four patterns produced by four combinations of two hypotheses (guilty versus not guilty) and two types of evidence (positive implicating guilty versus negative implicating not guilty). However, it is also assumed that these four dimensions can be viewed from three different perspectives: a naive perspective, the prosecutor's perspective, or the defense perspective. Consider the condition in which the prosecutor presents before the defense. The naive perspective represents the state of belief about the hypotheses and evidence from the judge's personal perspective and before any facts are known about the case, which is used to produce the first judgment. Assuming the prosecutor presents first, then the prosecutor's perspective represents the state of belief when the judge views the evidence from the prosecutor's arguments and after the first piece of evidence is presented, which is used to produce the second judgment. Assuming the defense presents second, then the defense's perspective represents the judge's state of belief when viewing the defense arguments and after the second piece of evidence is presented, which is used to produce the third judgment.

4.2.4.1 Unitary transformations

Before we can determine the probabilities for guilt after each piece of evidence, we need to specify the relationships among the naive basis, the prosecutor basis, and the defense basis. According to our quantum model, the same belief state $|S\rangle$ can be represented by three choices for the basis of the four-dimensional space:

$$|S\rangle = n_{G+} \cdot |N_{G+}\rangle + n_{G-} \cdot |N_{G-}\rangle + n_{\bar{G}+} \cdot |N_{\bar{G}+}\rangle + n_{\bar{G}-} \cdot |N_{\bar{G}-}\rangle,$$
$$= p_{G+} \cdot |P_{G+}\rangle + p_{G-} \cdot |P_{G-}\rangle + p_{\bar{G}+} \cdot |P_{\bar{G}+}\rangle + p_{\bar{G}-} \cdot |P_{\bar{G}-}\rangle,$$
$$= d_{G+} \cdot |D_{G+}\rangle + d_{G-} \cdot |D_{G-}\rangle + d_{\bar{G}+} \cdot |D_{\bar{G}+}\rangle + d_{\bar{G}-} \cdot |D_{\bar{G}-}\rangle,$$

where for each basis, the index $G+$ represents the pattern (guilty, positive evidence), $G-$ represents the pattern (guilty, negative evidence), $\bar{G}+$ represents the pattern (not guilty, positive evidence), and $\bar{G}-$ represents the pattern (not guilty, negative evidence). Each basis corresponds to a 4×1 column matrix of amplitudes: $|S\rangle$ can be represented by the 4×1 coordinate matrix n with respect to the naive basis, $|S\rangle$ can also be represented by the 4×1 coordinate matrix p in the prosecutor basis, and finally $|S\rangle$ can be represented by the 4×1 coordinate matrix d in the defense basis, where

$$n = \begin{bmatrix} n_{G+} \\ n_{G-} \\ n_{\bar{G}+} \\ n_{\bar{G}-} \end{bmatrix}, \quad p = \begin{bmatrix} p_{G+} \\ p_{G-} \\ p_{\bar{G}+} \\ p_{\bar{G}-} \end{bmatrix}, \quad d = \begin{bmatrix} d_{G+} \\ d_{G-} \\ d_{\bar{G}+} \\ d_{\bar{G}-} \end{bmatrix}.$$

Recall from Chapter 2 that a unitary matrix U is used to transform from one set of coordinates defined by a first basis into another set of coordinates defined by a second basis. Also as described in Chapter 2, a unitary matrix must satisfy the unitary property $U^\dagger U = I = U U^\dagger$ to preserve lengths and inner products between basis vectors. We want the basis vectors to remain unit length and pairwise orthogonal. One unitary matrix U_{pn} is required to transform the neutral coordinates into the prosecutor coordinates, $p = U_{pn} \cdot n$. A second unitary matrix U_{dn} is required to transform the neutral coordinates into the defense coordinates, $d = U_{dn} \cdot n$. Note that $n = U_{pn}^\dagger \cdot p$ and $d = U_{dn} \cdot n$, and so $d = U_{dn} \cdot U_{pn}^\dagger \cdot p = U_{dp} \cdot p$ determines the transformation from the prosecutor coordinates into the defense coordinates and $p = U_{dp}^\dagger \cdot d$ determines the transformation from the defense coordinates into the prosecutor's coordinates. In sum, we need to specify only the two unitary matrices U_{pn} and U_{dn}. Next we describe how to construct these unitary matrices.

Recall again from Chapter 2 that any unitary matrix can be constructed from a Hermitian matrix, $H = H^\dagger$, by the complex matrix exponential transformation $U = \exp(-i \cdot x \cdot H)$, where x is a parameter. Trueblood and Busemeyer (2010) used a Hermitian matrix that was previously developed for an earlier psychological application involving four-dimensional vector spaces (Pothos & Busemeyer, 2009). Chapters 8 and 9 discuss these unitary matrices in more detail (see also the section on Pauli matrices in Appendix D), and later in this chapter we show how this works with examples. For now, we simply assume that the Hermitian matrix H is constructed from two components, $H = H_1 + H_2$, defined by

$$H_1 = \begin{bmatrix} 1 & 1 & 0 & 0 \\ 1 & -1 & 0 & 1 \\ 0 & 0 & 1 & 1 \\ 0 & 0 & 1 & -1 \end{bmatrix}, \quad H_2 = \begin{bmatrix} 1 & 0 & 1 & 0 \\ 0 & -1 & 0 & 1 \\ 1 & 0 & -1 & 0 \\ 0 & 1 & 0 & 1 \end{bmatrix}. \tag{4.1}$$

The matrix H_1 rotates amplitudes to favor either the presence of positive evidence or negative evidence and the matrix H_2 rotates beliefs toward guilt when positive evidence is present and rotates beliefs toward innocence when negative evidence is present. Together these two matrices coordinate beliefs about evidence and hypotheses. The parameter x determines the degree of rotation and this is a free parameter in the model. We allow a different parameter value of x for U_{pn} versus U_{dn}. We also allow a different parameter value of x for strong and weak evidence. Altogether this produces four free parameter values for x, one for each combination of the four types of evidence WP, SP, WD, SD. This way of assigning parameters to evidence is the same kind of assumption used to fit parameters to the averaging model.

Now we are prepared to derive the judgment probabilities following each piece of evidence. The predictions are worked out initially for the condition in which prosecution evidence is presented before the defense. Later we summarize the equations for both orders of presentation.

4.2.4.2   Naive perspective

The initial state $|S\rangle$, before any evidence is presented, is represented in terms of the basis for the naive perspective (this is analogous to setting a Bayesian prior):

$$|S\rangle = n_{G+} \cdot |N_{G+}\rangle + n_{G-} \cdot |N_{G-}\rangle + n_{\bar{G}+} \cdot |N_{\bar{G}+}\rangle + n_{\bar{G}-} \cdot |N_{\bar{G}-}\rangle.$$

Like the averaging model, this initial state is designed to reproduce the mean of the first judgment before any evidence is presented. (This is also analogous to setting the prior in a Bayesian model.) This is achieved by setting the coordinates of the initial state, with respect to the naive basis, equal to the 4×1 matrix of amplitudes:

$$n = \begin{bmatrix} n_{G+} \\ n_{G-} \\ n_{\bar{G}+} \\ n_{\bar{G}-} \end{bmatrix} = \begin{bmatrix} \sqrt{0.459/2} \\ \sqrt{0.459/2} \\ \sqrt{0.541/2} \\ \sqrt{0.541/2} \end{bmatrix} \tag{4.2}$$

The probability of guilt for the first judgment, before any evidence is presented, is obtained by first projecting this state onto the subspace spanned by the guilty basis vectors, which equals $n_{G+} \cdot |N_{G+}\rangle + n_{G-} \cdot |N_{G-}\rangle$, and then computing the squared length, which equals $J(G) = |n_{G+}|^2 + |n_{G-}|^2 = 0.459$.

4.2.4.3   Prosecution perspective

Suppose the prosecutor presents the first piece of evidence and the judge changes to view the evidence from the prosecutor perspective. The initial state $|S\rangle$, before any evidence is presented, is represented in terms of the prosecutor basis as

$$|S\rangle = p_{G+} \cdot |P_{G+}\rangle + p_{G-} \cdot |P_{G-}\rangle + p_{\bar{G}+} \cdot |P_{\bar{G}+}\rangle + p_{\bar{G}-} \cdot |P_{\bar{G}-}\rangle.$$

The amplitudes for the prosecutor basis can be obtained by transforming the amplitudes from the naive basis given in Eq. (4.2)

$$p = \begin{bmatrix} p_{G+} \\ p_{G-} \\ p_{\bar{G}+} \\ p_{\bar{G}-} \end{bmatrix} = U_{pn} \cdot n.$$

To get a concrete idea of this change in state, suppose we set $x_p = 1.2393$ in the formula for the unitary matrix $U_{pn} = \exp(-i \cdot x_p \cdot H)$, where H is defined in Eq. (11.4), and n is given by Eq. (4.2) to produce $p = U_{pn} \cdot n$. Then the squared magnitudes of the amplitudes equal

$$
\begin{bmatrix}
|p_{G+}|^2 \\
|p_{G-}|^2 \\
|p_{\bar{G}+}|^2 \\
|p_{\bar{G}-}|^2
\end{bmatrix}
=
\begin{bmatrix}
0.7413 \\
0.0926 \\
0.1105 \\
0.0556
\end{bmatrix}.
$$

The prosecutor presents positive evidence favoring guilt, and so we need to revise the initial state vector on the basis of this evidence. First we project $|S\rangle$ onto the subspace for positive evidence spanned by $\{|P_{G+}\rangle, |P_{\bar{G}+}\rangle\}$ and then we normalize this projection to produce

$$
|S_+\rangle = \frac{p_{G+} \cdot |P_{G+}\rangle + 0 \cdot |P_{G-}\rangle + p_{\bar{G}+} \cdot |P_{\bar{G}+}\rangle + 0 \cdot |P_{\bar{G}-}\rangle}{\sqrt{|p_{G+}|^2 + |p_{\bar{G}+}|^2}}. \tag{4.3}
$$

The amplitudes for the revised state, conditioned on the positive evidence provided by the prosecutor, then equal

$$
p_+ = \frac{1}{\sqrt{|p_{G+}|^2 + |p_{\bar{G}+}|^2}}
\begin{bmatrix}
p_{G+} \\
0 \\
p_{\bar{G}+} \\
0
\end{bmatrix}. \tag{4.4}
$$

The judged probability of guilt for the second judgment, after the first piece of evidence, is obtained by projecting the state $|S_+\rangle$ onto the subspace for guilt spanned by $\{|P_{G+}\rangle, |P_{G-}\rangle\}$ and squaring its length, which equals

$$
J(G|P+) = || \, |P_{G+}\rangle\langle P_{G+}|S_+\rangle + |P_{G-}\rangle\langle P_{G-}|S_+\rangle \, ||^2
$$

$$
= || \, \frac{p_{G+}}{\sqrt{|p_{G+}|^2 + |p_{\bar{G}+}|^2}} \cdot |P_{G+}\rangle||^2 = \frac{|p_{G+}|^2}{|p_{G+}|^2 + |p_{\bar{G}+}|^2}.
$$

Using the numerical example described above, the probability of guilt following the positive evidence by the prosecution equals $\frac{|p_{G+}|^2}{|p_{G+}|^2 + |p_{\bar{G}+}|^2} = \frac{0.7413}{0.7413 + 0.1105} = 0.8703$, which equals the prediction under the quantum model for the second judgment with the strong prosecution in Table 4.1.

4.2.4.4   Defense perspective

Suppose the second piece of evidence is presented by the defense, in which case the judge changes the view to the defense perspective. The revised state $|S_+\rangle$, following the first piece of evidence, is represented in terms of the basis for the defense as

$$|S_+\rangle = d_{G+} \cdot |D_{G+}\rangle + d_{G-} \cdot |D_{G-}\rangle + d_{\bar{G}+} \cdot |D_{\bar{G}+}\rangle + d_{\bar{G}-} \cdot |D_{\bar{G}-}\rangle.$$

This defense state corresponds to a 4×1 matrix of amplitudes:

$$d_+ = \begin{bmatrix} d_{G+} \\ d_{G-} \\ d_{\bar{G}+} \\ d_{\bar{G}-} \end{bmatrix} = U_{dp} \cdot p_+.$$

To get a concrete idea of this change in state, suppose we set $x_p = 1.2393$ in $U_{pn} = \exp(-i \cdot x_p \cdot H)$ and we set $x_d = -3.8324$ in $U_{dn} = \exp(-i \cdot x_d \cdot H)$, where H is defined in Eq. (4.1), and p_+ is given by Eq. (4.4). Then the squared magnitudes of the coordinates of d_+ equal

$$\begin{bmatrix} |d_{G+}|^2 \\ |d_{G-}|^2 \\ |d_{\bar{G}+}|^2 \\ |d_{\bar{G}-}|^2 \end{bmatrix} = \begin{bmatrix} 0.5002 \\ 0.2124 \\ 0.0964 \\ 0.1909 \end{bmatrix}.$$

The defense presents negative evidence, and so the defense state is revised by projecting $|S_+\rangle$ onto the subspace spanned by $\{D_{G-}, D_{\bar{G}-}\}$, which produces the state of belief after both pieces of evidence

$$|S_{+,-}\rangle = \frac{0 \cdot |D_{G+}\rangle + d_{G-} \cdot |D_{G-}\rangle + 0 \cdot |D_{\bar{G}+}\rangle + d_{\bar{G}-} \cdot |D_{\bar{G}-}\rangle}{\sqrt{|d_{G-}|^2 + |d_{\bar{G}-}|^2}}.$$

The amplitudes with respect to the defense basis, conditioned on both pieces of evidence, then equal

$$d_{+,-} = \frac{1}{\sqrt{|d_{G-}|^2 + |d_{\bar{G}-}|^2}} \begin{bmatrix} 0 \\ d_{G-} \\ 0 \\ d_{\bar{G}-} \end{bmatrix}. \tag{4.5}$$

The judged probability of guilt, following both pieces of evidence, is obtained from the squared length of the projection of the last state on subspace spanned by $\{D_{G+}, D_{G-}\}$, which equals

$$J(G|P+, D-) = \| |D_{G+}\rangle\langle D_{G+}|S_+\rangle + |D_{G-}\rangle\langle D_{G-}|S_{+,-}\rangle \|^2$$

$$= \| \frac{d_{G-}}{\sqrt{|d_{G-}|^2 + |d_{\bar{G}-}|^2}} \cdot |D_{G-}\rangle \|^2 = \frac{|d_{G-}|^2}{|d_{G-}|^2 + |d_{\bar{G}-}|^2}.$$

Continuing with the numerical example, the probability of guilt following both pieces of evidence equals $\frac{|d_{G-}|^2}{|d_{G-}|^2 + |d_{\bar{G}-}|^2} = \frac{0.2124}{0.2124 + 0.1909} = 0.5266$, which equals the quantum model prediction in Table 4.1 for the strong prosecution followed by the strong defence.

4.2.4.5   Summary of quantum model

To summarize, we first select parameters, x_p and x_d, which are used to compute the two unitary matrices $U_{pn} = \exp(-i \cdot x_p \cdot H)$ and $U_{dn} = \exp(-i \cdot x_d \cdot H)$ with H defined by Eq. (4.1), and then we compute $U_{dp} = U_{dn} U_{pn}^{\dagger}$ and $U_{pd} = U_{dp}^{\dagger}$. We form two projector matrices, one that projects on the coordinates for guilty and another that projects on the coordinates for the positive evidence:

$$
P_G = \begin{bmatrix} 1 & 0 & 0 & 0 \\ 0 & 1 & 0 & 0 \\ 0 & 0 & 0 & 0 \\ 0 & 0 & 0 & 0 \end{bmatrix}, \quad
P_+ = \begin{bmatrix} 0 & 0 & 0 & 0 \\ 0 & 1 & 0 & 0 \\ 0 & 0 & 0 & 0 \\ 0 & 0 & 0 & 1 \end{bmatrix}.
$$

We start with the naive initial state n defined by Eq. (4.2). For the prosecutor–defense order, we transform to the prosecutor coordinates $p = U_{pn} \cdot n$, revise the state for the positive prosecutor evidence as $p_+ = \frac{P_+ \cdot p}{||P_+ \cdot p||}$, and then compute the probability of guilt given the positive evidence, $||P_G \cdot p_+||^2$. Then we transform to the defense coordinates $d_+ = U_{dp} \cdot p_+$, revise the state again for the negative defense evidence $d_{+,-} = \frac{(I-P_+) \cdot d_+}{||(I-P_+) \cdot d_+||}$, and then compute the probability of guilt given both pieces of evidence, $||P_G \cdot d_{+,-}||^2$. For the defense–prosecutor order, we transform to the defense coordinates $d = U_{dn} \cdot n$, revise the state for the negative defense evidence as $d_- = \frac{(I-P_+) \cdot d}{||(I-P_+) \cdot d||}$, and then compute the probability of guilt given the negative evidence, $||P_G \cdot d_-||^2$. Then we transform to the prosecutor coordinates $p_- = U_{pd} \cdot d_-$, revise the state again for the positive prosecutor evidence $p_{-,+} = \frac{P_+ \cdot p_-}{||(P_+ \cdot p_-||}$, and then compute the probability of guilt given both pieces of evidence, $||P_G \cdot p_{-,+}||^2$.

The quantum model requires fitting four parameters, a pair $(x_{p,s}, x_{d,s})$ for strong evidence and another pair $(x_{p,w}, x_{d,w})$ for weak evidence, to the 12 conditions in Table 4.1. We fit the four parameters by minimizing the SSE between the predicted and observed mean probability judgments for each of the 12 conditions plus the initial judgment, which produced SSE $= 0.0058$ (standard deviation of the error $= 0.022$, $R^2 = 0.9986$). The predicted values are displayed in the last two columns of Table 4.1. This quantum model provides a very accurate fit, and it is clearly a better fit than the averaging model. Note that the quantum model correctly predicts all of the recency effects and it also correctly reproduces ordering of the probabilities across all conditions. The only place where the model makes a noticeable error is for the SP condition, where it overestimates the strength of this evidence.

4.2.5   Conclusions from the quantitative test

There were two purposes for this quantitative test of the quantum model. One was to provide a detailed example showing how to construct a vector space and unitary transformations relating different incompatible bases. The second was to provide a quantitative test that compares the quantum model with another heuristic model, the averaging model, for explaining order effects on inference. The averaging model was chosen for comparison because it was the strongest candidate for explaining conjunction–disjunction errors, and it was also designed specifically to explain recency effects observed in inference tasks.

Both the quantum model and the averaging model used the same initial belief, and both models were allowed to fit a separate parameter to the SP, WP, SD, and WD types of evidence. Thus, both models had the same number of parameters (although the relative complexity of these models remains unknown). The models were fit to 12 different conditions in Table 4.1, which provides a challenging data set with strong recency effects. It is not so easy to fit these 12 conditions, because the averaging model did not even succeed in reproducing the correct ordering across all the conditions. The quantum model succeeded in producing a very accurate fit to all 12 conditions. We do not want to conclude that we have proved that the quantum model is true, or even that the averaging model is false. What we conclude is that this quantitative test makes a convincing case for considering the quantum model to be a viable new candidate for modelling human inference and it deserves to enter the model-testing fray.

4.3 Compatibility and quantum rationality

Both of the applications in this chapter relied heavily on the idea that it is important to introduce a distinction between compatible and incompatible representations of events when describing human judgments. More accurately, we should say "reintroduce" this distinction, because Bohr actually got the idea of complementarity from William James. Human judges may be capable of using either compatible or incompatible representations, and they are not constrained or forced to use just one. The use of compatible representations produces judgments that agree with the classic and Bayesian laws of probability, whereas the use of incompatible representations produces violations. But the latter may be necessary to deal with deeply uncertain situations (involving unknown joint probabilities), where one needs to rely on simple incompatible representations to *construct* sequential conjunctive probabilities *coherently* from quantum principles. Compatible representations may only become available after a person gains sufficient experience with joint observations of the variables to form a good estimate of the joint probabilities (Nilsson, 2008). In fact, both types of representations, compatible and incompatible, may be available to the judge, and the context of a problem may trigger the use of one or the other (Reyna & Brainerd, 1995). More advanced versions of quantum probability theory (using a Fock space, which is analogous to a hierarchical Bayesian-type model) provide principles for combining both types of representations (Aerts, 2009).

Bayesian models of cognition are claimed to be founded on a rational basis (Oaksford & Chater, 2009). In fact, Bayes' rule is derived from Kolmogorov's axioms for classic probability theory. Quantum models of cognition are based on von Neumann's axioms, which reduce to classic theory when all the variables are assumed to be compatible. So why do we need to use incompatible events, and is this not irrational? In fact, the physical world obeys quantum principles and incompatible events are an essential part of nature. Nevertheless, there are clear circumstances where everyone agrees that the events should be treated classically (such as randomly sampling balls from urns). However, it is harder to argue what is rational for cases like the Linda story, because one cannot refer to any empirical relative frequencies for a singular or unique event. Furthermore, it remains an empirical question whether quantum or Bayesian methods are more useful for modelling probabilities of very complex sequences when the joint probabilities are largely unknown. Also, incompatible events may be essential for understanding our commonly occurring but nevertheless very complex human interactions. For instance, when trying to judge something as uncertain as winning an argument with another person, the likelihood of success may depend on using incompatible representations that allow viewing the same facts from different perspectives.

The main aspect of quantum theory which makes it successful relates to order effects in probability computations. Order effects arise in quantum theory because it is a geometric theory: probabilities are computed from projections to different subspaces. But, as we have shown, it is typically the case that the order with which these projections occur can affect the eventual outcome. Empirical findings on human judgment indicate strong order effects as well, and it is for this reason that quantum theory appears to provide an intuitive and parsimonious explanation for such findings.

5
Quantum-inspired models of
concept combinations

Consider the concept combination "pet human." In word association experiments, human subjects often produce the associate "slave" in relation to this combination. The striking aspect of this associate is that it is not produced as an associate of "pet" or "human" in isolation. In other words, the associate "slave" cannot be recovered from the constituent concepts. Such examples have been used in both cognitive science and philosophy to argue that concept combinations have a *non-compositional* semantics. This chapter will feature how various non-compositional accounts of concept combinations can be provided from quantum theory. Quantum theory is a theory which caters for the modelling of non-compositionality because the state of a quantum entangled system cannot be constructed from the states of its individual subsystems. Utilizing probabilistic methods developed for analyzing composite systems in quantum theory, we show that it is possible to classify concept combinations as having "classically compositional," "pseudo-classically non-compositional," or "non-classically non-compositional" semantics by determining whether the joint probability distribution modelling the combination is factorizable or not.

5.1   Concept combinations and cognition

The principle of semantic compositionality states the meaning of a (syntactically complex) whole is a function only of the meanings of its (syntactic) parts together with the manner in which these parts were combined (Pelletier, 1994). Whether the semantics of concepts are compositional, or not, has been somewhat of a battleground. On the one hand, there are authors like Fodor (1994) who are adamant that concepts are, and must be, compositional, but this position stands in contrast with the computational linguist Zadrozny (1994), who produced a theorem suggesting that: "the standard definition of compositionality is formally vacuous." Many authors tend to use arguments relying upon compositionality, even as they admit that there may be something non-compositional about the semantics of concept combinations (Weiskopf, 2007). There are good reasons for this state of affairs. A compositional semantics allows the semantics of higher order structures to be constructed by combining the semantics of its constituent parts. This view of modelling semantics has become firmly established in a number of disciplines, including logic, linguistics, cognition and computer science, and a long track record of success has left modelling almost habitually compositional. For example, in a recent article defining and evaluating various vector-based approaches for modelling concept combinations, all approaches studied were compositional (Mitchell & Lapata, 2010). Indeed, just asking the question of how to model semantics in a *non-compositional* way has an oddly unfamiliar ring to it. Moreover, there are no obvious ways to address this question, save perhaps by adopting a connectionist approach (Goschke & Koppelberg, 1991).

The compositional approach to semantics is often assumed to have originated from Gottlob Frege - it is sometimes labeled as "Frege's principle" (Pelletier, 1994). However, it is both a curious and little known fact that it is extraordinarily difficult to find this principle clearly stated in his writings, and it can even be doubted whether he expressed it at all (Pelletier, 2001). This has not stopped the principle being viewed as obviously being true (or at least very useful), hence the tremendous impact of the principle in the fields just mentioned. We agree with Pelletier (1994) that the principle is underspecified in a number of ways; for example, what meaning is, what counts as a (syntactic) part, what counts as a syntactic complex, and how combination is defined. This underspecification naturally allows a lot of room in setting the dividing line between compositionality and non-compositionality. This chapter attempts to clarify the position of this dividing line by means of a suite of sophisticated tools that have already been developed for analyzing non-compositionality within quantum theory. These tools can be applied to the analysis of concepts, and provide theoretically justified grounds for deciding whether a particular concept combination can be considered in terms of the semantics of its constituent parts. Specific cases will be discussed where concept combinations can be shown to be non-compositional using these analytical methods.

5.1.1   Cognitive theories of conceptual combination

A fundamental aspect of everyday language comprehension is the interpretation of compound phrases through conceptual combination (Costello & Keane, 2000). Concept combinations cover a broad range of compound phrases ranging from the everyday "black cat" to novel compound nominals such as "cactus fish."

While the assumption that the semantics of concept combinations are compositional has been found problematic (Medin & Shoben, 1988; Hampton, 1997), virtually all researchers have at least assumed a weak form of compositionality in which the initial combination process begins with separate meanings, but is supplemented later by external contextual information (Swinney *et al.*, 2007). For example, in Wisniewski's (1996) dual process model of conceptual combination, there is a competition between relation linking (e.g., "zebra crossing" as a crossing for zebras) and property mapping processes (e.g., "zebra crossing" as a striped crossing) to form the compound meaning. This process is affected by the similarity of the constituent concepts, with similar concepts (e.g., "elephant horse") more likely to result in a property interpretation (e.g., a large horse), and dissimilar concepts (e.g., "elephant box") more likely to result in a relational interpretation (e.g., a box for holding elephants). According to Wisniewski (1996) this is because similar concepts share many dimensions (four legs, similar shape, etc. in the case of elephant and horse) and thus are easier to combine by mapping one property to another. These processes are all compositional, in the sense that they rely almost exclusively on properties of the individual concepts. It is only later that background knowledge is drawn upon to infer the possible emergent properties of the new concept. Thus, an "elephant box" could be deemed as likely to be made of a strong material such as wood, and hopefully to contain air-holes. As evidence for this form of weak compositionality in conceptual combination, Swinney *et al.* (2007) showed that for adjectival combinations such as "boiled celery" the properties of the individual words such as "green" are activated before emergent properties such as "soft." However, for the combination "apartment dog," apartment modifies the "habitat" dimension of dog rather than its "size" (a dog the size of an apartment), which in turn shows that background knowledge also plays a role in early combinatory processes such as slot selection (Murphy, 1988).

Fodor (1994) is perhaps the most strident advocate of compositionality in cognition:

> It is extremely plausible that the productivity and systematicity of language and thought are both to be explained by appeal to the productivity and systematicity of mental representations, and that mental representations are systematic and productive because they are compositional. The idea is that mental representations are constructed by the application of a finite number of combinatorial principles to a finite basis of (relatively or absolutely) primitive concepts

Such thoughts are echoed in computational models of word meaning. It is common in cognitive science, as well as in fields such as computational linguistics, information retrieval, and machine learning, to employ dimensional representations in the form of vectors to represent individual words. For example, words are represented as high-dimensional vectors computed from a corpus of electronic text, as in the latent semantic analysis model (Landauer & Dumais, 1997). However, there is surprisingly little research about how specific vector representations corresponding to individual concepts should be composed. Recently, a number of approaches were examined using the principle of compositionality as the guiding principle (Mitchell & Lapata, 2010).

The phenomenon of emergent associates described above in relation to examples such as "pet human" have been used, however, as evidence for the semantics of concept combinations to be non-compositional (Hampton, 1997). In the wake of this, there have been various quantum models developed to account for non-compositional semantics. This chapter will present some of the prominent models, which can be broadly distinguished by whether quantum interference is being employed or whether concept combinations are being modelled as composite quantum systems.

5.2   Non-compositional models of concept combinations based in quantum interference

Concept combinations can be broadly classified into two types (Hampton, 1997). First there are combinations that have an intersective semantics; for example, the meaning of "black cat" is the intersection of black objects and objects that are cats. Intersective semantics is compositional, as the semantics of "black cat" is determined solely in terms of the semantics of the constituent concepts "black" and "cat." It is tempting to assume most concept combinations can be modelled this way. The study of intersective combinations in cognitive science has revealed, however, that the semantics of concept combinations is not always intersective. For example, in "astronaut pen," the intersection of "astronaut" and "pen" is empty; therefore, its semantics is vacuous (Gärdenfors, 2000; Weiskopf, 2007). To address this problem by using a fuzzy notion on intersection leads to the problem known as overextension; for example, "guppy" overextends the intersection of "pet fish," because "guppy" is not typically judged a "pet" or a "fish," but is readily judged as a prototypical "pet fish." The "pet fish" example, then, revolves around how prototypicality behaves under conjunction.

Gabora and Aerts (2002) were the first to attempt a comprehensive theory of conceptual representation using quantum theory. A substantial body of work developing quantum-like models of concept combinations based on prototype theory has subsequently arisen. An important underlying assumption is that concepts change continuously under influence of context, and this change is described as a change of the state of the concept. The theory "is essentially a contextual theory, which is one of the reasons why we can model the concepts in the way a quantum entity is described by the mathematical formalism of quantum mechanics, which is a contextual physical theory describing physical entities whose states change under influence of contexts of measurement" (Aerts, 2009).

First, an object i is assumed to have a graded membership $\mu_i(A)$ with respect to a concept A. In other words, the semantics of A is extensional; that is, defined by a set of objects, where membership is graded. For example, Hampton (1988) employed the scale $\{-3, -2, -1, 0, +1, +2, +3\}$, where $+3$ indicates a rating of the highest degree of membership of the category. This scale is then normalized by appropriately mapping the range -3 to $+3$ onto a probability scale ranging from 0 to 1. This scheme can be extended to conjunctions with $\mu_i(A \text{ and } B)$ denoting the graded membership of the conjunction of concepts A and B. A fuzzy notion of intersection is formalized: $\mu_i(A \text{ and } B) = \min(\mu_i(A), \mu_i(B))$. Overextension occurs when $\mu_i(A \text{ and } B) > \min(\mu_i(A), \mu_i(B))$. The "observed weight" of the conjunction c is the difference: $\Delta_c = \mu_i(A \text{ and } B) - \min(\mu_i(A), \mu_i(B))$. In addition, the "Kolmogorovian conjunction factor" is defined as $k_c = 1 - \mu_i(A) - \mu_i(B) + \mu_i(A \text{ and } B)$.

Aerts (2009: Theorem 3) proves that the membership weights $\mu_i(A)$, $\mu_i(B)$ and $\mu_i(A \text{ and } B)$ of an item i with respect to concepts A, B and the conjunction of A and B can be modelled by classical probability theory if and only if $\Delta_c < 0$, (i.e., there is no overextension), and $k_c \geq 0$. The significance of this result is that it formalizes the boundary condition where classical probability is an appropriate modelling framework for concept combinations ($k_c \geq 0$). In addition, it formalizes the condition where intersective semantics is appropriate ($\Delta_c < 0$). In other words, when the latter condition fails, then the concept combination cannot be modelled by intersective semantics and, therefore, has a non-compositional semantics. When the conditions are not satisfied, a model based on quantum superposition and interference is proposed (Aerts, 2009).

As an example (see Hampton (1988)) take the word "peppercorn." When evaluated as a member of "food" it received a normalized weight of 0.875; and when it was evaluated as a member of "plant" it received a value of 0.6207; but when evaluated as the combination "food plant" it was attributed a normalized value of 0.7586. For this example, we have the concepts $A =$ "food" and $B =$ "plant," and the item $i =$ "peppercorn." Drawing on the data presented above, $\mu_i(A) = 0.875$, $\mu_i(B) = 0.6207$, and $\mu(A \text{ and } B) = 0.7586$. Therefore,

$$\Delta_c = \mu_i(A \text{ and } B) - \min(\mu_i(A), \mu_i(B))$$
$$= 0.7586 - 0.6207$$
$$= 0.1379.$$

Similarly,

$$k_c = 1 - \mu_i(A) - \mu_i(B) + \mu(A \text{ and } B)$$
$$= 1 - 0.875 - 0.6207 + 0.7586$$
$$= 0.2629.$$

As $\Delta_c > 0$, the concept combination cannot be modelled by classical probability theory.

In a simple version of the quantum model (Aerts, 2009), concepts A and B are represented as states $|A\rangle$, $|B\rangle \in \mathbf{C}^3$ of a three-dimensional complex Hilbert space. The concept combination is modelled by the superposition of concepts A and B: $|A \text{ and } B\rangle = \frac{1}{2}(|A\rangle + |B\rangle)$. In particular, the amplitudes with respect to a canonical basis are chosen specifically to reproduce the observed data as follows:

$$|A\rangle \to \psi_A = \left(\sqrt{a}, 0, \sqrt{1-a}\right)^\dagger$$

$$|B\rangle \to \psi_B = e^{i\beta} \cdot \left(\sqrt{\frac{(1-a)(1-b)}{a}}, \sqrt{\frac{a+b-1}{a}}, -\sqrt{1-b}\right)^\dagger$$

$$|A \text{ and } B\rangle \to \psi_{A \wedge B} = \frac{1}{\sqrt{2}}(\psi_A + \psi_B).$$

The constants a and b are related to the membership function according to the following mutually exclusive and complete conditions:

$$\mu_i(A) + \mu_i(B) \leq 1 \Rightarrow a = 1 - \mu_i(A), b = 1 - \mu_i(B)$$
$$\mu_i(A) + \mu_i(B) > 1 \Rightarrow a = \mu_i(A), b = \mu_i(B).$$

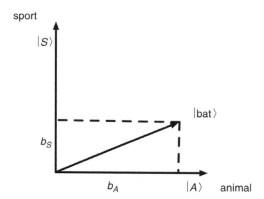

Figure 5.1 The word "bat" represented in a two-dimensional vector space.

under investigation (i) has more than one distinct sense and (ii) that the senses are related. Both of these aspects are addressed when "bat" is modelled in a two-dimensional Hilbert space, the basis vectors of which correspond to the two possible senses. The relationship between the senses is that they are assumed to be orthogonal, as illustrated in Figure 5.1. The vector in Figure 5.1 can be assumed to have a length of one, which means that it can represent the probability that one of the two senses of "bat" will be recalled. Such probabilities are obtained by considering how much the vector projects onto the basis vectors which correspond to the two possible senses: sport (denoted $|S\rangle$) or animal (denoted $|A\rangle$), where the lengths b_A and b_S in Figure 5.1 are the square-root terms: $b_S^2 + b_A^2 = 1$. Thus, the probability of a particular sense being recalled is related to a projected length along the relevant basis vector: $b_S = \sqrt{p_s}$ and $b_A = \sqrt{p_a}$.

Such a quantum-like representation can model the ambiguity of a free association experiment very naturally as a quantum superposition of the two senses (Aerts & Czachor, 2004; Widdows, 2004; Bruza & Cole, 2005; Aerts & Gabora, 2005; Gabora et al., 2008; Bruza et al., 2009c; Aerts, 2009):

$$|bat\rangle = b_S|S\rangle + b_A|A\rangle. \tag{5.1}$$

Here, b_S and b_A are scalars representing the likelihood of the sport or animal senses being produced in a free association experiment. Such a framework can be extended to model the combinations of words. Quantum theory uses the tensor product to model composite systems and we will show how concept combinations can be modelled in the same way. Consider Figure 5.2, which depicts two systems A and B. System A is in state $|u\rangle = a_0|0\rangle + a_1|1\rangle$ and system B is in state $|v\rangle = b_0|0\rangle + b_1|1\rangle$. For the purposes of the example, we shall take A and B to be photons, which can be measured to reveal a polarization of either "up" (denoted $|1\rangle$) or "down" ($|0\rangle$) when sent through a polarizer and toward a detecting apparatus. In this case, $|a_1|^2$ is a scalar which reflects the probability of the photon in state $|u\rangle$ will have a polarization of "up" after measurement at the

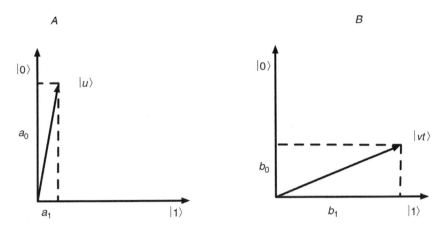

Figure 5.2 The separate state spaces of two interacting quantum systems, A and B.

apparatus. Conversely, $|a_0|^2$ corresponds to the probability the photon will have polarization "down" after measurement. The state of the composite system $A \otimes B$ can be obtained by taking the tensor product of the states of the individual photons:

$$|u\rangle \otimes |v\rangle = (a_0|0\rangle + a_1|1\rangle) \otimes (b_0|0\rangle + b_1|1\rangle) \tag{5.2}$$

$$= a_0b_0|00\rangle + a_1b_0|10\rangle + a_0b_1|01\rangle + a_1b_1|11\rangle, \tag{5.3}$$

where the new notation $|i\rangle \otimes |j\rangle = |ij\rangle$ is introduced as a shorthand. Observe how the state of this combined system is represented in a new, larger vector space with basis vectors $\{|00\rangle, |01\rangle, |10\rangle, |11\rangle\}$. These basis vectors, or "basis states," represent all possible measurement outcomes for the combined system. For example, the basis state $|11\rangle$ may represent the photon in system A and the photon in system B both being found with a polarization of "up." The scalars of the combined system are still related to probabilities, but now in a four-dimensional space: $|a_0b_0|^2 + |a_0b_1|^2 + |a_1b_0|^2 + |a_1b_1|^2 = 1$. Thus, the probability $|a_0b_0|^2$ now corresponds to the probability the state represented by Eq. (5.2) will give an outcome $|00\rangle$ (both photons in the system with polarization "down") upon measurement. The same approach can be followed to model concept combinations as composite systems (see Figure 5.3).

Recall that the word "bat" can be represented as a superposition between two senses "sport" ($|S\rangle$) and "animal" ($|A\rangle$), as depicted in Figure 5.1. The same can be said for the concept "boxer" (see Table 5.2 where, once again, the associates relevant to the sport sense of "boxer" are in bold), and the tensor product corresponding to Eq. (5.3) can be equivalently written in matrix form:

$$|\text{boxer}\rangle \otimes |\text{bat}\rangle \to \begin{array}{c} |A\rangle \\ |S\rangle \end{array} \begin{pmatrix} a_Ab_A & a_Abs \\ a_sb_A & a_sbs \end{pmatrix}. \tag{5.4}$$

Table 5.2 Free association probabilities for the word "boxer"

Associate	Probability
fighter	**0.14**
gloves	**0.14**
fight	**0.09**
dog	0.08
shorts	**0.07**
punch	**0.05**
Tyson	**0.05**
...	...

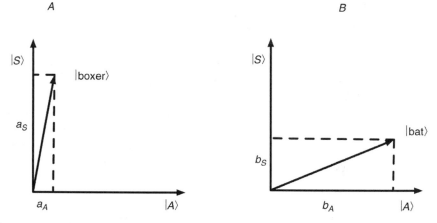

Figure 5.3 The separate state spaces of two interacting quantum systems, A (boxer) and B (bat).

This matrix representation is advantageous as it provides a simple way in which to understand non-compositional systems. If the state of a quantum system is factorizable, then the system is compositional in the sense it can be expressed as a product of states corresponding to the separate subsystems. A composite quantum system that is not factorizable is deemed *non-compositional*, and termed *entangled*.

By way of illustration, consider the state of the composite system corresponding to "boxer bat" to be $x|AS\rangle + y|SA\rangle$, where $x^2 + y^2 = 1$. Such a state could be represented similarly to Eq. (5.4), but now has the following form:

$$
\begin{array}{cc}
 & \begin{array}{cc} |A\rangle & |S\rangle \end{array} \\
\begin{array}{c} |A\rangle \\ |S\rangle \end{array} & \begin{pmatrix} 0 & x \\ y & 0 \end{pmatrix}
\end{array}. \tag{5.5}
$$

This state represents a situation where a human subject would respond with one of only two possible interpretations corresponding to the states $|AS\rangle$ and

$|SA\rangle$ with respective probabilities x^2 and y^2, such that $x^2 + y^2 = 1$. The state $|SA\rangle$ would represent a subject who attributes a sport sense to "boxer" and an animal sense to "bat," which corresponds to an interpretation like "a small furry black animal with boxing gloves on." The basis state $|AS\rangle$, on the other hand, represents an animal sense for "boxer" (i.e., a breed of dog) and a sport sense for "bat." In this case the interpretation could be a "toy bat for a boxer dog" or the more animal unfriendly "a bat to beat boxer dogs with." Ultimately, the human subject would settle on one of the two interpretations represented by either $|AS\rangle$ or $|SA\rangle$.

The state represented in Eq. (5.5) is non-compositional because it cannot be factorized into individual vectors $|\text{boxer}\rangle \in A$ and $|\text{bat}\rangle \in B$. The proof of this claim proceeds by way of contradiction and requires only some basic arithmetic. Assume (5.5) *is* factorizable into the required individual states. If so, they can be represented respectively as $|\text{boxer}\rangle = a_A|A\rangle + a_S|S\rangle \in A$ and $|\text{bat}\rangle = b_A|A\rangle + b_S|S\rangle \in B$ for arbitrary constants a_A, a_S, b_A, b_S such that the product has the form

$$|\text{boxer}\rangle \otimes |\text{bat}\rangle = a_A b_A|AA\rangle + a_A b_S|AS\rangle + a_S b_A|SA\rangle + a_S b_S|SS\rangle.$$

Note the combined state in Eq. (5.5) has the form

$$0|AA\rangle + x|AS\rangle + y|SA\rangle + 0|SS\rangle, \tag{5.6}$$

meaning that either ($a_A = 0$ or $b_A = 0$) and either ($a_S = 0$ or $b_S = 0$). The fact that $a_A b_S = x$ with $x > 0$ implies that $a_A > 0$ and $b_S > 0$. Similarly, $a_S b_A = y$ with $y > 0$ implies $a_S > 0$ and $b_A > 0$. If $a_A > 0$ then this must mean that $b_A = 0$ to realize a zero component for the basis state $|AA\rangle$; but this cannot be, because b_A must be greater than zero. Hence, no coefficients a_A, a_S, b_A, b_S can be found such that (5.6) is satisfied. ∎

Put simply, such a result means that if the concept combination "boxer bat" has a state that is represented by the form depicted in (5.5) then it cannot be factorized (decomposed) into two states, where one corresponds to "boxer" and the other to "bat."

There are other possibilities for motivating the basis states and using the tensor product to model the concept combination as a composite system. We saw previously that an object i has a graded membership $\mu_i(A)$ with respect to concept A. Blutner (2009) models A as a state $|A\rangle$ in a Hilbert space spanning orthogonal basis vectors $|i\rangle$ as a superposition of its weighted instances:

$$|A\rangle = \sum_{i \in A} \mu_i(A)|i\rangle.$$

Similarly, the concept B is modelled by the state $|B\rangle = \sum_{j \in B} \mu_j(B)|j\rangle$. This is very similar to the approach taken in this section, but where the basis states correspond to instances of a concept rather than senses.

The tensor product of the two states $|A\rangle, |B\rangle$ defines the space in which the concept combination AB will be modelled:

$$|A\rangle \otimes |B\rangle = \sum_{i \in A, j \in B} x_{ij}(|i\rangle \otimes |j\rangle), \tag{5.7}$$

which is more conveniently written as

$$|A\rangle \otimes |B\rangle = \sum_{i \in A, j \in B} x_{ij}(|ij\rangle), \tag{5.8}$$

In other words, the concept combination AB is modelled in a vector space of dimension $|A| \times |B|$ and with basis vectors $\{|ij\rangle | i \in A, j \in B\}$.

Blutner (2009) proposes to model the concept combination AB as an entangled state via a "diagonalization operation" Δ, the effect of which is to adjust the weights of the tensor product via a function $\delta(\cdot, \cdot)$:

$$\Delta(|A\rangle \otimes |B\rangle) = \sum_{i \in A, j \in B} \delta(i, j)x_{ij}(|ij\rangle). \tag{5.9}$$

As the resulting state $\psi = \Delta(|A\rangle \otimes |B\rangle)$ is entangled, the adjustment of the weights $\delta(i, j)$ in the tensor product is done in such a way that the state is not factorizable. In other words, the semantics of the concept combination AB are rendered non-compositional.

To illustrate the intended effect of entangled states of the form in Eq. (5.9), consider the concept combination "striped apple." Let i be an instance, and consider the following propositions:

P1 i is "striped"

P2 i is an "apple"

P3 i is a "striped apple."

Hampton (1997) argues this combination is problematic for intersective semantics because "striped" and "apple" are contradictory. Therefore, an apple that had stripes would be a better exemplar of a "striped apple" (P3) than either of the component propositions P1 and P2 simply because apples do not generally have stripes and striped objects are usually not apples. Thus, P3 should have a higher truth value than P1 or P2. This fact confounds the minimum rule seen earlier for modelling intersective semantics: $\mu_i(\text{striped and apple}) = \min(\mu_i(\text{striped}), \mu_i(\text{apple}))$. The effect of the weighting function δ realizes an entangled state that follows the required intuition (see Figure 5.4).

The Blutner (2009) model just described was influenced by another model motivated from a quantum-theoretic view of concepts called SCOP. The state–context–property (SCOP) model is historically the first quantum-like model of concepts which was developed to address the phenomenon of emergent properties with respect to concept combinations (Gabora & Aerts, 2002). SCOP is a

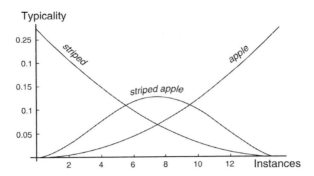

Figure 5.4 Weighting of instances with regard to the concepts "striped," "apple," and "striped apple" and the typicality function μ (from Blutner (2009)).

sophisticated model which has been developed and applied in a subsequent series of papers (Aerts & Gabora, 2005; Gabora *et al.*, 2008). We will not treat SCOP in all its detail, but instead provide a high-level overview of how SCOP models concept combinations, in particular with respect to compositional semantics.

In SCOP, concepts are viewed as category structures and instances of concepts are assumed to have a graded membership to a category. Concept combinations are then modelled using the tensor product as was shown earlier in Eq. (5.9). Instead of using a weighting function Δ to model the composition, SCOP uses projection operators which model how context affects the respective concepts A and B. In SCOP, each concept (e.g., "fish") is assumed to have a prototypical, or "ground," state. The ground state is formalized as a function μ which maps instances of the concept to a graded membership value. For example, in the ground state of "fish," μ(guppy) would be relatively low when compared with instances such as "herring," "goldfish," or "trout" (see Aerts and Gabora (2005: Table 3)). When "fish" is seen in context, e.g., $e =$ "The fish is a pet," then the graded membership μ(guppy) increases. The effect of context e on the state $|A\rangle$ modelling concept A is represented by the projector $\mathbf{P}_e^A$. Assuming $|A\rangle$ models the ground state of concept A and $|B\rangle$ models the ground state of concept B, context e is applied to a concept combination AB as follows:

$$\left(\mathbf{P}_e^A \otimes \mathbf{P}_e^B\right)\left(|A\rangle \otimes |B\rangle\right) = \left(\mathbf{P}_e^a|A\rangle \otimes \mathbf{P}_e^b|B\rangle\right).$$

The previous formula shows how the context affects the ground states of the individual concepts A and B. Note, however, that this state reflects a compositional semantics, as it is a product of two states both of which have been subjected to the influence of context via the projection operator. Aerts and Gabora (2005) conclude that such a product state models a set of specific intersective interpretations. For example, assume $e =$ "The fish is a pet" and the concept combination "pet fish." The product state $\mathbf{P}_e^{\text{pet}}|\text{pet}\rangle \otimes \mathbf{P}_e^{\text{fish}}|\text{fish}\rangle$ has the corresponding intuition: the pet being a fish and the fish being a pet. For example, one may interpret "pet" as a goldfish and "fish" as a "guppy." It is when the state of combination under the influence of context results in both "pet" and "fish" being interpreted as "guppy" that the semantics is non-compositional. This is because such behavior is typical of quantum entangled states, which, as we have seen, are not decomposable into states corresponding to the individual subsystems (see Eq. (5.5)). Aerts and Gabora (2005) provide an account of such entangled states using density matrices, but we will not deal with them here.

SCOP is a geometric model of conceptual semantics. Cognitive science features many models which are geometric in the sense words, or concepts, are represented as vectors. A significant number of these models are termed semantic space models. (The connection between these models and quantum theory is covered in Chapter 7.) The appeal of vector representations of concepts is their ability to represent meaning by using distributional information assuming words occurring within similar contexts are semantically similar. Despite their widespread use, vector-based models typically represent *individual* concepts, and methods for constructing representations of combinations of concepts have only begun to receive attention (Mitchell & Lapata, 2010). In addition, vector-based approaches have been developed in isolation to symbolically driven grammatical approaches to language. This divide has been bridged by using pregroups as a unification mechanism (Coecke *et al.*, 2010). Pregroups can be used to formalize the structure of natural language but also share a common structure with vector spaces and tensor products, when viewed from the perspective of category theory. The category theory used is an application of a categorical framework originally developed to reason about quantum phenomena. More specifically, the meaning of a word is represented by a vector in a vector space, the grammatical role is a type in a pregroup, and the tensor product of vector spaces paired with the pregroup composition is used for the composition of (meaning, type) pairs. This approach unifies the symbolic and vector-based approaches for natural language, and thus goes beyond the modelling of concept combinations. There are, however, a few points to be made with respect to the semantics of concept combinations. The first is the approach can be viewed as being largely compositional. However, consider a `subject-verb-object` structure. Coecke *et al.* (2010) argue the meaning of the verb will need to interact with the meaning of both the object and subject, so it cannot be decomposed into "three disconnected entities." This inability to decompose the structure is at odds with the principle of compositionality which, as stated at the beginning of this chapter, involves parts, and hence *decomposition* of the complex expression is assumed. In addition, viewing the subject, object, and verb as interacting is aligned with the model presented earlier in which concepts are modelled as interacting quantum systems. In both cases, tensor products are the formal mechanism to model the interactions.

5.4 Probabilistic approaches for analyzing the compositionality of concept combinations

Superposition states such as that represented in Eq. (5.2)–(5.5) are never directly observed in quantum experiments. What is observed corresponds to a

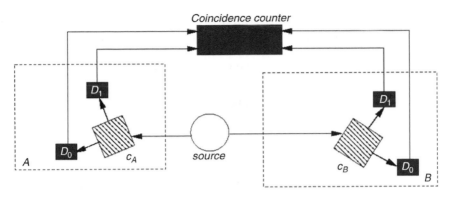

Figure 5.5 An experimental scenario testing for the non-decomposability of an entangled system of two polarized photons. A source emits two entangled photons that travel to polarizers at c_A and c_B. In each of the regions A and B, either detector D_0 (polarization is "down") or D_1 (polarization is "up") clicks, and this is recorded at a coincidence counter.

particular basis state which the system is deemed to have "collapsed" onto. As we saw in Chapter 2, quantum theory supplies the probability that the particular outcome will be observed. In addition, quantum theory provides a well-developed set of analytical tools that can be used to determine whether the state of a system of interest can be validly decomposed into separate subsystems. These will now be explored in relation to their applicability for determining the non-compositionality of concept combinations.

In a psychological experiment, a superposition is merely a word that can be interpreted using a number of different senses, while an entangled cognitive state is merely one which is highly biased toward one subset of interpretative senses. Finally, collapse is merely the process by which a subject decides upon a particular interpretation in the context of a set of cues and stimuli. Thus, when presented to a human subject, "boxer bat" elicits *one specific interpretation*, which is seen as an outcome of the experiment.

There is a substantial body of literature discussing the probabilistic basis upon which certain quantum systems can be considered as separable. (See, for example, (Dickson, 1998) for a good overview.) Probability theory must be used because, depending upon its experimental setting, a quantum system will give an outcome x_i from among a set of possibilities $\{x_1, x_2, \dots\}$, leading to a statistical result for an ensemble of similarly prepared systems. When two supposedly separate quantum systems A and B are each measured, they can sometimes yield a set of outcomes indicating a link between them which defies compositional analysis.

Of particular interest to our current argument is when two supposedly separate quantum systems A and B are each measured. For example, consider the scenario in Figure 5.5, which represents a case where photons, which are particles of light, are specially prepared in an entangled state and then allowed to separate, one photon flying off to region A and the other to region B. Photons have an observable property termed polarization, which can be measured using the analyzers positioned at c_A and c_B. Depending upon both the state that was prepared initially and the orientation of analyzers, this experiment will result in one of the detectors (D_0 or D_1) in region A recording that the photon was incident at it and one of those at region B making a similar observation. An entangled (i.e., non-decomposable) state will exhibit correlations between the two apparently separated photons. Indeed, if the state is entangled, then the joint probability distribution across A and B is *not* factorizable. However, the converse does not hold; if the joint probability distribution of a similar system is not factorizable then this does not imply that the state *must necessarily be* entangled. Even though Winsberg and Fine (2003) have suggested that a non-entangled quantum system *must have* a factorizable formalization, the less contentious converse view is that factorizability implies compositionality (Bruza *et al.*, 2011).

In what follows, the Cereceda (2000) analysis of composite quantum systems will be employed to an analysis of bi-ambiguous concept combinations. The term "bi-ambiguous" has been coined to reflect the fact that both concepts in the combination AB are homographs. For the purposes of the development to follow, each concept is assumed to have two senses. (Recall the "boxer bat" example discussed above). The senses of such a concept can be labeled as *dominant* or *subordinate*, because subjects usually exhibit a natural predisposition toward the recall of one sense. The distinction between the two can be inferred from free association norms such as those discussed above. For example, the dominance of the sport sense of "boxer" is clearly evident in Table 5.2. It should be noted, however, that the distinction between "dominant" and "subordinate" senses is not necessary for the theory presented below; rather, it is an aid to the explanation of the following analysis.

In quantum entanglement experiments, the data collected are frequently used to generate a set of joint probability distributions corresponding to different measurement settings. Thus, for the experiment depicted in Figure 5.5, the polarizers c_A and c_B are reoriented to a new combination of measurement settings for four different cases. Human subjects can be similarly reoriented through the use of priming. Thus, if a human subject is first shown the word "vampire" and subsequently asked to interpret the combination "boxer bat," then they may be biased toward interpreting the animal sense of "bat." Priming also allows for an experimental control of the general context in which concept combinations are presented. This is important because in the everyday world concept combinations appear in the context of other words, which affects how the concepts are ultimately interpreted.

As the concept combinations are bi-ambiguous, the interpretation of the combination AB can be described in terms of four dichotomous random variables, **A1**, **A2**, **B1**, **B2**, corresponding to priming conditions across the two senses. The numbers 1 and 2 correspond to the dominant and subordinate senses of the respective concepts A and B. These random variables range over the two values $\{+1, -1\}$. In quantum physics the value $+1$ corresponds to the photon having polarization "up" when measured by the polarizer, whereas the value -1 signifies a measurement outcome of polarization "down." This intuition carries across into the interpretation of concepts as follows: $\mathbf{A1} = +1$ means when the dominant sense of concept A was first primed, and concept A was indeed subsequently interpreted in its dominant sense by the human subject (spin "up"). Conversely, $\mathbf{A1} = -1$ means the dominant sense of concept A was primed but was not interpreted in its dominant sense (spin "down"). Similar relationships hold for $\mathbf{A2}$, $\mathbf{B1}$, and $\mathbf{B2}$.

Following Cereceda's analysis, there are 16 joint probabilities corresponding to interpretations of concepts A and B across the various priming conditions:

$$p_1 \equiv p(\mathbf{A1} = +1, \mathbf{B1} = +1), \qquad p_2 \equiv p(\mathbf{A1} = +1, \mathbf{B1} = -1)$$
$$p_3 \equiv p(\mathbf{A1} = -1, \mathbf{B1} = +1), \qquad p_4 \equiv p(\mathbf{A1} = -1, \mathbf{B1} = -1)$$
$$p_5 \equiv p(\mathbf{A1} = +1, \mathbf{B2} = +1), \qquad p_6 \equiv p(\mathbf{A1} = +1, \mathbf{B2} = -1)$$
$$p_7 \equiv p(\mathbf{A1} = -1, \mathbf{B2} = +1), \qquad p_8 \equiv p(\mathbf{A1} = -1, \mathbf{B2} = -1)$$
$$p_9 \equiv p(\mathbf{A2} = +1, \mathbf{B1} = +1), \qquad p_{10} \equiv p(\mathbf{A2} = +1, \mathbf{B1} = -1)$$
$$p_{11} \equiv p(\mathbf{A2} = -1, \mathbf{B1} = +1), \qquad p_{12} \equiv p(\mathbf{A2} = -1, \mathbf{B1} = -1)$$
$$p_{13} \equiv p(\mathbf{A2} = +1, \mathbf{B2} = +1), \qquad p_{14} \equiv p(\mathbf{A2} = +1, \mathbf{B2} = -1)$$
$$p_{15} \equiv p(\mathbf{A2} = -1, \mathbf{B2} = +1), \qquad p_{16} \equiv p(\mathbf{A2} = -1, \mathbf{B2} = -1)$$

These 16 probabilities can be considered in four blocks of four probabilities, each block corresponding to a particular polarizer setting, e.g., p_1, p_2, p_3, and p_4 together form the joint distribution for $p(\mathbf{A1}, \mathbf{B1}) = \{p(\mathbf{A1} = +1, \mathbf{B1} = +1), p(\mathbf{A1} = +1, \mathbf{B1} = -1), p(\mathbf{A1} = -1, \mathbf{B1} = +1), p(\mathbf{A1} = -1, \mathbf{B1} = -1)\}$. These 16 probabilities can be set out in the following array:

$$
A \quad
\begin{array}{cc}
 & \\
\mathbf{A1} \begin{array}{c} +1 \\ -1 \end{array} \\
\\
\mathbf{A2} \begin{array}{c} +1 \\ -1 \end{array}
\end{array}
\left(
\begin{array}{cc|cc}
p_1 & p_2 & p_5 & p_6 \\
p_3 & p_4 & p_7 & p_8 \\
\hline
p_9 & p_{10} & p_{13} & p_{14} \\
p_{11} & p_{12} & p_{15} & p_{16}
\end{array}
\right) = P_{AB}. \qquad (5.10)
$$

with column headers B: $\mathbf{B1}$ ($+1$, -1) and $\mathbf{B2}$ ($+1$, -1).

Observe how the matrix P_{AB} in Eq. (5.10) is complete, in that it covers all possible priming conditions across the respective senses of the concepts. In what follows, P_{AB} will be used as the basis for determining whether a concept combination is compositional or not.

5.4.1 Compositional semantics

The first case arises when the joint probability distribution across the random variables is factorizable. Historically, quantum theory investigated "hidden variable theories" in order to explain experimental results emerging from the probabilistic framework represented in the matrix of probabilities P_{AB}. For example,

Fine refers to the system of inequalities that must be satisfied as the Bell–Clauser–Horne inequalities, as these can be traced back to original work of the physicists Bell (1987) and Clauser and Horne (1974), but we will adhere to the more frequently used "Clauser–Horne" (CH) designation. Written out in full they have the following form:

$$-1 \leq p(A1, B1) + p(A1, B2) + p(A2, B2) - p(A2, B1) - p(A1) - p(B2) \leq 0 \tag{5.14}$$

$$-1 \leq p(A2, B1) + p(A2, B2) + p(A1, B2) - p(A1, B1) - p(A2) - p(B2) \leq 0 \tag{5.15}$$

$$-1 \leq p(A1, B2) + p(A1, B1) + p(A2, B1) - p(A2, B2) - p(A1) - p(B1) \leq 0 \tag{5.16}$$

$$-1 \leq p(A2, B2) + p(A2, B1) + p(A1, B1) - p(A1, B2) - p(A2) - p(B1) \leq 0. \tag{5.17}$$

These differ from the CHSH inequality in that prior probabilities $p(Ai)$ and $p(Bj)$ are required. ($p(Ai)$ is shorthand for $p(\mathbf{Ai} = +1)$.) In quantum entanglement experiments, one approach taken to determine such priors is to compute the ratio of "polarization up" observations at an analyzer to the total number of photons in the experiment (Clauser & Horne, 1974). For example, if there are n subjects, this equates to the ratio of the number of times subjects interpret a concept A or B in its dominant sense (s1), or subordinate sense (s2), with respect to n:

$$p(A1) = \frac{N(A = s1)}{n}, \tag{5.18}$$

$$p(A2) = \frac{N(A = s2)}{n}, \tag{5.19}$$

$$p(B1) = \frac{N(B = s1)}{n}, \tag{5.20}$$

$$p(B2) = \frac{N(A = s2)}{n}. \tag{5.21}$$

5.5 Empirical examples of the non-compositionality of concept combinations

The previous section has provided analytical means to analyze the compositionality of bi-ambiguous concept combinations. Three novel bi-ambiguous concept combinations will be used as examples: "boxer bat," "spring plant," and "ring pen." The following is a summary of experiments reported in Bruza et al. (2012).

Participants completed a web-based task in which they provided an interpretation for the bi-ambiguous concept combinations. The combinations were only seen once by each participant. Before being asked to interpret the concept combination, each participant was presented a priming word (e.g., "vampire") bat

			B2(ball)		**B1**(vampire)	
			+1	−1	+1	−1
	A2(dog)	+1	0	0.89	0.42	0.46
		−1	0	0.11	0	0.12
boxer						
	A1(fighter)	+1	0	0.67	0.61	0.30
		−1	0	0.13	0	0.09

Figure 5.6 "Boxer bat" $(n = 108)$.

which they were asked to classify as "natural" or "non-natural." The goal of the classification task was to activate the prime in memory. Two senses were primed for each concept in the combination, meaning there were four priming conditions. For example, in relation to the concept combination "boxer bat," "fighter" is used to prime the sport sense of "boxer" (denoted $A1$), "dog " is used to prime the animal sense of "boxer" (denoted $A2$), "ball" is used to prime the sport sense of "bat" (denoted $B1$) and "vampire" is used to prime the animal sense of "bat" (denoted $B2$). Participants were divided into four groups with each group being subjected to one of the four priming conditions. After priming, subjects were asked to interpret the concept combination; for example, "a furry black animal with boxing gloves on." After supplying their interpretation of the concept combination, participants were then asked to detail which sense they chose for each concept in the combination. For example, in relation to the concept "bat" the options were: (1) an animal, (2) a piece of sporting equipment, or (3) other (which the subjects was asked to explicitly specify). In order to allow a cleaner mapping to quantum theory, only data gathered under options 1 and 2 were considered.

5.5.1   Illustrations of the non-compositionality analysis

Figure 5.6 depicts the empirical results for "boxer bat" in a matrix form of 16 joint probabilities derived from the four priming conditions across the senses of each constituent concept. For example, $P(\mathbf{A1} = +1, \mathbf{B2} = -1)$ denotes the probability that "boxer" was interpreted in the sport sense when primed for that sense (via "fighter") and "bat" was not interpreted in the sport sense when primed for that sense (via "ball"). Observe how each of the primes is associated with a corresponding random variable. The CHSH inequality (5.12) is not violated ($\Delta = 1.95$, $n = 108$). Hence, "boxer bat" is deemed to be classically compositional.

5.5.1.1   "Spring plant"

Figure 5.7 depicts the empirical results for the bi-ambiguous concept combination "spring plant." In this case the CHSH inequality is not violated ($\Delta = 2$, $n = 136$), but is on the limit of holding. The concept combination "spring plant

			B2(factory)		B1(seed)	
			+1	−1	+1	−1
A2(coil)	+1		0.51	0	0.9	0
	−1		0	0.49	0	0.1
A1(summer)	+1		0.87	0	0.98	0
	−1		0	0.13	0	0.02

spring (row label, left of matrix)

Figure 5.7 "Spring plant" ($n = 136$).

pen

			B2(pig)		B1(ink)	
			+1	−1	+1	−1
A2(oval)	+1		0.49	0	0.69	0
	−1		0	0.51	0	0.31
A1(diamond)	+1		0.21	0	0.26	0
	−1		0.03	0.76	0.33	0.41

ring (row label, left of matrix)

Figure 5.8 "Ring pen" ($n = 132$).

plant" is therefore "classically compositional." Notice how the probability mass resides on the diagonals of the four component joint distributions. Positive diagonal values imply that when the concept "spring" is interpreted as a season, the concept "plant" is always interpreted as vegetation. Conversely, when the concept "spring" is interpreted as a coil, the concept "plant" is always interpreted as a "factory." In other words, the senses of the two words are maximally "classically" correlated.

5.5.1.2   "Ring pen"

Figure 5.8 depicts the the empirical results for the concept combination "ring pen." The CHSH inequality is violated for this concept combination ($\Delta = 2.61$, $n = 132$). This implies the concept combination "ring pen" has a non-classical non-compositional semantics.

It is revealing to examine why "ring pen" displays this behavior when "spring plant" does not. "Ring pen" shows a similar structure to "spring plant"; there is a strong correlation between the senses under priming, as seen by the probability mass concentrating on the diagonals. For example, when "ring" is interpreted in its shape sense, "pen" is interpreted as an enclosure; for example, "a round shaped enclosure for animals to be kept in." Conversely, when "ring" is interpreted as jewelry, "pen" is interpreted as some sort of a writing instrument; for example, "a miniature pen worn as a ring." The joint distribution in the bottom right quadrant is what crucially differentiates "ring pen" from the probabilistic signature of "spring plant." In this quadrant the interpretation of "ring" crosses over ($p_{15} = p(\mathbf{A1} = -1, \mathbf{B1} = +1) = 0.33$). This gives a significant probability on the reverse diagonal ($p_{14} + p_{15}$) which pushes the CHSH inequality above

2 (see Eq. 5.12). The crossover is due to "ring" being interpreted both as a "shape" and as "jewelry," while "pen" is interpreted as a writing instrument; for example " curly plastic novelty writing implement" in addition to "a miniature pen worn as a ring." This crossover does not happen with the perfectly correlated senses of "spring plant."

Detailed empirical studies on 12 concept bi-ambiguous combinations showed that most have non-classical non-compositional semantics (Bruza *et al.*, 2011).

5.5.2 Broader reflections on the analysis of non-compositionality using the CH and CHSH inequalities

We shall briefly reflect in this section about the scope and ramifications of the analysis methods when applied to concept combinations, and what they imply for the relationship between compositionality and factorization.

In quantum theory, violation of the CHSH inequality, or the CH system of inequalities, determines a strict dividing line between "classical" and "non-classical" compositionality. In formal terms, compositionality is expressed by a factorization of the joint probability distribution. Shimony (2009) details how the CHSH inequality can be constructed using two probabilistic assumptions, from which the factorization of the joint probability distribution can be derived. We will now provide the essential details of this derivation, as it provides a framework for the deeper exploration of the manner in which the factorization of a joint distribution relates to compositionality.

Let $\mathbf{A}$ and $\mathbf{B}$ be random variables ranging over $\{+1, -1\}$ and α_i, β_j, i, $j \in \{1, 2\}$, be a set of four primes (or measurement settings). In quantum theory, $\mathbf{A}$ and $\mathbf{B}$ denote outcomes at two separated sides of an experiment (see Figure 5.5) and α_i, β_j are analyzer settings. As was the case in the above analysis, $\mathbf{A} = +1$ means that concept A has been interpreted in its dominant sense and α_1 denotes the prime used to prime the dominant sense of concept A. When considering how a concept is interpreted, one could assume that only four elements are involved; thus, $p(\mathbf{A}|\alpha_i, \beta_j, \mathbf{B})$ would denote the probability of an interpretation of concept A given the primes α_i, β_j and some interpretation of B. Similarly, concept B has a probability of being interpreted given by $p(\mathbf{B}|\alpha_i, \beta_j, \mathbf{A})$. Now, with the help of the following two assumptions, Shimony (2009) derived a factorization condition.

1. An "outcome independence" (OI) assumption, which is taken to imply that the outcome at one wing of a quantum entanglement experiment is independent of the outcome at the other wing. In terms of concept combinations, OI is equivalent to stating that the interpretation of a concept is independent of how the other concept was interpreted:

$$p(\mathbf{A}|\alpha_i, \beta_j, \mathbf{B}) = p(\mathbf{A}|\alpha_i, \beta_j), \tag{5.22}$$

$$p(\mathbf{B}|\alpha_i, \beta_j, \mathbf{A}) = p(\mathbf{B}|\alpha_i, \beta_j). \tag{5.23}$$

2. A "parameter independence" (PI) assumption, which states that the analyzer settings are independent of each other. In terms of concept combinations, this assumption implies that the primes only affect their designated concept; for example, the primes α_i only affect concept A and the primes β_j only affect concept B:

$$p(\mathbf{A}|\alpha_i, \beta_j) = p(\mathbf{A}|\alpha_i), \tag{5.24}$$

$$p(\mathbf{B}|\alpha_i, \beta_j) = p(\mathbf{B}|\beta_j). \tag{5.25}$$

The analysis of quantum experiments is generally based upon a consideration of probability distributions of the form $p(\mathbf{A}, \mathbf{B}|\alpha_i, \beta_j)$, but it can be shown that OI and PI together generate a factorization of this distribution which greatly simplifies such an analysis:

$$p(\mathbf{A}, \mathbf{B}|\alpha_i, \beta_j) = \underbrace{p(\mathbf{A}|\alpha_i)}_{A}\underbrace{p(\mathbf{B}|\beta_j)}_{B}. \tag{5.26}$$

This factorization was originally formulated by Bell with the inclusion of a local hidden variable λ, which if known would allow the "decoupling" of A and B making them "locally explicable" (Bell, 1987):

$$p(\mathbf{A}, \mathbf{B}|\alpha_i, \beta_j, \lambda) = p(\mathbf{A}|\alpha_i, \lambda)p(\mathbf{B}|\beta_j, \lambda). \tag{5.27}$$

The notion of "locally explicable" can be understood as: (i) each system A and B possessing its own distinct state and (ii) the joint state of the two systems is wholly determined by these separate states (Winsberg & Fine, 2003). Clearly, this definition of "locally explicable" shows marked similarity to the principle of compositionality.

Violation of the CHSH inequality means that the decomposition expressed in Eq. (5.27) is not possible. This in turn raises the question of which assumptions, "outcome independence" (OI) and/or "parameter independence" (PI) have failed, a question which has been quite extensively debated in the quantum physics literature (Maudlin, 1994; Dickson, 1998: chapter 6). We will not enter this debate, but simply state that parameter independence is unlikely to hold for conceptual combination, whereas it is assumed to hold for the collapse interpretation of quantum theory (Bruza et al., 2012).

Regardless of the assumptions underpinning the factorization equation (5.27), violation of a CHSH or CH inequality is generally taken to imply that there is no hidden variable which can make such a factorization possible (Fine, 1982a; Griffiths, 2002) for a physical quantum system. However, it seems appropriate to ask whether the factorization expressed in (5.27) is the only one appropriate to concept combinations. This is where the result of Fine's theorem 3 (discussed in Section 5.4.3) becomes particularly important, as, unlike (5.27), its proof is not based on an assumption of factorizability. When the CH system of inequalities is violated a joint probability distribution across $\mathbf{A1}$, $\mathbf{A2}$, $\mathbf{B1}$, $\mathbf{A2}$ cannot be constructed, and the possibility of finding any factorization, however expressed, is ruled out. This is a powerful result.

We can further add to our understanding of compositionality by considering the manner in which the probabilistic methods developed in quantum theory have recently been applied in the analysis of a biased two-penny game (Iqbal & Abbot, 2009). The biased two-penny game is one in which players A and B each have two biased coins, similar to the way in which concepts A and B might be biased toward a particular set of interpretations (Bruza *et al.*, 2010). In contrast to the work presented here, which considered whether the joint probability distribution (5.11) or (5.27) was factorizable, quantum game approaches define compositionality in terms of whether the matrix of probabilities P_{AB} is factorizable. Thus, this approach would consider the concept combination AB as compositional if there exist column vectors P_A and P_B describing probability distributions modelling concepts A and B such that $P_A P_B^T = P_{AB}$, where there exists an r, r', s, s' such that

$$P_A^T = (r, (1 - r), r', (1 - r')) \qquad (5.28)$$
$$P_B^T = (s, (1 - s), s', (1 - s')), \qquad (5.29)$$

which implies that the concept combination can be modelled in terms of its constituent concepts A and B. If the rank of matrix P_{AB}, rank(P_{AB}) > 1, then this is a sufficient condition to rule out compositionality (Bruza *et al.*, 2010). However, such a result naturally suggests a new form of non-compositional behavior. In particular, when the the matrix P_{AB} is not compositional, but the CHSH inequality is not violated, then the concept combination could be deemed to be "pseudo-classically" non-compositional, a term which has emerged from quantum game theory. In such a situation, the game cannot be modelled with reference to its individual players A and B, but the game is not quantum-like entangled (since the CHSH value $|\Delta| \leq 2$). (When this analysis is applied to the concept combinations "boxer bat" and "spring plant" these exhibit "pseudo-classical" non-compositional semantics.)

Both the CHSH and CH inequalities can be employed for the analysis of the (non-)compositionality of concept combinations. We summarize the relative advantages of each analysis method. The CHSH inequality has the advantage of providing a useful explanatory technique, which can be used to understand (non-)compositional semantics as was illustrated in Section 5.5.1. In addition, the CHSH inequality has a maximal theoretical bound, which allows the degree of violation to be expressed in the absence of any method to determine whether a violation is significant or not. The CH inequalities provide a particularly strong non-compositionality result via Fine's theorems (Fine, 1982a, 1982b). In addition, the CH system of inequalities relies on prior probabilities which can be used to easily include data where the analyzer fails to make a detection. The analogue in concept combinations is when a subject attributes a sense to a concept that was not one according to the dominant or subordinate senses that were anticipated.

Finally, it is important to note that since the CHSH and CH inequalities are both based on conventional probability theory, it is non-controversial to apply them outside of quantum physics (Aerts *et al.*, 2000; Khrennikov, 2010).

In quantum physics, empirical violation of these inequalities has been used to prove that two particles are quantum entangled. In a series of papers, an analogous approach has been taken to prove, or at least argue, that concepts are quantum-like entangled in cognition (Aerts *et al.*, 2000, 2005; Gabora & Aerts, 2002; Aerts & Gabora, 2005; P. D. Bruza et al., 2009; Aerts & Sozzo, 2011). Another way to interpret such violations is in terms of the limits placed on the ability to model phenomena within a single probability distribution. We saw above via Fine's theorem that violation of the CH inequalities equates with the impossibility of the pairwise joint distributions to be constructed from a single probability distribution defined by the four random variables. Khrennikov (2010) describes such a situation as probabilistic incompatibility. Probabilistic compatibility means that it is possible to construct a joint probability distribution across the random variables. Khrennikov states that George Boole was the first to study probabilistic compatibility. Khrennikov (2010: footnote p. 26) further states the Russian mathematician Vorob'ev solved the general probability of probabilistic compatibility, but his results were ignored:

> The main problem of the classical probabilistic community was concentration on mathematical problems related to a single Kolmogorov space, especially various limit theorems. In such a situation, even the idea that something could not be embedded in such a space was not particularly welcome. Vorob'ev's works were not highly estimated by the Soviet probabilistic community (which was one of the strongest in the world) and, as a result, not by the international community either.

Rather than intriguing speculation about whether concepts are entangled, perhaps the real significance of quantum-like approaches to modelling concepts is raising the question of whether conceptual semantics, and language more generally, can be validly modelled in a single probability space – something which is currently taken as obviously being true.

6
An application of quantum theory to conjoint memory recognition

One of the goals of quantum cognition and decision is to explain findings that seem paradoxical from a classic probability point of view. This is important to justify the introduction of this new theory. So far we have used the theory to explain paradoxical findings from research on human probability judgments and conceptual combinations. These are both considered higher level cognitive functions that involve more complex reasoning. What about more primitive cognitive functions such as memory recognition? Do paradoxical findings with respect to classic probability theory occur in this basic area of cognition? If so, how can a quantum model help to explain these findings over and above current explanations? This chapter presents a new application of quantum theory to a puzzling phenomenon observed in human memory recognition called the episodic overdistribution (EOD) effect (Brainerd & Reyna, 2008). First we describe the phenomena and explain why it is a puzzle, and then we present a quantum solution to the puzzle and compare it with previous memory recognition models.

6.1 Episodic overdistribution effect

In the conjoint–recognition paradigm, participants are rehearsed on a single set T of memory targets (e.g., each member is a short description of an event). After a delay, a recognition test phase occurs, during which they are presented with a series of test probes that consist of trained targets from T, related non-targets from a different set R of distracting events (e.g., each member is a new event that has some meaningful relation to a target event), and an unrelated set U of non-target items (e.g., each member is completely unrelated to the targets). During the memory test phase, three different types of recognition instructions are employed: the first is a verbatim instruction (V) that requires one to accept or not accept only exact targets from T; the second is a gist instruction (G) that requires one to accept or not accept only related non-targets from R; the third is an instruction to accept verbatim or gist items $(V$ or $G)$–that is, it requires one to accept or not accept probes from either T or R. Hereafter, V represents the event "accept as a target from T," G represents the event "accept as a non-target from R" and V or G represents the event "accept as either a target from T or a related non-target from R." Note that $T \cap R = \varnothing$, and so logically V and G are supposed to be mutually exclusive events. Also, logically the event V or G should equal the event $V \cup G$, but this remains an empirical question.

First consider memory test trials that employ a test probe belonging to the target set T. If the verbatim question is asked, then the probability of accepting the target is formally defined by the conditional probability $p(V|T)$; if the gist question is asked, then the probability of accepting the target is formally defined by the probability $p(G|T)$; finally, if the verbatim or gist question is asked, then this is formally defined by the probability $p(V$ or $G|T)$. Logically, a probe x comes from T or G but not both, implying that $p(V$ or $G|T) = p(V|T) + p(G|T)$. The difference, $\text{EOD}(T) = p(V|T) + p(G|T) - p(V$ or $G|T)$ is an EOD effect. Brainerd and Reyna (2008) observed EOD effects obtained from 116 different experimental conditions, and 90% of the 116 studies produced a positive effect.

Next consider the memory test trials that employ a test probe belonging to the related set R. If the verbatim question is asked, then the probability of accepting the probe is formally defined by $p(V|R)$; if the gist question is asked, then the probability of accepting the probe is formally defined by $p(G|R)$; finally, if the verbatim or gist question is asked, then the probability of accepting the probe is formally defined by $p(V$ or $G|R)$. Once again, the test probe came from T or G but not both, implying that $p(V$ or $G|R) = p(V|R) + p(G|R)$. The EOD for related non-targets is defined by the difference $\text{EOD}(R) = p(V|R) + p(G|R) - p(V$ or $G|R)$. The observed EOD effects obtained from 165 different experimental conditions reported by Brainerd and Reyna (2008) revealed 90% of 165 studies produced a positive effect.

There are some other interesting and important facts reported in Brainerd and Reyna (2008). First, the EOD effect is often larger than $p(V$ or $G)$ when the latter is small in size; for example the largest positive $\text{EOD} = 0.40$ occurred when $p(V$ or $G) = 0.20$. Second, the EOD is usually positive, but 10% actually produce negative EOD effects and occasionally the negative effects are quite large (e.g., $\text{EOD} = -0.20$). Third, the sum of the probability for the verbatim plus the probability for the gist is greater than one for 17% of the conditions when the probe came from a target T, and for 7% of the conditions when the probe came from a related non-target R.

Table 6.1 contains the means from six experimental conditions reported in an earlier article (Brainerd et al., 1999), which will be used to evaluate the fit of the quantum model. The rows labeled Obs contain the real data and rows labeled Pred contain the predictions of the quantum model described later. There are nine columns of data. The columns labeled V|T, G|T, and B|T contain the probabilities for the verbatim, gist, both (verbatim or gist) questions when the probe came from the studied target list T, the columns labeled V|R, G|R, B|R contain probabilities for the verbatim, gist, both (verbatim or gist) questions when the probe came from list R, and the columns labeled V|U, G|U, B|U contain probabilities for the verbatim, gist, both (verbatim or gist) questions

Table 6.1 Quantum model fit to Brainerd *et al.* (1999) results[a]

Cond	Source	$V\|T$	$G\|T$	$B\|T$	$V\|R$	$G\|R$	$B\|R$	$V\|U$	$G\|U$	$B\|U$
1	Obs	0.52	0.16	0.60	0.40	0.56	0.68	0.10	0.24	0.32
1	Pred	0.52	0.16	0.62	0.36	0.56	0.58	0.10	0.24	0.28
2	Obs	0.74	0.09	0.82	0.28	0.67	0.65	0.06	0.18	0.28
2	Pred	0.74	0.11	0.86	0.32	0.67	0.71	0.03	0.18	0.30
3	Obs	0.63	0.13	0.76	0.37	0.72	0.77	0.10	0.23	0.34
3	Pred	0.63	0.14	0.78	0.38	0.72	0.77	0.07	0.23	0.35
4	Obs	0.79	0.12	0.84	0.18	0.70	0.77	0.11	0.22	0.30
4	Pred	0.79	0.15	0.90	0.24	0.70	0.78	0.06	0.22	0.43
5	Obs	0.74	0.13	0.82	0.15	0.64	0.71	0.20	0.23	0.32
5	Pred	0.74	0.16	0.87	0.22	0.64	0.75	0.10	0.23	0.46
6	Obs	0.79	0.12	0.83	0.52	0.68	0.70	0.20	0.24	0.34
6	Pred	0.79	0.14	0.88	0.57	0.68	0.68	0.15	0.24	0.25
Avg	Obs	0.70	0.13	0.78	0.32	0.66	0.71	0.13	0.22	0.32
Avg	Q Pred	0.70	0.16	0.83	0.35	0.66	0.71	0.07	0.22	0.33
Avg	Q Err	0	0.02	0.04	0.05	0	0.04	0.04	0	0.07
Avg	CM Err	0	0	0	0	0.45	0.21	0	0.06	0.06
Avg	DP Err	0.02	0	0.01	0	0.02	0.02	0	0	0

[a]Note: the response probabilities for probes taken from set U are actually predictions from the dual process model.

Table 6.2 Mean EOD

Source	T	R	U
Obs	0.048	0.265	0.035
Q Pred	0.028	0.297	−0.036

when the probe came from list U.[1] The last pair of rows were obtained by averaging across the six experimental conditions.

The mean EOD effect averaged across these six conditions is shown in Table 6.2. The column labeled V shows the average EOD when the probe was a target from T, the column labeled R contains the average EOD when the probe was a related non-target from R, and the column labeled U shows the results for probes taken from unrelated non-targets in U.

6.2   Classic probability

Let us first examine these results from a classic probability theory perspective. Suppose we assume that V is the event "accept probe under V instructions,"

---

[1]Brainerd *et al.* (1999) did not report the probabilities for responses to probes from set U. Instead, they reported the predictions from the response bias estimates. Consequently, we are using the predictions instead of the real data for these probabilities for probes from set U.

G is an event "accept probe under G instructions," V or G is an event "accept probe under V or G instructions," and also assume that the latter equals the union of these two events so that V or $G = V \cup G$. We will denote the type of probe by $x \in \{T, R, U\}$ so that, for example, $p(V$ or $G|x)$ represents the probability of accepting a probe as verbatim or gist given the probe actually came from population x. Then according to classic probability theory, $p(V$ or $G|x) = p(V \cup G|x) = p(V|x) + p(G|x) - p(V \cap G|x)$ and EOD $= p(V|x) + p(G|x) - p(V \cup G|x) = p(V \cap G|x)$. So the EOD measures the joint probability that the probe says yes it is from T and yes it is from R. But according to the experimenter's instruction, the categories V,G are mutually exclusive and so logically $p(V \cap G|x) = 0 =$ EOD. Then, either the participants are not following the instructions or they are not following classic probability theory.

Suppose we assume that participants are not following instructions but they are obeying classic probability theory. Then, first of all, classic probability theory requires $0 \leq p(V \cap G|x) =$ EOD, and we should never observe negative EOD effects. Yet negative effects do occur for 10% of the conditions reviewed in Brainerd and Reyna (2008), and sometimes they are as negative as -0.20. For example, in Table 6.1, a negative EOD effect occurred for probes taken from the non-related non-target distribution U for conditions 2 and 3, although they are small in size. Second, classic probability theory requires $p(V \cap G|x) =$ EOD $\leq p(V \cup G|x) = p(V$ or $G|x)$, and we should never obtain EOD effects that exceed the probability of agreeing to G or V. However, Brainerd and Reyna (2008) found that the EOD often exceeded $p(V$ or $G|x)$ when the latter was relatively small in size.

If we try to fit the classic model to data in Table 6.2, then we would simply set $p(V \cup G|x) = p(V|x) + p(G|x) -$ EOD. This would work in all cases except for conditions 2 and 3 for the unrelated non-target probe, for in these two cases the EOD is negative.

6.2.1   Classic probability model with Markov constraint

Alternatively, we could try to fit a realistic but slightly more restricted version of the classic probability model that also incorporates a Markov constraint. For probes taken from the target set T, we simply set

$$p(V|T) = p(V|T)$$
$$p(G|T) = p(V|T) \cdot p(G|V) + p(\bar{V}|T) \cdot p(G|\bar{V})$$
$$p(V \text{ or } G|T) = p(V|T) + p(\bar{V}|T) \cdot p(G|\bar{V}).$$

This part perfectly fits three parameters $\{p(V|T), p(G|V), p(G|\bar{V})\}$ to three data points. Next consider the model for probes from related non-targets from set R:

$$p(V|R) = p(V|R)$$
$$p(G|R) = p(V|R) \cdot p(G|V) + p(\bar{V}|R) \cdot p(G|\bar{V})$$
$$p(V \text{ or } G|T) = p(V|R) + p(\bar{V}|R) \cdot p(G|\bar{V}).$$

This second part of the model perfectly fits the first data point, but it must predict the next two reusing the two conditional probabilities $\{p(G|V), p(G|\bar{V})\}$ estimated from the set T. Finally, consider the model for the unrelated non-targets in U:

$$p(V|U) = p(V|U)$$
$$p(G|U) = p(V|U) \cdot p(G|V) + p(\bar{V}|U) \cdot p(G|\bar{V})$$
$$p(V \text{ or } G|T) = p(V|U) + p(\bar{V}|U) \cdot p(G|\bar{V}).$$

This third part of the model introduces only one new parameter $p(V|U)$ and it must predict the next two data points.

This model produces the mean absolute prediction errors shown in Table 6.1 in the row labeled CM Err. As we can see in the table, this model makes terrible predictions for the "gist" and for the "verbatim or gist" questions under the related non-target condition for set R, and so it has to be rejected.[2]

In sum, a classic probability model cannot explain positive EOD effects if we assume participants obey instructions. Even if participants are not obeying instructions, it cannot explain the occasional negative EOD effects that occur, and it cannot explain EOD effects that exceed $p(V \text{ or } G|x)$ which occur when the latter is small. Also, if we impose a Markov constraint on the model, it does an extremely poor job of predicting the data that are not used as model parameters.

6.3 Cognitive models

Two cognitive models are applicable to this paradigm. One is the signal detection model (Rotello *et al.*, 2004) and the other is the dual process model (Jacoby, 1991). We consider the signal detection model first.

6.3.1 Signal detection model

Figure 6.1 illustrates the basic idea. Suppose the probe is described by two features: one is its strength on a gist dimension and another is its strength on a verbatim dimension. When a probe of type x is presented, it produces a sample point X in this two-dimensional space. The probe is assigned to one of three categories depending on whether it falls into one of three subsets. The

---

[2]If we use the probabilities from the related non-target probes in set R to derive the conditional probabilities for $p(V|G)$ and $p(V|\bar{G})$ and we use these conditionals to make predictions, then the prediction errors are much larger for the "verbatim" question.

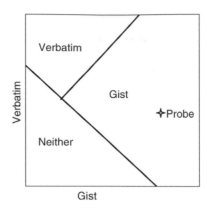

Figure 6.1 Two-dimensional signal-detection model. The vertical dimension represents the verbatim feature and the horizontal dimension represents the gist feature. The lines indicate category bounds. The star is a probe in the gist category.

two-dimensional space is assumed to be partitioned into three mutually exclusive and exhaustive subsets: one subset, C_V, is used to categorize the probe as a verbatim item, a second subset C_G is used to categorize the probe as a gist item, and a third subset C_U is used to categorize the probe as neither of these two. According to this model, $p(V \text{ or } G|x) = p(X \in C_V \cup X \in C_G|x) = p(X \in C_V|x) + p(X \in C_G|x)$. If we further assume that the category boundaries for categorizing probes do not change across instructions so that $p(X \in C_V) = p(V|x)$ and $p(X \in C_G) = p(G|x)$, then this model is the same as the classic probability model that assumes participants follow instructions, and it predicts zero EOD effects. To explain EOD effects we would need to allow the category boundaries to change across instructions – we would need three different versions of Figure 6.1 with one category overlapping another across figures. But then all the explanation for the results depends on these arbitrary changes in the category bounds across instructions, and this does not leave any degrees of freedom for testing the model with the conjoint memory recognition data.

6.3.2 Dual process model

The dual process model was modified and extended by Brainerd *et al.* (1999) for the conjoint memory recognition paradigm. First we consider the original idea underlying the dual process model, and then we add extra assumptions for response bias.

6.3.3 Original model

Let us first consider the model for the case when the probe is a target from set T. The model for the recognition process is a simple Markov model as illustrated

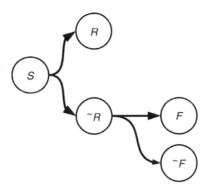

Figure 6.2 Dual process model for a probe from the target set T. From the start, the state can transit to recollect (p_T) or not; if the probe is not recollected, the state can transit to familiar (q_T) or not. Under verbatim instructions, the probe is accepted if recollected or familiar.

in Figure 6.2. From the initial state S in the figure, the process can transit to a recollect state labeled R with probability p_T, and with probability $1 - p_T$ it moves to the not recollect state labeled $\tilde{R}$ in the figure. From the not recollect state the process can move to the familiar state labeled F with probability q_T or move to the not familiar state labeled $\tilde{F}$ with probability $1 - q_T$. For the verbatim instructions, the probe is accepted if it enters state R or if it enters state F. For the gist instructions, the probe is accepted only in state F. For the verbatim or gist instruction, the probe is accepted in state R or state F. From this Markov process, we can derive the following probabilities of accepting a probe from T:

$$p(V|T) = p_T + (1 - p_T) \cdot q_T$$

$$p(G|T) = (1 - p_T) \cdot q_T$$

$$p(V \text{ or } G|T) = p_T + (1 - p_T) \cdot q_T.$$

The same process is used for probes taken from the related non-target set R, but the transition probabilities change, so that we obtain the equations

$$p(V|R) = p_R + (1 - p_R) \cdot q_R$$

$$p(G|R) = (1 - p_R) \cdot p_R$$

$$p(V \text{ or } G|R) = p_R + (1 - p_R) \cdot q_R.$$

This original version of the dual process model predicts EOD because for $x \in \{T, R\}$:

$$\text{EOD}(T) = \Pr(V|x) + \Pr(G|x) - \Pr(V \text{ or } G|x)$$

$$= (1 - p_x) \cdot q_x.$$

This dual process model also violates classic probability theory because it implies that $p(V|x) = p(V$ or $G|x)$, but according to classic probability $p(V|x) \leq p(V \cup G|x)$ and the inequality must be strict in this case. Empirically, it is the case that $p(V|x) < p(V$ or $G|x)$ as can be seen for all the cases in Table 6.1. So this needs to be fixed.

6.3.4   Bias model

The model is fixed by adding a new guessing state to the model with a bias factor. If the process does not recollect the probe and the probe is not familiar, then there is a probability of entering a guess state that accepts the probe anyway. The probability of entering the guess state depends on the instructions. When this guess state is included in the model, the equations are changed as follows for probes of type $x \in \{T, R\}$:

$$p(V|x) = p_x + (1 - p_x) \cdot q_x + b_V \cdot (1 - p_x)(1 - q_x),$$

$$p(G|x) = (1 - p_x) \cdot p_x + b_G \cdot (1 - p_x)(1 - q_x),$$

$$p(V \text{ or } G|x) = p_x + (1 - p_x) \cdot q_x + b_{VG} \cdot (1 - p_x)(1 - q_x).$$

For non-related non-targets from U, the recognition process never enters the recollection or familiar state, and it is simply assumed that the probabilities are generated from probabilities of entering the guessing state:

$$p(V|U) = b_V$$

$$p(G|U) = b_G$$

$$p(V \text{ or } G|U) = b_{VG}.$$

Altogether this model has seven free parameters $\{p_T, q_T, p_R, q_R, b_V, b_G, b_{VG}\}$ which are used to explain nine data points (each row with nine columns in Table 6.1) which leaves two degrees of freedom for testing the model. When the model is fit to the data, the chi-square tests for significant violations are not statistically significant, indicating a close fit. The predictions from the dual process model are not shown here but they are presented in Brainerd et $al.$ (1999: Table 6.2). The mean absolute prediction errors for each condition, averaged across the six studies, are shown in Table 6.1 in the row labeled DP Err. As can be seen, the prediction errors are very small. (They must be zero for the unrelated non-targets because the "data" used in this table for these conditions are actually the predictions themselves. The article did not report the real data points.)

This seems to be a questionable way to predict differences between the V instructions versus the V or G instructions – by the response bias alone. In order to produce higher probabilities for V or G compared with V instructions, the model requires $b_{VG} > b_V$. Furthermore, the only way that the dual process model can produce negative EOD effects is also by the bias terms. In conclusion, the bias terms are needed to do a lot of the explaining in this model, but the

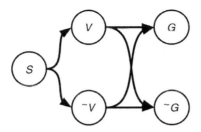

Figure 6.3 Quantum model for probes from the target set T. Starting from state S, the process can travel though states V or not V to arrive at states G or not G.

bias parameters are simply free parameters. This is a serious problem for the dual process model.

6.4 Path diagram quantum model

Here we consider a very simple path diagram quantum model for the conjoint recognition paradigm. We could use the geometric approach to describe this model, as we did in the previous two chapters. But instead, in this chapter, we will use a path diagram description. The two give equivalent results, but in this case it is easier to work with a simple path diagram.

6.4.1 Analysis of probes from trained targets

The basic idea is illustrated in Figure 6.3. Consider the condition when the probe is selected from a target set T. Under this condition we assume verbatim information is available first and is processed before gist. The person can transit directly from state S in the figure to state V, or the person can also pass through states V or $\tilde{V}$ in the figure to reach state G.

6.4.1.1 Probability of accepting a probe from T as verbatim

The start state $|S_T\rangle$ (labeled S in the figure) depends on the fact that the probe came from set T. From this state, the person can transit directly to the verbatim state $|V\rangle$ (labeled V in the figure) with amplitude $\langle V|S_T\rangle$. Then the probability of accepting the probe from T under the verbatim instruction simply equals $p(V|T) = |\langle V|S_T\rangle|^2$ and the probability of not accepting the probe equals $1- |\langle V|S_T\rangle|^2$.

6.4.1.2 Probability of accepting a probe from T as gist

Under the gist instruction, the probability of starting at state $|S_T\rangle$ and ending at state $|G\rangle$ simply equals $|\langle G|S_T\rangle|^2$ and the probability of not accepting it as gist equals $1 - |\langle G|S_T\rangle|^2$. However, for our model analysis, we need to decompose this in terms of the paths shown in Figure 6.3. There are two paths starting from state $|S_T\rangle$ and ending at state $|G\rangle$ to consider. One path is to transit from $|S_T\rangle \to |V\rangle$ with amplitude $\langle V|S_T\rangle$ and then transit from $|V\rangle \to |G\rangle$ with path amplitude $\langle G|V\rangle$, which produces a path amplitude equal to the product $\langle G|V\rangle\langle V|S_T\rangle$. The other path is $|S_T\rangle \to |\bar{V}\rangle \to |G\rangle$, which has a path amplitude equal to $\langle G|\bar{V}\rangle\langle \bar{V}|S_T\rangle$. The person is only asked to answer the gist question, and so the two verbatim states (accept or reject) do not need to be resolved for this question. That is, the person does not have to decide whether verbatim or not is true to answer the gist question. Therefore, the amplitude for the two indeterminate paths to make the transition $|S_T\rangle \to |G\rangle$ follows the law of total amplitude,

$$\langle G|S_T\rangle = \langle G|V\rangle\langle V|S_T\rangle + \langle G|\bar{V}\rangle\langle \bar{V}|S_T\rangle,$$

and the probability of accepting the probe from T as gist equals

$$\left|\langle G|S_T\rangle\right|^2 = \left|\langle G|V\rangle\langle V|S_T\rangle + \langle G|\bar{V}\rangle\langle \bar{V}|S_T\rangle\right|^2.$$

6.4.1.3   Probability of accepting a probe from T as verbatim or gist

Now consider the probability for the $V\,\text{or}\,G$ question when the probe is taken from set T. To answer the $V\,\text{or}\,G$ question, the person first needs to resolve whether or not the probe is verbatim and then whether or not the probe is gist. The probability of accepting under the $V\,\text{or}\,G$ question equals the probability of accepting the probe as verbatim plus the probability that it is not accepted as verbatim but it is accepted as gist, $p(V\,\text{or}\,G|T) = p(V|T) + p(\bar{V}|T) \cdot p(G|\bar{V})$. We already determine that $p(V|T) = |\langle V|S_T\rangle|^2$ and the amplitude for the transition from $|\bar{V}\rangle \to |G\rangle$ equals $\langle G|\bar{V}\rangle$, and so the probability of this transition equals $p(G|\bar{V}) = |\langle G|\bar{V}\rangle|^2$.

In summary, we have the following three equations for each question when probes are taken from the target set T:

$$p(V|T) = \left|\langle V|S_T\rangle\right|^2, \tag{6.1}$$

$$p(G|T) = \left|\langle G|V\rangle\langle V|S_T\rangle + \langle G|\bar{V}\rangle\langle \bar{V}|S_T\rangle\right|^2,$$

$$p(V\,\text{or}\,G|T) = \left|\langle V|S_T\rangle\right|^2 + \left|\langle \bar{V}|S_T\rangle\right|^2 \cdot \left|\langle G|\bar{V}\rangle\right|^2$$

$$= 1 - \left|\langle \bar{G}|\bar{V}\rangle\langle \bar{V}|S_T\rangle\right|^2.$$

Using the observed data, we can set $\langle V|S_T\rangle = \sqrt{p(V|T)}$ and $\langle \bar{V}|S_T\rangle = \sqrt{p(\bar{V}|T)}$. But we cannot observe $\langle G|V\rangle$ or $\langle G|\bar{V}\rangle$ in this particular paradigm, and so we need to determine these two transition amplitudes somehow. We will do this later, after we have finished the rest of the model equations.

6.4.2   Analysis of probes from non-targets

Now we consider the condition when the probe is selected from a non-target set, either R or U. Under these conditions, we assume that gist information is

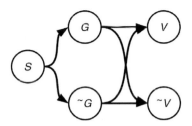

Figure 6.4 Quantum model for probe from a non-target set. Gist is processed before verbatim.

available first and is processed before verbatim. The basic idea is illustrated in Figure 6.4. Accordingly, the person can transit directly from state S in the figure to state G. The person can also pass through states G or $\tilde{G}$ in the figure to reach state V.

6.4.2.1 Probability of accepting a probe from set R

When the probe is selected from set R, the initial state $|S_R\rangle$ is determined by the properties of this set. Now we follow the same principles used earlier to derive the choice probabilities, except that we assume gist is processed before verbatim. This leads to the following set of equations for the three types of questions:

$$p(G|R) = |\langle G|S_R\rangle|^2, \tag{6.2}$$
$$p(V|R) = |\langle V|G\rangle\langle G|S_R\rangle + \langle V|\bar{G}\rangle\langle \bar{G}|S_R\rangle|^2,$$
$$p(V\,\text{or}\,G|R) = |\langle G|S_R\rangle|^2 + |\langle \bar{G}|S_R\rangle|^2 \cdot |\langle V|\bar{G}\rangle|^2$$
$$= 1 - |\langle \bar{V}|\bar{G}\rangle\langle \bar{G}|S_R\rangle|^2.$$

We can set $\langle G|S_R\rangle = \sqrt{p(G|R)}$ and $\langle \bar{G}|S_R\rangle = \sqrt{p(\bar{G}|R)}$. However, we still need to determine $\langle V|\bar{G}\rangle$ and $\langle V|G\rangle$, which will be done after we consider the equations for probes from the unrelated non-targets from set U.

6.4.2.2 Probability of accepting a probe from set U

When the probe is selected from set U, the initial state $|S_U\rangle$ is determined by the properties of this set. Once again, we follow the same principles used earlier to derive the choice probabilities, assuming that gist is processed before verbatim. This leads to the following set of equations for the three types of questions:

$$p(G|U) = |\langle G|S_U\rangle|^2,$$
$$p(V|U) = |\langle V|G\rangle\langle G|S_U\rangle + \langle V|\bar{G}\rangle\langle \bar{G}|S_U\rangle|^2,$$
$$p(V\,\text{or}\,G|U) = |\langle G|S_U\rangle|^2 + |\langle \bar{G}|S_U\rangle|^2 \cdot |\langle V|\bar{G}\rangle|^2.$$
$$= 1 - |\langle \bar{V}|\bar{G}\rangle\langle \bar{G}|S_U\rangle|^2.$$

Once again we can set $\langle G|S_U \rangle = \sqrt{p(G|U)}$ and $\langle \bar{G}|S_U \rangle = \sqrt{p(\bar{G}|R)}$, but once again we need to determine the amplitudes for the transitions $\langle V|G \rangle$ and $\langle V|\bar{G} \rangle$.

6.4.3 Unitary transformation matrices

At this point, we need to determine both of the 2×2 unitary transition matrices shown in Figures 6.3 and 6.4, which determine the transitions from the pair of $\{|V\rangle, |\bar{V}\rangle\}$ pair of states to the pair of $\{|\bar{G}\rangle, |G\rangle\}$ pair of states (for Figure 6.3), and also in the opposite direction (for Figure 6.4):

$$U_{GV} = \begin{bmatrix} \langle G|V \rangle & \langle G|\bar{V} \rangle \\ \langle \bar{G}|V \rangle & \langle \bar{G}|\bar{V} \rangle \end{bmatrix}, \ U_{VG} = \begin{bmatrix} \langle V|G \rangle & \langle V|\bar{G} \rangle \\ \langle \bar{V}|G \rangle & \langle \bar{V}|\bar{G} \rangle \end{bmatrix}.$$

Recall that a unitary matrix must be orthonormal – the rows and columns must have length one, the columns must be orthogonal to each other, and the rows must be orthogonal to each other.[3] For example, $U_{GV} \cdot U_{GV}^{\dagger} = I$, which implies that U_{GV} must satisfy the constraints $|\langle G|V \rangle|^2 + |\langle \bar{G}|V \rangle|^2 = 1$, $|\langle G|\bar{V} \rangle|^2 + |\langle \bar{G}|\bar{V} \rangle|^2 = 1$, $|\langle G|V \rangle|^2 + |\langle G|\bar{V} \rangle|^2 = 1$, $|\langle \bar{G}|V \rangle|^2 + |\langle \bar{G}|\bar{V} \rangle|^2 = 1$, as well as $\langle G|V \rangle^* \cdot \langle G|\bar{V} \rangle - \langle \bar{G}|V \rangle^* \cdot \langle \bar{G}|\bar{V} \rangle = 0$ and $\langle G|V \rangle \cdot \langle \bar{G}|V \rangle^* - \langle G|\bar{V} \rangle \cdot \langle \bar{G}|\bar{V} \rangle^* = 0$. The upshot is that only a single transition amplitude is needed to construct each matrix. In particular, to determine U_{GV}, we estimate $\langle G|\bar{V} \rangle$ as a free parameter and set $\langle G|V \rangle = \sqrt{1 - |\langle G|\bar{V} \rangle|^2} = \langle \bar{G}|\bar{V} \rangle$ and $\langle \bar{G}|V \rangle = -\langle G|\bar{V} \rangle^*$. However, the transition amplitude $\langle G|\bar{V} \rangle$ is a complex number, and so let us express it as $\langle G|\bar{V} \rangle = |\langle G|\bar{V} \rangle| \cdot e^{i\theta}$. Then this single amplitude produces two free parameters. The same procedure can be done for the matrix U_{VG}.

6.4.4 State representation

One important remaining question concerns the relations between the two unitary matrices U_{GV} and U_{VG}. The answer depends on the dimension of the state space that we assume. There are two simple choices.

One is to assume that the states in Figure 6.3 are the same as the states in Figure 6.4. Then we are postulating a two-dimensional quantum model with the initial state represented by

$$|S\rangle = |V\rangle\langle V|S\rangle + |\bar{V}\rangle\langle \bar{V}|S\rangle = |G\rangle\langle G|S\rangle + |\bar{G}\rangle\langle \bar{G}|S\rangle,$$

and this holds for all probes including both target and non-target probes. Under this assumption, the law of reciprocity applies so that $U_{VG} = U_{GV}^{\dagger}$ and so we only need one transition amplitude to determine both unitary matrices. We could choose $\langle G|\bar{V} \rangle = |\langle G|\bar{V} \rangle| \cdot e^{i\theta}$ to construct U_{GV} and then set $\langle V|\bar{G} \rangle =$

---

[3]This is necessary if we want the path diagram model to be consistent with a geometric model. These constraints also imply that the transition matrix is doubly stochastic. However, it is not absolutely necessary to make the amplitude model agree with the geometric model (Khrennikov, 2010).

$\langle G|\bar{V}\rangle^* = |\langle G|\bar{V}\rangle| \cdot e^{-i\theta}$ to construct U_{VG}. This makes a very nice and simple model; we tried this, but it fits the unrelated non-target data very poorly. So we have to reject this simple model.

A second assumption is that the states in Figure 6.3 are not the same as the states in Figure 6.4, and instead they form a four-dimensional model with the initial state represented by

$$|S\rangle = |V_T\rangle\langle V_T|S\rangle + |\bar{V}_T\rangle\langle \bar{V}_T|S\rangle + |V_N\rangle\langle V_N|S\rangle + |\bar{V}_N\rangle\langle \bar{V}_N|S\rangle$$
$$= |G_T\rangle\langle G_T|S\rangle + |\bar{G}_T\rangle\langle \bar{G}_T|S\rangle + |G_N\rangle\langle G_N|S\rangle + |\bar{G}_N\rangle\langle \bar{G}_N|S\rangle.$$

The state $|V_T\rangle$ represents accepting a target as verbatim, $|\bar{V}_T\rangle$ represents rejecting a target as verbatim, $|V_N\rangle$ represents accepting a non-target as verbatim, and $|\bar{V}_N\rangle$ represents rejecting a non-target as verbatim. The state $|G_T\rangle$ represents accepting a target as gist, $|\bar{G}_T\rangle$ represents rejecting a target as gist, $|G_N\rangle$ represents accepting a non-target as gist, and $|\bar{G}_N\rangle$ represents rejecting a non-target as gist.

When the probe is from the target set T we impose the constraint $\langle V_N|S_T\rangle = \langle \bar{V}_N|S_T\rangle = 0$ and when the probe is from a non-target set we impose the constraint $\langle G_T|S_N\rangle = \langle \bar{G}_T|S_N\rangle = 0$, and the complete transition matrix for the entire 4×4 space is described by

$$U = \begin{bmatrix} U_{GV} & 0 \\ 0 & U_{VG}^\dagger \end{bmatrix} = \begin{bmatrix} \langle G_T|V_T\rangle & \langle G_T|\bar{V}_T\rangle & 0 & 0 \\ \langle \bar{G}_T|V_T\rangle & \langle \bar{G}_T|\bar{V}_T\rangle & 0 & 0 \\ 0 & 0 & \langle G_N|V_N\rangle & \langle G_N|\bar{V}_N\rangle \\ 0 & 0 & \langle \bar{G}_N V_N\rangle & \langle \bar{G}_N|\bar{V}_N\rangle \end{bmatrix}.$$

Under this assumption, U_{VG} and U_{GV} are not related, and so each one requires fitting a separate transition amplitude. With this four-dimensional model, we need to construct U_{VG} using the amplitude $\langle G|\bar{V}\rangle = |\langle G|\bar{V}\rangle| \cdot e^{i\theta}$ and we need to construct U_{GV} using another amplitude, $\langle V|\bar{G}\rangle = |\langle V|\bar{G}\rangle| \cdot e^{i\phi}$. This generates four free parameters.

We chose a compromise solution to fit the quantum model. We assumed the four-dimensional space model but we equated the phases for the two unitary matrices, $\phi = \theta$, so that both matrices are constructed from three parameters: U_{GV} is constructed using the amplitude $\langle G|\bar{V}\rangle = |\langle G|\bar{V}\rangle| \cdot e^{i\theta}$ and U_{VG} is constructed using amplitude $\langle V|\bar{G}\rangle = |\langle V|\bar{G}\rangle| \cdot e^{i\theta}$, and the three free parameters are $\{|\langle G|\bar{V}\rangle|, |\langle V|\bar{G}\rangle|, \theta\}$.

6.4.5 Purpose of the phase

What is the purpose of the phase θ in this quantum model? Consider the set of three equations in 6.1 for the verbatim, gist, and "verbatim or gist" questions when the probe comes from a target set T. The probability for the verbatim question only depends on the squared magnitude of the transition amplitude $\langle V|S_T\rangle$ and the phase has no effect. Next consider the probability for the "verbatim or gist" question. This equation involves computing the squared magnitude of two transition amplitudes: one is $|\langle V|S_T\rangle|^2$, for which the phase has no effect, and the other is $|\langle G|V\rangle|^2$, and again the phase has no effect. So the phases of the amplitudes are not involved in either the verbatim question or the "verbatim or gist" question.

The phase has an important effect on the gist question for probes from the target set T, and this occurs because (see Chapter 2)

$$
\begin{aligned}
|\langle G|S_T\rangle|^2 &= \left|\langle G|V\rangle\langle V|S_T\rangle + \langle G|\bar{V}\rangle\langle\bar{V}|S_T\rangle\right|^2 \\
&= \left|\langle G|V\rangle\langle V|S_T\rangle\right|^2 + \left|\langle G|\bar{V}\rangle\langle\bar{V}|S_T\rangle\right|^2 \\
&\quad + 2\cdot\left|\langle G|V\rangle\langle V|S_T\rangle\langle G|\bar{V}\rangle\langle\bar{V}|S_T\rangle\right|\cdot\cos(\theta).
\end{aligned}
$$

Thus, the phase θ enters into the interference term when we express the probability for accepting the gist in terms of the transitions through the two verbatim states. If we set $\cos(\theta) = 0$, or in other words we set $\theta = \pi/2$ or $\theta = 3\pi/2$ or $\theta = -\pi/2$ or $\theta = -3\pi/2$ or any whole number multipliers of these values, then the phase goes to zero and the law of total amplitude produces the same result as the law of total probability.

Let us analyze the effect of phase on the $\mathrm{EOD}(T)$ for probes taken from T. The quantum model predicts that $p(V\,\mathrm{or}\,G|T) = p(V|T) + p(\bar{V}|T)\cdot p(G|\bar{V})$ and so

$$
\begin{aligned}
\mathrm{EOD}(T) &= p(V|T) + p(G|T) - p(V\,\mathrm{or}\,G|T) \\
&= p(G|T) - p(\bar{V}|T)\cdot p(G|\bar{V}) \\
&= p(V|T)p(G|V) + p(\bar{V}|T)p(G|\bar{V}) - p(\bar{V}|T)\cdot p(G|\bar{V}) \\
&\quad + 2\cdot\left|\langle G|V\rangle\langle V|S_T\rangle\langle G|\bar{V}\rangle\langle\bar{V}|S_T\rangle\right|\cdot\cos(\theta) \\
&= p(V|T)p(G|V) + 2\cdot\left|\langle G|V\rangle\langle V|S_T\rangle\langle G|\bar{V}\rangle\langle\bar{V}|S_T\rangle\right|\cdot\cos(\theta).
\end{aligned}
$$

If $\cos(\theta) = 0$, then $\mathrm{EOD}(T) = p(V|T)\cdot p(G|V)$, which is simply the probability of accepting verbatim and then accepting gist. Therefore, the phase can increase or decrease the EOD effect depending on the sign of the interference. If the interference is negative, then the EOD is reduced below what one would expect from the probability of accepting verbatim and then gist. That is, if the interference is negative, then the EOD is reduced down toward zero, which is what one would expect if participants were following instructions.

6.4.6   Quantum model parameters and model fit

Now we summarize the six parameters used to fit the quantum model. First, we set $\langle V|S_T\rangle = \sqrt{p(V|T)}$ and $\langle \bar{V}|S_T\rangle = \sqrt{1 - |\langle V|S_T\rangle|^2}$, $\langle G|S_R\rangle = \sqrt{p(G|R)}$ and $\langle \bar{G}|S_R\rangle = \sqrt{1 - |\langle G|S_R\rangle|^2}$, and $\langle G|S_U\rangle = \sqrt{p(G|U)}$ and $\langle \bar{G}|S_U\rangle = \sqrt{1 - |\langle G|S_U\rangle|^2}$. This uses three parameters to fit three data points. Next we fit the three parameters $|\langle G|\bar{V}\rangle|$, $|\langle V|\bar{G}\rangle|$, and θ to the remaining six data points in each row of Table 6.1 using an approximate maximum likelihood method.[4] This produces three degrees of freedom for testing the model within each row; or a total of $6 \times 3 = 18$ degrees of freedom for the entire table.

The predictions from this model are shown in Table 6.1. As can be seen in the table, the model predictions are not perfect but they are reasonably accurate and reproduce the basic qualitative patterns. Also, the model correctly predicts EOD effects for both the targets and the related non-targets, and the predicted effect is larger for the related non-targets, which accurately reflects the observed results for these six studies. The quantum model predicts a small negative EOD effect on average for the unrelated non-targets. Although a negative EOD effect did empirically occur for conditions 2 and 3 in Table 6.1, on average the EOD effect was positive for the unrelated non-targets.

It is also interesting to note that the estimated phase for each of the six conditions consistently produced a negative cosine (mean $\cos(\theta) = -0.85$), or in other words a negative interference effect, which reduces the EOD toward zero. This could be interpreted as reflecting an adjustment of the probability for accepting verbatim and gist down toward zero to satisfy the demand that these answers be mutually exclusive.

6.5   Comparison of models

If we compare the average absolute errors in Table 6.1, we see that the quantum model produces significantly more accurate predictions than the classic model under the Markov assumptions for the related non-targets in R. The quantum model does have an advantage because it uses six parameters to fit nine data points, whereas the classic model with the Markov assumption uses only five to fit nine, but the improvement produced by the one additional parameter in the quantum model is clearly worthwhile.

The dual process model, extended to include bias factors, provides a better fit to the data than the simple quantum model developed in this chapter. However, the dual process model uses seven parameters to fit each row which leaves only two degrees of freedom to test the model, whereas the quantum model used six parameters to each row which leaves three degrees of freedom to test the model. Thus, there are model complexity issues that need to be resolved. However, the more important point concerns the way the two models explain the results for the "verbatim or gist" question.

The only way that the dual process model can explain why $p(V \operatorname{or} G|T) > p(V|T)$ is by assuming that the bias for $V \operatorname{or} G$ is greater than the bias for V. So the bias is doing most of the work in this model. The quantum model assumes a more logical approach – it must predict $p(V \operatorname{or} G|T) > p(V|T)$ because of the logic entailed by the question: the person accepts "verbatim or gist" either if the verbatim question is accepted or if the verbatim question is rejected and

---

[4]This is only an approximate for two reasons. One is that we do not know the exact sample sizes for each observation. The second is that we have to use the bias parameter estimates in place of the real data for the unrelated non-target conditions.

the gist question is accepted. Thus, the quantum model is forced to predict that $p(V \text{ or } G|T) = p(V|T) + p(\bar{V}|T) \cdot p(G|\bar{V}) > p(V|T)$. It is not a result of fitting parameters to data.

6.6   Concluding comments

Let us review some of the main points of this chapter. First of all, the EOD effect is another interesting example of a finding that appears puzzling from a classic probability theory point of view. The probability of answering yes to the question "Is the probe verbatim or gist?" does not add up to what you would expect from applying the OR rule of classic probability theory to a pair of mutually exclusive events. There is a well-established model, called the dual processing model, which has been used to explain these findings. The dual process model is a Markov model, but its predictions do not obey the OR rule of classic probability. In fact, the core assumptions of this model predict that the probability of a positive response to the "verbatim only" question should equal the probability of a positive response to the "verbatim or gist" question. This produces the EOD effect. However, in order to explain the fact that the probability of positive response to the "verbatim or gist" question is empirically larger than the probability for the "verbatim only" question, the dual process model has to add a larger bias parameter for the "verbatim or gist" question compared with the "verbatim only" question. We explored the application of a quantum model to this problem in some detail for three reasons. One is to apply the theory to a brand new domain, which is memory recognition. The second is to work out the application in some detail in order to provide an example that may be useful for future applications. A final reason was to seek a more satisfactory answer for the puzzling finding regarding the EOD effect. We tried to argue that the quantum model provides a more natural interpretation for the "verbatim or gist" question compared with the dual processing model.

7
Quantum-like models of human semantic space

A connection between quantum theory and human memory came out of cybernetics research in the early 1950s (von Foerster, 1950). It was not until modelling the activation of a word in human memory did the connection begin to appear in mainstream psychological literature. Target word activation was speculated as being similar to quantum entanglement because the target word and its associative network were being activated "in synchrony," the core intuition behind the "spooky-action-at-a-distance" formula (Nelson *et al.*, 2003). This chapter begins by developing a quantum-like model of the human mental lexicon and compares it against other memory models. Specific attention is paid to how these models describe the activation of a word in memory in the context of the extra- and intra-list cuing tasks. The chapter then covers how quantum theory can be applied to model human semantic space.

7.1   The human mental lexicon

A mental lexicon refers to the words that comprise a language, and its structure is defined here by the associative links that bind this vocabulary together. Such links are acquired through experience and the vast and semi-random nature of this experience ensures that words within this vocabulary are highly interconnected, both directly and indirectly through other words. For example, the word *planet* becomes associated with *earth*, *space*, *moon*, and so on, and within this set, *moon* can become linked to *earth* and *star*. Words are so associatively interconnected with each other they meet the qualifications of a "small world" network wherein it takes only a few associative steps to move from any one word to any other in the lexicon (Steyvers & Tenenbaum, 2005). Because of such connectivity, individual words are not represented in long-term memory as isolated entities but as part of a network of related words. However, depending upon the context in which they are used, words can take on a variety of different meanings, and this is very difficult to model (Gabora *et al.*, 2008).

Much evidence shows that, for any individual, seeing or hearing a word activates words related to it through prior learning. As illustrated in Figure 7.1, seeing *PLANET* activates the associates *earth*, *moon*, and so on, because *planet–earth*, *planet–moon*, *moon–space* and other associations have been acquired in

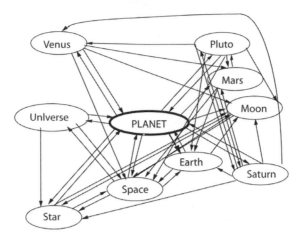

Figure 7.1 Planet's associative structure (from Nelson and McEvoy (2005)).

the past. This activation aids comprehension, is implicit, and provides rapid, synchronous access to associated words.

Understanding how such activation affects memory requires a map of links among known words, and free association provides one reliable means for constructing such a map (Nelson *et al.*, 2004). In free association, words are presented to large samples of participants who produce the first associated word to come to mind. The probability or strength of a preexisting link between words is computed by dividing the production frequency of a response word by its sample size. For example, the probabilies that *planet* produces *earth* and *mars* are 0.61 and 0.10, respectively, and we say that *earth* is a more likely or a stronger associate of *planet* than *mars*. This attempt to map the associative lexicon soon made it clear that some words produce more associates than others. This feature is called "set size" and it indexes a word's associative dimensionality (Nelson & McEvoy, 1979; Nelson *et al.*, 1992). Finally, mapping the lexicon also revealed that the associates of some words are more interconnected than others. Some words have many such connections (e.g., *moon–space*, *earth–planet*), whereas some have none, and this feature is called "connectivity" (Nelson *et al.*, 2003). Experiments have shown that link strengths between words, the set size, and connectivity of individual words have powerful effects on recall.

7.1.1 Recall tasks

In extralist cuing, participants typically study a list of to-be-recalled target words shown on a monitor for 3 s each (e.g., *planet*). The study instructions ask them to read each word aloud when shown and to remember as many as possible, but participants are not told how they will be tested until the last word is shown. The test instructions indicate that new words, the test cues,

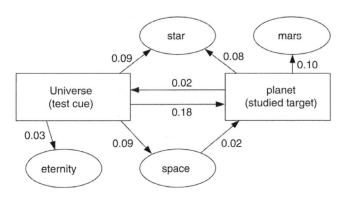

Figure 7.2 Links that join the test cue and target and competing associates that do not. (Adapted from Nelson and McEvoy (2005)).

will be shown and that each test cue (e.g., *universe*) is related to one of the target words just studied. These cues are not present during study (hence, the name extralist cuing). As each cue is shown, participants attempt to recall its associatively related word from the study list.

In intralist cuing, the word serving as the test cue is presented with its target during study (e.g., *universe planet*). Participants are asked to learn the pairing, but otherwise the two tasks are the same.

These tasks allow for many variations in the learning and testing conditions and in the associative characteristics of the words studied and their test cues. For example, the to-be-recalled target words can be systematically selected for either task from the norms based on their individual associative structures. With other variables controlled, half of the targets in the study list could be high and half could be low in associative connectivity. Similarly, half could have small or large set sizes. The potential effects of some feature of the human mental lexicon are investigated by selecting words that systematically differ in that characteristic to determine how it affects recall. Extralist cuing experiments show that recall varies with the nature of the test cue and the target as individual entities and with the linking relationships that bind them together. The cue–target relationship can vary in strength in one or in all of four different ways. Figure 7.2 shows *planet* as a studied target, with *universe* as the test cue. As can be seen, cue-to-target strength is 0.18 and target-to-cue strength is 0.02. These two links directly connect the cue and target, and stronger links increase the probability of correct recall. Recall also varies with indirect links (Nelson *et al.*, 1997). Recall is higher when mediated links (*universe → space → planet*) and shared associate links are present (both *universe* and *planet* produce *star* as an associate). Finally, with cue–target strength controlled, other findings show that target words having higher levels of associative connectivity (more associate-to-associate links) are more likely to be recalled (Nelson *et al.*, 1998). In contrast, target words with greater dimensionality or set size are less likely to be recalled (Nelson *et al.*, 1992). Figure 7.2 shows two associates, one linked to the cue

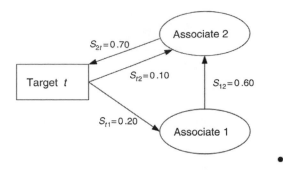

Figure 7.3 A hypothetical target with two associates and single associate-to-target and associate-to-associate links. From Nelson *et al.* (2003) (reprinted/adapted with permission).

(*eternity*) and one linked to the target (*mars*). These associates do not link the cue and the target together and are likely to compete with the target and hinder recall.

The positive effects of the target's associative connectivity and the negative effects of its set size occur even though attention is never drawn to the associates at any time. Furthermore, the effects of connectivity and set size in the extralist cuing task are not produced by confounding word attributes, nor are they found only with particular types of participants or conditions (Nelson *et al.*, 1993a; Gee *et al.*, 1999; Nelson & Goodmon, 2002). Both effects are evident regardless of target frequency, concreteness, and number of target meanings. The effects are found for young and old participants, under very fast and very slow presentation rates, as well as under incidental and intentional learning and testing conditions. Standard psychological explanations have generally failed to explain how associative structure has such robust effects on recall. Quantum theory is offering a promising alternative (Nelson & McEvoy, 2007; P. D. Bruza et al., 2009).

7.1.2   Spooky-action-at-a-distance

Figure 7.3 shows a hypothetical target having two target-to-associate links. There is also an associate-to-associate link between Associates 1 and 2, and an associate-to-target link from Associate 2 to the Target t. The values on the links indicate relative strengths estimated via free association. Nelson *et al.* (2003) have investigated reasons for the more likely recall of words having more associate-to-associate links. Two competing explanations for why associate-to-associate links benefit recall have been proposed.

The first is the "spreading activation" equation, which is based on the classic idea that activation spreads through a fixed associative network, weakening with conceptual distance (e.g., Collins and Loftus (1975)):

$$S(t) = \sum_{i=1}^{n} S_{ti} S_{it} + \sum_{i=1}^{n} \sum_{j=1}^{n} S_{ti} S_{ij} S_{jt} \tag{7.1}$$

$$= (0.10 \times 0.70) + (0.20 \times 0.60 \times 0.70) \tag{7.2}$$

$$= 0.154, \tag{7.3}$$

where n is the number of associates and $i \neq j$. $S(t)$ denotes the strength of implicit activation of target t due to study, S_{ti} target-to-associate activation strength, S_{it} associate-to-target activation strength (resonance), and S_{ij} associate-to-associate activation strength (connectivity). Multiplying link strengths produces the weakening effect. Activation ostensibly travels from the target to and among its associates and back to the target in a continuous chain, and the target is strengthened by activation that returns to it from preexisting connections involving two- and three-step loops. More associate-to-associate links create more three-step loops and theoretically benefit target recall by increasing its activation strength in long-term memory. Importantly, note that the effects of associate-to-associate links are contingent on the number and strength of associate-to-target links because they allow activation to return to the target. If associate-to-target links were absent, even the maximum number of associate-to-associate links would have no effect on recall because activation could not return to the target.

In contrast, in the "spooky-action-at-a-distance" equation, the target activates its associative structure "in synchrony" (Nelson et al., 2003):

$$S(t) = \sum_{i=1}^{n} S_{ti} + \sum_{i=1}^{n} S_{it} + \sum_{i=1}^{n} \sum_{j=1}^{n} S_{ij} \tag{7.4}$$

$$= 0.20 + 0.10 + 0.70 + 0.60 \tag{7.5}$$

$$= 1.60, \tag{7.6}$$

where $i \neq j$; S_{ti}, target-to-associate i strength; S_{it}, associate i-to-target strength (resonance); S_{ij}, associate i-to-associate j strength (connectivity). This equation assumes that each link in the associative set contributes additively to the target's activation strength. The beneficial effects of associate-to-associate links are not contingent on associate-to-target links. Stronger target activation is predicted when there are many associate-to-associate links even when associate-to-target links are absent. In fact, associate-to-target links are not special in any way. Target activation strength is solely determined by the sum of the link strengths within the target's associative set, regardless of origin or direction. The curious labeling of this equation mirrors Einstein's comment on quantum entanglement implying non-local effects between spatially separated particles. The intuition behind the spooky-action-at-a-distance equation reflects this intuition as it formalizes the notion that links between a target's associates affect its recall even when they are "distant" from the target. Evidence for this intuition is found in Figure 7.4, which shows the results of an extralist cuing experiment with cue-to-target strength set at a moderate level. Recall is more

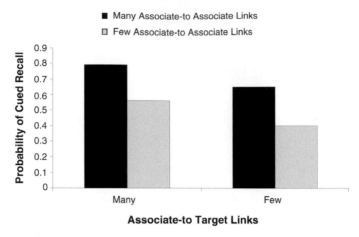

Figure 7.4 Probability of cued recall as a function of the numbers of associate-to-target and associate-to-associate links.

likely when target words have more associate-to-associate links (connectivity) and more associate-to-target links (resonance). Most importantly for theory development, these variables have additive effects. Associate-to-associate links promote recall which does not depend necessarily on associate-to-target links, indicating that the spreading activation rule provides an inadequate explanation for why the existence of associate-to-associate links facilitates recall. Spreading activation cannot explain why the link between *earth → moon* facilitates the recall of *planet* when given *universe* as a test cue. This is because even though there is a link *planet → earth* and *earth → moon*, spreading activation requires the link *moon → planet* to contribute to the activation of *planet*. As *moon → planet* does not exist, no activation of *planet* can proceed via the link *earth → moon*. We will gradually introduce a quantum-like model which will address this weakness of the spreading activation model.

The meaning of the target is uncertain in the extralist cuing task because there is no specific semantic context made available during study to bias the meaning of the target. In contrast, the meaning of the target is more certain in the intralist cuing task because a meaningful and interactive context word is presented. Extant findings are consistent with this interpretation. Nelson *et al.* (1993a) compared recall in the two tasks where targets or context word–target word pairs were studied for 3 s, followed by an immediate cued recall test. Figure 7.5 shows effects of target connectivity were apparent in the extralist cuing task but not in the intralist cuing task. Studying the pair *universe–planet* completely eliminated the influence of links between *moon–space*, *moon–earth*, and so on. A possible explanation for this difference motivated from quantum theory is given in (Bruza *et al.*, 2009c). We saw in Section 5.3 how a word can be modelled in a quantum-like way as a superposed state. In the intralist task, the test cue is presented during study with the target and serves as the sole context for the target (and the reverse). If studying a target word in the presence of

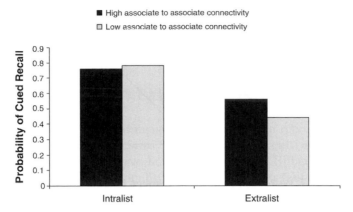

Figure 7.5 Effects of associate-to-associate connectivity as a function of cuing task. (Experiment 1 in Nelson *et al.* (1993b), reprinted/adapted with permission.)

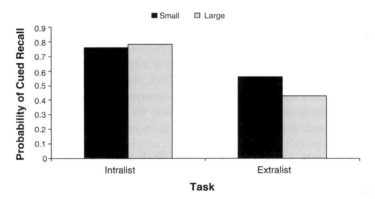

Figure 7.6 Target set size effects as a function of cuing task. (Experiment 1 in Nelson *et al.* (1993b), reprinted/adapted with permission.)

an associatively related word causes its superposed state to collapse (e.g., see Bruza and Cole (2005)), one would expect the effects of associative connectivity to be reduced and perhaps even eliminated, and this is what Figure 7.5 exhibits. The same can be hypothesized in relation to dimensionality. Figure 7.6 shows that the effects of target dimensionality, or set size, are present in the extralist cuing, but not in the intralist cuing task.

7.2 Words, context and Hilbert space

In Chapter 2 it was shown how the choice of basis vectors is fundamentally important in formulating a quantum model. Right at the core of measurement in quantum theory is a recognition of the context of the system as important

the more associates there are, the higher the dimensionality of the Hilbert space is. However, it does not cater for the interconnectivity of the associate network around t_i. The next section will demonstrate how the associative network around a target word can be modelled as a composite quantum system.

7.3 An analysis of spooky-activation-at-a-distance in terms of a composite quantum system

Nelson and McEvoy (2007) stated the connection between spooky-action-at-a-distance formula and quantum entanglement as follows: "The activation-at-a-distance rule assumes that the target is, in quantum terms, entangled with its associates because of learning and practicing language in the world. Associative entanglement causes the studied target word to simultaneously activate its associate structure." The goal of this section is to show how this intuition can be formalized in terms of a composite quantum system. Recall that both set size and associative connectivity have been demonstrated time and again as having robust effects on the probability of recall. Therefore, it is important that the quantum model is able to cater for the set size and connectivity effects described at length in the introduction to this chapter. As the spooky-action-at-a-distance formula sums link strengths irrespective of direction, it expresses the intuition that a target with a large number of highly interconnected associates should translate into a high activation level during study.

Table 7.1 is a matrix representation of the associative network of the hypothetical target t shown in Figure 7.3. The bottom line of the matrix represents the degree to which a word is activated by its immediate neighborhood. As a simple illustrative approximation, the nonzero free association probabilities are averaged:

$$p_{a_2} = \frac{\Pr(a_2|t) + \Pr(a_2|a_1)}{2} \tag{7.10}$$

$$= \frac{0.1 + 0.6}{2} \tag{7.11}$$

$$= 0.35. \tag{7.12}$$

Table 7.1 Matrix corresponding to hypothetical target shown in Figure 7.3. Free association probabilities are obtained by finding the row of interest (the cue) and running across to the associate word obtained.

	t	a_1	a_2
t		0.2	0.1
a_1			0.6
a_2	0.7		
	$p_t = 0.7$	$p_{a_1} = 0.2$	$p_{a_2} = 0.35$

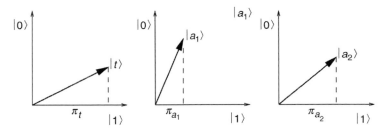

Figure 7.8 Three-bodied quantum system of words. The projection of the qubit onto the $|1\rangle$ basis relates to the probabilities in Table 7.1 via the change of variables below.

The assumption behind both spreading activation and spooky-action-at-a-distance is that free association probabilities determine the strength of activation of a word during study; they only differ in the way this activation strength is computed. Viewing free association probabilities in matrix form allows us to consider the system in Figure 7.3 as a many-bodied quantum system modelled by three qubits. Figure 7.8 depicts this system as a set of qubits; each word is in a superposed state of being activated $|1\rangle$, or not $|0\rangle$, in memory. Note how each summed column in Table 7.1 with a nonzero probability leads to a qubit. For ease of exposition in the following analysis, we shall change variables. The probabilities depicted in Table 7.1 are related to the probability densities of Figure 7.8 by taking their square root: e.g., $\pi_t^2 = p_t$. Using such a change of variables, the state of the target word t would be written as

$$|t\rangle = \sqrt{\bar{p_t}}|0\rangle + \sqrt{p_t}|1\rangle = \bar{\pi}_t|0\rangle + \pi_t|1\rangle, \tag{7.13}$$

where the probability of recall due to free association is $p_t = \pi_t^2$, and $\bar{p}_t = 1 - p_t = \bar{\pi}_t^{\,2}$ represents the probability of a word not being recalled. Thus, the states of the individual words are represented as follows in order to avoid cluttering the analysis with square root signs:

$$|t\rangle = \bar{\pi}_t|0\rangle + \pi_t|1\rangle \tag{7.14}$$

$$|a_1\rangle = \bar{\pi}_{a_1}|0\rangle + \pi_{a_1}|1\rangle \tag{7.15}$$

$$|a_2\rangle = \bar{\pi}_{a_2}|0\rangle + \pi_{a_2}|1\rangle, \tag{7.16}$$

where $\bar{\pi}_t = \sqrt{1 - \pi_t^2}, \bar{\pi}_{a_1} = \sqrt{1 - \pi_{a_1}^2}$, and $\bar{\pi}_{a_2} = \sqrt{1 - \pi_{a_2}^2}$. It was shown in Section 5.3 how a concept combination could be modelled as a composite quantum system. The same approach is again adopted to model the state $|\psi_t\rangle$ of target t by employing the tensor product of the individual states:

$$|\psi_t\rangle = |t\rangle \otimes |a_1\rangle \otimes |a_2\rangle \tag{7.17}$$

$$= (\bar{\pi}_t|0\rangle + \pi_t|1\rangle) \otimes (\bar{\pi}_{a_1}|0\rangle + \pi_{a_1}|1\rangle) \otimes (\bar{\pi}_{a_2}|0\rangle + \pi_{a_2}|1\rangle) \tag{7.18}$$

$$= \bar{\pi}_t \bar{\pi}_{a_1} \bar{\pi}_{a_2} |000\rangle + \pi_t \bar{\pi}_{a_1} \bar{\pi}_{a_2} |100\rangle + \bar{\pi}_t \pi_{a_1} \bar{\pi}_{a_2} |010\rangle + \pi_t \pi_{a_1} \bar{\pi}_{a_2} |110\rangle$$
$$+ \bar{\pi}_t \bar{\pi}_{a_1} \pi_{a_2} |001\rangle + \pi_t \bar{\pi}_{a_1} \pi_{a_2} |101\rangle + \bar{\pi}_t \pi_{a_1} \pi_{a_2} |011\rangle + \pi_t \pi_{a_1} \pi_{a_2} |111\rangle$$
$$\tag{7.19}$$

The introduction detailed how free association probabilities can be used to compute the strength of activation of target t during study. Hence, $|111\rangle$ represents the state in which all respective qubits collapse onto their state $|1\rangle$. In other words, $|111\rangle$ denotes the state of the system in which words t, a_1, and a_2 have all been *activated* due to study of target t. The probability of observing this is given by taking the square of the product $\pi_t \pi_{a_1} \pi_{a_2}$. Conversely, the state $|000\rangle$ corresponds to the basis state in which none of the words have been activated.

The product state $|\psi_t\rangle$ of the three-bodied composite system depicted in Eq. (7.19) does not capture Nelson and McEvoy's intuition that the studied target word t simultaneously activates its entire associative structure. This intuition suggests target t activates its associates in synchrony; when target t is studied it activates *all* of its associates, or none at all. In order to model this intuition, the state $|\psi_t\rangle$ is assumed to evolve into an entangled state $|\psi_t'\rangle$ of the form

$$|\psi_t'\rangle = \sqrt{p_0}|000\rangle + \sqrt{p_1}|111\rangle. \tag{7.20}$$

This formula expresses a superposed state in which the entire associative structure is activated ($|111\rangle$) or not at all ($|000\rangle$). The question remains how to ascribe values to the probabilities p_0 and p_1. In quantum theory these values would be determined by the unitary dynamics evolving the product state $|\psi_t\rangle$ into the entangled state $|\psi_t'\rangle$. One approach is to assume the lack of activation of the target is determined by lack of activation of any of the associates (Bruza *et al.*, 2009c). That is,

$$p_0 = \bar{p}_t \bar{p}_{a_1} \bar{p}_{a_2}, \tag{7.21}$$

$$p_1 = 1 - p_0 = 1 - \bar{p}_t \bar{p}_{a_1} \bar{p}_{a_2}. \tag{7.22}$$

Consequently, the remaining probability mass contributes to the activation of the associative structure as a whole. Departing from the assumption of an entangled state, the probability p_1 corresponds to Nelson and McEvoy's intuition of the strength of activation of target t in synchrony with its associative network:

$$p_1 = 1 - \bar{p}_t \bar{p}_{a_1} \bar{p}_{a_2} \tag{7.23}$$

$$= 1 - (1 - p_t)(1 - p_{a_1})(1 - p_{a_2}) \tag{7.24}$$

$$= 1 - (1 - 0.7)(1 - 0.2)(1 - 0.35) \tag{7.25}$$

$$= 0.844. \tag{7.26}$$

It is interesting to note that the strength of activation p_1 lies between spreading activation and spooky-action-at-a-distance. Based on a substantial body of empirical evidence, Nelson *et al.* (2003) have argued persuasively that spreading activation *underestimates* strength of activation. Conversely, Bruza *et al.* (2009c) hypothesized that the probability of activation using the entanglement model (Eqs. (7.20) and (7.22)) may lie between spreading activation (Eq. (7.1)) and spooky-action-at-a-distance (Eq. (7.4)).

A detailed empirical analysis over 4068 extralist test cases revealed that this hypothesis does not hold and the entanglement model tends to overestimate the level of activation of a target word (Galea *et al.*, 2011). The overestimation is caused by the naive assumption behind Eq. (7.22) in which the probability of non-activation of a target is defined as a product of the probabilities of non-activation of all of its associates (p_0 in Eq. (7.22)). Even though this makes intuitive sense, one can see in this equation that, as dimensionality increases, the product of probabilities computing probability of non-activation of the target (p_0) will approach zero and hence the probability of activation of the target $p_1 = 1 - p_0$ will approach one. Therefore, the overestimation of activation will be particularly pronounced for targets with larger set size. Despite the overestimation, the errors of the entanglement model are normally distributed. In addition, the entanglement model is robust as the error distribution is stable across different topologies of associative network, a feature which does not hold for both the spooky-action-at-a-distance and spreading activation models. Therefore, the prospects for further development of entanglement models of target activation are encouraging.

One way to address this overestimation is to find a constructive means to evolve the product state $|\psi_t\rangle$ (7.19) into the entangled state $|\psi_t'\rangle$ (7.20). Chapter 8 will show how dynamics in quantum theory can be applied to dynamics in decision making. Another approach is to draw on theory developed in the field of quantum computing. Formally, a unitary transformation U is needed such that

$$U|\psi_t\rangle = |\psi_t'\rangle.$$

In the context of the example, the product state $|\psi_t\rangle$ can be written as the following column matrix:

$$|\psi_t\rangle \rightarrow \begin{bmatrix} \alpha_{000} \\ \alpha_{001} \\ \alpha_{010} \\ \alpha_{011} \\ \alpha_{100} \\ \alpha_{101} \\ \alpha_{110} \\ \alpha_{111} \end{bmatrix} = \begin{bmatrix} 0.3949684 \\ 0.2898275 \\ 0.1974842 \\ 0.1449138 \\ 0.6033241 \\ 0.4427189 \\ 0.3016621 \\ 0.2213549 \end{bmatrix},$$

where using the values in Table 7.1: $\alpha_{000} = \bar{\pi}_t \bar{\pi}_{a_1} \bar{\pi}_{a_2} = 0.3949684, \ldots, \alpha_{111} = \pi_t \pi_{a_1} \pi_{a_2} = 0.2213549$ correspond to activation levels in the product state (7.19). On the other hand, the entangled state ψ_t' has the form

$$|\psi_t'\rangle \rightarrow \begin{bmatrix} \beta_{000} \\ 0 \\ 0 \\ 0 \\ 0 \\ 0 \\ 0 \\ \beta_{111} \end{bmatrix},$$

where $\beta_{000}^2 = p_0$ and $\beta_{111}^2 = p_1$ (see Eq. (7.20)). It will be shown in Section 10.3.4 how the unitary transformation U can be constructed from C–H gates developed in quantum computing. The form of such a unitary transformation, denoted U_{CH}, is

$$U_{\mathrm{CH}} = \begin{bmatrix} H & \mathbf{0} \\ \mathbf{0} & H \cdot Z \end{bmatrix},$$

where H is a Hadamard gate and Z is a gate which changes signs. (See Section 10.3.4 for more details.) As the running example deals with an eight-dimensional space, a second-order Hadamard transformation is therefore required:

$$H_2 = \frac{1}{2} \begin{bmatrix} 1 & 1 & 1 & 1 \\ 1 & -1 & 1 & -1 \\ 1 & 1 & -1 & -1 \\ 1 & -1 & -1 & 1 \end{bmatrix}.$$

The corresponding Z-gate has the following form:

$$Z = \begin{bmatrix} 1 & 0 & 0 & 0 \\ 0 & -1 & 0 & 0 \\ 0 & 0 & -1 & 0 \\ 0 & 0 & 0 & 1 \end{bmatrix}.$$

The U_{CH} transform produces an entangled state when the amplitudes in ψ_t are uniform. One way to accommodate this property is by averaging the probabilities of activation where t is not recalled, i.e., across $|000\rangle, |001\rangle, |010\rangle, |011\rangle$, and averaging the probabilities of activation corresponding to when target t is recalled, i.e., across $|100\rangle, |101\rangle, |110\rangle, |111\rangle$. Therefore, in terms of the running example, the product state ψ_t could be uniformly primed as follows:

$$|\psi_t\rangle \rightarrow \begin{bmatrix} \sqrt{\frac{1}{4}\left(\alpha_{000}^2 + \alpha_{001}^2 + \alpha_{010}^2 + \alpha_{011}^2\right)} \\ \sqrt{\frac{1}{4}\left(\alpha_{000}^2 + \alpha_{001}^2 + \alpha_{011}^2 + \alpha_{011}^2\right)} \\ \sqrt{\frac{1}{4}\left(\alpha_{000}^2 + \alpha_{001}^2 + \alpha_{011}^2 + \alpha_{011}^2\right)} \\ \sqrt{\frac{1}{4}\left(\alpha_{000}^2 + \alpha_{001}^2 + \alpha_{011}^2 + \alpha_{011}^2\right)} \\ \sqrt{\frac{1}{4}\left(\alpha_{100}^2 + \alpha_{101}^2 + \alpha_{110}^2 + \alpha_{111}^2\right)} \\ \sqrt{\frac{1}{4}\left(\alpha_{100}^2 + \alpha_{101}^2 + \alpha_{110}^2 + \alpha_{111}^2\right)} \\ \sqrt{\frac{1}{4}\left(\alpha_{100}^2 + \alpha_{101}^2 + \alpha_{110}^2 + \alpha_{111}^2\right)} \\ \sqrt{\frac{1}{4}\left(\alpha_{100}^2 + \alpha_{101}^2 + \alpha_{110}^2 + \alpha_{111}^2\right)} \end{bmatrix} = \begin{bmatrix} 0.2738613 \\ 0.2738613 \\ 0.2738613 \\ 0.2738613 \\ 0.4183300 \\ 0.4183300 \\ 0.4183300 \\ 0.4183300 \end{bmatrix}.$$

Finally, applying the unitary transformation U_{CH} to ψ_t produces the following entangled state:

$$|\psi_t'\rangle \rightarrow \begin{bmatrix} \beta_{000} \\ 0 \\ 0 \\ 0 \\ 0 \\ 0 \\ 0 \\ \beta_{111} \end{bmatrix} = \begin{bmatrix} 0.5477226 \\ 0 \\ 0 \\ 0 \\ 0 \\ 0 \\ 0 \\ 0.8366600 \end{bmatrix}.$$

Therefore, the probability of the target t activating its associate network in synchrony (see Figure 7.3) is $p_1 = \beta_{111}^2 = 0.7$. This is considerably less than the probability of 0.844 determined by Eq. (7.22). Even though this is one example, such an approach has the potential to address the overestimation problem caused by the naive assumption underlying (7.22).

7.3.1   Summary

This section illustrated how the human mental lexicon can be modelled using quantum theory. It has been shown how words in memory can be viewed as superposed states in a Hilbert space. In the memory literature, context is sometimes represented as a vector such as in the matrix model of memory (Humphreys *et al.*, 1989a) and more recently in a holographic model of the human mental lexicon (Jones & Mewhort, 2007). In the quantum model presented here, context is essentially modelled just like it is in quantum physics: the context of the experiment is a particular choice and orientation of a measuring apparatus. This boils down to a particular choice of basis. We have shown a spectrum of possibilities for chosing bases; for example, a two-dimensional basis corresponding to "recalled," "not recalled" to bases whereby the basis vectors correspond to associates, or senses, of the given word being modelled. Particles in a composite quantum system may become entangled, which, broadly speaking, means the state of the composite system cannot be expressed as a tensor product of the states of the respective particles. The particles are "non-separable." A key difference in quantum-like models of the human mental lexicon when compared with memory models published in the memory literature, such as the well-known spreading activation model, is the assumption that words in memory may be non-separable. We have shown by assuming entanglement of words in memory that there is some theoretical justification for the spooky-action-at-a-distance-model (Nelson *et al.*, 2003). Although Einstein eschewed non-separable effects as "spooky," later experiments showed that the state of a particle measured at one location instantly affects the state of an entangled particle at a more distant location. In this section, non-separable effects refer to remote links in a target's semantic network that aid its recall and recognition; for example, the "Pluto–Venus" link increases the probability that the word *planet* will be recalled. Current understanding attributes this effect to the connectivity of the links in the target's neighborhood, but in the quantum model just presented it is the entangled state modelling the network which allows the activation of the target to activate all its associates "in synchrony."

7.4   The quantum mechanics of semantic space

Aerts and Czachor (2004) were the first to establish a formal connection between quantum theory and semantic space models used in applied cognition and computational linguistics. These models are typically run across a corpus of electronic text and produce representations of words in a high-dimensional space. Even though specific details of the models may differ, they all feature a remarkable level of compatibility with a variety of human information processing tasks, such as semantic word association. Therefore, there is some justification to believe such models capture some of the cognitive semantics of words.

We begin this chapter by illustrating the connection between quantum theory and semantic space by using the Hyperspace Analogue to Language (HAL) model (Lund & Burgess, 1996; Burgess *et al.*, 1998). HAL produces representations of words in a high-dimensional space that seem to correlate well with the equivalent human representations. For example, "...simulations using HAL accounted for a variety of semantic and associative word priming effects that can be found in the literature...and shed light on the nature of the word relations found in human word-association norm data" (Lund & Burgess, 1996).

Given an N-word vocabulary, HAL computes an $N \times N$ matrix constructed by moving a window of length l over the corpus by one word increment, ignoring punctuation, sentence, and paragraph boundaries (see Figure 7.9). All words within the window are considered as co-occurring with the last word in the window with a strength inversely proportional to the distance between the words. Each row i in the matrix represents accumulated weighted associations of word i with respect to other words which preceded i in a context window.

Table 7.2 A simple semantic space computed by HAL

	arms	ig	of	pres	reag	scand	the
arms	0	3	4	1	2	0	5
ig	0	0	0	4	5	0	0
of	0	5	0	3	4	0	0
pres	0	0	0	0	0	0	0
reag	0	0	0	5	0	0	0
scand	5	2	3	0	1	0	4
the	0	4	5	2	3	0	0

```
def calculate_hal(documents, n)
  HAL = 2DArray.new()
  for d in documents {
    for i in 1 .. d.len {
      for j in max(1,i-n) .. i-1 {
        HAL[d.word(i),d.word(j)] += n+1-(i-j)
}}}
  return HAL
end
```

Figure 7.9 Algorithm to compute the HAL matrix for a collection of documents. It is assumed that the documents have been pruned of stop words and punctuation.

Conversely, column i represents accumulated weighted associations with words that appeared after i in a window. For example, consider the text "President Reagan ignorant of the arms scandal," with $l = 5$, the resulting HAL matrix H would be as in Table 7.2.

If word precedence information is considered unimportant the matrix $S = H + H^\mathrm{T}$ denotes a symmetric matrix in which $S[i,j]$ reflects the strength of association of word i seen in the context of word j, irrespective of whether word i appeared before or after word j in the context window. The column vector S_j represents the strengths of association between j and other words seen in the context of the sliding window: the higher the weight of a word, the more it has lexically co-occurred with j in the same context(s). For example, Figure 7.10 illustrates the vector representation for "Reagan" taken from a matrix S computed from a corpus of 21578 Reuters[3] news feeds taken from the year 1988. (The weights in the table are not normalized.) Highly weighted associations reflect prototypical aspects of Reagan in his presidential role dealing with Congress, tax, vetoes, etc. In addition, the more highly weighted associations reflect default associations; for example, "president" and "administration."

[3] The Reuters-21578 collection is standard test collection which has been used for research into automatic text classification.

> president (5259), administration (2859), trade (1451), house (1426), budget
> (1023), congress (991), bill (889), tax (795), veto (786), white (779),
> japan (767), senate (726), iran (687), billion (666), dlrs (615), japanese
> (597), officials (554), arms (547), tariffs (536) ...

Figure 7.10 Example representation of the word "Reagan."

Associations with lower weights seem to reflect the trade war with Japan
("japan", "tariffs") and the Iran–Contra scandal ("Iran", "arms"). In other
words, the representation of Reagan represents a superposition of different senses
of the word "Reagan," as was shown in Section 5.3 with the concept "bat." In
this case, however, the senses are not being derived from free association data,
but by an algorithm run over a corpus of electronic text (Novakovich *et al.*,
2009).

HAL is an exemplar of a growing ensemble of computational models emerging
from cognitive science and computational linguistics, which generally fall under
the label "semantic space" (Lund & Burgess, 1996; Landauer & Dumais, 1997;
Patel *et al.*, 1997; Burgess *et al.*, 1998; Lowe, 2000, 2001; Landauer *et al.*, 1998;
Schütze, 1998; Levy & Bullinaria, 1999; Sahlgren, 2002; 2006, Jones *et al.*, 2006;
Bullinaria & Levy, 2007; Jones & Mewhort, 2007; Sahlgren *et al.*, 2008; Widdows
& Cohen, 2008; Bruza & De Vine, 2010).

7.4.1   Bridging semantic space and quantum mechanics

HAL exemplifies how a semantic space model assigns each word in a given
vocabulary a point in a finite-dimensional vector space. Lowe (2001) formalizes
a semantic space model as a quadruple $\langle A, G, F, M \rangle$ where:

- G is a set of m basis elements.

- A is a function which maps the co-occurrence frequencies between words
  in a vocabulary V and the basis elements so each $w \in V$ is represented by
  a vector $(A(g_1, w), \ldots, A(g_m, w))$.

- F is a function which maps pairs of vectors onto a continuous-valued
  quantity. The interpretation of F is often "semantic similarity" between
  the two vectors in question.

- M is a transformation which takes one semantic space and maps it into
  another; for example, via dimensional reduction

A semantic space S is an instance of the range of the function A. That
is, S is an $m \times n$ matrix where the columns $\{1, \ldots, n\}$ correspond to vector
representations of words. A typical method for deriving the vocabulary V is
to tokenize the corpus from which the semantic space is computed and remove
non-information bearing words such as "the," "a," etc. The letters u, v, w will
be used to identify individual words.

The interpretation of the basis elements corresponding to the rows $\{1\ldots m\}$ depends on the type of semantic space in question. Table 7.2 illustrates that HAL produces a square matrix in which the basis elements are words in the vocabulary V, so $S[u, w], u \in G$, represents the strength of co-occurrence of word w in the context of basis element (a word) u. In contrast, a row in the semantic space models produced by latent semantic analysis (Landauer *et al.*, 1998) corresponds to a text item; for example, a whole document, a paragraph, or even a fixed window of text. The value $S[t, w], t \in G$, denotes the salience of word w in text t. Information-theoretic approaches are sometimes used to compute salience.

For reasons of a more straightforward embedding of semantic space into quantum theory, we will focus on square, symmetric semantic spaces ($m = n$). A column vector in S corresponds to the ket $|w\rangle$:

$$|w\rangle \rightarrow \begin{pmatrix} w_1 \\ \vdots \\ w_n \end{pmatrix}. \tag{7.27}$$

Conversely, a row vector $v = (v_1, \ldots, v_n)$ is denoted by the bra $\langle v|$. In a nutshell, a ket $|w\rangle$ describes the state of "meaning" of a word w in semantic space S.

7.4.2   Superposed states of words in semantic space

Consider the following traces of text from the Reuters-21578 collection:

- *President Reagan was ignorant about much of the Iran arms scandal.*

- *Reagan says U.S. to offer missile treaty.*

- *Reagan seeks more aid for Central America.*

- *Kemp urges Reagan to oppose stock tax.*

Each of these is a window which HAL will process accumulating weighted word associations in relation to the word "Reagan." In other words, included in the HAL vector for "Reagan" are associations dealing with the Iran–Contra scandal, missile treaty negotiations with the Soviets, stock tax, etc. The point is, when HAL runs over the full collection, the vector representation for "Reagan" ends up corresponding to a superposition of basis states, whereby a basis state corresponds to a particular "sense" or "characteristic meaning" of "Reagan." For example, Reagan in the political sense, in the sense dealing with the Iran–Contra scandal, etc.

Consider once again the HAL matrix H computed from the text "President Reagan ignorant of the arms scandal." As mentioned before, $S = H + H^{\mathrm{T}}$ is a real symmetric matrix. Consider a set of y text windows of length l which are centred around a word w. Associated with each such text window $j, 1 \leq j \leq m$, is a semantic space S_j. It is assumed that the semantic space is N-dimensional, whereby the N dimensions correspond to a fixed vocabulary V as above. The semantic space around word w, denoted by S_w, can be calculated by the sum

$$S_w = \sum_{j=1}^{y} S_j. \tag{7.28}$$

The above formula provides a toehold for computing a semantic space in terms of a sum of semantic spaces: each constituent semantic space corresponds to a specific sense of the concept w. By way of illustration, let the word w be "Reagan" and assume there are a total of y traces centred on the word "Reagan," x of which deal with the Iran–Contra issue. These x traces can be used to construct a semantic space using Eq. (7.28). Let S_i denote this semantic space. Its associated probability $p_i = \frac{x}{y}$. Assume the word w has m senses. As each sense i represents a particular state of w, each can be represented as a semantic space S_i with an associated probability:

$$S_w = p_1 S_1 + \ldots + p_m S_m, \tag{7.29}$$

where $p_1 + \ldots + p_m = 1$.

This formula expresses that the semantic space around a concept w can be conceived of as a linear combination of semantic spaces around senses of w. The formula is intuitively close to quantum theory, where a density matrix (see Appendix B) corresponding to a superposed state can be expressed as a weighted combination of density matrices corresponding to basis states. There is no requirement that the state vectors of the pure states are orthogonal to one another. (This is an alternative approach to modelling a word than that presented in Section 5.3, where the senses of a concept were modelled as orthogonal basis states.)

As mentioned in the introduction (Section 7.4), there are various semantic space models presented in the literature. Each will involve a different rendering as a density matrix. The method adopted in this illustration rests on the intuition that the ket $|e_i\rangle$ in each semantic space S_i of Eq. (7.29) corresponds to a state vector representing a sense of word w. A density matrix ρ_i can be formed by the product $|e_i\rangle\langle e_i|$. Building on this, a density matrix ρ_w corresponding to the semantic space S_w can be constructed as follows:

$$\rho_w = p_1 \rho_1 + \ldots + p_m \rho_m. \tag{7.30}$$

Importantly, no assumption of orthogonality has been made. This approach to representing a semantic space contrasts approaches using the spectral decomposition of the semantic space (Aerts & Czachor, 2004; Aerts & Gabora, 2005). As the semantic space S_w is a symmetric matrix it is, therefore, Hermitian. The spectral decomposition theorem (Section 2.4.9) allows S_w to be defined as follows:

$$S_w = \sum_{i=1}^{n} |e_i\rangle \lambda_i \langle e_i| \tag{7.31}$$

$$= \sum_{i=1}^{n} \lambda_i |e_i\rangle \langle e_i| \tag{7.32}$$

$$= \lambda_1 |e_1\rangle \langle e_1| + \ldots + \lambda_n |e_n\rangle \langle e_n|. \tag{7.33}$$

This equation parallels the one given in Eq. (7.30). The eigenvalues λ_i relate to the probabilities of the associated eigenvectors. Each eigenvector $|e_i\rangle$ contributes to the linear combination via the density matrix $|e_i\rangle \langle e_i|$. The eigenvectors $|e_i\rangle$ of S_w should ideally correspond to the senses of word w. Unfortunately, this does not bear out in practice when singular value decomposition is used (Bruza & Cole, 2005; Novakovich *et al.*, 2009).

7.4.3 The collapse of meaning in the light of context

"The starting point is that, for some concepts, the meaning of the concept is determined by the *context* in which it occurs" (Gärdenfors, 2000: 119). Context effects manifest in relation to contrast classes. Consider, "red" in the following combinations: "red book," "red wine," "red hair," "red skin," "red soil." Gärdenfors argues contrast classes generate conceptual subspaces; for example, skin colors form a subspace of the space generated by colors in general. In other words, each of the combinations involving "red" results in a separate subspace representing the particular quality of "red"; for example, the quality of "red" would actually be "purple" when "red" is seen in the context of "wine."

Quantum collapse of a state and the collapse of meaning in the presence of context relates to Gärdenfors' intuitions in the following way. A concept w is represented as a semantic space S_w. Context acts like a quantum measurement which projects S_w into a (sub)space. By way of illustration, consider "Reagan" in the context of "Iran." For the purposes of discussion, assume there are two possible senses. The first deals with the Iran–Contra scandal and the other deals with the hostage crisis at the American embassy in Teheran. In some cases the resulting space will be a subspace, like in the Iran–Contra subspace of the Reagan space, but context may not always result in the collapse onto the basis state because the context may not be sufficient to fully resolve the sense in question. This phenomenon marks a clear distinction between the quantum modelling of words on semantic space and orthodox quantum theory, where measurement of a quantum system results in the collapse of the superposed state of the system onto a basis state. The matrix model of human memory similarly contains the notion of superposed memory states, and it has been argued (emphasis ours), "The superposition of memory traces in a vector bundle resulting from a memory retrieval has often been considered to be a noisy signal that needs to be 'cleaned up' [i.e., full collapse onto a basis state as in quantum theory]. The point we make here is that this is *not necessarily so* and that the superposition of vectors [after retrieval] is a powerful process that adds to the flexibility of memory processes." (Wiles *et al.*, 1994). This suggests a less stringent notion of collapse of the meaning of a word is required than that maintained within standard quantum theory, which will now be developed in respect to the matrix model of memory.

7.4.3.1   A quantum-like matrix model of memory

Consider a concept w considered in the light of some context; for example, other words. The context is denoted generically by x. The effect of context x is brought about by the operator $\mathbf{P}_x$. Following on from the preceding section, $\mathbf{P}_x$ is required to model a partial collapse of meaning with respect to the senses of w, which are not necessarily orthogonal to each other. The operator $\mathbf{P}_x$ is formally not a projection operator which is both idempotent and Hermitian (see Section 2.3.10), but nevertheless does have the intuition that after the operator is applied, the result is a subspace of meaning. Assuming the density matrix ρ_w corresponds to a concept w, the collapse of meaning in the light of context x is characterized by the following equation:

$$\mathbf{P}_x \rho_w \mathbf{P}_x^\dagger = \mathbf{P}_x(p_1\rho_1 + \ldots + p_m\rho_m)\mathbf{P}_x^\dagger = \rho_w^x, \qquad (7.34)$$

where ρ_w^x is the state of w after the "collapse" of its meaning.

   If $\mathbf{P}_x$ is orthogonal to a sense $|e_i\rangle$ represented by the density matrix $\rho_i = |e_i\rangle\langle e_i|$, then $\mathbf{P}_x$ projects this sense onto the zero point in the Hilbert space. If the projection $\mathbf{P}_x$ is not orthogonal to a sense $|e_i\rangle$, then it has the effect of retrieving those senses out of the combination expressed in Eq. (7.34). This is not unlike the notion of a cue which probes human memory. Cues can be used to access memory in two ways: via *matching* or *retrieval* processes. Matching entails the "comparison of the test cue(s) with the information stored in memory" (Humphreys *et al.*, 1989b: 41). This process measures the similarity of the cue(s) and the memory representation. The output of this process is a scalar quantity (i.e., a single numeric value representing the degree or strength of the match).

   The intuition we will attempt to develop is that collapse of word meaning due to context is akin to a cued-recall retrieval operation driven by the operator $\mathbf{P}_x$ on a given density matrix corresponding to the state of a word's meaning.[4] The probability of collapse is the scalar quantity resulting from matching.

   In the matrix model of memory (Humphreys *et al.*, 1989b), memory representations can include items, contexts, or combinations of items and contexts (associations). Items can comprise stimuli, words, or concepts. Each item is modelled as a vector of feature weights. Feature weights are used to specify the degree to which certain features form part of an item. There are two possible levels of vector representation for items. These include:

---

[4] In semantic space models, the meaning of a word is flexible as it derives from the underlying corpus – if the corpus changes, so do the meanings of words (McArthur, 2006).

- modality-specific peripheral representations (e.g., graphemic or phonemic representations of words);

- modality-independent central representations (e.g., semantic representations of words).

In our case, our discussion will naturally focus on the latter due to the assumption that semantic spaces deliver semantic representations of words. For example, the "Reagan" vector $|r\rangle$ from the semantic space S_r illustrates a "modality-independent central representation."

Context can be conceptualized as a mental representation (overall holistic picture) of the context in which items or events have occurred (e.g., "Reagan" in the context of "Iran"). Context is also modelled as a vector of feature weights. Following from this, context x is assumed to be represented by a ket $|x\rangle$. In the case of the running example, the "Iran" vector $|i\rangle$ drawn from the semantic space S_i could be employed as a context vector.

Memories are associative by nature and unique representations are created by combining features of items and contexts. Several different types of associations are possible (Humphreys *et al.*, 1989b). The association of interest here is a two-way association between a word $|w\rangle$ and a context $|x\rangle$. In the matrix model of memory, an association between context and a word is represented by an outer product: $|w\rangle\langle x|$. Seeing a given word (a target) in the context of other words (cue) forms an association which probes memory. Observe with respect to the running example how the probe $|r\rangle\langle i|$ embodies both the cue of the probe "Iran" and the target "Reagan."

In the light of the above brief digression into a matrix model of human memory, one possibility is to formalize the operator $\mathbf{P}_x$ as the probe $|w\rangle\langle x|$. The object being probed is a density matrix, which is not a superposition of memory traces but of semantic spaces hinged around a particular word or concept. Equation (7.29) and its density matrix equivalent (7.30) reflect this superposition; however, in this case the traces, in their raw form, are windows of text centred around w.

In short, viewing the collapse of meaning in terms of retrieval and matching processes in memory refines the collapse (7.34) as follows. Let $|w\rangle$ be a target concept and $|x\rangle$ be the context. First, collapse of meaning is characterized by projecting the probe into the memory corresponding to the state of the target word w. The collapse equates with retrieving a new state of meaning reflecting the change of meaning of w in light of the context:

$$\mathbf{P}_x \rho_w \mathbf{P}_x^\dagger = |w\rangle\langle x|\rho_w|x\rangle\langle w| = \rho_w^x. \tag{7.35}$$

The probability p of collapse is assumed to be a function of the match between the probe $\mathbf{P}_x$ and the memory ρ_w:

$$p = \langle x|\rho_w|w\rangle. \tag{7.36}$$

Motivating the collapse of meaning by means of the matrix model of memory introduces a deviation from standard quantum theory. After application of the

probe $\mathbf{P}_x = |w\rangle\langle x|$, the the state after the collapse, denoted ρ_w^x, is not guaranteed
to be a density matrix. This deviation from standard quantum theory is not
solely a technical issue. It may well be that there are different qualities of probe.
For example, "Reagan" in the context of "Iran" intuitively involves a projection
of the global "Reagan" semantic space onto a subspace dealing with "Iran."
(This is what the probe $\mathbf{P}_x$ attempts to model.) On the other hand, consider
"lion" in the context of "stone." In this case, the result after the application of
the context would seem to be considerably outside the "lion" space, as a "stone
lion" does not share many of the attributes of a living one. An alternative view
is to model "stone lion" as a concept combination and mechanisms such as the
tensor product can be used, as was shown in Section 5.3.

7.4.4   The probability of collapse

It is illustrative to examine how in the light of the running example the scalar
value resulting from the matching process determines the probability of collapse
(7.36) and denoted by $\langle i|\rho_r|r\rangle$.

First, the effect of the cue "Iran" via the context vector $|i\rangle$ is shown. The
"memory" to be probed derives from the target "Reagan" and is denoted by
the density matrix ρ_r:

$$\langle i|\rho_r = \langle i|(p_1\rho_1 + \ldots + p_m\rho_m)$$
$$= p_1\langle i|\rho_1 + \ldots + p_m\langle i|\rho_m.$$

Recall that each of the m constituent density matrices ρ_i derives from a particular sense of "Reagan" denoted e_i. Therefore, the previous equation can be
written as

$$\langle i|\rho_r = p_1\langle i|(|e_1\rangle\langle e_1|) + \ldots + p_m\langle i|(|e_m\rangle\langle e_m|)$$
$$= p_1(\langle i|e_1\rangle)\langle e_1| + \ldots + p_m(\langle i|e_m\rangle)\langle e_m|$$
$$= p_1\cos\theta_1\langle e_1| + \ldots + p_m\cos\theta_m\langle e_m|.$$

The salient facet of the last line is those senses that are not orthogonal to
the context vectors will be retrieved ($\cos\theta_i > 0$) and will contribute to the
probability of collapse. This accords with the intuitions expressed in the previous
section. In the running example, these senses were denoted $|e_c\rangle$ and $|e_h\rangle$. So,

$$\langle i|\rho_r = p_c\cos\theta_c\langle e_c| + p_h\cos\theta_h\langle e_h|.$$

A second aspect of the matching is post multiplying with the target vector
"Reagan," denoted $|r\rangle$:

$$(p_c\cos\theta_c\langle e_c| + p_h\cos\theta_h\langle e_h|)|r\rangle = p_c\cos\theta_c(\langle e_c|r\rangle) + p_h\cos\theta_h(\langle e_h|r\rangle)$$
$$= p_c\cos\theta_c\cos\psi_c + p_h\cos\theta_h\cos\psi_h$$
$$= p_cm_c + p_hm_h.$$

The angle $\cos\psi$ reflects how strongly the sense correlates with the given target. It can be envisaged as a measure of significance of the given sense with the target $|r\rangle$. An example of $|r\rangle$ would be to use the normalized vector computed from Figure 7.10 as the "modality-independent central representation" of Reagan. The scores due to matching of the probe with memory are reflected by the scalars m_c and m_h. These are modified by associated probabilities of the respective senses. Finally, the two terms are added to return a single scalar quantifying the probability of collapse.

7.4.5 Summary and reflections

The preceding development has centred around providing an account of the collapse of meaning in the light of context within a matrix model of human semantic space. It is important that the formalization rests on non-orthogonal density matrices. The approach presented here draws inspiration from a cue which probes human memory and describes collapse of meaning in terms of memory cues. The notion of a "probe" is not foreign to quantum mechanics. The most useful probes of the various wave functions of atoms and molecules are the various forms of spectroscopy. In spectroscopy, an atom or molecule starting with some wave function (represented by a density matrix) is probed with light, or some other particle. The light interacts with the molecule and leaves it in another state. This process is analogous to the probing of memory just described.

7.5 The distance between semantic spaces

Traditionally, semantic space theory employs different metrics to measure the distance between vector representations of words – the closer the distance, the more semantically related the words are assumed to be. These metrics have been used in various empirical studies; for example, to correlate human semantic word association norms with associations computed from a semantic space model. The modelling of semantic spaces as density matrices (Hermitian operators) has led to some useful theoretical developments for determining the distance between semantic spaces (Zuccon *et al.*, 2009).

We will begin by considering the distance between two semantic spaces, each of the same dimension. Let S_u and S_v be n-dimensional semantic spaces (see Section 7.1). In addition, the $\mathbf{P}_u$ and $\mathbf{P}_v$ are projection operators associated with S_u and S_v, respectively. For example, using spectral decomposition (7.33):

$$S_u = \lambda_1 |u_1\rangle\langle u_1| + \ldots + \lambda_n |u_n\rangle\langle u_n|.$$

Therefore, the projector $\mathbf{P}_u$ corresponding to semantic space S_u is defined as a sum of projectors with respect to the basis $\{|u_1\rangle, \ldots, |u_n\rangle\}$:

$$\mathbf{P}_u = |u_1\rangle\langle u_1| + \ldots + |u_n\rangle\langle u_n|.$$

Definition 7.1 *The chordal Grausmannian distance d_c between two n-dimensional semantic spaces S_u and S_v with respective projectors $\mathbf{P}_u$ and $\mathbf{P}_v$ is given by*

$$d_c(\mathbf{P}_u, \mathbf{P}_v) = \sqrt{n - \mathrm{tr}(\mathbf{P}_u \mathbf{P}_v)}.$$

The chordal distance provides a stepping stone to measure the distance between semantic spaces of differing dimensionality. First, the L_2-Hausdorf distance, which measures the minimal distance between a vector $|u_i\rangle$ and a subspace V by

$$d_{\mathrm{H}}(|u_i\rangle, V) = \min ||\,|u_i\rangle - |v\rangle||, \tag{7.37}$$

where $|v\rangle \in V$ and $||\cdot||$ is the L_2 distance. Hausdorf distance can be used to define a distance between two n-dimensional semantic subspaces.

Definition 7.2 *The distance $d_s(S_u, S_v)$ between two n-dimensional semantic spaces S_u and S_v is given by*

$$d_s(S_u, S_v) = \sqrt{\sum_{i=1}^{n} d_{\mathrm{H}}(|u_i\rangle, S_v)^2}, \tag{7.38}$$

where $\{|u_1\rangle, \ldots, |u_n\rangle\}$ is the basis for S_u.

This definition can be extended to semantic spaces of differing dimensionality. Assume S_v is m-dimensional with basis $\{|v_1\rangle, \ldots, |v_m\rangle\}$, then

$$d_s(S_u, S_v) = \sqrt{\max(m, n) - \sum_{i=1}^{n} \sum_{j=1}^{m} \langle u_i | v_j \rangle}. \tag{7.39}$$

The last equation can be used to define a corresponding similarity measure:

$$\mathrm{sim}(S_u, S_v) = 1 - \frac{d_s(S_u, S_v)}{\sqrt{\max(m, n)}}. \tag{7.40}$$

This last equation was employed on semantic space models computed from collections of relevant and non-relevant documents in relation to a query topic. Semantic spaces associated with relevant documents (R) were on average at a closer distance to each other than semantic spaces computed from non-relevant documents (N). The separation between (R) and (N) was not as distinct when Euclidean distance was used (Zuccon *et al.*, 2009).

8

What about quantum dynamics?
More advanced principles

What about a process theory? How does quantum theory explain changes in confidence across time or how does quantum theory predict the time that it takes to make a decision? So far we have only made use of the structural part of quantum theory introduced in Chapter 2. This chapter introduces some of the basic principles for quantum dynamics.

It is useful to compare quantum dynamics with Markov dynamics (Howard, 1971). Markov theory is a general mathematical framework for describing probabilistic-dynamic systems, which is commonly used in all areas of cognitive and decision sciences. For example, it is the mathematical basis that underlies random walk/diffusion models of decision making (Busemeyer & Diederich, 2009), or stochastic models of information processing (Townsend & Ashby, 1983), or multinomial processing tree models of memory retrieval (Batchelder & Reiffer, 1999), or the even more general field of stochastic processes (Bhattacharya & Waymire, 1990).

Quantum theory provides an alternative general mathematical framework for describing probabilistic-dynamic systems (Gudder, 1979). However, quantum theory is similar in many ways to Markov theory, and so if you already know Markov theory, then it will be easy to learn about quantum dynamics too. This chapter introduces the Kolmogorov forward equation used to describe time evolution in Markov models, as well as the quantum analogue – the Schrödinger equation – which describes time evolution in quantum models. This chapter examines the similarities and differences between these two types of evolution, and why they are both useful for cognitive and decision modelling. However, we are not doing physics, and so parameters such as the Planck constant used to describe physical phenomena are replaced by cognitive parameters used to represent human behavioral phenomena. We present quantum and Markov models side by side, making it possible to see exactly where these two theories agree and disagree.

This chapter is organized around three applications. The first is an application to bistable perception (Atmanspacher & Filk, 2010), the second is an application to a categorization and decision-making task (Busemeyer et al., 2006a), and the third is an application to random walk models of signal detection

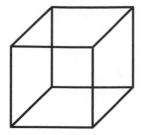

Figure 8.1 Necker cube figure used to produce bistable perception.

(Busemeyer *et al.*, 2006a; Fuss & Navarro, 2008). The first application is simpler because it is based on the analysis of a two-dimensional perceptual system, the second extends the ideas to a system with noisy or biased measurements, and the third application is most complex and describes how to model systems with a large number of ordered states. The first application describes a method for testing of a fundamental property of classical probability theory called the temporal Bell inequality; the second application provides a method for testing the law of total probability, which lies at the foundation of all Markov models, and the law of double stochasticity which is the basis for quantum theory.

8.1   Bistable perception application

Atmanspacher and his colleagues formulated a quantum model of bistable perception for the bistable image produced by viewing the Necker-cube ambiguous figure (Figure 8.1 Atmanspacher *et al.*, 2004). Here we present a modified version of their model, which is inspired by their model but not the same in all details.

The Necker figure is a cube projected onto a two-dimensional plane, which permits one to view the cube as having one of two different orientations. At any moment, the perceiver sees only one of the two orientations, but the orientation spontaneously flips every few moments to the opposite orientation.[1] In experiments, the switching rate is observed by asking the perceiver to press a button every time the orientation appears to flip. By observing the switches across time, one can obtain the dwell times between flips and obtain a distribution of dwell times. The empirical distributions tend to have the shape of a gamma distribution. The mean of the distribution depends on factors such as turning the stimulus off for an interval of time. The many empirical results supporting

---

[1] Chapter 5 considered applications of quantum theory to ambiguous words such as "bat." Usually some context (e.g., baseball versus vampire) is presented to fix the meanings of an ambiguous word. Perhaps the meanings of these ambiguous words also flip across time without some context to fix their meaning.

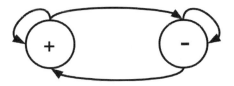

Figure 8.2 Two-state transition diagram for perception of the Necker cube.

the quantum model are summarized in detail in Atmanspacher and Filk (2010) and not provided here. Our goal here is to use this example to introduce quantum dynamics and the reader is referred to the Atmanspacher and Filk (2010) article for a detailed analysis of the model with respect to the experimental findings.

Although we work with simple two-dimensional models in this section, the basic equations are expressed using matrix algebra. The use of matrix algebra allows the same equations to be generalized and also used for $N > 2$-dimensional systems.

8.1.1 Markov model

It is useful to examine the Markov model side by side with the quantum model to see exactly what makes the quantum model so different. Also, it is important to compare Markov models with quantum models with respect to their ability to predict empirical findings.

8.1.1.1 State representation

First let us consider a two-dimensional Markov model for this process as illustrated in Figure 8.2. This model assumes that the perceptual system can be in one of two states at each moment in time – a plus state denoted $|+\rangle$ representing one of the orientations or a minus state denoted $|-\rangle$ representing the other orientation.

A single realization or sample path or trajectory produced by the Markov process starts in some initial state, either $|S(0)\rangle = |+\rangle$ or $|S(0)\rangle = |-\rangle$, and jumps back and forth across time from a clear plus state to a clear minus state. See Figure 8.3 for an example of a single trajectory for a Markov process. In the figure, the system is in a minus state at time 2, plus state at time 4, and minus state again at time 7.

The state definitely starts in a plus state or it definitely starts in a minus state. In Figure 8.3 it starts in the plus state, but in general we do not know which it is for any given sample path, and so we represent this uncertainty by assigning an initial probability distribution across these two possibilities, denoted $\phi_+(0)$ for plus and $\phi_-(0)$ for minus, and $\phi_+(0) + \phi_-(0) = 1$.

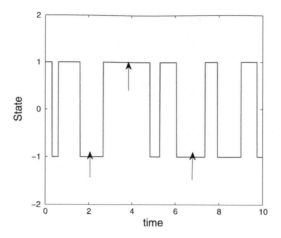

Figure 8.3 A single trajectory produced by the two-state Markov process.

8.1.1.2 State transitions

To cast this model of the perceptual system in matrix form, we define the initial probability distribution by a 2×1 state probability matrix

$$\phi(0) = \begin{bmatrix} \phi_+(0) \\ \phi_-(0) \end{bmatrix},$$

with the first coordinate representing plus, $|+\rangle$, and the second coordinate representing minus, $|-\rangle$. If the system is known to start from the plus state, then $\phi_+(0) = 1$; if the system is known to be in the minus state, then $\phi_-(0) = 1$; and if the state is unknown, then $\phi_+(0) + \phi_-(0) = 1$. From the plus state at time zero, the perceptual system can transit after some period of time t_1 to the minus state with a transition probability $T_{-,+}(t_1, 0)$ or it could remain in the plus state with transition probability $T_{+,+}(t_1, 0)$ and these two transition probabilities must sum to one (read the subscripts $T_{-,+}$ from right $+$ to left $-$). From the minus state at time zero, the system can transit after some period of time t_1 to the plus state with a transition probability $T_{+,-}(t_1, 0)$ or it could remain in the minus state with transition probability $T_{-,-}(t_1, 0)$ and these two transition probabilities must also sum to one. These four transition probabilities form a 2×2 transition matrix $T(t_1, 0)$. It is called a stochastic matrix because the entries are positive and sum to unity with a column:

$$T(t_1, 0) = \begin{bmatrix} T_{+,+}(t_1, 0) & T_{+,-}(t_1, 0) \\ T_{-,+}(t_1, 0) & T_{-,-}(t_1, 0) \end{bmatrix}.$$

The matrix product of the transition matrix times the initial probability distribution at time zero produces the updated distribution across the two states at time t_1:

$$\phi(t_1) = T(t_1, 0) \cdot \phi(0)$$

$$= \begin{bmatrix} T_{+,+}(t_1,0) & T_{+,-}(t_1,0) \\ T_{-,+}(t_1,0) & T_{-,-}(t_1,0) \end{bmatrix} \cdot \begin{bmatrix} \phi_+(0) \\ \phi_-(0) \end{bmatrix}$$

$$\begin{bmatrix} \phi_+(t_1) \\ \phi_-(t_1) \end{bmatrix} = \begin{bmatrix} T_{+,+}(t_1,0) \cdot \phi_+(0) + T_{+,-}(t_1,0) \cdot \phi_-(0) \\ T_{-,+}(t_1,0) \cdot \phi_+(0) + T_{-,-}(t_1,0) \cdot \phi_-(0) \end{bmatrix}.$$

This Markov equation follows directly from the *law of total probability*. The Markov model must obey this law, but the quantum model does not have to obey this rule. Therefore, the quantum model is not a special case of a Markov model.

Given the state at time t_1, we can update again using the transition matrix $T(t_2, t_1)$ that describes the probabilities of transitions for the period of time from t_1 to t_2:

$$\phi(t_2) = T(t_2, t_1) \cdot \phi(t_1)$$

$$= T(t_2, t_1) \cdot T(t_1, 0) \cdot \phi(0).$$

For many applications it is reasonable to assume that the transition matrix remains stationary so that $T(t_1 + t, t_1) = T(t_2 + t, t_2)$, in which case only the duration t of the time period is important. In this case we simply write the transition matrix as $T(t)$, in which case the distribution at time t_2 equals

$$\phi(t_2) = T(t_2) \cdot \phi(0).$$

$$= T(t_2 - t_1) \cdot T(t_1) \cdot \phi(0).$$

The first line in the above pair of equations simply follows from the original definition of the stationary transition matrix, but combining these two equations implies that the transition matrix obeys the semi-group property of dynamic systems,

$$T(t + u) = T(t) \cdot T(u) = T(u) \cdot T(t),$$

from which one can derive the following differential equation, called the Kolmogorov forward equation, that describes the time evolution of the transition matrix (see Bhattacharya and Waymire (1990: Section 4.2))

$$\frac{\mathrm{d}T(t)}{\mathrm{d}t} = K \cdot T(t).$$

as well as the time evolution of the probability distribution over states (simply multiply both sides on the right by $\phi(t)$):

$$\frac{\mathrm{d}\phi(t)}{\mathrm{d}t} = K \cdot \phi(t).$$

The 2×2 matrix K is called the intensity matrix, which is used to construct the transition matrix as a function of processing time duration. The intensity matrix must satisfy the following constraints to guarantee that the solution is a transition matrix: the off-diagonal entries must be positive but the sum of the elements within a column must equal zero. For a 2×2 matrix we require

$$K = \begin{bmatrix} -k_1 & k_2 \\ k_1 & -k_2 \end{bmatrix} = k_1 \cdot \begin{bmatrix} -1 & k \\ 1 & -k \end{bmatrix}, \quad k = \frac{k_2}{k_1}.$$

Choosing the coefficients in the intensity matrix is a critical part of building a Markov model. The parameter $k = k_2/k_1$ increases the rate of switching from minus to plus. Often, the values of these parameters are estimated from the data to maximize fit.

The solution to the Kolmogorov forward equation is the matrix exponential function

$$T(t) = e^{tK},$$

$$\phi(t) = e^{tK} \cdot \phi(0).$$

and this can be checked by taking the derivative: $\frac{\mathrm{d}}{\mathrm{d}t} e^{tK} = K \cdot e^{tK}$.

For the two-state model, we can derive a simple formula for the transition matrix $T(t) = e^{tK}$ by using the eigenvector representation of $K = Q \cdot \Lambda \cdot Q^{-1}$, where Q is a matrix of eigenvectors and Λ is a diagonal matrix of eigenvalues.[2]

$$Q = \begin{bmatrix} k & -1 \\ 1 & 1 \end{bmatrix}, \quad \Lambda = \begin{bmatrix} 0 & 0 \\ 0 & -(1+k) \cdot k_1 \end{bmatrix},$$

$$K = \begin{bmatrix} k & -1 \\ 1 & 1 \end{bmatrix} \cdot \begin{bmatrix} 0 & 0 \\ 0 & -(1+k) \cdot k_1 \end{bmatrix} \cdot \begin{bmatrix} \frac{1}{1+k} & \frac{1}{1+k} \\ -\frac{1}{1+k} & \frac{k}{1+k} \end{bmatrix}.$$

Using this representation for K we obtain

$$T(t) = e^{tK}$$

$$= \begin{bmatrix} k & -1 \\ 1 & 1 \end{bmatrix} \cdot \begin{bmatrix} e^0 & 0 \\ 0 & e^{-(1+k)k_1 t} \end{bmatrix} \cdot \begin{bmatrix} \frac{1}{1+k} & \frac{1}{1+k} \\ -\frac{1}{1+k} & \frac{k}{1+k} \end{bmatrix},$$

$$= \frac{1}{1+k} \cdot \begin{bmatrix} k + e^{-(1+k)k_1 t} & k - k \cdot e^{-(1+k)k_1 t} \\ 1 - e^{-(1+k)k_1 t} & 1 + k \cdot e^{-(1+k)k_1 t} \end{bmatrix}.$$

If we assume that $\phi_+(0) = \phi_-(0) = 0.50$, then we obtain the following probability for a plus state at time t:

---

[2] Note that K is not symmetric and the eigenvectors are not orthogonal, so we need to use the inverse of the eigenvector matrix on the right-hand side. See Chapter 2 on matrix algebra. This result was obtained from Mathematica by defining the matrix K symbolically and then using the Eigenvector[K] and Eigenvalue[K] and the Inverse[K] functions.

$$\phi_+(t) = \frac{k + e^{-(1+k)k_1 t} + k - k \cdot e^{-(1+k)k_1 t}}{2 \cdot (1+k)}$$

$$= \frac{k \cdot \left(1 - e^{-(1+k)k_1 t}\right) + k + e^{-(1+k)k_1 t}}{2 \cdot (1+k)}$$

$$= \frac{k}{1+k} \cdot \left(1 - e^{-(1+k)k_1 t}\right) + \frac{-k \cdot \left(1 - e^{-(1+k)k_1 t}\right) + k + e^{-(1+k)k_1 t}}{2 \cdot (1+k)}$$

$$= \frac{k}{1+k} \cdot \left(1 - e^{-(1+k)k_1 t}\right) + \frac{1}{2} \cdot e^{-(1+k)k_1 t}.$$

8.1.1.3   Response probabilities

Using the state transition probabilities described above, we can derive response probabilities at various time points from the Markov model. A response refers to a measurement that the perceiver makes or reports regarding the interpretation of the figure at some point in time. The response "plus orientation" at time t is denoted $R(t) = +$, and the response "minus orientation" at time t is $R(t) = -$. The mapping between states and responses for the Markov model can be represented by the two state-response transition matrices

$$M_- = \begin{bmatrix} 0 & 0 \\ 0 & 1 \end{bmatrix}, \ M_+ = \begin{bmatrix} 1 & 0 \\ 0 & 0 \end{bmatrix}.$$

In the following, it will also be convenient to use the 1×2 matrix $L = \begin{bmatrix} 1 & 1 \end{bmatrix}$ to perform summation across states. Using these matrices, the probability of observing a "plus" at time t equals the product

$$p(R(t) = +) = L \cdot M_+ \cdot T(t) \cdot \phi(0).$$

It is worth pointing out that the state-response matrix M_+ does not commute with the transition matrix $T(t)$ and so the order of operations must be maintained.

What happens to the distribution over the states after we observed a "plus" response at time t? Before the measurement at time t, the state is represented by the distribution $\phi(t) = [\phi_+(t), \phi_-(t)]^\dagger$; but immediately after the measurement, and observing the state, the distribution is revised to become[3]

$$\phi_+ = \frac{M_+ \cdot \phi(t)}{p(R(t) = +)}$$

$$= \frac{1}{p(R(t) = +)} \cdot \begin{bmatrix} \phi_+(t) \\ 0 \end{bmatrix} = \begin{bmatrix} 1 \\ 0 \end{bmatrix}.$$

Thereafter, we have $p(t + h | R(t) = +) = T(h) \cdot \phi_+$. The distribution after time t is then used to determine the response probabilities for later observations. For

---

[3] One could interpret this as the "collapse" of the Markov state after measurement.

example, the probability of a "minus" response at time t_2 given a "plus" at time t_1 equals

$$p(R(t_2) = - \,|R(t_1) = +) = L \cdot M_- \cdot T(t_2 - t_1) \cdot \phi_+.$$

Now let us consider the joint probabilities for more complex sequences. First, the joint probability of "plus" at t_1 and "minus" at t_2 equals

$$p(R(t_1) = + \cap R(t_2) = -)$$
$$= p(R(t_2) = - \,|R(t_1) = +) \cdot p(R(t_1) = +)$$
$$= L \cdot M_- \cdot T(t_2 - t_1) \cdot \phi_+ \cdot p(R(t_1) = +)$$
$$= L \cdot M_- \cdot T(t_2 - t_1) \cdot M_+ \cdot \phi(t_1)$$
$$= L \cdot M_- \cdot T(t_2 - t_1) \cdot M_+ \cdot T(t_1) \cdot \phi(0).$$

By repeated application of the above principle, the probability of a more complex sequence of responses, such as, for example, "minus" at time t_1 and "plus" at time t_2 and "minus" at time t_3 can be computed very easily (operating from right to left on the right-hand side):

$$p(R(t_1) = - \cap R(t_2) = + \cap R(t_3) = -) \tag{8.1}$$
$$= p(R(t_1) = -, \ R(t_2) = +, \ R(t_3) = -)$$
$$= L \cdot M_- \cdot T(t_3 - t_2) \cdot M_+ \cdot T(t_2 - t_1) \cdot M_- \cdot T(t_1) \cdot \phi(0).$$

Hereafter we will use the shorter notation $(R(t_1) = -, \ R(t_2) = +, \ R(t_3) = -)$ for a sequence of events rather than the longer notation $(R(t_1) = - \cap R(t_2) = + \cap R(t_3) = -)$.

8.1.1.4   Numerical example

Let us take a numerical example by setting $k_1 = 1 = k_2$ to examine the transition probability from a positive state at time zero to a negative state at time t. This choice of parameters for the intensity matrix makes it equally likely to switch from plus to minus and vice versa. In this simple case, we can derive a simple solution: $T_{-,+}(t) = \frac{1}{2}\left(1 - e^{-2t}\right) = T_{+,-}(t)$. However, to continue using our more general matrix methods, we computed the transitions using the matrix exponential function $T = \text{expm}(t*K)$ in Matlab for a range of t values. The dashed line in Figure 8.4 shows the transition probability $T_{-,+}(t)$ from plus to minus as a function of time for this Markov model. The dashed curve illustrates the exponential growth toward an equilibrium at 0.50 predicted by the Markov model.

Let us examine another important prediction of the Markov model again using $k_1 = 1 = k_2$ (unbiased switching). Suppose the system starts in the plus state $|+\rangle$ and we take a sequence of measurements, once after each time period Δt. How long will it take before we observe a switch to the minus state? The mean time to wait equals the time period for each observation times

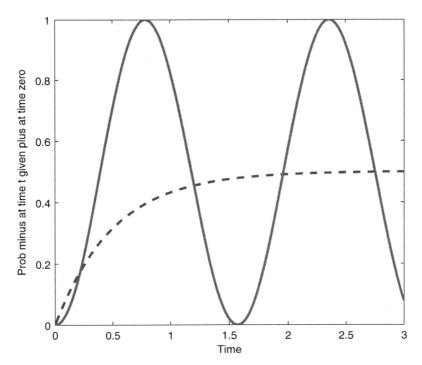

Figure 8.4 Transition probabilities for the Markov (dashed line) and quantum (solid line).

the expected number of observations, $\text{MT} = E(N) \cdot \Delta t$, so we need to determine the $E(N)$. The probability of staying in state $|+\rangle$ for a single observation is $p(R(\Delta t) = + | R(0) = +) = T_{+,+}(\Delta t)$ (which again we compute using $\texttt{T = expm(dt*K)}$ in Matlab). The probability of staying for $n-1$ consecutive plus observations and then switching to minus on the next step equals

$$p(R_1 = +, R_2 = +, \ldots, R_{n-1} = +, R_n = -)$$

$$= L \cdot (M_- \cdot T(\Delta t)) \cdot (M_+ \cdot T(\Delta t))^{n-1} \cdot \phi(0)$$

$$= T_{-,+}(\Delta t) \cdot (T_{+,+}(\Delta t))^{(n-1)}.$$

The expectation or mean number of observations that are required to observe a switch equals[4]

$$E(N) = \sum_{n=1}^{\infty} n \cdot (T_{+,+}(\Delta t))^{(n-1)} \cdot T_{-,+}(\Delta t) = \frac{1}{T_{-,+}(\Delta t)}.$$

---

[4]The solution on the right-hand side is obtained by using the well-known fact for geomtric series that $\sum_{n=1}^{\infty} n \cdot p^{n-1} = \frac{1}{(1-p)^2}$ for $0 < p < 1$.

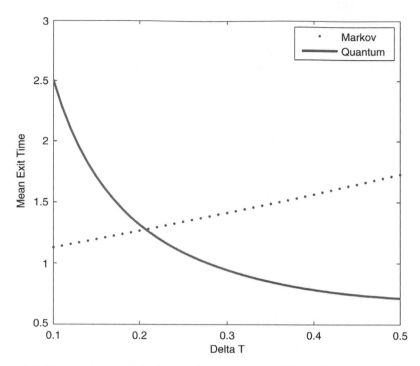

Figure 8.5 Comparison of Markov and quantum models with regard to the mean time to switch as a function of time between observations.

Therefore, the mean time to wait for a switch equals $\mathrm{MT} = E(N) \cdot \Delta t = \frac{\Delta t}{T_{-,+}(\Delta t)}$. The interesting prediction that we want to examine is how the mean time to wait for a switch varies depending on the time period Δt between each observation. The dotted line in Figure 8.5 shows the prediction for the Markov model – the line is increasing with increases in Δt. Alternatively, this means that if we *decrease* the observation interval toward zero $\Delta t \rightarrow 0$ (i.e., we increase the frequency of our observations), then this has the effect of decreasing the time we need to wait to see a change from plus to minus. Later we will contrast this prediction with the quantum model.

Before we conclude our review of the Markov model, we need to emphasize one point concerning the interpretation of the distribution $\phi(t)$ across time. What exactly does this distribution represent? To understand this, imagine running a computer simulation a billion times to generate an ensemble of trajectories. Each individual trajectory looks like some variation of Figure 8.3. The probability distribution $\phi(t)$ represents the ensemble average across all these individual trajectories. If we randomly sampled one trajectory and looked to see whether or not it is in the $|+\rangle$ state at time t, then $\phi_+(t)$ is the probability that this occurs.

8.1.2   Quantum model

The quantum model is very similar to the Markov model in many ways, and so
once you learn Markov models you already know a lot about quantum models.
But as we shall see below, these models also differ with respect to some critical
properties.

8.1.2.1   State representation

Now we consider a two-dimensional quantum model for the perceptual processing of the Necker cube, and we again use the idea illustrated in Figure 8.2.
We assume that the perceptual system can be observed in one of two states: a
plus state denoted $|+\rangle$ associated with one of the orientations or a minus state
denoted $|-\rangle$ associated with the other orientation. But now we define these
two states as two orthonormal basis vectors spanning a two-dimensional Hilbert
space. The quantum process starts in a superposition of the two basis states
$|S(0)\rangle = \psi_+(0) \cdot |+\rangle + \psi_-(0) \cdot |-\rangle$, where $\psi_+(0)$ is the amplitude corresponding
to the plus state, $\psi_-(0)$ is the amplitude for the minus state, and $|\psi_+(0)|^2 +$
$|\psi_-(0)|^2 = 1$. If $\psi_+(0) = 1$ then the system starts in a state equal to $|+\rangle$; al-
ternatively, if $\psi_-(0) = 1$ then the system starts in a state equal to $|-\rangle$. But a
remarkable property of the quantum model is that it does not have to start in a
strictly plus state or a strictly minus state (as required by the Markov model),
and instead it can start out in a superposed or indefinite state. Also, the state
does not jump discretely back and forth across time from a clear plus to a clear
minus. Instead, the superposed wave state evolves continuously across time until
a measurement is taken. Figure 8.6 illustrates the evolution of the amplitude
$\psi_-(t)$ for a single quantum process across time. Notice that it has a corkscrew
oscillation pattern. This amplitude represents the potential for the $|-\rangle$ to be
observed at each moment; but there is also an amplitude $\psi_+(t)$ giving the po-
tential for $|+\rangle$ to be observed at each moment. So both states have a potential
to occur at each moment for a single process. Therefore, the quantum model
does not produce a classic trajectory – that is, it does not produce a definite
state at each point in time. Instead, a *single* process undergoes a continuous
evolution of an indefinite (superposed) state.

8.1.2.2   State transitions

The initial state vector can be represented by the initial amplitudes using a
2×1 amplitude matrix

$$\psi(0) = \begin{bmatrix} \psi_+(0) \\ \psi_-(0) \end{bmatrix},$$

with the first coordinate representing the plus and the second coordinate representing the minus. If the system is known to be in the plus state, then $\psi_+(0) = 1$;
and if the system is known to be in the minus state, then $\psi_-(0) = 1$; and if

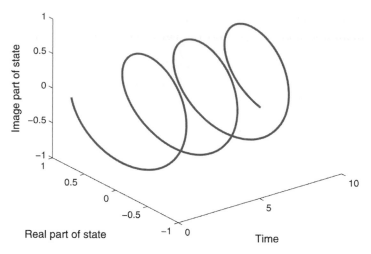

Figure 8.6 The real and imaginary parts of the amplitude for the minus state plotted as a function of time for the two-dimensional quantum model.

the state is unknown, then $|\psi_+(0)|^2 + |\psi_-(0)|^2 = 1$. From the plus state at time zero, the perceptual system can transit after some period of time t_1 to be observed at the minus state with transition amplitude $U_{-,+}(t_1,0)$ or it could remain in the plus state with transition amplitude $U_{+,+}(t_1,0)$ and the squared magnitudes of these two transition amplitudes must sum to one. From the minus state at time zero, the system can transit after some period of time t_1 to be observed at the plus state with a transition amplitude $U_{+,-}(t_1,0)$ or it could remain in the minus state with transition amplitude $U_{-,-}(t_1,0)$ and the squared magnitudes of these two transition amplitudes must also sum to one. These four transition amplitudes form a 2×2 amplitude matrix:

$$U(t_1,0) = \begin{bmatrix} U_{+,+}(t_1,0) & U_{+,-}(t_1,0) \\ U_{-,+}(t_1,0) & U_{-,-}(t_1,0) \end{bmatrix}.$$

But the matrix $U(t_1,0)$ must be a unitary matrix to preserve lengths and inner products, so that $U(t_1,0)^\dagger U(t_1,0) = I = U(t_1,0)U(t_1,0)^\dagger$ (see Chapter 2). This implies that, if we compute the squared magnitudes of the entries in the unitary matrix

$$\begin{bmatrix} |U_{+,+}(t_1,0)|^2 & |U_{+,-}(t_1,0)|^2 \\ |U_{-,+}(t_1,0)|^2 & |U_{-,-}(t_1,0)|^2 \end{bmatrix},$$

then this forms a transition probability matrix which must be *doubly stochastic* (both rows and columns sum to one; see Chapter 2). Recall that Markov models must be stochastic (elements within a column sum to one), but the elements in the rows do not have to sum to one. This double stochasticity property only holds for the quantum model; the Markov model does not have to obey this rule. This is an important empirically testable property of the quantum model, and from this we can see that the Markov model is not a special case of the quantum model. The Markov model must obey the law of total probability and the quantum model must obey the law of double stochasticity. They obey different laws.

The matrix product of the unitary matrix times the initial amplitude distribution at time zero produces the updated amplitude distribution across the two states at time t_1:

$$\psi(t_1) = U(t_1, 0) \cdot \psi(0)$$

$$= \begin{bmatrix} U_{+,+}(t_1, 0) & U_{+,-}(t_1, 0) \\ U_{-,+}(t_1, 0) & U_{-,-}(t_1, 0) \end{bmatrix} \cdot \begin{bmatrix} \psi_+(0) \\ \psi_-(0) \end{bmatrix}$$

$$\begin{bmatrix} \psi_+(t_1) \\ \psi_-(t_1) \end{bmatrix} = \begin{bmatrix} U_{+,+}(t_1, 0) \cdot \psi_+(0) + U_{+,-}(t_1, 0) \cdot \psi_-(0) \\ U_{-,+}(t_1, 0) \cdot \psi_+(0) + U_{-,-}(t_1, 0) \cdot \psi_-(0) \end{bmatrix}.$$

This is the law of total amplitude, which follows directly from Feynman's second rule for quantum probability (see Chapter 2). Given the state at time t_1, we can update again using the unitary matrix $U(t_2, t_1)$ that describes the amplitudes for transitions for the period of time from t_1 to t_2:

$$\psi(t_2) = U(t_2, t_1) \cdot \psi(t_1)$$

$$= U(t_2, t_1) \cdot U(t_1, 0) \cdot \psi(0).$$

Once again, for many applications it is reasonable to assume that the unitary matrix remains stationary so that $U(t_1 + t, t_1) = U(t_2 + t, t_2)$, in which case only the duration of the time period t is important. In this case we simply write the unitary matrix as $U(t)$, in which case the distribution of amplitudes at time t_2 equals

$$\psi(t) = U(t_2) \cdot \psi(0)$$

$$= U(t_2 - t_1) \cdot U(t_1 - 0) \cdot \psi(0).$$

The first line in the above pair of equations simply follows from the original definition of the stationary unitary matrix. But once again we see that, when we combine these two equations, together they imply that the unitary matrix also obeys the semi-group property of dynamic systems (see Hughes (1989: Section 3.10)):

$$U(t + u) = U(t) \cdot U(u) = U(u) \cdot U(t),$$

from which one can derive the following differential equation, called the Schrödinger equation,[5] that describes the time evolution of the unitary operator:

$$\frac{dU(t)}{dt} = -i \cdot H \cdot U(t),$$

---

[5] Erwin Schrödinger discovered this equation in 1926 about the same time that Heisenberg discovered his matrix equation, and shortly afterwards Schrödinger proved that the two were mathematically identical.

$$p(R(t_1) = +, R(t_2) = -)$$

$$= p(R(t_2) = - \mid R(t_1) = +) \cdot p(R(t_1) = +)$$

$$= ||M_- \cdot U(t_2 - t_1) \cdot \psi_+||^2 \cdot p(R(t_1) = +)$$

$$= ||M_- \cdot U(t_2 - t_1) \cdot M_+ \cdot \psi(t_1)||^2$$

$$= ||M_- \cdot U(t_2 - t_1) \cdot M_+ \cdot U(t_1) \cdot \psi(0)||^2.$$

Repeated application of the above principle allows us to compute the probability of more complex sequences of responses, such as, for example, "minus" at time t_1 and "plus" at time t_2 and "minus" at time t_3 (operating from right to left on the right-hand side):

$$p(R(t_1) = -, R(t_2) = + R(t_3) = -) \tag{8.2}$$

$$= ||M_- \cdot U(t_3 - t_2) \cdot M_+ \cdot U(t_2 - t_1) \cdot M_- \cdot U(t_1) \cdot \psi(0)||^2.$$

8.1.2.4   Numerical example

To see how this model behaves, we examine a special case produced by setting $h_1 = 0$ and $h_2 = 2$. This is the Hamiltonian used by Atmanspacher and Filk (2010) to produce a harmonic oscillator. In this simple case, we can derive the following simple solution for the transition from the plus state to the minus state after a period of time t: $|U_{-,+}(t)|^2 = \sin(2 \cdot t)^2 = |U_{+,-}(t)|^2$. However, to continue using our more general matrix methods, we computed the unitary matrix using the matrix exponential function `U = expm(-i*t*H)` in Matlab for a range of t values. The solid line in Figure 8.4 shows the transition probability for the quantum model. As can be seen, this probability oscillates from zero to one gradually across time according to a squared sine function. Consequently, the temporal dynamics of the quantum model are quite different than the Markov model. However, if we average over a large time window, then the two models produce similar average response probabilities.

Let us compare another important prediction of the quantum model with the Markov model, again using $h_1 = 0$ and $h_2 = 2$ (harmonic oscillator). As before, suppose the system starts in the plus state $|+\rangle$ and we take a sequence of measurements, once after each time period Δt. How long will it take before we observe a switch to the minus state? The probability of staying in state $|+\rangle$ for a single observation is $p(R(\Delta t) = + \mid R(0) = +) = |U_{+,+}(\Delta t)|^2$ (which again we compute using `U = expm(-i*dt*H)` in Matlab). The probability of staying plus for $n - 1$ consecutive observations and then switching to minus on the next step equals

$$p(R_1 = +, R_2 = +, \ldots, R_{n-1} = +, R_n = -)$$

$$= \left\| (M_- \cdot U(\Delta t)) \cdot (M_+ \cdot U(\Delta t))^{n-1} \cdot \psi(0) \right\|^2$$

$$= |U_{-,+}(\Delta t)|^2 \cdot |U_{+,+}(\Delta t)|^{2 \cdot (n-1)}.$$

Therefore, the mean number of observations that are required to observe a switch equals

$$E(N) = \sum_{n=1}^{\infty} n \cdot |U_{+,+}(\Delta t)|^{2 \cdot (n-1)} \cdot |U_{-,+}(\Delta t)|^2 = \frac{1}{|U_{-,+}(\Delta t)|^2},$$

and the mean time to wait for a switch equals $MT = E(N) \cdot \Delta t = \frac{\Delta t}{|U_{-,+}(\Delta t)|^2}$. Once again, the prediction that we want to examine is how the mean time to wait for a switch varies depending on the time period Δt between each observation. The solid line in Figure 8.5 shows the prediction for the quantum model – the curve is decreasing with increases in Δt! This means that if we decrease the observation interval toward zero $\Delta t \to 0$ (i.e., we increase the frequency of our observations), then this has the effect of *increasing* the time we need to wait to see a change from plus to minus. This predicted effect is called the quantum Zeno effect after the famous Greek philosopher who pondered on the question about "a watched arrow that never seems to move."

As we mentioned earlier, Atmanspacher and Filk (2010) review many empirical findings that accord with their model which are not described here. They also describe additional theoretical assumptions, such as, for example, allowing time dependence of the h_2 parameter in the Hamiltonian matrix H, and the latter is a key assumption required for fitting a gamma-distributed dwell time distribution.

This concludes our presentation of the quantum model. Although there are many formal similarities between Markov and quantum models, we see in Figure 8.4 that they behave quite differently. Of course, these predictions are only for highly specific versions of each model.[7] Is it possible to test them more generally? The next section describes a very general test that distinguishes the two models.

8.1.3 Temporal Bell inequality

How can we tell the difference between a Markov process and a quantum process? In this section, we describe a fundamental test that can be used to distinguish between the two classes of models, called the temporal Bell inequality test (Atmanspacher & Filk, 2010).[8] This test involves three experimental conditions, experienced on different experimental sessions, given to the same person. Each condition requires a pair of measurements of the perceptual system. In condition C_1, the orientation of the Necker cube is measured at times t_1 and t_2

---

[7]For example, another quantum model for binocular rivalry is presented by Manousakis (2009).

[8]The Bell inequality was first formulated by the physicist John Bell in 1966 (see Chapter 5). The temporal Bell inequality (Leggett & Garg, 1985) is a simple variant of the more famous but slightly more complex Bell inequality. The latter requires two systems and an interaction that produces a correlation between the two systems, and different types of tests are done on the separated systems to obtain the joint probabilities. The inequality presented here only requires a test of one system at different time points. See Peres (1998) or Hughes (1989) for a description of the original Bell inequality. See Chapter 5 for more details.

Table 8.1 Eight patterns produced by classic trajectories

State at t_1	State at t_2	State at t_3	Joint prob.	C_1	C_2	C_3
+1	+1	+1	$p(+++)$	0	0	0
+1	+1	−1	$p(++-)$	0	1	1
+1	−1	+1	$p(+-+)$	1	1	0
+1	−1	−1	$p(+--)$	1	0	1
−1	+1	+1	$p(-++)$	1	0	1
−1	+1	−1	$p(-+-)$	1	1	0
−1	−1	+1	$p(--+)$	0	1	1
−1	−1	−1	$p(---)$	0	0	0

after the onset of the stimulus, and a "same or different" judgment is recorded. In condition C_2, the orientation is measured at times t_2 and t_3 and another "same or different" judgment is recorded. Finally, for condition C_3, the orientation is measured at times t_1 and t_3 and a third "same or different" judgment is obtained.

Figure 8.3 illustrates the basic predictions of any two-state classic stochastic process model, including Markov models. At each time point, a single trajectory is in exactly one orientation state. In Figure 8.3, the example trajectory passes through state −1 at $t_1 = 2$, state +1 at time $t_2 = 4$, and state −1 at $t_3 = 7$. The first judgment, which compares times 2 and 4, is scored $C_1 = 1$ for being different at these two time points; the second judgment, comparing times 4 and 7, is scored $C_2 = 1$ for being different; and the third judgment, comparing times 2 and 7, is scored $C_3 = 0$ for being the same at these two time points. This single trajectory produces a pattern of responses 110 (shown in Table 8.1 under C_1, C_2, C_3) to the three conditions. Each trajectory that we sample passes through one of eight possible patterns, as shown in Table 1.

The probability of sampling a pattern from the entire ensemble of trajectories is represented by the column labeled "Joint prob." For example, $p(-+-)$ is the probability of the "minus, plus, minus" pattern produced in Figure 8.3. The temporal Bell inequality is based on total probabilities summed across the rows of Table 8.1 for each condition. Column C_1 represents the condition under which the perception is tested at times t_1 and t_2. The rows within column C_1 contain a one if t_1 and t_2 produce a difference for that row pattern; for example, the second row has a zero because the states at t_1 and t_2 are the same. Column C_2 represents the condition under which the perception is tested at times t_2 and t_3. The rows in column C_2 contain a one if t_2 and t_3 produce a difference judgment; for example, the second row has a one because the states at t_2 and t_3 are different. Column C_3 represents the condition under which the perception is tested at times t_1 and t_3. Finally, the rows of column C_3 contain a one if the row pattern produces a difference for times t_1 and t_3; for example, the second row has a one because t_1 and t_3 are different. If we multiply the column score (zero or one) by the corresponding joint probability and sum across the rows within a column, then we obtain the total probability of a *difference* for each column condition, denoted $p(D|C_j)$. The key property to notice is that, for every row where C_3 has a one, there is also a one in a row for either the column C_1 or C_2. Consequently, we arrive at the following temporal Bell inequality:

$$p(D|C_1) = p(+ - +) + p(+ - -) + p(- + +) + p(- + -)$$

$$p(D|C_2) = p(+ + -) + p(+ - +) + p(- + -) + p(- - +)$$

$$p(D|C_3) = p(+ + -) + p(+ - -) + p(- + +) + p(- - +)$$

$$p(D|C_1) + p(D|C_2) - p(D|C_3) = 2 \cdot (p(+ - +) + p(- + -)) .$$

The last line implies the temporal Bell inequality

$$p(D|C_1) + p(D|C_2) \geq p(D|C_3).$$

In other words, classic probability theory requires that the probability of a change from time t_1 to t_2 plus the probability of a change from time t_2 to t_3 must equal or exceed the probability of a change from time t_1 to t_3.

This is a very general test of classic stochastic process models that assume that a single trajectory is sampled from the same ensemble of trajectories for all three conditions.[9] No assumptions are made about the form of the joint probability distribution other than the assumption that the same distribution holds for all three conditions. For example, the events may have arbitrary marginal probabilities and arbitrary dependencies. Let us compare the Markov and quantum models for this inequality, starting with the Markov model.

Consider condition C_2 for example. First, note that $p(D|C_2) = p(R(t_2) = +, R(t_3) = -) + p(R(t_2) = -, R(t_3) = +)$. It is instructive to see exactly why the Markov model obeys the temporal Bell inequality. According to the Markov model,

$$p(R(t_2) = +, \ R(t_3) = -)$$

$$= L \cdot M_- \cdot T(t_3 - t_2) \cdot M_+ \cdot T(t_2) \cdot \phi(0)$$

$$= L \cdot M_- \cdot T(t_3 - t_2) \cdot M_+ \cdot T(t_2 - t_1) \cdot I \cdot T(t_1) \cdot \phi(0)$$

$$= L \cdot M_- \cdot T(t_3 - t_2) \cdot M_+ \cdot T(t_2 - t_1) \cdot (M_+ + M_-) \cdot T(t_1) \cdot \phi(0)$$

and the next line is the key step:

$$= L \cdot M_- \cdot T(t_3 - t_2) \cdot M_+ \cdot T(t_2 - t_1) \cdot M_+ \cdot T(t_1) \cdot \phi(0)$$

$$+ L \cdot M_- \cdot T(t_3 - t_2) \cdot M_+ \cdot T(t_2 - t_1) \cdot M_- \cdot T(t_1) \cdot \phi(0)$$

$$= p(+ + -) + p(- + -).$$

Following the same line of reasoning, $p(R(t_2) = -, \ R(t_3) = +) = p(+ - +) + p(- - +)$. This is just the law of total probability, which decomposes the joint

---

[9]This test of the temporal Bell is analogous to the test of the triangle inequality property implied by random utility models (Regenwetter et al., 2010).

probability for two events into the sum of the joint probabilities for three events. Furthermore, this decomposition of the joint probability for two events into the sum of the joint probabilities for three events is implied by the Markov model for both $p(D|C_1)$ and $p(D|C_2)$ as well. Therefore, the law of total probability obeyed by the Markov model implies the temporal Bell inequality. Let us check with a numerical example. If we set $P(0) = \begin{bmatrix} 0.5 & 0.5 \end{bmatrix}^{\dagger}$, set $k_1 = 1 = k_2$ in the intensity matrix K (as we did to generate the dashed line in Figure 8.4), and set $t_1 = 0.25$, $t_2 = 0.5$, and $t_3 = 0.75$, then we obtain $p(D|C_1) = 0.28$, $p(D|C_2) = 0.28$, $p(D|C_3) = 0.45$, which satisfies the temporal Bell inequality. (The Matlab program used to compute these probabilities is given in Appendix G).

Now let us look at the predictions of the quantum model. The quantum model obeys the law of total amplitude rather than the law of total probability, and this allows it to violate the temporal Bell inequality. Let us see how this works for condition 2 again:

$$p(R(t_2) = +, \ R(t_3) = -)$$

$$= ||M_- \cdot U(t_3 - t_2) \cdot M_+ \cdot U(t_2) \cdot \psi(0)||^2$$

$$= ||M_- \cdot U(t_3 - t_2) \cdot M_+ \cdot U(t_2 - t_1) \cdot I \cdot U(t_1) \cdot \psi(0)||^2$$

$$= ||M_- \cdot U(t_3 - t_2) \cdot M_+ \cdot U(t_2 - t_1) \cdot (M_+ + M_-) \cdot U(t_1) \cdot \psi(0)||^2$$

$$= ||\psi(+ + -) + \psi(- + -)||^2$$

and here is where the violation occurs:

$$\neq ||\psi(+ + -)||^2 + ||\psi(- + -)||^2,$$

where the inequality in the last line follows because the left-hand side produces an interference term which is missing on the right-hand side. This last result shows that the joint probability for two events cannot be decomposed into the sum of the joint probabilities for three events. Let us check with another numerical example (again, the Matlab program is in Appendix G). If we set $\psi(0) = \begin{bmatrix} \sqrt{0.5} & \sqrt{0.5} \end{bmatrix}^{\dagger}$, set $h_1 = 0$ and $h_2 = 2$ (as we did to generate the solid line in Figure 8.4), and set $t_1 = 0.25$, $t_2 = 0.50$, and $t_3 = 0.75$, then the quantum model predicts $p(D|C_1) = 0.23$, $p(D|C_2) = 0.23$, and $p(D|C_3) = 0.71$, which produces a large violation of the temporal Bell inequality.

So far, this experiment has not been conducted, and so we do not know if the temporal Bell inequality is violated or not in the Necker cube perception task. It is not a perfect test, because one could argue that the conditions change the three-event joint probabilities somehow, but this argument must be supported by a mathematical model of how this change occurs. Otherwise it remains an empirically empty claim. Now let us turn to look at higher dimensional Markov and quantum models, and we consider another way to test the law of total probability and double stochasticity.

Table 8.2 Category–decision-making task results

Type face	$p(G)$	$p(A|G)$	$p(B)$	$p(A|B)$	$p_T(A)$	$p(A)$	t	p
Wide	0.84	0.35	0.16	0.52	0.37	0.39	0.5733	0.5716
Narrow	0.17	0.41	0.83	0.63	0.59	0.69	2.54	0.018

Figure 8.7 Example faces used in a categorization–decision experiment. The left two are from narrow category and the right two are from wide category.

8.2 Categorization decision-making application

Townsend *et al.* (2000) introduced a new paradigm to study the interactions between categorization and decision making. Initially, this paradigm was used to test a Markov model; subsequently, this paradigm was extended for comparisons of both Markov and quantum models (Busemeyer *et al.*, 2009). In a categorization–decision task, on each trial, participants are shown pictures of faces, which vary along two dimensions (face width and lip thickness). See Figure 8.7 for examples.

Two different distributions of faces are used: on average, a "narrow" face distribution has a narrow width and thick lips; on average, a "wide" face distribution has a wide width and thin lips. The participants are asked to categorize the faces as belonging to either a "good" guy or "bad" guy group, and/or they are asked to decide whether to take an "attack" or "withdraw" action. The participants are informed that "narrow" faces had a 0.60 probability to come from the "bad guy" population and "wide" faces had a 0.60 chance to come from the "good guy" population. The participants were usually (probability 0.70) rewarded for attacking "bad guys" and they were usually (probability 0.70) rewarded for withdrawing from "good guys." The primary manipulation was produced by using the following two test conditions, presented across a series of trials, to each participant. In the C-then-D condition, participants made a categorization followed by an action decision; in the D-alone condition, participants only made an action decision. The experiment included a total of 26 participants, but each participant provided 51 observations for the C–D condition for a total of $26 \times 51 = 1326$ observations, and each person produced 17 observations for the D-alone condition, producing $17 \times 26 = 442$ total observations. The results are shown in Table 8.2.

fit the categorization results, and set $T_{AB} = p(A|B) = 0.63$ and $T_{AG} = p(A|W) = 0.41$ to fit the transition probabilities. This uses three parameters; but there are four data points, so there is one degree of freedom left to test the model. The last degree of freedom comes from the constraint imposed by the law of total probability. The Markov model predicts that $p_T(A) = p(A)$. Table 8.2 shows that this prediction is severely violated for the narrow faces (but only mildly violated for the wide faces). So this particular Markov model cannot account for the narrow face interference effect. It could be modified by assuming that the transition matrix changes across tasks, but then the model is no longer empirically testable.

8.2.2 Quantum model

In Chapter 1, we briefly introduced a simple two-dimensional quantum model for this task. Recall Figure 1.2, which is reproduced here as Figure 8.8. Here we again assume that there are two category states $C = \{|G\rangle, |B\rangle\}$ and two action states $D = \{|A\rangle, |W\rangle\}$. We assume that C and D represent two different sets of orthonormal basis vectors within the same two-dimensional space. In other words, the events described by C are incompatible with the events described by D. The state of the quantum system can be expressed in either basis as $|S\rangle = \psi_B \cdot |B\rangle + \psi_G \cdot |G\rangle = \psi_A \cdot |A\rangle + \psi_W \cdot |W\rangle$.

Once again it is assumed that the presentation of the face generates an initial superposition state in the two-dimensional space. For the C-then-D task, the decision maker resolves the initial state into one of the categorization states in C and then transfers to one of the states in D to select an action. For the D-alone task, the initial state remains unresolved and passes through both category states in C to arrive at a final choice of an action from set D.

The initial state, described in terms of the categorization basis, is the 2×1 column vector

$$\psi_I = \begin{bmatrix} \psi_B \\ \psi_G \end{bmatrix},$$

which contains the initial amplitudes for the category states (which depend on the type of face). The probability of initially observing the "good" category equals $p(G) = |\psi_G|^2$, and similarly $p(B) = |\psi_B|^2$, and so the squared length of ψ_I must equal one. The 2×2 unitary matrix

$$U = \begin{bmatrix} u_{AB} & u_{AG} \\ u_{WB} & u_{WG} \end{bmatrix}$$

contains the amplitudes for transiting from each category state to each action state. This is a unitary matrix, $U^\dagger U = UU^\dagger = I$, so that it preserves the unit-length property of the state. More specifically, the requirement $U^\dagger U = I$ implies

$$|u_{AB}|^2 + |u_{WB}|^2 = 1,$$

$$|u_{AG}|^2 + |u_{WG}|^2 = 1,$$

$$u_{AG}^* \cdot u_{AB} + u_{WG}^* \cdot u_{WB} = 0,$$

and the requirement $UU^\dagger = I$ implies

$$|u_{AB}|^2 + |u_{AG}|^2 = 1,$$

$$|u_{WB}|^2 + |u_{WG}|^2 = 1,$$

$$u_{AB} \cdot u_{WB}^* + u_{AG} \cdot u_{WG}^* = 0,$$

The transition probabilities observed under the C-then-D condition are determined by the squared magnitudes of the entries in the unitary matrix. Specifically, $T_{ij}(u_{ij}) = |u_{ij}|^2$ is the probability of observing an action i given that a previous category response j was observed. As can be seen from the above constraints, a unitary matrix produces a transition matrix $T(U)$ that is doubly stochastic: both the rows and columns of the transition matrix generated by U sum to one (Peres, 1998).

The final amplitude of taking each action under the D-alone condition is given by the matrix product

$$\psi_F = U \cdot \psi_I = \begin{bmatrix} \psi_B \cdot u_{AB} + \psi_G \cdot u_{AG} \\ \psi_B \cdot u_{WB} + \psi_G \cdot u_{WG} \end{bmatrix} = \begin{bmatrix} \psi_A \\ \psi_W \end{bmatrix},$$

which can be interpreted as the *law of total amplitude* (Gudder, 1988). The probability of making an "attack" decision in the D-alone condition equals

$$\begin{aligned} |\psi_A|^2 &= |\psi_B \cdot u_{AB} + \psi_G \cdot u_{AG}|^2 \\ &= (\psi_B \cdot u_{AB} + \psi_G \cdot u_{AG})(\psi_B \cdot u_{AB} + \psi_G \cdot u_{AG})^* \\ &= |\psi_B|^2 |u_{AB}|^2 + |\psi_G|^2 |u_{AG}|^2 \\ &\quad + 2 \cdot \mathrm{Re}\left[(\psi_B \cdot u_{AB}) \cdot (\psi_G \cdot u_{AG})^*\right] \\ &= p_G \cdot T_{AG} + p_B \cdot T_{AB} + \mathrm{Int}_A. \end{aligned}$$

In other words, the quantum prediction differs from the Markov prediction by an interference term

$$\begin{aligned} \mathrm{Int}_A &= 2 \cdot \mathrm{Re}\left[(\psi_B \cdot u_{AB}) \cdot (\psi_G \cdot u_{AG})^*\right] \\ &= 2 \cdot |\psi_G| \cdot |u_{AG}| \cdot |\psi_B| \cdot |u_{AB}| \cdot \cos(\theta), \end{aligned}$$

where θ is the phase of the complex number $(\psi_G \cdot u_{AG}) \cdot (\psi_B \cdot u_{AB})^*$ (see Chapter 2). The law of total amplitude produces a probability that violates the law of total probability because of the interference term, which can be positive or negative. If the interference term is zero (i.e., $\cos(\theta) = 0$), then the probability produced by the law of total amplitude agrees with the law of total probability.

Using the same arguments as above, the probability of making a "withdraw" decision in the D-alone condition must equal

$$p(W) = |\psi_W|^2 = |\psi_B \cdot u_{WB} + \psi_G \cdot u_{WG}|^2$$

$$= |\psi_B|^2 |u_{WB}|^2 + |\psi_G|^2 |u_{WG}|^2$$

$$+ 2 \cdot \text{Re}\left[(\psi_B \cdot u_{WB}) \cdot (\psi_G \cdot u_{WG})^*\right]$$

$$= p_G \cdot T_{WG} + p_B \cdot T_{WB} + \text{Int}_W.$$

The constraints on the unitary matrix force the interference terms to be negatively related:

$$\text{Int}_A = 2 \cdot \text{Re}\left[(\psi_B \cdot u_{AB}) \cdot (\psi_G \cdot u_{AG})^*\right]$$

$$= 2 \cdot \text{Re}\left[\psi_B \cdot \psi_G^* \cdot u_{AB} \cdot u_{AG}^*\right]$$

$$= -2 \cdot \text{Re}\left[\psi_B \cdot \psi_G^* \cdot u_{WG}^* \cdot u_{WB}\right]$$

$$= -\text{Int}_W.$$

8.2.2.1   Empirical test of double stochasticity

Let us examine how well this model accounts for the observed data in Table 8.2. To fit the narrow face data, we set $|u_{AB}|^2 = 0.60$, which implies that $|u_{AG}|^2 = 0.40$ (which approximates the observed probabilities $p(A|B) = 0.63$ and $p(A|G) = 0.41$, respectively). We also set $|\psi_G|^2 = 0.17$, which exactly reproduces $p(G) = 0.17$. Finally, if we set $\cos(\theta) = 0.333$, then this model produces $|\psi_A|^2 = 0.69 = p(A)$, which reproduces the data obtained from condition D-alone. Note that the use of $\cos(\theta) = 0.333$ implies that complex amplitudes are required to fit the data.

Is this model empirically testable? Yes, because the model uses only three parameters $(u_{AG}|^2, |\psi_G|^2, \cos(\theta))$ to fit four data points in Table 8.2 for each type of face, leaving one degree of freedom to test the model for each face condition. In fact, the single degree of freedom from each condition comes from the double stochasticity constraint imposed by the unitary matrix. In particular, for any simple *two*-dimensional quantum model, the transition matrix must satisfy the equality $|u_{WG}|^2 = 1 - |u_{WB}|^2 = |u_{AB}|^2$. This constraint is approximately satisfied by the observed transition matrix for the narrow face data.

$$T_{\text{Narrow}} = \begin{bmatrix} 0.63 & 0.41 \\ 0.37 & 0.59 \end{bmatrix}.$$

Unfortunately, the quantum model fails to explain the wide face data. The observed transition matrix more strongly violates double stochasticity:

$$T_{\text{Wide}} = \begin{bmatrix} 0.52 & 0.35 \\ 0.48 & 0.65 \end{bmatrix}.$$

Note that, for the wide face data, the observed values, $p(W|G) = 0.65$ and $p(A|B) = 0.52$, are far apart, but according to the quantum model they are required to be equal. In summary, this two-dimensional quantum model fails because it requires the law of double stochasticity, which is violated for the wide face data. Let us consider a hybrid model, called a quantum noise model, which is a blend of Markov and quantum models.

8.2.3 Markov and quantum noise models

The preceding Markov and quantum models assumed that the states were directly observable. In other words, it was assumed that the response directly reveals the state. However, there may be many situations in which a measurement does not faithfully reflect the underlying state. For example, if a person is asked about a sensitive issue (e.g., Do you abuse drugs?), they may be biased against truthfully reporting their state. Or a person could simply make an honest error (e.g., intend to say yes but push a wrong button for no). The violation for the wide face condition of the categorization–decision experiment may be caused by a bias against attacking wide faces even if the person thinks it is from the "bad" category.

Now we explore the possibility that the states are mapped into responses by some "noisy" process that allows measurement "errors" or "biases" to partially hide the true state. When measurements are noisy, it becomes important to introduce a distinction between states and observed responses. To do this, the categorization response is denoted by a variable C that can take on labels b or g for choosing the "bad" or "good" category, respectively; and these responses are used to infer the states $|G\rangle$ and $|B\rangle$. The choice response for an action is denoted by a variable D that can take on labels a or w for the choice of attack and withdraw actions, respectively; and these choices reflect the action states $|A\rangle$ and $|W\rangle$. The "noise" could represent response errors or response biases.

8.2.3.1 Hidden Markov model

First consider including noise into the Markov model. This is called a hidden Markov model because the state is no longer directly observable, and it has to be inferred from noisy observations. The noisy measurement is achieved by introducing a probabilistic response map from states to responses (Rabiner, 1989). The following two matrices map category states into category responses

$$M_{\mathrm{b}} = \begin{bmatrix} m_{\mathrm{b}B} & 0 \\ 0 & m_{\mathrm{b}G} \end{bmatrix}, \ M_{\mathrm{g}} = \begin{bmatrix} m_{\mathrm{g}B} & 0 \\ 0 & m_{\mathrm{g}G} \end{bmatrix}.$$

For example, if the person enters the category state $|B\rangle$, there is a probability $m_{\mathrm{b}B}$ of responding that the face is "bad", and there is a probability $m_{\mathrm{g}B}$ of responding that the face is "good." The next two matrices map action states to choices of each action:

$$M_{\mathrm{a}} = \begin{bmatrix} m_{\mathrm{a}A} & 0 \\ 0 & m_{\mathrm{a}W} \end{bmatrix}, \ M_{\mathrm{w}} = \begin{bmatrix} m_{\mathrm{w}A} & 0 \\ 0 & m_{\mathrm{w}W} \end{bmatrix}.$$

For example, if the person is in the state $|A\rangle$, then the person may actually choose to attack with probability $m_{\mathrm{a}A}$, but the person may instead choose to

withdraw with a probability m_{wA}. To guarantee that the categorization response probabilities sum to unity, we require that $M_b + M_g = I$, where I is the
identity matrix; to require the action response probabilities to sum to unity, we
require that $M_a + M_w = I$. In other words, $m_{wA} = 1 - m_{aA}$ and $m_{aW} = 1 - m_{wW}$.
This model reduces to the original Markov model without noise when we set
$m_{bB} = 1 = m_{gG}$ and $m_{aA} = 1 = m_{wW}$. Again, it is convenient to define a row
vector $L = \begin{bmatrix} 1 & 1 \end{bmatrix}$ which is used to sum across states.

Using these definitions, we can compute the following response probabilities.
The probability that a face is categorized $C = g$ equals

$$p(C = g) = L \cdot M_g \cdot \phi_I.$$

If we observe the $C = g$ category response, then the probability distribution
across inference states is revised by Bayes' rule to become

$$\phi_g = \begin{bmatrix} p(G|C = g) \\ p(B|C = g) \end{bmatrix} = \frac{M_g \cdot \phi_I}{p(C = g)} = \frac{1}{p(C = g)} \begin{bmatrix} \phi_B \cdot m_{gB} \\ \phi_G \cdot m_{gG} \end{bmatrix}.$$

As the above equation shows, the categorization response changes the distribution across inference states. The probability of choosing action $D = a$ given that
we observe a categorization response $C = g$ equals

$$p(D = a|C = g) = L \cdot M_a \cdot T \cdot \phi_g.$$

The probability that the face is first categorized as a "bad guy" and then the
person attacks equals

$$p(C = b, D = a) = L \cdot M_a \cdot T \cdot M_b \cdot \phi_I.$$

The probability that the face is first categorized as a "good guy" and then the
person attacks equals

$$p(C = g, D = a) = L \cdot M_a \cdot T \cdot M_g \cdot \phi_I.$$

In fact, the probability for more complex sequences of responses, as shown in
Eq. (8.1) continues to apply to hidden Markov models even when noisy measurements are included.

Let us see if adding this new feature helps the Markov model to explain the
interference effect found with the categorization–decision task. The probability
of attacking under the decision-alone condition equals

$$\begin{aligned}
p(D = a) &= L \cdot D_a \cdot T \cdot \phi_I \\
&= L \cdot M_a \cdot T \cdot I \cdot \phi_I \\
&= L \cdot M_a \cdot T \cdot (M_b + M_g) \cdot \phi_I \\
&= L \cdot M_a \cdot T \cdot M_b \cdot \phi_I + L \cdot M_a \cdot T \cdot M_g \cdot \phi_I \\
&= p(C = b, D = a) + p(C = g, D = a) \\
&= p_T(D = a).
\end{aligned}$$

In summary, this model still satisfies the law of total probability, which of course fails to explain the interference effects found with the categorization decision-making task.

8.2.4 Quantum noise model

On the one hand, the two-dimensional Markov model failed because the interference effects violate the law of total probability. On the other hand, the two-dimensional quantum model failed because the observed transition matrices violate double stochasticity. An interesting idea is to combine the two classes of models and form a quantum Markov model. The following is a new model inspired by – but much simpler than – a model proposed by Accardi et $al.$ (2009). It assumes that the noisy measurements are used to assess the hidden quantum states.

The present model assumes that the quantum states are not directly observable because of measurement "errors" or "noise." As before, it is important to distinguish between states and observed responses. Once again, the categorization response is denoted by a variable C that can take on labels b or g for choosing the "bad" or "good" category, respectively; and the choice response for an action is denoted by a variable D that can take on labels a or w for the choice of attack and withdraw actions, respectively.

The choices are represented by measurement operators (Gardiner, 1991) that map states in observed responses. The two noisy measurement operators for categorizing a face as a "bad guy" or a "good guy" are defined by

$$M_b = \begin{bmatrix} \sqrt{m_{bB}} & 0 \\ 0 & \sqrt{m_{bG}} \end{bmatrix}, \; M_g = \begin{bmatrix} \sqrt{m_{gB}} & 0 \\ 0 & \sqrt{m_{gG}} \end{bmatrix}.$$

For example, if the person is in the inference state $|B\rangle$, then the person may actually categorize the face as "bad" with probability m_{bB}, but the person may instead categorize the face as good with probability m_{gB}. The two noisy measurement operators for choosing to attack or withdraw actions are defined by

$$M_a = \begin{bmatrix} \sqrt{m_{aA}} & 0 \\ 0 & \sqrt{m_{aW}} \end{bmatrix}, \; M_w = \begin{bmatrix} \sqrt{m_{wA}} & 0 \\ 0 & \sqrt{m_{wW}} \end{bmatrix}.$$

For example, if the person is in action state $|A\rangle$, then the person may choose to attack with probability m_{aA}, but instead the person may choose to withdraw with probability m_{wA}. This model reduces to the original quantum model without noise when we set $m_{bB} = 1 = m_{gG}$ and $m_{aA} = 1 = m_{wW}$. These two measurement operators form a complete set because they satisfy the completeness property $M_b^\dagger M_b + M_g^\dagger M_g = I$ and $M_a^\dagger M_a + M_w^\dagger M_w = I$ needed to guarantee that the choice probabilities sum to one across actions. In other words, $m_{wA} = 1 - m_{aA}$ and $m_{aW} = 1 - m_{wW}$.

Using these definitions, we can compute the following response probabilities. The probability that a face is categorized $C = g$ equals

$$p(C = g) = ||M_g \cdot \psi_I||^2.$$

If we observe the $C = g$ category response, then the amplitude distribution across inference states is revised by a quantum version of Bayes' rule (Gardiner, 1991) to become

$$\psi_g = \begin{bmatrix} \psi(B|C = g) \\ \psi(G|C = g) \end{bmatrix} = \frac{M_g \cdot \psi_I}{\sqrt{p(C = g)}} = \frac{1}{\sqrt{p(C = g)}} \begin{bmatrix} \psi_B \cdot \sqrt{m_{gB}} \\ \psi_G \cdot \sqrt{m_{gG}} \end{bmatrix}.$$

As the above equation shows, the categorization response changes the amplitude distribution across inference states, but it does not completely resolve all uncertainty, and the state remains in superposition. The probability of choosing action $D = a$ given that we observe a categorization response $C = g$ equals

$$p(D = a|C = g) = \left\| M_a \cdot U \cdot \psi_g \right\|^2.$$

Finally, the probability to attack for the D-alone condition equals

$$p(D = a) = \left\| M_a \cdot U \cdot \psi_I \right\|^2.$$

The probability that the face is first categorized as a "good guy" and then the person attacks equals

$$p(C = g, D = a) = \left\| M_a \cdot U \cdot M_g \cdot \psi_I \right\|^2.$$

The probability that the face is first categorized as a "bad guy" and then the person attacks equals

$$p(C = b, D = a) = \left\| M_a \cdot U \cdot M_b \cdot \psi_I \right\|^2.$$

In fact, the probability for more complex sequences of responses as shown in Eq. (8.2) continues to apply even when noisy measurements are included.

8.2.4.1   Empirical application

Now let us see if we can construct a version of the quantum noise model that can account for both the narrow and wide face results. To do this without introducing too many parameters so that we can still test the model, we need to impose some simplifying assumptions. We start by assuming noise or bias in the action that is observed but no noise or bias in the categorization measurement so that

$$M_g = \begin{bmatrix} 1 & 0 \\ 0 & 0 \end{bmatrix}, \ M_b = \begin{bmatrix} 0 & 0 \\ 0 & 1 \end{bmatrix},$$

$$M_a = \begin{bmatrix} \sqrt{m_{aA}} & 0 \\ 0 & \sqrt{m_{aW}} \end{bmatrix}, \ M_w = \begin{bmatrix} \sqrt{m_{wA}} & 0 \\ 0 & \sqrt{m_{wW}} \end{bmatrix}.$$

We also parameterize the unitary matrix as follows (where the parameter u is a probability between zero and one):

$$U = \begin{bmatrix} \sqrt{u} & \sqrt{1 - u} \cdot e^{i\theta} \\ -\sqrt{1 - u} \cdot e^{-i\theta} & \sqrt{u} \end{bmatrix}.$$

Then the probabilities for each category response equal

$$p(C = b) = |\psi_B|^2, \ p(C = g) = |\psi_G|^2.$$

The amplitudes for the states conditioned on each category response are

$$\psi_b = \begin{bmatrix} 1 \\ 0 \end{bmatrix}, \ \psi_g = \begin{bmatrix} 0 \\ 1 \end{bmatrix}.$$

Then the observed conditional probabilities equal

$$p(D = a|C = b) = \|M_a \cdot U \cdot \psi_b\|^2 = m_{aA} \cdot u + m_{aW} \cdot (1 - u),$$
$$p(D = w|C = g) = \|M_w \cdot U \cdot \psi_g\|^2 = m_{wA} \cdot (1 - u) + m_{wW} \cdot u.$$

These two conditional probabilities are no longer equal; instead, the difference equals

$$p(D = a|C = b) - p(D = w|C = g) = (m_{aA} - m_{wW}).$$

For example if we set $m_{aA} < m_{wW}$, then $p(D = a|C = b) < p(D = w|C = g)$. Finally, the probability of attack equals

$$p(D = a) = \|M_a \cdot U \cdot \psi_I\|^2$$

$$= m_{aA} \cdot \left| \psi_B \cdot \sqrt{u} + \psi_G \cdot \sqrt{1-u} \cdot e^{i\theta} \right|^2$$

$$+ m_{aW} \cdot \left| \psi_G \cdot \sqrt{u} - \psi_B \cdot \sqrt{1-u} \cdot e^{-i\theta} \right|^2$$

$$= m_{aA} \cdot \left(|\psi_B|^2 \cdot u + |\psi_G|^2 \cdot (1-u) + 2 \cdot |\psi_B| \cdot |\psi_G| \cdot \sqrt{1-u}\sqrt{u} \cdot \cos(\theta) \right)$$

$$+ m_{aW} \cdot \left(|\psi_G|^2 \cdot u + |\psi_B|^2 \cdot (1-u) - 2 \cdot |\psi_B| \cdot |\psi_G| \cdot \sqrt{1-u}\sqrt{u} \cdot \cos(\theta) \right)$$

$$= p(C = b) p(D = a|C = b) + p(C = g) p(D = a|C = g)$$

$$+ m_{aA} \cdot \text{Int}_A - m_{aW} \cdot \text{Int}_A$$

$$= p_T(D = a) + (m_{aA} - m_{aW}) \cdot \text{Int}_A,$$

$$\text{Int}_A = 2 \cdot |\psi_B| \cdot |\psi_G| \cdot \sqrt{1-u}\sqrt{u} \cdot \cos(\theta).$$

The last line also shows that $m_{aA} = m_{aW}$ results in no interference effect.

This model can now account for both the narrow and wide face results. To account for the wide face data, we set $m_{wW} = 1$, $m_{wA} = 0.13$, $\psi_g = \sqrt{0.84}$, $u = 0.5977$, $\theta = 0.5130 \cdot \pi$, which then exactly reproduces the wide face data. To account for the narrow face data, we set $m_{aW} = 1$, $m_{aW} = 0.04$, $\psi_g = \sqrt{0.83}$, $u = 0.6146$, $\theta = 0.4105 \cdot \pi$, which then exactly reproduces the wide face data. The problem is that this model requires the same number of parameters as data points, which leaves no degrees of freedom left to test the model. In view of the limitations of all the two-dimensional models reviewed above, Busemeyer *et al.* (2009) proposed a four-dimensional version of the quantum model. However, we will wait until the next chapter to present this model, where it is described in detail and where we applied it to some other puzzling phenomena from decision research. At this point, we will turn to our last application to a signal detection task.

8.3   Random walk signal detection model

Signal detection is a decision task in which a human operator monitors noisy information for a potential target (e.g., scanning an image for bombs at an airport security check point, or scanning a chest X-ray for malignant tumors). Incoming information provides uncertain and conflicting evidence, but at some point in time a decision must be made, and the sooner the better. Incorrectly deciding that a target is present (i.e., a false alarm) could result in needless costs, but incorrectly deciding that a target is absent (i.e., a miss) could cause harm. Sampling information could also be costly, and so the decision maker needs to balance expected loss from incorrect decisions with costs of sampling new information. The goal of a psychological theory about this process is to describe the probability of making each choice, the confidence ratings assigned to these decisions, and the distribution of time that it takes to make the decision (Vickers, 1979).

Random walk models are a common way of modelling the decision process for this task. These models have their roots in Bayesian sequential sampling theory (DeGroot, 2004), according to which the decision maker accumulates the log likelihood evidence for the hypotheses (target present or absent) across time (Laming, 1968). But the psychological versions do not necessarily assume optimal integration of information (Link, 1992). Markov-type random walk models of signal detection have been studied in psychology for over 50 years, and during this time many variations have been developed and fine tuned, and they have achieved a high degree of success for fitting choice and response time distributions (Ratcliff & Smith, 2004). Quantum random walk models of signal detection are relatively new – one variation was developed by Busemeyer *et al.* (2006a) and another was developed by Fuss and Navarro (2008).[10] Below we present a simple version of the Markov random walk model that allows a direct comparison with the quantum model, and we present the Busemeyer *et al.* version of the quantum model because it builds on the ideas presented earlier in this chapter. The Fuss and Navarro model uses a more general density operator representation of the quantum state, which is presented in the appendix.

Figure 8.9 illustrates the basic idea. This figure displays only seven levels of confidence: -3 (strong confidence signal is absent), -2 (moderate confidence signal is absent), -1 (weak confidence signal is absent), 0 (uncertain), $+1$ (weak confidence signal is present), $+2$ (moderate confidence signal is present), $+3$ (strong confidence signal is present). However, the model can be easily extended

---

[10]The Busemeyer *et al.* version is based on Feynman *et al.*'s (1966: Ch. 16) crystal model. The Fuss and Navarro version is based on Aharonov *et al.*'s (1993) quantum random walk model.

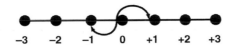

Figure 8.9 Random walk model for seven levels of confidence. Transitions occur between adjacent levels.

to a much larger number of confidence levels (e.g., 101 to more closely approximate a continuum). The essential idea of a random walk model is that, when an information source is presented, the person samples evidence from the source at each moment in time, and this evidence changes the level of confidence regarding the two hypotheses. Confidence drifts up or down to nearby confidence levels depending on the information sampled during each moment, and the process continues until a positive threshold is crossed to generate a plus response (decide signal is present) or a negative threshold is crossed to generate a minus response (decide signal is absent).

8.3.1 State representation

Initially, we will assume that the Markov and quantum models are based on a set of $m = 7$ states $C = \{|-3\rangle, |-2\rangle, |-1\rangle, |0\rangle, |+1\rangle, |+2\rangle, |+3\rangle\}$ representing the seven levels of confidence in Figure 8.9. We use seven states just to make the example simple. All of the equations below are expressed by matrices that do not depend on the number of states, and so they can be applied to systems with an arbitrarily large number of states (e.g., $m = 101$) as well.

8.3.1.1 Markov model

According to the Markov model, the decision maker can only be in exactly one of the seven possible states $|x\rangle$ for $x \in \{-3, -2, -1, 0, +1, +2, +3\}$ at each moment in time. The process steps from the current state to an adjacent state, and this walking up and down the confidence scale continues until an observation is made that produces a response. The initial probability distribution over the seven states is represented by a 7×1 matrix $\phi(0)$. For example, the initial distribution may be uniformly distributed by setting $\phi_x(0) = 1/7$. This probability distribution represents the probability of sampling one of the seven states to start a trajectory.

8.3.1.2 Quantum model

According to the quantum model, the seven states are represented by seven orthonormal basis vectors $|x\rangle$ for $x \in \{-3, -2, -1, 0, +1, +2, +3\}$ that span a seven-dimensional Hilbert space. The decision maker starts out in a superposition state, $|S(0)\rangle = \sum_x \psi_x(0) \cdot |x\rangle$, which is a linear combination of the seven orthonormal basis vectors. This superposition state evolves continuously across time until an observation is made that produces a response. The quantum model starts with an initial amplitude distribution over the seven states represented by the 7×1 matrix $\psi(0)$. For example, the initial distribution may be uniformly distributed by setting $\psi_x(0) = 1/\sqrt{7}$. This amplitude distribution represents the potential for all seven states to start the process in parallel.

8.3.2 State transitions

8.3.2.1 Markov model

The intensity matrix for the seven-state Markov model is defined by the 7×7 tri-diagonal matrix

$$
K =
\begin{bmatrix}
-\alpha & \beta_- & 0 & 0 & 0 & 0 & 0 \\
\alpha & -\alpha & \beta_- & 0 & 0 & 0 & 0 \\
0 & \beta_+ & -\alpha & \beta_- & 0 & 0 & 0 \\
0 & 0 & \beta_+ & -\alpha & \beta_- & 0 & 0 \\
0 & 0 & 0 & \beta_+ & -\alpha & \beta_- & 0 \\
0 & 0 & 0 & 0 & \beta_+ & -\alpha & \alpha \\
0 & 0 & 0 & 0 & 0 & \beta_+ & -\alpha
\end{bmatrix}
\quad \text{transit to} \quad
\begin{bmatrix}
-3 \\ -2 \\ -1 \\ 0 \\ +1 \\ +2 \\ +3
\end{bmatrix} .
$$

The entry within cell k_{ij} of K represents the transition rate to row state i from column state j (the confidence values corresponding to the row states are listed on the right-hand side of the matrix). The parameter $\beta_+ > 0$ determines the rate of increase in confidence across time, and the parameter $\beta_- > 0$ determines the rate of decrease and $-\alpha = -(\beta_+ + \beta_-)$ returns the state to its current location. The transition matrix again obeys the forward Kolmogorov equation

$$
\frac{\mathrm{d}}{\mathrm{d}t} T(t) = K \cdot T(t),
$$

$$
T(t) = e^{tK},
$$

and the probability distribution over states at time t obeys the Kolmogorov forward equation

$$
\frac{\mathrm{d}}{\mathrm{d}t} \phi(t) = K \cdot \phi(t),
$$

$$
\phi(t) = e^{tK} \cdot \phi(0)
$$

This simple example only uses seven states, but all of these equations apply equally well to an arbitrary number of states.[11]

---

[11] If we set $\beta_+ = \frac{1}{2} \cdot \left(\frac{\sigma^2}{\Delta^2} + \frac{\mu}{\Delta} \right)$ and $\beta_- = \frac{1}{2} \cdot \left(\frac{\sigma^2}{\Delta^2} - \frac{\mu}{\Delta} \right)$, where $x(t)$ equals the confidence level at time t, Δ equals the size of the step, μ is the mean step, and σ^2 is the variance of the step, then as $\Delta \to 0$, the number of states becomes infinite and this process converges to the process governed by the Kolmogorov foward equation $\frac{\partial}{\partial t} \phi_x(t) = \frac{\sigma^2}{2} \cdot \frac{\partial^2}{\partial x^2} \phi_x(t) - \mu \cdot \frac{\partial}{\partial x} \phi_x(t)$. See Busemeyer *et al.* (2006a).

8.3.2.2   Quantum model

The Hamiltonian for the seven-state quantum model is defined by 7×7 tri-diagonal Hermitian matrix[12]

$$
H = \begin{bmatrix}
\mu_{-3} & \sigma^2 & 0 & 0 & 0 & 0 & 0 \\
\sigma^2 & \mu_{-2} & \sigma^2 & 0 & 0 & 0 & 0 \\
0 & \sigma^2 & \mu_{-2} & \sigma^2 & 0 & 0 & 0 \\
0 & 0 & \sigma^2 & \mu_0 & \sigma^2 & 0 & 0 \\
0 & 0 & 0 & \sigma^2 & \mu_{+1} & \sigma^2 & 0 \\
0 & 0 & 0 & 0 & \sigma^2 & \mu_{+2} & \sigma^2 \\
0 & 0 & 0 & 0 & 0 & \sigma^2 & \mu_{+3}
\end{bmatrix} \quad \text{transit to} \quad \begin{bmatrix} -3 \\ -2 \\ -1 \\ 0 \\ +1 \\ +2 \\ +3 \end{bmatrix}.
$$

The entry in cell h_{ij} of H represents amplitude diffusing to row state i from column state j (the confidence values corresponding to the row states are shown on the right-hand side of the matrix). The parameter σ^2 determines the diffusion rate out of a basis state and the parameter μ_x determines the diffusion rate back into a basis state $|x\rangle$. The diagonal values correspond to the potential function in the Schrödinger equation. We use a linear increasing potential function, $\mu_x = \beta \cdot x$ that corresponds to a constant positive force. Other potential functions, such as for example a quadratic function, could also be used. The unitary matrix obeys the differential equation

$$
\frac{\mathrm{d}}{\mathrm{d}t} U(t) = -i \cdot H \cdot U(t)
$$

$$
U(t) = \mathrm{e}^{-itH}
$$

and the amplitude distribution at time t obeys the Schrödinger equation

$$
\frac{\mathrm{d}}{\mathrm{d}t} \psi(t) = -i \cdot H \cdot \psi(t)
$$

$$
\psi(t) = \mathrm{e}^{-itH} \cdot \psi(0).
$$

Once again these equations are not limited to seven states, and they all apply to an arbitrarily large number of states.[13]

8.3.3   Confidence ratings

At this point we can derive important predictions that distinguish the Markov and quantum models for confidence. As we shall see, the Markov model must obey the law of total probability and the quantum model must obey the law

---

[12]Note that adding a constant to the diagonal of H has no observable effect. If $H_1 = H + k \cdot I$, then $||\mathrm{e}^{-iH_1} \cdot \psi||^2 = ||\mathrm{e}^{-i(H+kI)} \cdot \psi||^2$ and because H and $k \cdot I$ commute it follows that $||\mathrm{e}^{-i(H+kI)} \cdot \psi||^2 = ||\mathrm{e}^{-iH} \cdot \mathrm{e}^{-ikI} \cdot \psi||^2 = ||\mathrm{e}^{ik} \cdot \mathrm{e}^{-iH} \cdot \psi||^2 = |\mathrm{e}^{-ik}|^2 \cdot ||\mathrm{e}^{-iH} \cdot \psi||^2$.

[13]If we let $x(t)$ equal the confidence level at time t, Δ equal the size of the step, and σ^2 equal the variance of the step, then as $\Delta \to 0$ this process converges to the process governed by the Schrödinger equation $-i\frac{\partial}{\partial t}\psi_x(t) = \frac{\sigma^2}{2} \cdot \frac{\partial^2}{\partial x^2}\psi_x(t) - \mu_x \cdot \psi(t)$. See Busemeyer *et al.* (2006a).

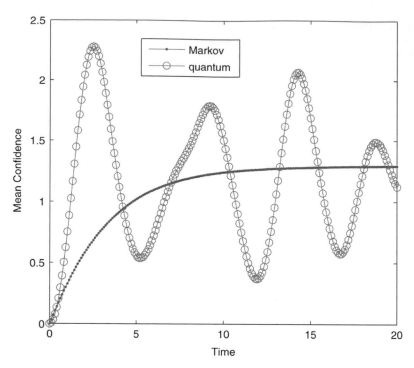

Figure 8.10 Mean confidence (on a -3 to $+3$ scale) as a function of deliberation time for the Markov and quantum models.

of double stochasticity. According to the Markov model, confidence jumps from one level to the next across time to produce a definite trajectory. According to the quantum model, confidence is represented by a superposition over all the levels that evolves continuously across time. Both models provide predictions for the probability of observing a particular level of confidence at each moment.

8.3.3.1   Mean confidence

Let us first examine how the mean confidence changes across time.[14] To do this, set $\phi_x(0) = 1/7$ for all seven states and $\beta_+ = 1.25$, $\beta_- = 0.75$ for the Markov model, and examine the evolution of the probability distribution across time according to the Kolmogorov forward equation, $T(t) = e^{tK}$. Then the mean confidence at time t equals $E(x(t)) = \sum_x \phi_x(t) \cdot x$, which produces the predictions shown as the line with the dots in Figure 8.10. As can be seen, the Markov model predicts that confidence gradually increases toward an equilibrium state around 1.25 on the -3 to $+3$ scale. The probability distribution for the Markov model behaves like sand blown by strong winds. The pile starts out equally spread out across the scale, but then the wind blows the pile

---

[14]The Matlab program used to compute the following predictions is provided in Appendix G.

up against the barrier on the right, and as more and more sand piles up on the right, the sand eventually forms an equilibrium distribution piled up on the right.

To examine the predictions of the quantum model, set $\psi_x(0) = 1/\sqrt{7}$ for all seven states, $\mu_x = x/3$ for $x = -3, -2-1, 0, 1, 2, 3$ and $\sigma^2 = 1$, and examine the evolution of the amplitude distribution across time using the Schrödinger equation, $U(t) = e^{-itH}$. The mean confidence at time t equals $E(x(t)) = \sum_x |\psi_x(t)|^2 \cdot x$, which produces the predictions shown as the open circles in Figure 8.10. As can be seen, the quantum model predicts that confidence rises and then oscillates around the mean level of 1.25. The quantum model behaves like water blown by strong winds. The water starts out equally spread out across the scale, but then the wind blows the water toward the barrier on the right, and eventually the waves crash up against the barrier and recoil back toward the left, but again the winds continue to blow the waves back toward the barrier on the right, producing an oscillating pattern.

It is not known at this time which of these two predictions is correct, and perhaps this depends on the nature of the signal detection task. Tasks involving simple sources of information providing relatively unambiguous information may produce a monotonic increase in confidence with time as predicted by the Markov model. Other tasks involving more ambiguous information may cause confidence to waver systematically across time. In fact, evidence for oscillation in attention has been described by Large and Jones (1999). A strong test requires using a dense time grid across a wide range of times to pick up the oscillation pattern. If we only observe two or three time points it will be difficult to see the oscillation pattern. For example, if we only observe time points 0, 1, and 2, then both models predict a rise in confidence. This test is difficult to do without first fitting the models to data because the unit of the time scale must be estimated from the data. The test below does not suffer these difficulties.

8.3.3.2   Laws of total probability and double stochasticity

There is a simple and parameter-free method for testing Markov and quantum models that only requires two conditions. For condition C2, we obtain two confidence ratings, at two different time points, say t_1 and $t_2 = t_1 + t$. For condition C1, we obtain a confidence rating at time t_2 only. Let us first examine the law of total probability for each model by comparing $p(R(t_2) = x|C1)$ with $p(R(t_2) = x|C2)$ for each confidence level x.

First we examine the Markov model. Define M_x as the state-response probability transition matrix for responding with confidence level x from each Markov state, and we require $\sum_x M_x = I$ so that the probabilities sum to one across all confidence levels. For example, M_x can be defined as an indicator matrix with zeros everywhere except a one in the diagonal corresponding to the row representing confidence level x. Also define L as a 1×7 matrix filled with ones which is used to sum across states. Then according to the Markov model

which can result in one of three responses: positive (i.e., a positive threshold is crossed, so stop processing and decide signal is present), negative (i.e., a negative threshold is crossed, so stop processing and decide signal is not present), or neither (i.e., the current state remains within threshold and so continue evidence accumulation).

8.3.4.1 Hidden Markov model

Recall that it is important to distinguish the states from the responses because of possible measurement errors. Thus, the process is a hidden Markov process. Given the current state, the probability of deciding positive, negative, or neither is determined by three different 7×7 state-response transition matrices: M_+, which represents the noisy detection for crossing the positive threshold; M_-, which represents the noisy detection for crossing the negative threshold; and M_N, which represents the decision to continue processing evidence. The "positive" response matrix M_+ has zero in all cells except for the diagonal cells in the rows corresponding to positive levels of confidence, which have transition probabilities m_x for rows with $x > 0$. For example, using the seven-state model, if we set $m_{+3} = 1$ and $m_{+2} = 0 = m_{+1}$, then the person will decide to stop and say signal present only if a threshold level of confidence equal to $+3$ is found during a check on the state. But if $m_{+3} = 0.5 = m_{+2}$ and $m_{+1} = 0$, then the person has only a 50% chance of stopping on state $+3$, but there is also a 50% chance of stopping on state $+2$. The "negative" response matrix M_- has zero in all cells except for the negative diagonal cells m_x for $x < 0$. For example, if we set $m_{-3} = 1$ and $m_{-2} = 0 = m_{-1}$, then the person will decide to stop and say signal absent only if confidence level -3 is observed during a check on the current Markov state. The "neither" response matrix equals $M_N = I - M_+ - M_-$, so that $M_+ + M_- + M_N = I$. This is necessary to guarantee that the response probabilities sum to unity.

To compute the response probabilities, it is convenient to define L as a 1×7 row matrix full of ones which simply sums the probabilities across states. The probability of stopping at time $T = n \cdot \Delta t$ and deciding signal present equals the probability of responding "neither" on the first $n-1$ checks and then responding "plus" on the next check. This equals

$$p(T = n \cdot \Delta t \cap R(T) = +) = L \cdot M_+ \cdot T(\Delta t) \cdot [M_N \cdot T(\Delta t)]^{n-1} \cdot \phi(0).$$

Similarly, the probability of stopping at time $T = n \cdot \Delta t$ and deciding signal absent equals the probability of responding "neither" on the first $n - 1$ checks and then responding "negative" on the next check. This equals

$$p(T = n \cdot \Delta t \cap R(T) = -) = L \cdot M_- \cdot T(\Delta t) \cdot [M_N \cdot T(\Delta t)]^{n-1} \cdot \phi(0).$$

Let us take a look at the distribution of stopping times predicted by the Markov type of model. To obtain a closer approximation to a continuous-state model, we used $m = 101$ levels of confidence rather than only $m = 7$. The initial state was set equal to $\phi_x(0) = 1/9$ for $x = 0, \pm 1, \pm 2, \pm 3, \pm 4$. Also,

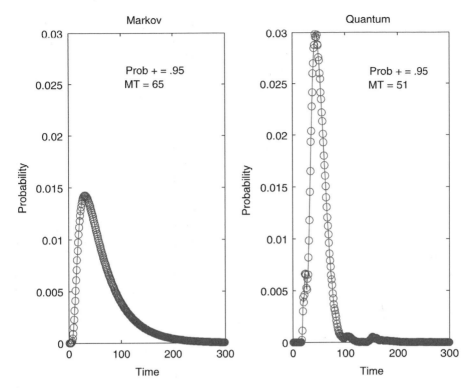

Figure 8.11 Comparison of Markov and quantum random walk models with regard to the distribution of stopping times for a signal detection task.

we set $m_x = 0.25$ for $x \in \{40, 41, \ldots, 50\}$ to define M_+ and $m_x = 0.25$ for $x \in \{-50, -49, \ldots, -40\}$ to define M_- for the state-response transition matrices for responding signal present and signal absent. The intensity matrix was defined by setting $\beta_- = 9.765$ and $\beta_+ = 10.325$ (which was chosen to produce high accuracy within about 100 time steps), and finally we set $\Delta t = 1$ for the time period of each step. The left panel of Figure 8.11 shows the shape of the distribution for the Markov model. In this case the probability of responding "plus" for signal present is 0.95 and the mean number of steps needed to make the decision equals 65.

8.3.4.2 Quantum noise model

The quantum model also allows for measurement or observation errors to occur (Gardiner, 1991: Ch. 2). Given the current state, the amplitude for deciding positive, negative, or neither is determined by three different state-response transition amplitude matrices: M_+, representing the noisy observation of crossing the positive threshold; M_-, which represents the noisy observation of crossing the negative threshold; and M_N, which represents the observation that the threshold has not been crossed so that continued processing evidence is required. The "positive" response matrix M_+ has zero in all cells except for the diagonal cells corresponding to positive levels of confidence, which have amplitudes $\sqrt{m_x}$ for $x > 0$. The "negative" response matrix M_- has zero in all cells except for the diagonal cells corresponding to negative levels of confidence, which have amplitudes $\sqrt{m_x}$ for $x < 0$. The "neither" state-response matrix M_N is a diagonal matrix that must satisfy the completeness property $M_+^\dagger \cdot M_+ + M_-^\dagger \cdot M_- + M_N^\dagger \cdot M_N = I$. This is required to guarantee that the response probabilities sum to unity. For example, using the seven-state model, if we set $m_{+3} = 1$ and $m_{+2} = 0 = m_{+1}$ in M_+, and we set $m_{-3} = 1$ and $m_{-2} = 0 = m_{-1}$ in M_-, and we set $M_N = I - M_+ - M_-$, then these three state-response transition amplitude matrices are three orthogonal projection matrices; but this eliminates any measurement or observation errors. However, if we set $\sqrt{m_{+3}} = \sqrt{0.8} = \sqrt{m_{+2}}$, and $\sqrt{m_{-3}} = \sqrt{0.8} = \sqrt{m_{-2}}$, and $M_N = \mathrm{diag}[\sqrt{0.2}, \sqrt{0.2}, 1, 1, 1, \sqrt{0.2}, \sqrt{0.2}]$, then these are no longer orthogonal projection matrices, but instead they are linear measurement operators that still satisfy the completeness requirement, and they allow for measurement errors.

The probability of stopping at time $T = n \cdot \Delta t$ and deciding signal present equals the probability of responding "neither" on the first $n - 1$ checks and then responding "plus" on the next check. This equals

$$p(T = n \cdot \Delta t \cap R(T) = +) = ||M_+ \cdot U(\Delta t) \cdot [M_N \cdot U(\Delta t)]^{n-1} \cdot \psi(0)||^2.$$

Similarly, the probability of stopping at time $T = n \cdot \Delta t$ and deciding signal absent equals the probability of responding "neither" on the first $n - 1$ checks and then responding "negative" on the next check. This equals

$$p(T = n \cdot \Delta t \cap R(T) = -) = ||M_- \cdot U(\Delta t) \cdot [M_N \cdot U(\Delta t)]^{n-1} \cdot \psi(0)||^2.$$

Now let us take a look at the distribution of stopping times predicted by this quantum model. As much as possible, we used the same parameters as used by the Markov model to make a comparison between the two models. Again, we want to obtain a close approximation to a continuous-state model, and so we used $m = 101$ levels of confidence. The initial state was set equal to $\psi_x(0) = \sqrt{1/9}$ for $x = 0, \pm1, \pm2, \pm3, \pm4$. We set $\sqrt{m_x} = \sqrt{0.25}$ for $x \in \{40, 41, \ldots, 50\}$ to define M_+ and $\sqrt{m_x} = \sqrt{0.25}$ for $x \in \{-50, -49, \ldots, -40\}$ to define M_- for the state-response transition matrices for responding signal present and signal absent. The Hamiltonian matrix was defined by setting $\mu_x = 2 \cdot x$ for $x = -101, -100, \ldots, 100, 101$ and $\sigma^2 = 1$ (which produce high accuracy within about 100 time steps), and finally we set $\Delta t = 1$ for the time period of each step. The right panel of Figure 8.11 shows the shape of the distribution for the quantum model. In this case the probability of responding "plus" for signal present equals 0.95 and the mean number of steps needed to make the decision equals 51.

Both distributions have a fast rise and a long tail, producing a distribution skewed to the right. However, the quantum distribution is compressed relative to the Markov; consequently, in this example, the quantum model reached a high 0.95 level of accuracy quicker than the Markov model. Fuss and Navarro speculated that quantum decision processes may reach decisions faster because of the parallel nature of the evidence accumulation process produced by using a superposition state. This is an interesting question for future research. The quantum model also exhibits some small multi-modal behavior as a result of the oscillations produced by the unitary operator. However, the multiple modes might not be detected if there is noise present (see Fuss and Navarro (2008) for more analysis of this point). Busemeyer *et al.* (2006a) compared the fits of these quantum and Markov models with empirical choice probabilities and response time distributions reported in Ratcliff and Smith (2004). Although the quantum model provided reasonable fits to the data, the Markov model provided more accurate fits. Clearly, this is a new area of research for quantum modelling and more work needs to be done to improve the quantum model at this point.

One important direction that needs more exploration is to incorporate other sources of noise into the quantum random walk model. The model presented here only allowed for noise entering through measurement errors. But this does not include environmental noise that enters directly into dynamics. More advanced quantum noise models have been developed for this purpose (e.g., Gardiner, 1991; Percival, 1998; Nielsen and Chuang, 2000). Fuss and Navarro (2008) applied these more advanced quantum noise models to their quantum random walk model and found that this type of noise produces distributions that become smoother and more similar to the Markov process.

This concludes our introduction to quantum dynamics. Appendix E describes the Fuss and Navarro model. It also presents quantum dynamics based on a density matrix representation of the quantum state, and it describes how to inject quantum noise operations directly into the dynamic process. The next chapter presents a detailed analysis of a Hamiltonian that was specially designed for a quantum account of paradoxical findings from decision research.

9

What is the quantum advantage? Applications to decision making

Can quantum theory provide new answers to puzzling results from decision research that have resisted formal explanations so far? This chapter presents several new contributions that quantum theory provides to decision research. However, in order to locate where quantum theory can make an important new contribution, we first need to provide some necessary background on decision theory and what has already been accomplished.

Decision science is a highly developed field that has produced a variety of sophisticated mathematical theories (Gilboa, 2009; Wakker, 2010). Some of these theories are *rational* theories, which prescribe optimal ways to make decisions. Others are *psychological* theories that describe the way people actually make decisions.

One of the most important rational decision theories is von Neumannn and Morgenstern's *expected utility (EU) theory* (von Neumann & Morgenstern, 1944).[1] Expected utility theory is designed for decisions *under risk*; that is, a choice among actions defined as an objective probability distribution over possible payoffs. An important extension of (EU) theory is Savage's (1954) *subjective expected utility (SEU) theory*. This extends utility theory to decisions *under uncertainty*; that is, a choice among actions defined as functions that map uncertain events into payoffs, and the events may not have objective probabilities. A more general theory designed for decisions under both uncertainty and risk was presented by Anscombe and Aumann (1963). All of these theories are rational, in the sense that they are based on a small set of compelling axioms and the prescribed action logically follows from the axioms. An important feature of rational decision theories is that they rely on the assignment of probabilities to events according to rules that obey the Kolmogorov axioms.

Unfortunately, human behavior does not obey the rational axioms of EU theory or SEU theory. Decision researchers have designed a specific type of decisions under risk in which people systematically produce violations of the EU axioms (Allais, 1953); they have also designed a specific type of decisions under uncertainty in which people systematically produce violations of the SEU

---

[1] John von Neumann was a brilliant mathematician who not only axiomatized quantum physics, but also axiomatized EU, and if that is not enough, he was also the architect of our modern-day computers.

axioms (Ellsberg, 1961). These two behavioral violations of rational decision making are called the Allais and Ellsberg paradoxes, respectively.

Descriptive theories were developed to account for these paradoxical findings. One of the most influential descriptive theories is called *prospect theory* (Kahneman & Tversky, 1979; Tversky & Kahneman, 1990). Prospect theory accounts for the Allais and Ellsberg paradoxes by replacing Kolmogorov probabilities with decision weights that are nonlinear and non-additive. The best model remains in considerable debate because new paradoxes have been found which violate the axioms of prospect theory (Birnbaum, 2008). So the hunt for an adequate descriptive theory of decision making continues.

Recently, several general quantum models of decision making have been proposed to account for the Allais and Ellsberg paradoxes (La Mura, 2009; Yukalov & Sornette, 2010). Later in this chapter, a quantum model for the Ellsberg paradox is briefly outlined. However, it is difficult to show a significant advantage for quantum theories over previous descriptive theories for the Allais and Ellsberg phenomena. The previous descriptive theories already do a fairly good job explaining the main findings.

To show an advantage, quantum theorists need to attack problems that have stubbornly resisted formal explanations by traditional decision theorists. To accomplish this goal, this chapter focuses on two other puzzling phenomena from decision research: one is called the disjunction effect, which violates an axiom of SEU theory (Tversky & Shafir, 1992); another is called dynamic inconsistency, which violates axioms required for backward induction analysis of multistage decisions (Cubitt *et al.*, 1998; Busemeyer *et al.*, 2000). A dynamic quantum model provides a simple account of both findings. Furthermore, this same model also accounts for the interference effect of categorization on decision making discussed in Chapter 8.

9.1   Allais and Ellsberg paradoxes

There are various versions of the Allais paradox. In the simplest version, a person is presented with two choices. The first is a choice between option A ($1 million for sure) versus option B (0.80 probability of winning $5 million or else nothing). The second is a choice between option A′ (0.10 probability of winning $1 million or else nothing) versus option B′ (0.08 probability of winning $5 million or else nothing). What should a decision maker choose?

According to expected utility theory (von Neumann & Morgenstern, 1944), a rational decision maker should choose the action that maximizes expected utility:

$$\text{EU}(\text{act}) = \sum_i p(E_i) \cdot u(\text{act}|E_i),$$

where $p(E_i)$ is the probability that event E_i occurs and $u(\text{act}|E_i)$ is the utility of the payoff that is obtained by choosing an action if event E_i occurs. The expected utility for option A is simply $u(\$1M)$ and the expected utility of option B is

Table 9.1 Ellsberg choice sets

Action	R	B	G
First pair			
A	$100	0	0
B	0	$100	0
Second pair			
A′	$100	0	$100
B′	0	$100	$100

$(0.80) \cdot u(\$5M)$. Therefore, A preferred to B implies $u(\$1M) > (0.80) \cdot u(\$5M)$. However, if we multiply both sides by 0.10 then we obtain the inequality $(0.10) \cdot u(\$1M) > (0.10) \cdot (0.80) \cdot u(\$5M) = (0.08) \cdot u(\$5M)$, and so the person should also prefer option A′ over option B′. In other words, EU theory assumes that preferences are independent of a common probability factor that applies to both options. Most people choose option A over B when presented with the first choice; but contrary to EU theory, they change and prefer option B′ over A′ for the second choice. This is called a violation of the independence axiom of EU theory.

Prospect theory replaces the probabilities $p(E_i)$ in the EU formula with decision weights, $w(p(E_i))$, that are a nonlinear function of the probabilities. The prospect value of option A remains $u(\$1M)$, but the prospect value of option B becomes $w(0.80) \cdot u(\$5M)$; also, the prospect value of option A′ equals $w(0.10) \cdot u(\$1M)$ and the prospect value of option B′ equals $w(0.08) \cdot u(\$5M)$. Prospect theory accounts for the Allais preference pattern by assuming that $w(0.08) > w(0.10) \cdot w(0.80)$.

There are different versions of what is generally called the "Ellsberg paradox," and here we consider the version shown in Table 9.1.

The decision maker is told that a ball will be randomly sampled from an urn and the color of the ball determines the payoff for each action. The urn contains red, blue, and green balls. The urn is known to contain 100 red balls and 200 other balls, but the exact number of blue and green balls is unknown. Consider the first pair of choices between actions A and B in Table 9.1. If A is chosen and a red ball is selected, then the person wins $100; otherwise the person gets zero. If B is chosen and a blue ball is selected, then the person wins $100; otherwise the person gets zero. Next consider the second pair of choices. If A′ is chosen, then the person wins $100 when either the red or green ball is selected; otherwise nothing. If B′ is chosen, then the person wins $100 if either the blue or green ball is selected; otherwise nothing.

These two pairs of choices were designed to test Savage's (1954) axiom called the "sure thing" principle. This principle concerns a preference relation between two actions, denoted $A \succeq B$, which is interpreted as "A is preferred or is indifferent to B." This principle states the following: if $A \succeq B$ when event X occurs, and $A \succeq B$ when event X does not occur $(\bar{X})$, then $A \succeq B$ when event X is unknown.

Consider the first pair in Table 9.1. If $\bar{G}$ occurs it is not clear what to do about A versus B, but assume for the moment that $A \succeq B$. If G occurs instead, then it follows that $A \succeq B$ because A gives the same payoff as B. Therefore, according to the "sure thing" principle, $A \succeq B$ even when G is unknown. Next consider the second pair in Table 9.1. Now if $\bar{G}$ occurs, then A' is exactly the same as A and B' is exactly the same as B; so given that $A \succeq B$, it follows that $A' \succeq B'$. If G occurs, then it follows that $A' \succeq B'$ because A' gives the same payoff as B'. Therefore, according to the "sure thing" principle, $A' \succeq B'$ even when G is unknown. If we change the original assumption for the first pair to $B \succeq A$ when event $\bar{G}$ occurs, then the "sure thing" principle implies that $B' \succeq A'$. In sum, the sure thing principle implies that if $A \succeq B$ then $A' \succeq B'$ or if $B \succeq A$ then $B' \succeq A'$.

This consistency of preference across choice pairs is necessary for SEU theory for the following reason. According to SEU theory, the decision maker chooses the action that maximizes subjective expected utility:

$$\text{SEU}(\text{act}) = \sum_i p(E_i) \cdot u(\text{act}|E_i),$$

where $p(E_i)$ is the subjective or personal probability assigned to event E_i and $u(\text{act}|E_i)$ is the utility of the payoff produced by that action when event E_i occurs. For the Ellsberg problems, if $A \succ B$ then $\text{SEU}(A) = p(R) \cdot u(\$100) > p(B) \cdot u(\$100) = \text{SEU}(B)$, which implies $p(R) > p(B)$, which implies $\text{SEU}(A') = p(R) \cdot u(\$100) + p(G) \cdot u(\$100) > p(B) \cdot u(\$100) + p(G) \cdot u(\$100) = \text{SEU}(B')$, which finally implies $A' \succ B'$. The common consequence entailed by event G cancels out and has no effect, which makes the choice between A versus B identical to the choice between A' versus B'. In short, if $p(R) \geq p(B)$ then $A \succeq B$ and $A' \succeq B'$, but if $p(B) \geq p(R)$ then $B \succeq A$ and $B' \succeq A'$. The Ellsberg paradox refers to the fact that empirical research on the Ellsberg problems in Table 9.1 systematically finds that, for the first pair, people most frequently choose A over B; but these same people reverse for the second pair and most frequently choose B' over A' (Camerer & Weber, 1992).

Prospect theory accommodates the Ellsberg paradox finding by using non-additive decision weights as follows (Tversky & Fox, 1995). For the first pair, the prospect weighted utility for A equals $w(R) \cdot u(\$100)$ and the weighted utility of B equals $w(B) \cdot u(\$100)$, which implies $w(R) > w(B)$. But for the second pair, the weighted utility of A' equals $w(R \cup G) \cdot u(\$100)$ and the weighted utility of B' equals $w(B \cup G) \cdot u(\$100)$. To explain the findings, it follows that $w(R \cup G) < w(B \cup G)$, which requires that w is non-additive for mutually exclusive events, $w(X \cup Y) \neq w(X) + w(Y)$ for $X \cap Y = \varnothing$.

Most researchers accept these findings regarding the Allais and Ellsberg paradoxes as evidence that the principles of expected utility theory have been systematically violated. However, two methodological issues are often ignored. One is that the EU principles are statements about the preferences for an individual decision maker and the empirical results are based on choices averaged across individuals. Only if we assume homogeneity across individuals can we conclude that the evidence implies a violation of the EU principles – yet homogeneity is not a reasonable assumption. Alternatively, one could argue that a violation of an EU principle occurs whenever an individual produces a choice pattern of choosing act A on the first pair and then choosing act B' on the second pair. But then we encounter the second methodological issue – choice is probabilistic and so a single choice pattern by an individual provides an unreliable measure of the underlying preference relations (Luce, 2000). In fact, Camerer (1989) found that the participants in his experimental tests of utility models changed their choices in nearly one out of every three trials even when real payoffs were used. Given the probabilistic nature of choice, a test of utility principles requires one to estimate the *probability* of choice patterns for each person. Greater attention to individual differences and statistical methodology is required to make a convincing argument that an axiom is violated (Regenwetter *et al.*, 2010).

9.1.1   Projective expected utility theory

La Mura (2009) proposed an axiomatic foundation for a quantum theory of decision making under uncertainty, which he then used to account for the Allais and Ellsberg paradoxes.[2] Here, we briefly summarize the theory and describe its application to the Ellsberg paradox.

Suppose X is a risky action that produces real valued payoffs $x_1, \ldots, x_n$ with probabilities $p_1, \ldots, p_n$ respectively. These n probabilities can be mapped into a unit-length $n \times 1$ amplitude column matrix ψ with element $\sqrt{p_i}$ in row i of ψ so that $\psi^\dagger \cdot \psi = 1$. The evaluation of this risky action is made on the basis of an $n \times n$ Hermitian utility matrix, denoted U, that has a spectral decomposition $U = \sum u(x_i) \cdot V_i \cdot V_i^\dagger$, where the eigenvalue $u(x_i)$ equals the utility of payoff x_i and V_i is the ith eigenvector of U. The projective expected utility (PEU) for risky action X corresponding to the amplitude matrix ψ equals

$$\text{PEU}(\psi) = \psi^\dagger \cdot U \cdot \psi \tag{9.1}$$

$$= \psi^\dagger \left(\sum_i u(x_i) \cdot V_i \cdot V_i^\dagger \right) \psi$$

$$= \sum_i u(x_i) \cdot (\psi^\dagger \cdot V_i) \cdot \left(V_i^\dagger \cdot \psi \right)$$

$$= \sum_i u(x_i) \cdot \left| \psi^\dagger \cdot V_i \right|^2 .$$

The last line is a weighted utility model with the weight of outcome x_i determined by $\left| \psi^\dagger \cdot V_i \right|^2$. The act producing the largest PEU is chosen most frequently. Note that if U is restricted to be a diagonal matrix, then the matrix V of eigenvectors is simply an identity matrix, which implies $\left| \psi^\dagger \cdot V_i \right|^2 = p_i$ so that PEU theory reduces to the von Neumann and Morgenstern EU theory. In terms of

---

[2]It is a quantum extension of the Anscombe and Aumann (1963) theory.

quantum concepts, U is an observable and PEU is the mean of this observable (see Chapter 2).

An alternative way to interpret PEU theory is the following. When presented with a risky action with payoffs $x_1, \ldots, x_n$ and probabilities $p_1, \ldots, p_n$, the person forms a state vector $|\psi\rangle$ that is expressed with respect to an orthonormal basis $\{V_i, i = 1, n\}$ such that

$$|\psi\rangle = \sum_i \langle V_i | \psi \rangle \cdot |V_i\rangle.$$

Then the term $\left|\psi^\dagger \cdot V_i\right|^2 = \left|\langle V_i | \psi \rangle\right|^2$ appearing in Eq. (9.1) is the subjective decision weight assigned to the utility $u(x_i)$. It is important to note, however, that this decision weight is determined partly by the outcome probabilities that enter into ψ, but also partly by the eigenvector V_i that is obtained from the utility operator U. The inner product $\langle V_i | \psi \rangle$ measures the correlation of the beliefs determined by ψ with the evaluation eigenvector V_i associated with eigenvalue $u(x_i)$ of the utilty operator U.

For decisions under uncertainty, different states of the world may exist, $\{|s_j\rangle, j = 1, m\}$ and the amplitude matrix ψ now depends on the state of the world $|s_j\rangle$. To reflect this dependence, we now define ψ_j as the $n \times 1$ column matrix of amplitudes conditional on state $|s_j\rangle$. Suppose there are m possible states, $|s_j\rangle$; each state has an amplitude equal to ϕ_j (a scalar). The combined risk and uncertainty amplitude matrix is an $(n \cdot m) \times 1$ column matrix Ψ

$$\Psi = \begin{bmatrix} \phi_1 \cdot \psi_1 \\ \cdot \\ \phi_j \cdot \psi_j \\ \cdot \\ \phi_m \cdot \psi_m \end{bmatrix},$$

and the PEU equals

$$\mathrm{PEU}(\Psi) = \Psi^\dagger \cdot (I \otimes U) \cdot \Psi$$

$$= \sum_j |\phi_j|^2 \cdot \left(\psi_j^\dagger \cdot U \cdot \psi_j\right)$$

$$= \sum_j |\phi_j|^2 \cdot \mathrm{PEU}(\psi_j).$$

In the first line of the above equation, the Kronecker product is used to form the $(n \cdot m) \times (n \cdot m)$ utility matrix $(I \otimes U)$. This simply makes m copies of U down the diagonal of an identity matrix (see Chapter 2 on matrix algebra).

9.1.2 Application to Ellsberg paradox

To apply this theory to the Ellsberg paradox, note that there are only two payoffs $\{\$100, 0\}$, and so the theory begins with with a 2×2 Hermitian utility matrix to represent these two payoffs (assume α is a real-valued free parameter):

$$U = \begin{bmatrix} 1 & a \\ a & 0 \end{bmatrix}.$$

The number of red balls is known, but there is uncertainty about the number of blue and green balls. Therefore, the decision maker needs to consider various possible distributions of blue and green balls. For simplicity, consider three equally likely possibilities: all blue balls, equal number of blue and green balls, and all green balls.

Consider the first pair involving a choice between A versus B. For option A, the number of red balls is known so that the exact probability to win is $1/3$ and the distribution of blue or green does not matter. Because there is no uncertainty about the probabilities of payoffs for option A we obtain

$$\mathrm{PEU}(A) = \begin{bmatrix} \sqrt{1/3} & \sqrt{2/3} \end{bmatrix} \cdot \begin{bmatrix} 1 & a \\ a & 0 \end{bmatrix} \cdot \begin{bmatrix} \sqrt{1/3} \\ \sqrt{2/3} \end{bmatrix}$$

$$= \frac{1}{3} + a \cdot \frac{\sqrt{8}}{3} = \frac{1}{3} + a \cdot \frac{\sqrt{72}}{9}.$$

For option B, the number of blue balls is unknown and the payoffs for B depend on the number of blue balls, so we must use the mixture across possible states:

$$\mathrm{PEU}(B) = \frac{1}{3} \cdot \left(\frac{2}{3} + a \cdot \frac{\sqrt{8}}{3} \right) + \frac{1}{3} \cdot \left(\frac{1}{3} + a \cdot \frac{\sqrt{8}}{3} \right) + \frac{1}{3} \cdot 0$$

$$= \frac{1}{3} + 2 \cdot a \cdot \frac{\sqrt{8}}{9} = \frac{1}{3} + a \cdot \frac{\sqrt{32}}{9}.$$

If $a > 0$, then $\mathrm{PEU}(A) > \mathrm{PEU}(B)$.

Now consider the second pair involving a choice between A′ versus B′. For option B′, the number of blue and green balls is known, so that the exact probability to win is $2/3$ and the distribution of blue or green does not matter. Because there is no uncertainty about the probabilities of the payoffs for option B′ we obtain

$$\mathrm{PEU}(B') = \begin{bmatrix} \sqrt{2/3} & \sqrt{1/3} \end{bmatrix} \cdot \begin{bmatrix} 1 & a \\ a & 0 \end{bmatrix} \cdot \begin{bmatrix} \sqrt{2/3} \\ \sqrt{1/3} \end{bmatrix}$$

$$= \frac{2}{3} + a \cdot \frac{\sqrt{8}}{3} = \frac{6}{9} + a \cdot \frac{\sqrt{72}}{9}.$$

For option A′, the number of green balls is unknown and the payoffs for A′ depend on the number of green balls, so we must use the mixture across possible states:

$$\mathrm{PEU}(A') = \frac{1}{3} \cdot \left(\frac{1}{3} + a \cdot \frac{\sqrt{8}}{3} \right) + \frac{1}{3} \cdot \left(\frac{2}{3} + a \cdot \frac{\sqrt{8}}{3} \right) + \frac{1}{3} \cdot 1$$

$$= \frac{6}{9} + a \cdot 2 \cdot \frac{\sqrt{8}}{9} = \frac{6}{9} + a \cdot \frac{\sqrt{32}}{9}.$$

If $a > 0$, then $\text{PEU}(B') > \text{PEU}(A')$. If $a = 0$, then there are no differences in preferences at all. According to this model, the off-diagonal element of the utility matrix is the critical parameter for determining approach or avoidance of uncertainty. If $a > 0$, then there is an advantage for the risky action over the uncertain action.

La Mura (2009) also demonstrates how the PEU model can account for the Allais paradox, but we refer the reader to the original article for those details. In short, quantum models of decision making can accommodate the Allais and Ellsberg paradoxes. But so can non-additive weighted utility models, and so these paradoxes do not point to any unique advantage for the quantum model. The phenomena addressed next provide some new and important advantages.

9.2 The disjunction effect

One of the most puzzling findings in decision research is the disjunction effect (Tversky & Shafir, 1992).[3] The original studies were designed to test Savage's "sure thing" principle of rational decision theory (Savage, 1954). According to the sure thing principle, if under state of the world X you prefer action A over B, and if under the complementary state of the world X̄ you also prefer action A over B, then you should prefer action A over B even when you do not know the state of the world.

9.2.1 Two-stage gambling paradigm

Tversky and Shafir (1992) experimentally investigated this principle by presenting students with a target gamble that had an equal chance of winning $200 or losing $100 (they used hypothetical money). This gamble has a positive expected value equal to $50, but when Tversky and Shafir (1992) ran a study with $N = 75$ students who were asked whether or not they would like to play this gamble, only 33% chose to play. This indicates that the students were risk averse; but this is not yet a violation of the "sure thing" principle.

In order to test the "sure thing" principle, the target gamble was used in a two-stage game. A total of $N = 98$ students were asked to imagine that they had already played the target gamble once, and now they were asked whether or not they wished to play the same gamble a second time. The key result is based on the decision for the second play, after finishing the first play. The first experiment included three conditions, and all three conditions were presented to each person, but the conditions were separated by a week and mixed with other decision problems to produce independent decisions. In one condition, the students were informed that they had already won the first gamble; in a second condition, they were informed that they had lost the first gamble; and

---

[3]The disjunction effect described in this chapter is not the same effect as the disjunction fallacy described in Chapter 4. The disjunction effect concerns a decision-making error, while the disjunction fallacy concerns a probability judgment error. Although the two findings are quite different, both can be understood as arising from quantum interference effects.

Table 9.2 Results from the two-stage gambling task

Study	Known win	Known loss	Unknown	N^a
Tversky & Shafir	0.69	0.58	0.37	169
Tversky & Shafir[b]	0.73	0.63	0.79	144
Kühberger et al.	0.72	0.47	0.48	188
Lambdin & Burdsal	0.63	0.45	0.41	165
Average	0.68	0.50	0.42	
Quantum model	0.72	0.52	0.38	

[a] N refers to the number of choices included in each proportion.
[b] Not predicted to produce a disjunction effect.

in a third condition, they did not know the outcome of the first gamble. If they thought they won the first gamble, the majority (69%) chose to play again; if they thought they had lost the first gamble, then again the majority (59%) chose to play again; but if they did not know whether they had won or lost, then the majority chose not to play (only 36% wanted to play again). Tversky and Shafir (1992) ran a second study to replicate the first study by using three independent groups of students, with each group receiving only one condition, and the results of the second study closely replicated the first study.[4] The average results of these first two studies are shown in the first row labeled "Tversky & Shafir" of Table 9.2.

The psychological explanation for this finding is people fail to follow through on consequential reasoning. When the person knows they have won the first gamble, then a reason to play again arises from the fact that they have extra house money with which to play. When the person knows they have lost the first gamble, then a reason to play again arises from the fact that they need to recover for their losses. When the person does not know the outcome of the first play, these reasons fail to arise.[5]

Tversky and Shafir (1992) also ran two other studies that were not predicted to produce a disjunction effect. A third study used a design in which all three conditions were presented at once (rather than being separated by weeks); in this case, the target gamble was chosen *more* frequently than both known conditions. Presumably, presentation of all conditions at once makes the reasons for choosing the gamble more apparent. A fourth study added $400 to the first-stage gamble, but kept the second-stage gamble the same as the original target gamble; in this case, the target gamble was chosen with the *same* high frequency as the two

---

[4] Some researchers question whether it is meaningful to test the "sure thing" principle using independent groups of participants for each condition, because this does not permit one to establish whether or not the reversal occurs within a single person (Lambdin & Burdsal, 2007).

[5] People have argued that the low probability of taking the gamble for the unknown condition is caused by uncertainty avoidance as in the Ellsberg paradox. On the contrary, the probability of winning in the second stage is known to be exactly 0.50 for both known and unknown conditions. Furthermore, the uncertainty about the first gamble outcome for the unknown condition cannot be avoided by choosing to reject the second-stage gamble. The win or loss from the first stage remains unknown even when the second-stage gamble is rejected.

known conditions. Presumably, adding \$400 made all outcomes positive and so there was always a single reason for choosing the gamble rather than two conflicting reasons. The average results of these other two studies are shown in the second row labeled "Tversky & Shafir" of Table 9.2.

There have been several attempts to replicate the disjunction effect using the two-stage gambling paradigm, but the reliability of the results remains somewhat controversial. Kühberger *et al.* (2001) conducted four studies using the two-stage gamble paradigm. The first study by Kühberger *et al.* was a direct replication of the second study by Tversky and Shafir (1992) (using an independent groups design); the second study used smaller payoffs; the third study presented all three conditions at once to each person (as in the third study by Tversky and Shafir (1992)), and the last study used small but *real* payoffs. In all of these studies, the unknown condition produced a choice frequency that was approximately equal to the known loss condition and both were much less frequently chosen than the known win condition. The average results of these four studies are shown in the third row labeled "Kühberger *et al.*" of Table 9.2. Kühberger *et al.* (2001) concluded that they did not find a disjunction effect.

The most recent replication of the disjunction effect was reported by Lambdin and Burdsal (2007), who conducted three studies using the original target gamble and two other different target gambles. In these studies, on average, the known win produced the highest frequency of taking the gamble on the second play, and the unknown condition produced a slightly lower frequency of taking the gamble on the second play as compared with the known loss condition. The average results of these three studies are shown in the fourth row labeled "Lambdin & Burdsal" of Table 9.2.

In summary, if we average across the first, third and fourth rows (excluding the second row that was not predicted to produce the effect), then the average of all the results produces a disjunction effect shown in the row labeled "average."

9.2.2 Prisoner dilemma paradigm

Another paradigm, called the prisoner dilemma (PD) paradigm, was used by Shafir and Tversky (1992) to investigate the disjunction effect. In all PD games, the two players need to decide independently whether to cooperate with the opponent or to defect against the other. Table 9.3 shows a typical payoff matrix for a PD game. In this example, if you cooperate and your opponent defects you win 5 points and your opponent wins 25 points (later exchanged for *real* money in these experiments). No matter what the other player does, an individual player always gains more when he defects; this makes defection the dominant option when the game is played only once against a given opponent (one-shot PD).

In the Shafir and Tversky (1992) study, a total of 80 participants were involved and each person played six PD games for real money mixed in with many other games. The human player was told that they were playing another human opponent, when in fact the choices were programmed ahead of time. They found that when a player was informed that the opponent defected, then in 97% of the

Table 9.3 Prisoner dilemma game

	You defect	You cooperate
Opponent defects	Y:10 O:10	Y:5 O:25
Opponent cooperates	Y:25 O:5	Y:20 O:20

games the player defected; if the player was informed that the other opponent cooperated, then in 84% of the games the player defected; but if the player did not know what the opponent chose, then the player defected in only 63% of games.

Several other studies were conducted to replicate and extend the disjunction effect using the PD game. The first was by Rachel Croson (1999). A total of 80 participants played two PD games for *real* money, and half were required to predict what the opponent would do and half were not asked to make this prediction. For the first payoff matrix, of the players who made predictions, 55% predicted defection. Players who made predictions decided to defect in a total of 45% of the games; players who did not make predictions decided to defect in only 22.5% of the games. The second payoff condition by Croson used an asymmetric variation on the payoffs used in the PD game. For the second payoff condition, of the players who made predictions, 58% predicted defection. In this second study, players who made predictions decided to defect in 57.5% of the trials, and players who did not make predictions decided to defect only in 37.5% of the games.

More recently, a very close replication of Shafir and Tversky (1992) was obtained by Merv Matthews (Busemeyer *et al.*, 2006b). A total of 88 students played six PD games (mixed in with many other games) for *real* money against a *computer* agent. When told that the agent defected, the players defected in 92.4% of the games; when told that the agent cooperated, the players defected in 83.6% of the games; but when the agent's action was unknown, the players defected in 64.9% of the games.

Other studies also found evidence for disjunction effects using the PD paradigm (Li & Taplan, 2002; Hristova & Grinberg, 2008). Table 9.4 provides a summary of all of the disjunction effects using the PD paradigm. In summary, the PD paradigm has produced a robust disjunction effect.

9.2.3   Theoretical implications of the disjunction effect

9.2.3.1   Sure thing principle

At this point, it is important to distinguish between the empirical finding of a "disjunction effect" and its implications for the "sure thing" principle. The "disjunction effect" is an empirical finding in which the proportion taking the target gamble under the unknown condition falls below both of the proportions taking the target gamble under each of the known conditions. Usually, this is also interpreted as a violation of the "sure thing" principle. But as pointed out earlier, the latter is complicated by two methodological issues. One is that the

Table 9.4 Summary of disjunction effect with PD game

Study	Known defect	Known cooperation	Unknown	N^a
Shafir & Tversky	0.97	0.84	0.63	444
Croson[b]	0.67	0.32	0.30	80
Li & Taplan[c]	0.82	0.77	0.72	90
Matthew	0.91	0.84	0.66	528
Histrova & Grinberg	0.97	0.93	0.88	20
Average	0.87	0.74	0.64	
Quantum model	0.82	0.72	0.65	

[a] N refers to the number of choices included in each proportion.
[b] Average results from first two payoff matrices.
[c] Average results from all seven payoff matrices.

"sure thing" principle is a statement about an individual decision maker and the empirical results concern choices averaged across individuals. Only if we assume homogeneity across individuals can we conclude that the evidence indicates a violation of the "sure thing" principle.

Instead of comparing choice proportions averaged across individuals, one could argue that a violation of the "sure thing" principle occurs only if a particular choice pattern occurs – that is, the same person takes the target gamble under both known conditions, but then rejects the target gamble under the unknown condition (Lambdin & Burdsal, 2007). In fact, this was the most common choice pattern reported by Tversky and Shafir (1992), and this type of pattern was also the most common in the PD paradigm by Shafir and Tversky (1992). Unfortunately, here we encounter the second methodological issue. This simple definition of a violation is flawed because single choices are unreliable, and a single choice cannot establish a preference relation. In fact, Tversky and Shafir (1992) ran a separate study with $N = 95$ students to estimate choice reliability by presenting the same target gamble to each student on two different occasions (several weeks apart), and 19% changed their choice across replications. Given the probabilistic nature of choice, a test of the "sure thing" principle requires one to estimate the *probability* choice patterns across conditions for each person. As noted earlier, this methodological problem is not unique to disjunction effect, and the same issue can be raised with the interpretation of the findings from the Allais and Ellsberg paradoxes.

9.2.3.2 Law of total probability

The disjunction effect can be interpreted as an *interference* effect for the following reason. Recall that an interference effect is a violation of the law of total probability. First consider the two-stage gambling paradigm. Define G as the event "taking" the second gamble, $\bar{G}$ is the event "not taking" the second gamble, W is the event "imagine winning the first gamble," and L is the event "imagine losing the first gamble." In the unknown condition, the player has to *imagine* the outcome (W, L) first, and then chooses G or $\bar{G}$ according to the imagined outcome. Define $p(W)$ as the probability that the person imagines winning the first gamble and $p(L)=1-p(W)$ is the probability to imagine losing the first gamble. Whatever the value of $p(W)$ in the unknown condition, the total probability should be a weighted average of the two known conditions: $p_T(G)=p(W)\cdot p(G|W)+p(L)\cdot p(G|L)$. According to this reasoning, $p_T(G)$ must lie in between the two known probabilities. Empirically it is found that $p(G|W) > p(G|L)$, which requires that $p(G|W) \geq p_T(G) \geq p(G|L)$. However, the results show that the empirical probability of gambling for the unknown condition, denoted $p(G)$, actually falls below the probability for the known loss condition. Therefore, we have $p(G) < p(G|L) < p_T(G) < p(G|W)$, which implies a negative interference effect.

The same argument holds for the PD game results by Shafir and Tversky (1992). Define A_D as the event "player defects," A_C is the event "player co-operates," B_D is the event "imagine opponent defects," and B_C is the event "imagine opponent cooperates." In the unknown condition, suppose the player *imagines* the outcome (B_D, B_C) first and then chooses A_D or A_C according to the imagined outcome. Define $p(B_D)$ as the probability that the person imagines the opponent defects and $p(B_C)=1-p(B_D)$ is the probability to imagine the opponent cooperates. Whatever the value of $p(B_D)$ in the unknown condition, the total probability should be a weighted average of the two known conditions: $p_T(A_D)=p(B_D)\cdot p(A_D|B_D)+p(B_C)\cdot p(A_D|B_C)$. According to this reasoning, $p_T(A_D)$ must lie in between the two known probabilities. Empirically it is found that $p(A_D|B_D) > p(A_D|B_C)$, which requires that $p(A_D|B_D) \geq p_T(A_D) \geq p(A_D|B_C)$. The probability of defecting when the opponent was known to defect was very high (0.97), and so was the probability of defecting when the opponent was known to cooperate (0.84); but the probability of defecting under the unknown condition was lower than both of the known conditions (0.63). The replication by Matthews in Table 9.4 produced almost the same results. No weighted average of the high percentages from the two known conditions can equal the low average for the unknown condition, and so this again is a negative interference effect.

9.2.3.3 Double stochasticity

The disjunction effect also has implications for double stochasticity. The 2×2 transition matrices formed by the conditional probabilities shown in Tables 9.2 and 9.4 are *not* doubly stochastic. For example, consider the results from the Tversky and Shafir (1992) gambling study shown in the first row of Table 9.2. We can form a 2×2 transition matrix (from events win, lose in the first stage to events gamble, not gamble in the second stage) as follows:

$$T = \begin{bmatrix} p(G|W) & p(G|L) \\ p(\bar{G}|W) & p(\bar{G}|L) \end{bmatrix} = \begin{bmatrix} 0.65 & 0.55 \\ 0.35 & 0.45 \end{bmatrix},$$

and this transition matrix is clearly not doubly stochastic because the rows sum to greater than one. Consider also the results from Shafir and Tversky (1992) shown in Table 9.4. The 2×2 transition matrix (from events opponent defects, cooperates to events player defects, cooperates) as follows:

$$T = \begin{bmatrix} p(A_D|B_D) & p(A_D|B_C) \\ p(A_C|B_D) & p(A_C|B_C) \end{bmatrix} = \begin{bmatrix} 0.97 & 0.84 \\ 0.03 & 0.12 \end{bmatrix},$$

which once again is clearly not doubly stochastic.

These results imply that one cannot use a two-dimensional quantum model with noise-free measurements to account for these results. One either needs to use a two-dimensional quantum–Markov model with noisy measurements (see Chapter 8) or a higher dimensional quantum model. A four-dimensional quantum model is developed below. The four-dimensional quantum model produces a 4×4 transition matrix that must be doubly stochastic, but the 2×2 matrix of conditional probabilities generated by the four-dimensional quantum model is no longer predicted to be doubly stochastic.

9.3 Markov and quantum models of the disjunction effect

The original explanation for the disjunction effect was a psychological idea based on the failure of consequential reasoning under the unknown condition. Tversky and Shafir (1992) explained the finding in terms of choice based on reasons as follows. Consider, for example, the two-stage gambling problem. If the person knew they had won, then they had extra house money with which to play and for this reason they chose to play again; if the person knew they had lost, then they needed to recover their losses and for this other reason they chose to play again; but if they did not know the outcome of the game, then these two reasons did not emerge into their minds. Why not? If the first play is unknown, it must definitely be either a win or a loss, and it cannot be anything else. In the PD game, the opponent has only two possible choices: defect or cooperate. So the mystery is why these reasons do not emerge for the unknown condition. If choice is based on reasons, then the unknown condition has *two* good reasons. Somehow these two good reasons cancel out to produce no reasons at all! This is analogous to wave interference where two waves meet with one wave rising while the other wave is falling so they cancel out. This analogy generates an interest in exploring quantum models.

The psychological explanation given by Tversky and Shafir (1992) is quite consistent with a formal quantum model for the effect. Busemeyer *et al.* (2006a) originally suggested a quantum interference interpretation for the disjunction effect; since that time, various quantum models for this effect have been proposed, each one ultimately explaining the effects by interference terms, which includes Pothos and Busemeyer (2009), Khrennikov and Haven (2009), Aerts (2009), Yukalov and Sornette (2010), and Accardi *et al.* (2009). We cannot describe all of these various quantum models for the disjunction effect in detail within this chapter. Instead, we give a detailed presentation of the Pothos

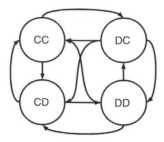

Figure 9.1 Transition diagram of a four-state model. Transitions can occur between any of the four circular states.

and Busemeyer model because it provides an example of a dynamic quantum model like those discussed in Chapter 8. The other models are summarized in Appendix F. Also see Cheon and Takahashi (2010) for analysis of the boundary conditions for quantum models under the unknown condition.

Before we present the dynamic quantum model, one distinct advantage over traditional utility models can be pointed out from the beginning. Quantum decision models are fundamentally probabilistic – they provide quantitative predictions for the *probability* that one option is chosen over another. In fact, the empirical results are choice frequencies, even for a single individual person. Traditional utility theories are deterministic – they can only specify an algebraic preference relation – and they are unable to make quantitative predictions for probability of choice. Cognitive psychologists have developed Markov models of choice behavior, which are also probabilistic (Townsend & Ashby, 1983). Therefore, we systematically compare the quantum model with a comparable Markov model. The model is described for the PD game, but the same exact model can be applied to the two-stage gamble. The presentation of the models is made according to four simple steps.

9.3.1   Step 1: representation of beliefs and actions

The PD game involves a set of four mutually exclusive and exhaustive outcomes $\{B_D A_D, B_D A_C, B_C A_D, B_C A_C\}$, where, for example, $B_C A_D$ symbolizes the event in which the player believes the opponent will cooperate but the player intends to act by defecting. Both the Markov and quantum models assume that these four events correspond to four mutually exclusive and exhaustive belief–action states of the decision maker $\{|B_D A_D\rangle, |B_D A_C\rangle, |B_C A_D\rangle, |B_C A_C\rangle\}$. Figure 9.1 illustrates some of the possible transitions between the four states.

The Markov model assumes that a person starts in exactly one circle in Figure 9.1, but we do not know which one it is, and so we assign probabilities of starting at each one. So at the beginning of a game, the initial probability of starting out in one of these four states is defined by a probability distribution represented by the 4×1 matrix

$$\phi(0) = \begin{bmatrix} \phi_{\text{DD}} \\ \phi_{\text{DC}} \\ \phi_{\text{CD}} \\ \phi_{\text{CC}} \end{bmatrix},$$

where, for example, ϕ_{CD} is the probability of starting in state $|B_{\text{C}}A_{\text{D}}\rangle$. This probability distribution satisfies the constraint $L \cdot \phi = 1$, where $L = \begin{bmatrix} 1 & 1 & 1 & 1 \end{bmatrix}$.

The quantum model assumes that at the beginning of a game the person has some potential to be in every circle in Figure 9.1. So the person's state is a superposition of the four orthonormal basis states

$$|\psi\rangle = \psi_{\text{DD}} \cdot |B_{\text{D}}A_{\text{D}}\rangle + \psi_{\text{DC}} \cdot |B_{\text{D}}A_{\text{C}}\rangle + \psi_{\text{CD}} \cdot |B_{\text{C}}A_{\text{D}}\rangle + \psi_{\text{CC}} \cdot |B_{\text{C}}A_{\text{C}}\rangle$$

and the initial state corresponds to an amplitude distribution represented by the 4×1 column matrix

$$\psi(0) = \begin{bmatrix} \psi_{\text{DD}} \\ \psi_{\text{DC}} \\ \psi_{\text{CD}} \\ \psi_{\text{CC}} \end{bmatrix},$$

where, for example, $|\psi_{\text{CD}}|^2$ is the probability of observing state $|B_{\text{C}}A_{\text{D}}\rangle$ initially. The squared length of ψ must equal one: $\psi^\dagger \cdot \psi = 1$.

9.3.2 Step 2: inferences based on prior information

For both models, information about the opponent's action at time t_1 changes the initial state at time $t = 0$ into a new state at time t_1. For the Markov model, if the opponent is known to defect, then the probability distribution across states changes to

$$\phi(t_1) = \frac{1}{\phi_{\text{DD}} + \phi_{\text{DC}}} \begin{bmatrix} \phi_{\text{DD}} \\ \phi_{\text{DC}} \\ 0 \\ 0 \end{bmatrix} = \begin{bmatrix} \phi_{\text{D}} \\ 0 \end{bmatrix}.$$

The initial probability that the opponent defects (before given the information) equals $(\phi_{\text{DD}} + \phi_{\text{DC}})$, and so the 2×1 matrix ϕ_{D} is the conditional probability distribution across actions given the opponent defects, which sums to one. If the opponent is known to cooperate, then the state changes to

$$\phi(t_1) = \frac{1}{\phi_{\text{CD}} + \phi_{\text{CC}}} \begin{bmatrix} 0 \\ 0 \\ \phi_{\text{CD}} \\ \phi_{\text{CC}} \end{bmatrix} = \begin{bmatrix} 0 \\ \phi_{\text{C}} \end{bmatrix}.$$

The initial probability that the opponent cooperates (before given the information) equals $(\phi_{\text{CD}} + \phi_{\text{CC}})$, and so the 2×1 matrix ϕ_{C} is the conditional probability distribution across actions given that the opponent cooperates, which also sums to one. For the unknown condition, the state remains the same as the initial state:

$$\phi(t_1) = \phi(0)$$

$$= \begin{bmatrix} (\phi_{DD} + \phi_{DC}) \cdot \phi_D \\ (\phi_{CD} + \phi_{CC}) \cdot \phi_C \end{bmatrix}$$

$$= (\phi_{DD} + \phi_{DC}) \cdot \begin{bmatrix} \phi_D \\ 0 \end{bmatrix} + (\phi_{CD} + \phi_{CC}) \cdot \begin{bmatrix} 0 \\ \phi_C \end{bmatrix}.$$

The last line expresses the initial distribution for the unknown condition as a mixed state produced by a weighted average of the distributions for the two known conditions.

For the quantum model, if the opponent is known to defect, the amplitude distribution across states changes to

$$\psi(t_1) = \frac{1}{\sqrt{|\psi_{DD}|^2 + |\psi_{DC}|^2}} \begin{bmatrix} \psi_{DD} \\ \psi_{DC} \\ 0 \\ 0 \end{bmatrix} = \begin{bmatrix} \psi_D \\ 0 \end{bmatrix}. \tag{9.2}$$

The initial probability that the opponent defects (before given any information) equals $\left(|\psi_{DD}|^2 + |\psi_{DC}|^2 \right)$, and so the 2×1 matrix ψ_D is the conditional amplitude distribution across actions given that the opponent defects, which has a squared length equal to one. If the opponent is known to cooperate, then the state changes to

$$\psi(t_1) = \frac{1}{\sqrt{|\psi_{CD}|^2 + |\psi_{CC}|^2}} \begin{bmatrix} 0 \\ 0 \\ \psi_{CD} \\ \psi_{CC} \end{bmatrix} = \begin{bmatrix} 0 \\ \psi_C \end{bmatrix}. \tag{9.3}$$

The initial probability that the opponent cooperates (before given any information) equals $\left(|\psi_{CD}|^2 + |\psi_{CC}|^2 \right)$, and so the 2×1 matrix ψ_C is the conditional amplitude distribution across actions given that the opponent cooperates, which also has a squared length equal to one. For the unknown condition, it remains the same as the initial state:

$$\psi(t_1) = \psi(0)$$

$$= \begin{bmatrix} \sqrt{|\psi_{DD}|^2 + |\psi_{DC}|^2} \cdot \psi_D \\ \sqrt{|\psi_{CD}|^2 + |\psi_{CC}|^2} \cdot \psi_C \end{bmatrix}$$

$$= \sqrt{|\psi_{DD}|^2 + |\psi_{DC}|^2} \cdot \begin{bmatrix} \psi_D \\ 0 \end{bmatrix} + \sqrt{|\psi_{CD}|^2 + |\psi_{CC}|^2} \cdot \begin{bmatrix} 0 \\ \psi_C \end{bmatrix}.$$

The last line expresses the initial state for the unknown condition as a superposition formed by a weighted sum of the amplitude distributions for the two known conditions.

9.3.3 Step 3: strategies based on payoffs

For both models, the decision maker must evaluate the payoffs in order to select an appropriate action, which changes the previous state at time t_1 into a final state at time t_2. The evolution of the state during this time period corresponds to the thought process leading to a decision.

For the Markov model, the state evolution obeys a Kolmogorov forward equation driven by a 4×4 intensity matrix K (described below):

$$\frac{d}{dt}\phi(t) = K \cdot \phi(t),$$

which has a matrix exponential solution (see the section on matrix algebra in Chapter 2)

$$\phi(t_2) = e^{Kt} \cdot \phi(t_1)$$

for $t = t_2 - t_1$. The state to state transition matrix is defined by

$$T(t) = e^{tK}$$

with $T_{ij}(t) = p[\text{transiting to state } i \text{ at time } t_2 \text{ given being in state } j \text{ at time } t_1]$.

The off-diagonal elements of the intensity matrix K are positive and the diagonal elements of K are negative so that the columns of K sum to zero, which then guarantees that the columns of T sum to one, which finally guarantees that $\phi(t)$ always sums to unity. Initially, we assume

$$K = K_1 = \begin{bmatrix} K_D & \mathbf{0} \\ \mathbf{0} & K_C \end{bmatrix}, \tag{9.4}$$

$$K_D = \begin{bmatrix} -1 & k_D \\ 1 & -k_D \end{bmatrix}, \quad K_C = \begin{bmatrix} -1 & k_C \\ 1 & -k_C \end{bmatrix}.$$

The 2×2 intensity matrix K_D applies when the player believes that the opponent will defect, and the other 2×2 matrix K_C applies when the player believes the opponent will cooperate. (Recall that the intensity matrix K_D was analyzed in detail in Chapter 8.) The parameter k_D is a function of the difference between the payoffs for defecting relative to cooperating given that your opponent defects, and k_C is a function of the difference between payoffs for defecting relative to cooperating given that your opponent cooperates. The intensity matrix transforms the state probabilities to favor either defection or cooperation, depending on the payoffs for each belief state.

For the quantum model, the state evolution obeys a Schrödinger equation driven by a 4×4 Hamiltonian matrix H (described below):

$$\frac{d}{dt}\psi(t) = -i \cdot H \cdot \psi(t),$$

which has a matrix exponential solution

$$\psi(t_2) = e^{-iHt} \cdot \psi(t_1)$$

for $t = t_2 - t_1$. The unitary matrix is defined by

$$U(t) = e^{-itH},$$

which determines the transition probabilities according to $T_{ij}(t) = |U_{ij}(t)|^2 = p[$observing state i at time t_2 given that state j was observed at time $t_1]$.

The Hamiltonian matrix H is a Hermitian matrix, $H^\dagger = H$, so that U is a unitary matrix, $U^\dagger U = I$, which finally guarantees that $\psi(t)$ always has unit length. Also, the unitary property implies that the transition matrix T generated from U is doubly stochastic; that is, both the rows and columns of T sum to one. Initially, we assume

$$H = H_1 = \begin{bmatrix} H_{\rm D} & \mathbf{0} \\ \mathbf{0} & H_{\rm C} \end{bmatrix}, \tag{9.5}$$

$$H_{\rm D} = \frac{1}{\sqrt{1 + h_{\rm D}^2}} \begin{bmatrix} h_{\rm D} & 1 \\ 1 & -h_{\rm D} \end{bmatrix}, \quad H_{\rm C} = \frac{1}{\sqrt{1 + h_{\rm C}^2}} \begin{bmatrix} h_{\rm C} & 1 \\ 1 & -h_{\rm C} \end{bmatrix}.$$

The 2×2 Hamiltonian matrix $H_{\rm D}$ applies when the player believes that the opponent will defect, and the other 2×2 matrix $H_{\rm C}$ applies when the player believes the opponent will cooperate. (Recall that the Hamiltonian matrix $H_{\rm D}$ was analyzed in detail in Chapter 8 and in Appendix D on Pauli matrices). The parameter $h_{\rm D}$ is a function of the difference between the payoffs for defecting relative to cooperating given that your opponent defects, and $h_{\rm C}$ is a function of the difference between payoffs for defecting relative to cooperating given that your opponent cooperates. The Hamiltonian matrix transforms the state probabilities to favor either defection or cooperation, depending on the payoffs for each belief state.

For both models, the utility parameters $(k_{\rm D}, h_{\rm D})$, used when the opponent defects, are assumed to be determined by $u(x_{\rm DD} - x_{\rm DC})$, where $x_{\rm DD}$ is the payoff for defecting if the opponent defects, $x_{\rm DC}$ is the payoff for cooperating if the opponent defects, and u is a monotonically increasing utility function. Similarly, the utility parameters under the belief that the opponent will cooperate $(k_{\rm C}, h_{\rm C})$ are assumed to be determined by $u(x_{\rm CD} - x_{\rm CC})$, where $x_{\rm CD}$ is the payoff for defecting if the opponent cooperates, $x_{\rm CC}$ is the payoff for cooperating if the opponent cooperates, and again u is a monotonically increasing function. For example, given the payoffs in Table 9.1, $x_{\rm DD} = 10$, $x_{\rm DC} = 5$, $x_{\rm CD} = 25$, and $x_{\rm CC} = 20$ so that $u(x_{\rm DD} - x_{\rm DC}) = u(5) = u(x_{\rm CD} - x_{\rm CC})$. In particular, for the payoff matrix shown in Table 9.1, $k_{\rm D} = k_{\rm C} = k$ is determined by $u(5)$ and $h_{\rm D} = h_{\rm C} = h$ is also determined by $u(5)$. In this case, $K_{\rm D} = K_{\rm C}$ and $H_{\rm D} = H_{\rm C}$.

For both models, a decision corresponds to a measurement of the state at time t_2. For both models we use the measurement matrix that picks out the defect states for each belief about the opponent:

$$M = \begin{bmatrix} M_1 & \mathbf{0} \\ \mathbf{0} & M_2 \end{bmatrix}, \tag{9.6}$$

$$M_1 = \begin{bmatrix} 1 & 0 \\ 0 & 0 \end{bmatrix}, \quad M_2 = \begin{bmatrix} 1 & 0 \\ 0 & 0 \end{bmatrix}.$$

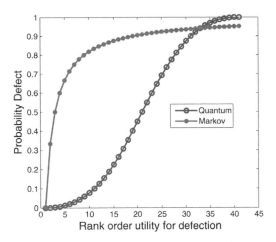

Figure 9.2 Probability of defection plotted as a function of the rank order value of the utility for defecting.

For the Markov model, using $L = \begin{bmatrix} 1 & 1 & 1 & 1 \end{bmatrix}$, the probability of defecting at time $t_2 = t_1 + t$ equals

$$p(D) = L \cdot M \cdot e^{tK} \cdot \phi(t_1), \tag{9.7}$$

For the quantum model, the probability of defecting at time $t_2 = t_1 + t$ equals

$$p(D) = ||M \cdot e^{-itH} \cdot \psi(t_1)||^2. \tag{9.8}$$

Let us see how these models behave at this point. In order to do this we need to choose a processing time t parameter for the Markov and quantum models. We are not fitting decision times, and so this parameter was chosen to produce a choice probability that reaches its maximum for each model. For the quantum model, we can see from Chapter 8 (also see the appendix) that this time point equals $t = \frac{\pi}{2}$. For the Markov model, $t = 100$ was satisfactory for producing asymptotic results. Hereafter, $t = \frac{\pi}{2}$ will always be used for the quantum model in this chapter. The predictions are based on Eq. (9.7) or (9.8) which can be easily computed in Matlab using the `expm` function. For example, after defining the matrices `M`, `H`, and `Psi`, and defining the time constant `t`, the following two steps can be used to compute the quantum model prediction: `PD = M*expm(-i*t*H)*Psi; PD = PD'*PD`. The predictions for the quantum model were computed by setting $\psi_i(t_1) = \frac{1}{2}$ for all four rows, $t = \frac{\pi}{2}$, and allowing h to range from -1 to $+1$ in equal steps. The predictions for the Markov model were computed by setting $\phi_i(t_1) = \frac{1}{4}$ for all four rows, and $t = 100$, and allowing k to range from 0 to 20 in equal steps.

As can be seen in Figure 9.2, both models produce a monotonically increasing probability of defection as a function of the utility for defecting. The Markov model produces an exponential growth to a limit at one (with sufficiently large utilities) and the quantum model produces an S-shaped growth in probability of defection as a function of the utility.

At this point of model development, the evolution of states during the period of time t_1 to time t_2 depends solely on the payoffs, while the beliefs about the opponent's action remain fixed. The intensity matrix in Eq. (9.4) only operates on the actions and it leaves the belief state intact, and the same is true for the Hamiltonian in Eq. (9.5). To see this more clearly, consider the evolution for the quantum model. Recall that $|\psi_{DD}|^2 + |\psi_{DC}|^2$ represents the player's probability that the opponent will defect and ψ_D is a 2×1 matrix containing the amplitude for each action conditioned on believing the opponent will defect ($||\psi_D||^2 = 1$); also recall that $|\psi_{CD}|^2 + |\psi_{CC}|^2$ is the player's probability that the opponent will cooperate and ψ_C is a 2×1 matrix containing the amplitude for each action conditioned on believing the opponent will cooperate ($||\psi_C||^2 = 1$). The final state $\psi(t_2)$ equals

$$\psi(t_2) = e^{-itH} \cdot \psi(0) \tag{9.9}$$

$$= \begin{bmatrix} e^{-itH_D} & 0 \\ 0 & e^{-itH_C} \end{bmatrix} \cdot \begin{bmatrix} \sqrt{|\psi_{DD}|^2 + |\psi_{DC}|^2} \cdot \psi_D \\ \sqrt{|\psi_{CD}|^2 + |\psi_{CC}|^2} \cdot \psi_C \end{bmatrix}$$

$$= \begin{bmatrix} \sqrt{|\psi_{DD}|^2 + |\psi_{DC}|^2} \cdot e^{-itH_D} \cdot \psi_D \\ \sqrt{|\psi_{CD}|^2 + |\psi_{CC}|^2} \cdot e^{-itH_C} \cdot \psi_C \end{bmatrix}.$$

The last line shows that the unitary operator e^{-itH_D} rotates the two actions but it leaves the squared length of ψ_D equal to one; similarly, the unitary operator e^{-itH_C} rotates the two actions but it leaves the squared length of ψ_C equal to one. Thus, the probability of believing the opponent will defect for the final state $\psi(t_2)$ remains the same as it was for the initial state $\psi(0)$. More intuitively, if the player is told that the opponent has defected, then this information is never questioned, and the player remains believing that the opponent will defect until the decision is made. Alternatively, if the player does not know the opponent's action and initially thinks it is equally likely that the opponent will defect or cooperate, then the player remains in this same equally likely belief state until a decision is made. Only the states associated with the player's defect or cooperate actions, separately for each belief, are changed.

Under this assumption neither the Markov nor the quantum model can produce a disjunction effect. To see why this is true for the quantum model, consider the predictions for the unknown condition. Referring back to Eq. (9.9),

$$||M \cdot \psi(t_2)||^2 = \left\| \begin{bmatrix} \sqrt{|\psi_{DD}|^2 + |\psi_{DC}|^2} \cdot M_1 \cdot e^{-itH_D} \cdot \psi_D \\ \sqrt{|\psi_{CD}|^2 + |\psi_{CC}|^2} \cdot M_2 \cdot e^{-itH_C} \cdot \psi_C \end{bmatrix} \right\|^2$$

$$= \left(|\psi_{\mathrm{DD}}|^2 + |\psi_{\mathrm{DC}}|^2\right) \cdot ||M_1 \cdot \mathrm{e}^{-itH_{\mathrm{D}}} \cdot \psi_{\mathrm{D}}||^2$$

$$+ \left(|\psi_{\mathrm{CD}}|^2 + |\psi_{\mathrm{CC}}|^2\right) \cdot ||M_2 \cdot \mathrm{e}^{-itH_{\mathrm{C}}} \cdot \psi_{\mathrm{C}}||^2.$$

Note that $||M_1 \cdot \mathrm{e}^{-itH_{\mathrm{D}}} \cdot \psi_{\mathrm{D}}||^2$ equals the probability of defecting when the opponent is known to defect and $||M_2 \cdot \mathrm{e}^{-itH_{\mathrm{C}}} \cdot \psi_{\mathrm{C}}||^2$ equals the probability of defecting when the opponent is known to cooperate. Therefore, the last line expresses the probability of defecting for the unknown condition as a weighted average of the two known conditions. This cannot produce a disjunction effect. One additional stage is needed to account for the disjunction effect.

9.3.4　Step 4: strategies based on evaluations of both beliefs and payoffs

To explain the disjunction effect, it is important to allow the decision maker to change beliefs about the opponent's action during the deliberation period between time t_1 and time t_2. For example, the player may become suspicious about the experimenter's information concerning the opponent's move during this period of time. More generally, the player may tend to change their beliefs to be consistent with their own actions (Festinger, 1957). In the case of the PD game, this motivates a change of beliefs about what the opponent will do in a direction that is consistent with the person's intended action. In other words, if a player chooses to cooperate, then he/she would tend to think that the other player will cooperate as well. Shafir and Tversky (1992) proposed the same idea, but in terms of a personal bias for "wishful thinking." So an evolutionary operator is introduced that produces changes in beliefs too. Although changes in beliefs can be implemented in both Markov and quantum models, we shall see that it does not help the Markov model, and only the quantum model explains the disjunction effect.

For the Markov model, an intensity matrix that produces a change of beliefs in the direction of wishful thinking is

$$K_2 = \begin{bmatrix} -1 & 0 & d & 0 \\ 0 & 0 & 0 & 0 \\ 1 & 0 & -d & 0 \\ 0 & 0 & 0 & 0 \end{bmatrix} + \begin{bmatrix} 0 & 0 & 0 & 0 \\ 0 & -d & 0 & 1 \\ 0 & 0 & 0 & 0 \\ 0 & d & 0 & -1 \end{bmatrix}. \tag{9.10}$$

The first matrix in this sum produces transitions in beliefs toward the opponent defecting when the player plans to defect and the second matrix produces transitions in beliefs toward the opponent cooperating when the player plans to cooperate. To see how this works, notice that

$$\frac{\mathrm{d}}{\mathrm{d}t}\phi(t) = K_2 \cdot \phi(t)$$

$$= \begin{bmatrix} d \cdot \phi_{\mathrm{CD}} - \phi_{\mathrm{DD}} \\ \phi_{\mathrm{CC}} - d \cdot \phi_{\mathrm{DC}} \\ \phi_{\mathrm{DD}} - d \cdot \phi_{\mathrm{CD}} \\ d \cdot \phi_{\mathrm{DC}} - \phi_{\mathrm{CC}} \end{bmatrix}.$$

If $d > 1$ then the rate of increase for the first and last rows is greater than the middle two rows. For example, if we set $\phi_i(0) = 1/4$ for all four rows, $d = 10$, and $t = 10$, then

$$\phi(10) = \mathrm{e}^{10K_2} \cdot \phi(0) = \begin{bmatrix} 0.45 \\ 0.05 \\ 0.05 \\ 0.45 \end{bmatrix}.$$

By itself, Eq. (9.10) is an inadequate description of behavior in PD game, because it cannot explain how preferences vary with payoffs. We need to combine Eqs. (9.4) and (9.10) to produce an intensity matrix $K = K_1 + K_2$. Accordingly, for the Markov model, the final state at time t_2 is determined by

$$\phi(t_2) = \mathrm{e}^{t(K_1 + K_2)} \cdot \phi(t_1). \tag{9.11}$$

The probability of defecting at time t_2 is then given by $p(D) = L \cdot M \cdot \phi(t_2)$, with $\phi(t_2)$ defined by Eq. (9.11).

For the quantum model, a Hamiltonian that produces a change of beliefs in the direction of wishful thinking is

$$H_2 = \frac{-c}{\sqrt{2}} \begin{bmatrix} 1 & 0 & 1 & 0 \\ 0 & 0 & 0 & 0 \\ 1 & 0 & -1 & 0 \\ 0 & 0 & 0 & 0 \end{bmatrix} + \frac{-c}{\sqrt{2}} \begin{bmatrix} 0 & 0 & 0 & 0 \\ 0 & -1 & 0 & 1 \\ 0 & 0 & 0 & 0 \\ 0 & 1 & 0 & 1 \end{bmatrix}. \tag{9.12}$$

The first matrix in this sum produces transitions in beliefs toward the opponent defecting when the player plans to defect and the second matrix produces transitions in beliefs toward the opponent cooperating when the player plans to cooperate. To see how this works, notice that

$$\frac{\mathrm{d}}{\mathrm{d}t}\psi(t) = -i \cdot H_2 \cdot \psi(t)$$

$$= i \cdot \frac{c}{\sqrt{2}} \begin{bmatrix} \psi_{\mathrm{DD}} + \psi_{\mathrm{CD}} \\ \psi_{\mathrm{CC}} - \psi_{\mathrm{DC}} \\ \psi_{\mathrm{DD}} - \psi_{\mathrm{CD}} \\ \psi_{\mathrm{DC}} + \psi_{\mathrm{CC}} \end{bmatrix}.$$

If $c > 0$, then the rate of increase for the first and last rows is greater than the middle two rows. For example, if we set $\psi_i(0) = 1/2$ for all four rows, $c = 1$, and

$t = \frac{\pi}{2}$, then this produces squared magnitudes for each of the four coordinates equal to the values on the right-hand side of the arrow:

$$\psi\left(\frac{\pi}{2}\right) = e^{-i\frac{\pi}{2}H_2} \cdot \psi(0) \rightarrow \begin{bmatrix} 0.50 \\ 0.00 \\ 0.00 \\ 0.50 \end{bmatrix}.$$

Once again, by itself, Eq. (9.12) is an inadequate description of behavior in PD games, because it cannot explain how preferences vary with payoffs. We need to combine Eqs. (9.5) and (9.12) to produce a Hamiltonian matrix $H = H_1 + H_2$. Accordingly, for the quantum model, the final state at time t_2 is determined by

$$\psi(t_2) = e^{-it(H_1 + H_2)} \cdot \psi(t_1). \tag{9.13}$$

The probability of defecting at time t_2 is then given by $p(D) = ||M \cdot \psi(t_2)||^2$, with $\psi(t_2)$ defined above by Eq. (9.13).

9.3.5 Model predictions

On the basis of the assumptions described above, we can derive the following general (parameter-free) implications from both models.

9.3.5.1 Markov predictions

First we examine the predictions for the Markov model. Essentially, it is impossible for the Markov model to produce the disjunction effect. The proof is straightforward. Consider the following prediction for the unknown condition:

$$p(D|UK) = L \cdot M \cdot e^{t(K_1+K_2)} \cdot \phi(t_1)$$

$$= L \cdot M \cdot e^{t(K_1+K_2)} \left((\phi_{DD} + \phi_{DC}) \cdot \begin{bmatrix} \phi_D \\ 0 \end{bmatrix} + (\phi_{CD} + \phi_{CC}) \cdot \begin{bmatrix} 0 \\ \phi_C \end{bmatrix} \right)$$

$$= (\phi_{DD} + \phi_{DC}) \cdot L \cdot M \cdot e^{t(K_1+K_2)} \cdot \begin{bmatrix} \phi_D \\ 0 \end{bmatrix}$$

$$+ (\phi_{CD} + \phi_{CC}) \cdot L \cdot M \cdot e^{t(K_1+K_2)} \cdot \begin{bmatrix} 0 \\ \phi_C \end{bmatrix}.$$

The final probabilities obtained from the Markov model are a linear transformation of the initial probabilities. Furthermore, the predictions for the two known cases are

$$p(D|KD) = L \cdot M \cdot e^{t(K_1+K_2)} \cdot \begin{bmatrix} \phi_D \\ 0 \end{bmatrix},$$

$$p(D|KC) = L \cdot M \cdot e^{t(K_1+K_2)} \cdot \begin{bmatrix} 0 \\ \phi_C \end{bmatrix}.$$

It follows that the prediction of the Markov model for the unknown condition can be expressed as

$$p(D|UK) = (\phi_{\mathrm{DD}} + \phi_{\mathrm{DC}}) \cdot p(D|KD) + (\phi_{\mathrm{CD}} + \phi_{\mathrm{CC}}) \cdot p(D|KC). \qquad (9.14)$$

Therefore, the Markov model must predict that the probability for the unknown case is a weighted average of the probabilities for the two known cases. It continues to obey the law of total probability and it cannot produce the disjunction (interference) effect.

Markov models have been widely applied in understanding human choice behavior (Busemeyer & Townsend, 1993). Accordingly, one can naturally wonder whether it is possible to salvage the Markov model. First, recall that the Markov model fails even when we allow for "wishful thinking" in this model. Second, the analyses above hold for any initial state $\phi(0)$ and any intensity matrix K (not just the ones used above to motivate the model), but they are based on two key assumptions: the same initial state $\phi(0)$ is used to begin the process for all three conditions and the same intensity matrix K is used across both known and unknown conditions. However, we can relax even these assumptions. Even if the initial state is not the same across conditions, the Markov model must predict that the marginal probability of defecting in the unknown condition (whatever mixture is used) is a convex combination of the two probabilities conditioned on the known action of the opponent. This prediction is violated in the data of Tables 9.2 and 9.4. Furthermore, even if we change intensity matrices across conditions (using the K_1 intensity matrix for known conditions and using the $K_1 + K_2$ matrix for the unknown condition), the Markov model continues to satisfy the law of total probability because this change has absolutely no effect on the predicted probability of defection (the K_2 matrix does not change the defection rate). Thus, our tests of the Markov model are very robust.

9.3.5.2 Quantum predictions

Next we examine the predictions for the quantum model. Consider the following prediction for the unknown condition:

$$\psi(t_1) = \left(\sqrt{|\psi_{\mathrm{DD}}|^2 + |\psi_{\mathrm{DC}}|^2} \cdot \begin{bmatrix} \psi_{\mathrm{D}} \\ \mathbf{0} \end{bmatrix} + \sqrt{|\psi_{\mathrm{CD}}|^2 + |\psi_{\mathrm{CC}}|^2} \cdot \begin{bmatrix} \mathbf{0} \\ \psi_{\mathrm{C}} \end{bmatrix} \right)$$

$$p(D|UK) = ||M \cdot \mathrm{e}^{-it(H_1+H_2)} \cdot \psi(t_1)||^2$$

$$= ||\sqrt{|\psi_{\mathrm{DD}}|^2 + |\psi_{\mathrm{DC}}|^2} \cdot M \cdot \mathrm{e}^{-it(H_1+H_2)} \cdot \begin{bmatrix} \psi_{\mathrm{D}} \\ \mathbf{0} \end{bmatrix}$$

$$+ \sqrt{|\psi_{\mathrm{CD}}|^2 + |\psi_{\mathrm{CC}}|^2} \cdot ||M \cdot \mathrm{e}^{-it(H_1+H_2)} \cdot \begin{bmatrix} \mathbf{0} \\ \psi_{\mathrm{C}} \end{bmatrix} ||^2.$$

Note that while the final amplitude distribution is a linear transformation of the initial amplitude distribution, the final probability distribution is a nonlinear transformation because probabilities are obtained by squaring the amplitudes. Furthermore, the predictions for the two known cases are

$$p(D|KD) = \left\| M \cdot e^{-it(H_1+H_2)} \cdot \begin{bmatrix} \psi_D \\ 0 \end{bmatrix} \right\|^2,$$

$$p(D|KC) = \left\| M \cdot e^{-it(H_1+H_2)} \cdot \begin{bmatrix} 0 \\ \psi_C \end{bmatrix} \right\|^2.$$

Therefore, prediction for the unknown condition can be re-expressed as

$$p(D|UK) = \left(|\psi_{DD}|^2 + |\psi_{DC}|^2 \right) \cdot p(D|KD) + \left(|\psi_{CD}|^2 + |\psi_{CC}|^2 \right) \cdot p(D|KC)$$

$$+ \sqrt{|\psi_{DD}|^2 + |\psi_{DC}|^2} \cdot \sqrt{|\psi_{CD}|^2 + |\psi_{CC}|^2} \cdot \text{Int}_D,$$

where Int_D is defined as the following inner product of two non-orthogonal vectors:

$$V_D = M \cdot e^{-it(H_1+H_2)} \cdot \begin{bmatrix} \psi_D \\ 0 \end{bmatrix} \qquad (9.15)$$

$$V_C = M \cdot e^{-it(H_1+H_2)} \cdot \begin{bmatrix} 0 \\ \psi_C \end{bmatrix}$$

$$\text{Int}_D = V_D^\dagger \cdot V_C + V_C^\dagger \cdot V_D.$$

Note that two state vectors for the two known conditions, defined by Eqs. (9.2) and (9.3), are orthogonal; but after they are transformed by $M \cdot e^{-it(H_1+H_2)}$ as in Eq. (9.15) they become non-orthogonal. The inner product must be negative to produce negative interference and account for the disjunction effect.

The quantum model was fit to the average data separately for Tables 9.2 and 9.4. (The program used to generate predictions from the model is provided in Appendix G). The predictions for the quantum model were computed by setting $\psi_i(t_1) = \frac{1}{2}$ for all four rows to make the initial state equally likely, $t = \frac{\pi}{2}$ to allow the choice probability to reach maximum across time, and estimating two free parameters, h and c. For the two-stage gambling task, the best fitting parameters were $h = 0.4841$ and $c = 1.7375$, which produced the following predictions for the probability of taking the gamble (also shown in the last row in Table 9.2): $p(G|KW) = 0.72$ for the known win condition, $p(G|KL) = 0.52$ for the known loss condition, and $p(G|UK) = 0.38$ for the unknown condition. This closely reproduces the results shown in Table 9.2. For the PD paradigm, the best fitting parameters were $h = 0.5263$ and $c = 2.2469$, which produced the following predictions for the probability of defecting (also shown in the last row of Table 9.4): $p(D|KD) = 0.82$ when the opponent was known to defect, $p(D|KC) = 0.72$, when the opponent was known to cooperate, and $p(D|UK) = 0.65$ when the opponent's action was unknown. This closely reproduces the results shown in Table 9.4.

In summary, the dynamic quantum model provides a formal quantitative account for this puzzling finding that has resisted explanations by traditional

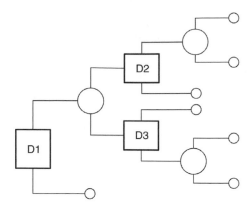

Figure 9.3 Two-stage gamble decision tree. D1 represents the decision to play the first gamble. D2 is the decision to play the second gamble after winning the first. D3 is the decision to play the second gamble after losing the first.

decision theories. Further tests with more conditions are needed to build confidence in this model. So far we have only accomplished fitting three data points using two free parameters (although they are difficult data points to fit). What is needed is a larger experiment using more conditions to provide more degrees of freedom for testing this model and comparing it with competing models. The next section provides such a test.

9.4   Dynamic consistency

Most complex decisions involve planning for the future across sequences of actions and events. For example, making a decision about a difficult medical procedure involves forming contingency plans for possible negative consequences. Optimal strategies for planning multistage decisions usually rely on backward induction procedures that require planning from the last stage and working backwards to the current stage (von Winterfeldt & Edwards, 1986). This requires the current decision to be based on plans for future decisions. Dynamic consistency is a critical assumption entailed by this planning process. A decision maker is dynamically consistent if the decision maker actually carries out the planned action once that decision is realized (Machina, 1989). If the plan is not carried out, then the optimality of the earlier decisions is compromised.

Consider the example shown in Figure 9.3, which is a decision tree with two stages. Suppose D1 is a decision to perform a knee surgery or not. If no surgery is performed (choosing down from D1), then the decision ends and the person lives with a damaged knee. If surgery is performed, the surgery could be successful (up at the circular node) or not (down at the circular node). If the surgery succeeds, the person is faced with another decision at node D2, which is to resume playing tennis or not (which damaged the knee in the first place); and if the person does decide to play tennis again (chooses up at D2) then she faces another gamble with her knee. If the surgery is unsuccessful, the person faces the decision node D3, which is to decide whether or not to try the surgery again; which in turn could succeed or fail. Thus, the decision at node D1 depends on what the person plans to do for example at node D2. In particular, surgery may only seem worthwhile if the person wants to play tennis with the successfully repaired knee. If the person chooses to do the surgery because she plans to play tennis again, then, following successful surgery, the person should go ahead with the plan and play tennis to be dynamically consistent. Otherwise what was the point of taking the chance and doing the surgery in the first place? If, instead, the person with the successfully repaired knee changes her mind and decides not to take any more chances with it, then she is dynamically inconsistent.

It is not so surprising that a person might be dynamically inconsistent in a very complex situation such as deciding about surgery. The person making the decision at one point in time is not the same as the person facing decisions at later points in time (Strotz, 1956). The person with a damaged knee at an early point in time is not the same anymore as the person with the repaired knee at a later point in time. But can people at least be dynamically consistent on shorter time scales involving less complicated decisions? There is an accumulating body of empirical evidence showing that people have difficulty planning ahead (Hey & Knoll, 2007) and they are dynamically inconsistent even with very simple choice situations and short time horizons (Cubitt *et al.*, 1998; Busemeyer *et al.*, 2000). Below we analyze in detail one set of findings regarding dynamic inconsistency originally reported by Barkan and Busemeyer (1999) and later replicated and extended by Barkan and Busemeyer (2003).

Barkan and Busemeyer (1999) used a two-stage gambling paradigm to study dynamic consistency, which was similar to the one used by Tversky and Shafir (1992) to study the disjunction effect. A total of 100 people participated and each person played the four gambles shown in Table 9.5 twice. Each gamble had an equal chance of producing a win or a loss. The columns labeled "win" and "loss" indicate the points that could be won or lost for each gamble (each point was worth one cent). For each gamble in Table 9.5, the person was forced to play the first round and then, contingent on the outcome of the first round, they were given a choice whether or not to play the second round with the same gamble.

This two-stage decision can be represented by the decision tree shown in Figure 9.3, except that the person was forced to go up at decision node D1. While still at node D1, however, the person was asked to make plans at nodes D2 and D3 contingent on each outcome of the first play. Contingent on winning the first round, the person had to select a plan at node D2 to take or reject the gamble again; contingent on losing the first round, the person had to make another plan at node D3 to take or reject the gamble again. Then the first-stage gamble was actually played out and the win or loss was revealed. After experiencing the win (actually arriving at node D2) the person made a final decision to take or reject; and after experiencing a loss (actually arriving at node D3) the person also had to decide whether to take or reject the gamble a

Table 9.5 Barkan and Busemeyer (1999) dynamic inconsistency effect

Win	Lose	Plan win	Plan loss	Final win	Final loss	$p(W)$
80	−100	0.25	0.26	0.20	0.35	0.64
80	−40	0.76	0.72	0.69	0.73	−0.19
200	−100	0.68	0.68	0.60	0.75	0.43
200	−40	0.84	0.86	0.76	0.89	0.31

second time. The plan and the final decision were made equally valuable because the experimenter randomly selected either the planned action or the final action to determine the final payoff. Table 9.5 shows the main results.[6]

The first two columns of Table 9.5 show the payoffs of the four gambles; the next two columns show the probability of choosing to take the gamble on the second stage contingent on planning for a win or loss on the first play, and the next two columns show the probability to take the second gamble after actually experiencing a win or a loss on the first play. (The last column labeled $p(W)$ is discussed below.) First note that there was little or no difference between the plans contingent on winning or losing the first play. However, a dynamic inconsistency effect occurred because people changed substantially and system-atically away from their plans on the final decision. Actually winning the first stage produced a decrease in probability of taking the gamble (compare the Plan and Final columns for Win), and actually losing the first play produced an increase in probability (compare the Plan and Final columns for Loss).

Furthermore, the results provide additional evidence for interference effects based on the following reason. If the person makes the planned choice by pre-dicting the first-stage outcome and choosing on the basis of this prediction, then the probability of choosing the gamble on the plan should be a weighted average of the probabilities of choosing the gamble after winning and losing. Define W as the event "win first play" and L as the event "lose first play" and define T as the event "take second-stage gamble," and define R as the event "reject the second stage gamble." Then the total probability for planning to take the gam-ble is given by the law of total probability formula: $p(T|\text{plan}) = p(W) \cdot p(T|W) + p(L) \cdot p(T|L)$. We obtain estimates of $p(T|W), p(T|L)$ from the final decision, which can be used to estimate the single unknown parameter $p(W)$ from the data. If the model is correct, a common probability $p(W)$ for the event win the first play should be operating across all payoff conditions. On the contrary, as shown in the last column of Table 9.5, this weighted average model fails because the estimate of $p(W)$ given to the win condition changes dramatically, depend-ing on the payoff conditions. In fact, the negative weight for the (80, −40) payoff condition reflects a small disjunction effect, in which case the average probabil-ity for the plan (which equals 0.74) is greater than both final probabilities (0.69 for final win and 0.73 for final loss).

---

[6]The plan win and plan loss results are actually the average across the elaborated and partial plan conditions in Barkan and Busemeyer (1999).

Table 9.6 Barkan and Busemeyer (2003) dynamic inconsistency results

Win	Loss	EV	Outcome	Obs plan	Pred plan	Obs final	Pred final
200	220	−10	W	0.46	0.43	0.34	0.35
180	200	−10	W	0.45	0.43	0.35	0.35
200	200	0	W	0.59	0.60	0.51	0.49
120	100	10	W	0.70	0.63	0.62	0.53
140	100	20	W	0.62	0.67	0.54	0.57
200	140	30	W	0.63	0.71	0.53	0.60
200	120	40	W	0.74	0.73	0.68	0.62
200	100	50	W	0.79	0.74	0.70	0.64
80	100	−10	L	0.36	0.38	0.44	0.48
100	120	−10	L	0.47	0.39	0.63	0.49
100	100	0	L	0.63	0.57	0.64	0.64
200	180	10	L	0.57	0.66	0.69	0.71
160	140	10	L	0.68	0.65	0.69	0.70
200	160	20	L	0.67	0.69	0.72	0.73
160	100	30	L	0.65	0.70	0.73	0.73
180	100	40	L	0.68	0.72	0.80	0.75
200[a]	100	50	L	0.85	0.74	0.82	0.76

[a] This was a practice problem presented first before all other problems.

It is interesting to compare the results found in Table 9.5 with those from Table 9.2. In Table 9.2, a large increase in probability of taking the gamble occurred after imagining a win on the first stage; and a smaller increase in probability of taking the gamble occurred after imagining a loss, compared with the unknown condition. In Table 9.5, experiencing a real gain decreased the probability of taking the gamble; and experiencing a real loss increased the probability of taking the gamble, compared with the plan condition.

Barkan and Busemeyer (2003) replicated and extended these results with a larger design. A total of 100 people participated and each person played the 17 gambles shown in Table 9.6 twice. The column labeled EV indicates the expected value of the gamble. The results are shown in Table 9.6. The probability of taking the gamble during the planning stage is shown for each gamble under the column labeled "Obs plan";[7] the probability of taking the gamble during the final stage is shown under the column labeled "Obs final." Changes in probabilities down the rows of the table show the effect of the expected value on the probability of taking the gamble. The difference between the planned and final columns indicates the effect of dynamic inconsistency. Notice that following a win (the first eight rows) the probability of taking the gamble at the final stage was always smaller than the probability of taking the gamble at the planning

[7] There was little or no difference in the planned probability of taking the gamble, contingent on each outcome of the first gamble, and so the results shown here are the average across the two outcomes. See Barkan and Busemeyer (2003) for the complete results listed separately for each contingent outcome.

stage. In other words, participants changed their minds and became more risk averse after experiencing a win compared with planning for a win. Notice that following a loss (the last nine rows) the probability of taking the gamble at the final stage was always smaller than the probability of taking the gamble at the planning stage. In other words, participants changed their minds and became more risk-seeking after experiencing a loss compared with planning for a loss.

What are explanations for the dynamic inconsistency effects found in Tables 9.5 and 9.6? Tversky and Shafir (1992) proposed a model from prospect theory that allowed different utility functions to be used for the planned and final decisions. Yukalov and Sornette (2009) proposed an alternative idea based on interference effects that occur during the planning stage. Next we compare the fit of a model based on prospect theory to the fit of a model based on quantum theory for these results.

9.4.1 Reference point change model based on prospect theory

Barkan and Busemeyer (2003) tried to account for these results by using a model based on prospect theory originally proposed by Tversky and Shafir (1992) to account for the disjunction effect. The essential idea is that the decision maker ignores the planned wins or losses, but is later affected by the experienced wins or losses. Consider a generic gamble G that produces a win equal to x_W or a loss equal in magnitude to x_L with equal probability. In prospect theory, the utility function for an outcome x is often represented by $u(x) = x^a$ for $x \geq 0$, and $u(x) = -b \cdot |x|^a$ for $x < 0$. The parameter a is used to model risk aversion and it usually has a value between zero and one; the parameter b is used to model loss aversion and usually it has a value greater than one.

During the planning stage, it is assumed that people ignore the planned outcome of the first gamble and simply compute a utility for playing the second gamble based solely on the payoffs for the second gamble:

$$u(G|\text{Plan}) = (0.50) \cdot x_W^a - (0.50) \cdot b \cdot x_L^a. \tag{9.16}$$

The choice for the plan is based on the comparison of the utility of gambling on the second play to status quo (a zero outcome), $D_P = u(G|\text{Plan}) - 0$.

Following the experience of a win, the person includes the win from the first gamble into the evaluation of the payoffs for the second gamble and uses the following utility function:

$$u(G|\text{Win}) = (0.50) \cdot (x_W + x_W)^a + (0.50) \cdot (x_W - x_L)^a, \text{ if } (x_W - x_L) > 0, \tag{9.17}$$

$$u(G|\text{Win}) = (0.50) \cdot (x_W + x_W)^a - (0.50) \cdot b \cdot |(x_W - x_L)|^a, \text{ if } (x_W - x_L) < 0.$$

The choice after experiencing a win is based on the comparison of the utility of gambling again on the second play to the utility of keeping the amount of the win from the first gamble, $D_W = u(G|\text{Win}) - x_W^a$.

Following the experience of a loss, the person includes the loss from the first gamble into the evaluation of the payoffs for the second gamble and uses the following utility function:

$$u(G|\text{Loss}) = (0.50) \cdot (x_W - x_L)^a - (0.50) \cdot b \cdot (x_L + x_L)^a, \text{ if } (x_W - x_L) > 0, \tag{9.18}$$

$$u(G|\text{Loss}) = -(0.50) \cdot b \cdot |(x_W - x_L)|^a$$
$$- (0.50) \cdot b \cdot (x_L + x_L)^a, \text{ if } (x_W - x_L) < 0.$$

The choice after experiencing a loss is based on the comparison of the utility of gambling again on the second play to the utility of keeping the amount of the loss from the first gamble, $D_L = u(G|\text{Loss}) - x_L^a$.

Essentially, the reference point for evaluating gains and losses changes in this model. For example, during the plan, the possibility of losing $100 on the second gamble is evaluated as a loss (because any payoff below zero is considered a loss). But after finding out that $200 was won on the first play, then the possibility of losing $100 on the second play is evaluated as a reduced gain (any payoff below $-200 is now considered a loss). In short, dynamic inconsistency arises from the use of different utility functions, defined by different reference points, for plans versus final decisions.

So far, this model is deterministic and cannot produce choice probabilities. To convert these utilities into probabilities, it is common to use a logistic function, which produces the following probabilities to play the second gamble for each of the three conditions:

$$p(T|\text{Plan}) = \frac{1}{1 + e^{-dD_P}}$$

$$p(T|\text{Win}) = \frac{1}{1 + e^{-dD_W}}$$

$$p(T|\text{Loss}) = \frac{1}{1 + e^{-dD_L}},$$

where d is a parameter that adjusts the sensitivity of choice probability to the utility of the gamble.

This model has three free parameters (a, b, d) that were fit to the 34 data points in Table 9.6 (17 plan probabilities and 17 final probabilities). The best fitting parameters (minimizing sum of squared error) are $a = 0.8683$, $b = 0.9223$, and $d = 2.6980$. It is odd that the loss aversion parameter b is less than one. The model produced an $\text{SSE} = 0.1322$, which converts into an $R^2 = 0.7745$. In other words, 77% of the variance in the data was recovered by the model with three parameters. The R^2 is based on the sample data, and it is a biased estimate when applied to the population data. Often an adjusted R^2 is used to estimate of the proportion predicted in the population rather than in the sample, which penalizes models with more parameters. The prospect model produced and adjusted $R^2 = 0.7599$, or in other words an estimate of 76% for the population data.

9.4.2   Model based on quantum theory

The dynamic quantum model developed for the disjunction effect was used again to account for the dynamic inconsistency effect shown in Table 9.5. The essential idea is that the decision maker uses a consistent utility function for plans and final decisions and always incorporates the outcomes from the first stage into the decision for the second stage, but the planned decision is made from a superposition state over possible first-stage outcomes.

The two-stage game involves a set of four mutually exclusive and exhaustive outcomes $\{B_W A_T, B_W A_R, B_L A_T, B_L A_R\}$, where, for example, $B_W A_T$ symbolizes the event "win the first stage" and "take the second-stage gamble," and $B_L A_R$ represents the event "lose the first stage" and "reject the second-stage gamble." These four events correspond to four mutually exclusive and exhaustive basis states $\{|B_W A_T\rangle, |B_W A_R\rangle, |B_L A_T\rangle, |B_L A_R\rangle\}$. The state of the decision maker is a superposition over these four orthonormal basis states:

$$|\psi\rangle = \psi_{WT} \cdot |B_W A_T\rangle + \psi_{WR} \cdot |B_W A_R\rangle + \psi_{LT} \cdot |B_L A_T\rangle + \psi_{LR} \cdot |B_L A_R\rangle.$$

The initial state is represented by a 4×1 column matrix $\psi(0)$ containing elements ψ_{ij} $i = W, L$ and $j = T, R$, which is the amplitude distribution over the four basis states. Initially, during the planning stage, an equal distribution is assumed, so that $\psi(0)$ has elements $\psi_{ij} = 1/2$ for all four entries. The state following experience of a win is updated to ψ_W, which has $1/\sqrt{2}$ in the first two entries and zeros in the second two. The state following experience of a loss is updated to ψ_L, which has $1/\sqrt{2}$ in the last two entries and zeros in the first two.

Evaluation of the payoffs causes the initial states to evolve into final states according to the Schrödinger equation, and the Hamiltonian that drives the Schrödinger equation is again defined by the sum of two parts, $H = H_1 + H_2$, where

$$H_1 = \begin{bmatrix} \frac{h_W}{\sqrt{1+h_W^2}} & \frac{1}{\sqrt{1+h_W^2}} & 0 & 0 \\ \frac{1}{\sqrt{1+h_W^2}} & \frac{-h_W}{\sqrt{1+h_W^2}} & 0 & 0 \\ 0 & 0 & \frac{h_L}{\sqrt{1+h_L^2}} & \frac{1}{\sqrt{1+h_L^2}} \\ 0 & 0 & \frac{1}{\sqrt{1+h_L^2}} & \frac{-h_L}{\sqrt{1+h_L^2}} \end{bmatrix}, \quad H_2 = \frac{-c}{\sqrt{2}} \begin{bmatrix} 1 & 0 & 1 & 0 \\ 0 & -1 & 0 & 1 \\ 1 & 0 & -1 & 0 \\ 0 & 1 & 0 & 1 \end{bmatrix}.$$

The upper right corner of H_1 is defined by the payoffs given a win and the bottom right corner of H_1 is defined by the payoffs given a loss (this is described in more detail below). The matrix H_2 is defined as in Eq. (9.12) earlier. Referring to H_2, the parameter c is a free parameter that allows changes in beliefs during the decision process.

The utilities for taking the gamble are mapped into the parameters h_W and h_L in H_1, and the latter must be scaled between -1 and $+1$. To accomplish this, the parameter h_W used to define H_1 is defined as

$$h_W = \frac{2}{1 + e^{-D_W}} - 1,$$

where D_W is defined by Eq. (9.17). The parameter h_L used to define H_2 is defined as

$$h_L = \frac{2}{1 + e^{-D_L}} - 1,$$

where D_L is defined by Eq. (9.18).

The projection matrix $M = \mathrm{diag}\,[1, 0, 1, 0]$ is used to map states into the response for taking the gamble on the second stage. The probability of planning to take the second-stage gamble equals

$$p(T|\text{Plan}) = ||M \cdot e^{-i(H_1+H_2)t} \cdot \psi(0)||^2.$$

The probability of taking the second-stage gamble following the experience of a win equals

$$p(T|\text{Win}) = ||M \cdot e^{-i(H_1+H_2)t} \cdot \psi_W||^2.$$

The probability of taking the second-stage game following the experience of a loss equals

$$p(T|\text{Loss}) = ||M \cdot e^{-i(H_1+H_2)t} \cdot \psi_L||^2.$$

In sum, this quantum model has only three parameters: a and b are used to determine the utilities in Eqs. (9.17) and (9.18) in the same way as used in the prospect model; the third is the parameter c for changing beliefs (for reasons given earlier, the time for deliberation is set equal to $t = \frac{\pi}{2}$). These three parameters were fit to the 34 data points in Table 9.6, and the best fitting parameters (minimizing sum of squared error) are $a = 0.7101$, $b = 2.5424$, and $c = -4.4034$. The risk-aversion parameter is a bit below one as expected, and the loss parameter b exceeds one, as it should be. Note that the belief-changing parameter c has the opposite sign when applied to Table 9.6 as the previous application to Table 9.2, but note that the data from this experiment also turn out in the opposite direction as found in the Tversky and Shafir (1992) gambling experiment. The model produced an SSE $= 0.1035$, which converts into an $R^2 = 0.8234$. In other words, 82% of the variance in the data was recovered by the model with three parameters. The adjusted $R^2 = 0.8120$, or in other words 81% for the population.

If we force $c = 0$ then the quantum model is no longer "quantum like" because there is no interference. In this case, the model reduces to an equal-weight version of the weighted average model discussed in relation to Table 9.5, which satisfies the law of total probability. (An equal-weight model is reasonable, because the actual probability of winning was 0.50 for all gambles.) This model was fit to the results in Table 9.6 by using only two parameters, a and b, for the quantum model (with $c = 0$), and it produced SSE $= 0.1259$ and $R^2 = 0.7854$. To evaluate whether or not the extra parameter c is useful, we computed the adjusted R^2 for each model. The adjusted R^2 penalizes models with more parameters. The adjusted $R^2 = 0.7787$ for the two-parameter model with $c = 0$ still falls below the adjusted R^2 for the three-parameter quantum model, and so the c parameter is making a useful contribution in this application.

In summary, if we compare the three models using adjusted R^2, then we find that the three-parameter quantum model did best by reproducing 81% of the

Table 9.7 Category–decision-making task results

Type face	$p(G)$	$p(A|G)$	$p(B)$	$p(A|B)$	$p_T(A)$	$p(A)$
Wide	0.84	0.35	0.16	0.52	0.37	0.39
Quantum	0.84	0.35	0.16	0.57	0.39	0.44
Narrow	0.17	0.41	0.83	0.63	0.59	0.69
Quantum	0.17	0.39	0.83	0.61	0.57	0.74

variance, the two-parameter quantum model (essentially a weighted-averaging model) did second best, reproducing 78%, and the reference point change model from prospect theory reproduced the lowest with 76%. This does not prove that the quantum model is right or even better than the reference point change model for all of these types of gambling situations. But it does demonstrate that the quantum model can perform as well or better than traditional decision models when fitting a large amount of data using a small number of parameters.

The quantum model provides a fundamentally different explanation for the dynamic inconsistency effects compared with the prospect theory model. The prospect model accounts for the effect by using different utility functions for the planned and final stages. The quantum model assumes that the same utility functions are used for the planned and final stages, and dynamic inconsistency arises from interference effects that occur during the uncertain planned stage of decision making (Yukalov & Sornette, 2009).

9.5   Interference of categorization on decisions

The dynamic quantum model, which was designed for the disjunction effect, also provides a good account of the interference effect of categorization on decision making (Busemeyer *et al.*, 2009), which was discussed in Chapter 8. Recall that, in this task, decision makers are shown a face that comes from either a "bad" guy or "good" guy poplulation, and the decision maker has to decide to "attack" or "withdraw." There are two conditions: in the C-then-D condition the person categorizes first and then decides, and the D-alone condition the person only decides an action. The results are reproduced in Table 9.7. The rows for the "wide" face represent the "good" population of faces and the rows for the "narrow" face represent the "bad" population. The columns first show the probabilities for the C-then-D condition: the probability of categorizing the face as a "good" guy, the probability of "attacking" given that the face was categorized as a "good" guy, the probability of categorizing the face as a "bad" guy, the probability of "attacking" given the face was categorized as a "bad" guy, and the total probability for "attacking" under the C-then-D condition, $p_T(A) = p(G)p(A|G) + p(B)p(A|B)$. The last column shows the probability of "attack" for the D-alone condition.

The same Markov and quantum models described earlier can be applied to this task as follows. The task involves a set of four mutually exclusive and exhaustive outcomes $\{C_G D_A, C_G D_W, C_B D_A, C_B D_W\}$, where for example $C_G D_A$

symbolizes the event in which the player infers that the face came from the "good" population and decides to "attack." Both Markov and quantum models assume that these four events correspond to four mutually exclusive and exhaustive belief–action states of the decision maker $\{|C_G D_A\rangle, |C_G D_W\rangle, |C_B D_A\rangle, |C_B D_W\rangle\}$.

As we showed earlier (see the arguments leading to Eq. (9.14)), the four-dimensional Markov model must continue to satisfy the law of total probability. Therefore, it cannot predict the interference effects (that is, the differences between $p_T(A)$ and $p(A)$) shown in Table 9.7. Therefore, we will only present the quantum model.

The quantum model again assumes a four-dimensional vector space spanned by four orthonormal basis vectors represented by the four previously mentioned states, so that the decision maker's state vector can be expressed as

$$|\psi\rangle = \psi_{GA} \cdot |C_G D_A\rangle + \psi_{GW} \cdot |C_G D_W\rangle + \psi_{BA} \cdot |C_B D_A\rangle + \psi_{BW} \cdot |C_B D_W\rangle.$$

With respect to this basis, the state corresponds to the 4×1 column vector ψ. The initial state before categorization equals $\psi_I = \sqrt{\frac{1}{2}} \left[\sqrt{p(G)}, \sqrt{p(G)}, \sqrt{p(B)}, \sqrt{p(B)} \right]^\dagger$. If the face is categorized as a "good" guy, then the initial state reduces to $\psi_B = \sqrt{\frac{1}{2}} [1, 1, 0, 0]^\dagger$, and if the face is categorized as a "bad" guy, then the initial state reduces to $\psi_G = \sqrt{\frac{1}{2}} [0, 0, 1, 1]^\dagger$. The final state is obtained from the initial state by a unitary transformation,

$$\psi_F = e^{-itH} \cdot \psi_I,$$

where H is the Hamiltonian that is described below. The probability of "attacking" equals

$$p(A) = \|M \cdot \psi_F\|^2,$$

where the response map for "attack" is defined as $M = \text{diag}[1, 0, 1, 0]$. The Hamiltonian H is defined by two parts $H = H_1 + H_2$, where

$$H_1 = \begin{bmatrix} \frac{-h_G}{\sqrt{1+h_G^2}} & \frac{1}{\sqrt{1+h_G^2}} & 0 & 0 \\ \frac{1}{\sqrt{1+h_G^2}} & \frac{h_W}{\sqrt{1+h_G^2}} & 0 & 0 \\ 0 & 0 & \frac{h_B}{\sqrt{1+h_B^2}} & \frac{1}{\sqrt{1+h_B^2}} \\ 0 & 0 & \frac{1}{\sqrt{1+h_B^2}} & \frac{-h_B}{\sqrt{1+h_B^2}} \end{bmatrix}, \quad H_2 = \frac{c}{\sqrt{2}} \begin{bmatrix} -1 & 0 & 1 & 0 \\ 0 & 1 & 0 & 1 \\ 1 & 0 & 1 & 0 \\ 0 & 1 & 0 & -1 \end{bmatrix}.$$

The 2×2 submatrix in the upper left corner of H_1 rotates the amplitudes in the direction to favor "withdraw" when the face is categorized as a "good" guy; the 2×2 submatrix in the lower right corner of H_1 rotates the amplitudes in the opposite direction to favor "attack" when the face is categorized as a "bad" guy. The second part H_2 rotates inferences for the "good" population to match "withdraw" actions and rotates inferences for the "bad" population to match "attack" actions. For example, if we set $\frac{c}{\sqrt{2}} = \frac{0.9417}{\sqrt{2}}$, then $e^{-i(\pi/2)H_2} \cdot [1,1,1,1]^{\dagger}/2$ produces squared amplitudes equal to $[0.0021, 0.4979, 0.4979, 0.0021]$, so that the face is believed to be "good" when the decision is to "withdraw" and the face is believed to be "bad" when the decision is to "attack."

The model was fit to the data in Table 9.7 as follows (the program used to compute the predictions is presented in Appendix G). To eliminate one parameter, we fixed $h_B = 1$, and for reasons given earlier the time for deliberation is set equal to $t = \frac{\pi}{2}$. We then fit three parameters to the four data points for each face condition. For the wide face data, we set $\sqrt{p(G)} = \sqrt{0.84}$, $h_G = 0.4638$, and $c = 0.8516$. For the narrow face data we set $\sqrt{p(G)} = \sqrt{0.17}$, $h_G = -0.3106$, and $c = 0.9417$. These parameters produced the predictions shown in the rows labeled quantum in Table 9.7. Although the fits are not perfect, they reproduce the main pattern of results for both face conditions.

9.6 Concluding comments

This chapter started by briefly reviewing traditional decision theory and the puzzling findings known as the famous Allais and Ellsberg paradoxes of decision making. A quantum utility model was presented that is capable of accommodating these results. But this is well-covered territory, and many traditional weighted utility models can also account for these findings.

In order to demonstrate an advantage for quantum models, this chapter focused more on two other puzzling findings from decision research. One is the disjunction effect, which has been interpreted as a violation of the "sure thing" principle of rational decision making. The other is the finding of dynamic inconsistency between planned and final actions. At present, only quantum models have provided a formal and quantitative account of the disjunction effect results. This chapter presented a dynamic quantum model which successfully accounted for the disjunction effect. But past studies of the disjunction effect included only three, albeit difficult to explain, data points, and so a stronger test of the dynamic quantum model with more data points was needed. An experiment investigating dynamic inconsistency provided a stronger quantitative test of the dynamic quantum model using a high ratio of data points per parameter. The dynamic quantum model was compared with a more traditional "reference point change" model based on prospect theory and the quantum model performed better at predicting the dynamic inconsistency effects than the reference point change model. These two initial successes build confidence that the dynamic quantum decision model provides a viable new way to understand human decision making.

Furthermore, the same dynamic quantum model was also successfully applied to a completely different application – the interference of categorization on decision making discussed in Chapter 8. A distinct advantage of the quantum model is its ability to provide a general and accurate account of such diverse and puzzling decision-making phenomena.

10

How to model human information processing using quantum information theory

How can quantum theory be used to model human performance on complex information processing tasks? Quantum computing and quantum information theory is relatively new, but it is already a highly developed field (Nielsen and Chuang, 2000). The concept of a quantum computer was introduced by Feynman in 1982 (Feynman, 1982). Soon afterwards, a universal quantum computer was formulated by David Deutsch in 1989 using quantum gates, which he demonstrated could perform computations not possible with classic Turing machines, including generating genuine random numbers and performing parallel calculations within a single register. Subsequently, new quantum algorithms were discovered by Peter Schor in 1984 and Lov Grover in 1997 that could solve important computational problems, such as factoring and searching, faster than any known Turing machine. However, all of these accomplishments were designed for actual quantum computers, and only very small versions have been realized so far. Moreover, if we are not working under the assumption that the brain is a quantum computer, then what has all of this to do with information processing by humans?

The answer is that quantum information processing theory provides new and powerful principles for modelling human performance. Currently, there are three general approaches to modelling information processing with humans. One is based on production rule systems such as used in Act-R (Anderson, 1993), EPIC (Meyer & Kieres, 1997), and Soar (Laird *et al.*, 1987); a second is neural network (Grossberg, 1982) and connectionist network (Rumelhart & McClelland, 1986) models; and a third is Bayesian models (Griffiths *et al.*, 2008). Although there are some hybrid models such as Clarion (Sun *et al.*, 2001) that employ a combination of approaches, quantum information processing models naturally integrate all three approaches into a single unified framework. Let us see how this works, starting from simple examples and working toward more complex ones.

10.1   Information represented by qubits

10.1.1   Single qubit

Information processing theory concerns information, and so first we define the information used in quantum information processing. Suppose A is some proposition such as:

> There is smoke in the hallway.

According to classic information processing theory, this proposition can be represented by a single bit $|A\rangle$ that can be assigned only one of two possible states: $|A\rangle = |0\rangle \to$ false versus $|A\rangle = |1\rangle \to$ true. In classic probability theory, we assign probabilities to the event that A is true versus the event that A is false. The corresponding concept in quantum information processing is a superposition of true and false states, which is a unit-length vector in a two-dimensional Hilbert space:

$$|A\rangle = \alpha_0 \cdot |0\rangle + \alpha_1 \cdot |1\rangle, \tag{10.1}$$

where α_0, α_1 are possibly complex numbers such that $|\alpha_0|^2 + |\alpha_1|^2 = 1$. The two basis vectors $\{|0\rangle \to \begin{bmatrix} 1 & 0 \end{bmatrix}^\dagger, |1\rangle \to \begin{bmatrix} 0 & 1 \end{bmatrix}^\dagger\}$ are orthogonal and each one is unit length, and this basis is referred to as the *computational* basis. The 2×1 column vector

$$|A\rangle \to \alpha = \begin{bmatrix} \alpha_0 \\ \alpha_1 \end{bmatrix}$$

represents the qubit $|A\rangle$ with respect to this computational basis. The projector for the event that A is true equals $|1\rangle\langle 1|$, which corresponds to the indicator matrix $P_A = \text{diag} \begin{bmatrix} 0 & 1 \end{bmatrix}$ that picks out the second coordinate from α. The probability that event A is true equals the squared projection $||P_A \cdot \alpha||^2 = |\alpha_1|^2$. Obviously, the matrix corresponding to the projector $|0\rangle\langle 0|$ for event A is false is $\text{diag} \begin{bmatrix} 1 & 0 \end{bmatrix}$ and the probability that A is false equals $||P_{\bar{A}} \cdot \alpha||^2 = |\alpha_0|^2$. As we shall see later, it is not necessary to work with qubits in the computational basis, but this is a convenient way to begin to understand quantum information processing.

10.1.2   Multiple qubits

Now suppose B is another proposition such as "there is an emergency." This new event B could be compatible or incompatible with the earlier event A, but for now we will assume that it is compatible with event A. According to classic information processing theory, these two propositions can be represented by a pair of events $|AB\rangle$ that can be assigned only one of four possible states: $|00\rangle, |01\rangle, |10\rangle, |11\rangle$, and classic probability theory assigns a probability to each of these four states. The corresponding concept in quantum information processing is a superposition of these four states, which is a unit length vector in a four-dimensional Hilbert space:

$$|AB\rangle = \alpha_{00} \cdot |00\rangle + \alpha_{01} \cdot |01\rangle + \alpha_{10} \cdot |10\rangle + \alpha_{11} \cdot |11\rangle, \tag{10.2}$$

where $\alpha_{00}, \alpha_{01}, \alpha_{10}, \alpha_{11}$ are possibly complex numbers such that $|\alpha_{00}|^2 + |\alpha_{01}|^2 + |\alpha_{10}|^2 + |\alpha_{11}|^2 = 1$. The four basis vectors $\{|00\rangle, |01\rangle, |10\rangle, |11\rangle\}$ are orthogonal and each one is unit length, and this basis is again referred to as the *computational* basis. For example, the basis vector $|01\rangle$ represents the event A is false and B is true, which corresponds to $\begin{bmatrix} 0 & 1 & 0 & 0 \end{bmatrix}^\dagger$ with respect to the computational basis. The projector for this event is $|01\rangle\langle 01|$, which corresponds to the matrix $P_{\bar{A}B} = \text{diag}\begin{bmatrix} 0 & 1 & 0 & 0 \end{bmatrix}$ when using the computational basis, which picks out the second coordinate from α. The 4×1 column vector

$$|AB\rangle \to \alpha = \begin{bmatrix} \alpha_{00} \\ \alpha_{01} \\ \alpha_{10} \\ \alpha_{11} \end{bmatrix}$$

represents the person's beliefs about a pair of events $|AB\rangle$ with respect to this computational basis. The general state $|AB\rangle$ may be "entangled" or "separable" depending on the amplitudes α_{ij}: if $\alpha_{ij} = a_i \cdot b_j$ for all i, j, then the state is separated and otherwise it is entangled. A separated state corresponds to statistically independent events in classic probability theory and an entangled state corresponds to statistically dependent events in classic probability. The projection onto the event A is false and B is true equals

$$P_{\bar{A}B} \cdot \alpha = \begin{bmatrix} 0 \\ \alpha_{01} \\ 0 \\ 0 \end{bmatrix}.$$

The probability of this event then equals ($\bar{A}$ refers to not A)

$$p(\bar{A} \wedge B) = ||P_{\bar{A}B} \cdot \alpha||^2 = |\alpha_{01}|^2.$$

10.1.3   Tensor products of basis vectors

More formally, the basis for multiple qubits is formed by an operation called a tensor product of the bases for the individual qubits. Suppose the pair of events {A is true, A is false} is represented by the pair of orthonormal basis vectors $\{|1_A\rangle, |0_A\rangle\}$ that span a two-dimensional Hilbert space with coordinates $|1_A\rangle \to \begin{bmatrix} 0 & 1 \end{bmatrix}^\dagger$ and $|0_A\rangle \to \begin{bmatrix} 1 & 0 \end{bmatrix}^\dagger$; suppose another pair of events {B is true, B is false} is represented by another pair of orthonormal basis vectors $\{|1_B\rangle, |0_B\rangle\}$ that span a different two-dimensional Hilbert space with coordinates $|1_B\rangle \to \begin{bmatrix} 0 & 1 \end{bmatrix}^\dagger$ and $|0_B\rangle \to \begin{bmatrix} 1 & 0 \end{bmatrix}^\dagger$; then the four combinations of events $\{A \wedge B, A \wedge \bar{B}, \bar{A} \wedge B, \bar{A} \wedge \bar{B}\}$ are represented by a four-dimensional tensor product space spanned by $\{|0\rangle \otimes |0\rangle, |0\rangle \otimes |1\rangle, |1\rangle \otimes |0\rangle, |1\rangle \otimes |1\rangle\}$, where $|i\rangle \otimes |j\rangle$ is the tensor product between two vectors. (In Chapter 5 the same approach was used to model the combination of two concepts.) The tensor product space is not the same as the cross-product space because the former contains all the linear combinations of all of the vectors in the latter. For brevity, the tensor product $|i\rangle \otimes |j\rangle$ is sometimes written as $|i\rangle |j\rangle$, or even shorter as $|ij\rangle$. The coordinates of the tensor product are obtained as follows:

$$|i\rangle \rightarrow \begin{bmatrix} a_1 \\ a_2 \end{bmatrix}, |j\rangle \rightarrow \begin{bmatrix} b_1 \\ b_2 \end{bmatrix},$$

$$|i\rangle \otimes |j\rangle \rightarrow \begin{bmatrix} a_1 \\ a_2 \end{bmatrix} \otimes \begin{bmatrix} b_1 \\ b_2 \end{bmatrix} = \begin{bmatrix} a_1 \cdot \begin{bmatrix} b_1 \\ b_2 \end{bmatrix} \\ a_2 \cdot \begin{bmatrix} b_1 \\ b_2 \end{bmatrix} \end{bmatrix} = \begin{bmatrix} a_1 \cdot b_1 \\ a_1 \cdot b_2 \\ a_2 \cdot b_1 \\ a_2 \cdot b_2 \end{bmatrix}.$$

Note that the tensor product of two basis vectors produces a separable state (i.e., one that is not entangled). We saw in Section 5.3 that this is not possible with entangled states. For example, the tensor product corresponding to the event "A is true and B is false" equals

$$|10\rangle = |1\rangle \otimes |0\rangle = \begin{bmatrix} 0 \\ 1 \end{bmatrix} \otimes \begin{bmatrix} 1 \\ 0 \end{bmatrix} = \begin{bmatrix} 0 \\ 0 \\ 1 \\ 0 \end{bmatrix}.$$

The Kronecker product of linear operators is used to operate on individual qubits in quantum information processing. Using abstract vector notation,

$$(\mathbf{U}_1 \otimes \mathbf{U}_2)\,(|A\rangle \otimes |B\rangle) = \mathbf{U}_1|A\rangle \otimes \mathbf{U}_2|B\rangle.$$

The tensor product of gates applies a gate separately to each qubit within a tensor product of qubits. The coordinates of a Kronecker product are obtained as follows (also see Chapter 2):

$$\mathbf{U}_1 \rightarrow U_1 = \begin{bmatrix} u_{11} & u_{12} \\ u_{21} & u_{22} \end{bmatrix}$$

$$\mathbf{U}_2 \rightarrow U_2 = \begin{bmatrix} v_{11} & v_{12} \\ v_{21} & v_{22} \end{bmatrix}$$

$$U_1 \otimes U_2 = \begin{bmatrix} u_{11} \cdot U_2 & u_{12} \cdot U_2 \\ u_{21} \cdot U_2 & u_{22} \cdot U_2 \end{bmatrix}$$

$$= \begin{bmatrix} u_{11} \cdot v_{11} & u_{11} \cdot v_{12} & u_{12} \cdot v_{11} & u_{12} \cdot v_{12} \\ u_{11} \cdot v_{21} & u_{11} \cdot v_{22} & u_{12} \cdot v_{21} & u_{12} \cdot v_{22} \\ u_{21} \cdot v_{11} & u_{21} \cdot v_{12} & u_{22} \cdot v_{11} & u_{22} \cdot v_{12} \\ u_{21} \cdot v_{21} & u_{21} \cdot v_{22} & u_{22} \cdot v_{21} & u_{22} \cdot v_{22} \end{bmatrix}.$$

Recall from Chapter 2 that the Kronecker product is associative and distributive but not commutative, so that $(U_1 \otimes U_2) \otimes U_3 = U_1 \otimes (U_2 \otimes U_3)$ and $U_1 \otimes (U_2 + U_3) = U_1 \otimes U_2 + U_1 \otimes U_3$ but $U_1 \otimes U_3 \neq U_3 \otimes U_1$. In Matlab, the Kronecker product is computed using `kron(U1,U2)`. All of these ideas can be extended to three or more propositions, as shown later in this chapter.

10.2 Rules formed by control U gates

10.2.1 Not gates

A gate is a unitary operator that changes one state into another. An important unitary operation in quantum computing is to reverse the amplitudes assigned to the true and false states. First consider a single qubit represented by Eq. (10.1). The unitary operator denoted $\mathbf{X}$, called the Not gate, changes a true state into a false state and changes a false state into a true state. It is defined by the following operation on the basis states:

$$\mathbf{X}|0\rangle = |1\rangle, \; \mathbf{X}|1\rangle = |0\rangle$$

$$|A\rangle = \alpha_0 \cdot |0\rangle + \alpha_1 \cdot |1\rangle$$

$$\mathbf{X}|A\rangle = \alpha_0 \cdot \mathbf{X}|0\rangle + \alpha_1 \cdot \mathbf{X}|1\rangle$$

$$= \alpha_0 \cdot |1\rangle + \alpha_1 \cdot |0\rangle.$$

With respect to the computational basis, this unitary operator is represented by the matrix

$$\mathbf{X} \to X = \begin{bmatrix} 0 & 1 \\ 1 & 0 \end{bmatrix}, \; X \cdot \begin{bmatrix} \alpha_0 \\ \alpha_1 \end{bmatrix} = \begin{bmatrix} \alpha_1 \\ \alpha_0 \end{bmatrix}.$$

Note that $X^\dagger \cdot X = I = X \cdot X^\dagger$ so that X is unitary, and also $X^\dagger = X$ so that X is Hermitian, and finally $X \cdot X = X^2 = I$.

Sometimes it is useful to make a partial flip; for example, change the state part way from true to false. As shown in Chapter 8 and in Appendix D on Pauli matrices, this can be done by using the unitary matrix $U(t) = e^{-itX}$ with X defined as it is for the Not gate; as t ranges from $t = 0$ to $t = \frac{\pi}{2}$ the probability for flipping from the false to the true state grows from zero to one. Note that $U\left(\frac{\pi}{2}\right) = -i \cdot X$ and the common phase factor $-i$ has no effect on the final squared magnitudes used to determine the probabilities of events ($|-i|^2 = 1$).

Next consider two qubits represented by Eq. (10.2). Suppose we wish to flip the first qubit and leave the second intact. This is done by using the Kronecker product as follows (see Section 2.3 on matrix algebra section):

$$\alpha = \begin{bmatrix} \begin{bmatrix} \alpha_{00} \\ \alpha_{01} \end{bmatrix} \\ \begin{bmatrix} \alpha_{10} \\ \alpha_{11} \end{bmatrix} \end{bmatrix} = \begin{bmatrix} \phi_0 \\ \phi_1 \end{bmatrix}, \; \phi_0 = \begin{bmatrix} \alpha_{00} \\ \alpha_{01} \end{bmatrix}, \; \phi_1 = \begin{bmatrix} \alpha_{10} \\ \alpha_{11} \end{bmatrix}.$$

$$(X \otimes I) \cdot \alpha = \begin{bmatrix} 0 & I \\ I & 0 \end{bmatrix} \cdot \begin{bmatrix} \phi_0 \\ \phi_1 \end{bmatrix} = \begin{bmatrix} \phi_1 \\ \phi_0 \end{bmatrix} = \begin{bmatrix} \begin{bmatrix} \alpha_{10} \\ \alpha_{11} \end{bmatrix} \\ \begin{bmatrix} \alpha_{00} \\ \alpha_{01} \end{bmatrix} \end{bmatrix}.$$

This Kronecker product is computed in Matlab using `kron(X,eye(2))`, where X is previously defined as `X = [0 1; 1 0]`. Alternatively, we can flip the second qubit as follows:

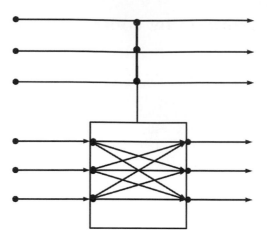

Figure 10.1 Diagram of a control U gate. The top three lines are the control inputs which determine whether or not to apply the U gate to the bottom three target outputs.

$$(I \otimes X) \cdot \alpha = \begin{bmatrix} X & \mathbf{0} \\ \mathbf{0} & X \end{bmatrix} \cdot \begin{bmatrix} \phi_0 \\ \phi_1 \end{bmatrix} = \begin{bmatrix} X \cdot \phi_0 \\ X \cdot \phi_1 \end{bmatrix} = \begin{bmatrix} \begin{bmatrix} \alpha_{01} \\ \alpha_{00} \end{bmatrix} \\ \begin{bmatrix} \alpha_{11} \\ \alpha_{10} \end{bmatrix} \end{bmatrix}.$$

This product is computed in Matlab using `kron(eye(2),X)`. Both qubits are flipped by the matrix

$$(X \otimes X) \cdot \alpha = \begin{bmatrix} \mathbf{0} & X \\ X & \mathbf{0} \end{bmatrix} \cdot \begin{bmatrix} \phi_0 \\ \phi_1 \end{bmatrix} = \begin{bmatrix} \begin{bmatrix} \alpha_{11} \\ \alpha_{10} \end{bmatrix} \\ \begin{bmatrix} \alpha_{01} \\ \alpha_{00} \end{bmatrix} \end{bmatrix}.$$

This product is computed in Matlab using `kron(X,X)`.

10.2.2   If–then rules and the C-Not gate

In classic information processing models, a sequence of condition–action production rules are used to perform complex tasks. Quantum computing uses controlled U gates to achieve the same purpose. A control U gate consists of a set of control input lines and a set of target output lines. If the control lines are satisfied then a unitary operator is applied to the target lines. Otherwise the targets remain unchanged (see Figure 10.1). The C-Not gate is particularly effective when there is a default non-action, which needs to flipped – from off to on – when a certain condition is present.

Consider the following simple example:

If there is an emergency then "activate the alarm" and otherwise do not take any action.

As before, we use B to represent the event "there is an emergency" and we use X to represent the action "activate the alarm." The abstract form of the rule is then "if B then do X." To represent this situation, we use a pair of qubits to form the following superposition state:

$$|BX\rangle = \alpha_{00} \cdot |00\rangle + \alpha_{01} \cdot |01\rangle + \alpha_{10} \cdot |10\rangle + \alpha_{11} \cdot |11\rangle.$$

The first qubit represented by B is called the control qubit and the second qubit represented by X is called the target qubit. The coefficients assigned to the basis vectors represent the state *before* applying the rule. For example, before applying the rule, the probability that the alarm is already active $\left(|\alpha_{01}|^2 + |\alpha_{11}|^2\right)$ should be near zero; likewise, the probability that the alarm is not already active $\left(|\alpha_{00}|^2 + |\alpha_{10}|^2\right)$ should initially be near one.

The control U gate for this rule operates on the basis vectors as follows:

$$\mathbf{U}_{\text{CN}} \cdot |00\rangle = |00\rangle$$

$$\mathbf{U}_{\text{CN}} \cdot |01\rangle = |01\rangle$$

$$\mathbf{U}_{\text{CN}} \cdot |10\rangle = |11\rangle$$

$$\mathbf{U}_{\text{CN}} \cdot |11\rangle = |10\rangle.$$

Nothing is changed if the control qubit equals $|0\rangle$, and the target qubit is flipped from off to on when the control qubit equals $|1\rangle$. The resulting action on the state $|BX\rangle$ equals

$$\mathbf{U}_{\text{CN}}|BX\rangle = \alpha_{00} \cdot \mathbf{U}_{\text{CN}}|00\rangle + \alpha_{01} \cdot \mathbf{U}_{\text{CN}}|01\rangle + \alpha_{10} \cdot \mathbf{U}_{\text{CN}}|10\rangle + \alpha_{11} \cdot \mathbf{U}_{\text{CN}}|11\rangle$$

$$= \alpha_{00} \cdot |00\rangle + \alpha_{01} \cdot |01\rangle + \alpha_{10} \cdot |11\rangle + \alpha_{11} \cdot |10\rangle.$$

This control U gate can be represented by matrix operations using the computational basis as follows:

$$|BX\rangle \to \alpha = \left[\begin{bmatrix} \alpha_{00} \\ \alpha_{01} \\ \alpha_{10} \\ \alpha_{11} \end{bmatrix}\right] = \begin{bmatrix} \phi_0 \\ \phi_1 \end{bmatrix}$$

$$\mathbf{U} \to U_{\text{CN}} = \begin{bmatrix} I & \mathbf{0} \\ \mathbf{0} & X \end{bmatrix}, \ I = \begin{bmatrix} 1 & 0 \\ 0 & 1 \end{bmatrix}, \ X = \begin{bmatrix} 0 & 1 \\ 1 & 0 \end{bmatrix}$$

$$\beta = U_{\text{CN}} \cdot \alpha = \begin{bmatrix} I & \mathbf{0} \\ \mathbf{0} & X \end{bmatrix} \cdot \begin{bmatrix} \phi_0 \\ \phi_1 \end{bmatrix} = \begin{bmatrix} I \cdot \phi_0 \\ X \cdot \phi_1 \end{bmatrix}$$

$$= \left[\begin{bmatrix} 1 & 0 \\ 0 & 1 \\ 0 & 1 \\ 1 & 0 \end{bmatrix} \cdot \begin{bmatrix} \alpha_{00} \\ \alpha_{01} \\ \alpha_{10} \\ \alpha_{11} \end{bmatrix}\right] = \begin{bmatrix} \alpha_{00} \\ \alpha_{01} \\ \alpha_{11} \\ \alpha_{10} \end{bmatrix} = \begin{bmatrix} \beta_{00} \\ \beta_{01} \\ \beta_{10} \\ \beta_{11} \end{bmatrix}.$$

Essentially, the target qubit is flipped when the control qubit is in the true state. The matrix X simply flips the coordinates of the last two rows of α to form the new state β. After applying the rule, the probability that B is true and action X is taken now equals $|\beta_{11}|^2 = |\alpha_{10}|^2$, but the probability that B is false and action X is taken remains equal to the initial value $|\beta_{01}|^2 = |\alpha_{01}|^2$. From the fact that X is unitary and the fact that I is unitary, it follows that U_{CN} is also unitary. This particular control U gate formed by using the Not gate is called the controlled Not gate or C-Not gate. The C-Not gate is both Hermitian and unitary (and reversible) because $U_{CN} = U_{CN}^{\dagger}$ and $U_{CN} \cdot U_{CN} = I$.

Notice that the C-Not gate acts like an if–then production rule, but it also acts like a connectionist network that maps a distributed representation of input amplitudes α directly into a distributed representation of output amplitudes β. It has the advantage of both approaches to information processing – it is easy to describe its function but it also deals naturally with fuzzy and uncertain information.

10.2.2.1   Inference followed by C-Not

Now let us consider a slightly more complex scenario:

> If smoke is detected, then infer whether or not there is an emergency, and if there is an emergency, then decide whether or not to activate the alarm.

In this case, Lüder's rule is used to update the state and afterwards a C-Not gate is used to take an appropriate action. As before, proposition A is used to represent presence of smoke, proposition B is used to represent the emergency, and X is used to represent activating the fire alarm. To represent this situation, three qubits are used, one for A, one for B, and a third for X, to form an initial state, which is a vector in an eight-dimensional Hilbert space

$$|ABX\rangle = \alpha_{000} \cdot |000\rangle + \alpha_{001} \cdot |001\rangle + \alpha_{010} \cdot |010\rangle + \alpha_{011} \cdot |011\rangle \qquad (10.3)$$

$$+ \alpha_{100} \cdot |100\rangle + \alpha_{101} \cdot |101\rangle + \alpha_{110} \cdot |110\rangle + \alpha_{111} \cdot |111\rangle.$$

For example, the basis vector $|100\rangle$ represents the case where A is true (smoke is present) but B is false (there is no emergency) and X is false (fire alarm is not active). Again, these coefficients represent the state before observing events A and B and before the rule is applied (e.g., before seeing smoke and knowing whether or not there is an emergency, and so the alarm is initially off). In this case, it is usually assumed that the action is not true (the alarm is not active) *before* observations are made or rules are applied so that $|\alpha_{000}|^2 + |\alpha_{010}|^2 + |\alpha_{100}|^2 + |\alpha_{110}|^2$ is close to one and $|\alpha_{001}|^2 + |\alpha_{011}|^2 + |\alpha_{101}|^2 + |\alpha_{111}|^2$ is close to zero.

This C-Not gate flips the third target qubit representing the action state X from off to on whenever the second control qubit representing event B is true, and otherwise it leaves the state unchanged. For the state given in Eq. (10.3), the matrix that performs this operation is as follows

$$
U_X = I \otimes U_{\mathrm{CN}} = \begin{bmatrix} U_{\mathrm{CN}} & 0 \\ 0 & U_{\mathrm{CN}} \end{bmatrix} = \begin{bmatrix} I & 0 & 0 & 0 \\ 0 & X & 0 & 0 \\ 0 & 0 & I & 0 \\ 0 & 0 & 0 & X \end{bmatrix},
$$

$$
\alpha = \begin{bmatrix} \phi_{00} \\ \phi_{01} \\ \phi_{10} \\ \phi_{11} \end{bmatrix}, \quad \phi_{ij} = \begin{bmatrix} \alpha_{ij0} \\ \alpha_{ij1} \end{bmatrix}
$$

$$
\beta = U_X \cdot \alpha = \begin{bmatrix} I \cdot \phi_{00} \\ X \cdot \phi_{01} \\ I \cdot \phi_{10} \\ X \cdot \phi_{11} \end{bmatrix} = \begin{bmatrix} \alpha_{000} \\ \alpha_{001} \\ \alpha_{011} \\ \alpha_{010} \\ \alpha_{100} \\ \alpha_{101} \\ \alpha_{111} \\ \alpha_{110} \end{bmatrix} = \begin{bmatrix} \beta_{000} \\ \beta_{001} \\ \beta_{010} \\ \beta_{011} \\ \beta_{100} \\ \beta_{101} \\ \beta_{110} \\ \beta_{111} \end{bmatrix}.
$$

In this case, the identity matrix operates on the first qubit and the C-Not gate operates on the last two qubits. This operation is computed in Matlab using $Ux = kron(eye(2),Ucn))$, where Ucn is previously defined as the control Not matrix.

Let us examine the sequence of events for this scenario. The initial state before observing event A and before the rule is applied is given by α in Eq. (10.3). If event A (smoke) is observed to be true, then Lüder's rule is used to update the state: the initial state α is projected onto the subspace for this event using the matrix P_A corresponding to the projector $|100\rangle\langle100| + |101\rangle\langle101| + |110\rangle\langle110| + |111\rangle\langle111|$, and normalized to produce the inference about the emergency state given that smoke is present:

$$
\alpha_A = \frac{P_A \cdot \alpha}{||P_A \cdot \alpha||}.
$$

The matrix P_A simply picks out the last four rows of α, and the result is normalized. Next, the "if–then" rule is applied by using the C-Not gate to flip the action from off to on if there is an emergency:

$$
\beta_A = U_X \cdot \alpha_A.
$$

Finally, the decision to activate the alarm is based on the projection $\gamma = P_X \cdot \beta_A$ based on the matrix P_X representing the projector $|001\rangle\langle001| + |011\rangle\langle011| + |101\rangle\langle101| + |111\rangle\langle111|$ for activating the alarm:

$$\|\gamma\|^2 = \|P_X \cdot \beta_A\|^2 = \frac{\|P_X \cdot U_X \cdot P_A \cdot \alpha\|^2}{\|P_A \cdot \alpha\|^2} \tag{10.4}$$

$$= \frac{|\beta_{101}|^2 + |\beta_{111}|^2}{|\beta_{100}|^2 + |\beta_{101}|^2 + |\beta_{110}|^2 + |\beta_{111}|^2}$$

$$= \frac{|\alpha_{101}|^2 + |\alpha_{110}|^2}{|\alpha_{100}|^2 + |\alpha_{101}|^2 + |\alpha_{111}|^2 + |\alpha_{110}|^2}.$$

If we assume that the smoke makes it very likely that an emergency is present so that $\left(|\alpha_{110}|^2 + |\alpha_{111}|^2\right)$ is very high and $\left(|\alpha_{100}|^2 + |\alpha_{101}|^2\right)$ is very low, and if it is very unlikely that the alarm was active before learning about the event A so that $\left(|\alpha_{100}|^2 + |\alpha_{110}|^2\right)$ is very high and $\left(|\alpha_{101}|^2 + |\alpha_{111}|^2\right)$ is very low, then the probability of activating the alarm after observing smoke will be close to one.

The information processing for this example is captured by the sequence of matrix operations given in Eq. (10.4). On the one hand, the above equation can be viewed as a production rule sequence that starts with an initial state α, observes event A and makes an inference about event B using P_A, then applies a rule using U_X, and finally makes a decision based on P_X. Alternatively, the combined matrix $W = (P_X \cdot U_X \cdot P_B)$ can be viewed as a simple connectionist network that takes the input α and filters it through W to produce an output γ, which is then used to determine the final decision. Also, the decision depends on probabilistic inference about event B using information about event A, just like a Bayesian model of cognition.

10.2.3   Logical rules and the Toffoli gate

Now consider a conjunctive rule such as:

> If there is an emergency and there is smoke then activate the fire alarm, otherwise do nothing with the fire alarm.

As before, we use proposition A to represent presence of smoke, proposition B to represent the emergency, and X to represent activating the fire alarm. The abstract form of this rule is "if A and B then do X." To represent this situation, three qubits are again used, one for A, one for B, and a third for X, to form an initial state which is a vector in an eight-dimensional Hilbert space:

$$|ABX\rangle = \alpha_{000} \cdot |000\rangle + \alpha_{001} \cdot |001\rangle + \alpha_{010} \cdot |010\rangle + \alpha_{011} \cdot |011\rangle$$

$$+ \alpha_{100} \cdot |100\rangle + \alpha_{101} \cdot |101\rangle + \alpha_{110} \cdot |110\rangle + \alpha_{111} \cdot |111\rangle.$$

For example, the basis vector $|100\rangle$ represents the case where A is true (an emergency is present) but B is false (there is no smoke) and X is false (fire alarm is not active). The first two qubits are the control qubits and the last qubit is the target. Again, the coefficients represent the state before observing events A and

B (e.g., before seeing smoke and before knowing about an emergency). In this case, it is usually assumed that the action is not taken *before* the observation is made (the alarm is initially off) so that $|\alpha_{000}|^2 + |\alpha_{010}|^2 + |\alpha_{100}|^2 + |\alpha_{110}|^2$ is close to one and $|\alpha_{001}|^2 + |\alpha_{011}|^2 + |\alpha_{101}|^2 + |\alpha_{111}|^2$ is close to zero.

The control U gate for this rule operates on the basis vectors as follows:

$$\mathbf{U} \cdot |110\rangle = |111\rangle$$

$$\mathbf{U} \cdot |111\rangle = |110\rangle$$

otherwise

$$\mathbf{U} \cdot |ABX\rangle = |ABX\rangle.$$

The third qubit is flipped when the first two control qubits are in the true state, otherwise nothing is changed. Therefore, the resulting action on the state $|ABX\rangle$ equals

$$\mathbf{U}|ABX\rangle = \alpha_{000} \cdot |000\rangle + \alpha_{001} \cdot |001\rangle + \alpha_{010} \cdot |010\rangle + \alpha_{011} \cdot |011\rangle$$

$$+ \alpha_{100} \cdot |100\rangle + \alpha_{101} \cdot |101\rangle + \alpha_{110} \cdot |111\rangle + \alpha_{111} \cdot |110\rangle.$$

This control U gate can be represented by matrix operations using the computational basis as follows:

$$U_T = \begin{bmatrix} I & 0 & 0 & 0 \\ 0 & I & 0 & 0 \\ 0 & 0 & I & 0 \\ 0 & 0 & 0 & X \end{bmatrix}, \quad \alpha = \begin{bmatrix} \phi_{00} \\ \phi_{01} \\ \phi_{10} \\ \phi_{11} \end{bmatrix}, \quad \phi_{ij} = \begin{bmatrix} \alpha_{ij0} \\ \alpha_{ij1} \end{bmatrix}$$

$$\beta = U_T \cdot \alpha = \begin{bmatrix} I \cdot \phi_{00} \\ I \cdot \phi_{01} \\ I \cdot \phi_{10} \\ X \cdot \phi_{11} \end{bmatrix} = \begin{bmatrix} \alpha_{000} \\ \alpha_{001} \\ \alpha_{010} \\ \alpha_{011} \\ \alpha_{100} \\ \alpha_{101} \\ \alpha_{111} \\ \alpha_{110} \end{bmatrix} = \begin{bmatrix} \beta_{000} \\ \beta_{001} \\ \beta_{010} \\ \beta_{011} \\ \beta_{100} \\ \beta_{101} \\ \beta_{110} \\ \beta_{111} \end{bmatrix}.$$

The final probability of activating the alarm, given that A and B are true, equals

$$\frac{|\beta_{111}|^2}{|\beta_{111}|^2 + |\beta_{110}|^2} = \frac{|\alpha_{110}|^2}{|\alpha_{110}|^2 + |\alpha_{111}|^2},$$

which will be near one because $|\alpha_{111}|^2$ is assumed to be near zero (i.e., the alarm is initially not active). The conjunctive control U gate is called a Toffoli gate. Like the C-Not gate, the Toffoli gate is also Hermitian and unitary: $U_T^\dagger = U_T$ and $U_T \cdot U_T = I$.

Next consider a disjunctive rule such as

> If there is smoke *or* there is an emergency then activate the alarm, otherwise do nothing.

This is logically equivalent to

> If there is no smoke *and* there is no emergency then do nothing, otherwise activate the alarm.

Again, it is assumed that the alarm is not activated before the rule is applied (the target is initially turned off). Then the control U gate to execute this disjunction rule is

$$U_{\mathrm{D}} = (X \otimes X \otimes I) \cdot U_{\mathrm{T}} \cdot (X \otimes X \otimes X) = \begin{bmatrix} I & 0 & 0 & 0 \\ 0 & X & 0 & 0 \\ 0 & 0 & X & 0 \\ 0 & 0 & 0 & X \end{bmatrix}$$

$$\beta = U_{\mathrm{D}} \cdot \alpha = \begin{bmatrix} I \cdot \phi_{00} \\ X \cdot \phi_{01} \\ X \cdot \phi_{10} \\ X \cdot \phi_{11} \end{bmatrix} = \begin{bmatrix} \alpha_{000} \\ \alpha_{001} \\ \alpha_{011} \\ \alpha_{010} \\ \alpha_{101} \\ \alpha_{100} \\ \alpha_{111} \\ \alpha_{110} \end{bmatrix} = \begin{bmatrix} \beta_{000} \\ \beta_{001} \\ \beta_{010} \\ \beta_{011} \\ \beta_{100} \\ \beta_{101} \\ \beta_{110} \\ \beta_{111} \end{bmatrix}.$$

The process starts on the right and works toward the left. The first matrix on the right $(X \otimes X \otimes X)$ reverses the third (target qubit) from off to on; reverses the truth state of the second control qubit; and reverses the truth state of the first control qubit. The center matrix U_{T} applies the Toffoli gate to select the appropriate action for the third target qubit. The matrix on the left $(X \otimes X \otimes I)$ resets the first two control qubits to their original states. The probability of activating the alarm after applying the disjunction rule is obtained by projecting the state after the rule, represented by β, onto the active or true state of the third target qubit using the matrix P_X corresponding to the projector $|001\rangle\langle 001| + |011\rangle\langle 011| + |101\rangle\langle 101| + |111\rangle\langle 111|$:

$$\|P_X \cdot \beta\|^2 = |\beta_{001}|^2 + |\beta_{011}|^2 + |\beta_{101}|^2 + |\beta_{111}|^2$$

$$= |\alpha_{001}|^2 + |\alpha_{010}|^2 + |\alpha_{100}|^2 + |\alpha_{110}|^2.$$

Assuming that the alarm is initially off, then $|\alpha_{001}|^2$ is close to zero. Therefore, the alarm will activate with a probability that is determined by $|\alpha_{110}|^2 + |\alpha_{100}|^2 + |\alpha_{010}|^2$; in other words, it is likely to be activated if the first or the second control qubit is true. The disjunction gate can be computed in Matlab using

U1 = kron(X,kron(X,X))), U2 = kron(X,kron(X,eye(2))), defining Utof as the Toffoli gate, and then computing Ud = U2*Utof*U1;.

Other logical rules can be formed using the ideas described above. For another example, consider an exclusive or XOR such as "if A is true and B is false or B is true and A is false, then activate action X." Assuming that the action X is initially inactive, the following control U gate performs this rule:

$$U_1 = (X \otimes I \otimes I) \cdot U_T \cdot (X \otimes I \otimes I),$$

$$U_2 = (I \otimes X \otimes I) \cdot U_T \cdot (I \otimes X \otimes I),$$

$$U_{\mathrm{XOR}} = U_2 \cdot U_1 = \begin{bmatrix} I & 0 & 0 & 0 \\ 0 & X & 0 & 0 \\ 0 & 0 & X & 0 \\ 0 & 0 & 0 & I \end{bmatrix},$$

$$\beta = U_{\mathrm{XOR}} \cdot \alpha = \begin{bmatrix} I \cdot \phi_{00} \\ X \cdot \phi_{01} \\ X \cdot \phi_{10} \\ I \cdot \phi_{11} \end{bmatrix} = \begin{bmatrix} \alpha_{000} \\ \alpha_{001} \\ \alpha_{011} \\ \alpha_{010} \\ \alpha_{101} \\ \alpha_{100} \\ \alpha_{110} \\ \alpha_{111} \end{bmatrix} = \begin{bmatrix} \beta_{000} \\ \beta_{001} \\ \beta_{010} \\ \beta_{011} \\ \beta_{100} \\ \beta_{101} \\ \beta_{110} \\ \beta_{111} \end{bmatrix}.$$

Moving from right to left, the first matrix U_1 activates the target if the first qubit is false and the second qubit is true, while the second matrix U_2 activates the target if the first qubit is true and the second qubit is false. The probability of activating the target for the XOR rule is

$$||P_X \cdot \beta||^2 = |\beta_{001}|^2 + |\beta_{011}|^2 + |\beta_{101}|^2 + |\beta_{111}|^2$$

$$= |\alpha_{001}|^2 + |\alpha_{010}|^2 + |\alpha_{100}|^2 + |\alpha_{111}|^2.$$

Assuming that the target is initially not active so that $|\alpha_{001}|^2 + |\alpha_{011}|^2 + |\alpha_{101}|^2 + |\alpha_{111}|^2$ is close to zero, then the probability of activating the target is determined by $|\alpha_{010}|^2 + |\alpha_{100}|^2$ as desired for the XOR rule. This is computed in Matlab by defining U1 = kron(X,kron(eye(2),eye(2))), U2 = kron(eye(2),kron(X,eye(2))), Utof is the Toffoli gate, and Uxor = (U2*Utof*U2)*(U1*Utof*U1).

What if we reversed the order and defined $U_{\mathrm{XOR}} = U_1 \cdot U_2$? The answer is that the order does not matter because the matrices U_1 and U_2 commute. The matrix $(I \otimes X \otimes I)$ also commutes with the matrix $(X \otimes I \otimes I)$, but the matrix U_T does not commute with the previous two matrices. Once again, it is worth noting that all of these logical gates, which are based on the Toffoli gate, act like an if–then production rule, but they also act like connectionist networks that map input amplitudes directly into output amplitudes.

10.2.4   Multiple action rules

More complex rules entailing multiple actions can be formed by building on the previous ideas. Consider the following example:

> If there is smoke and no cries for help, then activate the fire alarm; if there is no smoke and cries for help, then call 911; if there is smoke and cries for help, then activate the fire alarm and call for help; otherwise do nothing.

This rule involves four events: event A represents the presence of smoke, event B represents the presence of cries for help, the action X represents activating the fire alarm, and the action Y represents calling 911. Four qubits are used to represent these four events and the initial state is represented by the following vector in a 16-dimensional Hilbert space:

$$|ABXY\rangle = \alpha_{0000} \cdot |0000\rangle + \alpha_{0001} \cdot |0001\rangle + ... + \alpha_{1110} \cdot |1110\rangle + \alpha_{1111} \cdot |1111\rangle.$$

For example, the state $|0101\rangle$ represents the situation in which there is no smoke but there are cries for help so the fire alarm is not activated but 911 is called. It is assumed that initially the alarm is not active and 911 has not been called so that $\alpha_{ij10} = \alpha_{ij01} = \alpha_{ij11}$ are close or equal to zero.

In this case, the first two qubits are control qubits and the last two qubits are target qubits. For this situation, the control U gate is defined by

$$U_{\text{CU}} = \begin{bmatrix} I \otimes I & 0 & 0 & 0 \\ 0 & I \otimes I & 0 & 0 \\ 0 & 0 & I \otimes I & 0 \\ 0 & 0 & 0 & U_X \otimes U_Y \end{bmatrix}. \tag{10.5}$$

The first part of the rule "if there is smoke and no cries for help then activate the fire alarm" is accomplished by applying the gate

$$U_X = X, \ U_Y = I$$

$$U_1 = (I \otimes X \otimes I \otimes I) \cdot U_{\text{CU}} \cdot (I \otimes X \otimes I \otimes I).$$

The second part of the rule "if there is no smoke but there are cries for help then call 911" is accomplished by applying the gate

$$U_X = I, \ U_Y = X$$

$$U_2 = (X \otimes I \otimes I \otimes I) \cdot U_{\text{CU}} \cdot (X \otimes I \otimes I \otimes I).$$

The third part of the rule "if there is smoke and cries for help then activate the fire alarm and call for help" is accomplished by the applying gate

$$U_X = X, \ U_Y = X$$

$$U_3 = U_{\text{CU}}.$$

Finally, the entire complex rule is accomplished by

$$U_{\mathrm{On}} = U_3 \cdot U_2 \cdot U_1 = \begin{bmatrix} I \otimes I & 0 & 0 & 0 \\ 0 & I \otimes X & 0 & 0 \\ 0 & 0 & X \otimes I & 0 \\ 0 & 0 & 0 & X \otimes X \end{bmatrix},$$

$$\alpha = \begin{bmatrix} \phi_{00} \\ \phi_{01} \\ \phi_{10} \\ \phi_{11} \end{bmatrix}, \quad \phi_{ij} = \begin{bmatrix} \alpha_{ij00} \\ \alpha_{ij01} \\ \alpha_{ij10} \\ \alpha_{ij11} \end{bmatrix},$$

$$\beta = U_{\mathrm{On}} \cdot \alpha = \begin{bmatrix} I \otimes I \cdot \phi_{00} \\ I \otimes X \cdot \phi_{01} \\ X \otimes I \cdot \phi_{10} \\ X \otimes X \cdot \phi_{11} \end{bmatrix}.$$

This control U gate has the following effect: the first group of four amplitudes, corresponding to no smoke and no cries, remains unchanged; the second group of four amplitudes, corresponding to no smoke but cries are heard, has the amplitudes for the second action (911) flipped from off to on; the third group of four amplitudes, corresponding to smoke present but no cries heard, has the first action (alarm) flipped from off to on; and the fourth group of four amplitudes, corresponding to smoke and cries heard, has both actions flipped from off to on. In particular, when smoke and cries are present

$$X \otimes X \cdot \phi_{11} = \begin{bmatrix} \alpha_{1111} \\ \alpha_{1110} \\ \alpha_{1101} \\ \alpha_{1100} \end{bmatrix} = \begin{bmatrix} \beta_{1100} \\ \beta_{1101} \\ \beta_{1110} \\ \beta_{1111} \end{bmatrix}$$

so that if smoke and cries are present, then the probability of activating the alarm and calling 911 equals

$$\frac{|\beta_{1111}|^2}{|\beta_{1111}|^2 + |\beta_{1110}|^2 + |\beta_{1101}|^2 + |\beta_{1100}|^2}$$

$$= \frac{|\alpha_{1100}|^2}{|\alpha_{1111}|^2 + |\alpha_{1110}|^2 + |\alpha_{1101}|^2 + |\alpha_{1100}|^2},$$

which is close to one because $|\alpha_{1111}|^2 + |\alpha_{1110}|^2 + |\alpha_{1101}|^2$ is assumed to be close to zero.

The three matrices U_1, U_2, U_3 all commute, and so we can change the order of matrix multiplication without changing the result. Here, we see again that a complex collection of rules can all be represented within a simple permutation matrix that acts like a simple connectionist network mapping input amplitudes into output amplitudes.

Finally, suppose that the smoke and cries are later observed to be absent, so that it is appropriate to turn both the alarm and call to 911 off. In this case, we assume that the alarm is still on and the call to 911 is still active but the smoke and cries are no longer present so we wish to turn off both alarms. The following gate, based again on the control U gate U_{CU} defined in Eq. (10.5), accomplishes this task:

$$U_X = X,\ U_Y = X,$$

$$U_3 = U_{\mathrm{CU}},$$

$$U_{\mathrm{Off}} = (X \otimes X \otimes I \otimes I) \cdot U_3 \cdot (X \otimes X \otimes I \otimes I),$$

$$U_{\mathrm{Off}} = \begin{bmatrix} X \otimes X & 0 & 0 & 0 \\ 0 & I \otimes I & 0 & 0 \\ 0 & 0 & I \otimes I & 0 \\ 0 & 0 & 0 & I \otimes I \end{bmatrix},$$

$$\beta = U_{\mathrm{Off}} \cdot \alpha = \begin{bmatrix} (X \otimes X) \cdot \phi_{00} \\ (I \otimes I) \cdot \phi_{01} \\ (I \otimes I) \cdot \phi_{10} \\ (I \otimes I) \cdot \phi_{11} \end{bmatrix},$$

We are assuming that $\|\phi_{00}\|^2 = 1$; that is, the smoke and cries are not present anymore. Focusing on this case,

$$(X \otimes X) \cdot \phi_{00} = \begin{bmatrix} \alpha_{0011} \\ \alpha_{0010} \\ \alpha_{0001} \\ \alpha_{0000} \end{bmatrix} = \begin{bmatrix} \beta_{0000} \\ \beta_{0001} \\ \beta_{0010} \\ \beta_{0011} \end{bmatrix}.$$

So the probability that the alarm and call to 911 are both turned off equals

$$\frac{|\beta_{0000}|^2}{|\beta_{0000}|^2 + |\beta_{0001}|^2 + |\beta_{0010}|^2 + |\beta_{0011}|^2}$$

$$= \frac{|\alpha_{0011}|^2}{|\alpha_{0000}|^2 + |\alpha_{0001}|^2 + |\alpha_{0010}|^2 + |\alpha_{0011}|^2}.$$

Recall that we are assuming that the alarm and call to 911 were both still on before the rule was applied so that the probability that they are now both turned off is close to one.

More generally, if the control U gate has m control qubits and n target qubits then the matrix for this gate will be $2^{m+n} \times 2^{m+n}$ and it will have the form

$$U_{\mathrm{C}} = \begin{bmatrix} I & 0 \\ 0 & U \end{bmatrix},$$

where I is a $2^{m+n} - 2^n$ identity matrix and U is a $2^n \times 2^n$ unitary operator.

10.3 Evaluations represented by plus–minus states

10.3.1 Single event

The qubit is a two-dimensional state that is conventionally defined with respect to the computational basis $\{|0\rangle, |1\rangle\}$, and these two basis states are associated with the operational meaning that some event is true versus false. However, we are not limited to this basis, and another useful basis for representing states in the two-dimensional Hilbert space is a plus–minus basis, $\{|+\rangle, |-\rangle\}$, which can take on a different operational meaning that some event is positive versus negative.[1] The plus–minus states are defined by

$$|+\rangle = \frac{1}{\sqrt{2}} \left(|0\rangle + |1\rangle\right),$$

$$|-\rangle = \frac{1}{\sqrt{2}} \left(|0\rangle - |1\rangle\right).$$

Note that $\| \, |+\rangle \, \|^2 = 1$ and $\| \, |-\rangle \, \|^2 = 1$ and $\langle +|-\rangle = 0$, so that $\{|+\rangle, |-\rangle\}$ forms another orthonormal basis. The coordinates for the plus–minus basis vectors, expressed in terms of the computational basis, are

$$|+\rangle \rightarrow \frac{1}{\sqrt{2}} \begin{bmatrix} 1 \\ 1 \end{bmatrix}, \; |-\rangle \rightarrow \frac{1}{\sqrt{2}} \begin{bmatrix} 1 \\ -1 \end{bmatrix}.$$

Any arbitrary state $|A\rangle$ in the two-dimensional Hilbert space can be represented with respect to either the computational basis or the the plus–minus basis:

$$|A\rangle = \alpha_0 \cdot |0\rangle + \alpha_1 \cdot |1\rangle,$$

$$\beta_+ = \langle +|A\rangle = \frac{1}{\sqrt{2}} \left(\alpha_0 + \alpha_1\right),$$

$$\beta_- = \langle -|A\rangle = \frac{1}{\sqrt{2}} \left(\alpha_0 - \alpha_1\right),$$

$$|A\rangle = \beta_+ \cdot |+\rangle + \beta_- \cdot |-\rangle,$$

$$\alpha_0 = \langle 0|A\rangle = \frac{1}{\sqrt{2}} \left(\beta_+ + \beta_-\right),$$

$$\alpha_1 = \langle 1|A\rangle = \frac{1}{\sqrt{2}} \left(\beta_+ - \beta_-\right).$$

---

[1] For example, Blutner and Hochnadel (2010) developed an ingenious quantum model of Jung's personality theory. In their quantum model, the computational basis represents a question about a preference for using one of two possible "rational" psychological functions (thinking versus feeling), and the plus/minus basis represents a question about a preference for using one of two possible "irrational" psychological functions (sensation versus intuition). These questions are empirically measured using the Myers–Briggs personality test.

Table 10.1 Probabilities for various combinations of two test results made by assuming initial state is plus

	Plus–minus measured first			True–false measured first	
	$|0\rangle$	$|1\rangle$		$|+\rangle$	$|-\rangle$
$|+\rangle$	$1 \cdot (0.5)$	$1 \cdot (0.5)$	$|0\rangle$	$(0.5)\,(0.5)$	$(0.5)\,(0.5)$
$|-\rangle$	0	0	$|1\rangle$	$(0.5)\,(0.5)$	$(0.5)\,(0.5)$

The relation between the two sets of coordinates is given by

$$\begin{bmatrix} \beta_+ \\ \beta_- \end{bmatrix} = \frac{1}{\sqrt{2}} \begin{bmatrix} 1 & 1 \\ 1 & -1 \end{bmatrix} \cdot \begin{bmatrix} \alpha_0 \\ \alpha_1 \end{bmatrix} = \frac{1}{\sqrt{2}} \begin{bmatrix} \alpha_0 + \alpha_1 \\ \alpha_0 - \alpha_1 \end{bmatrix},$$

$$\begin{bmatrix} \alpha_0 \\ \alpha_1 \end{bmatrix} = \frac{1}{\sqrt{2}} \begin{bmatrix} 1 & 1 \\ 1 & -1 \end{bmatrix} \cdot \begin{bmatrix} \beta_+ \\ \beta_- \end{bmatrix} = \frac{1}{\sqrt{2}} \begin{bmatrix} \beta_+ + \beta_- \\ \beta_+ - \beta_- \end{bmatrix}.$$

Notice that if $|0\rangle$ is observed, then $\langle +|0\rangle = \langle -|0\rangle = \frac{1}{\sqrt{2}}$ and there is an equal chance of later observing $|+\rangle$ or $|-\rangle$, and the same is true if $|1\rangle$ is observed. Likewise, if $|+\rangle$ is observed, then $\langle 0|+\rangle = \langle 1|+\rangle = \frac{1}{\sqrt{2}}$ and there is an equal chance of later observing $|0\rangle$ or $|1\rangle$; and the same is true if $|-\rangle$ is observed.

Changing a basis as we just did, from the computational basis to the plus–minus basis, is precisely where quantum theory departs from traditional Bayesian models of cognition. It turns out to be impossible to build a consistent 2×2 joint probability distribution formed by crossing the true,false pair with the plus,minus pair because the results are order dependent. This is shown in Table 10.1, which was constructed by assuming that the initial state before any measurements starts out as a $|+\rangle$. If we examine the joint probabilities obtained by first measuring plus–minus and second measuring true–false, then we obtain the 2×2 table of probabilities shown on the left: starting from the plus state, a measurement of plus–minus produces plus with probability one; and given the plus state, when this is followed by a measurement of true–false, then the probability of true equals 0.50 and the probability of false equals 0.50. This produces the first row labeled $|+\rangle$ on the left-hand side of Table 10.1, and the second row labeled $|-\rangle$ is zero because it is impossible to produce a minus state when we start from the plus state. If we now examine the joint probabilities obtained by first measuring true–false and second measuring plus–minus, then we obtain the 2×2 table of probabilities shown on the right. Again starting from the plus state, a measurement of true–false produces false with probability 0.50; and given the false state, when this is followed by a measurement of plus–minus, the probability of plus equals 0.50 and the probability of minus equals 0.50. This produces the first row labeled $|0\rangle$ on the right-hand side of Table 10.1, and the same reasoning applies to produce the second row labeled $|1\rangle$ in the right-hand table of Table 10.1.

The plus state is a superposition of true and false, which is not the same as a probability mixture of true and false states. The plus state $|+\rangle$ is a pure quantum state (it is a vector in the Hilbert space). This pure plus state produces the following statistics: if we ask whether the event is true or false, then there is a 0.50 probability that the answer is true; but if we ask whether the event is positive or negative, then there is a 1.0 probability that the answer is positive. This is not the same as incorrectly describing this state as a mixed state. If the state is a mixed state, then the state is either the vector $|0\rangle$ with probability 0.50 or the the vector $|1\rangle$ with probability 0.50. This mixed state produces a different set of statistics: if we ask whether the event is true or false, then there is a 0.50 probability of observing a true answer (which agrees with the pure plus state); but if we ask whether the event is positive or negative, then there is again a 0.50 probability of observing a positive response (which disagrees with a pure plus state). This follows from the fact that, in this mixed state, there is a 0.50 probability that the current state is the vector $|0\rangle$; and given this $|0\rangle$ state, there is a 0.50 probability of observing a plus response. There is also a 0.50 probability that the current state is the vector $|1\rangle$; and given the $|1\rangle$ state, there is a 0.50 probability of observing a plus response. Classic probability theory only has mixed states, but quantum theory allows for pure superposition states.

10.3.2 Hadamard gate

The gate $\mathbf{H}$ that transforms true–false states into plus–minus states is called the Hadamard gate. The plus–minus states are obtained by a transformation $\mathbf{H}$ of the true–false states defined by

$$|+\rangle = \mathbf{H}|0\rangle = \frac{1}{\sqrt{2}}\left(|0\rangle + |1\rangle\right)$$

$$|-\rangle = \mathbf{H}|1\rangle = \frac{1}{\sqrt{2}}\left(|0\rangle - |1\rangle\right)$$

It follows from the relation between the coordinates that the matrix representation of the Hadamard gate, with respect to the computational basis, equals

$$\mathbf{H} \to H = \begin{bmatrix} \langle+|0\rangle & \langle+|1\rangle \\ \langle-|0\rangle & \langle-|1\rangle \end{bmatrix} = \frac{1}{\sqrt{2}} \begin{bmatrix} 1 & 1 \\ 1 & -1 \end{bmatrix}.$$

Note that $H^\dagger = H$ so that H is Hermitian and $H \cdot H = I$ so that H is unitary.

The Hadamard gate also changes a plus state, in which true versus false answers are equally likely, into a state that is certain to produce a false response; the Hadamard gate changes the minus state, in which true versus false answers are equally likely, into a state that is certain to produce a true response. In particular,

$$\mathbf{H}|+\rangle = |0\rangle, \ \mathbf{H}|-\rangle = |1\rangle,$$

$$H \cdot \frac{1}{\sqrt{2}} \begin{bmatrix} 1 \\ 1 \end{bmatrix} = \begin{bmatrix} 1 \\ 0 \end{bmatrix}, \ H \cdot \frac{1}{\sqrt{2}} \begin{bmatrix} 1 \\ -1 \end{bmatrix} = \begin{bmatrix} 0 \\ 1 \end{bmatrix}.$$

On the one hand, if a question about an event produces an observation that this event is true, then the plus versus minus answers for this same event are completely uncertain. On the other hand, if an event is observed to be in the plus state, then the true versus false answers to this same event are completely uncertain. Using this representation, one cannot be certain that the same event is true and positive at the same time.

The sign of a state assigned to a qubit can be changed by the $\mathbf{Z}$ gate:

$$\mathbf{Z} \rightarrow Z = \begin{bmatrix} 1 & 0 \\ 0 & -1 \end{bmatrix},$$

$$\mathbf{Z}|0\rangle = |0\rangle, \ \mathbf{Z}|1\rangle = -|1\rangle,$$

$$\mathbf{Z}|+\rangle = |-\rangle, \ \mathbf{Z}|-\rangle = |+\rangle.$$

The matrix Z is Hermitian and unitary: $Z^{\dagger} = Z$ and $Z \cdot Z = I$. The $\mathbf{Z}$ operation can be used with the Hadamard gate to reverse the effect of the Hadamard gate:

$$H \cdot Z = \frac{1}{\sqrt{2}} \begin{bmatrix} 1 & 1 \\ 1 & -1 \end{bmatrix} \cdot \begin{bmatrix} 1 & 0 \\ 0 & -1 \end{bmatrix} = \frac{1}{\sqrt{2}} \begin{bmatrix} 1 & -1 \\ 1 & 1 \end{bmatrix}.$$

In this case,

$$\mathbf{HZ}|+\rangle = \mathbf{H}|-\rangle = |1\rangle,$$

$$\mathbf{HZ}|-\rangle = \mathbf{H}|+\rangle = |0\rangle.$$

Note that $Z \cdot H \neq H \cdot Z$, so that Z and H do not commute and the order of multiplication matters. The product $(H \cdot Z)$ is not Hermitian, but it is unitary: $(H \cdot Z)^{\dagger} \neq (H \cdot Z)$ but $(H \cdot Z)^{\dagger} \cdot (H \cdot Z) = Z \cdot H \cdot H \cdot Z = I$ and $(H \cdot Z) \cdot (H \cdot Z)^{\dagger} = H \cdot Z \cdot Z \cdot H = I$.

The matrices representing the projector $|+\rangle\langle+|$ for the plus event and the projector $|-\rangle\langle-|$ for the minus event can be defined with respect to the computational basis as follows:

$$|+\rangle\langle+| \rightarrow P_{+} = \frac{1}{2} \begin{bmatrix} 1 \\ 1 \end{bmatrix} \cdot \begin{bmatrix} 1 & 1 \end{bmatrix} = \frac{1}{2} \begin{bmatrix} 1 & 1 \\ 1 & 1 \end{bmatrix},$$

$$|-\rangle\langle-| \rightarrow P_{-} = \frac{1}{2} \begin{bmatrix} 1 \\ -1 \end{bmatrix} \cdot \begin{bmatrix} 1 & -1 \end{bmatrix} = \frac{1}{2} \begin{bmatrix} 1 & -1 \\ -1 & 1 \end{bmatrix}.$$

Recall that the projector for the event true is $P_0 = \text{diag} \begin{bmatrix} 0 & 1 \end{bmatrix}$ and the projector for false is $P_0 = \text{diag} \begin{bmatrix} 1 & 0 \end{bmatrix}$. It is easy to show that the true–false projectors do not commute with the plus–minus projectors. For example, first asking whether the event is a plus and then asking whether the event is true does not produce the same probabilities as the reverse order:

$$P_1 \cdot P_{+} - P_{+} \cdot P_1 = \frac{1}{2} \begin{bmatrix} 0 & -1 \\ 1 & 0 \end{bmatrix}.$$

In other words, questions about an event being true versus false are incompatible with questions about the same event being positive or negative.

Sometimes it is desirable to move part way from equally likely to produce an increase in probability for one action over another but not complete certainty. Chapter 9 and the section on Pauli matrices in Appendix D discuss this problem. This can be achieved by using the unitary operator $U(t) = e^{-itH}$; as t ranges from $t = 0$ to $t = \pi/2$ the probability for the true state increases according to an S-shaped function from 0.50 to 1.0. Note that $U\left(\frac{\pi}{2}\right) = -i \cdot H$, and the common phase factor $-i$ has no effect.

10.3.3 Multiple events

Kronecker products of the Hadamard gate can be applied to states from higher dimensional spaces to form a state with equal probabilities assigned to all basis states. Consider a four-dimensional Hilbert space spanned by the computational basis for two qubits $\{|00\rangle, |01\rangle, |10\rangle, |11\rangle\}$. Set the initial state to $|00\rangle = |0\rangle \otimes |0\rangle$. Then apply the Kronecker product of the Hadamard gate to this state to form

$$(\mathbf{H} \otimes \mathbf{H})(|0\rangle \otimes |0\rangle) = \mathbf{H}|0\rangle \otimes \mathbf{H}|0\rangle$$

$$= \left(\frac{1}{\sqrt{2}}(|0\rangle + |1\rangle)\right) \otimes \left(\frac{1}{\sqrt{2}}(|0\rangle + |1\rangle)\right)$$

$$= \frac{1}{\sqrt{4}}(|00\rangle + |01\rangle + |10\rangle + |11\rangle).$$

Using the matrix representation with respect to the computational basis:

$$H \otimes H = \frac{1}{\sqrt{2}}\begin{bmatrix} 1 & 1 \\ 1 & -1 \end{bmatrix} \otimes \frac{1}{\sqrt{2}}\begin{bmatrix} 1 & 1 \\ 1 & -1 \end{bmatrix}$$

$$= \frac{1}{\sqrt{4}}\begin{bmatrix} 1 & 1 & 1 & 1 \\ 1 & -1 & 1 & -1 \\ 1 & 1 & -1 & -1 \\ 1 & -1 & -1 & 1 \end{bmatrix}$$

$$(H \otimes H) \cdot \begin{bmatrix} 1 \\ 0 \\ 0 \\ 0 \end{bmatrix} = \frac{1}{\sqrt{4}}\begin{bmatrix} 1 \\ 1 \\ 1 \\ 1 \end{bmatrix}.$$

More generally, if we define $H^1 = H$ and $H^{n+1} = H \otimes H^n$ then H^n transforms the state $|00..0\rangle$ into a superposition with each amplitude equal to $\frac{1}{\sqrt{n}}$.

More complex higher dimensional states can be formed using tensor products of both the computational and plus–minus bases.[2] Suppose event A represents

---

[2] Once again, an example is the quantum model of Jung's personality proposed by Blutner and Hochnadel (2010). The question about introversion versus extroversion is represented in the computational basis. This is combined by the tensor product with the question about sensation versus intuition, which is represented in the plus/minus basis.

taking an action and event B represents the consequence of this action. Suppose we wish to judge whether the event of taking the action is true or false and we wish to evaluate whether the consequence of taking the action is positive or negative. This state can be represented by a vector in the four-dimensional space as follows:

$$|AB\rangle = \gamma_{0+}|0+\rangle + \gamma_{0-}|0-\rangle + \gamma_{1+}|1+\rangle + \gamma_{1-}|1-\rangle.$$

The unit-length vector

$$\gamma = \begin{bmatrix} \gamma_{0+} \\ \gamma_{0-} \\ \gamma_{1+} \\ \gamma_{1-} \end{bmatrix} = \begin{bmatrix} \phi_0 \\ \phi_1 \end{bmatrix}$$

represents this state with respect to the following basis formed by tensor products of the basis vectors for the individual events:

$$|0+\rangle \rightarrow \begin{bmatrix} 0 \\ 1 \end{bmatrix} \otimes \begin{bmatrix} \frac{1}{\sqrt{2}} \\ \frac{1}{\sqrt{2}} \end{bmatrix},$$

$$|0-\rangle \rightarrow \begin{bmatrix} 0 \\ 1 \end{bmatrix} \otimes \begin{bmatrix} \frac{1}{\sqrt{2}} \\ \frac{-1}{\sqrt{2}} \end{bmatrix},$$

$$|1+\rangle \rightarrow \begin{bmatrix} 0 \\ 1 \end{bmatrix} \otimes \begin{bmatrix} \frac{1}{\sqrt{2}} \\ \frac{1}{\sqrt{2}} \end{bmatrix},$$

$$|1-\rangle \rightarrow \begin{bmatrix} 0 \\ 1 \end{bmatrix} \otimes \begin{bmatrix} \frac{1}{\sqrt{2}} \\ \frac{-1}{\sqrt{2}} \end{bmatrix}.$$

Each of these basis vectors remains unit length and each pair of basis vectors remains orthogonal. The probability that the event "action is taken" is true then equals

$$||(P_1 \otimes I) \cdot \gamma||^2 = ||\phi_1||^2.$$

The probability that the consequence is positive then equals

$$||(I \otimes P_+) \cdot \gamma||^2 = ||P_+ \cdot \phi_0||^2 + ||P_+ \cdot \phi_1||^2$$

and the probability that the action is taken and the consequence is positive equals

$$||(P_1 \otimes P_+) \cdot \gamma||^2 = ||P_+ \cdot \phi_1||^2.$$

This tensor product representation allows one to simultaneously evaluate whether an event is true or false and whether the consequence of the event is positive or negative.

10.3.4   C-H gates

The control Hadamard (C-H) gate is particularly effective when there are two equally strong competing actions, and a cue is used to decide which action to choose. Consider the following simple example:

> If there is smoke in the left wing then exit out the right, but if there is smoke in the right wing then exit out the left.

The abstract form of the rule is then "if cue equals CL then do action XR; if cue equals CR then do action XL." To represent this situation, the following superposition state is used:

$$|CX\rangle = \alpha_{00} \cdot |00\rangle + \alpha_{01} \cdot |01\rangle + \alpha_{10} \cdot |10\rangle + \alpha_{11} \cdot |11\rangle.$$

The first qubit represented by C is called the control qubit and the second qubit represented by X is the target qubit. In this situation, $|00\rangle$ represents the case in which cue CL is observed and the wrong action XL is taken, $|01\rangle$ represents the case in which cue CL is observed and the appropriate action XR is taken, $|10\rangle$ represents the case in which cue CR is observed and the correct action XL is taken, and $|11\rangle$ represents the case in which the other cue CR is observed and the wrong action XR is taken. The coefficients assigned to the basis vectors represent the state *before* applying the rule. Now it is assumed that, before seeing the cue and before applying the rule, the probability of each action is approximately equally likely so that $(|\alpha_{01}|^2 + |\alpha_{11}|^2) \approx (|\alpha_{00}|^2 + |\alpha_{10}|^2)$. This initial state can be prepared by applying the Hadamard gate to $|0\rangle$:

$$(\mathbf{I} \otimes \mathbf{H})(|C\rangle \otimes |0\rangle) = |C\rangle \otimes \mathbf{H}|0\rangle = |C\rangle \otimes |+\rangle = |C+\rangle.$$

The C-H gate is defined by the matrix

$$U_1 = X \otimes I,$$

$$U_{\mathrm{L}} = \begin{bmatrix} I & 0 \\ 0 & H \end{bmatrix}, \ U_{\mathrm{R}} = \begin{bmatrix} I & 0 \\ 0 & H \cdot Z \end{bmatrix},$$

$$U_{\mathrm{CH}} = U_{\mathrm{L}} \cdot (U_1 \cdot U_{\mathrm{R}} \cdot U_1),$$

$$U_{\mathrm{CH}} = \begin{bmatrix} I & \mathbf{0} \\ \mathbf{0} & H \end{bmatrix} \cdot \begin{bmatrix} \mathbf{0} & I \\ I & \mathbf{0} \end{bmatrix} \cdot \begin{bmatrix} I & \mathbf{0} \\ \mathbf{0} & H \cdot Z \end{bmatrix} \cdot \begin{bmatrix} \mathbf{0} & I \\ I & \mathbf{0} \end{bmatrix}$$

$$= \begin{bmatrix} H \cdot Z & \mathbf{0} \\ \mathbf{0} & H \end{bmatrix}.$$

The matrix U_{CH} first checks for cue CL and applies the Hadamard to perform action XR if cue CL is present; if this does not happen, then it flips the cue back to its original value to check for cue CR and applies the reversed Hadamard to perform action XL if cue CR is present. Note that the U_{CH} gate is unitary but not Hermitian because $H \cdot Z$ does not commute. However, $U_{\mathrm{L}} \cdot (U_1 \cdot U_{\mathrm{R}} \cdot U_1) = (U_1 \cdot U_{\mathrm{R}} \cdot U_1) \cdot U_{\mathrm{L}}$, so the order that we apply the check does not matter.

The effect of this gate on the initial state is shown below:

$$
\alpha = \left[\begin{bmatrix} \alpha_{00} \\ \alpha_{01} \\ \alpha_{10} \\ \alpha_{11} \end{bmatrix} \right] = \begin{bmatrix} \phi_0 \\ \phi_1 \end{bmatrix},
$$

$$
\beta = U_{\mathrm{CH}} \cdot \alpha = \begin{bmatrix} H \cdot Z & \mathbf{0} \\ \mathbf{0} & H \end{bmatrix} \cdot \begin{bmatrix} \phi_0 \\ \phi_1 \end{bmatrix} = \begin{bmatrix} H \cdot Z \cdot \phi_0 \\ H \cdot \phi_1 \end{bmatrix}
$$

$$
= \frac{1}{\sqrt{2}} \begin{bmatrix} \alpha_{00} - \alpha_{01} \\ \alpha_{00} + \alpha_{01} \\ \alpha_{10} + \alpha_{11} \\ \alpha_{10} - \alpha_{11} \end{bmatrix} = \begin{bmatrix} \beta_{00} \\ \beta_{01} \\ \beta_{10} \\ \beta_{11} \end{bmatrix}.
$$

If the cue is observed to be CL (e.g., smoke in the left wing), then given this information, the probability of taking the appropriate action XR (e.g., exit out the right wing) equals

$$
\frac{|\beta_{01}|^2}{|\beta_{00} + \beta_{01}|^2} = \frac{|\alpha_{00} + \alpha_{01}|^2}{|\alpha_{00} + \alpha_{01}|^2 + |\alpha_{00} - \alpha_{01}|^2}.
$$

The above probability will be near one whenever $\alpha_{00} \approx \alpha_{01}$ is initially the case. If the initial state is equally likely so that $\alpha_E = \begin{bmatrix} 1/2 & 1/2 & 1/2 & 1/2 \end{bmatrix}^\dagger$, then the final state after applying the U_{CH} gate equals $\beta = U_{\mathrm{CH}} \cdot \alpha_E = \begin{bmatrix} 0 & 1/\sqrt{2} & 1/\sqrt{2} & 0 \end{bmatrix}$, which is one of the famous entangled Bell states used in quantum computing. Thus, the U_{CH} gate turns a separated state into an entangled state.

10.4   State–action sequences

Agent–environment interactions produce sequences of states and actions across time. This more complex situation can be represented by combining a quantum information processing (QIP) model of the agents with a partially observable Markov decision processes (POMDP) model of the environment (Littman, 2009) (see Figure 10.2).

The POMDP is a discrete time model of the environment, which is formed by specifying four different finite sets: one containing a set E of environmental states, a second containing a set A of actions, a third containing a set O of observations, and a fourth containing a set of rewards R. The POMDP model also includes the three classic probability functions: a transition probability function $P_E : E \times A \times E \rightarrow [0,1]$ that takes a state and an action at one step in time and probabilistically selects a new state for the next step in time; an observation probability function $P_O : E \times A \times O \rightarrow [0,1]$ that takes a state and action and probabilistically selects an observation; a reward function $P_R : E \times A \times R \rightarrow [0,1]$ that takes a state and action and probabilistically delivers a reward or punishment.

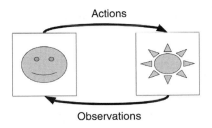

Figure 10.2 Agent–environment interaction model.

The quantum model is a model of the agent. The agent model consists of a unit-length state vector $|\psi\rangle$ of finite dimension that represents the agent's beliefs over the environmental states, actions, and observations, and a set of control U gates that are used to select actions on the basis of the agent state $|\psi\rangle$.

The two models work together as follows. At the beginning time point, the agent starts in a superposed state over the environment and observations and actions, makes an observation, projects the state vector onto the subspace consistent with the observation, and normalizes the projection using Lüder's rule to produce the initial state $|\psi_0\rangle$. Then the agent selects a control U gate that determines the action from the current state. The action selected by the agent is applied in conjunction with the environmental state to the POMDP model to change the environmental state, generate the next set of observations available to the agent, and the reward delivered to the agent. The action of the agent produces uncertainty about the environmental states, observations, and actions that were changed by the last action, and so the agent makes a new observation, projects the state onto the subspace consistent with the new observation, and normalizes to produce the updated state $|\psi_1\rangle$. This agent action–belief state change process continues until the final stage of the decision process. The rewards delivered by the POMDP model are used to learn the appropriate control U gates to apply for each agent state, and this topic is treated in the next chapter.

10.4.1 Example application

Suppose an agent is trying to escape a building that is on fire. The following POMDP model is assumed for the environment: there is a hallway without an exit, which branches off into wings with exits on the left and right. However, one (initially unknown) exit is blocked by fire that is producing smoke in the wings. The POMDP model for the environment can be represented in a simple manner by 12 states produced by combining six locations ("hall," "branch point," "left wing," "right wing," "left exit," "right exit") with two hypotheses about the blocked exit (left exit is blocked, right exit is blocked). Also, to keep things simple, suppose the agent has six mutually exclusive and exhaustive actions (turn left, turn right, move forward, move backward, stop, and check for smoke). Finally, suppose that checking for smoke produces four possible observations:

see smoke in the left wing, see smoke in the right wing, see no smoke, see smoke in both wings. It is assumed in this simple example that the state transition function is deterministic for all states and actions. For example, if the state is hallway and the action is move forward to branch point, then the new state will locate the agent at the branch point. The probability of observing smoke in a wing is assumed to depend on whether or not the exit for that wing is blocked by fire.

The agent model for this example assumes that the agent can directly observe the current location in the building and the current action. That is, the agent always knows the current location in the building and the current action. (A more general model would allow the location of the agent in the building to be inferred from other observations, but we omit this to keep the example fairly simple.) The blocked exit is uncertain and it must be inferred from observing smoke in a wing, and so only this observation needs to be included in the observation set. The four observations (smoke versus no smoke in each wing) can be represented by two qubits $|o_1 o_2\rangle$, with $o_i = 0, 1$, $i = 1, 2$. The vector $|00\rangle$ represents no smoke in either wing, $|01\rangle$ represents smoke in the right wing and not the left, $|10\rangle$ represents smoke in the left wing and not the right, $|11\rangle$ represents smoke in both wings. This produces four basis vectors that span a four-dimensional space.

The information about location of the agent can be represented using four qubits, with the first three qubits representing the location of the agent in the building and the last representing the hypothesis about the location of the blocked exit. The six locations in conjunction with the hypothesis that the "left exit is blocked" are defined by eight basis vectors $|s_1 s_2 s_3 0\rangle$, for $s_i = 0, 1$ and $i = 1, 2, 3$: $|0000\rangle$ corresponds to "location is hallway and left exit is blocked," $|0010\rangle$ corresponds to "location is branch point and left exit is blocked," $|0100\rangle$ corresponds to "location is left wing and left exit is blocked," $|0110\rangle$ corresponds to "location is right wing and left exit is blocked," $|1000\rangle$ corresponds to "location is left exit and left exit is blocked," $|1010\rangle$ corresponds to "location is right exit and left exit is blocked." The remaining two basis vectors, $|1100\rangle$ and $|1110\rangle$, are not used and so they are always assigned zero amplitude. Using a similar coding scheme, the six locations in conjunction with the hypothesis that the "right exit is blocked" are represented by the remaining eight basis vectors $|s_1 s_2 s_3 1\rangle$, for $s_i = 0, 1$ and $i = 1, 2, 3$ and $s_3 = 0, 1$. This produces a total of $2^4 = 16$ basis vectors spanning a 16-dimensional space, although four basis vectors are never used.

Six actions can be represented by three qubits. However, it is necessary to distinguish between the current action state and the new action states. So we need to double the number of action states by using three qubits for the current action state and another three qubits for the new action state. The three qubits for the current action states form eight basis vectors $|a_1 a_2 a_3\rangle$, with $a_j = 0$ or 1 for $j = 1, 2, 3$: $|000\rangle$, corresponds to stop, $|001\rangle$ corresponds to check for smoke, $|010\rangle$ corresponds to turn left, $|011\rangle$ corresponds to turn right, $|100\rangle$ corresponds to move forward, and $|101\rangle$ represents move backward. The remaining two basis vectors, $|110\rangle$ and $|111\rangle$, are not used and so they are always assigned zero amplitude. The three qubits for the new action state form another eight basis vectors $|n_1 n_2 n_3\rangle$, with $n_j = 0$ or 1 for $j = 1, 2, 3$, and these are defined in the same manner as the current action states. This produces a total of $2^3 2^3 = 2^6$ basis vectors, but 24 are are never used.

The complete basis for the agent system is then formed by all of the tensor products of the observation basis vectors with the location basis vectors and action basis vectors. Altogether there are 2 (observation) + 4 (environmental state) + 3 (current action) + 3 (new action) qubits, which produces a vector $|\psi\rangle$ within a $2^2 \times 2^4 \times 2^3 \times 2^3 = 2^{12}$-dimensional Hilbert space. The complete quantum state is a linear combination of these tensor product basis vectors:

$$|\psi\rangle = \sum \psi_i \cdot |o_1 o_2\rangle \otimes |s_1 s_2 s_3 s_4\rangle \otimes |a_1 a_2 a_3\rangle \otimes |n_1 n_2 n_3\rangle,$$

with the summation ranging across $o_i = 0, 1$ for $i = 1, 2$ and $s_j = 0, 1$ for $j = 1, 2, 3$ and $a_k = 0, 1$ for $k = 1, 2, 3$ and $n_m = 0, 1$ for $m = 1, 2, 3$. The state $|\psi\rangle$ is represented by a $2^{12} \times 1$ column matrix ψ that contains the amplitudes assigned to each of the 2^{12} basis vectors. However, as shown below, this is a very sparse matrix, and only a few of these basis vectors are ever used at one time in the analysis. (The matrix operations for these sparse matrices can easily be computed using sparse matrix operators in matrix programming languages such as Matlab.)

The sequence of actions are performed by control U gates defined on this 2^{12} Hilbert space. The first nine qubits are control qubits and the last three qubits are target qubits. To work with this high-dimensional space, we define I as a 2×2 identity matrix and we denote $I^1 = I$ and $I^{n+1} = I \otimes I^n$; X is the 2×2 Not gate and we denote $X^1 = X$ and $X^{n+1} = X \otimes X^n$, H is the Hadamard gate and we denote $H^1 = H$ and $H^{n+1} = H \otimes H^n$. Also, we define I_n as the $n \times n$ identity matrix with $n = 2^{12} - 2^3$. We usually start each new step with $n_k = 0$ for $k = 1, 2, 3$; that is, the new action is set to $|000\rangle$, representing "stopped" before the gate is applied.

For example, suppose the agent is in the hallway and is stopped and the agent observes this situation (e.g., applies a measurement at this point). Then the state of the agent becomes equal to the normalized projection onto the subspace consistent with observing $s_1 = 0$, $s_2 = 0$, $s_3 = 0$ for the hallway location and observing $a_1 = 0$, $a_2 = 0$, $a_3 = 0$ for the currently stopped action, which produces the initial state

$$|\psi_0\rangle = \psi_{000} \cdot |00\rangle |0000\rangle |000\rangle |000\rangle + \psi_{010} \cdot |01\rangle |0000\rangle |000\rangle |000\rangle$$
$$+ \psi_{100} \cdot |10\rangle |0000\rangle |000\rangle |000\rangle + \psi_{110} \cdot |11\rangle |0000\rangle |000\rangle |000\rangle$$
$$+ \psi_{001} \cdot |00\rangle |0001\rangle |000\rangle |000\rangle + \psi_{011} \cdot |01\rangle |0001\rangle |000\rangle |000\rangle$$
$$+ \psi_{101} \cdot |10\rangle |0001\rangle |000\rangle |000\rangle + \psi_{111} \cdot |11\rangle |0001\rangle |000\rangle |000\rangle.$$

The agent is in a superposition over the possible observations about smoke and hypotheses about the blocked exit. For example, ψ_{011} is the amplitude associated with the observation of no smoke in the left wing and smoke in the right wing and the right exit is blocked. The initial state is normalized so that $\langle \psi_0 | \psi_0 \rangle = 1$.

From this state, the following rule is appropriate: if the agent is in the hallway and stopped, then move forward. Therefore, from this state, we need to turn on the value of n_1 corresponding to the new target action, which is to move forward to the branch point. This is accomplished by applying the following control U gate to the initial state:

$$U_1 = I^2 \otimes \left(X^3 \otimes I\right) \otimes I^6,$$

$$U_2 = X \otimes I^2,$$

$$U_3 = \begin{bmatrix} I_n & \mathbf{0} \\ \mathbf{0} & U_2 \end{bmatrix},$$

$$\psi_1 = U_1 \cdot U_3 \cdot U_1 \cdot \psi_0.$$

The state of the agent after applying the gate equals

$$|\psi_1\rangle = \psi_{000} \cdot |00\rangle|0000\rangle|000\rangle|100\rangle + \psi_{010} \cdot |01\rangle|0000\rangle|000\rangle|100\rangle$$
$$+ \psi_{100} \cdot |10\rangle|0000\rangle|000\rangle|100\rangle + \psi_{110} \cdot |11\rangle|0000\rangle|000\rangle|100\rangle$$
$$+ \psi_{001} \cdot |00\rangle|0001\rangle|000\rangle|100\rangle + \psi_{011} \cdot |01\rangle|0001\rangle|000\rangle|100\rangle$$
$$+ \psi_{101} \cdot |10\rangle|0001\rangle|000\rangle|100\rangle + \psi_{111} \cdot |11\rangle|0001\rangle|000\rangle|100\rangle.$$

From this state, if the agent makes a decision (e.g., applies a measurement) to select the new action, then the next action is certain to be "move forward."

After taking the move forward action, the agent is moved to the branch point. Suppose the appropriate action is to stop at the branch point. Applying a control U gate to produce this change in state results in the state (we skip the details of the control U gate for this step)

$$|\psi_2\rangle = \psi_{000} \cdot |00\rangle|0010\rangle|100\rangle|000\rangle + \psi_{010} \cdot |01\rangle|0010\rangle|100\rangle|000\rangle$$
$$+ \psi_{100} \cdot |10\rangle|0010\rangle|100\rangle|000\rangle + \psi_{110} \cdot |11\rangle|0010\rangle|100\rangle|000\rangle$$
$$+ \psi_{001} \cdot |00\rangle|0011\rangle|100\rangle|000\rangle + \psi_{011} \cdot |01\rangle|0011\rangle|100\rangle|000\rangle$$
$$+ \psi_{101} \cdot |10\rangle|0011\rangle|100\rangle|000\rangle + \psi_{111} \cdot |11\rangle|0011\rangle|100\rangle|000\rangle.$$

After stopping and observing this action, the state changes to

$$|\psi_3\rangle = \psi_{000} \cdot |00\rangle|0010\rangle|000\rangle|000\rangle + \psi_{010} \cdot |01\rangle|0010\rangle|000\rangle|000\rangle$$
$$+ \psi_{100} \cdot |10\rangle|0010\rangle|000\rangle|000\rangle + \psi_{110} \cdot |11\rangle|0010\rangle|000\rangle|000\rangle$$
$$+ \psi_{001} \cdot |00\rangle|0011\rangle|000\rangle|000\rangle + \psi_{011} \cdot |01\rangle|0011\rangle|000\rangle|000\rangle$$
$$+ \psi_{101} \cdot |10\rangle|0011\rangle|000\rangle|000\rangle + \psi_{111} \cdot |11\rangle|0011\rangle|000\rangle|000\rangle.$$

At this point, the agent must turn left versus right and so the agent's state becomes a superposition over the new left and right actions. This superposition is obtained by turning on the second to last qubit and applying the Hadamard gate to the last qubit to change the last qubit from a false state into a plus state:

$$U_4 = I^2 \otimes I^4 \otimes I^3 \otimes (I \otimes X \otimes H),$$

$$\psi_4 = U_4 \cdot \psi_3.$$

The new state equals

$$
\begin{aligned}
|\psi_4\rangle = {}& \psi_{000} \cdot |00\rangle|0010\rangle|000\rangle|01\rangle|+\rangle + \psi_{010} \cdot |01\rangle|0010\rangle|000\rangle|01\rangle|+\rangle \\
& + \psi_{100} \cdot |10\rangle|0010\rangle|000\rangle|01\rangle|+\rangle + \psi_{110} \cdot |11\rangle|0010\rangle|000\rangle|01\rangle|+\rangle \\
& + \psi_{001} \cdot |00\rangle|0011\rangle|000\rangle|01\rangle|+\rangle + \psi_{011} \cdot |01\rangle|0011\rangle|000\rangle|01\rangle|+\rangle \\
& + \psi_{101} \cdot |10\rangle|0011\rangle|000\rangle|01\rangle|+\rangle + \psi_{111} \cdot |11\rangle|0011\rangle|000\rangle|01\rangle|+\rangle.
\end{aligned}
$$

The appropriate action is to check for smoke at this point, and suppose we observe smoke in the left wing and not in the right wing. Then the state is updated by using Lüder's rule to produce

$$c = \frac{1}{\sqrt{\left|\psi_{100}\right|^2 + \left|\psi_{101}\right|^2}},$$

$$
\begin{aligned}
|\psi_5\rangle = {}& \left(\frac{\psi_{100}}{c}\right) \cdot |10\rangle|0010\rangle|000\rangle|01\rangle|+\rangle \\
& + \left(\frac{\psi_{101}}{c}\right) \cdot |10\rangle|0011\rangle|000\rangle|01\rangle|+\rangle.
\end{aligned}
$$

This update in beliefs about the location of the blocked exit corresponds to a Bayesian update that occurs in a POMDP model.

Finally, we need to apply a gate that selects the appropriate action depending on the value of the smoke cue that we observe. The control H gate used to accomplish this objective is defined by

$$U_L = \begin{bmatrix} I_n & \mathbf{0} \\ \mathbf{0} & I \otimes I \otimes H \end{bmatrix},$$

$$U_R = \begin{bmatrix} I_n & \mathbf{0} \\ \mathbf{0} & I \otimes I \otimes H \cdot Z \end{bmatrix},$$

$$U_5 = (I \otimes X) \otimes (X^2 \otimes I) \otimes X \otimes I^6,$$

$$U_6 = (I \otimes X) \otimes (X^2 \otimes I) \otimes I \otimes I^6,$$

$$\psi_6 = (U_6 \cdot U_L \cdot U_6) \cdot (U_5 \cdot U_R \cdot U_5) \cdot \psi_5.$$

After applying this control H gate, the state changes to

$$|\psi_6\rangle = \left(\frac{\psi_{100}}{c}\right) \cdot |10\rangle|0010\rangle|000\rangle|01\rangle|1\rangle$$
$$+ \left(\frac{\psi_{101}}{c}\right) \cdot |10\rangle|0011\rangle|000\rangle|01\rangle|0\rangle.$$

The state of the agent is now entangled so that if the left exit is blocked ($s_4 = 0$), then the next action is to exit out the right ($n_1 = 0, n_2 = 1, n_3 = 1$), and if the right exit is blocked ($s_4 = 1$), then the next action is to exit out the left ($n_1 = 0, n_2 = 1, n_3 = 0$). The smoke is not a perfectly reliable indicator of the blocked exit, and so the agent remains superposed between the two hypotheses. At this point the agent would need to make a decision by projecting on one of the two hypotheses. The probability of projecting onto the hypothesis that the left exit is blocked equals $\left|\frac{\psi_{100}}{c}\right|^2$. If this measurement produces a decision that the left exit is blocked, then the agent applies a right turn action and moves forward down the right wing. In this way the agent proceeds to exit out the right and stop.

In summary, a sequence of actions and events can be modelled in much the same manner as a partially observable Markov decision process. The unique features of quantum theory only come into play when non-commuting projectors are used to update the state (which did not occur in this simple example). An issue that was ignored in this presentation was the problem of learning the appropriate or optimal action for each state. A quantum reinforcement learning algorithm is presented in the next chapter to accomplish this learning task.

10.5　Concluding comments

Quantum information processing is accomplished by updating the state after observations using Lüder's rule and then applying a sequence of control U gates to perform actions. All QIP is captured by the sequence of matrix operations. On the one hand, these matrix products can be viewed as production rule sequences that start with an initial state, observe some events, make inferences using Lüder's rule, and then apply rules using control U gates, and then choose actions. Alternatively, the combined matrix can be viewed as a connectionist network that takes the input and filters it to produce an output, which is then used to determine the final actions. Quantum information processing has the advantage of both approaches to information processing – it is easy to describe its function like a production rule but it also deals naturally with fuzzy and uncertain and noisy information like a distributed connectionist network. Also, the decisions depend on probabilistic inferences about events using observations in a manner similar to a Bayesian model of cognition. The main difference between the quantum and Bayesian methods occurs when we change the basis used to define a sequence of measurements (such as changing from the computational "true versus false" basis to the plus–minus basis).

11
Can quantum systems learn? Quantum updating

Learning is a critical aspect of any intelligent cognitive system. How can this be done within a QIP approach? This is a relatively new field, but some progress has already been achieved (Ivancevic & Ivancevic, 2010). There are at least three ways to accomplish learning using quantum principles. One way is to update the agent's belief state based on experience (Schack *et al.*, 2001), as done in Bayesian learning models (Griffiths *et al.*, 2008). A second way is to update the weights in a unitary matrix using gradient descent of an error function (Zak & Williams, 1998), as done in connectionist learning models (Rumelhart & McClelland, 1986). A third way is to update the amplitudes assigned to control U gate actions based on rewards and punishments (Dong *et al.*, 2010), as done with reinforcement learning algorithms (Sutton & Barto, 1998). This chapter reviews all three approaches.

11.1 Quantum state updating based on experience

For the first type of quantum learning model, consider how to update an agent's belief state based on experience. In Chapter 4 we presented a quantum model for probability judgments, and in that chapter the initial belief state denoted $|\psi\rangle$ was given or assumed to be already known in advance – when new facts were presented, inferences were made from the known state $|\psi\rangle$ using Lüder's rule. However, where does this initial state $|\psi\rangle$ come from? Now we examine how this initial state $|\psi\rangle$ can be learned or estimated from experience. Principles borrowed from quantum state tomography can be used to model the estimation of a quantum state (Schack *et al.*, 2001).

11.1.1 Quantum Bayes nets

Recall from Chapter 4 that a state vector can be used to represent a person's beliefs about combinations of values for a set of features (features are also called variables). Suppose there are four features labeled u, v, w, x, and, for simplicity, suppose each feature is binary valued with values $\{0, 1\}$. To be more concrete, suppose variable u represents the presence ($u = 1$) or absence ($u = 0$) of a genetic disposition for a neural disease. The latter can influence v which represents the presence or absence of a malfunctioning neural system. The variable w represents the presence or absence of an environmental stress, and w together with v influence the variable x, which represents the presence or absence of a psychopathological state. All combinations of the binary values for the four features form a total set of 16 unique event patterns.

For now we assume that all four features are compatible, in which case we can represent the belief state for these four binary variables by a vector $|\psi\rangle$ within an $n = 16$-dimensional Hilbert space spanned by 16 orthonormal basis vectors:

$$|\psi\rangle = \sum_{ijkl} \psi_{ijkl} \cdot |u_i v_j w_k x_l\rangle. \tag{11.1}$$

Each basis vector $|u_i v_j w_k x_l\rangle$ represents a combination of the binary values from the four variables. In particular, $|u_0 v_1 w_0 x_1\rangle$ represents the occurrence of the event that $u = 0$ and $v = 1$ and $w = 0$ and $x = 1$ (i.e., the event that there is no genetic predisposition, but there is a presence of a malfunctioning neural system, and there is no environmental stress, but psychopathological state is present). The coordinate ψ_{ijkl} assigned to a basis vector determines the probability amplitude for a combination of feature values. For example, ψ_{0101} represents the probability amplitude assigned to the combination of feature values $u = 0$, $v = 1, w = 0, x = 1$ (i.e., the probability amplitude that there is no genetic predisposition, but there is a presence of a malfunctioning neural system, and there is no environmental stress, but psychopathological state is present). The 16×1 matrix $\psi = [\psi_{ijkl}]$ contains all 16 coordinates for all 16 probability amplitudes ψ_{ijkl}, $i, j, k, l \in \{0, 1\}$, assigned to the 16 basis vectors.

The problem of learning a quantum state from experience is analogous to learning the probabilities in a Bayesian causal network (Pearl, 1988). Quantum Bayes nets can be used to represent dependencies among variables that define the basis for a quantum state (Tucci, 1995).[1] Consider, for example, the acyclic "causal" network shown in Figure 11.1. This represents one possible causal model for describing the causal relations among variables u, v, w, x.

Using Figure 11.1 as the basis for our model, we can assign probability amplitudes to ψ in this network using quantum principles analogous to principles used in Bayesian networks (Tucci, 1995). The basic idea is that any classic Bayes net can be extended to a quantum Bayes net by replacing the probabilities in the classic model with amplitudes in the quantum model. For our example in Figure 11.1, we can set

$$\psi_{ijkl} = \psi(u = i) \cdot \psi(v = j | u = i) \cdot \psi(w = k) \cdot \psi(x = l | v = j, w = k). \tag{11.2}$$

In the above expression we define $\psi(u = i)$ as the probability amplitude assigned to value i of variable u with the constraint $\sum_i |\psi(u = i)|^2 = 1$; we define $\psi(v = j | u = i)$ as the conditional probability amplitude of value j for variable v given that variable u is observed to have value i, with the constraint

---

[1] Also see Tucci (1997). The quantum Bayes nets developed by Tucci are acyclic. However, La Mura and Swiatczak (2007) extended the quantum model to include cyclic networks.

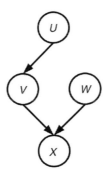

Figure 11.1 Example of a causal network in which variable u influences variable v, and both variables v and w influence variable x.

$\sum_j |\psi(v = j|u = i)|^2 = 1$ for each i; we define $\psi(w = k)$ as the probability amplitude for value k of variable w, with the constraint $\sum_k |\psi(w = k)|^2 = 1$; and we define $\psi(x = l|v = j, w = k)$ as the conditional probability amplitude that variable x has value l given that variable v is observed to have value j and variable w is observed to have value k, with the constraint $\sum_l |\psi(x = l|v = j, w = k)|^2 = 1$ for each pair of values for j, k. These constraints on the probability amplitudes guarantee that $||\psi^2|| = 1$. As shown below, the conditional amplitudes of Eq. (11.2) generate probabilities that are consistent with the results derived by applying Lüder's rule to the original amplitudes in Eq. (11.1) after observing the conditioning events.

The standard quantum probability rules are applied to this state to generate all the required marginal and conditional event probabilities needed to make inferences from the network shown in Figure 11.1. Consider, for example, the conditional probability $p(x = 1|v = j, w = k)$. Starting from basic quantum principles, we define a projector for observing the event $v = j$ as $P_{v=j}$, which corresponds to a 16×16 indicator matrix that picks out the amplitudes corresponding to the event $v = j$ from ψ in Eq. (11.1). We also define a projector for event $w = k$ as $P_{w=k}$, which corresponds to another 16×16 indicator matrix that picks out the amplitudes corresponding to event $w = k$ from ψ in Eq. (11.1). Recall that, according to Lüder's rule, if we observe the events $v = j$ and $w = k$, then the state changes from the initial state ψ to the revised state:

$$\psi_{v=j,w=k} = \frac{P_{v=j} \cdot P_{w=k} \cdot \psi}{||P_{v=j} \cdot P_{w=k} \cdot \psi||} = \frac{P_{v=j} \cdot P_{w=k}\psi}{\sqrt{p(v = j, w = k)}},$$

and note that

$$p(v = j, w = k) = ||P_{v=j} \cdot P_{w=k} \cdot \psi||^2$$

$$= \sum_i \sum_l |\psi(u = i)|^2 \cdot |\psi(v = j|u = i)|^2 \cdot |\psi(w = k)|^2$$

$$\cdot |\psi(x = l|v = j, w = k)|^2$$

$$= \sum_i |\psi(u=i)|^2 \cdot |\psi(v=j|u=i)|^2 \cdot |\psi(w=k)|^2$$

$$\cdot \sum_l |\psi(x=l|v=j,w=k)|^2$$

$$= \sum_i |\psi(u=i)|^2 \cdot |\psi(v=j|u=i)|^2 \cdot |\psi(w=k)|^2 \cdot 1,$$

so that the probability of observing $x=1$ after observing the other two events $v=j$ and $w=k$ equals

$$p(x=1|v=j,w=k) = \left\| P_{x=1} \cdot \psi_{v=j,w=k} \right\|^2$$

$$= \frac{\left\| P_{x=1} \cdot P_{v=j} \cdot P_{w=k} \cdot \psi \right\|^2}{\left\| P_{v=j} \cdot P_{w=k} \cdot \psi \right\|^2}$$

$$= \frac{\left\| P_{x=1} \cdot P_{v=j} \cdot P_{w=k} \cdot \psi \right\|^2}{p(v=j,w=k)}$$

$$= \frac{\left(\sum_i |\psi(u=i)|^2 \cdot |\psi(v=j|u=i)|^2 \cdot |\psi(w=k)|^2 \right) \cdot |\psi(x=1|v=j,w=k)|^2}{p(v=j,w=k)}$$

$$= \frac{p(v=j,w=k) \cdot |\psi(x=1|v=j,w=k)|^2}{p(v=j,w=k)} = |\psi(x=1|v=j,w=k)|^2.$$

The last line proves that $|\psi(x=1|v=j,w=k)|^2$ equals the same probability as obtained by applying Lüder's rule to Eq. (11.1) after observing the events $v=j$ and $w=k$. As another example, suppose we learn that $u=1$; and consider the conditional probability $p(x=1|u=1)$. Then this conditional probability equals

$$p(x=1|u=1) = \frac{\left\| P_{x=1} \cdot P_{u=1} \cdot \psi \right\|^2}{\left\| P_{u=1} \cdot \psi \right\|^2} = \frac{\sum_j \sum_k |\psi_{1jk1}|^2}{|\psi(u=1)|^2}$$

$$= \sum_j \sum_k |\psi(v=j|u=1)|^2 \cdot |\psi(w=k)|^2 \cdot |\psi(x=1|v=j,w=k)|^2.$$

Alternatively, we can compute the probability of $u=1$ given $x=1$:

$$p(u=1|x=1) = \frac{\left\| P_{u=1} \cdot P_{x=1} \cdot \psi \right\|^2}{\left\| P_{x=1} \cdot \psi \right\|^2}$$

$$= \frac{\left\| P_{u=1} \cdot P_{x=1} \cdot \psi \right\|^2}{\left\| (P_{u=0} + P_{u=1}) \cdot P_{x=1} \cdot \psi \right\|^2}$$

$$= \frac{\left\| P_{u=1} \cdot P_{x=1} \cdot \psi \rangle \right\|^2}{\left\| P_{u=0} \cdot P_{x=1} \cdot \psi \right\|^2 + \left\| P_{u=1} \cdot P_{x=1} \cdot \psi \right\|^2}$$

$$= \frac{\left\| P_{u=1} \cdot \psi \right\|^2 \left\| P_{x=1} \cdot \psi_{u=1} \right\|^2}{\left\| P_{u=0} \cdot \psi \right\|^2 \left\| P_{x=1} \cdot \psi_{u=0} \right\|^2 + \left\| P_{u=1} \cdot \psi \right\|^2 \left\| P_{x=1} \cdot \psi_{u=1} \right\|^2}$$

$$= \frac{p(u=1) \cdot p(x=1|u=1)}{\sum_i p(u=i) \cdot p(x=1|u=i)}.$$

As can be seen from the above examples, inference is performed with squared amplitudes in a manner directly analogous to Bayesian causal networks used in psychological theories of causal reasoning (Griffiths *et al.*, 2008).

Why derive probabilities from amplitudes if squared magnitudes of amplitudes simply reproduce the same results as using probabilities directly? The answer is that amplitudes become critical as soon as we introduce a new set of incompatible features. For example, suppose the basis $|u_i v_j w_k x_l\rangle$ is used to evaluate the probabilities generated by the variables in Figure 11.1 from an impersonal perspective of an institution (e.g., an expert providing opinions for the medical insurance industry) and the coordinates for this basis are represented by the amplitudes in ψ. Alternatively, suppose another orthonormal basis $|u_i' v_j' w_k' x_l'\rangle$ is used to evaluate the same events shown in Figure 11.1, but now from a personal perspective concerning the specific life of a single individual (e.g., providing judgments about a highly familiar patient) and the coordinates for this basis are represented by the amplitudes in $\phi = U \cdot \psi$. Suppose an expert is asked to evaluate whether a "genetic disposition is present" from the impersonal perspective of an insurance industry ($u = 1$), given that "psychopathological behavior is present" from the personal perspective of a single individual ($x' = 1$); or in other words, $p(u = 1|x' = 1)$. According to a quantum inference model, this probability is obtained by the following three steps. First, the personal basis $|u_i' v_j' w_k' x_l'\rangle$ is used to represent the belief state $|\psi\rangle$, which assigns the amplitudes according to ϕ. This belief state is updated on the basis of the fact that the personal event $x' = 1$ is observed by picking out the coordinates in ϕ corresponding to the event $x' = 1$ using the projector $P_{x'=1}$ and normalizing the result to produce the conditional amplitudes

$$\phi_{x'=1} = \frac{P_{x'=1}\phi}{\sqrt{p(x'=1)}}.$$

Then the basis is changed to $|u_i v_j w_k x_l\rangle$ in order to evaluate the impersonal insurance industry perspective, and this basis reassigns amplitudes according to the transformation

$$\psi_{x'=1} = U^\dagger \cdot \phi_{x'=1}.$$

Finally, the probability of $u - 1$ from the impersonal perspective given that $x' = 1$ is observed from the personal perspective equals

$$p(u = 1|x' = 1) = \left\| P_{u=1} \psi_{x'=1} \right\|^2.$$

In sum, by using amplitudes and unitary transformations, quantum theory provides a simple way to represent two different causal belief systems – one from a personal perspective and one from an impersonal perspective, and it also provides a simple and efficient way to evaluate sequences of evidence obtained from these different perspectives. Changes in the basis used to evaluate events produce non-commutative events that lead to order effects (see Chapters 3 and 4) and interference effects (see Chapter 9) and entanglement effects (see Chapters 5 and 7) that are difficult to explain using standard (Kolmogorov and Bayesian) probability theory.

11.1.2   Updating amplitudes based on experience

The amplitudes for a causal network are learned on the basis of observations generated by the causal network. Suppose we need to learn the probability amplitude vector

$$\alpha = \begin{bmatrix} \alpha_0 \\ \alpha_1 \end{bmatrix} = \begin{bmatrix} \psi\left(x = 0 | v = j, w = k\right) \\ \psi\left(x = 1 | v = j, w = k\right) \end{bmatrix},$$

with the constraint that $\|\alpha\|^2 = 1$. The set of all possible α forms a sphere with unit radius called the Bloch sphere (Nielsen and Chuang, 2000). Our prior distribution places probabilities on each point on this Bloch sphere. The prior probability density assigned to each point on the Bloch sphere is denoted $p(\alpha)$.

First, suppose α is known and we obtain N identical and independent observations on variable x (conditioned on observed values for $u = j, v = k$). The results are summarized by the pair of data points $R = (n_0, n_1)$, where n_0 is the number of times we observe $x = 0$ and n_1 is the number of times we observe $x = 1$, so that $N = n_0 + n_1$. According to the quantum model, the probability of obtaining $R = (n_0, n_1)$ given the state α equals the binomial distribution

$$p(n_0, n_1 | \alpha) = \binom{N}{n_1} \cdot \left(|\alpha_1|^2\right)^{n_1} \cdot \left(|\alpha_0|^2\right)^{n_0}.$$

The posterior probability of α given the observations in R is obtained by Bayes' rule (Schack *et al.*, 2001):

$$p(\alpha | n_0, n_1) = \frac{p(\alpha) \cdot p(R|\alpha)}{\int p(R|\alpha) p(\alpha) \, d\alpha}.$$

One commonly used prior is defined by uniform sphere integration. In this case the updating rule becomes (Jones, 1991)

$$p(\alpha | n_0, n_1) = (N + 1) \cdot \binom{N}{n_1} \cdot \left(|\alpha_1|^2\right)^{n_1} \cdot \left(|\alpha_0|^2\right)^{n_0}$$

(see Equation 23 in Jones (1991)).

Alternatively, we could assume a much more restrictive prior. In particular, we could assume that α is initially restricted to real values so that $\alpha_1 =$

$= \sqrt{p(x=1|v=j, w=k)}$. Then we can use a beta distribution $B(a+1, b+1)$ with a, b positive integers and $M = a + b$ to define the prior (Kruschke, 2010):

$$p(\alpha_1^2) = (M+1) \cdot \binom{M}{a} \cdot (\alpha_1^2)^a \cdot (\alpha_0^2)^b.$$

Using this beta prior, the posterior distribution equals

$$p(\alpha_1^2|n_0, n_1) = (N+M+1) \cdot \binom{N+M}{n_1+a} \alpha_1^{2(n_1+a)} \cdot \alpha_0^{2(n_0+b)}.$$

If we now wish to change variables from α_1^2 to α_1, then we have to use the change in rate $\left|\frac{\partial \alpha_1^2}{\partial \alpha_1}\right| = 2 \cdot \alpha_1$ to form the transformed density $p(\alpha_1|R) = 2 \cdot p(\alpha_1^2|R) \cdot \alpha_1$.

In summary, according to quantum probability theory, amplitudes are basic and probabilities are derived from amplitudes. Learning the state for a quantum network requires estimating the amplitudes for the nodes in the causal network from experience. In particular, for the causal network shown in Figure 11.1, learning involves estimating the amplitudes for $\psi(u=i)$, $\psi(v=j|u=i)$, $\psi(w=k)$, and $\psi(x=l|v=j, w=k)$ from experience.

Quantum theory also allows new causal belief networks to be formed by unitary transformations of the basis. However, this raises the following question: How does a person learn a unitary transformation that changes from one basis to the next? This issue is addressed in the next section.

11.2 Weight updating based on gradient descent learning

For a second type of quantum learning model, consider learning the "connection weights" u_{jk} in a unitary matrix U based on experience with pairs of input and output probability amplitude distributions, analogous to the learning of input–output activation patterns by a connectionist learning model. This idea has been used as the basis for quantum neural network learning models (Kouda *et al.*, 2005).[2]

The basic idea is illustrated in Figure 11.2 for the special case of a four-dimensional Hilbert space. Information is presented to a person (represented by S in the figure) and this information generates a belief state $|\psi\rangle$ which can be used to answer various kinds of questions. For example, S may contain information about the health of an individual. In the figure, this belief state is initially interpreted with respect to the four basis vectors C_1 to C_4. For example, C_1 to C_4 could represent four possible answers to questions about a person's health status when evaluated from an impersonal perspective of an institution such as an insurance company. This input basis assigns an amplitude distribution ψ to

---

[2] An alternative way to learn with quantum neural nets is to use a Grover (1997) amplitude amplification algorithm (Ventura & Martinez, 2000). An application of the Grover algorithm is presented in the next section on reinforcement learning.

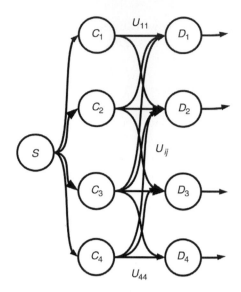

Figure 11.2 The inputs into C_1 to C_4 are connected to the outputs D_1 to D_4 by the connection weights u_{ij}.

the four events, so that the probability of observing an event corresponding to C_j equals $|\psi_j|^2$. Later this information is reinterpreted with respect to another set of four basis vectors D_1 to D_4. For example, D_1 to D_4 could represent four possible answers to questions about a person's health status when evaluated from a personal perspective about a single individual. The evaluator eventually learns a connection u_{jk} between each of four input basis vectors C_j and each of the four output basis vectors D_k to form a connection weight matrix U. These connection weights u_{jk} are eventually used to map the input amplitude distribution ψ across C_1 to C_4 into the output amplitude distribution ϕ across D_1 to D_4 by a simple linear combination rule $\phi_k = \sum_j u_{jk} \cdot \psi_j$. The final probability of observing an event corresponding to D_k is the squared magnitude $|\phi_k|^2$. Thus, the amplitudes are mapped in a simple linear manner but the observed event probabilities are related in a nonlinear manner.[3] Before presenting the learning model, we need to discuss more specifically the feedback information that is used for training in this learning task.

In general, a probability amplitude assigned to a basis vector is a complex number, $\phi_j = |\phi_j| \cdot e^{i\theta_j}$, with a magnitude $|\phi_j|$ and phase $e^{i\theta_j}$. The probability of the event pattern equals the squared magnitude $|\phi_j|^2$. A key assumption for this learning model is that a person can report a probability for each event pattern, which is determined from the squared magnitude of the amplitude assigned to its basis vector. This implies that an individual is aware of the

---

[3] A possible neural interpretation of the connection weight matrix is provided in Chapter 12. However, this transformation is closely related to Fourier transformations that are used to model features in the auditory and visual systems.

magnitude $|\phi_j|$ of an amplitude for a basis vector. However, we do not assume that a person is aware or able to report the phase information $e^{i\theta_j}$ about a probability amplitude. In quantum theory, only the probabilities (and thus the magnitude of the amplitude) are directly measurable, and the phase only has indirect effects that are expressed through the observed response probabilities.

When a piece of information is presented, the person initially represents the input with respect to the $|C_j\rangle$ basis and represents the information by an $N \times 1$ matrix $\psi = \left[\sqrt{p_j}\right]$, for $j = 1, \ldots, N$, where p_j equals the probability assigned to basis vector $|C_i\rangle$, with $\psi^\dagger \psi = 1$. When the person views this same information from the perspective of the $|D_j\rangle$ basis, the person experiences an $N \times 1$ matrix $\bar{\phi}$ containing the absolute values $\bar{\phi} = \left[|\phi_j|\right]$. Therefore, we assume that the person experiences input–output pairs $(\psi, \bar{\phi})$ across trials, and from these pairs the associative learning system gradually forms connections U that map ψ into ϕ. After training, the person is able to generate an appropriate output ϕ when given any new input ψ. Suppose the person experiences a sequence of input–output pairs $(\psi_t, \bar{\phi}_t)$ and there is a unitary matrix U such that $\phi_t = U \cdot \psi_t$. Define the estimate of the unitary transformation after t trials of experience as $\hat{U}_t$. The next predicted output generated by this estimate is denoted $\hat{\phi}_{t+1}$, which is an $N \times 1$ matrix containing only the magnitudes of the coordinates of the transformed input amplitudes $\hat{U}_t \cdot \psi_{t+1}$. The squared distance between the observed output and the prediction equals

$$F_t = \left\| \bar{\phi}_t - \hat{\phi}_t \right\|^2$$

$$= \left\| \bar{\phi}_t \right\|^2 + \left\| \hat{\phi}_t \right\|^2 - \left(\bar{\phi}_t^\dagger \cdot \hat{\phi}_t + \hat{\phi}_t^\dagger \cdot \bar{\phi}_t \right)$$

$$= 2 - \left(\bar{\phi}_t^\dagger \cdot \hat{\phi}_t + \hat{\phi}_t^\dagger \cdot \bar{\phi}_t \right)$$

and $R_t = \left(\bar{\phi}_t^\dagger \cdot \hat{\phi}_{t+1} + \hat{\phi}_{t+1}^\dagger \cdot \bar{\phi}_t \right)$ is twice the cosine of the angle between the target and the prediction. A trial-by-trial learning algorithm is formed by updating the estimate of the unitary matrix in a direction that maximizes the increase in this cosine (Toronto & Ventura, 2006).[4]

Recall from Chapter 2 that any unitary matrix can be expressed as a matrix exponential of a Hamiltonian matrix, $U = e^{-iH}$, where $H^\dagger = H$ is an $N \times N$ Hermitian matrix with elements $h_{jk} = h_{kj}^*$. Hereafter, we will assume that H is real so that $h_{jk} = h_{kj}$ (but note that $U = e^{-iH}$ is still a complex matrix and the phase makes its critical impact here). Under the latter constraint, the learning

---

[4]The algorithm below is closely related to the earlier one developed by Toronto and Ventura (2006) with the following important differences: Toronto and Ventura did not form the unitary from a Hamiltonian and so their transformation is not required to be unitary; they did not restrict the target output to contain only the magnitude of an amplitude and instead they assumed that both phase and magnitude are provided as feedback; they used a batch rather than trial-by-trial updating algorithm.

algorithm can be re-expressed in terms of the gradient of R_t with respect to the real values in H:

$$\nabla_t = \frac{\partial R_t(H)}{\partial H} = \left[\frac{\partial R_t}{\partial h_{jk}}\right].$$

In the above definition of the gradient, ∇_t is an $N \times N$ matrix with element $\delta_{jk} = \frac{\partial R_t}{\partial h_{jk}}$ in row j for $j = 1, \ldots, N$ and column k for $k = 1, \ldots, j$ and we require $\delta_{kj} = \delta_{jk}$ so that H remains symmetric. (This gradient is computed by a numerical finite-difference method in the program provided in Appendix G). Then the learning algorithm can be described by

$$H_t = H_{t-1} + s \cdot \nabla_t \tag{11.3}$$

$$\hat{U}_t = \mathrm{e}^{-iH_t}$$

and finally $\bar{\phi}_t$ contains the absolute values of the coordinates in $\hat{U}_t \cdot \psi_t$. The learning rate parameter s is a real-valued scalar. One additional step can be added to this algorithm – the previous estimate of H_{t-1} is changed to the new estimate H_t after trial t if and only if $R(H_t) > R(H_{t-1})$. In other words, only improvements in performance are accepted.

11.2.1   Example application

To examine how well this learning model works, consider the problem of learning the 4×4 unitary matrix described in Chapter 4, which was used to explain the order effects on inference in a juror decision task. The unitary matrix used in Chapter 4 was formed from the following Hamiltonian:

$$H = \begin{bmatrix} \frac{h}{\sqrt{1+h^2}} + \frac{-\gamma}{\sqrt{2}} & \frac{1}{\sqrt{1+h^2}} & \frac{-\gamma}{\sqrt{2}} & 0 \\ \frac{1}{\sqrt{1+h^2}} & \frac{-h}{\sqrt{1+h^2}} + \frac{\gamma}{\sqrt{2}} & 0 & \frac{-\gamma}{\sqrt{2}} \\ \frac{-\gamma}{\sqrt{2}} & 0 & \frac{h}{\sqrt{1+h^2}} + \frac{\gamma}{\sqrt{2}} & \frac{1}{\sqrt{1+h^2}} \\ 0 & \frac{-\gamma}{\sqrt{2}} & \frac{1}{\sqrt{1+h^2}} & \frac{-h}{\sqrt{1+h^2}} + \frac{-\gamma}{\sqrt{2}} \end{bmatrix}. \tag{11.4}$$

The unitary matrix was then obtained by the matrix exponential $U = \mathrm{e}^{-i\left(\frac{\pi}{2}\right)H}$. Recall from Chapter 4 that this unitary matrix was used to describe the change in basis used to make inferences in a juror decision task when evidence was viewed from either a defense on a prosecutor perspective.

The following procedure was used to sample input distributions. Each input amplitude distribution ψ_t was formed by randomly sampling N coordinates from a uniform distribution between zero and one and then normalizing the amplitudes so that $\psi_t^\dagger \cdot \psi_t = 1$.

The initial estimate for the unitary matrix was set equal to an identity matrix, $\hat{U}_0 = I$. This produced the first predicted output amplitude distribution for the first trial equal to $\bar{\phi}_1 = I \cdot \psi_1$. This initial prediction was then compared with the first target produced by the absolute values of the coordinates of $\phi_1 = U \cdot \psi_1 = \mathrm{e}^{-i\left(\frac{\pi}{2}\right)H} \cdot \psi_1$ with H defined in Eq. (11.4). The first prediction and

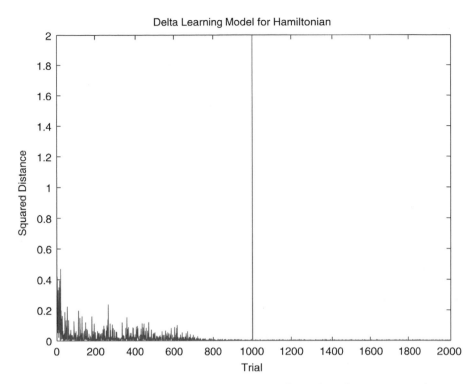

Figure 11.3 Squared distance between target and predicted output as a function training trial. The vertical line indicates where learning stopped and transfer testing began.

target were used to generate the initial squared distance $\left\|\bar{\phi}_1 - \hat{\phi}_1\right\|^2$, and the latter squared distance was used to start the learning algorithm.

Thereafter, the learning algorithm in Eq. (11.3) was applied for 1000 trials with $s = 0.25$. After 1000 trials, the step was set to zero to stop learning and the unitary matrix trained up to trial 1000 was then used to make predictions for the next 1000 trials. (The Matlab computer program used to calculate the results is provided in Appendix G.)

Figure 11.3 illustrates the efficiency of this learning model for the parameter values $h = 0.5167$ and $\gamma = 2.3109$ for Eq. (11.4). The squared distance rapidly drops from a starting value of 2 to a much lower value near 0.10 and it is eventually driven to zero. This result is typical for hundreds of simulations using these same parameters. Very similar results were also obtained by varying the parameters for the Hamiltonian and varying the step size s.

It is interesting to compare the target transition matrix T generated by the target U matrix with the estimated transition matrix $\hat{T}$ generated by the final estimate $\hat{U}$ after very extensive training (10,000 training trials). Each entry $T_{jk} = |\langle D_k | C_j \rangle|^2$ of the transition matrix contains the probability of transiting from a column input basis state $|C_j\rangle$ to a row output basis state $|D_k\rangle$. The target transition matrix is generated by taking the squared magnitudes of the cells in $U = \mathrm{e}^{-iH}$ with H defined by Eq. (11.4), and the estimated transition matrix is generated by taking the squared magnitudes of the cells in $\hat{U} = \mathrm{e}^{-iH_t}$ where H_t is the Hamiltonian learned from Eq. (11.3) after $t = 10,000$ trials. The target transition matrix is displayed below on the left as the matrix T and the estimate is displayed on the right as the matrix $\hat{T}$:

$$
T = \begin{bmatrix} 0.4825 & 0.0631 & 0.1307 & 0.3238 \\ 0.0631 & 0.4825 & 0.3238 & 0.1307 \\ 0.1307 & 0.3238 & 0.2874 & 0.2581 \\ 0.3238 & 0.1307 & 0.2581 & 0.2874 \end{bmatrix},
$$

$$
\hat{T} = \begin{bmatrix} 0.4845 & 0.0633 & 0.1290 & 0.3232 \\ 0.0633 & 0.4823 & 0.3252 & 0.1292 \\ 0.1290 & 0.3252 & 0.2880 & 0.2579 \\ 0.3232 & 0.1292 & 0.2579 & 0.2898 \end{bmatrix}.
$$

Comparing the two transition matrices, it can be seen that the estimate is very close to the target after extensive training. In fact, it was already reasonably close after only 1000 trials.

In sum, Eq. (11.3) provides a learning model to estimate a unitary matrix that transforms probability amplitudes expressed in one basis into probability amplitudes expressed in another basis. This learning model is new and it has not been empirically tested yet. However, it could be tested by training human learners with pairs of input and output probability distributions, and finally testing the human learners by presenting only the input distribution and asking the learner to generate the output distribution.

How can a person learn which unitary transform to use for different circumstances or situations? This is an issue that was raised earlier in Chapter 10. The next learning algorithm describes how to learn to apply control U gates to learn complex condition–action sequences.

11.3   Quantum reinforcement learning

For the third type of quantum learning, consider updating the amplitudes assigned to control U gate actions based on rewards and punishments, as done with reinforcement learning algorithms. A quantum reinforcement learning model for accomplishing this task was first proposed by Dong et al. (2008). The algorithm is based on the quantum information search algorithm originally proposed by Grover (1997). The quantum reinforcement learning algorithm does not require a quantum computer – instead, it can be directly used to learn to perform practical sequential decision-making tasks. The basic ideas are summarized below. First we review the basic concepts of the Markov decision-learning paradigm used in machine learning (Sutton & Barto, 1998) and then we describe the quantum reinforcement learning model.

11.3.1 Markov decision process paradigm

As described in Chapter 10, a POMDP consists of four sets: the first is a set $E = \{e_1, \ldots, e_n\}$ of environmental states, the second is a set $A = \{a_1, \ldots, a_m\}$ of mutually exclusive and exhaustive actions, the third is a set O of observations, and the fourth is a set R of rewards. In this chapter, for simplicity, we restrict the discussion to a Markov decision process (MDP) in which the states are directly observable, so that we do not distinguish between the sets E and O and dispense with the set O. The MDP also includes the two classic probability functions: a transition probability function $P_E : E \times A \times E \to [0,1]$ that takes an environmental state and an action at one step in time and probabilistically selects a new state for the next step in time; and a reward function $P_R : E \times A \times R \to [0,1]$ that takes a state and action and probabilistically delivers a reward or punishment. The agent applies a policy, which specifies the appropriate action to take for each state. The goal of a reinforcement learning algorithm is to learn a policy that maximizes the future discounted expected rewards.

In particular, the popular Q-learning algorithm works as follows (see Sutton and Barto (1998)). Define the estimate of the expected discounted future rewards for each state and action at time t as $Q(e_j, a_k, t)$. Suppose the last action taken at time t changed the state to e and the immediate reward $r(t)$ was obtained. Then the new estimate for each state is updated according to

$$Q(e_j, a_k, t+1) = (1 - \eta) \cdot Q(e_j, a_k, t) + \eta \cdot \left[r(t) + \gamma \cdot \max_l Q(e, a_l, t) \right],$$

where η is a learning rate parameter and γ is a discount rate parameter. The term in square brackets is the Q-learning "reward" signal. Then the next action is probabilistically selected based on its expected future reward value (see Sutton and Barto (1998)). However, standard reinforcement learning algorithms suffer some problems, including slow learning in complex environments and sensitivity to parameters that balance exploration versus exploitation of the environment in the action selection rule. Therefore, new ideas for improving performance are still greatly needed in this area.

11.3.2 Quantum action selection

The basic idea is that the current environmental state puts the agent in a superposition state over the set of possible actions. The superposition state is a vector in an m-dimensional space spanned by m orthonormal basis vectors denoted $|a_k\rangle$, $k = 1, \ldots m$, and each basis vector corresponds to one of the actions. If the current state is e_j, then the superposition state over actions is

$$|\psi_j\rangle = \sum_{k=1}^{m} \psi_{jk} \cdot |a_k\rangle,$$

with two constraints on the amplitudes: $\psi_{jk} = 0$ for any action that is not available from state e_j and, given the previous constraint, we also require $|\psi_j\rangle$ to remain unit length. Then the probability of taking action a_k from state e_j equals $|\psi_{jk}|^2$. The key new idea is the learning rule for amplifying the amplitudes ψ_{jk} that experience high rewards. To describe this algorithm we will ignore the basis states assigned zero amplitudes, because their actions are impossible from a given state, and consider only the basis states that correspond to possible actions. Hereafter, the $m \times 1$ matrix ψ will refer to the amplitudes for m actions and each action is assumed to be a potential choice.

11.3.3   Amplitude amplification

The amplitude amplification algorithm is an extension by Brassard and Hoyer of Grover's (1997) search algorithm (Hoyer, 2000). The algorithm begins with any arbitrary initial amplitude distribution represented by the $m \times 1$ matrix ψ_0, but it is common to start with $\psi_{jk} = \frac{1}{\sqrt{m}}$ for m actions from state e_j. Define ψ_t as the $m \times 1$ matrix of amplitudes after experiencing t trials of training. Suppose action a_j was chosen on the last trial t. The amplitude for action a_j is amplified or attenuated in proportion to reward $[r(t) + \gamma \cdot \max_l Q(e, a_l, t)]$ experienced by taking that action. This is done as follows.

Define A_k as an $m \times 1$ matrix with zeros in every row except the row k corresponding to action a_k, which is set equal to one. This is essentially the coordinates corresponding to the basis vector $|a_k\rangle$. Next define the following two matrices:

$$Q_1 = I - \left(1 - e^{i\phi_1}\right) \cdot \left(A_k \cdot A_k^\dagger\right),$$

$$Q_2 = \left(1 - e^{i\phi_2}\right) \cdot \left(\psi_t \cdot \psi_t^\dagger\right) - I,$$

where ϕ_1, ϕ_2 are two learning parameters that control the amount of amplification or attenuation. The matrix Q_1 flips the sign of the target action and the matrix Q_2 inverts all the amplitudes around the average amplitude, and together these to act to amplify the target while having no effect (except normalization) on the non-targets. Then the new amplitude distribution is formed by

$$\psi_{t+1} = (Q_2 \cdot Q_1)^L \cdot \psi_t, \qquad (11.5)$$

where the matrix power L indicates the integer number of applications of the update used on a single trial. The key idea of the learning algorithm is to relate the reward $[r(t) + \gamma \cdot \max_l Q(e, a_l, t)]$ to the parameters ϕ_1, ϕ_2, and L applied after each trial. One option is to fix $\phi_1 = \phi_2 = \pi \approx 3.1416$ and allow L to be the integer value of $c \cdot [r(t) + \gamma \cdot \max_l Q(e, a_l, t)]$, where $c > 0$ is a free parameter (Dong et al., 2008). This essentially produces the original Grover updating algorithm. However, this restricts the algorithm to discrete jumps in amplitudes, and it is too restrictive for small numbers of actions. Another option is to set $L = 1$ and restrict $\phi_1 = \phi_2 = \phi \cdot \pi \approx \phi \cdot 3.1416$ and vary ϕ in proportion to $c \cdot [r(t) + \gamma \cdot \max_l Q(e, a_l, t)]$ within a range that gives monotonic change in amplitude. The latter method is illustrated in the following two examples.

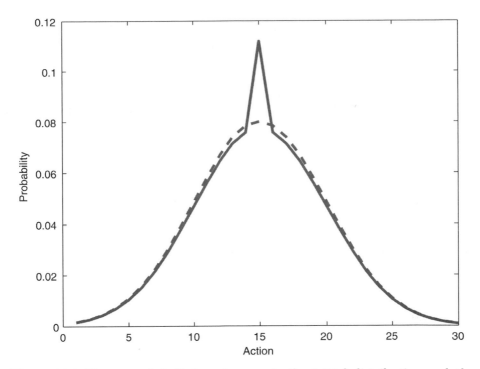

Figure 11.4 The smooth bell-shaped curve is the initial distribution and the curve with the spike is the distribution after amplification of action 15.

11.3.4   Examples of amplitude amplification

Two examples are provided below to illustrate how amplitude amplification works. Figure 11.4 depicts the amplification produced with $L = 1$ and $\phi = 0.15$ ($\phi_1 = \phi_2 = 0.15\pi$) for $m = 30$ actions and action 15 was updated. The initial distribution ψ_0 was approximately normally distributed, and the amplified distribution is shown with the spike at action 15. As can be seen, a single update modifies the selected action and leaves the remaining amplitudes the same except for renormalization. The computer code used to produce Figure 11.4 is presented in Appendix G.

Figure 11.5 shows the effect of varying $\phi_1 = \phi_2 = \phi \cdot \pi$ on the probability for the updated action. In this example, there are only $m = 3$ actions, and we set $L = 1$ and $\psi_k = \frac{1}{\sqrt{3}}$ initially so that the initial probability equals $\frac{1}{3}$. The top curve shows the amplification effect as a function of ϕ within the range $[1, 2]$ and note that $\phi = 1$ corresponds to $\phi_1 = \phi_2 = \pi$. The curve tends to oscillate and repeat itself if the range is extended. In this range, one could assume that ϕ is proportional to the reward signal.

Dong *et al.* (2010) extensively tested and compared the performance of the quantum reinforcement learning model with a standard reinforcement model using the popular "ϵ-greedy" algorithm (the best option is selected with probability

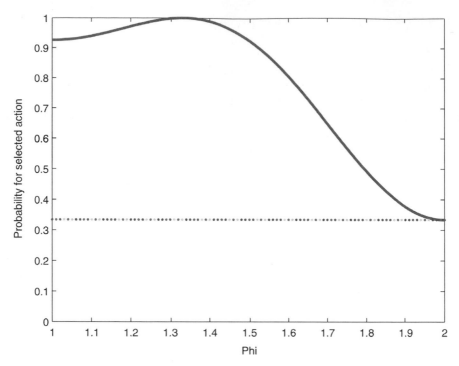

Figure 11.5 The top curve shows the probability assigned to the selected action after amplification; the bottom straight line is the probability before amplification. The difference is the amplification effect.

$1 - \epsilon$ and otherwise choice is random). The learning speeds for the two models were compared for different types of navigation environments (an artificial Markov world, a simulated robot navigation problem, and a real robot navigation problem) using a variety of learning rate parameters for the reinforcement learning model.[5] On the basis of these simulations and robotic experiments they reported that (a) the quantum reinforcement algorithm tended to reach convergence on the optimal solution faster than the traditional reinforcement learning model and, perhaps more importantly, (b) performance of the quantum reinforcement learning model was fairly robust with respect to variations in the learning rate parameter for reinforcement learning, whereas the performance of the traditional model was very sensitive to this learning parameter and worked well only within a restricted range. They concluded that the quantum action selection model improved performance by applying a more robust balance between exploration and exploitation. Amplitude amplification has also been used by Franco (2009b) to model human judgments.

---

[5]Dong *et al.* used a temporal difference learning model rather than a Q-learning model in their work. However, S.N. Balakrishan and K. Rajagopal (personal communication) replicated the original simulations by Dong and found that the Q-learning model works better.

11.4 Summary of learning models

This chapter addresses a fairly new topic on quantum learning models. Three different types of learning models were presented. One was Bayesian updating of quantum belief states (amplitudes) based on experience with independent and identically distributed observations on the values of variables. The second was to learn a unitary map between an input probability distribution (that describes the beliefs according to one set of basis vectors) into an output probability distribution (that describes the belief states by another set of basis vectors). In this case, learning was based on a gradient descent error function that measured the discrepancy between the predicted and the observed output probability distributions. The third type was a quantum reinforcement learning model that used an amplitude amplification algorithm (analogous to the Grover search algorithm) to update the probability amplitudes for actions in a Markov decision environment. Given the early stage of this research, the proposed models are designed to inspire future research rather than to be accepted as well-supported empirical models. Much more experimental and theoretical research needs to be done to extend these models, test their validity, and compare them with more traditional learning models.

12
What are the future prospects for quantum cognition and decision?

Quantum theory has inspired many new ideas for understanding cognition and decision making. Given the nascent state of this field, many new challenges still remain. What are the strengths and unique contributions of these ideas? What are likely next steps in its development? How can it be applied to practical problems in cognitive science? Is this a rational or an irrational system of reasoning? What, if any, are its connections to neuroscience? Should the hard problem of consciousness be considered? These are questions that we try to address in this chapter, albeit at times in a limited way. We end with a debate with a fictitious skeptic (actually previous reviewers) of these ideas. Let us start by reviewing what we have covered so far.

12.1 Contributions to cognition and decision

We begin by summarizing the conclusions reached in previous chapters regarding the usefulness of quantum theory for modelling phenomena in cognition and decision. Chapter 1 provided some motivation and Chapter 2 provided a theoretical introduction to quantum theory. Chapter 3 presented a quantum model to account for question order effects on survey research. An exact and parameter-free test was derived from the model, which produced surprisingly accurate predictions for results obtained from three different large Gallup poll survey studies. Chapter 4 described a quantum model of probability judgments to account for findings that produce violations of classic probability theory, including conjunction and disjunction fallacies and order effects on inference. This chapter also compared the quantitative predictions of a quantum model with a traditional heuristic judgment model, and the quantum model was found to produce more accurate predictions. Chapter 5 examined whether or not decompositional models are sufficient for modelling the semantics of conceptual combinations. New experimental findings reported in this chapter indicate that conceptual combinations behave like quantum entangled particles in the sense the joint probability distribution across the component concepts is not factorizable. Chapter 6 developed a quantum model to explain a puzzling finding from memory recognition called the EOD – the probability for recognizing a disjunction of two mutually exclusive test items falls below the sum of the component probabilities. The predictions of the quantum model were quantitatively compared with the predictions of a more traditional Markov model previously proposed to explain these findings. Although the two models produced approximately equal fits, we argued that the quantum model provided a better interpretation of the results. Chapter 7 used quantum entanglement to model how a target word is activated in synchrony with its associates during a memory experiment. In addition, it was shown how quantum theory can be applied to model human semantic space, in particular how context effects may be modelled. Chapters 8 and 9 presented applications of quantum theory to decision making. The quantum model was shown to provide a simple account of a violation of rational decision theory called the "sure thing principle." Furthermore, the predictions of a quantum model were quantitatively compared with the predictions of a traditional model of decision making, and the quantum model once again produced more accurate predictions. Chapters 10 and 11 made the argument that QIP models provide a natural way to integrate production rule systems, connectionist neural networks, and Bayesian probabilistic reasoning systems.

The contributions of these chapters can be placed within two higher level perspectives: the first seven chapters present quantum theory as the *way that a cognitive system forms beliefs about events*; the last four chapters present quantum theory as a *dynamic probabilistic system for evolving beliefs and preferences for actions across time*.

12.1.1 Summary of part 1

An unusual feature of quantum probability theory is that probabilities of events are generated from a geometric structure. Two amazing advantages follow from using a geometric structure.

The first is the ability to rotate from one basis to another for contextualizing and interpreting events. This affords a cognitive system great flexibility in answering questions about all sorts of events, ranging from questions about whether a law is ethical to whether a scientific hypothesis is true, simply by rotating the perspective for evaluation. This unique capability of changing the basis (perspective) for describing and evaluating events is not possible using traditional (including Bayesian) probability theory, and so in this regard quantum probability theory is more expressive than its traditional, "classical" counterpart. However, this extra flexibility comes at some cost, because events described from different perspectives may be *incompatible*; that is, they cannot be viewed simultaneously, and instead they must be evaluated sequentially. Also, deciding on a definite position for one perspective forces one to become indefinite from a different perspective. Consequently, the resolution or measurement of one event disturbs the likelihood of the second, producing order effects. Although the dependence on order of measurement may seem innocuous, it turns out to cause violations of the fundamental *law of total probability*. This violation has a signature that appears throughout the cognitive and decision sciences, including the empirical findings of question order effects in surveys, conjunction and disjunction fallacies in probability judgments, violations of the sure thing principle in decision making, overextension effects in conceptual semantics, and overdistribution effects in memory recognition. Viewed from the perspective of quantum theory, these seemingly paradoxical findings are simply a natural consequence of the flexibility of a geometric approach to probability. A quantum cognitive system provides coherent (with respect to the quantum axioms) answers to questions about almost any situation it needs to confront.

A second advantage of using a geometric structure is that it allows cognitive systems to be modelled in a non-compositional, as well as compositional, way. More precisely, concept combinations can be modelled like quantum *entangled* states such that the cognitive semantics attributed to a conceptual combination cannot be recovered from the semantics of the component concepts. Following a similar intuition, word association networks in human memory can be modelled as entangled composite quantum systems. An entangled quantum state is a curious situation in which it can become impossible to construct a complete joint distribution over atoms that can be used to compose all the pairwise distributions between parts. While entangled states generate probabilistic dependencies between pairs of outcomes analogous to pairwise joint probabilities in classical probability theory, these entangled states are capable of producing dependencies that are so strong that they violate the so-called Bell inequalities which prescribe a boundary condition for maximal classical (anti-)correlation. In other words, the cognitive system in question is non-compositional in nature. Research on conceptual combinations and word associations (Chapters 5 and 7) show that violations of the Bell inequalities do in principle occur. Consequently, these violations call into question the predominant program of reductionism in cognitive science.

12.1.2   Summary of part 2

While quantum theory is a probabilistic theory, it is also a dynamic information processing theory. The dynamic part is built from what are called unitary transition operators. Unitary operators generate an evolution of beliefs across time, and they also guide behavior according to "condition–action" types of rules. Unitary operators are specially designed to be length preserving in order to fit into the requirements of the geometric structure of quantum probability theory.

An important consequence of unitary evolution is that the whole concept of state change in a quantum dynamical system is completely different than what we are used to thinking about with classical dynamic probabilistic models, such as for example the popular Markov model. According to classic dynamic models, at each moment in time during evolution the cognitive system is in some *definite* state that determines whether some property is either true (and not false) or false (and not true). Consequently, the cognitive system is restricted to follow a *single* path or trajectory produced by moving from one definite state to another across time, analogous to the motion of a particle. The theoretical situation is completely different with a quantum dynamic model. At each moment in time during evolution, the cognitive system is in a *superposition* state–this is an enigmatic state in which it is impossible to say that a property is true, but at the same time it is impossible to say that a property is false. Consequently, the cognitive system has the intriguing potential to be following any of the paths at once like a wave moving across time in parallel across all positions. That is until the moment when a decision is made, which forces the system to resolve uncertainty and select a definite position (also known as state collapse or state reduction). This essential difference in dynamics results in two important properties for distinguishing quantum from Markov systems.

The first property concerns the transition probabilities from one state to another over time used by quantum versus Markov systems. On the one hand, Markov transitions continue to be constrained by the law of total probability, but the quantum model is not. On the other hand, the unitary operator for the quantum model is constrained to obey the law of double stochasticity, but the Markov model is not. Which dynamic is correct depends on whether cognitive systems obey the law of total probability or the law of double stochasticity. Evidence is presented for the latter in Chapters 8 and 9, but clearly more research is needed before any strong conclusions can be reached on this important issue.

The second property concerns the existence of a single joint distribution for describing all combinations of events across time. According to classic dynamic models, such as the Markov model, the probabilities for pairs of events across time can all be reconstructed (using the law of total probability) from one unified joint probability distribution that describes the distribution across all paths. This is not true for quantum dynamic systems. Measurements produce disturbances in the state so that the probabilities from pairs of observations can no longer be reconstructed from a common joint distribution across all paths. In other words, violations of the temporal version of the Bell (CHSH) inequality are predicted to occur. To date, this has not yet been empirically tested, and it remains an important issue for future research.

The second part of the book also expands the view of quantum theory by presenting it as a very general information processing framework capable of learning and performing complex rules and actions. In fact, QIP systems can be viewed as a way to integrate three different traditional information processing approaches. First, quantum systems can be programmed using "if–then" control U gates to perform like production rule systems. Second, the unitary operator representation of control U gates allows these gates to be compiled into content addressable–parallel activation processors just like connectionist systems. Finally, quantum information systems provide a formal and coherent procedure for processing uncertainty and updating probabilities just like Bayesian models of cognition. Clearly, this advanced stage of theorizing for quantum cognition is more speculative and needs more experimental verification. However, it is important to understand that quantum theory is comparable to other major modelling approaches in terms of its expressivity and computational power.

12.1.3   Previous research strategy

We recognize that it is not easy to convince others to learn and accept these new ideas without some compelling theoretical and empirical reasons for doing so. That is why it is important for quantum theory to be applied to unsolved puzzles and paradoxes that are very difficult or nearly impossible to explain with more traditional theories. Each of Chapters 3 through 9 addressed phenomena that have resisted satisfactory accounts by traditional cognitive models, and in each case a relatively simple quantum model was capable of accommodating the findings. Moreover, in some cases, including Chapters 4, 5, 6, and 9, precise quantitative tests and comparisons were used to show the advantage of quantum models over more traditional models. Of course, we do not intend to claim that quantum theory is superior to traditional models at this early stage of development, but put forward the view that quantum models should be considered as a serious alternative for modelling in cognition and decision.

12.2   Directions for future research

There are many broader issues to address that provide new directions for future research. Below is a list of ideas we think have high potential, but they are not necessarily ordered in terms of importance.

1. More research is required that directly tests fundamental quantum properties. In previous chapters, we focused primarily on tests of fundamental properties of classic probability models, including the law of total probability and the Bell (CHSH) inequality. To be balanced, research is needed which designs tests of quantum properties such as the law of reciprocity (discussed in Chapters 2 and 3) and the law of double stochasticity (discussed in Chapters 8 and 9). Another important property to test is the Heisenberg inequality described at the end of Chapter 2 (Atmanspacher *et al.*, 2002). To test the uncertainty principle, it would be useful to develop models for graded types of rating scales rather than the binary choices. Graded scales allow one to independently manipulate both the mean and the variance of the responses. In this way it is possible to vary conditions and examine whether a decrease in variance for one rating scale corresponds to an increase in variance for another scale so that the product of variances exceeds the uncertainty bound.

2. Develop clearer methods for determining a priori whether or not two questions (variables or observables) are compatible versus incompatible. The issue of the compatibility between two measures plays a critical role in all quantum applications. So far, compatibility has been determined post hoc; e.g., order dependence implicates incompatibility. Much stronger predictions could be made if compatibility could be decided prior to measurement, and then used to predict when order effects occur. At the end of Chapters 3 and 4 we discussed some initial ideas about how to determine a priori whether or not two variables are compatible.

3. Develop quantum models for confidence ratings and choice response time. The three most important dependent measures in cognitive science and decision making are choice, decision time, and confidence ratings. Most of the quantum models developed in this book were designed for binary choice. Some preliminary work toward developing a quantum random walk model was presented in Chapter 9. The quantum random walk provides a unified model for choice, confidence rating, and response time. However, at this early stage of development, the current quantum random walk models do not fit as well as the traditional random walk models (Busemeyer *et al.*, 2006a). Much more experimental and theoretical work needs to be done to develop these models (Fuss & Navarro, 2008).

4. Expand the theory into new empirical domains in cognition and decision. One important area that affords a quantum investigation is the topic of similarity judgments. Recently, Pothos and Busemeyer (2011) followed up earlier ideas proposed by Sloman (1993) to use projections for modelling similarity judgments. Another important area that has high prospects is the topic of causal reasoning. This topic has been successfully addressed by Bayesian models, but if order effects occur in this domain, then that could motivate an investigation of quantum models (Trueblood & Busemeyer, 2012). A third area is to introduce quantum models into the field of social cognition and social interactions. For example, the context-dependent construal of emotions (Schachter & Singer, 1962) is a topic that may benefit from quantum modelling.

5. Theoretically examine what makes a quantum model different from a traditional cognitive model. Many cognitive models use vectors in multidimensional feature spaces as cognitive representations of perceptual objects and semantic concepts, such as for example exemplar models of categorization (Nosofsky, 1988). These traditional cognitive models also use similarity between vectors in this feature space to determine probability of responding. Furthermore, cognitive models are not necessarily constrained to obey the laws of classic probability theory (e.g., see the dual process model discussed in Chapter 6). Clearly, these models share many of the same assumptions as the quantum models. Exactly what properties are critical for distinguishing a quantum model from a traditional cognitive model? For example, Chapter 7 examines a traditional matrix model of memory (Humphreys *et al.*, 1989a) and explores its relation to quantum concepts. One aspect that distinguishes quantum models from current models of cognitive systems is that quantum theory offers the possibility to model cognitive phenomena in a noncompositional way. The traditional matrix model of memory just mentioned is compositional, as the tensors used to construct it are product states, and hence factorizable. Quantum theory allows us to extend such models into non-compositional structures; however, for this purpose a suitable dynamics needs to be developed. Chapter 7 provided an initial illustration of how the model of a target word's associative structure can be

transformed into an entangled state, but more research is necessary for other transformations.

6. Explore relations with other generalized theories of uncertainty. This includes theories such as the Dempster–Shafer belief function theory (Shafer, 1976) or fuzzy logic theory (Zadeh, 1965) or intuitionist probability theory (Narens, 2007). Belief function theory has become popular in artificial intelligence (Halpern & Fagin, 1992), fuzzy reasoning has attracted decision researchers (Wallsten *et al.*, 1992) and psychologists (Reyna & Brainerd, 1995), and intuitionist models have been used to model probability judgments (Narens, 2009). How do these theories overlap and what are the strengths and weaknesses of each approach?

7. Develop and test models for quantum systems that integrate learning and memory with decision models. The end of Chapter 11 described some initial steps along these lines, but given the importance of combining learning, memory, and decision making for cognitive science, much more needs to be done on this topic. The quantum reinforcement learning model (Dong *et al.*, 2010) described in Chapter 11 has been most thoroughly examined, but only on the basis of computer simulations that compare learning rates for the quantum model and traditional reinforcement learning models. These models still need to be compared with human learning data.

8. Develop stronger linkages to quantum game theory. Research in game theory is distinguished from individual decision-making research by the introduction of multiple agents with possibly conflicting goals. Chapters 8 and 9 of this book only covered issues related to individual decision making. However, there is a large and growing field of quantum game theory initiated by Meyer (1999) and Eisert *et al.* (1999) (see also Piotrowski and Sladkowski (2002)). Many of the theoretical applications initiated by quantum game theory require the use of a physical quantum computer to provide quantum strategies. But more recently, work has appeared in which traditional game theory is extended by assuming that the agents hold quantum beliefs about their opponents (Lambert-Mogiliansky & Busemeyer, 2009). The latter type of work is more relevant to quantum cognition and decision research because these applications to game theory do not require quantum computers for implementation. In addition, the structural similarity between a biased two-penny game and modelling bi-ambiguous concepts combinations was recently brought to light (Bruza *et al.*, 2010).

12.3   Practical applications of quantum cognition

One potentially important area of application for quantum cognition is the field of information retrieval (IR) (van Rijsbergen, 2004). In fact, some initial success in this direction has been made by using quantum projection methods to represent retrieval cues that require negation, conjunction, and disjunction (Widdows & Bruza, 2007).

More importantly, the field of information retrieval lacks suitable user models of how users interact with the system. These interactions are based on decisions which are cognitively situated; for example, whether or not a document is relevant, or which terms to use in order to reformulate the query. Fallacies of decision making are likely to be active in this setting. For example, the conjunction fallacy may be manifest in decisions of topical relevance. Unsurprisingly, topic models such as latent Dirichlet allocation (Griffiths et $al.$, 2007) adhere to the following conjunctive property as it is based on classical probability: $p(z_i, z_j|d) \leq p(z_i|d)$, where z_i, z_j correspond to two topics and d is a document. Just like in the conjunction fallacy exemplified by the Linda example, it may well be that the user may judge $p(z_i, z_j|d) > p(z_i|d)$ particularly when topics z_i, z_j are both topically related to the information needed. As a consequence, decisions made by the system about topics are at odds with what the user would expect, potentially resulting in the loss of retrieval precision.

Decisions on topical relevance may involve incompatibility – certainty about the relevance of a topic may lead to uncertainty about the decision of the relevance of another topic. In other words, decisions about the relevance of topics may interfere – a user-related phenomenon that is acknowledged in various ways in the literature, but which is only beginning to receive serious consideration (e.g., Zuccon et $al.$, 2010). The same can be said for modelling relevance in IR. Relevance is generally conceived to have various dimensions; e.g., topical relevance (is the document topically related to my query?), trust (do I trust the author?), sentiment (does the information appeal to me?). These dimensions are considered to be more or less orthogonal, but it is easy to imagine the presence of interference effects (e.g., Wang et $al.$, 2010). In a quantum approach, relevance could be modelled by projecting a person's state vector onto various subspaces, each corresponding to a dimension of relevance, but where the subspaces may be incompatible and hence imply the presence of interference effects within relevance judgments. For example, with the emergence of Web 2.0 there are many online discussion fora in which the sentiment dimension of relevance is clearly evident in relation to controversial topics. It is easy to imagine that strong sentiment may interfere with decisions of topical relevance in relation to some strident on-line debate. The theory provided in Chapter 4 could be applied and extended to provide more cognitively motivated models of relevance, which conceivably could have computational counterparts in actual IR systems. Some initial steps in this direction have already been taken by incorporating interference effects in document ranking (Zuccon & Azzopardi, 2010).

The effectiveness of IR systems has only been in small increments for some time. This has led a growing number of researchers in the field to believe that the effectiveness of systems has basically "hit the wall," and major advances are only possible with sufficiently good models of users. An important aspect of such models is reliably modelling information-related decisions. The theory and models presented in this book could provide useful input to the development of such models, not only for IR, but also for other information processing systems.

Another potentially important area of application is the the field of non-monotonic reasoning (NMR). Previous work has successfully provided an impressive account of human practical reasoning at the symbolic level of cognition in which information is represented as logical propositions. We feel that the symbolic characterization of practical reasoning is only part of the picture.

Gärdenfors (2000: 127) argues that one must go under the symbolic level of cognition. In this vein, he states,

> ...information about an object may be of two kinds: *propositional* and *conceptual*. When the new information is propositional, one learns new *facts* about the object, for example, that x is a penguin. When the new information is conceptual, one *categorizes* the object in a new way, for example, x is *seen as* a penguin instead of as just a bird.

Gärdenfors' mention of "conceptual" refers to the conceptual level of a three-level model of cognition (Gärdenfors, 2000). How information is represented varies greatly across the different levels. The sub-conceptual level is the lowest level within which information is carried by a connectionist representation. Within the uppermost level information is represented symbolically. It is the intermediate, *conceptual level*, or *conceptual space*, which is of particular relevance to this book. Within this level, properties and concepts have a geometric representation in a dimensional space.

Chapter 5 explored some of the connections by means of a quantum-like model of concept combinations. What is yet to be satisfactorily explored is the connection with practical reasoning. Inference at the symbolic level is typically a linear, deductive process. Within conceptual space, inference takes on a decidedly associational character because associations are often based on similarity (e.g., semantic or analogical similarity), and notions of similarity are naturally expressed within a dimensional space. For example, Gärdenfors states that a natural interpretation of defaults represented at the symbolic level is to view them as "relations between concepts," e.g., the default associated with "Reagan" is "president." These relations change under context, as was shown in Chapter 7. When "Reagan" is seen in the context of "Iran," the default association is "scandal." The whole question of inference becomes more challenging with concept combinations such as "pet human." In word association experiments, human subjects readily produce the associate "slave" in relation to this combination. The striking aspect of this associate is that it is not produced as an associate of "pet," or "human" in isolation. In other words, the associate "slave" seems to be emergent. Such emergent associations are prevalent, sometimes having a highly creative character, and cognitive science is largely silent about how we produce them. An intriguing line of further research involves exploring how non-compositional conceptual semantics (Chapter 5) relates to such emergent inferences. Quantum approaches are starting to make some inroads in this regard

(Aerts & Gabora, 2005; Gabora *et al.*, 2008). A related question is how such emergent associates relate to a creative mode of practical inference known as abduction (Gabbay & Woods, 2005).

12.4   Quantum rationality

How does one determine whether a system of reasoning is rational? There are at least two ways to do this, and neither is perfect. One approach is to demand a set of axioms that guide the behavior of the system and then a judgment is made whether each of these axioms is reasonable. For example, expected utility theory of decision making (von Neumann & Morgenstern, 1944) is considered to be a rational theory of decision making because it is based on a small set of compelling axioms. A second way is to empirically examine the predictions derived from the system and evaluate their accuracy. Kolmogorov's theory of probability is often justified on the basis of the fact that it produces the correct relative frequencies for many simple experiments.

The problem with the first method is that each axiom in a set can appear to be reasonable, yet the entire system can be logically inconsistent, as demonstrated for example by Arrow's famous impossibility theorem for group decision making. The problem with the second method is that all theories and models are wrong to some extent and in some situations. For example, Kolmogorov's theory breaks down with experiments in particle physics. Consequently, when using the second method, we need to enter into the extremely difficult process of deciding which theory is more accurate and under what situations.

Quantum probability theory is based on a small and coherent set of axioms (actually there are numerous ways to axiomatize the theory). The axioms are primarily based on defining events in terms of subspaces, and then Gleason's theorem forces the particular rule for computing the probabilities. When all the events are compatible, quantum probabilities satisfy the same properties as classic probabilities and meet the same rational standards in this restricted case. The main question of rationality arises when incompatible events become involved.

With respect to accuracy, there is no question about the supremacy of quantum over Newtonian physics (although Newtonian physics remains applicable in many situations). The question addressed here is whether a human judge would be more or less accurate at predicting daily life events when relying on a quantum probability system as compared with the classic Kolmogorov system. The answer here might depend on the situation. If one is predicting something simple such as the face of a coin when it is flipped or the number on a die when it is cast, it is certainly better to use a classic probability model (or, equivalently, a quantum model that treats the events as compatible). If one is predicting something more complex and significant, such as the behavior of another person, then (as we have tried to show in this book) it may be better to use a quantum system. If one is predicting the behavior of some even more complex highly interconnected multi-agent mixed human–machine system, it is really unclear at this point which is better. For such complex systems the joint probabilities for all the events are either unknown or ill-defined. These types of complex systems contain many hidden factors and unobserved variables. Under these conditions, quantum statistical models might provide more accurate predictions than classic statistical models that rely heavily on strong conditional independence assumptions.

As pointed out by several physicists,[1] quantum theory was designed for complex situations in which one cannot observe all of the variables at once that are needed to fully understand the behavior of a system. Only partial information about the system can be observed at any moment in time, and the statistics that are observed summarize the results of many hidden interactions. Despite this restriction on information that we can obtain about the system, the probabilities from partial and coarse observations are related in a systematic manner and follow coherent laws. The strength of quantum theory is its capability of representing all of these statistical relations in a simple and systematic manner.

Kolmogorov (1933/1950) actually understood very well the limits of a theory built upon the tight restrictions of Boolean logic. He clearly pointed out that his axioms apply to a sample space from a *single* experiment, and different experiments require *new* sample spaces. The Boolean structure was not intended to be carried over all of these different experiments. However, he never built a theory to connect these sample spaces from different experiments back together, and his predecessors stressed models that forced everything into a single sample space. Quantum theory was designed to account for multiple experiments (Gudder, 1988) by using only a partial Boolean structure. It provides a coherent theory that connects the sample spaces from different experiments together into a unified probabilistic account.

As Herb Simon (Simon, 1957) pointed out long ago, human limitations and boundaries must always be considered when evaluating rationality. In earlier chapters we have argued that the cognitive system is constantly faced with a tremendously complex task. It must be prepared to answer all kinds of questions ranging from science, to ethics, to sports, and even romance, without any idea of what the entire joint probability distribution is like. One way to achieve this ability in a resourceful and efficient way is to form new descriptions of events for each topic by changing the perspective (basis) used to evaluate them. Within any fixed N-dimensional space, there is an infinite number of perspectives one can choose, which provides a vast number of ways to describe events, and this may be an effective way of dealing with the complex task that the cognitive system faces. For some environments it may be more efficient to represent some variables in an incompatible way, but for other environments it may be more effective to represent other variables in a compatible way. So the key to bounded rationality is learning when to represent variables as compatible versus incompatible in order to maximize accuracy, efficiency, and generalizability (Gigerenzer, 2000).

---

[1] See for example Aerts (2011), Graben and Atmanspacher (2008), Khrennikov (2007), and Yukalov and Sornette (2010).

12.5   Neuroscience and quantum theory

As mentioned in the first chapter of this book, at this early stage, researchers applying quantum principles to cognition and decision making are primarily concerned with understanding *human behavior*. Their goal is to develop new applications of the *core mathematical* principles of quantum theory to behavioral research findings; that is, they motivate the use of quantum models as innovative abstractions of existing problems. These abstractions have the character of idealizations in the sense there is no claim as to the validity of the idealization "on the ground." For example, work on quantum-like models on the human mental lexicon (Chapter 7) involves modelling words in human memory as entangled systems. There is no associated claim as to whether there is physical quantum entanglement going on somewhere in the brain. This may seem like a cop out, but is not that different to other idealizations employed in science. For example, in models of neural dynamics, the activity of large populations is often idealized as continuous, even though individual neurons are discretely firing. Quantum cognition research remains agnostic toward the so-called "quantum mind" hypothesis which is highly contentious. In this way, the quantum cognition program has the same goals as the Bayesian cognition program, which is also concerned primarily with understanding human behavior. However, the current focus on behavior does not preclude the eventual building of bridges to neuroscience in the future, and this section gives some general ideas about how such bridges could possibly be built.

A great deal of theoretical effort has been invested in neurophysiological models of the brain inspired in one way or another by quantum theory. Below is a brief description of four different theories. Only the first two theories, the Penrose–Hameroff theory and the Beck–Eccles theory, actually posit quantum physical effects in the brain that have meaningful relations to higher level cognition and decision. The third theory, initiated by Ricciardi–Umezawa, uses quantum field theory as a tool for deriving macroscopic physical brain states, and the last theory by de Barros and Suppes proposes that classic neural oscillators underlie the quantum statistics observed in behavior.

12.5.1   Two quantum brain models of consciousness

Before discussing the first two theories, let us point out two related issues concerning the scientific effort to build quantum computers. There is great interest in building quantum computers because they hold the promise of solving complex problems much faster than our current computers by taking advantage of the parallel computations afforded by superposition states (Nielsen & Chuang, 2000). The human brain also seems capable of performing very complex tasks with amazing speed and facility. This suggests the hypothesis that perhaps the brain can achieve this performance because it is some type of quantum computer? However, one of the main difficulties with building quantum computers is to keep the quantum systems isolated so that they do not interact with the environment. Environmental interaction causes decoherence; that is, the state evolves from a desired superposition state into an undesired mixed state. This also becomes an important issue for quantum brain computations – How can quantum computations possibly occur in a wet and hot and noisy brain environment without rapid decoherence?

The Penrose (1989)–Hameroff (1998) theory has attracted the most attention and debate. Their solution to the decoherence problem is that important quantum brain computations occur inside microtubules that lie within the protection of the cytoskeleton of a neuron. The microtubules are interconnected at the gap junctions of dendrites, and these connections extend throughout the cortex to produce a coherent entangled quantum state. The collapse of the quantum superposition state within the microtubules can trigger axonal spikes and govern behavior. This state reduction also generates a conscious experience. The frequency of collapse is synchronized within the gamma range of an EEG (approximately one collapse every 25 ms; that is, 40 Hz). In between collapses, the quantum state evolves unconsciously according to unitary evolution. Hameroff and his colleagues provide more details about the possible neurophysiological mechanisms underlying these connections between quantum theory and consciousness (Woolf & Hameroff, 2001). However, the theory has been criticized because a detailed analysis of decoherence times in the brain indicates that the decoherence time is extremely fast – so fast that it would be nearly impossible to perform any meaningful computations (Tegmark, 2000); but see the reply of Hagan et al. (2002). Subsequently, there have been other rebuttals and replies to this issue, but the general opinion seems to be that this remains a highly speculative idea. Criticisms have also appeared in the cognitive science literature (Litt et al., 2006), but again there is a reply (Hameroff, 2007).

Beck and Eccles (1992) proposed a detailed quantum model of the chemical process called exocytosis that occurs during polarization at the synaptic clef of a single neuron. The relevance of this theory for cognition is based on the idea that consciousness occurs in the dendrites, and that conscious intentions can enter into the quantum state reduction process at a dendrite. While it is certainly plausible that quantum physics is involved with this basic chemical reaction process, the question about how these micro-level details scale up to affect macro-level cognitive processing remains unanswered. So while this theory may remain a viable model of the chemical process for exocytosis, its implications for cognition and decision making remain vague.

12.5.2 A quantum field theory of memory

Ricciardi and Umezawa (1967) formulated a quantum field theoretical model of memory. (Quantum field theory is a very extensive generalization of quantum mechanics that provides the most precisely tested theory of elementary particles and solid state physics, but this theory goes beyond what is covered in this book.) The original theoretical effort was followed up by Jibu and Yasue (1995) and Vitiello (1995), who included effects of dissipation, chaos, and quantum noise (see also Pribram (1993) for related work; and see Vitiello (2001) for a readable introduction.) A hallmark of quantum field theory is to provide a mechanism for generating ordered states in many-body systems.[2] In this application, quantum field theory provides a mathematical framework from which a standard classical description of brain activity can be derived. The dynamically ordered states represent "memory states" of coherent activity in neuronal assemblies. These memory states are inequivalent representations of ground states in quantum fields, and classical activity of correlated neuronal assemblies emerge from spontaneous symmetry breaking of quantum fields. The wave packet in this quantum field application does not describe probability amplitudes, but rather it is a collective mode that sustains a field of neural activity, which gives rise to observable fields of electroencephalographic potentials recorded from the scalp (EEGs) and electrophysiologically recorded action potentials. Quantum field theory is argued to be the only theoretical tool capable of explaining the dynamic origin of long-range correlations, their stability, the multiplicity of stable states, and their rapid formation and dissolution. Empirical support for the theory is based on its account of EEG signals that exhibit diverse intermittent spatial patterns of waves, which repeatedly resynchronize in the beta and gamma ranges in very short time lags over very long distances (Freeman & Vitiello, 2006). This model also accounts for the scale-free features observed in the brain functional activity, establishing a link between the fractal behavior and the coherence of the correlated neuronal assemblies (Vitiello, 2009). Unfortunately, this theory has received insufficient attention from researchers in mainstream neuroscience.

12.5.3 A neural model of interference

Recently, de Barros and Suppes (2009) proposed an alternative way to relate neuroscience to quantum theory. Interference effects can occur in behavior without requiring quantum physical effects in the brain. More specifically, they propose that the underlying neurophysiological processes are neural assemblies of synchronized neural oscillators, but these neural oscillators produce wave mechanical type interference effects, and perhaps the latter can be modelled efficiently using quantum theory. They point out that neural oscillations can be observed by recording an EEG (Freeman, 1979), and cortical oscillations may propagate in the cortex as if they are waves (Nunez & Srinivasan, 2006). Synchronized cortical oscillations in different regions of the cortex are related to cognitive processes and perhaps even consciousness (Ward, 2003).

The basic idea is that networks of excitatory and inhibitory neurons generate oscillations in populations of membrane potentials of an interconnected network across time. The firing of shunting interneurons inhibits a network of neurons for a period of time during which they cannot fire; but this inhibition eventually wears off, allowing excitatory inputs to activate these same neurons. Neurons that are synchronized with activation recover from inhibition as activation is applied, while neurons that are not synchronized remain unavailable for

---

[2]It may come as a surprise to many readers to know that quantum field theory is not limited to the microscopic world, but is in fact responsible for explaining the organization of macro objects in warm environments such as the familiar magnet (Blasone *et al.*, 2011).

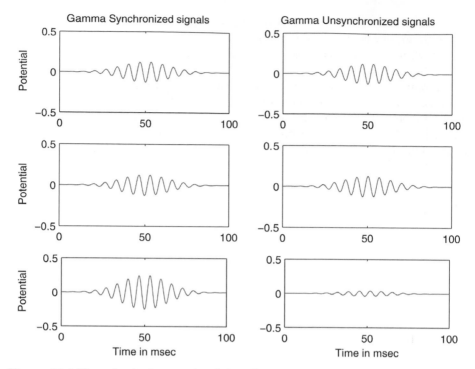

Figure 12.1 Hypothetical example of the effect of synchronization of input presynaptic neurons on a target post-synaptic neuron. The inputs are synchronized on the left and unsynchronized on the right. Bottom panels show the superposition effect.

activation. As illustrated in Figure 12.1, a superposition of synchronized presynaptic inputs has greater impact on their post-synaptic target neurons. On the one hand, if two neural systems oscillate in phase, their synchronized waves combine constructively to strengthen activation above each separate system at the critical time points when they are released from inhibition. See left panel of Figure 12.1. On the other hand, if the two neural systems oscillate out of phase, then their unsynchronized waves combine destructively and remain below each separate system (Suppes *et al.*, 2011). See right panel of Figure 12.1.

The quantum state of a cognitive system is considered to be a working memory state (Baddeley, 1992), which is used to evaluate beliefs and preferences under the context provided by the current situation. The activation pattern produced by assemblies of synchronized neural oscillators could be used to serve as mechanisms for neurally coding the magnitudes of the amplitudes that describe the quantum state. The current context serves as a cue for retrieving or activating a working memory state in long-term memory (Atkinson & Shiffrin, 1968). Unitary operators and projection operators represent the long-term memory associations of a quantum cognitive system. Projection operations in a quantum model can be performed by a matched filter type of neural network. The unitary transformation can be performed by connectionist-type networks that associate input to output patterns. The main issue is whether the brain has developed neural coding systems capable of computing the types of transformations required by unitary operators.

As pointed out in Chapter 2 (see Section 2.3.9.1), unitary operators essentially perform a type of Fourier transformation of inputs into outputs that code amplitude and phase information for a spectrum of frequencies.[3] There is substantial evidence that the brain uses both amplitude and phase coding (Fries *et al.*, 2007) to coordinate cortical computations that subserve high-level cognitive functions (Fries, 2009).

12.5.4   Standing uncommitted

In summary, there are several competing ideas about how to build bridges between neuroscience and quantum theory. But quantum cognition and decision researchers generally remain uncommitted and not bound to any one of these ideas. Instead, by focusing on human behavior, work in quantum cognition and decision can proceed and inform future advances on the neurophysiological underpinnings.

12.6   The hard problem of consciousness

Why do we have conscious experiences and what causes these experiences? These are hard questions to answer, and there is a very extensive philosophical literature on the topic (Chalmers, 1996). In this section, we briefly discuss the relevance of consciousness for quantum cognition and decision.[4]

As mentioned in Chapter 1, there are long-standing connections between quantum theory and consciousness. This connection began with some prominent quantum theorists, such as von Neumann and Wigner, speculating that human observation is essential for quantum state reduction. Later, Stapp and Penrose became advocates for a quantum physical model of the brain, and they stepped forward to tackle the hard problem of understanding when and why we have conscious experiences. Both argue for a strong correlation between conscious experience and quantum state collapse (state reduction) that occurs in the brain when a decision is reached. However, they differ on the causal direction. On the one hand, Stapp (2009) argues for the causal effect that conscious experience has on physical state reduction, which implies that mind can somehow influence matter. On the other hand, Penrose (1989) argues that quantum state reduction causes a conscious experience. Matter influences mind by producing

---

[3]The complex exponential used in unitary and Fourier transformations simply provides a mathematically efficient tool for combining pairs of sine and cosine functions, and the latter are used to determine the amplitude and phase at each frequency.

[4]See the excellent article by Atmanspacher (2011) for a review of efforts to relate quantum theory and consciousness.

an experience that cannot be computed algorithmically. A comparison of the two positions is presented by Schwartz *et al.* (2005).

12.6.1   Where does consciousness enter into traditional cognitive and decision theories?

In cognitive science, discussions of ideas about consciousness often arise in connection with research on the important topic of attention (Pashler, 1998). Although they are distinct concepts, a strong link between attention and consciousness was strongly forged very early by William James (James, 1890). The behavioral revolution in psychology that occurred in the 1920s cut off almost all discussion of conscious events, and this prohibition persisted until the cognitive revolution that occurred in the 1960s. Even today the topic of consciousness remains a dubious topic somewhat on the fringe of research in cognitive science and decision making.

Rather than addressing the hard problem on the origins of conscious experience, cognitive theorists are concerned with the easier problems of identifying the kind of cognitive processes that are available to consciousness as well as how much conscious attention various kinds of tasks require. For example, the automatic versus controlled theory of information processing (Shiffrin & Schneider, 1977) posits that complex tasks with varied input and output mappings require slow serial processing, large attentional resources, and conscious control, whereas simple tasks with consistent mappings can become automated and performed unconsciously in a fast and parallel manner without requiring attentional resources. In addition, cognitive psychologists have proposed different types of reasoning systems that are related to conscious attention – an associative system in which one is unaware of the process and only aware of the result and a rule-based system that involves awareness of both process and result (Sloman, 1996). Decision scientists have also proposed different types of human decision-making processes that are related to conscious deliberation – some individuals tend to rely more on unconscious intuitive processes, while others tend to rely more on conscious analytic processes (Hammond, 1987; Epstein *et al.*, 1992; Stanovich & West, 2000). Social cognition research has focused on the role of conscious awareness in attitude formation. This research examines the different types of information that are processed either implicitly (relatively unconsciously) versus explicitly (relatively consciously) during attitude information (Smith & Decoster, 2000; Rydell *et al.*, 2006). In the field of learning, there remains debate whether learning can only take place with awareness or whether learning can occur without awareness (Dulany *et al.*, 1984).

12.6.2   Where does consciousness enter into quantum cognition and decision?

Consciousness is not necessarily a central topic in quantum cognition and decision research either. However, as pointed out in Chapter 1, the idea of state reduction (state collapse) is central. State reduction refers to the process of making a decision by resolving an indeterminate (superposition) state into a determinant state, and updating the resolved state according to Lüder's rule. For example, initially we may be uncertain about whether an event is true or not, but after learning some new facts, the uncertainty is resolved into a definite value of truth; or initially we are uncertain about which course of action to take, but after evaluating the consequences we resolve this indecision into a definite course of action. Quantum cognition and decision researchers must be able to identify the conditions that cause the decision to resolve the superposition state.

Stapp, Penrose and Hameroff have all argued that humans remain unconscious during unitary state evolution and state reduction entails a conscious experience. Generally, this seems like a compelling idea, and in fact something along these lines was assumed in the previous chapters. But on further thought this tight connection between state reduction and consciousness comes under question for two reasons. First, humans are aware of their indecision and uncertainty before reaching a decision, and they are able to assess this indecision by reporting confidence ratings or probability estimates. Second, decisions are sometimes reached without any conscious awareness of why or when it happened. A person may suddenly realize that an issue has been resolved without knowing when or how it got resolved. Memory is a confounding factor in this issue, because one might easily forget a previously experienced conscious resolution. In short, the connection between consciousness and state reduction remains an empirical question.

Measurement is assumed to cause state reduction, but what constitutes a measurement in cognition and decision? Consider a juror on a jury evaluating conflicting evidence regarding a crime. Before making up his or her mind, the juror is indefinite or superposed with regard to guilt or innocence. After deliberation, if the juror is asked to make an irreversible and consequential decision, and the juror finally decides and commits to a guilty verdict, then a state reduction could occur. But during deliberation, if the juror is simply asked for an intermediate assessment and inconsequential judgment of likelihood of guilt, then this judgment could leave the person in the same indefinite state as before the judgment. Unlike subatomic particles in quantum physics, it seems possible for humans to assess their superposition state without disturbing it.

Often, it is assumed that if a person is asked a question by an outsider and the person responds with an answer, then this implies that the person's state has been "measured." That is, the person has resolved an indefinite state into a definite state that matches the answer. While this may often be true, it is not necessarily the case. If a man asks his wife if he gained weight over the holidays, she may answer "no" without resolving any uncertainty about his weight simply to avoid hurting his feelings. A response (measurement) may not always induce a conscious resolution of uncertainty. In this case, the response is a only noisy measure of state change. Quantum noise models (as discussed in Chapter 8) may be required under many circumstances. Quantum noise models were developed in physics to account for noisy measurements such as detectors failing to record an electron emission (Gardiner, 1991).

Cognitive and decision neuroscientists can now peek inside the brain during deliberation using functional magnetic resonance imaging (fMRI) and evoked response potentials (ERPs).[5] Do these neurophysiological measurements of the brain cause state reduction? For example, using ERP recordings from the scalp, an experimenter can record a voltage potential on each side of the head above the pre-motor areas that prepare for left- versus right-hand trigger movements. This ERP measure is called the lateralized readiness potential (Gratton *et al.*, 1988). If a choice is executed by a device triggered by the left or right hand, then the lateralized readiness potential provides an estimate of the neural preparation for movements to either hand. Indirectly, the lateralized readiness potential measures the preference state at each moment in time. Does this measurement cause a collapse and conscious resolution of a decision? Apparently not, because the lateralized readiness potential vacillates for an extended period before a decision is reached. As another example, fMRI scans can be used to observe activation of brain areas during ongoing decision processes before a decision is reached without stopping the process (Ahn *et al.*, 2011).

Suppose that no question is asked by an outsider and no decision is externally reported. Will the person remain in an indefinite state or can a person perform a "self-measurement" and store (record) the result in memory? Consider the juror example once again. Will the juror remain indefinite until he or she is forced by an outsider to commit and make an irreversible decision, or can the juror resolve this judgment by him or herself ahead of the commitment time? It seems reasonable to assume that the latter is not only possible but most common. As discussed in Chapter 8, if a person is given as much time as needed to make a choice, then periodic "self-measurements" of the state are needed to check and determine whether or not the reduced state has crossed a threshold for stopping deliberation and making a final decision.

The possibility of "self-measurement" raises interesting new psychological and philosophical issues for quantum theory that do not arise in classic theory. The issue is *not* just concerned with state reduction per se. Recall from Chapter 8 that both Markov and quantum models exhibit what could be interpreted as "state reduction" or "state collapse" following an observation – the probability (classic) or amplitude (quantum) distributions are updated according to the new observation in both Markov and quantum systems (using Bayes' rule for the former and Lüder's rule for the latter). Also recall from Chapter 8 that both Markov and quantum systems are non-commutative with respect to a sequence of measurements. Neither non-commutativity nor state reduction is unique to quantum theory! But there is a critical difference injected by using amplitudes as primitives rather than probabilities. The critical difference is that the act of measurement itself, even when ignoring its outcome, changes the future probabilities of events in the quantum model, but not in the Markov model. According to the Markov model, the total probability of some future event, *averaged over the possible values of a measurement*, remains the same as if no observation was made at all. According to the quantum model, the total probability of some

---

[5]We thank our colleague Professor Zheng Wang for raising the next question.

future event, *averaged over the possible values of the observed event*, is *not* the same as if no observation was made at all because of interference effects. Thus, self-measurements produce more fundamental changes in the cognitive system for quantum models compared with classic models. This gives humans the inexplicable power to change themselves (generate state reduction) by the nature and the timing of the questions (choice of measurements) that they ask themselves (Schwartz *et al.*, 2005).

In conclusion, the concept of measurement, resolution of indeterminacy, conscious decisions, and state reduction is much more subtle and complicated, as well as intriguing, with humans than it is with microscopic subatomic particles.

12.7 Can only misbegotten fallacies result from a marriage between quantum and cognition?

Reviewers tend to be skeptical of new ideas, such as applying quantum theory to cognition and decision. We agree that this is the proper scientific attitude to take. Reviewers are very useful for raising a number of interesting critical questions that have to be answered. These questions might also arise in the minds of readers, and so we end by providing some answers to some of these challenging questions.

Reviewer: The conceptual foundations of quantum mechanics are notoriously counter-intuitive, so why should this mathematics provide a way to explain people's intuitions? Of course, such a first reaction does not mean the idea is wrong, but the idea faces more than the usual burden of convincing skeptical readers. The central problem with quantum cognition is its avoidance of obvious conceptual questions about *why* one would posit a "quantum" explanation for human cognitive biases in the first place. I do not see how it is possible to avoid addressing the "elephant in the room" – i.e., what is the rationale for bringing QM into psychology at all!

Authors: Six extensive psychological reasons are presented in Chapter 1, and they are summarized at the beginning of this chapter as well. But it may be useful to point out one more reason. Quantum probability is *not* an exotic theory as many believe. (Perhaps the reputation for being an incomprehensible theory comes from some very complex mathematical applications experienced in college physics classes.) The essential quantum axioms are quite simple, and they are a few small steps away from classic Kolmogorov and Markov theory. However, those small steps are psychologically meaningful, and they provide the crucial steps needed to account for what seem to be paradoxes from the classic perspective.

Reviewer: The quantum probability framework is very flexible and can be used to describe almost any behavior with the appropriate set of additional background assumptions. If the motivation from the beginning is just to relax some assumptions in classical probability theory, it only feeds the reader's suspicion that this approach is going to be very hard to constrain or test in strong (falsifiable) ways. What is the added value? Obviously it is much more "flexible" than standard probability theory, so it can post hoc account for anomalies for standard probability theory. But, I was not convinced there was a special advantage to applying a probability theory originally invented to handle atomic and subatomic phenomena to human judgments. The question I kept struggling with was: Is the claim that the approach is "compatible" with these phenomena, or does it actually predict them?

Authors: Quantum theory is based on axioms from which one can mathematically derive numerous a-priori and parameter-free predictions. In particular, all quantum models must obey the law of double stochasticity and the law of reciprocity, and these constraints on the quantum model are *not* required by Markov models. The law of reciprocity was directly empirically tested in Chapter 3. Other strong predictions are derived for each of the phenomena covered in this book. For example, consider the conjunction and disjunction fallacies described in Chapter 4. The quantum model for these fallacies must predict that these errors only occur when one event has a high likelihood and the other has a low likelihood, zero errors should occur when the two probabilities are equal, no errors can occur for complementary events, these errors only occur if order effects also occur, no double conjunction errors can occur, and, finally, conjunction errors occur only when there is a positive dependency of the unlikely event on the likely event. Finally, Chapter 5 provides a clear dividing line for determining when conceptual semantics are compositional, or not.

Reviewer: The bottom line of my review is the same as before: I think the only way most readers will overcome the barriers to reading this book and make the investment needed to understand it is if it is clear that they will get enough "bang for their buck," that the mathematical framework has strong quantitative power to explain and predict people's judgments, and in particular judgments that other frameworks cannot account for in a compelling way.

Authors: This is a very important point and we have tried to address this point in the book by two strategies. First, we tackle phenomena that are so puzzling that they have resisted formal (mathematical) traditional accounts for many years. This includes, for example, the conjunction fallacy described in Chapter 4, how to model non-compositional conceptual semantics described in Chapter 5, and violations of the sure thing principle described in Chapter 9. Second, we provided several quantitative predictions and comparisons of these predictions with competing traditional models (using the same number of free parameters) and found the quantum model to be superior in most cases and equal in others. This includes model comparisons presented in Chapters 4, 6, and 9.

Reviewer: Quantum logic applies to events that are intrinsically incompatible (e.g., the position and momentum of a particle). The events described in cognitive experiments are not of this nature. As far as the world is concerned, one can simultaneously be a feminist and a bank teller. This part of our world is truly classical. If the human mind has to use quantum logic to judge events in a classical world, the misfit does not make the deviations less of a fallacy, and a person who makes it is not less wrong about it. So why do we need to use incompatible events, and is this not irrational? For all of the examples of cognitive biases that the authors introduce, and that interest them throughout the book, they are clearly biases about *the classical world*. To put it bluntly: if you believe that Linda is more likely to be a bank teller active in the feminist movement than a bank teller, then no appeal to quantum mechanics is going to save you!! You are simply mistaken.

Authors: Yes, we agree that the conjunction fallacy by itself is truly an error in an absolute sense. However, as we argued in Section 12.4 on "quantum rationality," human limitations and boundaries must always be considered when evaluating the rationality of an entire system when applied to a wide range of problems. The cognitive system is constantly faced with a tremendously complex task of answering all kinds of questions without any idea of the entire joint probability distribution. One way to achieve this ability in a coherent manner is to use incompatible representations. This may reflect an effective trade-off between dealing with a complex world while tolerating errors in artificially simplified cases.

Reviewer: What sets up the feature space representation? This seems essential to understanding how the quantum framework is to be applied. But, without specifying how the features are set up, the framework seems to have the capacity to explain almost anything, as in unconstrained feature-based models of similarity.

Authors: The problem of setting up the feature space is carried out by the same methods as used in Bayesian models. In a Bayesian model, first one needs to postulate a sample space that describes all the events that can occur (assume finite for simplicity). The cardinality of this set determines the number of elementary events in the sample space. Each elementary event in a Bayesian model is a combination of possible feature values. A single feature value is constructed from the union of feature combinations. The joint probabilities for these feature combinations are constructed from a Bayesian causal network. The same method is used in quantum theory. First, one postulates a Hilbert space and the (finite for simplicity) dimension determines the number of basis vectors. Each basis vector corresponds to a feature combination just like the Bayesian model. A subspace spanned by a subset of basis vectors represents a single feature value. The probability amplitudes for the feature combinations can be constructed from a quantum causal network as described in Chapter 11.

Reviewer: What cognitive meaning is represented by a state of belief $\psi_A = [1, 1, 1, 1]^\dagger / 2$ versus a state of belief $\psi_B = [-i, i, 1, -1]^\dagger / 2$?

Authors: The answer is there is essentially no difference in cognitive states – they both generate four equally likely events. Only the basis used to describe the coordinates has changed by an arbitrary phase factor. The cognitive belief state prior to a decision can always be expressed in terms of positive real amplitudes by transforming to an appropriate basis prior to measurement of the belief.

Reviewer: Let me point out simple predictions of the quantum model as concerns the conjunction of two incompatible events "U" (an unlikely event) and "L" (a likely event). The conjunction "L and then U" involves the sequence of projections PL followed by PU. This means that, conditional on the response "yes" to both of the questions "L and then U," the following probability predictions ensue: Prob("U"|"L and then U") = 1, Prob("L"|"L and then U") < 1. Note that the initially unlikely event "U" has now become certain and that answering yes to the question "L," given that "L and then U" was already confirmed, is less than certain.

Authors: We must predict that Prob("U"|"L and then U") = 1, provided you ask again immediately. If you wait for a while, then other thoughts or information can disturb the state and reduce this probability. In fact, the person can review the story facts and revise the state based on this review so that it returns to the initial state in the same way it was generated at the beginning. We must predict Prob("L"|"L and then U") < 1 provided that the person actually takes the time to go through the sequence of judgments again when asked immediately afterwards. But the person is not likely to make a new judgment at all, and instead the person will simply read off the earlier answer "L" from memory. In other words, the person may simply recall and repeat the previous answer instead of making an entirely new judgment. In fact, the person will wonder why the experimenter is repeating the same question, and will feel pressure to appear consistent and, therefore, simply recall the previous answer. Clearly, if the person just recalls an earlier answer then our quantum model does not apply at all. Our quantum model only models the judgment process, not reading or memory recall processes. If the person just recalls the answer and does not make a new judgment, then of course we expect that the person will just repeat the answer. The person has to make a new judgment for this prediction to hold, and this condition is likely to be violated.

Reviewer: My firm impression of "quantum cognition" is that it is neither quantum nor cognitive.

Authors: Our quantum approach to decision making embodies all the characteristics of a good cognitive theory: it is based on a coherent set of formal principles, the formal principles are related to specific assumptions about psychological process (notably, the existence of order effects and context dependence of judgments), and it leads to quantitative computational models which can parsimoniously account for both old and new empirical data. The form of quantum cognitive theories is very much like that of Bayesian ones, and of course the latter have been hugely influential in recent cognitive science. Thus, we are puzzled by the reviewer's sweeping dismissive comment and, indeed, his impression is not shared by everyone (Shiffrin, 2010).[6]

Afterthought: This reviewer is actually correct! Quantum cognition cannot be decomposed into the two simple composite parts of quantum plus cognition, and instead it is a new emergent and entangled concept.

---

[6]We thank our colleague Professor Emmanuel Pothos for these last comments.

Appendices

A   Notation

Below is a brief list of the notation used in this book. In general, the Dirac notation is used for abstract vectors and operators that are expressed in a co-ordinate free manner, and traditional matrix algebra notation is used when a vector or an operator is expressed in terms of coordinates of a specific basis.

N is the dimension of a Hilbert space

a, b, c, x, y, z are scalars which can be complex numbers

X, Y, P, Q are matrices

$\text{diag}[X]$ is a diagonal matrix formed from the $N \times 1$ column matrix X

α, β, γ are often used to represent $N \times 1$ column matrices of amplitudes

α_i is one coordinate value of α; that is, a single amplitude

$X^\dagger$ is the Hermitian transpose of X

X^{-1} is the inverse of the full rank matrix X

If α is an $N \times 1$ column matrix, then $\alpha^\dagger$ is an $1 \times N$ row matrix of conjugate values

$(\alpha^\dagger \cdot \beta)$ is the inner product of two $N \times 1$ column matrices (α, β)

$\psi \cdot \phi^\dagger$ is the outer product matrix of two $N \times 1$ column matrices (ψ, ϕ)

$\text{Tr}[X]$ is the trace of the square matrix X

$X \otimes Y$ is the Kronecker product of two matrices

$V = \{|V_i\rangle, i = 1, N\}$ orthonormal basis, or $W = \{|W_i\rangle, i = 1, N\}$ for another one

$|X\rangle$ is an abstract vector; it can be represented by a $N \times 1$ matrix α once you choose a basis

$|X\rangle \rightarrow \alpha$ means represent $|X\rangle$ by the $N \times 1$ matrix α of coordinates with respect to basis V

$|X\rangle \rightarrow \beta$ means represent $|X\rangle$ by the $N \times 1$ matrix β of coordinates with respect to another basis W

$\langle X|$ is the adjoint of $|X\rangle$, and if $|X\rangle \rightarrow \alpha$ then $\langle X| \rightarrow \alpha^\dagger$

$\langle X|Y\rangle$ is an inner product of two vectors

$|X\rangle\langle Y|$ is an outer product linear operator

A, B, C and such letters are used for events or subspaces

$\bar{B}$ represents negation or complement of B

$\mathbf{P}_A$ projector which is a linear operator

P_A matrix representation of the projector in some coordinate system with respect to some basis

$\mathbf{M}^{\dagger}$ adjoint of $\mathbf{M}$

$|X\rangle \otimes |Y\rangle$ tensor product of two vectors

B   Density matrix representation of states

Density matrices provide a more general way to represent a mixed quantum state. For example, a density matrix provides a simple way to represent probabilities generated by pooling or averaging responses across individuals who start in different states. It is also useful for situations in which a person makes a choice and we are interested in the expected state following the choice, averaged over all the possible choice outcomes. Finally, it is also required for quantum noise operations that inject noise directly into the quantum dynamics.

Before getting into this topic, we need to present one additional matrix operation that was not discussed in Chapter 2, which is called the trace of a matrix. The trace of X is equal to the sum of the diagonal elements of X: $\text{Tr}[X] = \sum_{i=1}^{n} x_{ii}$. The trace of a linear operator $\mathbf{X}$ equals the trace of any matrix representation of the operator. The trace of a Hermitian matrix $X^{\dagger} = X$ also equals the sum of its eigenvalues. The trace is a linear transformation: if X and Y are both $N \times N$ matrices then $\text{Tr}[aX + bY] = a\text{Tr}[X] + b\text{Tr}[Y]$. The trace of a product satisfies $\text{Tr}[X \cdot Y] = \text{Tr}[Y \cdot X]$ and this can be extended to higher products; for example, $\text{Tr}[(X \cdot Y) \cdot Z] = \text{Tr}[Z \cdot (X \cdot Y)] = \text{Tr}[X \cdot (Y \cdot Z)] = \text{Tr}[(Y \cdot Z) \cdot X]$, and so on. From the latter property it follows that the trace of a Hermitian matrix $X^{\dagger} = X$ also equals the sum of its eigenvalues: $\text{Tr}[X] = \text{Tr}[V \cdot \Lambda \cdot V^{\dagger}] = \text{Tr}[V^{\dagger} \cdot V \cdot \Lambda] = \text{Tr}[\Lambda]$, where V is the orthonormal matrix of eigenvectors and Λ is the diagonal matrix of eigenvalues. Note that a projector P satisfies $P \cdot P = P$, so that $\text{Tr}[P \cdot X \cdot P] = \text{Tr}[P \cdot P \cdot X] = \text{Tr}[P \cdot X] = \text{Tr}[X \cdot P]$. The trace of an outer product of a pair of $N \times 1$ matrices ψ and ϕ equals the inner product: $\text{Tr}[\psi \cdot \phi^{\dagger}] = (\phi^{\dagger} \cdot \psi)$, from which it follows that $\text{Tr}[\psi \cdot \psi^{\dagger}] = (\psi^{\dagger} \cdot \psi) = \|\psi\|^2$. The trace of a Hermitian transpose of X equals the conjugate of the trace of X: $\text{Tr}[X^{\dagger}] = (\text{Tr}[X])^*$.

B.1   Pure states

Suppose $|\psi\rangle = \sum \psi_j \cdot |j\rangle$ is a unit-length superposition state that lies within an N-dimensional Hilbert space spanned by the basis vectors $\{|j\rangle$, for $j = 1, \ldots, N\}$. The density operator corresponding to this state is the outer product operator $|\psi\rangle\langle\psi|$. This density operator is called the density for a pure state. A pure state is a superposition state (not simply a basis state), and it is distinguished later from a mixed state. With respect to the $\{|j\rangle, j = 1, \ldots, N\}$ basis, the state can be represented by the $N \times 1$ column matrix of amplitudes ψ which has amplitude ψ_j in the jth row. The density matrix corresponding to this state is formed by the outer product $\rho = \psi\psi^{\dagger}$. A density matrix for a pure state satisfies the properties of a projector $\rho^2 = \rho = \rho^{\dagger}$ as well as the completeness property $\text{Tr}[\rho] = 1$. Because $\rho^2 = \rho$, a pure state must also satisfy $\text{Tr}[\rho^2] = 1$, which is a key test of a pure state (as opposed to a mixed state described below).

Suppose P_A is the matrix representation of the projector that projects the state $|\psi\rangle$ onto the subspace representing event A so that the probability of this event equals $p(A) = ||P_A \cdot \psi||^2$. Exactly the same probability can be computed from the density matrix by the trace operation

$$p(A) = \text{Tr}[P_A \cdot \rho \cdot P_A] = \text{Tr}[\rho \cdot P_A] = \text{Tr}[P_A \cdot \rho],$$

which simply equals the sum of the diagonal elements of the matrix product $P_A \cdot \rho$. After observing the event A the state is revised to become

$$\psi_A = \frac{P_A \cdot \psi}{\sqrt{p(A)}},$$

$$\rho_A = \psi_A \psi_A^\dagger = \frac{P_A \cdot \rho \cdot P_A^\dagger}{p(A)}.$$

The state evolves according to the Schrödinger equation $\frac{d}{dt}\psi(t) = -i \cdot H \cdot \psi(t)$ and the density matrix evolves according to the Heisenberg equation

$$\begin{aligned}
\frac{d}{dt}\rho(t) &= \frac{d}{dt}\left(\psi(t)\psi(t)^\dagger\right) \\
&= \left(\frac{d}{dt}\psi(t)\right) \cdot \psi(t)^\dagger + \psi(t) \cdot \left(\frac{d}{dt}\psi(t)^\dagger\right) \\
&= -i \cdot H \cdot \psi(t) \cdot \psi(t)^\dagger + \psi(t) \cdot i \cdot \psi(t)^\dagger \cdot H \\
&= -i \cdot (H \cdot \rho - \rho \cdot H) = -i \cdot [H, \rho],
\end{aligned}$$

where $[A, B] = A \cdot B - B \cdot A$ is the commutator. The solutions to these equations are

$$\psi(t) = e^{-itH} \cdot \psi(0) = U(t) \cdot \psi(0),$$
$$\rho(t) = \psi(t)\psi(t)^\dagger = U(t) \cdot \rho(0) \cdot U(t)^\dagger.$$

B.2 Mixed states

The density matrix representation becomes very useful for the following problem. Suppose we perform an experiment on a group of individuals, and there are important individual differences, so we cannot assume each person begins in the same state. Suppose some proportion $p_i > 0$ of individuals begin in state $|\psi_i\rangle$ for $i = 1, \ldots, m$ individual differences with $\sum_i p_i = 1$. The density matrix provides a general way to represent this mixed state: $\rho = \sum_i p_i \cdot \rho_i$. Note that the mixed density is still Hermitian, $\rho^\dagger = \rho$, and the trace is a linear operation so that $\text{Tr}\left[\sum_i p_i \cdot \rho_i\right] = \sum_i p_i \cdot \text{Tr}[\rho_i] = 1$. But a mixed state satisfies the key property $\text{Tr}[\rho^2] < 1$, which distinguishes it from a pure state.

The probability of event A equals

$$p(A) = \sum_i p_i \cdot \|P_A \cdot \psi_i\|^2 = \sum_i p_i \cdot \mathrm{Tr}[\rho_i \cdot P_A]$$

$$= \mathrm{Tr}\left(\sum_i p_i \cdot \rho_i \cdot P_A\right) = \mathrm{Tr}[P_A \cdot \rho],$$

and the last expression provides a simpler and more compact way to express this probability. The evolution of the mixed state is most easily expressed by the density matrix because

$$\rho(t) = U(t) \cdot \rho(0) \cdot U(t)^\dagger$$

$$= U(t) \cdot \left(\sum_i p_i \cdot \rho_i(0)\right) \cdot U(t)^\dagger$$

$$= \sum_i p_i \cdot U(t) \cdot \rho_i(0) \cdot U(t)^\dagger$$

$$= \sum_i p_i \cdot \rho_i(t).$$

The density matrix is also useful for representing a state that occurs after a choice response R, but we are interested in the expectation of this state (averaged over the possible responses). For example, suppose ρ_0 is the state before a choice is made among m options. The state that is expected to result after this choice (averaged over the possible choices) equals $\rho_1 = \sum_i p(R = i) \cdot \rho_i$, where $\rho_i = \frac{P_i \cdot \rho_0 \cdot P_i^\dagger}{p(R=i)}$ is the state given choice of response $R = i$ and P_i is a projector onto the subspace for response $R = i$. This updated state simplifies to $\rho_1 = \sum_i P_i \cdot \rho_0 \cdot P_i^\dagger$.

Density matrices are indispensable for injecting quantum noise into the quantum dynamics. Let us consider one simple example called depolarization (see Nielsen and Chuang (2000): 379). The basic idea is that, during the period of time required for processing one of the steps of a cognitive or decision task, there is some probability p that the person is attentive and processes the task information, and there is some probability $(1 - p)$ that the person is inattentive and drifts off without direction. Formally, there is some probability p that during this step the state is updated according to the dynamics of the unitary operator $U(t)$ representing the task information, and there is some probability $(1 - p)$ that the state depolarizes to a state of equal probability for all responses. If ρ is the state before this information processing step and the period of processing equals t, then it is updated after this step to the new state

$$\rho(t) = p \cdot U(t) \cdot \rho \cdot U(t)^\dagger + (1 - p) \cdot \frac{I}{N},$$

where N is the dimension of ρ.

C Analysis of question order effects using density matrices

In Chapter 3 we derived an exact parameter-free q-test for the quantum model of question order effects, but we used a pure state $|\psi\rangle$ for a single individual to derive this test. Below, we derive the same result using a more general density matrix representation. Now we assume that the population of respondents is represented by a density operator ρ.[1] For example the density could represent the population mixture $\rho = \sum p_i \cdot |\psi_i\rangle\langle\psi_i|$, where $|\psi_i\rangle$ is a pure state and p_i is the proportion of the population that has this pure state. The yes answers to questions A and B are represented by projection operators M_A and M_B respectively and the no answers are represented by projectors $M_{\bar{A}} = I - M_A$ and $M_{\bar{B}} = I - M_B$ respectively. The empirically observed probability of answering a question A is denoted $p(A)$ and the probability predicted by the quantum model is denoted $Q(A)$.

First: Is question A true? The quantum probability of saying yes is defined by

$$Q(A) = \mathrm{Tr}\left[M_A \cdot \rho \cdot M_A\right]$$

and the new state after answering yes to this question equals

$$\rho_A = \frac{M_A \cdot \rho \cdot M_A}{Q(A)}.$$

Similarly, the probability of saying no equals

$$Q(\bar{A}) = \mathrm{Tr}\left[M_{\bar{A}} \cdot \rho \cdot M_{\bar{A}}\right]$$

and the new state after answering no to this question equals

$$\rho_{\bar{A}} = \frac{M_{\bar{A}} \cdot \rho \cdot M_{\bar{A}}}{Q(\bar{A})}.$$

Second: Is question B true (after giving an answer to question A)?

$$Q(B|A) = \mathrm{Tr}\left[M_B \cdot \rho_A \cdot M_B\right] = \frac{\mathrm{Tr}\left[M_B M_A \rho M_A M_B\right]}{Q(A)} = \frac{\mathrm{Tr}\left[(M_A M_B M_A)\,\rho\right]}{Q(A)},$$

$$Q(B|\bar{A}) = \mathrm{Tr}\left[M_B \cdot \rho_{\bar{A}} \cdot M_B\right] = \frac{\mathrm{Tr}\left[M_B M_{\bar{A}} \rho M_{\bar{A}} M_B\right]}{Q(\bar{A})} = \frac{\mathrm{Tr}\left[(M_{\bar{A}} M_B M_{\bar{A}})\,\rho\right]}{Q(\bar{A})}.$$

Following these definitions, the probability of yes to A and then yes to B equals

$$p(\mathrm{AyBy}) = Q(A)\, Q(B|A)$$

$$= Q(A) \cdot \frac{\mathrm{Tr}\left[(M_A M_B M_A)\,\rho\right]}{Q(A)} = \mathrm{Tr}\left[(M_A M_B M_A)\,\rho\right].$$

---

[1] Originally I derived the test for pure states. Thanks to Reinhard Blutner for suggesting that I prove this more generally using density operators rather than pure quantum states. The result we obtain here closely resembles a similar result found in Niestegge (2008).

Similarly, the probability of no to B and then yes to A equals

$$p(\text{BnAy}) = Q\left(\bar{B}\right) Q\left(A|\bar{B}\right)$$
$$= \text{Tr}\left[(M_{\bar{B}} M_A M_{\bar{B}})\,\rho\right].$$

The decomposition of question A in the non-comparative context effects is given below.

$$Q(A) = \text{Tr}\left[M_A \cdot \rho \cdot M_A\right]$$
$$= \text{Tr}\left[M_A \left(M_B + M_{\bar{B}}\right) \rho \left(M_B + M_{\bar{B}}\right) M_A\right]$$
$$= \text{Tr}\left[(M_A M_B \rho + M_A M_{\bar{B}} \rho)\left(M_B M_A + M_{\bar{B}} M_A\right)\right]$$
$$= \text{Tr}\left[\begin{array}{c} M_A M_B \rho M_B M_A + M_A M_{\bar{B}} \rho M_B M_A \\ + M_A M_B \rho M_{\bar{B}} M_A + M_A M_{\bar{B}} \rho M_{\bar{B}} M_A \end{array}\right]$$
$$= \text{Tr}\left[M_B M_A M_B \rho\right] + \text{Tr}\left[M_B M_A M_{\bar{B}} \rho\right]$$
$$\quad + \text{Tr}\left[M_{\bar{B}} M_A M_B \rho + M_{\bar{B}} M_A M_{\bar{B}} \rho\right]$$
$$= Q\left(B\right) Q(A|B) + Q\left(\bar{B}\right) Q\left(A|\bar{B}\right)$$
$$\quad + \text{Tr}\left[(M_B M_A M_{\bar{B}})\,\rho\right] + \text{Tr}\left[(M_B M_A M_{\bar{B}})^{\dagger} \rho\right]$$
$$= p(\text{ByAy}) + p(\text{BnAy}) + C_A$$
$$C_A = \text{Tr}\left[(M_B M_A M_{\bar{B}})\,\rho\right] + \text{Tr}\left[(M_B M_A M_{\bar{B}})^{\dagger} \rho\right].$$

Furthermore:

$$\text{Tr}\left[(M_B M_A M_{\bar{B}})\,\rho\right] = \text{Tr}\left[M_B M_A \left(I - M_B\right) \rho\right]$$
$$= \text{Tr}\left[M_B M_A \rho - M_B M_A M_B \rho\right]$$
$$= \text{Tr}\left[M_B M_A \rho\right] - p(\text{ByAy}),$$
$$\text{Tr}\left[(M_B M_A M_{\bar{B}})^{\dagger} \rho\right] = \text{Tr}\left[((I - M_B) M_A M_B)\,\rho\right]$$
$$= \text{Tr}\left[(M_A M_B)\,\rho - (M_B M_A M_B)\,\rho\right]$$
$$= \text{Tr}\left[(M_A M_B)\,\rho\right] - p(\text{ByAy}).$$

Combining these two produces

$$C_A = \text{Tr}\left[(M_A M_B + M_B M_A)\,\rho\right] - 2p(\text{ByAy}).$$

Similarly:

$$C_B = \text{Tr}\left[(M_B M_A + M_A M_B)\,\rho\right] - 2p(\text{AyBy}).$$

Note that the term $\text{Tr}\left[(M_B M_A + M_A M_B)\,\rho\right]$ is identical in both equations. Therefore:

$$C_A + 2p\left(\text{ByAy}\right) = C_B + 2p(\text{AyBy}),$$

which implies

$$
\begin{aligned}
0 &= [C_A + 2 \cdot Q(B)Q(A|B)] - [C_B + 2 \cdot Q(A)Q(B|A)] \\
&= [Q(A) - Q(B)Q(A|B) - Q(\overline{B})Q(A|\overline{B}) + 2 \cdot Q(B)Q(A|B)] \\
&\quad - [Q(B) - Q(A)Q(B|A) - Q(\overline{A})Q(B|\overline{A}) + 2 \cdot Q(A)Q(B|A)] \\
&= [Q(A) + Q(B)Q(A|B) - Q(\overline{B})Q(A|\overline{B})] \\
&\quad - [Q(B) + Q(A)Q(B|A) - Q(\overline{A})Q(B|\overline{A})] \\
&= [Q(A)Q(B|A) + Q(A)Q(\overline{B}|A) + Q(B)Q(A|B) - Q(\overline{B})Q(A|\overline{B})] \\
&\quad - [Q(B)Q(A|B) + Q(B)Q(\overline{A}|B) + Q(A)Q(B|A) - Q(\overline{A})Q(B|\overline{A})] \\
&= [Q(A)Q(\overline{B}|A) - Q(\overline{B})Q(A|\overline{B})] - [Q(B)Q(\overline{A}|B) - Q(\overline{A})Q(B|\overline{A})] \\
&= [Q(A)Q(\overline{B}|A) + Q(\overline{A})Q(B|\overline{A})] - [Q(B)Q(\overline{A}|B) + Q(\overline{B})Q(A|\overline{B})] = 0.
\end{aligned}
$$

This leads to the q-test of the quantum model. If the quantum model is correct, then we hypothesize that

$$
q = [p(\text{AyBn}) + p(\text{AnBy})] - [p(\text{ByAn}) + p(\text{BnAy})] = 0.
$$

This can be tested using a simple test for a difference between proportions for two groups, one getting question A first and the other getting question B first.

D Pauli matrices

Pauli matrices are commonly used to form unitary matrices for two-dimensional quantum systems. The Pauli matrices are named after Wolfgang Pauli, one of the founding fathers of quantum theory. They are defined as follows, along with their spectral decomposition:

$$
\sigma_x = \sigma_1 = \begin{bmatrix} 0 & 1 \\ 1 & 0 \end{bmatrix}
$$

$$
= (1) \cdot \begin{bmatrix} \frac{1}{\sqrt{2}} \\ \frac{1}{\sqrt{2}} \end{bmatrix} \cdot \begin{bmatrix} \frac{1}{\sqrt{2}} & \frac{1}{\sqrt{2}} \end{bmatrix} + (-1) \cdot \begin{bmatrix} \frac{1}{\sqrt{2}} \\ \frac{-1}{\sqrt{2}} \end{bmatrix} \cdot \begin{bmatrix} \frac{1}{\sqrt{2}} & \frac{-1}{\sqrt{2}} \end{bmatrix},
$$

$$
\sigma_y = \sigma_2 = \begin{bmatrix} 0 & -i \\ i & 0 \end{bmatrix}
$$

$$
= (1) \cdot \begin{bmatrix} \frac{1}{\sqrt{2}} \\ \frac{i}{\sqrt{2}} \end{bmatrix} \cdot \begin{bmatrix} \frac{1}{\sqrt{2}} & \frac{i}{\sqrt{2}} \end{bmatrix}^* + (-1) \cdot \begin{bmatrix} \frac{i}{\sqrt{2}} \\ \frac{1}{\sqrt{2}} \end{bmatrix} \cdot \begin{bmatrix} \frac{i}{\sqrt{2}} & \frac{1}{\sqrt{2}} \end{bmatrix}^*,
$$

$$
\sigma_z = \sigma_3 = \begin{bmatrix} 1 & 0 \\ 0 & -1 \end{bmatrix}
$$

$$
= (1) \cdot \begin{bmatrix} 1 \\ 0 \end{bmatrix} \cdot \begin{bmatrix} 1 & 0 \end{bmatrix} + (-1) \cdot \begin{bmatrix} 0 \\ 1 \end{bmatrix} \cdot \begin{bmatrix} 0 & 1 \end{bmatrix}.
$$

From these matrices we can form linear combinations to construct others, such as the Hadamard matrix:

$$H = \frac{1}{\sqrt{2}}(\sigma_x + \sigma_z) = \frac{1}{\sqrt{2}}\begin{bmatrix} 1 & 1 \\ 1 & -1 \end{bmatrix}.$$

Some important properties are

$$\sigma_i^\dagger = \sigma_i,$$
$$\sigma_i^2 = I,$$
$$\sigma_i\sigma_j + \sigma_j\sigma_i = 2 \cdot \delta_{ij},$$
$$\sigma_i\sigma_j - \sigma_j\sigma_i = 2 \cdot i \cdot \sigma_k.$$

A rotation of a two-dimensional state around the axis defined by the unit-length vector (with real values)

$$\eta = \begin{bmatrix} \eta_1 \\ \eta_2 \\ \eta_3 \end{bmatrix}, \quad \eta^\dagger \eta = 1,$$

is realized by the linear combination of Pauli matrices, which is defined as

$$\eta \cdot \sigma = \eta_1 \cdot \sigma_1 + \eta_2 \cdot \sigma_2 + \eta_3 \cdot \sigma_3$$
$$= \begin{bmatrix} \eta_3 & \eta_1 - i \cdot \eta_2 \\ \eta_1 + i \cdot \eta_2 & -\eta_3 \end{bmatrix}.$$

Suppose we include an additional parameter η_0 contributed by the identity matrix I to form

$$H = \eta_0 \cdot I + \eta_1 \cdot \sigma_1 + \eta_2 \cdot \sigma_2 + \eta_3 \cdot \sigma_3$$
$$= \begin{bmatrix} \eta_0 + \eta_3 & \eta_1 - i \cdot \eta_2 \\ \eta_1 + i \cdot \eta_2 & \eta_0 - \eta_3 \end{bmatrix}.$$

The unitary matrix U formed by H equals $U = e^{-iH} = e^{-i(\eta_0 I + \eta\sigma)}$. But note that I commutes with $\eta \cdot \sigma$ and so we can re-express the unitary matrix as

$$U = e^{-i(\eta_0 I + \eta\sigma)}$$
$$= e^{-i\eta_0 I} \cdot e^{-i\eta\sigma}$$
$$= e^{-i\eta_0} \cdot e^{-i\eta\sigma}.$$

The first term $e^{-i\eta_0}$ is a common phase factor that ultimately has no effect on the final probabilities, and so it can be ignored.

The matrix $\eta \cdot \sigma$ also has the property $(\eta \cdot \sigma)^2 = I$. Any Hermitian matrix A with the property $A^2 = I$ has eigenvalues equal to $+1$ or -1. This follows from the fact that

$$A^2 = \left(V \cdot \Lambda \cdot V^\dagger\right)\left(V \cdot \Lambda \cdot V^\dagger\right)$$
$$= V \cdot \Lambda^2 \cdot V^\dagger = I$$
$$\rightarrow \Lambda^2 = V^\dagger V = I$$
$$\rightarrow \lambda_i^2 = 1 \rightarrow \lambda_i = \pm 1.$$

Using this fact we can express

$$
\begin{aligned}
e^{i\theta A} &= V \cdot \text{diag}[..e^{i\theta(\pm 1)}..] \cdot V^\dagger \\
&= V \cdot \text{diag}[.. (\cos(\theta \cdot (\pm 1)) + i \cdot \sin(\theta \cdot (\pm 1)))..] \cdot V^\dagger \\
&= V \cdot \text{diag}[.. \cos(\theta \cdot (\pm 1))..] \cdot V^\dagger + i \cdot V \cdot \text{diag}[.. \sin(\theta \cdot (\pm 1))..] \cdot V^\dagger \\
&= \cos(\theta) V \cdot V^\dagger + i \cdot V \cdot \text{diag}[.. (\pm 1) \cdot \sin(\theta)..] \cdot V^\dagger \\
&= \cos(\theta) \cdot I + i \cdot \sin(\theta) \cdot V \cdot \Lambda \cdot V^\dagger \\
&= \cos(\theta) \cdot I + i \cdot \sin(\theta) \cdot A.
\end{aligned}
$$

We can apply the above result to the 2×2 matrix $\eta \cdot \sigma$ to obtain

$$
\begin{aligned}
e^{-i\theta\eta\sigma} &= \cos(\theta) \cdot \begin{bmatrix} 1 & 0 \\ 0 & 1 \end{bmatrix} - i \cdot \sin(\theta) \cdot \begin{bmatrix} \eta_3 & \eta_1 - i \cdot \eta_2 \\ \eta_1 + i \cdot \eta_2 & -\eta_3 \end{bmatrix} \\
&= \begin{bmatrix} \cos(\theta) - i \cdot \sin(\theta) \cdot \eta_3 & -i \cdot \sin(\theta) \cdot (\eta_1 - i \cdot \eta_2) \\ -i \cdot \sin(\theta) \cdot (\eta_1 + i \cdot \eta_2) & \cos(\theta) + i \cdot \sin(\theta) \cdot \eta_3 \end{bmatrix} \\
&= \begin{bmatrix} \cos(\theta) - i \cdot \sin(\theta) \cdot \eta_3 & -\sin(\theta) \cdot (i \cdot \eta_1 + \eta_2) \\ -\sin(\theta) \cdot (i \cdot \eta_1 - \eta_2) & \cos(\theta) + i \cdot \sin(\theta) \cdot \eta_3 \end{bmatrix}.
\end{aligned}
$$

If we multiply this matrix by an initial state ψ we obtain

$$
\phi = e^{-i\theta\eta\sigma} \cdot \psi = \begin{bmatrix} (\cos(\theta) - i \cdot \sin(\theta) \cdot \eta_3) \cdot \psi_1 - (\sin(\theta) \cdot (i \cdot \eta_1 + \eta_2)) \cdot \psi_2 \\ -(\sin(\theta) \cdot (i \cdot \eta_1 - \eta_2)) \cdot \psi_1 + (\cos(\theta) + i \cdot \sin(\theta) \cdot \eta_3) \cdot \psi_2. \end{bmatrix}.
$$

The first coordinate equals

$$
\phi_1 = (\cos(\theta) \cdot \psi_1 - \sin(\theta) \cdot \eta_2 \cdot \psi_2) - i \cdot \sin(\theta) \cdot (\eta_3 \cdot \psi_1 + \eta_1 \cdot \psi_2)
$$

and the squared magnitude of the first coordinate equals

$$
|\phi_1|^2 = |\cos(\theta) \cdot \psi_1 - \sin(\theta) \cdot \eta_2 \cdot \psi_2|^2 + \sin^2(\theta) \cdot |\eta_3 \cdot \psi_1 + \eta_1 \cdot \psi_2|^2.
$$

Recall that η is real and only ψ may be complex. If we also assume that ψ is real, then

$$
\begin{aligned}
|\phi_1|^2 &= |\cos(\theta) \cdot \psi_1|^2 + |\sin(\theta) \cdot \eta_2 \cdot \psi_2|^2 - 2 \cdot \cos(\theta) \cdot \psi_1 \cdot \sin(\theta) \cdot \eta_2 \cdot \psi_2 \\
&\quad + \sin^2(\theta) \cdot \left(|\eta_3 \cdot \psi_1|^2 + |\eta_1 \cdot \psi_2|^2 + 2 \cdot \eta_3 \cdot \psi_1 \cdot \eta_1 \cdot \psi_2 \right) \\
&= \cos^2(\theta) \cdot \psi_1^2 + \sin^2(\theta) \cdot \left(\eta_2^2 \cdot \psi_2^2 + \eta_3^2 \cdot \psi_1^2 + \eta_1^2 \cdot \psi_2^2 \right) \\
&\quad + 2 \cdot \left(\sin^2(\theta) \cdot \eta_3 \cdot \psi_1 \cdot \eta_1 \cdot \psi_2 - \cos(\theta) \cdot \psi_1 \cdot \sin(\theta) \cdot \eta_2 \cdot \psi_2 \right).
\end{aligned}
$$

In particular, if we set $\psi_1 = 1/\sqrt{2} = \psi_2$ then we obtain

$$|\phi_1|^2 = \frac{1}{2} + \eta_3 \cdot \eta_1 \cdot \sin^2(\theta) - \eta_2 \cdot \cos(\theta) \cdot \sin(\theta).$$

Now suppose we use the following Hamiltonian:

$$H = \frac{1}{\sqrt{1+h^2}} \begin{bmatrix} h & 1 \\ 1 & -h \end{bmatrix} = \frac{1}{\sqrt{1+h^2}} \cdot \sigma_1 + 0 \cdot \sigma_2 + \frac{h}{\sqrt{1+h^2}} \cdot \sigma_3.$$

Then the unitary matrix (with $\eta_2 = 0$) equals

$$U(t) = e^{-itH} = \frac{1}{\sqrt{1+h^2}} \cdot \begin{bmatrix} \cos(\theta) - i \cdot \sin(\theta) \cdot h & -i \cdot \sin(\theta) \\ -i \cdot \sin(\theta) & \cos(\theta) + i \cdot \sin(\theta) \cdot h \end{bmatrix}$$

Then we obtain the following probability:

$$|\phi_1|^2 = \frac{1}{2} + \frac{h}{\sqrt{1+h^2}} \cdot \frac{1}{\sqrt{1+h^2}} \cdot \sin^2(\theta)$$

$$= \frac{1}{2} + \frac{h}{1+h^2} \cdot \sin^2(\theta).$$

Thus, $|\phi_1|^2$ reaches its maximum (for the first time) at $\theta = \pi/2$, at which point $\sin^2(\theta) = 1$ and $|\phi_1|^2 = \frac{1}{2} + \frac{h}{1+h^2}$. Finally, if we set $h = 1$ (as it is in the Hadamard matrix), then

$$|\phi_1|^2 = \frac{1}{2} + \frac{1}{2} \cdot \sin^2(\theta).$$

In this case, at $\theta = \frac{\pi}{2}$, $\sin^2(\theta) = 1$ and $|\phi_1|^2 = 1$.

E   Quantum random walk

In Chapter 8 we presented a version of a quantum random walk model used by Busemeyer *et al.* (2006a). Here, we present a second version used by Fuss and Navarro, who based their ideas on the original Aharonov *et al.* (1993) theory. Suppose there are confidence levels: $x \in \{.., -2, -1, 0, 1, 2..\}$. The levels at or below $-m$ cross the threshold for responding signal absent and the levels at or above $+m$ cross the threshold for responding signal present. For example, $-m = -3$ for the lower threshold and $+m = +3$ for the upper threshold produces a total seven levels that lie at or within the bounds. This model uses a concept called chirality: the state of evidence can travel along two tracks – a left track that leads down to a response of signal absent and a right track that leads up to a response of signal present. The left track is represented by basis vectors $|L, x\rangle$ and the right track is represented by basis vectors $|R, x\rangle$. For example, $|R, +3\rangle$ could represent a strong level of confidence for signal present. The state is a superposition of these orthonormal basis vectors $|\psi\rangle = \sum_x \psi_{L,x}(t) \cdot |L, x\rangle +$

$\psi_{R,x}(t) \cdot |R, x\rangle$. For example, the initial state could be set by $\psi_{L,x} = \psi_{R,x} = 1/\sqrt{6}$ for $x = -1,\ 0,\ 1$. The state contains pairs of amplitudes, which are updated according to the pair of equations

$$\psi_x(t+1) = \begin{bmatrix} \psi_{L,x}(t+1) \\ \psi_{R,x}(t+1) \end{bmatrix} = e^{ik} \cdot \begin{bmatrix} s^* \cdot \psi_{L,x+1}(t) - r^* \cdot \psi_{R,x+1}(t) \\ s \cdot \psi_{R,x-1}(t) + r \cdot \psi_{L,x-1}(t) \end{bmatrix},$$

where s is the amplitude for staying in the same track (s^* is the complex conjugate of s) and r is the amplitude to reverse and switch tracks. If the state stays in the right track, then it systematically steps to the right (higher confidence in signal present); and if the state stays in the left track, then it systematically steps to the left (higher confidence signal is absent). The walk is probabilistic because the state can transfer from the right to the left track or the reverse. The transformation matrix formed by this updating rule can be described as follows. Define

$$U_L = e^{ik} \cdot \begin{bmatrix} 0 & 0 \\ -r^* & s^* \end{bmatrix}, \quad U_R = e^{ik} \cdot \begin{bmatrix} s & r \\ 0 & 0 \end{bmatrix}.$$

If there are $n = 7$ levels of confidence that lie at or within the bounds, with the first level $x = -3$ representing the threshold for responding signal absent and last level $x = +3$ representing the threshold for signal present, then the transformation matrix[2] is defined as

$$U = \begin{bmatrix} 0 & U_L & 0 & 0 & 0 & 0 & 0 \\ 0 & 0 & U_L & 0 & 0 & 0 & 0 \\ 0 & U_R & 0 & U_L & 0 & 0 & 0 \\ 0 & 0 & U_R & 0 & U_L & 0 & 0 \\ 0 & 0 & 0 & U_R & 0 & U_L & 0 \\ 0 & 0 & 0 & 0 & U_R & 0 & 0 \\ 0 & 0 & 0 & 0 & 0 & U_R & 0 \end{bmatrix}.$$

Once again, if we assume for example $n = 7$ levels of confidence at or within the bounds, then U is a 14×14 transformation matrix, and $\psi(t)$ is the 14×1 state at time t, and the state at the next step of the walk then equals $\psi(t+1) = U(t) \cdot \psi(t)$. The probability of observing the upper threshold at time t and choosing signal present equals $||\psi_{+3}(t)||^2$ and the probability of observing the lower threshold at time t and choosing signal absent equals $||\psi_{-3}(t)||^2$.

F   Alternative quantum models of the disjunction effect

Busemeyer *et al.* (2006a) originally suggested a quantum interference interpretation for the disjunction effect. Since that time, a list of various quantum models

---

[2]The entire matrix is not unitary and so the length of the state is not preserved. The amplitude distribution shrinks over time when it spills over the threshold.

for this effect have been proposed, each one ultimately explaining the effects by interference terms. This list includes Pothos and Busemeyer (2009), Khrennikov and Haven (2009), Aerts (2009), Yukalov and Sornette (2009), and Accardi *et al.* (2009). In Chapter 8 we describe the original Busemeyer *et al.* (2006a) idea as well as a quantum noise model. In Chapter 9 we describe the Pothos and Busemeyer (2009) model. Here, we describe the other models, starting with the simplest and working toward the more complex vesions.

For these presentations, we will use an example based on the PD paradigm. In this paradigm, B_D and B_C represent the player's belief that the opponent will defect or cooperate respectively, and A_D and A_C represent the player's action to defect or cooperate respectively, and the notation $p(A_D|B_C)$ represents the probability that the player decides to defect given that the opponent is known to cooperate.

F.1   Two-dimensional contextual probability model

Khrennikov and Haven (2009) proposed a "contextual" probability model. This is a generalization of the two-dimensional quantum model presented in Chapter 8 for the categorization and decision paradigm. Define ψ_0 as a 2×1 column matrix containing amplitudes representing the player's beliefs that the opponent will defect (first coordinate) or cooperate (second coordinate). Define ψ_1 as a 2×1 column matrix containing amplitudes representing the player's choice to defect (first coordinate) or cooperate (second coordinate). These two column matrices are related by a linear transformation V, which is a 2×2 matrix described below:

$$\psi_1 = V \cdot \psi_0$$

with

$$V = \begin{bmatrix} \sqrt{p(A_D|B_D)} & \sqrt{p(A_D|B_C)} \cdot e^{i\theta(\delta_1)} \\ \sqrt{p(A_C|B_D)} \cdot e^{i\theta(\delta_2)} & \sqrt{p(A_C|B_C)} \end{bmatrix}.$$

The matrix V is neither a transition matrix nor a unitary matrix.[3] The exponents

$$\theta(\delta_1) = \cos^{-1}\left(\frac{\delta_1}{2 \cdot |\langle A_D|B_D\rangle\langle B_D|S\rangle\langle A_D|B_C\rangle\langle B_C|S\rangle|}\right),$$

$$\theta(\delta_2) = \cos^{-1}\left(\frac{\delta_2}{2 \cdot |\langle A_C|B_D\rangle\langle B_D|S\rangle\langle A_C|B_C\rangle\langle B_C|S\rangle|}\right)$$

---

[3]One might try to interpret the two linear operators, $V_D = M_D \cdot V$ and $V_C = M_C \cdot V$ as positive operator valued measures for computing the probabilities of the actions, but this is not possible either because they do not satisfy the completeness requirement $S = V_D^\dagger V_D + V_C^\dagger V_C \neq I$. The diagonal elements are one and the real (cosine) component in the off-diagonal elements of S subtract to zero, but the complex (sine) component in the off-diagonal elements of S add to a nonzero value.

are chosen to reproduce the observed interference effects, δ_1 and δ_2, respectively. The above definitions imply

$$\delta_1 = 2\cos(\theta(\delta_1)) \cdot |\langle A_\mathrm{D}|B_\mathrm{D}\rangle\langle B_\mathrm{D}|S\rangle\langle A_\mathrm{D}|B_\mathrm{C}\rangle\langle B_\mathrm{C}|S\rangle|,$$
$$\delta_2 = 2\cos(\theta(\delta_2)) \cdot |\langle A_\mathrm{C}|B_\mathrm{D}\rangle\langle B_\mathrm{D}|S\rangle\langle A_\mathrm{C}|B_\mathrm{C}\rangle\langle B_\mathrm{C}|S\rangle|,$$
$$\delta_1 = -\delta_2.$$

In order to use the arccos function, we require

$$\frac{|\delta_1|}{2 \cdot |\langle A_\mathrm{D}|B_\mathrm{D}\rangle\langle B_\mathrm{D}|S\rangle\langle A_\mathrm{D}|B_\mathrm{C}\rangle\langle B_\mathrm{C}|S\rangle|} \le 1. \tag{F.1}$$

Otherwise the arccos function is replaced with the arccosh function; and instead of using the *complex* field, a field of *hyperbolic* numbers generated by a Clifford algebra is used (see section 4.5.1 in Khrennikov, 2010).

The transformed amplitudes equal

$$\begin{bmatrix} \langle A_\mathrm{D}|S\rangle \\ \langle A_\mathrm{C}|S\rangle \end{bmatrix} = \begin{bmatrix} \sqrt{p(A_\mathrm{D}|B_\mathrm{D})} \cdot \langle B_\mathrm{D}|S\rangle + \sqrt{p(A_\mathrm{D}|B_\mathrm{C})} \cdot e^{i\theta(\delta_1)} \cdot \langle B_\mathrm{C}|S\rangle \\ \sqrt{p(A_\mathrm{C}|B_\mathrm{D})} \cdot e^{i\theta(\delta_2)} \cdot \langle B_\mathrm{D}|S\rangle + \sqrt{p(A_\mathrm{C}|B_\mathrm{C})} \cdot \langle B_\mathrm{C}|S\rangle \end{bmatrix},$$

which produces final probabilities equal to

$$|\langle A_\mathrm{D}|S\rangle|^2 = p(A_\mathrm{D}|B_\mathrm{D}) \cdot p(B_\mathrm{D}) + p(A_\mathrm{D}|B_\mathrm{C}) \cdot p(B_\mathrm{C}) + \delta_1',$$
$$\delta_1' = 2 \cdot \mathrm{Re}\left(\sqrt{p(A_\mathrm{D}|B_\mathrm{D})} \cdot \langle B_\mathrm{D}|S\rangle \cdot \sqrt{p(A_\mathrm{D}|B_\mathrm{C})} \cdot e^{i\theta(\delta_1)} \cdot \langle B_\mathrm{C}|S\rangle\right)$$
$$= 2 \cdot \left|\sqrt{p(A_\mathrm{D}|B_\mathrm{D})} \cdot \langle B_\mathrm{D}|S\rangle \cdot \sqrt{p(A_\mathrm{D}|B_\mathrm{C})} \cdot \langle B_\mathrm{C}|S\rangle\right| \cdot \cos(\theta(\delta_1) + \phi_S),$$
$$|\langle A_\mathrm{C}|S\rangle|^2 = p(A_\mathrm{C}|B_\mathrm{D}) \cdot p(B_\mathrm{D}) + p(A_\mathrm{C}|B_\mathrm{C}) \cdot p(B_\mathrm{C}) + \delta_2',$$
$$\delta_2' = 2 \cdot \left|\sqrt{p(A_\mathrm{C}|B_\mathrm{D})} \cdot \langle B_\mathrm{D}|S\rangle \cdot \sqrt{p(A_\mathrm{C}|B_\mathrm{C})} \cdot \langle B_\mathrm{C}|S\rangle\right| \cdot \cos(\theta(\delta_2) + \phi_S).$$

The phase parameter ϕ represents the phase of the complex number $\langle B_\mathrm{D}|S\rangle^* \langle B_\mathrm{C}|S\rangle = |\langle B_\mathrm{D}|S\rangle \cdot \langle B_\mathrm{C}|S\rangle| \cdot e^{i\phi}$. If ψ_0 is restricted to be real, then $\phi = 0$ and $\delta_1' = \delta_1 = -\delta_2 = -\delta_2'$, so that the generalized quantum model exactly reproduces the observed interference effect. Even though this V transformation is not unitary, the probabilities continue to sum to one because $\delta_1 + \delta_2 = 0$; that is, as long as the initial state is restricted to real values. If the initial state is complex, then it is possible for $\delta_1' \ne \delta_1$, $\delta_2' \ne \delta_2$, $\delta_1' + \delta_2' \ne 0$ and $|\langle A_\mathrm{D}|S\rangle|^2 + |\langle A_\mathrm{C}|S\rangle|^2 \ne 1$. This should be no surprise, because V is not unitary. Khrennikov (2010) restricts ψ_0 to be real with unit length.

To see how this model works, let us apply it to one of the PD experiments. The data from the Shafir and Tversky (1992) study do not satisfy the constraint for the arccos, so let us choose the Croson study instead.[4] In this case,

---

[4]The hyperbolic model must be used for the Tversky and Shafir (1992) PD game results. See Khrennikov (2010: Ch. 7).

$p(B_D) = 0.54$, $p(A_D|B_D) = 0.68$, $p(A_D|B_C) = 0.17$, which produces $p_T(A_1) = 0.445$, and $p(A_D) = 0.225$, so $\delta_1 = 0.225 - 0.445 = -0.22 = -\delta_2$, and

$$
\begin{bmatrix}
\theta(\delta_1) = \arccos\left(\dfrac{-0.22}{2 \cdot \sqrt{0.68 \cdot 0.54 \cdot 0.17 \cdot 0.46}}\right) = 2.28 \\[2ex]
\theta(\delta_2) = \arccos\left(\dfrac{+0.22}{2 \cdot \sqrt{0.32 \cdot 0.54 \cdot 0.83 \cdot 0.46}}\right) = 1.13
\end{bmatrix},
$$

$$
V = \begin{bmatrix}
\sqrt{0.68} & \sqrt{0.17} \cdot e^{i(2.28)} \\
\sqrt{0.32} \cdot e^{i(1.13)} & \sqrt{0.83}
\end{bmatrix}
$$

If we set $\langle B_D|S \rangle = 1$, then $p(A_D|B_D) = |\langle A_D|B_D \rangle|^2 = 0.68$, and if we set $\langle B_C|S \rangle = 1$, then $p(A_D|B_C) = |\langle A_D|B_C \rangle|^2 = 0.17$, and if we set

$$
\psi_0 = \begin{bmatrix} \langle B_D|S \rangle \\ \langle B_C|S \rangle \end{bmatrix} = \begin{bmatrix} \sqrt{0.54} \\ \sqrt{0.46} \end{bmatrix},
$$

$$
\psi_1 = \begin{bmatrix} \langle A_D|S \rangle \\ \langle A_C|S \rangle \end{bmatrix} = V \cdot \psi_0 = \begin{bmatrix} \sqrt{0.68 \cdot 0.54} + \sqrt{0.17 \cdot 0.46} \cdot e^{i(2.28)} \\ \sqrt{0.32 \cdot 0.54} \cdot e^{i(1.13)} + \sqrt{0.83 \cdot 0.46} \end{bmatrix},
$$

$$
|\langle A_D|S \rangle|^2 = 0.225 ,
$$

$$
|\langle A_C|S \rangle|^2 = 0.775.
$$

This model exactly reproduces all of the data from the Croson study. Note, however, if we set

$$
\psi_0 = \begin{bmatrix} \sqrt{0.54} \cdot i \\ \sqrt{0.46} \end{bmatrix}
$$

then $|\langle A_D|S \rangle|^2 = 0.70$ and $|\langle A_C|S \rangle|^2 = 0.09$ which sums to less than one. Therefore, the V transformation only preserves length when ψ_0 is real.

Let us consider another example using the data from the disjunction effect produced by the two-stage game. In this case we set

$$
V = \begin{bmatrix}
\sqrt{0.69} & \sqrt{0.59} \cdot e^{i(2.03)} \\
\sqrt{0.31} \cdot e^{i(0.66)} & \sqrt{0.41}
\end{bmatrix}.
$$

If we set $\langle B_D|S \rangle = 1$, then $p(A_D|B_D) = |\langle A_D|B_D \rangle|^2 = 0.69$, and if we set $\langle B_C|S \rangle = 1$, then $p(A_D|B_C) = |\langle A_D|B_C \rangle|^2 = 0.59$, and if we set $\langle B_D|S \rangle = \frac{1}{\sqrt{2}} = \langle B_C|S \rangle$ then we obtain $p(A_D) = 0.36$, which exactly reproduces the two-stage gambling game results. This model can reproduce all of the results reviewed above as long as the trigonometric constraint (F.1) is satisfied. If this constraint is violated, then one must switch from complex numbers to hyperbolic numbers. In fact, the latter is required to fit the results from the PD game.

F.2 Three-dimensional quantum model

A three-dimensional quantum model of the disjunction effect was proposed by Aerts (2009). Now we assume that there are three mutually exclusive states of inference: $|B_D\rangle$ represents the inference that the opponent will defect, $|B_C\rangle$ represents the inference that the opponent will cooperate, and $|B_N\rangle$ represents neither of these two inferences. The person starts in the initial state $|S\rangle$, and the transition from this initial state to each inference state is represented by the unit-length initial amplitude distribution

$$\psi_0 = \begin{bmatrix} \langle B_D|S\rangle \\ \langle B_C|S\rangle \\ \langle B_N|S\rangle \end{bmatrix}.$$

From this initial state the person can transit to one of three action states: $|A_{D1}\rangle$ represents the action to defect using one reason, $|A_{D2}\rangle$ represents the action to defect using a second reason, and $|A_C\rangle$ represents the action to cooperate. The amplitude distribution across the action states is represented by

$$\psi_1 = \begin{bmatrix} \langle A_{D1}|S\rangle \\ \langle A_{D2}|S\rangle \\ \langle A_C|S\rangle \end{bmatrix} = U \cdot \psi_0.$$

The transitions from the initial amplitude distribution to the final amplitude distribution are generated by a 3×3 unitary matrix U:

$$U = \begin{bmatrix} \sqrt{a} & e^{i\beta} \cdot \sqrt{\frac{(1-a)(1-b)}{a}} & -\sqrt{\frac{(1-a)(a+b-1)}{a}} \\ 0 & e^{i\beta} \cdot \sqrt{\frac{a+b-1}{a}} & \sqrt{\frac{1-b}{a}} \\ \sqrt{1-a} & -e^{i\beta} \cdot \sqrt{1-b} & \sqrt{a+b-1} \end{bmatrix},$$

with $0 \le a$, $b < 1$ and β is a parameter designed to reproduce the interference effect:

$$\beta = \arccos\left[\frac{\delta_1}{\sqrt{(1-a)(1-b)}} \right].$$

This model requires that $a + b \ge 1$, as well as the trigonometric constraint

$$\frac{|\delta_1|}{\sqrt{(1-a)(1-b)}} \le 1. \tag{F.2}$$

The 3×3 unitary matrix U satisfies the unitary property $U^\dagger U = I = UU^\dagger$, and so it preserves length $||\psi_1|| = 1$. This implies that the transition matrix generated by this unitary matrix must be a 3×3 doubly stochastic transition matrix. But it is difficult to check the double stochasticity property, because the experiments only report a smaller collapsed version of this matrix (which collapses across states $\{|A_{D1}\rangle, |A_{D2}\rangle\}$. As shown below, the two-dimensional transition matrix generated by this three-dimensional unitary matrix does not satisfy double stochasticity.

The choice probabilities are determined by two projectors, one that projects onto the two defection action states and the other that projects onto the single cooperation state:

$$M_1 = \begin{bmatrix} 1 & 0 & 0 \\ 0 & 1 & 0 \\ 0 & 0 & 0 \end{bmatrix}, \ M_2 = \begin{bmatrix} 0 & 0 & 0 \\ 0 & 0 & 0 \\ 0 & 0 & 1 \end{bmatrix}.$$

Then the probability of defection equals

$$p(A_D) = ||M_1 \cdot \psi_1||^2 = ||M_1 \cdot U \cdot \psi_0||^2.$$

If the opponent is known to defect, then $\langle B_D|S \rangle = 1$, which produces $p(A_D|B_D) = a$; if the opponent is known to cooperate, then $\langle B_C|S \rangle = 1$, which produces $p(A_D|B_C) = \frac{(1-a)(1-b)}{a} + \frac{a+b-1}{a} = b$; if the opponent's action is unknown, then $\langle B_D|S \rangle = \frac{1}{\sqrt{2}} = \langle B_C|S \rangle$, which produces

$$p(A_D) = \frac{a+b}{2} + \sqrt{(1-a)(1-b)} \cos(\beta).$$

Note that this model does not require $p(A_D|B_C) = 1 - p(A_D|B_D)$ because $p(A_D|B_C) = b$ and $p(A_D|I_D) = a$, and these two parameters are functionally independent of each other.

The model runs into trouble with the Shafir and Tversky (1992) PD game results because it violates the trigonometric constraint (F.2). So let us see how this model works for the two-stage gambling game. In this case set $a = 0.69 = p(A_D|B_D)$, $b = 0.59 = p(A_D|B_C)$; then assuming $\langle B_D|S \rangle = \frac{1}{\sqrt{2}} = \langle B_C|S \rangle$ and setting $\beta = 0.7875 \cdot \pi$ produces $p(A_D) = 0.36$ for the unknown condition assuming, this exactly reproduces the results for the two-stage gamble.

F.3 Four-dimensional quantum model

A four-dimensional model for the disjunction effect was proposed by Yukalov and Sornette (2009). Once again, consider the PD paradigm. The model begins by assuming that the person initially represents the entire situation by a unit-length vector in a four-dimensional space:

$$\psi = \begin{bmatrix} \psi_{11} \\ \psi_{12} \\ \psi_{21} \\ \psi_{22} \end{bmatrix},$$

where ψ_{ij} is the amplitude for believing your opponent will take action i ($i = 1$ for believing the opponent will defect, $i = 2$ for believing the opponent will cooperate) and the player intends to take action j ($j = 1$ for player defects, $j = 2$ for player cooperates). For example, ψ_{21} is the amplitude to believe that the opponent will cooperate but the player intends to take the action to defect.

The total amplitude for the player to defect is based on a superposition of two amplitudes regarding beliefs about the opponent:

$$\phi_1 = k \cdot (\psi_{11} + \psi_{21}).$$

Likewise, the total amplitude for the player to cooperate is also based on a superposition of two amplitudes regarding beliefs about the opponent:

$$\phi_2 = k \cdot (\psi_{12} + \psi_{22}).$$

The probability that the player chooses to defect then equals $|\phi_1|^2$ and the probability that the player chooses to cooperate equals $|\phi_2|^2$. These two probabilities must sum to one, and this is accomplished by setting the normalizing coefficient to

$$k^2 = \frac{1}{|\phi_1|^2 + |\phi_2|^2},$$

which requires $|\phi_1|^2 + |\phi_2|^2 > 0$. Based on this answer for the normalizing coefficient, the probability of defecting equals

$$p(A_\mathrm{D}) = \frac{|\psi_{11} + \psi_{21}|^2}{|\psi_{11} + \psi_{21}|^2 + |\psi_{12} + \psi_{22}|^2}. \tag{F.3}$$

If the opponent is known to defect, then

$$\psi = \begin{bmatrix} a_1 \\ a_2 \\ 0 \\ 0 \end{bmatrix}$$

and $|a_1|^2 + |a_2|^2 = 1$, which implies $P(A_\mathrm{D}|B_\mathrm{C}) = |a_1|^2$; likewise, if the opponent is known to cooperate, then

$$\psi = \begin{bmatrix} 0 \\ 0 \\ b_1 \\ b_2 \end{bmatrix}$$

and $|b_1|^2 + |b_2|^2 = 1$, which implies $P(A_\mathrm{D}|B_\mathrm{C}) = |b_1|^2$. If the opponent is believed to be equally likely to defect or cooperate, then

$$\psi = \frac{1}{2} \cdot \begin{bmatrix} a_1 \\ a_2 \\ b_1 \\ b_2 \end{bmatrix}$$

and we use (F.3) to obtain

$$p(A_\mathrm{D}) = \frac{|a_1 + b_1|^2}{|a_1 + b_1|^2 + |a_2 + b_2|^2}.$$

To see how this works, first consider the PD game results. If we set $a_1 = \sqrt{0.97}$, $b_1 = \sqrt{0.84} \cdot e^{i \cdot 2.7934}$, then $k^2 = 23.1557$, which produces $p(A_\mathrm{D}|B_\mathrm{D}) = 0.97$ and $p(A_\mathrm{D}|B_\mathrm{C}) = 0.84$, and $p(A_\mathrm{D}) = 0.65$ reproducing the results from the PD game. Next, consider the two-stage gambling results. If we set $a_1 = \sqrt{0.69}$, $b_1 = \sqrt{0.59} \cdot e^{i\pi}$, then $k^2 = 367.2929$, which produces $p(A_\mathrm{D}|B_\mathrm{D}) = 0.69$ and $p(A_\mathrm{D}|B_\mathrm{C}) = 0.59$, and $p(A_\mathrm{D}) = 0.36$, reproducing the results from the two-stage gambling game.

G   Computer programs

G.1   Chapter 8: program used to test temporal Bell property

```
%%%%%%%%%%%%%%%%%%%%%%%%%%%%%%%%%%%%
%%%   Quantum Model
h = 2;  t = .25;
H =[ 0 1;
     1 0];
Mp = [1 0;
      0 0];
Mn = eye(2)-Mp;
S0 = sqrt([.5 .5])';
U = expm(-1i*t*h*H);
%%% Condition 1: Test at t1 and t2
     Pnp = Mn*U*Mp*U*S0; Pnp = Pnp'*Pnp;
     Ppn = Mp*U*Mn*U*S0; Ppn = Ppn'*Ppn;
     Pc1 = Pnp +Ppn;
%%% Condition 2:  Test at t2 and t3
     Pnp = Mn*U*Mp*U*U*S0; Pnp = Pnp'*Pnp;
     Ppn = Mp*U*Mn*U*U*S0; Ppn = Ppn'*Ppn;
     Pc2 = Ppn +Pnp;
%%%  Condition 3: Test at t1 and t3
     Pnp = Mn*U*U*Mp*U*S0; Pnp = Pnp'*Pnp;
     Ppn = Mp*U*U*Mn*U*S0; Ppn = Ppn'*Ppn;
     Pc3 = Pnp +Ppn;
disp(' Pc1 Pc2 Pc3 Diff')
disp([Pc1 Pc2 Pc3 (Pc3-Pc1-Pc2)])
%%% Markov model
k= 1;
K = [ -k  k;
       k -k];
```

```
P0 = [.5 .5]';
U = expm(t*K);
L = [1 1]';
%%% Condition 1: Test at t1 and t2
    Pnp = Mn*U*Mp*U*S0; Pnp = L'*Pnp;
    Ppn = Mp*U*Mn*U*S0; Ppn = L'*Ppn;
    Pc1 = Pnp +Ppn;
%%% Condition 2: Test at t2 and t3
    Pnp = Mn*U*Mp*U*U*S0; Pnp = L'*Pnp;
    Ppn = Mp*U*Mn*U*U*S0; Ppn = L'*Ppn;
    Pc2 = Pnp +Ppn;
%%% Condition 3: Test at  t1 and t3
    Pnp = Mn*U*U*Mp*U*S0; Pnp = L'*Pnp;
    Ppn = Mp*U*U*Mn*U*S0; Ppn = L'*Ppn;
    Pc3 = Ppn +Pnp;
disp(' Pc1 Pc2 Pc3 D')
disp([Pc1 Pc2 Pc3 (P3-P1-P2)])
%%%%%%%%%%%%%%%%%%%%%%%%%%%%%%%%%%%%%%
```

G.2 Chapter 8: program used to generate Figure 8.7

```
%%%%%%%%%%%%%%%%%%%%%%%%%%%%%%%%%%%%%%
% mean conf across time only seven states
clc
clear
%%% initial parameters
ns = 7;          % odd no. evidence states
ws = 3;          % ws = start width
tv = 0:.1:20;    % no time steps
nt = size(tv,2);
Mid = (ns+1)/2;
mv = -(Mid-1):(Mid-1);
%%%%  Quantum model
    mu = 1;          % drift rate
    ap = 1;          % diffusion
    % build start state
        S0 = zeros(ns,1);
        S0((Mid-ws):(Mid+ws)) = 1;
        S0 = S0./sqrt(S0'*S0);
    % build Hamiltonian
        b = mu*mv;
        a = ap*ones(ns,1);
        H = buildH(a,b,a);     % function given below
    % time loop
    PM1 = [];
    for n=1:nt
```

```
            t = tv(n);
            U = expm(-1i*t*H);
            St = U*S0;
            Mc = mv*(abs(St).^2);
            PM1 = [PM1 ; [n+1 Mc]];
        end
%%%% Markov model
        mu = .5; % drift rate
        var = 2; % diffusion
        % build start state
            S0 = zeros(ns,1);
            S0((Mid-ws):(Mid+ws)) = 1;
            S0 = S0./sum(S0);
        % build intensity matrix
            mk = ones(ns,1);
            b = -var*mk;
            a1 = .5*(var-mu)*mk;
            a2 = .5*(var+mu)*mk;
            K = buildK(a1,b,a2);    % function given below
        % time loop
        PM2=[];
        for n=1:nt
            t = tv(n);
            T = expm(t*K);
            Pt = T*S0;
            Mc = mv*Pt;
            PM2 = [PM2 ; [n+1 Mc]];
        end

    %%%%% Plot results
    plot(tv,PM2(:,2),'-o',tv,PM1(:,2),'.-')
        xlabel('Time')
        ylabel('Mean Confidence')
        legend('Markov','quantum')
    %%%% functions used in above program
    function H = buildH(a,b,c)
    % H = buildH(a,b,c)
    % m = number of states
    % a = off diag left
    % b = diag
    % c = off diag right
    m = size(a,1);
    H = zeros(m);
    H(1,[1 2])= [ b(1) c(1)];
    H(m,[m-1 m]) = [a(m) b(m)];
    for k = 2:(m-1)
```

```
K = [(k-1) k (k+1)] ;
H(k,K) = [a(k) b(k) c(k)];
end
function K = buildK(a,b,c)
% K = buildK(a,b,c)
% m = number of states
% a = off diag left
% b = diag
% c = off diag right
m = size(a,1);
K = zeros(m);
K([1 2],1)= [ b(1) -b(1)];
K([m-1 m], m) = [-b(m) b(m)];
for k = 2:(m-1)
    v = [(k-1) k (k+1)] ;
    K(v,k) = [a(k) b(k) c(k)];
end
%%%%%%%%%%%%%%%%%%%%%%%%%%%%%%%%%%%%%
```

G.3   Chapter 9: program to fit category decision data

```
% main program to fit categ dec int eff using Pothos Busemeyer model
    % three params
    clc
    clear
    % state is GA GW BA BW
    % data = [ p(Gc) p(D|Gc) p(Gd) p(D|Gd) p(D) ]
    % X = [ .84 .35 .16 .52 .39]'; % orig c-then-d wide
    % p = [ .4638 1 .8516]'; % fit shown in Table 2
    X = [ .17 .41 .83 .63 .69]'; % orig narr c-then-d
    p = [-.3106 1 .9417]';
    t = pi/2;
    mu1 = p(1); % good guy
    mu2 = p(2); % bad guy
    gam = p(3);
    Ha1 =(1/sqrt(1+(mu1.^2)))*kron([1 0 ; 0 0],[-mu1 1; 1 mu1]); % good guy
    Ha2 =(1/sqrt(1+(mu2.^2)))*kron([0 0 ; 0 1],[mu2 1; 1 -mu2]); % bad guy
    Ha = Ha1 + Ha2;
    Hc = (gam/sqrt(2))*( kron([-1 1;1 1],[1 0; 0 0])...
    + kron([1 1;1 -1],[0 0; 0 1]) );
    H = Ha + Hc;
    U = expm(-1i*t*H);
    X1 = [1 1 0 0]'; X1 = X1./sqrt(X1'*X1); % good guy
    X2 = [0 0 1 1]'; X2 = X2./sqrt(X2'*X2); % bad guy
    X3 = sqrt(X(1)).*X1 + sqrt(X(3)).*X2; X3 = X3./sqrt(X3'*X3); % un-
known
```

```
S1 = U*X1;
S2 = U*X2;
S3 = U*X3;
M = [1 0 0 0;
0 0 0 0
0 0 1 0
0 0 0 0];
P1 = M*S1; P1 = P1'*P1; % attack given good
P2 = M*S2; P2 = P2'*P2; % attack given bad
P3 = M*S3; P3 = P3'*P3; % attack unknown
P = [ X(1) P1 X(3) P2 P3]';
SSE = X-P; SSE = SSE'*SSE;
disp(' SSE good bad gam')
disp([SSE p'])
disp(' Data Pred')
X = [X(1:4) ; X(1)*X(2) + X(3)*X(4); X(5)];
P = [P(1:4) ; P(1)*P(2) + P(3)*P(4); P(5)];
disp([X P])
%%%%%%%%%%%%%%%%%%%%%%%%%%%%%%%%%%%%%%%
```

G.4   Chapter 11: program to learn a unitary matrix

```
% learn unitary using only abs of state
clear
clc
parmv = [.5167 2.3109];
% parmv = [.5935 1.743];
% parmv = [.5 0];
mu1 = 1/(1+exp(-parmv(1)));
mu2 = 1/(1+exp(-parmv(1)));
gam = parmv(2);
Ha1 = (1/sqrt(1+(mu1.^2)))*kron([1 0 ; 0 0],[mu1 1; 1 -mu1]);
Ha2 = (1/sqrt(1+(mu2.^2)))*kron([0 0 ; 0 1],[mu2 1; 1 -mu2]);
Ha = Ha1 + Ha2;
Hc = (-gam/sqrt(2))*( kron([1 1;1 -1],[1 0; 0 0])...
+ kron([-1 1;1 1],[0 0; 0 1]) );
H = Ha + Hc;
U = expm(-1i*(pi/2)*H);
s = size(U);
N = 2000;
sl = N/2;
He = eye(s);
F = 0;
del = .25; % .25
Fm = F;
for t = 1:N
```

```
        X = rand(s(1,1),1);
        X = X./sqrt(X'*X);
        Y = U*X;
        Y = abs(Y);
        Ht = He + (t<=sl).*del.*DerivU2(He,X,Y);
        Ut = expm(-1i.*(pi/2).*Ht);
        Yh = Ut*X;
        Yh = abs(Yh);
        Ft = real(Y'*Yh + Yh'*Y);
        He = (Ft>F).*Ht + (Ft<=F).*He;
        Ue = expm(-1i.*(pi/2).*He);
        Yh = Ue*X;
        Yh = abs(Yh);
        F = real(Y'*Yh + Yh'*Y);
        Fm = [Fm F];
end
disp('Final Distance')
disp(2-F)
Sl = zeros(N+1,1); Sl(sl+1)=2;
plot((0:N),2-Fm,(0:N),Sl)
xlabel('Trial')
ylabel('Squared Distance')
axis([0 N 0 2])
title('Delta Learning Model for Hamiltonian')
%%%%%%%%%%%%%%%%%%%
function DU = DerivU2(H,X,Y)
% function DU = DerivU2(H,X,Y)
h = .001;
s = size(H,1);
U = expm(-1i*(pi/2)*H);
Yh = U*X;
Yh = abs(Yh);
FU = Y'*Yh + Yh'*Y;
DU = zeros(s,s);
for j=1:s
    for k = 1:j
        Hc = H;
        Hc(j,k) = Hc(j,k)+h;
        Hc(k,j) = Hc(j,k);
        Uh = expm(-1i*(pi/2)*Hc);
        Yh = Uh*X;
        Yh = abs(Yh);
        FUh = Y'*Yh + Yh'*Y;
        DU(j,k) = (FUh-FU)./h;
        DU(k,j) = DU(j,k);
    end
end
```

```
%%%%%%%%%%%%%%%%%%%%%%%%%%%%%%%%%%%%%%%%
Program used to generate Figure 11.4
%%%%%%%%%%%%%%%%%%%%%%%%%%%%%%%%%%%%%%%%
% Amplitude amplification algorithm
clc
clear
N = 30; % number of actions
L = 1; % number of amplifications
a = 15; % chosen option
ph1 = .15*pi;
ph2 = ph1;
p1 = exp(1i*ph1);
p2 = exp(1i*ph2);
% X0 = ones(N,1)/sqrt(N);
seq = (1:N)'; mid = N/2;
X0 = exp( -((seq-mid)/10).^2 );
X0 = X0./sqrt(X0'*X0);
A = 1.*((1:N)'==a);
P1 = eye(N) - (1-p2)*(A*A');
P2 = (1-p1)*(X0*X0') - eye(N);
Q = P2*P1;
Y = (Q^L)*X0; YM = abs(Y).^2;
ph1 = seq;
plot(ph1,YM,'-','LineWidth',2)
hold on
plot(ph1,abs(X0(a)).^2,'.','LineWidth',3)
hold off
xlabel('Action')
ylabel('Probability for selected action')
axis([min(ph1) max(ph1) 0 1])
end
```

References

Accardi, L., Khrennikov, A. Y., & Ohya, M. (2009). Quantum Markov model for data from Shafir–Tversky experiments in cognitive psychology. *Open Systems and Information Dynamics*, **16**(4), 371–385.

Aerts, D. (2009). Quantum structure in cognition. *Journal of Mathematical Psychology*, **53**(5), 314–348.

Aerts, D. & Aerts, S. (1994). Applications of quantum statistics in psychological studies of decision processes. *Foundations of Science*, **1**, 85–97.

Aerts, D. & Czachor, M. (2004). Quantum aspects of semantic analysis and symbolic artificial intelligence. *Journal of Physics A–Mathematical and General*, **37**, L123–L132 (http://uk.arxiv.org/abs/quant-ph/0309022).

Aerts, D. & Gabora, L. (2005). A theory of concepts and their combinations II: A Hilbert space representation. *Kybernetes*, **34**, 192–221.

Aerts, D. & Sozzo, S. (2011). Quantum structure in cognition: why and how concepts are entangled (arXiv:1104.1322v1).

Aerts, D., Aerts, S., Broeckaert, J., & Gabora, L. (2000). The violation of Bell inequalities in the macroworld. *Foundations of Physics*, **30**, 1378–1414.

Aerts, D., Broekaert, J., & Gabora, L. (2005). A case for applying an abstracted quantum formalism to cognition. In *Mind in Interaction*, ed. M. Bickhard & R. Campbell. Amsterdam: John Benjamins.

Aerts, D., Broekaert, J., & Gabora, L. (2011). A case for applying an abstracted quantum formalism to cognition. *New Ideas in Psychology*, **29**, 136–146.

Aharonov, Y., Davidovich, L., & Zagury, N. (1993). Quantum random walks. *Physical Review A*, **48**, 1687–1690.

Ahn, W. Y., Krawitz, A., Kim, W., Busemeyer, J. R., & Brown, J. W. (2011). A model-based FMRI analysis with hierarchical Bayesian parameter estimation. *Journal of Neuroscience, Psychology, and Economics*, **4**(2), 95–110.

Allais, M. (1953). Le comportement de l'homme rationnel devant le risque: critique des postulats et axiomes de l'école américaine. *Econometrica*, **21**, 503–546.

Anderson, J. R. (1993). *Rules of the Mind.* Erlbaum.

Anscombe, F. J. & Aumann, R. J. (1963). A definition of subjective probability. *Annals of Mathematical Statistics*, **34**, 199–205.

Ashby, F. G. & Townsend, J. T. (1986). Varieties of perceptual independence. *Psychological Review*, **93**, 154–179.

Aspect, A. (1999). Bell's inequality test: more ideal than ever. *Nature*, **398**, 189–190.

Atkinson, R. C. & Shiffrin, R. M. (1968). Human memory: a proposed system and its control processes. In *The Psychology of Learning and Motivation*, ed. K. W. Spence & J. T. Spense. New York: Academic Press, pp. 89–195.

Atmanspacher, H. (2011). Quantum approaches to consciousness. In *Stanford Encyclopedia of Philosophy*, ed. E. N. Zalta.

Atmanspacher, H. & Filk, T. (2010). A proposed test of temporal nonlocality in bistable perception. *Journal of Mathematical Psychology*, **54**, 314–321.

Atmanspacher, H., & Romer, H., & Walach, H. (2002). Weak quantum theory: complementarity and entanglement in physics and beyond. *Foundations of Physics*, **32**, 379–406.

Atmanspacher, H., Filk, T., & Romer, H. (2004). Quantum zero features of bistable perception. *Biological Cybernetics*, **90**, 33–40.

Baaquie, B. E. (2004). *Quantum Finance: Path Integrals and Hamiltonians for Options and Interest Rates*. Cambridge University Press.

Baddeley, A. D. (1992). Working memory. *Science*, **255**, 556–559.

Barkan, R. & Busemeyer, J. R. (1999). Changing plans: dynamic inconsistency and the effect of experience on the reference point. *Psychological Bulletin and Review*, **10**, 353–359.

Barkan, R. & Busemeyer, J. R. (2003). Modeling dynamic inconsistency with a changing reference point. *Journal of Behavioral Decision Making*, **16**, 235–255.

Batchelder, W. H. & Reiffer, D. M. (1999). Theoretical and empirical review of multinomial process tree modeling. *Psychonomic Bulletin and Review*, **6**, 57–86.

Beck, F. & Eccles, J. (1992). Quantum apsects of brain activity and the role of consciousness. *Proceedings of the National Academy of Sciences of the USA*, **89**, 11357–11361.

Behera, L., Kar, I., & Elitzur, A. C. (2005). Recurrent quantum neural network model to describe eye tracking of moving target. *Foundations of Physics Letters*, **18**(4), 357–370.

Bell, J. (1987). Bertlmann's socks and the nature of reality. In *Speakable and Unspeakable in Quantum Mechanics*. Cambridge University Press.

Beltrametti, E. G. & Cassinelli, G. (1981). *The Logic of Quantum Mechanics. Encyclopedia of Mathematics and its Applications*, volume 15. Addison-Wesley.

Bhattacharya, R. N. & Waymire, E. C. (1990). *Stochastic Processes with Applications*. Wiley.

Birnbaum, M. (2008). New paradoxes of risky decision making. *Psychological Review*, **115**, 463–501.

Blasone, M., Jizba, P., & Vitiello, G. (2011). *Quantum Field Theory and its Macroscopic Manifestations*. London: Imperial College Press.

Blutner, R. (2009). Concepts and bounded rationality: an application of Niestegge's approach to conditional quantum probabilities. In *Foundations of Probability and Physics No. 5 – AIP Conference Proceedings*, vol. 1101, ed. L. Acardi, A. Y. Khrennikov, C. A. Fuchs, G. Jaeger, J.-A. Larsson, & S. Stenholm. American Institute of Physics, pp. 302–310.

Blutner, R. & Hochnadel, E. (2010). Two cubits for C.G. Jung's theory of personality. *Cognitive Systems Research*, **11**(3), 243–259.

Bohr, N. (1958). *Atomic Physics and Human Knowledge*. New York: Wiley.

Bordley, R. F. (1998). Quantum mechanical and human violations of compound probability principles: toward a generalized Heisenberg uncertainty principle. *Operations Research*, *46*, 923–926.

Bordley, R. & Kadane, J. B. (1999). Experiment-dependent priors in psychology. *Theory and Decision*, **47**(3), 213–227.

Brainerd, C. J. & Reyna, V. F. (2008). Episodic over-distribution: a signature effect of familiarity without recognition. *Journal of Memory and Language*, **58**, 765–786.

Brainerd, C. J., Reyna, V. F., & Mojardin, A. H. (1999). Conjoint recognition. *Psychological Review*, **106**(1), 160–179.

Bruza, P. & Cole, R. J. (2005). Quantum logic of semantic space: an exploratory investigation of context effects in practical reasoning. In *We Will Show Them: Essays in Honour of Dov Gabbay*, ed. S. Artemov, H. Barringer, A. S. d'Avila, L. C. Lamb, & J. Woods, College Publications, pp. 339–361.

Bruza, P. & De Vine, L. (2010). Semantic oscillations: encoding context and structure in complex valued holographic vectors. In *Quantum Informatics for Cognitive, Social, and Semantic Processes (QI 2010)*, ed. P. Bruza, W. Lawless, C. von Rijsbergen, D. Sofge, & D. Widdows. AAAI Press.

Bruza, P., Lawless, W., van Rijsbergen, C. J., & Sofge, D. (2007). *Proceedings of the AAAI Spring Symposium on Quantum Interaction*. AAAI Press.

Bruza, P., Lawless, W., van Rijsbergen, C. J., & Sofge, D. (2008). *Quantum Interaction: Proceedings of the Second Quantum Interaction Symposium*. London: College Publications.

Bruza, J. R., Busemeyer, P., & Gabora, L. (2009a). Introduction to the special issue on quantum cognition. *Journal of Mathematical Psychology*, **53**(5), 303–305.

Bruza, P., Sofge, D., Lawless, W., van Rijsbergen, C. J., & Klusch, M. (2009b). *Proceedings of the Third Quantum Interaction Symposium*. Springer.

Bruza, P., Kitto, K., Nelson, D., & McEvoy, C. (2009c). Is there something quantum-like in the human mental lexicon? *Journal of Mathematical Psychology*, **53**(5), 362–377.

Bruza, P. D., Kitto, K., Nelson, D., & McEvoy, C. (2009d). Extracting spooky-activation-at-a-distance from considerations of entanglement. In *Proceedings of the Third Quantum Interaction Symposium*, vol. 5494. Springer, pp. 71–83.

Bruza, P., Iqbal, A., & Kitto, K. (2010). The role of non-factorizability in determining "pseudo-classical" non-separability. In *Quantum Informatics for Cognitive, Social, and Semantic Processes (QI 2010)*, ed. P. Bruza, W. Lawless, C. van Rijsbergen, D. Sofge, & D. Widdows. AAAI Press.

Bruza, P., Kitto, K., Ramm, B., & Sitbon, L. (2012). The non-compositionality of concept combinations. *Cognitive Science*, Under review.

Bullinaria, J. A. & Levy, J. P. (2007). Extracting semantic representations from word co-occurrence statistics: a computational study. *Behavior Research Methods*, **39**(3), 510–526.

Burgess, C., Livesay, K., & Lund, K. (1998). Explorations in context space: words, sentences, discourse. *Discourse Processes*, **25**(2–3), 211–257.

Busemeyer, J. R. & Diederich, A. (2009). *Cognitive Modeling*. Sage.

Busemeyer, J. & Townsend, J. (1993). Decision field theory: a dynamic-cognitive approach to decision making in an uncertain environment. *Psychological Review*, **100**, 432–459.

Busemeyer, J. & Wang, Z. (2010). Quantum probability applied to the social and behavioral sciences. In *Proceedings of the First Interdisciplinary Chess Interactions Conference*, ed. C. Rangacharyulu & E. Haven World Scientific Publishing Company, pp. 115–125.

Busemeyer, J. R., Weg, E., Barkan, R., Li, X., & Ma, Z. (2000). Dynamic and consequential consistency of choices between paths of decision trees. *Journal of Experimental Psychology: General*, **129**, 530–545.

Busemeyer, J. R., Wang, Z., & Townsend, J. T. (2006a). Quantum dynamics of human decision making. *Journal of Mathematical Psychology*, *50*, 220–241.

Busemeyer, J. R., Matthews, M., & Wang, Z. (2006b). A quantum information processing explanation of disjunction effects. In *Proceedings of the 29th Annual Conference of the Cognitive Science Society and the 5th International Conference of Cognitive Science*, ed. R. Sun & N. Myake. Erlbaum, pp. 131–135.

Busemeyer, J. R., Wang, Z., & Lambert-Mogiliansky, A. (2009). Comparison of Markov and quantum models of decision making. *Journal of Mathematical Psychology*, **53**(5), 423–433.

Busemeyer, J. R., Pothos, E. M., Franco, R., & Trueblood, J. S. (2011). A quantum theoretical explanation for probability judgment errors. *Psychological Review*, **118**(2), 193–218.

Camerer, C. F. (1989). An experimental test of several generalized utility theories. *Journal of Risk and Uncertainty*, **2**, 61–104.

Camerer, C. F. & Weber, M. (1992). Recent developments in modeling preferences: uncertainty and ambiguity. *Journal of Risk and Uncertainty*, **5**, 325–370.

Carlson, B. W. & Yates, J. F. (1989). Disjunction errors in qualitative likelihood judgment. *Organizational Behavior and Human Decision Processes*, **44**, 368–379.

Caves, C. M., Fuchs, C. A., & Schak, R. (2002). Quantum probabilties as Bayesian probabilities. *Physical Review A*, **65**(2), 1–6.

Cereceda, J. (2000). Quantum mechanical probabilities and general probabilistic constraints for Einstein–Podolsky–Rosen–Bohm experiments. *Foundations of Physics Letters*, **13**(5), 427–442.

Chalmers, D. (1996). *The Conscious Mind*. Oxford University Press.

Cheon, T. & Takahashi, T. (2010). Interference and inequality in quantum decision theory. *Physics Letters A*, **375**, 100–104.

Clauser, J. & Horne, M. (1974). Experimental consequences of objective local theories. *Physical Review D*, **10**(2), 526–535.

Coecke, B., Sadrzadeh, M., & Clark, S. (2010). Mathematical foundations for a compositional distributional model of meaning. *Linguistic Analysis*, **36**(1–4), 345–384.

Collins, A. & Loftus, E. (1975). A spreading-activation theory of semantic processing. *Psychological Review*, **82**(6), 407–428.

Conte, E. (1983). Exploration of biological function by quantum mechanics. In *Proceedings 10th International Congress on Cybernetics*. Namur-Belgique, pp. 16–23.

Conte, E., Todarello, O., Federici, A., Vitiello, F., Lopane, M., & Khrennikov, A. (2007). Some remarks on an experiment suggesting quantum-like behavior of cognitive entities and formulation of an abstract quantum mechanical formalism to describe cognitive entity and its dynamics. *Chaos, Solitons, and Fractals*, **31**, 1076–1088.

Conte, E., Khrennikov, A. Y., Todarello, O., Federici, A., Mendolicchio, L., & Zbilut, J. P. (2009). Mental states follow quantum mechanics during perception and cognition of ambiguous figures. *Open Systems and Information Dynamics*, **16**, 1–17.

Costello, F. & Keane, M. (2000). Efficient creativity: constraint-guided conceptual combination. *Cognitive Science*, **24**(2), 299–349.

Croson, R. (1999). The disjunction effect and reason-based choice in games. *Organizational Behavior and Human Decision Processes*, **80**(2), 118–133.

Cubitt, R. P., Starmer, C., & Sugden, R. (1998). Dynamic choice and the common ratio effect: an experimental invesigation. *Economic Journal*, **108**, 1362–1380.

DeBarros, J. A. & Suppes, P. (2009). Quantum mechanics, interference, and the brain. *Journal of Mathematical Psychology*, **53**, 306–313.

DeGroot, M. H. (2004). *Optimal Statistical Decisons*. Wiley–IEEE.

Dickson, W. (1998). *Quantum Chance and Non-Locality*. Cambridge University Press.

Dirac, P. A. M. (1958). *The Principles of Quantum Mechanics*. Oxford University Press.

Dong, D., Chen, C., Li, H., & Tarn, T. J. (2008). Quantum reinforcement learning. *IEEE Transactions on Systems, Man, and Cybernetics, B: Cybernetics*, **38**(5), 1207–1220.

Dong, D., Chen, C., Chu, J., & Tarn, T. J. (2010). Robust quantum-inspired reinforcement learning for robot navigation. *IEEE/ASME Transactions on Mechatronics*, **17**(1), 1–12.

Dougherty, M. R. P., Gettys, C. F., & Odgen, E. E. (1999). Minverva-dm: a memory processes model for judgments of likelihood. *Psychological Review*, **106**(1), 180–209.

Dulany, D. E., Carlson, R. A., & Dewey, G. I. (1984). A case of syntactical learning and judgment: how conscious and how abstract? *Journal of Experimental Psychology: General*, **113**(4), 541–555.

Eisert, M., Wilkens, J., & Lewenstein, M. (1999). Quantum games and quantum strategies. *Physical Review Letters*, **83**, 3077–3080.

Ellsberg, D. (1961). Risk, ambiguity, and the savage axioms. *Quarterly Journal of Economics*, **75**, 643–669.

Engesser, K., Gabbay, D. M., & Lehmann, D. (2009). *Handbook of Quantum Logic and Quantum Structures*. Elsevier.

Epstein, S., Lipson, A., Holstein, C., & Huh, E. (1992). Irrational reactions to negative outcomes: evidence for two conceptual systems. *Journal of Personality and Social Psychology*, **62**, 328–339.

Feldman, J. M. & Lynch, J. G. (1988). Self-generated validity and other effects of measurement on belief, attitude, intention, and behavior. *Journal of Applied Psychology*, **73**(3), 421–435.

Festinger, L. (1957). *A Theory of Cognitive Dissonance*. Stanford University Press.

Feynman, R. P. (1982). Simulating physics with computers. *International Journal of Theoretical Physics*, **21**, 467–488.

Feynman, R. P., Leighton, R. B., & Sands, M. (1965). *Lectures on Physics: Quantum Mechanics*, volume III. Addison-Wesley.

Fine, A. (1982a). Hidden variables, joint probability and the Bell inequalities. *Physics Review Letters*, **48**(5), 291–295.

Fine, A. (1982b). Joint distributions, quantum correlations and commuting observables. *Journal of Mathematical Physics*, **23**(7), 1306–1310.

Fisk, J. E. (2002). Judgments under uncertainty: representativeness or potential surprise? *British Journal of Psychology*, **93**, 431–449.

Fodor, G. (1994). Concepts: a potboiler. *Cognition*, **50**, 95–113.

Franco, R. (2009a). The conjunctive fallacy and interference effects. *Journal of Mathematical Psychology*, **53**(5), 415–422.

Franco, R. (2009b). Quantum amplitude amplification algorithm: an explanation of availability bias. In *Quantum Interaction*, Lecture Notes in Computer Science, vol. 5494, ed. P. Bruza, D. Sofge, W. Lawless, K. van Rijsbergen, & M. Klusch. Springer, pp. 84–96.

Freeman, W. J. (1979). Nonlinear dynamics of paleocortex manifested in the olfactory EEG. *Biological Cybernetics*, **35**, 21–37.

Freeman, W. J. & Vitiello, G. (2006). Nonlinear brain dynamics as macroscopic manifestation of underlying many-body dynamics. *Physics of Life Reviews*, **3**, 93–118.

Fries, P. (2009). Neural gamma-band synchronization as a fundamental process in cortical computation. *Annual Reviews of Neuroscience*, **32**, 209–224.

Fries, P., Nikoli, D., & Singer, W. (2007). The gamma cycle. *Trends in Neuroscience*, **50**(7), 309–316.

Fuss, I. G. & Navarro, D. J. (2008). Partially coherent quantum models for human two-choice decisions. In *Proceedings of the Second Quantum Interaction Symposium*, ed. P. D. Bruza, W. Lawless, K. van Rijsbergen, D. A. Sofge, B. Coecke, & S. Clark. College Publications, pp. 75–82.

Gabbay, D. & Woods, J. (2005). *The Reach of Abduction: Insight and Trial*, vol. 2. Elsevier.

Gabora, L. & Aerts, D. (2002). Contextualizing concepts using a mathematical generalization of the quantum formalism. *Journal of Experimental Theoretical Artificial Intelligence*, **14**, 327–358.

Gabora, L., Rosch, E., & Aerts, D. (2008). Toward an ecological theory of concepts. *Ecological Psychology*, **20**, 84–116.

Galea, D., Bruza, P., Kitto, K., Nelson, D., & McEvoy, C. (2011). Modelling the activation of words in human memory: the spreading activation, spooky-activation-at-a-distance and the entanglement models compared. In *Proceedings of the Fifth Quantum Interaction Symposium (QI-2011)*. Springer.

Gärdenfors, P. (2000). *Conceptual Spaces: The Geometry of Thought*. MIT Press.

Gardiner, C. W. (1991). *Quantum Noise*. Springer.

Gavanski, I. & Roskos-Ewoldsen, D. R. (1991). Representativeness and conjoint probability. *Journal of Personality and Social Psychology*, **61**, 181 194.

Gee, N., Nelson, D., & Krawczyk, D. (1999). Is the connectedness effect a result of underlying network interconnectivity? *Journal of Memory and Language*, **40**(4), 479–497.

Gigerenzer, G. (2000). *Adaptive Thinking: Rationality in the Real World*. Oxford University Press.

Gilboa, I. (2009). *Theory of Decision under Uncertainty*. Cambridge University Press.

Gleason, A. M. (1957). Measures on the closed subspaces of a Hilbert space. *Journal of Mathematical Mechanics*, **6**, 885–893.

Goschke, T. & Koppelberg, D. (1991). The concept of representation and the representation of concepts in connectionist models. In *Philosophy and Connectionist Theory*, ed. W. Ramsey, S. Stich, & D. Rumelhart. Laurence Erlbaum, pp. 129–161.

Graben, P. B. & Atmanspacher, H. (2006). Complementarity in classical dynamical systems. *Foundations of Physics*, **36**, 291–306.

Graben, P. B. & Atmanspacher, H. (2008). Extending the philosophical significance of the idea of complementarity. In *Recasting Reality: Wolfgang Pauli's Philosophical Ideas and Contemporary Science*, ed. H. Atmanspacher & H. Primas. Berlin: Springer, pp. 99–113.

Gratton, G., Coles, M. G., Sirevaag, E. J., Erickson, C. J., & Donchin, E. (1988). Pre- and poststimulus activation of response channels: a psychophysiological analysis. *Journal of Experimental Psychology: Human Perception and Performance*, **14**, 331–344.

Griffiths, R. (2002). *Consistent Quantum Theory*. Cambridge University Press.

Griffiths, R. B. (2003). *Consistent Quantum Theory*. Cambridge University Press.

Griffiths, T., Steyvers, M., & Tenenbaum, J. (2007). Topics in semantic memory. *Psychological Review*, **114**(2), 211–244.

Griffiths, T. L., Kemp, C., & Tenenbaum, J. B. (2008). Bayesian models of cognition. *Cambridge Handbook of Computational Cognitive Modeling*, In ed. R. Sun. Cambridge University Press, pp. 59–100.

Grossberg, S. (1982). *Studies of Mind and Brain: Neural Principles of Learning, Perception, Development, Cognition, and Motor Control.* Reidel.

Grossberg, S. (2000). The complementary brain: unifying brain dynamics and modularity. *Trends in Cognitive Science,* **4**, 233–246.

Grover, L. K. (1997). Quantum mechanics helps in searching for a needle in a haystack. *Physical Review Letters,* **79**(2), 325–327.

Gudder, S. P. (1979). *Stochastic Methods in Quantum Mechanics.* Dover.

Gudder, S. P. (1988). *Quantum Probability.* Academic Press.

Gupta, S. & Zia, R. K. P. (2001). Quantum neural networks. *Journal of Computer and System Science,* **63**(3), 355–383.

Hagan, S., Hameroff, S., & Tuszynksi, J. (2002). Quantum computation in brain microtubles? Decoherence and biological feasibility. *Physical Reviews E,* **65**, 061901.

Halmos, P. R. (1993). *Finite-Dimensional Vector Spaces.* Springer.

Halpern, J. Y. & Fagin, R. (1992). Two views of belief: belief as generalized probability and belief as evidence. *Artificial Intelligence,* **54**, 275–317.

Hameroff, S. R. (1998). Quantum computation in brain microtubles? The Penrose–Hameroff "Orch Or" model of consciousness. *Philosophical Transactions of the Royal Society London (A),* **356**, 1869–1896.

Hameroff, S. R. (2007). The brain is both a neurocomputer and quantum computer. *Cognitive Science,* **31**, 1035–1045.

Hammond, K. R. (1987). Direct comparison of the efficacy of intuitive and analytic cognition in expert judgment. *IEEE Transactions on Systems, Man, and Cybernetics,* **SMC-17**(5), 753–770.

Hampton, J. (1988). Overextension of conjunctive concepts: evidence for a unitary model for concept typicality and class inclusion. *Journal of Experimental Psychology,* **14**(1), 12–32.

Hampton, J. (1997). Conceptual combination. In *Knowledge, Concepts, and Categories,* ed. K. Lamberts & D. Shank. MIT Press, pp. 133–160.

Hastie, R. & Park, B. (1988). The relationship between memory and judgment depends on whether the judgment is memory-based or on-line. *Psychological Review,* **93**, 258–268.

Haven, E. (2002). A discussion on embedding the Black–Scholes option pricing model in a quantum physics setting. *Physica A,* **304**, 507–524.

Heisenberg, W. (1958). *Physics and Philosophy.* Harper and Row.

Hey, J. D. & Knoll, J. A. (2007). How far ahead do people plan? *Economic Letters,* **96**, 8–13.

Histrova, E. & Grinberg, M. (2008). Disjunction effect in prisoner's dilemma: evidences from an eye-tracking study. In *Proceedings of the 30th Annual Conference of the Cognitive Science Society,* ed. B. Love, K. McCrae, & V. M. Sloutsky. Austin, TX: Cognitive Science Society.

Hogarth, R. & Einhorn, H. J. (1992). Order effects in belief updating: the belief adjustment modeling. *Cognitive Pschology,* **24**, 1–55.

Howard, R. A. (1971). *Dynamic Probabilistic Systems: Volume I Markov models.* John Wiley & Sons, Inc.

Hoyer, P. (2000). Arbitrary phases in quantum amplitude amplification. *Physical Review A*, **62**, 052304-1–052304-5.

Hughes, R. I. G. (1989). *The Structure and Interpretation of Quantum Mechanics*. Harvard University Press.

Humphreys, M., Bain, J., & Pike, R. (1989a). Different ways to cue a coherent memory system: a theory for episodic, semantic and procedural tasks. *Psychological Review*, **96**, 208–233.

Humphreys, M., Pike, R., Bain, J., & Tehan, G. (1989b). Global matching: a comparison of the Siam, Minerva II, matrix and Todam models. *Journal of Mathematical Psychology*, **33**, 36–67.

Iqbal, A. & Abbot, D. (2009). Non-factorizable joint probabilities and evolutionarily stable strategies in the quantum prisoner's dilemma game. *Physics Letters A*, **373**, 2537–2541.

Isham, C. (1995). *Lectures on Quantum Theory*. Imperial College Press.

Isham, C. (2004). *Lectures on Quantum Theory*. Imperial College Press.

Ivancevic, V. & Aidman, E. (2007). Life space foam: a medium for motivational and cognitive dynamics. *Physica A*, **382**, 616–630.

Ivancevic, V. G. & Ivancevic, T. T. (2010). *Quantum Neural Computation*. Springer.

Jacoby, L. L. (1991). A process dissociation framework: separating automatic from intentional uses of memory. *Journal of Memory and Language*, **30**, 513–541.

James, W. (1890). *The Principles of Psychology*. Dover.

Jibu, M. & Yasue, K. (1995). *Quantum Brain Dynamics and Consciousness*. Amsterdam: Benjamins.

Jones, K. R. W. (1991). Principles of quantum inference. *Annals of Physics*, **207**, 140–170.

Jones, M. & Mewhort, D. (2007). Representing word meaning and order information in a composite holographic lexicon. *Psychological Review*, **114**(1), 1–37.

Jones, M., Kintsch, W., & Mewhort, D. (2006). High-dimensional semantic space accounts of priming. *Journal of Memory and Language*, **55**, 534–552.

Kahneman, D., & Tversky, A. (1979). Prospect theory: an analysis of decision under risk. *Econometrica*, **47**, 263–291.

Khrennikov, A. Y. (1999). Classical and quantum mechanics on information spaces with applications to cognitive, psychological, social, and anomalous phenomena. *Foundations of Physics*, **29**, 1065–1098.

Khrennikov, A. Y. (2004). *Information Dynamics in Cognitive, Psychological, Social and Anomalous Phenomena*. Kluwer Academic.

Khrennikov, A. Y. (2007). Can quantum information be processed by macroscopic systems? *Quantum Information Processing*, **6**(6), 401–429.

Khrennikov, A. Y. (2010). *Ubiquitous Quantum Structure: From Psychology to Finance*. Springer.

Khrennikov, A. Y. & Haven, E. (2009). Quantum mechanics and violations of the sure thing principle: the use of probability interference and other concepts. *Journal of Mathematical Psychology*, **53**(5), 378–388.

Kolmogorov, A. N. (1933/1950). *Foundations of the Theory of Probability.* New York: Chelsea Publishing Co.

Kouda, N., Matsui, N., Nishimura, H., & Peper, F. (2005). Qubit neural network and its learning efficiency. *Neural Computation and Applications*, **14**, 114–121.

Kruschke, J. K. (2010). *Doing Bayesian Data Analysis: A Tutorial with R and BUGS.* Academic Press.

Kuhberger, A., Komunska, D., & Perner, J. (2001). The disjunction effect: does it exist for two-step gambles? *Organizational Behavior and Human Decision Processes*, **85**(2), 250–264.

Laird, J. E., Newell, A., & Rosenbloom, P. S. (1987). Soar: an architecture for general intelligence. *Artificial Intelligence*, **33**, 1–64.

Laloë, F. (2001). Do we really understand quantum mechanics? Strange correlations, paradoxes, and theorems. *American Journal of Physics*, **69**(6), 655–701.

Lambdin, C. & Burdsal, C. (2007). The disjunction effect reexamined: relevant methodological issues and the fallacy of unspecified percentage comparisons. *Organizational Behavior and Human Decision Processes*, **103**, 268–276.

Lambert-Mogiliansky, A. & Busemeyer, J. R. (2009). An exploration of type indeterminacy in strategic decision making. In *Quantum Interaction: Proceedings of the Third Quantum Interaction Symposium*, ed. P. Bruza, D. A. Sofge, W. Lawless, K. van Rijsbergen, & M. Klusch. Springer, pp. 113–128.

Lambert-Mogiliansky, A., Zamir, S., & Zwirn, H. (2009). Type indeterminacy: a model of the KT (Kahneman–Tversky)-man. *Journal of Mathematical Psychology*, **53**(5), 349–361.

Laming, D. R. (1968). *Information Theory of Choice Reaction Time.* Wiley.

La Mura, P. (2009). Projective expected utility. *Journal of Mathematical Psychology*, **53**(5), 408–414.

La Mura, P., & Swiatczak, L. (2007). Markov entanglement networks. In *Quantum Interaction*, ed. P. Bruza, W. Lawless, K. van Rijsbergen, & D. A. Sofge. AAAI Press.

Landauer, T. & Dumais, S. (1997). A solution to Plato's problem: the latent semantic analysis theory of acquisition, induction and representation of knowledge. *Psychological Review*, **104**, 211–240.

Landauer, T., Foltz, P., & Laham, D. (1998). An introduction to latent semantic analysis. *Discourse Processes*, **25**(2–3), 259–284.

Large, E. W. & Jones, M. R. (1999). The dynamics of attending: how people track time-varying events. *Psychological Review*, **106**, 119–159.

Leggett, A. J. & Garg, A. (1985). Quantum mechanics versus macroscopic realism: is the flux there when nobody looks? *Physical Review Letters*, **54**, 857–860.

Levy, J. & Bullinaria, J. (1999). Learning lexical properties from word usage patterns: which context words should be used? In *Connectionist Models of Learning, Development and Evolution: Proceedings of the Sixth*

Neural Computation and Psychology Workshop, ed. R. French & J. Sounge. Springer, pp. 273–282.

Li, S. & Taplin, J. (2002). Examining whether there is a disjunction effect in prisoner's dilemma games. *Chinese Journal of Psychology*, **44**(1), 25–46.

Link, S. W. (1992). *The Wave Theory of Difference and Similarity*. Earlbaum.

Litt, A., Eliasmith, C., Kroon, F. W., Weinsteing, S., & Thagard, P. (2006). Is the brain a quantum computer? *Cognitive Science*, **30**, 593–603.

Littman, M. L. (2009). A tutorial on partially observable Markov decision processes. *Journal of Mathematical Psychology*, **53**, 119–125.

Lowe, W. (2000). What is the dimensionality of human semantic space? In *Connectionist Models of Learning, Development and Evolution: Proceedings of the Sixth Neural Computation and Psychology Workshop*, ed. R. French & J. Sounge. Springer, pp. 303–311.

Lowe, W. (2001). Towards a theory of scmantic space. In J. D. Moore & K. Stenning (Eds.), *Proceedings of the Twenty-Third Annual Conference of the Cognitive Science Society*. Lawrence Erlbaum Associates, pp. 576–581.

Luce, R. D. (2000). *Utility of Gains and Losses*. Erlbaum.

Lund, K. & Burgess, C. (1996). Producing high-dimensional semantic spaces from lexical co-occurrence. *Behavior Research Methods, Instruments & Computers*, **28**(2), 203–208.

Machina, M. (1989). Dynamic inconsistency and non-expected utility models of choice under uncertainty. *Journal of Economic Literature*, **27**, 1622–1668.

Manousakis, E. (2009). Quantum formalism to describe binocular rivalry (arXiv, 0709, 4516v2).

Maudlin, T. (1994). *Quantum Non-Locality and Relativity: Metaphysical Intimations of Modern Physics*, Aristotelian Society Series, vol. 13. Blackwell.

McArthur, R. (2006). Computing with meaning by operationalising socio-cognitive semantics. Unpublished doctoral dissertation, Queensland University of Technology.

Medin, D. & Shoben, E. (1988). Context and structure in conceptual combination. *Cognitive Psychology*, **20**, 58–190.

Meyer, D. A. (1999). Quantum strategies. *Physical Review Letters*, **82**, 1052–1055.

Meyer, D. & Kieres, D. E. (1997). A computational theory of executive cognitive processes and multiple task performance. Part 1. Basic processes. *Psychological Review*, **104**, 2–65.

Mitchell, J. & Lapata, M. (2010). Composition in distributional models of semantics. *Cognitive Science*, **34**, 1388–1429.

Miyamoto, J. M., Gonzalez, R., & Tu, S. (1995). Compositional anomalies in the semantics of evidence. In *Decision Making from a Cognitive Perspective*, ed. J. R. Busemeyer, D. L. Medin, & R. Hastie. New York: Academic Press, pp. 1–50.

Moore, D. W. (2002). Measuring new types of question-order effects. *Public Opinion Quarterly*, **66**, 80–91.

Morier, D. M. & Borgida, E. (1984). The conjuction fallacy: a task specific phenomena? *Personality and Social Psychology Bulletin*, **10**, 243–252.

Murphy, G. (1988). Comprehending complex concepts. *Cognitive Science*, **12**, 529–562.

Narens, L. (2007). *Theories of Probability: An Examination of Logical and Qualitative Foundations*. World Scientific Publishing Company.

Narens, L. (2009). A foundation for support theory based on a non-Boolean event space. *Journal of Mathematical Psychology*, **53**, 399–407.

Nelson, D. & Goodmon, L. (2002). Experiencing a word can prime its accessibility and its associative connections to related words. *Memory & Cognition*, **30**, 380–398.

Nelson, D. & McEvoy, C. (1979). Encoding context and set size. *Journal of Experimental Psychology: Human Learning and Memory*, **5**(3), 292–314.

Nelson, D. & McEvoy, C. (2005). Implicitly activated memories: the missing links of remembering. In *Learning and Memory: Advances in Theory and Applications*, ed. C. Izawa & N. Ohta. New Jersey: Erlbaum, pp. 177–198.

Nelson, D. & McEvoy, C. (2007). Entangled associative structures and context. In *Proceedings of the AAAI Spring Symposium on Quantum Interaction*, ed. P. Bruza, W. Lawless, C. van Rijsbergen, & D. Sofge. AAAI Press.

Nelson, D., Schreiber, T., & McEvoy, C. (1992). Processing implicit and explicit representations. *Psychological Review*, **99**(2), 322–348.

Nelson, D., McEvoy, C., Janczura, G., & Xu, J. (1993a). Implicit memory and inhibition. *Journal of Memory and Language*, **32**, 667–691.

Nelson, D., Bennett, D., Gee, N., Schreiber, T., & McKinney, V. (1993b). Implicit memory: effects of network size and interconnectivity on cued recall. *Journal of Experimental Psychology: Learning, Memory and Cognition*, **19**(4), 747–764.

Nelson, D., Bennett, D., & Leibert, T. (1997). One step is not enough: making better use of association norms to predict cued recall. *Memory & Cognition*, **25**(6), 785–796.

Nelson, D., McKinney, V., Gee, N., & Janczura, G. (1998). Interpreting the influence of implicitly activated memories on recall and recognition. *Psychological Review*, **105**(2), 299–324.

Nelson, D., McEvoy, C., & Pointer, L. (2003). Spreading activation or spooky action at a distance? *Journal of Experimental Psychology: Learning, Memory and Cognition*, **29**(1), 42–52.

Nelson, D., McEvoy, C., & Schreiber, T. (2004). The University of South Florida, word association, rhyme and word fragment norms. *Behavior Research Methods, Instruments & Computers*, **36**, 408–420.

Nielsen, M. A. & Chuang, I. L. (2000). *Quantum Computation and Quantum Information*. Cambridge University Press.

Niestegge, G. (2008). An approach to quantum mechanics via conditional probabilities. *Foundations of Physics*, **38**, 241–256.

Nilsson, H. (2008). Exploring the conjunction fallacy within a category learning framework. *Journal of Behavioral Decision Making*, **21**, 471–490.

Nosofsky, R. M. (1988). Exemplar-based accounts of relations between classification, recognition, and typicality. *Journal of Experimental Psychology: Learning, Memory, and Cognition*, **14**, 700–708.

Novakovich, D., Bruza, P., & Sitbon, L. (2009). Inducing shades of meaning by matrix methods: a first step towards thematic analysis of opinion. In *Proceedings of the Third International Conference on Advances in Semantic Processing (Semapro'09)*. IEEE Press, pp. 86–91.

Nunez, P., & Srinivasan, R. (2006). *Electric Fields of the Brain: The Neurophysics of EEG*, 2nd edn. Oxford University Press.

Oaksford, M. & Chater, N. (2009). Précis of Bayesian rationality: the probabilistic approach to human reasoning. *Behavioral and Brain Sciences*, **32**, 69–120.

Pashler, H. (1998). *The Psychology of Attention*. MIT Press.

Patel, M., Bullinaria, J., & Levy, J. (1997). Extracting semantic representations from large text corpora. In *Connectionist models of Learning, Development and Evolution: Proceedings of the Fourth Neural Computation and Psychology Workshop*, ed. R. French & J. Sounge. Springer, pp. 199–212.

Payne, J., Bettman, J. R., & Johnson, E. J. (1992). Behavioral decision research: a constructive processing perspective. *Annual Review of Psychology*, **43**, 87–131.

Pearl, J. (1988). *Probabilistic Reasoning in Intelligent Systems: Networks of Plausible Inference*. Morgan Kaufmann.

Pelletier, J. (1994). The principle of semantic compositionality. *Topoi*, **13**, 11–24.

Pelletier, J. (2001). Did Frege believe Frege's principle? *Logic, Language and Information*, **10**(1), 87–114.

Penrose, W. (1989). *The Emperor's New Mind*. Oxford University Press.

Percival, I. (1998). *Quantum State Diffusion*. Cambridge University Press.

Peres, A. (1998). *Quantum Theory: Concepts and Methods*. Kluwer Academic.

Piotrowski, E. W. & Sladkowski, J. (2002). An invitation to quantum game theory. *International Journal of Theoretical Physics*, **42**, 1089–1099.

Pitowski, I. (1989). *Quantum Probability, Quantum Logic* (vol. 321 Lecture Notes in Physics). Springer.

Pothos, E. M. & Busemeyer, J. R. (2009). A quantum probability model explanation for violations of 'rational' decision making. *Proceedings of the Royal Society, B.*, **276**(1665), 2171–2178.

Pothos, E. M. & Busemeyer, J. R. (2011). A quantum probability explanation for violations of symmetry in similarity judgments. In *Proceedings of the Cognitive Science Society*.

Pribram, K. H. (1993). *Rethinking Neural Networks: Quantum Fields and Biological Data*. Erlbaum.

Primas, H. (2007). Non-Boolean descriptions for mind–matter problems. *Mind & Matter*, **5**(1), 7–44.

Rabiner, L. R. (1989). A tutorial on hidden Markov models and selected applications in speech recognition. *Proceedings of the IEEE*, **77**(2), 257–286.

Ratcliff, R., & Smith, P. (2004). A comparison of sequential sampling models for two-choice reaction time. *Psychological Review*, **111**, 333–367.

Regenwetter, M., Dana, J., & Davis-Stober, C. P. (2011). Transitivity of preferences. *Psychological Review*, **118**, 42–56.

Reyna, V. & Brainerd, C. J. (1995). Fuzzy-trace theory: an interim synthesis. *Learning and Individual Differences*, **7**, 1–75.

Ricciardi, L. M. & Umezawa, H. (1967). Brain and physics of many bodied problems. *Kybernetik*, **4**, 44–48.

Rotello, C. M., Macmillan, N. A., & Reeder, J. A. (2004). Sum-difference theory of remembering and knowing: a two-dimensional signal-detection model. *Psychological Review*, **111**(3), 588–616.

Rumelhart, D. E. & McClelland, J. L. (1986). *Parallel Distributed Processing: Explorations in the Microstructure of Cognition*. MIT Press.

Rydell, R. J., McConnell, A. R., & Mackie, D. M. (2006). Of two minds: forming and changing valence-inconsistent implicit and explicit attitudes. *Psychological Science*, **17**(11), 954–958.

Sahlgren, M. (2002). Towards a flexible model of word meaning. *AAAI Spring Symposium 2002*, March 25–27, Stanford University, Palo Alto, CA.

Sahlgren, M. (2006). The word-space model. Unpublished doctoral dissertation, Stockholm University.

Sahlgren, M., Holst, A., & Kanerva, P. (2008). Permutations as a means to encode order in word space. In *Proceedings of the 30th Annual Meeting of the Cognitive Science Society (Cogsci'08)*. Washington, DC.

Sakurai, J. J. (1994). *Modern Quantum Mechanics*. New York: Addison-Wesley.

Savage, L. J. (1954). *The Foundations of Statistics*. John Wiley & Sons.

Schack, R., Brun, T. A., & Caves, C. M. (2001). Quantum Bayes rule. *Physical Review A*, **64**, 014305-1–014305-4.

Schachter, S. & Singer, J. E. (1962). Cognitive, social, and physiological determinants of emotional state. *Psychological Review*, **69**(5), 379–399.

Schuman, H. & Presser, S. (1981). *Questions and Answers in Attitude Surveys: Experiments on Question Form, Wording, and Content*. New York: Academic Press.

Schütze, H. (1998). Automatic word sense discrimination. *Computational Linguistics*, **24**(1), 97–124.

Schwartz, J., Stapp, H., & Beauregard, M. (2005). Quantum physics in neuroscience and psychology: a neurophysical model of mind–brain interaction. *The Philosophical Transactions of the Royal Society B*, **360**(1458), 1309–1327.

Schwarz, N. (2007). Attitude construction: evaluation in context. *Social Cognition*, **25**, 638–656.

Shafer, G. (1976). *A Mathematical Theory of Evidence*. Princeton University Press.

Shafir, E. & Tversky, A. (1992). Thinking through uncertainty: nonconsequential reasoning and choice. *Cognitive Psychology*, **24**, 449–474.

Sherman, S. J. (1980). On the self-erasing nature of errors of prediction. *Journal of Personality and Social Psychology*, **39**, 210–221.

Shiffrin, R. M. (2010). Perspectives on modeling in cognitive science. *Topics in Cognitive Science*, **2**, 736–750.

Shiffrin, R. M. & Schneider, W. (1977). Controlled and automatic human information processing II: perceptual learning, automatic attending, and a general theory. *Psychological Review*, **84**, 127–190.

Shimony, A. (2009). Bell's theorem. In *The Stanford Encyclopedia of Philosophy*, Summer 2009 edn, ed. E. Zalta. Stanford University (http://plato.stanford.edu/archives/sum2009/entries/bell-theorem/).

Sides, A., Osherson, D., Bonini, N., & Viale, R. (2002). On the reality of the conjunction fallacy. *Memory and Cognition*, **30**, 191–198.

Simon, H. A. (1957). *Models of Man*. New York: Wiley.

Simpson, G. (1994). Context and the processing of ambiguous words. In *Handbook of Pyscholinguistics*, ed. M. Gernsbacher. Academic Press, pp. 359–374.

Sloman, S. A. (1993). Feature-based induction. *Cognitive Psychology*, **25**, 231–280.

Sloman, S. A. (1996). The empirical case for two systems of reasoning. *Psychological Bulletin*, **119**, 3–22.

Smith, E. R. & DeCoster, J. (2000). Dual process models in social and cognitive psychology: conceptual integration and links to underlying memory systems. *Personality and Social Psychology Review*, **4**, 108–131.

Stanovich, K. E. & West, R. F. (2000). Individual differences in reasoning: implications for the rationality debate. *Brain and Behavioral Sciences*, **23**, 645–726.

Stapp, H. P. (2009). *Mind, Matter, and Quantum Mechanics*, 3rd edn. Springer.

Steyvers, M. & Tenenbaum, J. (2005). Graph theoretic analysis of semantic networks: small worlds in semantic networks. *Cognitive Science*, **29**(1), 41–78.

Stolarz-Fantino, S., Fantino, E., Zizzo, D. J., & Wen, J. (2003). The conjunction effect: new evidence for robustness. *American Journal of Psychology*, **116**(1), 15–34.

Strang, G. (1980). *Linear Algebra and its Applications*. Academic Press.

Strotz, R. H. (1956). Myopia and inconsistency in dynamic utility maximization. *Review of Economic Studies*, **23**(3), 165–180.

Sun, R., Merril, E., & Peterson, T. (2001). From implicit skills to explicit knowledge: a bottom up model of skill learning. *Cognitive Science*, **25**(2), 203–244.

Suppes, P., de Barros, A., & Oas, G. (2011). Neural phase oscillator representations of behavioral stimulus response models. *Journal of Mathematical Psychology*, under review.

Sutton, R. & Barto, A. G. (1998). *Reinforcement Learning: An Introduction*. MIT Press.

Swinney, D., Love, T., Walenski, M., & Smith, E. (2007). Conceptual combination during sentence comprehension: evidence for compositional processes. *Psychological Science*, **18**(5), 397–400.

Tegmark, M. (2000). Importance of quantum decoherence in brain processes. *Physical Review E*, **61**(4), 4194–4206.

Toronto, N. & Ventura, D. (2006). Learning quantum operators from quantum state pairs. In *IEEE World Congress on Computational Intelligence*, pp. 2607–2612.

Tourangeau, R., Rasinski, K. A., & Bradburn, N. (1991). Measuring happiness in surveys: a test of the subtraction hypothesis. *Public Opinion Quarterly*, **55**(2), 255–266.

Tourangeau, R., Rips, L. J., & Rasinski, K. A. (2000). *The Psychology of Survey Response*. Cambridge University Press.

Townsend, J. T., Silva, K. M., Spencer-Smith, J., & Wenger, M. (2000). Exploring the relations between categorization and decision making with regard to realistic face stimuli. *Pragmatics and Cognition*, **8**, 83–105.

Townsend, J. T., & Ashby, G. F. (1983). *Stochastic Modeling of Elementary Psychological Processes*. Cambridge University Press.

Trueblood, J. S. & Busemeyer, J. R. (2011). A quantum probability model for order effects on inference. *Cognitive Science*, **35**(8), 1518–1552.

Trueblood, J. S. & Busemeyer, J. R. (2012). A quantum probability model of causal reasoning. *Frontiers in Cognitive Science*, in press.

Tucci, R. R. (1995). Quantum Bayesian nets. *International Journal of Modern Physics*, *B*, **9**, 295–337.

Tucci, R. R. (1997). Quantum Bayesian refs. arxivsquant-ph/9706039v1.

Tversky, A. & Fox, C. R. (1995). Weighing risk and uncertainty. *Psychological Review*, **102**(2), 269–283.

Tversky, A. & Kahneman, D. (1983). Extensional versus intuitive reasoning: The conjunctive fallacy in probability judgment. *Psychological Review*, **90**, 293–315.

Tversky, A. & Kahneman, D. (1990). Advances in prospect theory: cumulative representation of uncertainty. *Journal of Risk and Uncertainty*, **5**, 297–323.

Tversky, A. & Koehler, D. J. (1994). Support theory: a nonextensional representation of subjective probability. *Psychological Review*, **101**, 547–567.

Tversky, A. & Shafir, E. (1992). The disjunction effect in choice under uncertainty. *Psychological Science*, **3**, 305–309.

Van Rijsbergen, K. (2004). *The Geometry of Infomation Retrieval*. Cambridge University Press.

Ventura, D. & Martinez, T. (2000). Quantum associative memory. *Information Sciences*, **124**, 273–296.

Vickers, D. (1979). *Decision Processes in Perception*. Academic Press.

Vitiello, G. (1995). Dissipation and memory capacity in the quantum brain model. *International Journal of Modern Physics*, *B*, **9**, 973–989.

Vitiello, G. (2001). *My Double Unveiled*. Amsterdam: John Benjamins Publishing Co.

Vitiello, G. (2009). Fractals and the Fock–Bargmann representation of coherent states. In *QI2009*, ed. P. Bruza, D. Sofge, W. Lawless, K. van Rijsbergen,

& M. Klusch. Lecture Notes in Artificial Intelligence, vol. 5494. Springer, 6–16.

von Foerster, H. (1950). Quantum mechanical theory of memory. In *Cybernetics: Transactions of the Sixth Conference*, ed. H. von Foerster. Josiah Macy, Jr. Foundation, pp. 112–145.

Von Neumann, J. (1932/1955). *Mathematical Foundations of Quantum Theory*. Princeton University Press.

Von Neumann, J. & Morgenstern, O. (1944). *Theory of Games and Economic Behavior*. New Jersey: Princeton University Press.

Von Sidow, M. (2011). The Bayesian logic of frequency–based conjunction fallacies. *Journal of Mathematical Psychology*, **55**, 119–139.

Von Winterfeldt, D. & Edwards, W. (1986). *Decision Analysis and Behavioral Research*. Cambridge University Press.

Wakker, P. (2010). *Prospect Theory: For Risk and Ambiguity*. Cambridge University Press.

Wallsten, T., Budescu, D., & Zwick, R. (1992). Comparing the calibration and coherence of numerical and verbal probability judgments. *Management Science*, **39**, 176–190.

Wang, J., Song, D., Zh, Hou, Y., & Bruza, P. (2010). Explanation of relevance judgement discrepancy with quantum interference. In *Quantum Informatics for Cognitive, Social, and Semantic Processes (QI 2010)*, ed. P. Bruza, W. Lawless, C. von Rijsbergen, D. Sofge, & D. Widdows. AAAI Press.

Wang, Z. & Busemeyer, J. R. (2012). Explaining and predicting question order effects using a quantum probability model. Under review (http:mypage.in.edu/~jbusemeyer/quantum/QuestOrdEff.pdf).

Ward, L. M. (2003). Synchronous neural oscillations and cognitive processes. *Trends in Cognitive Science*, **7**(12), 553–559.

Wedell, D. H. & Moro, R. (2008). Testing boundary conditions for the conjunction fallacy: effects of response mode, conceptual focus, and problem type. *Cognition*, **107**, 105–136.

Weiskopf, D. (2007). Compound nominals, context and compositionality. *Synthese*, **156**, 161–204.

Widdows, D. (2004). *Geometry and Meaning*. CSLI Publications.

Widdows, D. & Bruza, P. (2007). Quantum information dynamics and open world science. In *Quantum Interaction*, ed. P. Bruza, W. Lawless, C. von Rijsbergen, & D. Sofge. AAAI Press.

Widdows, D. & Cohen, T. (2008). Semantic vector combinations and the synoptic gospels. In *Proceedings of the Third Quantum Interaction Symposium*, vol. 5494. Springer, pp. 251–264.

Wiles, J., Halford, G., Stewart, J., Humphreys, M., Bain, J., & Wilson, W. (1994). Tensor models: a creative basis for memory and analogical mapping. In *Artificial Intelligence and Creativity*, ed. T. Dartnall. Kluwer Academic Publishers, pp. 145–159.

Winsberg, E. & Fine, A. (2003). Quantum life: interaction, entanglement, and separation. *Journal of Philosophy*, **100**(2), 80–97.

Wisniewski, E. J. (1996). Construal and similarity in conceptual combination. *Journal of Memory and Language*, **35**(3), 435–453.

Woolf, N. J. & Hameroff, S. R. (2001). A quantum approach to visual consciousness. *Trends in Cognitive Science*, **5**, 472–478.

Wyer, R. (1976). An investigation of the relations among probability estimates. *Organizational Behavior and Human Performance*, **15**, 1–18.

Yukalov, V. I. & Sornette, D. (2008). Quantum decision theory as quantum theory of measurement. *Physical Letters A*, **372**, 6867–6871.

Yukalov, V. I. & Sornette, D. (2009). Physics of risk and uncertainty in quantum decision making. *European Physical Journal B*, **71**, 533–548.

Yukalov, V. I. & Sornette, D. (2010). Decision theory with prospect interference and entanglement. *Theory and Decision*, **70**, 283–328.

Zadeh, L. (1965). Fuzzy sets. *Information and Control*, **8**, 338–353.

Zadrozny, W. (1994). From compositional to systematic semantics. *Linguistics and Philosophy*, **17**(4), 329–342.

Zak, M. & Williams, C. P. (1998). Quantum neural nets. *International Journal of Theoretical Physics*, **37**, 651–684.

Zuccon, G. & Azzopardi, L. (2010). Using the quantum probability ranking principle to rank interdependent documents. In *Advances in Information Retrieval, 32nd European Conference on IR Research (ECIR 2010)*. Springer, pp. 357–369.

Zuccon, G., Azzopardi, L., & van Rijsbergen, C. (2009). Semantic spaces: measuring the distances between different subspaces. In *Proceedings of the Third Quantum Interaction Symposium*, vol. 5494. Springer, pp. 225–236.

Zuccon, G., Azzopardi, L., Hauff, C., & von Rijsbergen, C. (2010). Estimating interference in the QPRP for subtopic retrieval. In *Proceedings of the 32nd Annual ACM Conference of Research and Development in Information Retrieval (SIGIR 2004)*.

Index